WORKSHOPS IN COMPUTING
Series edited by C. J. van Rijsbergen

M. Z. Kwiatkowska, M. W. Shields, R. M. Thomas

Semantics for Concurrency

Proceedings of the International
BCS-FACS Workshop,

Sponsored by Logic for IT (S.E.R.C.),

23–25 July 1990, University of Leicester, UK

Springer-Verlag Berlin Heidelberg GmbH

Marta Zofia Kwiatkowska, BSc, MSc, PhD
Department of Computing Studies, University of Leicester
University Road, Leicester, LE1 7RH

Michael William Shields, BA, PhD
Engineering Electronic Laboratories, The University
Canterbury, Kent, CT2 7NT

Richard Monro Thomas, MA, MSc, DPhil
Department of Computing Studies, University of Leicester
University Road, Leicester, LE1 7RH

British Library Cataloguing in Publication Data
Semantics for currency: proceedings of the International BCS-FACS Workshop, 23–25 July 1990, University of Leicester
1. Computer systems. Parallel programming
I. Kwiatkowska M. Z. (Marta Zofia) *1957–* II. Shields, M. W. (Mike W.)
III. Thomas, R. M. (Richard Monro) *1952–*
004.35

Library of Congress Cataloging in Publication Data
International BCS-FACS Workshop (1990: University of Leicester) Semantics for concurrency:proceedings/International BCS-FACS Workshop:sponsored by S.E.R.C. "Logic for IT." University of Leicester, UK, 23–25 July 1990; editors, M.Z. Kwiatkowska, M.W. Shields, R.M. Thomas.
p. cm. – (Workshops in computing)
"Publishing in collaboration with the British Computer Society."
ISBN 978-3-540-19625-9 ISBN 978-1-4471-3860-0 (eBook)
DOI 10.1007/978-1-4471-3860-0
1. Parallel programming (Computer science)–Congresses. 2. Programming languages (Electronic computers)–Semantics–Congresses.
I. Kwiatkowska, M. Z. (Marta Z.), 1957– . II. Shields, M. W. (Michael William), 1950– . III. Thomas, R. M. (Richard Monro), 1952– . IV. S.E.R.C. "Logic for IT." V. British Computer Society. VI. Title. VII. Series
QA76.642.I5G 1990
005.2—dc20 90–10064 CIP

Originally published by Springer-Verlag Berlin Heidelberg New York in 1990

2128/3916–543210 Printed on acid-free paper

Preface

The semantics of concurrent systems is one of the most vigorous areas of research in theoretical computer science, but suffers from disagreement due to different, and often incompatible, attitudes towards abstracting non-sequential behaviour. When confronted with process algebras, which give rise to very elegant, highly abstract and compositional models, traditionally based on the interleaving abstraction, some argue that the wealth of contribution they have made is partially offset by the difficulty in dealing with topics such as fairness. On the other hand, the non-interleaving approaches, based on causality, although easing problems with fairness and confusion, still lack structure, compositionality, and the elegance of the interleaving counterparts. Since both these approaches have undoubtedly provided important contributions towards understanding of concurrent systems, one should concentrate on what they have in common, rather than the way they differ.

The International Workshop on Semantics for Concurrency held at the University of Leicester on 23–25 July 1990 was organised to help overcome this problem. Its main objective was *not* to be divisive, but rather to encourage discussions leading towards the identification of the positive objective features of the main approaches, in the hope of furthering common understanding. The Workshop met with an excellent response, and attracted contributions from all over the world. The result was an interesting and varied programme, which was a combination of invited and refereed papers. The invited speakers were:

Prof. dr. E. Best (Hildesheim University)
Prof. dr. A. Mazurkiewicz (Polish Academy of Sciences, Warsaw)
Prof. R. Milner (University of Edinburgh)
Dr. A. W. Roscoe (Oxford University)
Dr. J. J. M. M. Rutten (CWI Amsterdam)
Dr. C. Stirling (University of Edinburgh)

These Proceedings contain papers presented at the Workshop; they are listed in the same order as they appeared in the programme. There will also be a special issue of *Theoretical Computer Science* including some of the papers in this volume.

This Workshop would not have taken place without the enthusiasm and financial support of the Logic for IT initiative (Science and Engineering Research Council), Special Interest Group in the Formal Aspects of Computing Science of the British Computer Society (BCS-FACS), the University of Leicester and Hewlett-Packard Laboratories. Special thanks are due to the other two members of the Organising and Programme Committee, Mike Shields and Rick Thomas, and all the reviewers. Finally, thanks go to Jackie Macklin for all her assistance, especially with the mailing, Sandra Pearson, Paul Manning, Nick Measor, and everyone else who helped.

Leicester, UK
1990

Marta Kwiatkowska
Chair

Contents

A General Tableau Technique for Verifying Temporal Properties of Concurrent Programs (Extended Abstract)

Colin Stirling and David Walker
Department of Computer Science
University of Edinburgh
Edinburgh EH9 3JZ, U.K.

1 Introduction

Labelled transition systems provide convenient models for many computational systems. Their usefulness is due partly to their natural association with temporal logics which may be used to express interesting properties of systems. It is of course vital to be able not only to express properties of programs but also to determine whether they hold of them. In the case of finite-state systems, much work has been done on automatic model checking [4]. Algorithms are known for a variety of logics, and many have been implemented and used to study systems including communications protocols and digital circuits.

But many systems, for example many interesting concurrent programs, are not finite-state. Infinite-state systems are often treated by axiomatic methods [11]. Here we provide a general tableau technique, an extension of the model-theoretic methods which underpin model checking, for checking temporal properties expressed in the modal mu-calculus. The technique has been described and used for verifying properties of Petri Nets in [2], and for properties of CCS processes in [3]. Here we use it to study a concurrent while program and a CSP type program.

The paper is organized as follows. In Section 2 we discuss the interpretation of concurrent programs as labelled transition systems. The expression of temporal properties in the modal mu-calculus in considered in Section 3, while in Section 4 the general tableau technique is described. Section 5 contains the two examples, and in Section 6 we discuss some further issues.

2 Labelled Transition Systems

A wide range of computational systems may be conveniently modelled using labelled transition systems. A *labelled transition system* is a structure $\mathcal{T} = (\mathcal{P}, \{\xrightarrow{a} \mid a \in \mathcal{L}\})$ consisting of a set $\mathcal{P}$ (or $\mathcal{P}_\mathcal{T}$) of *points* together with a family of binary relations on $\mathcal{P}$ indexed by a set $\mathcal{L}$ (or $\mathcal{L}_\mathcal{T}$) of *labels*, the *sort* of $\mathcal{T}$. The points may represent configurations of a system, while the labels may carry information pertinent to transitions between configurations.

Among the systems which are naturally modelled using transition systems are programs expressed in concurrent while languages and CSP type languages. Transition systems are generated from programs when such languages are accorded structured operational interpretations [13]. The points consist of program phrases and state information. In a CSP type language, a label may indicate an ability to communicate along a certain channel. A compositional interpretation of a concurrent while language is possible if each program is understood in terms of its *potential computations*, those which arise when it is executed in parallel with other programs [1]. In this case the labels indicate whether a transition is due to the program or its environment.

Usually, rather than the possible transitions from one configuration to another it is the overall behaviour of a system which is of interest. This behaviour arises from the runs of the system, a *run* being a maximal path $E_0 \xrightarrow{a_0} E_1 \xrightarrow{a_1} \ldots$ through $\mathcal{T}$, where maximality means that either the path is infinite or from its final point no transition is possible.

In Section 5 we study in detail two examples. The first is an intricate concurrent while language program due to Knuth [8] intended to ensure mutual exclusion among a number of programs, while the second due to Pease, Shostak and Lamport [12] is a problem in which a number of communicating processes, some of which may be running on 'faulty' processors, are required to achieve a mutual agreement. In the next section we consider temporal properties of transition systems, illustrating the ideas by showing how to express certain properties of Knuth's program.

Well-formed programs of the following language, in which Knuth's program may be expressed, are interpreted as transition systems (here well-formed means that every label occurring in a goto labels a unique program):

$$p \ ::= \ \lambda \ \mid \ A \ \mid \ p_1;p_2 \ \mid \ \texttt{if}\ e\ \texttt{then}\ p \ \mid \ \texttt{while}\ e\ \texttt{do}\ p \ \mid \ p_1\|p_2 \ \mid \ L:p$$

Here λ is the empty program satisfying $\lambda;p = p = p;\lambda$ and $\lambda\|p = p = p\|\lambda$, A ranges over atomic programs including assignment and goto, e over expressions, and L over program labels. A configuration is a pair (p, m) with p a program and m a state, a partial function from variables to values. Transitions between configurations are given by a family of rules including the following:

- $(x := e, m) \xrightarrow{x:=e} (\lambda, m[v/x])$ where v is the value of e in m, and $[v/x]$ is the customary updating notation
- $(\texttt{goto}\ L, m) \xrightarrow{\texttt{goto}\ L} (L : p, m)$
- $(\texttt{if}\ e\ \texttt{then}\ p, m) \xrightarrow{e} (p, m)$ if the value of e in m is true
- if $(q, m) \xrightarrow{a} (q', m')$ then $(p\|q, m) \xrightarrow{a} (p\|q', m')$

The transition system arising from a program may be augmented to become the intended model of the program by adding the appropriate valuation. We may regard the CSP primitives as atomic programs and add rules to cater for them:

- $(c!e, m) \xrightarrow{c!e} (\lambda, m[v/x])$ where v is the value of e in m
- $(c?x, m) \xrightarrow{c?x} (\lambda, m[v/x])$ for any value v

- if $(p,m) \xrightarrow{c!e} (p',m')$ and $(q,m) \xrightarrow{c?x} (q',m')$ then $(p\|q,m) \xrightarrow{x:=e} (p'\|q',m')$

In the second example in Section 5 we shall assume a standard treatment of recursion.

The general version of Knuth's program allows an arbitrary number of concurrent components. [8] contains also a version for the case of two programs and it is this which we study. The program contains variables c_1, c_2 and k and may be written

$$p_1 \| p_2$$

where, letting j be the index of the other program, p_i is

```
while true do
        ns_i; {atomic program for noncritical section}
        L_i0 : c_i := 1;
        L_i1 : if k = i then goto L_i2;
        if c_j ≠ 0 then goto L_i1;
        L_i2 : c_i := 2;
        if c_j = 2 then goto L_i0;
        k := i;
        cs_i; {atomic program for critical section}
        k := j;
        c_i := 0
```

Usually, interest lies in the behaviour of a program when it is executed from one of a set of initial states. We often write such a set M_0.

3 Temporal Properties

A very rich and very succinct temporal logic for expressing properties of transition systems (subsuming standard linear and branching time logics including CTL*) is a slight extension of the modal mu-calculus. The syntax of formulae Φ is as follows:

$$\Phi \; ::= \; Q \;\mid\; \neg\Phi \;\mid\; \Phi_1 \wedge \Phi_2 \;\mid\; [K]\Phi \;\mid\; \nu Z.\Phi$$

where Q ranges over a set of atomic formulae, Z over propositional variables, and K over *subsets* of a label set $\mathcal{L}$. In the formula $\nu Z.\Phi$, $\nu Z.$ binds free occurrences of Z in Φ. A syntactic restriction on $\nu Z.\Phi$ is that each free occurrence of Z in Φ lies within the scope of an even number of negations. The modal mu-calculus is due to Pratt [14] and Kozen [9] (although it was introduced for a different purpose that its use here). Its use as a temporal logic is due to Emerson and Lei [6] and Larsen [10]. The slight extension here is that sets of labels may appear in the modalities $[K]$ instead of single labels.

Derived operators are defined in the familiar way: $tt \stackrel{\text{def}}{=} \nu Z.Z$; $ff \stackrel{\text{def}}{=} \neg tt$; $\Phi \vee \Psi \stackrel{\text{def}}{=} \neg(\neg\Phi \wedge \neg\Psi)$; $\langle K\rangle\Phi \stackrel{\text{def}}{=} \neg[K]\neg\Phi$; and $\mu Z.\Phi \stackrel{\text{def}}{=} \neg\nu Z.\neg\Phi[Z := \neg Z]$ where $\neg\Phi[Z := \neg Z]$ is the result of substituting $\neg Z$ for each free occurrence of Z. Further useful abbreviations (which also apply to the $\langle K\rangle$ modalities) are

$$\begin{aligned}
[-K]\Phi &\stackrel{\text{def}}{=} [\mathcal{L} - K]\Phi \\
[a_1,\ldots,a_n]\Phi &\stackrel{\text{def}}{=} [\{a_1,\ldots,a_n\}]\Phi \\
[-]\Phi &\stackrel{\text{def}}{=} [\mathcal{L}]\Phi
\end{aligned}$$

Formulae of this logic are interpreted on labelled transition systems (of sort $\mathcal{L}$) as follows. A model is a pair $(\mathcal{T}, \mathcal{V})$ where $\mathcal{T}$ is a transition system and $\mathcal{V}$ a valuation assigning sets of points to atomic formulae and to propositional variables: $\mathcal{V}(Q) \subseteq \mathcal{P}_{\mathcal{T}}$ and $\mathcal{V}(Z) \subseteq \mathcal{P}_{\mathcal{T}}$. We assume the customary updating notation: $\mathcal{V}[\mathcal{E}/Z]$ is the valuation $\mathcal{V}'$ which agrees with $\mathcal{V}$ except that $\mathcal{V}'(Z) = \mathcal{E}$. Finally the set of points of $\mathcal{T}$ having the property Φ in the model $(\mathcal{T}, \mathcal{V})$ is inductively defined as $\| \Phi \|_{\mathcal{V}}^{\mathcal{T}}$ (where for ease of notation we drop the index $\mathcal{T}$ which is assumed to be fixed):

$$
\begin{aligned}
\| Q \|_{\mathcal{V}} &\stackrel{\text{def}}{=} \mathcal{V}(Q) \\
\| Z \|_{\mathcal{V}} &\stackrel{\text{def}}{=} \mathcal{V}(Z) \\
\| \neg\Phi \|_{\mathcal{V}} &\stackrel{\text{def}}{=} \mathcal{P} - \| \Phi \|_{\mathcal{V}} \\
\| \Phi \wedge \Psi \|_{\mathcal{V}} &\stackrel{\text{def}}{=} \| \Phi \|_{\mathcal{V}} \cap \| \Psi \|_{\mathcal{V}} \\
\| [K]\Phi \|_{\mathcal{V}} &\stackrel{\text{def}}{=} \{E \in \mathcal{P} \mid \forall F \in \mathcal{P}. \forall a \in K. \text{ if } E \xrightarrow{a} F \text{ then } F \in \| \Phi \|_{\mathcal{V}}\} \\
\| \nu Z. \Phi \|_{\mathcal{V}} &\stackrel{\text{def}}{=} \bigcup\{\mathcal{E} \subseteq \mathcal{P} \mid \| \Phi \|_{\mathcal{V}[\mathcal{E}/Z]} \supseteq \mathcal{E}\}
\end{aligned}
$$

The expected clause for the derived operator $\mu Z. \Phi$ is:

$$\| \mu Z. \Phi \|_{\mathcal{V}} \stackrel{\text{def}}{=} \bigcap\{\mathcal{E} \subseteq \mathcal{P} \mid \| \Phi \|_{\mathcal{V}[\mathcal{E}/Z]} \subseteq \mathcal{E}\}$$

We assume that a temporal property is given by a *closed* formula (one without free variables) of the mu-calculus. Our interest is the expression and verification of crucial temporal properties of concurrent while, or CSP, programs as described in Section 2. In such a case our concern is whether a family of initial configurations $\mathcal{E}_0 = \{(p, m) \mid m \in M_0\}$ has the property Φ: that is, if $\mathcal{E}_0 \subseteq \| \Phi \|_{\mathcal{V}}^{\mathcal{T}}$ where $(\mathcal{T}, \mathcal{V})$ is the intended model of programs. There are various classifications of temporal properties of programs [11], relating almost exclusively to linear time logics. Prominent amongst these are *safety* and *liveness* properties. With respect to the mu-calculus a much more subtle classification can be given. Here we shall merely indicate some of the delicacy.

Consider safety first, that something bad, Φ, can never *become true*. This is expressed by the following formula (where Φ does not contain Z free): $\nu Z. \neg\Phi \wedge [-]Z$. This just expresses that $\neg\Phi$ is invariant: $\mathcal{E}_0 \subseteq \| \nu Z. \neg\Phi \wedge [-]Z \|_{\mathcal{V}}^{\mathcal{T}}$ just in case $\neg\Phi$ is true throughout every run from any point in $\mathcal{E}_0$. One elaboration is the more discriminating property that $\neg\Phi$ is invariant throughout every run which involves just K actions: $\nu Z. \neg\Phi \wedge [K]Z$. Another elaboration is to view safety as meaning: some bad actions never *happen*. If K is the subset of bad actions, then this property is given by the formula $\nu Z. [K]ff \wedge [-]Z$. The crucial safety property of Knuth's program, from Section 2, is a mixture of these notions: that it is not possible to execute both critical sections, given by the formula: $\nu Z. ([cs_1]ff \vee [cs_2]ff) \wedge [-]Z$.

Liveness covers a whole collection of features from simple eventualities to complex fairness properties. The basic eventuality, that something good, Φ, becomes true, is given by the formula $\mu Y. \Phi \vee ([-]Y \wedge \langle - \rangle tt)$. A simple elaboration of this is that K actions happen until Φ becomes true: $\mu Y. \Phi \vee ([K]Y \wedge \langle K \rangle tt)$. A different approach is to view the basic eventuality in terms of actions: eventually some good action *happens*. Let K be the good actions. The formula expressing that every run contains an action in K is: $\mu Y. [-K]Y \wedge \langle - \rangle tt$. This formula, in effect, states that each part of a run only involving actions not in K is well-founded. This very important distinction between *being true* and *happening* is not countenanced within the standard classifications of properties of programs. The crucial liveness property of Knuth's program is not easy to formalize because it is dependent on a fairness requirement. Count a fair run as one where both components contribute infinitely often. Liveness is that throughout any fair run if a component p_i requests entry into its critical section (by performing $c_i := 1$) then eventually cs_i happens. This requires us to build fairness into the formula expressing this property. Assume that the labels other than cs_i, the critical section of p_i, are partitioned into two disjoint sets K_1 and K_2 with K_i representing the actions that p_i may perform (but which p_j may not perform). The formula expressing liveness for p_i is Φ_i:

$$\begin{aligned}
\Phi_i &= \nu Z.[c_i := 1]\Phi'_i \wedge [-]Z \\
\Phi'_i &= \nu Z_1.\Psi_i \wedge [-cs_i]Z_1 \\
\Psi_i &= \mu X.[K_1](\nu Y.[K_2](\nu Y_1.X \wedge [-cs_i]Y_1) \wedge [-cs_i]Y)
\end{aligned}$$

This merely states that there cannot be a run where K_1 and K_2 actions happen infinitely often, and $c_i := 1$ happens without cs_i happening later. Such a property is not expressible within standard branching time logics such as CTL [7].

The mu-calculus is a very rich temporal logic. Besides liveness and safety properties, cyclic (or counting) properties can also be expressed. But it is essential that we can also verify such crucial properties of programs. When models are finite then one can use model checking techniques (as presented for the mu-calculus in [17], for instance). But in general, models are not finite. In these cases, axiomatic techniques are often used [11]. Here instead we shall provide a general tableau technique, a simple extension of the model-theoretic methods which underpin model checking, for checking temporal properties on infinite models. This technique has been described and used for verifying properties of Petri nets in [2], and for properties of CCS processes in [3].

4 The Tableau System

Assume a fixed mu-calculus model $(\mathcal{T}, \mathcal{V})$ where $\mathcal{T}$ is a transition system which may contain an infinite number of points. We wish to show that some set of points $\mathcal{E}$ has the temporal property Φ, that $\mathcal{E} \subseteq \| \Phi \|^{\mathcal{T}}_{\mathcal{V}}$. We present a tableau system for proving this, built on sequents of the form $\mathcal{E} \vdash_{\Delta} \Phi$ where Δ is a *definition list* which keeps track of unrolling of fixed point formulae. A definition is given as $U = \Psi$ where U is a propositional constant and Ψ a fixed point formula. A finite list Δ of definitions $(U_1 = \Psi_1, \ldots, U_n = \Psi_n)$ has the two properties: that each U_i is distinct, and that each Ψ_i can only mention propositional constants belonging to the set $\{U_1, \ldots, U_{i-1}\}$[1]. Lists of definitions can be extended: if U is not declared in Δ and Ψ only mentions constants declared in Δ then, $\Delta \cdot U = \Psi$ is the definition list that results from appending $U = \Psi$ to Δ. When Δ is a definition list and U is declared to be Ψ in Δ, then $\Delta(U) = \Psi$.

The rules of the tableau system below are inverse natural deduction style rules. The premise sequent is the goal to be achieved (that $\mathcal{E} \subseteq \| \Phi \|^{\mathcal{T}}_{\mathcal{V}}$) while the consequents are the subgoals. The rules are presented only for formulae in positive form (where

[1]We assume the interpretation of formulae relative to definition lists as in [17] by in effect treating constants as variables: if Δ is $(U_1 = \Psi_1, \ldots, U_n = \Psi_n)$ then $\| \Phi_\Delta \|^{\mathcal{T}}_{\mathcal{V}} = \| \Phi \|^{\mathcal{T}}_{\mathcal{V}_n}$ where $\mathcal{V}_0 = \mathcal{V}$ and $\mathcal{V}_{i+1} = \mathcal{V}_i[\| \Psi_{i+1} \|^{\mathcal{T}}_{\mathcal{V}_i} / U_{i+1}]$.

all negations are moved inwards by using the dual operators $\vee$, $\langle K\rangle$ and $\mu Y.$). We assume that σ ranges over $\{\nu,\mu\}$. In the rules for $\langle K\rangle$ we assume that f is a function from the set $\mathcal{E}$ to the set $f(\mathcal{E})$ such that for all $E \in \mathcal{E}$, $\exists a \in K.\, E \xrightarrow{a} f(E)$.

$$\wedge \qquad \frac{\mathcal{E} \vdash_\Delta \Phi_1 \wedge \Phi_2}{\mathcal{E} \vdash_\Delta \Phi_1 \qquad \mathcal{E} \vdash_\Delta \Phi_2}$$

$$\vee \qquad \frac{\mathcal{E} \vdash_\Delta \Phi_1 \vee \Phi_2}{\mathcal{E}_1 \vdash_\Delta \Phi_1 \qquad \mathcal{E}_2 \vdash_\Delta \Phi_2} \quad \mathcal{E} = \mathcal{E}_1 \cup \mathcal{E}_2$$

$$[K] \qquad \frac{\mathcal{E} \vdash_\Delta [K]\Phi}{\mathcal{E}' \vdash_\Delta \Phi} \quad \mathcal{E}' = \{E \mid \exists F \in \mathcal{E}.\, \exists a \in K.\, F \xrightarrow{a} E\}$$

$$\langle K\rangle \qquad \frac{\mathcal{E} \vdash_\Delta \langle K\rangle\Phi}{f(\mathcal{E}) \vdash_\Delta \Phi}$$

$$\sigma Z. \qquad \frac{\mathcal{E} \vdash_\Delta \sigma Z.\, \Phi}{\mathcal{E} \vdash_{\Delta'} U} \quad \Delta' = \Delta \cdot (U = \sigma Z.\, \Phi)$$

$$U \qquad \frac{\mathcal{E} \vdash_\Delta U}{\mathcal{E} \vdash_\Delta \Phi[Z := U]} \quad \Delta(U) = \sigma Z.\, \Phi$$

$$\text{Thin} \qquad \frac{\mathcal{E} \vdash_\Delta \Phi}{\mathcal{E}' \vdash_\Delta \Phi} \quad \mathcal{E}' \supseteq \mathcal{E}$$

To test if every point in $\mathcal{E}$ has the property Φ (relative to Δ) one has to achieve the goal $\mathcal{E} \vdash_\Delta \Phi$ by building a tableau, a proof tree whose root is labelled with the initial sequent. Sequents labelling the immediate successors of a node are determined by an application of one of the rules. The boolean, $[K]$ and $\langle K\rangle$ rules are straightforward. New constants are introduced when fixed point formulae are met, and then these are unfolded. The rule Thin allows the set of points to be enlarged, and is essential for completeness of the technique (and need only be applied to sequents with fixed point formulae).

An essential missing ingredient is when a node in a proof tree counts as a leaf. We assume that the rules above only apply to nodes that are not terminal. A node n labelled by the sequent $\mathcal{F} \vdash_\Delta \Psi$ is *terminal* if one of the following conditions holds:

1. $\mathcal{F} = \emptyset$
2. $\Psi = Q$ or $\Psi = \neg Q$
3. $\Psi = \langle K\rangle\Phi$ and $\exists F \in \mathcal{F}.\, \forall a \in K.$ not $(F \xrightarrow{a})$
4. $\Psi = U$ and $\Delta(U) = \sigma Z.\, \Phi$ and there is a node above n in the proof tree labelled $\mathcal{E} \vdash_{\Delta'} U$ with $\mathcal{E} \supseteq \mathcal{F}$.

A node fulfilling condition 4 is called a *σ-terminal*. A node fulfilling conditions 1 or 4 when $\sigma = \nu$ is said to be a *successful* terminal, whereas a node fulfilling 3 is *unsuccessful*. In the case of 2 success depends on the valuation $\mathcal{V}$ of the model: if $\mathcal{F} \subseteq \mathcal{V}(Q)$ when Ψ is Q, or $\mathcal{F} \subseteq \mathcal{P} - \mathcal{V}(Q)$ when Ψ is $\neg Q$ then it is successful; otherwise it is unsuccessful. The definition of a successful μ-terminal, a σ-terminal when $\sigma = \mu$, is intricate and requires some notation.

Suppose a node n is labelled by $\mathcal{E} \vdash_{\Delta} \Phi$ and n' labelled $\mathcal{E}' \vdash_{\Delta'} \Phi'$ is an immediate successor of n. We say that $E' \in \mathcal{E}'$ at n' is a *dependant* of $E \in \mathcal{E}$ at n if

- the rule applied to n is $\wedge$, $\vee$, $\sigma Z.$, U or Thin and $E = E'$, or
- the rule is $[K]$ and $E \xrightarrow{a} E'$ for some $a \in K$, or
- the rule is $\langle K \rangle$ and $E' = f(E)$.

Assume that the *companion* of a σ-terminal is that node above it which makes it a terminal. Next we define a *trail* to F at a μ-terminal n from E at its companion m to be a sequence of pairs of nodes and points $(n_1, E_1), \ldots, (n_k, E_k)$ with $(n_1, E_1) = (m, E)$ and $(n_k, E_k) = (n, F)$ such that for all i with $1 \leq i < k$ either

1. E_{i+1} at n_{i+1} is a dependant of E_i at n_i, or
2. n_i is the immediate predecessor of a σ-terminal node n' (where $n' \neq n$) whose companion is n_j for some $j \leq i$, and $n_{i+1} = n_j$ and E_{i+1} at n' is a dependant of E_i at n_i.

Then each companion node n of a μ-terminal node induces a preorder $\sqsubset_n$ by $F \sqsubset_n E$ if there is a trail to F at a node m from E at its companion n. (Notice that a node may be a companion of various μ-terminal nodes). A μ-terminal node is *successful* if the ordering induced by its companion node n is well-founded: that is, if there is no infinite descending chain

$$\ldots \sqsubset_n E_2 \sqsubset_n E_1 \sqsubset_n E_0$$

Finally we say that a tableau is *successful* if it is finite and all its leaves are successful terminals. The following theorem states that the tableau technique is both *sound* and *complete* for arbitrary (infinite) transition systems. (The proof is not given here.)

Theorem 1 $\mathcal{E} \vdash_{\Delta} \Phi$ is the root of a successful tableau on $(\mathcal{T}, \mathcal{V})$ iff $\mathcal{E} \subseteq \| \Phi \|_{\mathcal{V}}^{\mathcal{T}}$.

This tableau technique can therefore be used to verify temporal properties of concurrent systems on arbitrary data. As the technique is data independent it generalizes standard methods used in program logics which employ induction or appeal to reasoning on well-founded structures. We now apply it to concurrent while and CSP program examples.

5 Two Examples

We apply the tableau technique to two examples. First, we examine Knuth's program from Section 2. Recall the program $p_1 \| p_2$; where j represents the index of the other program, p_i is the following:

p_{i0}	**while true do**
p_{i1}	$\quad ns_i$;
p_{i2}	$\quad L_{i0} : c_i := 1$;
p_{i3}	$\quad L_{i1}$: **if** $k = i$ **then goto** L_{i2};
p_{i4}	$\quad$ **if** $c_j \neq 0$ **then goto** L_{i1} ;
p_{i5}	$\quad L_{i2} : c_i := 2$;
p_{i6}	$\quad$ **if** $c_j = 2$ **then goto** L_{i0} ;
p_{i7}	$\quad k := i$;
p_{i8}	$\quad cs_i$;
p_{i9}	$\quad k := j$;
p_{i10}	$\quad c_i := 0$

Here p_{i0} abbreviates the program p_i while, for instance, p_{i9} abbreviates the program $k := j; c_i := 0; p_i$. The initial configuration set $\mathcal{E}_0$ is defined as:

$$\{(p_{10} \| p_{20}, m) \mid m(c_i) = 0 \text{ and } (m(k) = 1 \text{ or } m(k) = 2)\}$$

The safety property, that both components cannot execute their critical sections concurrently, is given by the formula:

$$\Phi = \nu Z. ([cs_1]ff \vee [cs_2]ff) \wedge [-]Z$$

To prove that the program has this property we need to exhibit a successful tableau whose root is labelled by the sequent $\mathcal{E}_0 \vdash_{()} \Phi$ (where $()$ is the empty definition list). Let $\mathcal{E}$ be the following family of all *potential* configurations:

$$\{(p_{1x} \| p_{2y}, m) \mid 0 \leq x \leq 10 \wedge 1 \leq y \leq 10 \wedge m(c_i) \in \{0,1,2\} \wedge m(k) \in \{1,2\}\}$$

And let $\mathcal{F}$ be the set of failing configurations:

$$\{(p_{1x} \| p_{2y}, m) \mid (x > 6 \wedge y > 6) \text{ or } (x \geq 6 \wedge m(c_1) \neq 2) \text{ or } (y \geq 6 \wedge m(c_2) \neq 2)\}$$

Finally, let $\mathcal{E}_1 = \mathcal{E} - \mathcal{F}$ be the set of acceptable configurations. The successful tableau is as follows:

$$\dfrac{\mathcal{E}_0 \vdash_{()} \Phi}{\dfrac{\mathcal{E}_1 \vdash_{()} \Phi}{\dfrac{\mathcal{E}_1 \vdash_{\Delta} U}{\dfrac{\mathcal{E}_1 \vdash_{\Delta} ([cs_1]ff \vee [cs_2]ff) \wedge [-]U}{\dfrac{\mathcal{E}_1 \vdash_{\Delta} [cs_1]ff \vee [cs_2]ff}{\dfrac{\mathcal{E}_{11} \vdash_{\Delta} [cs_1]ff}{\emptyset \vdash_{\Delta} ff} \quad \dfrac{\mathcal{E}_{12} \vdash_{\Delta} [cs_2]ff}{\emptyset \vdash_{\Delta} ff}} \qquad \dfrac{\mathcal{E}_1 \vdash_{\Delta} [-]U}{\mathcal{E}_1' \vdash_{\Delta} U}}}}}$$

where Δ is $(U = \Phi)$.

Notice here the application of the rule Thin at the first step. The set $\mathcal{E}_{11}$ consists of the configurations in $\mathcal{E}_1$ with the feature:

$$\{(p_{1x} \| p_{2y}, m) \mid x \neq 8\}$$

and the set $\mathcal{E}_{12}$ is similar but with $y \neq 8$ instead. Clearly $\mathcal{E} = \mathcal{E}_{11} \cup \mathcal{E}_{12}$. The set $\mathcal{E}'_1 = \{\beta \mid \exists \alpha \in \mathcal{E}_1 . \exists a \in \mathcal{L}. \alpha \xrightarrow{a} \beta\}$. The proof is completed by showing that $\mathcal{E}'_1 \subseteq \mathcal{E}_1$ (as then the leaf labelled $\mathcal{E}'_1 \vdash_\Delta U$ is successful). The reader is invited to establish this straightforward property.

The liveness property is that throughout any fair run, if a component p_i requests entry to its critical section (by performing $c_1 := 1$), eventually cs_i happens. For component i this property is given by Φ_i:

$$\begin{aligned} \Phi_i &= \nu Z. [c_i := 1]\Phi'_i \wedge [-]Z \\ \Phi'_i &= \nu Z_1 . \Psi_i \wedge [-cs_i]Z_1 \\ \Psi_i &= \mu X. [K_1](\nu Y. [K_2](\nu Y_1 . X \wedge [-cs_i]Y_1) \wedge [-cs_i]Y) \end{aligned}$$

where K_i represents the actions that p_i may perform (but which p_j cannot perform) and $K_1 \cup K_2$ is all the labels except for cs_i. Again we need to provide a successful tableau, this time with root labelled $\mathcal{E}_0 \vdash_{()} \Phi_i$. As in the safety case we appeal to the set $\mathcal{E}_1$. In the tableau on the next page we let

$$\begin{aligned} \Psi'_i &= \nu Y. [K_2](\nu Y_1 . V \wedge [-cs_i]Y_1) \wedge [-cs_i]Y \\ \Psi''_i &= \nu Y_1 . V \wedge [-cs_i]Y_1 \end{aligned}$$

In the tableau $\mathcal{E}'_1$ is as in the safety case, and so the leaf labelled $\mathcal{E}'_1 \vdash_{\Delta_1} U_1$ is successful. Moreover, as $\mathcal{E}''_1 \subseteq \mathcal{E}'_1$, the leaves $\mathcal{E}''_1 \vdash_{\Delta_j} U_i$ are also successful. This means that we are left with showing that the ordering $\sqsubset_n$ induced by the companion node n of the leaf $\mathcal{E}_1 \vdash_{\Delta_5} V$ is well-founded. The proof of this relies on the sets $\mathcal{E}_3$ and $\mathcal{E}_4$:

$$\begin{aligned} \mathcal{E}_3 &= \{F \mid \exists E \in \mathcal{E}_1 . \exists a \in K_1 . E \xrightarrow{a} F\} \\ \mathcal{E}_4 &= \{F \mid \exists E \in \mathcal{E}_1 . \exists a \in K_2 . E \xrightarrow{a} F\} \end{aligned}$$

Any trail from node n to a leaf (which may pass through the leaves $\mathcal{E}''_1 \vdash_{\Delta_4} U_3$ or $\mathcal{E}''_1 \vdash_{\Delta_5} U_4$) must pass through both these sets. That is, $E \sqsubset_n F$ if $E \xrightarrow{a_1 w a_2} F$ where $a_1 \in K_1$ and $a_2 \in K_2$ and $w \in (K_1 \cup K_2)^*$. That $\sqsubset_n$ is well-founded is straightforward to establish as the reader can check.

The second example is much more involved. In [12] Pease, Shostak and Lamport study a problem in which a number of processes are required to reach a mutual agreement on a set of data values. The subtlety of the problem is that some of the processes may be running on 'faulty' processors, capable of producing spurious data. The paper contains an algorithm together with a proof that under certain conditions it ensures that the appropriate agreement is achieved. We give a concrete representation of the system of processes as a program in a CSP type language and use the tableau system as the basis for a proof that it enjoys some properties of interest. In establishing that certain tableaux are successful, some detailed and intricate analyses are required; in particular we recall the main proof from [12]. We

$$\mathcal{E}_0 \vdash_{()} \Phi_i$$

$$\mathcal{E}_1 \vdash_{()} \Phi_i$$

$$\mathcal{E}_1 \vdash_{\Delta_1} U_1$$

$$\mathcal{E}_1 \vdash_{\Delta_1} [c_i := 1]\Phi_i' \wedge [-]U_1$$

$\mathcal{E}_1 \vdash_{\Delta_1} [c_i := 1]\Phi_i'$	$\mathcal{E}_1 \vdash_{\Delta_1} [-]U_1$
$\mathcal{E}_2 \vdash_{\Delta_1} \Phi_i'$	$\mathcal{E}_1' \vdash_{\Delta_1} U_1$
$\mathcal{E}_1 \vdash_{\Delta_1} \Phi_i'$	
$\mathcal{E}_1 \vdash_{\Delta_2} U_2$	
$\mathcal{E}_1 \vdash_{\Delta_2} \Psi_i \wedge [-cs_i]U_2$	

$\mathcal{E}_1 \vdash_{\Delta_2} \Psi_i$	$\mathcal{E}_1 \vdash_{\Delta_2} [-cs_i]U_2$
n $\quad \mathcal{E}_1 \vdash_{\Delta_3} V$	$\mathcal{E}_1'' \vdash_{\Delta_2} U_2$
$\mathcal{E}_1 \vdash_{\Delta_3} [K_1]\Psi_i'$	
$\mathcal{E}_3 \vdash_{\Delta_3} \Psi_i'$	
$\mathcal{E}_1 \vdash_{\Delta_3} \Psi_i'$	
$\mathcal{E}_1 \vdash_{\Delta_4} U_3$	
$\mathcal{E}_1 \vdash_{\Delta_4} [K_2]\Psi_i'' \wedge [-cs_i]U_3$	

$\mathcal{E}_1 \vdash_{\Delta_4} [K_2]\Psi_i''$	$\mathcal{E}_1 \vdash_{\Delta_4} [-cs_i]U_3$
$\mathcal{E}_4 \vdash_{\Delta_4} \Psi_i''$	$\mathcal{E}_1'' \vdash_{\Delta_4} U_3$
$\mathcal{E}_1 \vdash_{\Delta_4} \Psi_i''$	
$\mathcal{E}_1 \vdash_{\Delta_5} U_4$	
$\mathcal{E}_1 \vdash_{\Delta_5} V \wedge [-cs_i]U_4$	

$\mathcal{E}_1 \vdash_{\Delta_5} V$	$\mathcal{E}_1 \vdash_{\Delta_5} [-cs_i]U_4$
	$\mathcal{E}_1'' \vdash_{\Delta_5} U_4$

where $\Delta_1 = (U_1 = \Phi_i)$, $\Delta_2 = \Delta_1 \cdot (U_2 = \Phi_i')$, $\Delta_3 = \Delta_2 \cdot (V = \Psi_i)$, $\Delta_4 = \Delta_3 \cdot (U_3 = \Psi_i')$ and $\Delta_5 = \Delta_4 \cdot (U_4 = \Psi_i'')$.

Figure 1: A tableau for $\mathcal{E}_0 \vdash_{()} \Phi_i$

suggest that the style of proof offered here allows a perspicuous account of certain aspects of the behaviour of the system to be presented.

Let P be a set of processes with $|P|= n$. Let $F \subseteq P$ be the set of faulty processes and $N = P - F$ the set of non-faulty processes. Assume that $|F|= f < \frac{n}{3}$; in [12] it is shown that the problem is insoluble if $f \geq \frac{n}{3}$. Let V be the set of data values.

Each process $p \in P$ contains variables x_p and y_{pq} for $q \in P$ (and other variables described below). Of interest is the behaviour of the system when executed from an initial state in $M_0 = \{m \mid \text{dom}(m) = \{x_p \mid p \in P\}\}$. The intention is that the variables y_{pq} be assigned values in such a way that a condition called *interactive consistency* [12] is achieved: it is required that

if $N(p)$ and $N(q)$ then for all r, $y_{pr} = y_{qr}$, and if, in addition, $N(r)$ then $y_{pr} = x_r$.

In order to achieve interactive consistency, a number $(f+1)$ of rounds of exchanges of data values amongst the processes take place. These exchanges are followed by an independent computation by each process p in which, on the basis of the data received, it assigns values to the y_{pq}. To describe the program a little notation is convenient: for $i \geq 0$ let $P_{\leq i} = \{w \in P^* \mid |w| \leq i\}$. In addition to those mentioned above, process p contains also variables x_{pw} for $w \in P_{\leq f+1}$. The idea is that the value assigned to $x_{p1\,p2\ldots pm}$ is the value which $p2$ tells $p1$ that $p3$ tells $p2$ that ... that pm tells $p(m-1)$ is the value of x_{pm}.

We may represent process p by the following program $T(p)$:

$$T(p) = R(p,1); \cdots; R(p, f+1); S(p)$$

where $R(p,i)$ describes p's part in the ith round of exchanges and $S(p)$ the final computation of the values of the y_{pq}. To describe $R(p,i)$ a little more notation is useful. For $q \in P$ and fixed i with $1 \leq i \leq f+1$ let $w[q,1], \ldots, w[q,K]$ be the lexicographical ordering of $\{w \in P^* \mid |w| = i \text{ and } w(1) = q\}$ where $w(1)$ is the first element of w and $K = n^{i-1}$. Then for $p \in N$ and $1 \leq i \leq f+1$ $R(p,i)$ is the program:

$$(\|_{j=1}^{K}(x_{pw[p,j]} := x_{w[p,j]}) \qquad (1)$$

$$\| \quad (\|_{q \neq p}(c_{qp}?x_{pw[q,1]}; \ldots; c_{qp}?x_{pw[q,K]}))$$

$$\| \quad (\|_{q \neq p}(c_{pq}!x_{w[p,1]}; \ldots; c_{pq}!x_{w[p,K]})) \qquad (2)$$

For $p \in F$ $R(p,i)$ differs only in that the values assigned in (1) and output in (2) may be arbitrary.

The program $S(p)$ is the call

$$S(p, P, f, \{x_{pw} \mid w \in P_{\leq f+1}\}, \{y_{pq} \mid q \in P\})$$

of the recursive procedure with body:

$y_{pp} := x_p$;
$\|_{q \neq p}($ if $(\exists v. \exists Q \subseteq P.\ |Q| > \frac{|P|+f}{2} \wedge \forall w \in Q_{\leq f}.\ x_{pwq} = v)$

```
        then y_pq := some such v { it will be uniquely determined }
    else (S(p, P − {q}, f − 1, {x_pw | w ∈ (P − {q})_≤f}, {z_pr | r ∈ P − {q}}) ;
        if (∃v. ∃R ⊆ P − {q}. |R| ≥ ⌊(|P|+f)/2⌋ ∧ ∀r ∈ R. p_pr = v)
            then y_pq := some such v { it will be uniquely determined }
        else y_pq := ⊥ { a default value }))
```

The final program π_0 is then

$$\pi_0 = ||_{p \in P} T(p)$$

Interest lies in the properties of the initial configurations in $\Pi_0 = \{(\pi_0, m_0) \mid m_0 \in M_0\}$ which we now investigate.

First we introduce atomic formulae $D(pwq)$ and $C(pwq)$ for $p, q \in P$ and $w \in P_{\leq f}$ such that in the intended interpretation

$$\begin{array}{lll}(\pi, m) \models D(pwq) & \text{iff} & x_{pwq} \in \text{dom}(m) \\ (\pi, m) \models C(pwq) & \text{iff} & m(x_{pwq}) = m(x_q)\end{array}$$

and let B be the formula

$$\bigwedge\{D(pwq) \Longrightarrow C(pwq) \mid N(pwq)\}$$

where $N(u)$ means $N(r)$ for all r in u.

We first show that B is invariant, i.e. that $\Pi_0 \models \nu Z. B \wedge [-]Z$, by establishing that the following tableau is successful:

$$\dfrac{\Pi_0 \vdash_{()} \nu Z. B \wedge [-]Z}{\dfrac{\Pi \vdash_{()} \nu Z. B \wedge [-]Z}{\dfrac{\Pi \vdash_{\Delta} U}{\dfrac{\Pi \vdash_{\Delta} B \wedge [-]U}{\begin{array}{cc}\Pi \vdash_{\Delta} B & \dfrac{\Pi \vdash_{\Delta} [-]U}{\Pi' \vdash_{\Delta} U} \\ \cdots & \end{array}}}}}$$

where Δ is $(U = \nu Z. B \wedge [-]Z)$, Π is the set of configurations reachable from configurations in Π_0, and Π' is the set of immediate successors of configurations in Π.

Certainly $\Pi' \vdash_{\Delta} U$ is a successful terminal as $\Pi' \subseteq \Pi$. Suppose that from $\Pi \vdash_{\Delta} B$ an unsuccessful terminal is reached. Then there is a shortest pwq such that $(\pi, m) \models D(pwq) \wedge \neg C(pwq)$ for some (π, m) reachable from some $(\pi_0, m_0) \in \Pi_0$. Let $r = wq(1)$. The only assignment to x_{pwq} is $x_{pwq} := x_{wq}$ if $r = p$, or it results from a communication $c_{rp}?x_{pwq} || c_{rp}!x_{wq}$ otherwise. In either case since $m(x_{wq}) = m(x_q)$ by minimality of pwq, it follows that $m(x_{pwq}) = m(x_q)$. Contradiction. Hence the tableau is successful. Note also that since each x_{pwq} is assigned a value only once, the truth of $D(pwq)$ and hence that of $C(pwq)$ is preserved once it is established.

Now let A be an atomic formula expressing interactive consistency in the intended interpretation:

$(\pi, m) \models A$ iff for all p, q, r, $y_{pq} \in \mathrm{dom}(m)$ and if $N(p)$, $N(q)$ and $F(r)$ then $m(y_{pr}) = m(y_{qr})$ and $m(y_{pq}) = m(x_q)$.

We show that interactive consistency is achieved by establishing that the following tableau is successful:

$$\dfrac{\dfrac{\dfrac{\dfrac{\Pi_0 \vdash_{()} \mu Y. A \vee ([-]Y \wedge \langle - \rangle tt)}{\Pi \vdash_{()} \mu Y. A \vee ([-]Y \wedge \langle - \rangle tt)}}{\Pi \vdash_{\Delta} V}}{\Pi \vdash_{\Delta} A \vee ([-]V \wedge \langle - \rangle tt)}}{\Pi_1 \vdash_{\Delta} A \qquad \dfrac{\Pi_2 \vdash_{\Delta} [-]V \wedge \langle - \rangle tt}{\dfrac{\Pi_2 \vdash_{\Delta} [-]V}{\Pi_2' \vdash_{\Delta} V} \quad \dfrac{\Pi_2 \vdash_{\Delta} \langle - \rangle tt}{g(\Pi_2) \vdash_{\Delta} tt}}}$$

where Δ is $(Y = \mu Y. A \vee ([-]Y \wedge \langle - \rangle tt))$, Π is the set of configurations reachable from configurations in Π_0, $\Pi_1 = \{(\pi, m) \mid (\pi, m) \models A\}$, $\Pi_2 = \Pi - \Pi_1$, Π_2' is the set of immediate successors of configurations in Π_2, and $g : \Pi_2 \longrightarrow g(\Pi_2)$ is a total function.

That $\Pi_1 \vdash_{\Delta} A$ is a successful terminal is immediate. The success of $\Pi_2' \vdash_{\Delta} V$ follows from the fact that $\Pi_2' \subseteq \Pi$ together with the observation that π_0 is a finite terminating program. Since if there is a trail from (π, m) at the companion to (π', m') at the terminal, $(\pi, m) \longrightarrow^* (\pi', m')$, it follows that the well-foundedness condition is met.

It remains to show that a suitable function g exists, or equivalently that if $(\pi_0, m_0) \longrightarrow^* (\pi, m) \not\longrightarrow$ then $(\pi, m) \models A$. By examining π_0 we observe that we must have $\pi = \lambda$ and hence $y_{pq} \in \mathrm{dom}(m)$ for all p, q. Notice also that, by an earlier remark, each configuration in a suffix of the run $(\pi_0, m_0) \longrightarrow^* (\pi, m)$ satisfies $D(pwq)$ and hence $C(pwq)$ provided $N(pwq)$. Hence it suffices to show that the procedures $S(p)$ achieve interactive consistency given the correct values of the x_{pwq} for $N(pwq)$.

The argument from [12] to establish this is as follows. The proof is by induction on f. If $f = 0$ the result is immediate since each y_{pq} is assigned the value of x_q as required. Suppose $f > 0$. Assume $N(p)$ and $N(q)$.

First note that $|N| > \frac{|P|+f}{2}$, since $|P| > 3f$, and $\forall w \in N_{\leq f}. m(x_{pwq}) = m(x_q)$. Moreover if $|Q| > \frac{|P|+f}{2}$ and $\forall w \in Q_{\leq f}. m(x_{pwq}) = v$, then since $N \cap Q \neq \emptyset$, $v = m(x_q)$. Hence in this case $m(y_{pq}) = m(x_q)$ as required.

Now suppose $F(r)$. If $|Q| > \frac{|P|+f}{2}$ and $\forall w \in Q_{\leq f}. m(x_{pwr}) = v$, and $|Q'| > \frac{|P|+f}{2}$ and $\forall w \in Q'_{\leq f}. m(x_{qwr}) = v'$, then since $Q \cap Q' \cap N \neq \emptyset$ it follows that $m(y_{pr}) = m(y_{qr})$. If Q, v are as above but no such Q', v' exist, than setting $R = Q - \{q\}$, $|R| \geq \lfloor \frac{|P|+f}{2} \rfloor$ and $\forall s \in R. \forall w \in P_{\leq f-1}. m(x_{qws}) = m(x_{qpws}) = m(x_{pws}) = v$ since $N(p)$, and so again $m(y_{pr}) = m(y_{qr})$. Similarly if Q', v' but no Q, v as above exist.

Finally if both $S(p)$ and $S(q)$ make recursive calls then by induction hypothesis for all s, $m(z_{ps}) = m(z_{qs})$, and hence it again follows that $m(y_{pr}) = m(y_{qr})$. This completes the proof.

6 Further Issues

It is often the case that in order to establish a liveness property of a system, a fairness or progress assumption is required. In the analysis of Knuth's program in Section 5, the appropriate assumption is incorporated into the temporal property. A natural alternative approach is to delimit a family of *admissible* runs through a transition system. This leads naturally to an *extended labelled transition system*, a structure $\mathcal{T} = (\mathcal{P}, \{\xrightarrow{a} \mid a \in \mathcal{L}\}, \Sigma)$ with Σ (or $\Sigma_{\mathcal{T}}$) the set of admissible runs through $\mathcal{T}$. Associated with such structures are temporal mu-calculi (in the terminology of [16]). A natural question is if the tableau system can be extended to these logics. Another important issue is modularity: can the tableau system underpin compositional logics of concurrency as presented in [1,15]? As exemplified in Section 5, the present technique involves global analyses of systems. The development of techniques to allow a less monolithic approach is an important problem. A further issue is the state space problem. The tableau system by grouping states into families avoids this problem. A useful area for examination is networks of similar processes [5]. Finally, the provision of machine support for applications of the tableau technique, a move from the fully automatic model checking of the finite-state case (as in [W18] for example) to machine-assisted proof, is worthy of investigation.

References

[1] H. Barringer, R. Kuiper and A. Pnueli, *Now You May Compose Temporal Logic Specifications*, in Proc. 16th Symp. Theory of Comp. ACM Press, 1984.

[2] J. Bradfield, *Proving Temporal Properties of Petri Nets*, to appear in Proc. of 11th International Conference on Applications and Theory of Petri Nets, Paris, June 1990.

[3] J. Bradfield and C. Stirling, *Verifying Temporal Properties of Procesees*, submitted for publication.

[4] E. Clarke, E. Emerson and A. Sistla, *Automatic Verification of Finite-State Systems Using Temporal Logic Specifications: a Practical Approach*, in Proc. 10th Annual ACM Symp. in Principles of Programming Languages, 1983.

[5] E. Clarke and O. Grumberg, *The Model Checking Problem for Concurrent Systems With Many Simple Processes*, in Procs. Temporal Logic in Specification, eds. B. Banieqbal, H. Barringer and A. Pnueli, Springer LNCS 398, 1989.

[6] E. Emerson and C.-L. Lei, *Efficient Model Checking in Fragments of the Propositional Mu-Calculus*, in Proc. 1st IEEE Symp. on Logic in Computer Science, 1986.

[7] E. Emerson and J. Srinivasan, *Branching Time Temporal Logic*, in Proc. Workshop on Linear Time, Branching Time and Partial Order in Logics and Models for Concurrency, eds. J. de Bakker, W.-P. de Roever and G. Rozenberg, Springer LNCS 354, 1989.

[8] D. Knuth, *Additional Comments on a Problem in Concurrent Program Control*, Comm. ACM, 9/5 1966.

[9] D. Kozen, *Results on the Propositional μ-calculus*, Theoretical Computer Science, 27 1983.

[10] K. Larsen, *Proof Systems for Hennessy-Milner Logic with Recursion*, to appear in Information and Computation.

[11] Z. Manna and A. Pnueli, *The Anchored Version of the Temporal Framework*, in Proc. Workshop on Linear Time, Branching Time and Partial Order in Logics and Models for Concurrency, eds. J. de Bakker, W.-P. de Roever and G. Rozenberg, Springer LNCS 354, 1989.

[12] M. Pease, R. Shostak and L. Lamport, *Reaching Agreement in the Presence of Faults*, Journal ACM, 27 1980.

[13] G. Plotkin, *A Structural Approach to Operational Semantics*, Technical Report DAIMI FN-19, University of Aarhus 1981.

[14] V. Pratt, *A Decidable Mu-Calculus*, in Proc. 22nd IEEE Foundations of Computer Science, 1981.

[15] C. Stirling, *A Generalization of Owicki-Gries's Hoare Logic for a Concurrent While Language*, Theoretical Computer Science 58 (1988).

[16] C. Stirling, *Modal and Temporal Logics*, chapter to appear in Handbook of Logic in Computer Science, OUP 1990.

[17] C. Stirling and D. Walker, *Local Model Checking in the Modal Mu-Calculus*, in Proc. Intl. Joint Conf. on Theory and Practice of Software Development, eds. J. Diaz and F. Orejas, Springer LNCS 351, 1989.

[18] D. Walker, *Automated Analysis of Mutual Exclusion Algorithms Using CCS*, Formal Aspects of Computing (1989) 1.

Traps, Free Choice and Home States[1]

(Extended Abstract)

Eike Best
Institut für Informatik, Universität Hildesheim, D-3200 Hildesheim

Ludmila Cherkasova
Computing Center, USSR Academy of Sciences, 630090 Novosibirsk

Jörg Desel
Institut für Informatik, Technische Universität München, D-8000 München

Javier Esparza
Institut für Informatik, Universität Hildesheim, D-3200 Hildesheim

1 Introduction

The free choice Petri net shown in Figure 1 has a live and bounded (even safe) marking which is not a home state; from any other reachable marking, it is impossible to reach the initial marking again. The net also has an unmarked trap $\{s_0, s_2, s_3, s_5, s_6\}$, that is, a set of places with the property that every output transition of the set is also an input transition of the set.

The full paper [1] presents a proof that the non-existence of an unmarked trap actually characterises the home state property. The present note introduces the basic notions, gives an outline of the proof and describes a series of related results and consequences.

We use the concepts of a Petri net, a marked net, a transition sequence, the set $[M\rangle$ of markings reachable from a given marking M, liveness, boundedness, safeness (1-boundedness) etc. in their usual meaning; the reader is referred, e.g., to [3]. A net (S, T, F) is free choice iff

$$\forall t_1, t_2 \in T, t_1 \neq t_2 \colon \ {}^\bullet t_1 \cap {}^\bullet t_2 \neq \emptyset \ \Rightarrow \ |{}^\bullet t_1| = 1 = |{}^\bullet t_2|.$$

Let $N = (S, T, F)$ be a net. We call a marking M a home state of N iff

$$\forall M' \in [M\rangle \colon \ M \in [M'\rangle.$$

[1]Work done partly within the Esprit Basic Research Action No.3148 D-E-M-O-N - Design Methods Based on Nets.

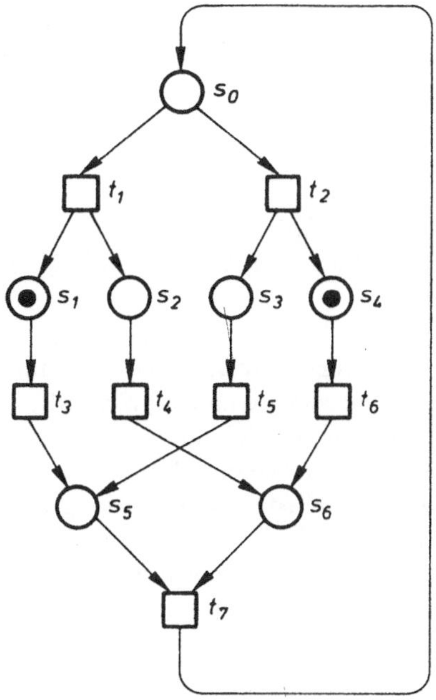

Figure 1: A basic example

Let $\Sigma = (S, T, F, M_0)$ be a net with an initial marking M_0. We call a marking M a home state of Σ iff

$$\forall M' \in [M_0\rangle\colon\ \ M \in [M'\rangle.$$

Remark 1.1

Note that there is a subtle difference between the home states of a net N in general (taking into account no initial marking) and the home states of a system Σ in particular (taking into account an initial marking M_0). Every home state of a system $\Sigma = (S, T, F, M_0)$ is also a home state of its underlying net $N = (S, T, F)$. But a home state of (S, T, F) may fail to be a home state of Σ because there might be a marking $M' \in [M_0\rangle$ such that $M \notin [M'\rangle$ (this is certainly true if $M \notin [M_0\rangle$, but it might also be true if $M \in [M_0\rangle$). The distinction is necessary to understand the connection between the various results to be explained below. ■ 1.1

Let (S, T, F) be a net. A set of places $Q \subseteq S$ is called a trap iff $Q \neq \emptyset$ and $Q^\bullet \subseteq {}^\bullet Q$. A set $Q \subseteq S$ is called unmarked (or marked) under a marking M iff $M(Q) = 0$ (respectively, $M(Q) > 0$). The salient property of a trap is that if it is marked once ($M(Q) > 0$) then it is marked always ($M'(Q) > 0$ for all $M' \in [M\rangle$).

2 The General Setting

First, we quote the main result from [1].

Theorem 2.1

Let $N = (S, T, F)$ be a free choice net and let M be a live and bounded marking of N. Then M is a home state of N if and only if every trap $Q \subseteq S$ is marked under M.

Proof: The direction ($\Rightarrow$) is very easy to prove. Assume that M is a marking of $N = (S, T, F)$ such that some trap $Q \subseteq S$ satisfies $M(Q) = 0$. By the strong connectedness of (S, T, F) (which follows from the liveness and boundedness of (S, T, F, M) [3]), every place of Q has at least one input transition. Hence by the liveness of (S, T, F, M), some marking $M' \in [M\rangle$ is reachable such that Q is marked under M'. Because a trap, once marked, remains marked, we have $M \notin [M'\rangle$. Hence M is not a home state.
The difficulties are buried in the proof of ($\Leftarrow$). This proof is given in [1].
■ 2.1

From [2, 7] we recall the following result:

Fact 2.2

Let $\Sigma = (S, T, F, M_0)$ be a free choice system with a live and bounded initial marking M_0. Then there is a marking $M \in [M_0\rangle$ which is a home state of Σ.
■ 2.2

This result cannot directly be interpreted as a consequence of Theorem 2.1, since it ensures the existence of a marking reachable from every successor of the initial marking, while from Theorem 2.1, it is only immediate that some reachable marking M exists which is reachable from every other marking in $[M\rangle$ (not necessarily $[M_0\rangle$). The existence of some reachable home state of N (rather than of Σ) follows from boundedness:

Fact 2.3

Let $\Sigma = (N, M_0)$ be a bounded system with the underlying net $N = (S, T, F)$. Then there is a marking $M \in [M_0\rangle$ such that M is a home state of N.

Proof: The strongly connected components $\{R_1, R_2, \ldots\}$ of the reachability graph of Σ can be partially ordered by the relation $R_i \preceq R_j$, meaning that a directed path leads from R_i to R_j. By the boundedness of Σ, the reachability graph is finite. Hence $\preceq$ has at least one maximal element. All markings in such an element are home states of N.
■ 2.3

As already mentioned, any home state of Σ is also a home state of N. For live and bounded free choice systems, we have a stronger result:

Fact 2.4

Let $\Sigma = (N, M_0)$ with $N = (S, T, F)$ be a live and bounded free choice system. Then M is a home state of Σ iff $M \in [M_0\rangle$ and M is a home state of N.

Proof: ($\Rightarrow$) is immediate: $M \in [M_0\rangle$ follows from $M_0 \in [M_0\rangle$, and then, $M' \in [M\rangle$ implies $M' \in [M_0\rangle$.
To prove ($\Leftarrow$), let $M \in [M_0\rangle$ be a home state of N. Let $\tilde{M}$ be a home state of Σ (which exists by Fact 2.2). Let $M' \in [M_0\rangle$ be arbitrary. Then $\tilde{M} \in [M'\rangle \cap [M\rangle$, since $\tilde{M}$ is a home state of Σ. Since $\tilde{M} \in [M\rangle$ and M is a home state of N, we have $M \in [\tilde{M}\rangle$. Since $\tilde{M} \in [M'\rangle$, we also have $M \in [M'\rangle$. This proves that M is also a home state of Σ. ∎ 2.4

Together, Fact 2.2 and Fact 2.4 show that the reachability graph of a live and bounded free choice system $\Sigma = (N, M_0)$ ends with a unique maximal (in the sense of $\preceq$) strongly connected component which equals the set of home states of Σ and also the set of home states of N which are reachable from $[M_0\rangle$. For this reason, we may speak merely of 'home state' from now on.
Finally, we state three consequences of Theorem 2.1. The first one shows that any transition sequence which contains every transition at least once must necessarily produce a home state. This property has been conjectured in [5] where it has been phrased in terms of well-behaved bipolar schemata which (under the translation given there) correspond to a class of live and bounded free choice nets.

Corollary 2.5

Let $\Sigma = (S, T, F, M_0)$ be a live and bounded free choice system. Let $M_0[\tau\rangle M$ with a transition sequence $\tau \in T^*$ such that every transition of T occurs at least once in τ. Then M is a home state.

Proof: By the liveness and boundedness of Σ, every place of S has at least one input transition. Hence during τ, every trap has been marked at least once. Since traps, once marked, cannot become unmarked, M must be a marking of (S, T, F) at which every trap is marked. The result follows with Theorem 2.1. ∎ 2.5

The second corollary shows that the home state property is monotonic.

Corollary 2.6

Let $N = (S, T, F)$ be a free choice net and let M be a live and bounded marking of N. If M is a home state then every marking M' with

$$\{s \in S \mid M(s) > 0\} \subseteq \{s \in S \mid M'(s) > 0\}$$

(which is true in particular if $M \leq M'$) is also a home state.

Proof: Immediate with Theorem 2.1 and the analogous monotonicity properties of liveness and boundedness for free choice nets (see [6]). ∎ 2.6

The monotonicity of the home state property can be used to define a procedure which allows the systematic derivation of all home states of a given structurally live and bounded free choice net from the live and bounded markings of its T-components [1].
The last corollary states that the home state property is polynomially decidable:

Corollary 2.7

Let $N = (S, T, F)$ be a free choice net such that all markings of N are bounded. Let M be a marking of N. Then it is decidable in polynomial time whether M is a home state of N.

Proof: (Sketch.) Using the algorithm of [4], it is possible to check in polynomial time whether or not M is live. If M is not live then M is not a home state (unless no transition is enabled at M, which is also easily determined in polynomial time). If M is live, Theorem 2.1 can be applied, and the methods of [4] can be adapted in the following way to check whether all traps are marked in polynomial time. The algorithm to check liveness [4] reduces the problem to a linear programming problem. The problem of finding all traps can be solved by an analogous linear programming problem, since traps are defined symmetrically to the structures which are examined in the algorithm for deciding liveness. ∎ 2.7

References

[1] E. Best, L. Cherkasova, J. Desel and J. Esparza: Traps, Free Choice and Home States. Informatik-Berichte Nr.5/90, Institut für Informatik, Universität Hildesheim (1990).

[2] E. Best and K. Voss: Free Choice Systems have Home States. Acta Informatica 21, 89–100 (1984).

[3] E. Best and J. Desel: Partial Order Behaviour and Structure of Petri Nets. To appear in: Formal Aspects of Computing Vol.2 (1990).

[4] J. Esparza and M. Silva: A Polynomial Time Algorithm to Decide Liveness of Bounded Free Choice Nets. Technical Report, Universidad de Zaragoza (1989).

[5] H.J. Genrich and P.S. Thiagarajan: A Theory of Bipolar Synchronization Schemes. Theoretical Computer Science 30, 241–318 (1984).

[6] W. Reisig: Petri Nets - an Introduction. Springer EATCS Monographs in Theoretical Computer Science Vol.4 (1985).

[7] W. Vogler: Live and Bounded Free Choice Nets have Home States. Petri Net Newsletters Vol. 32, published by GI (Gesellschaft für Informatik) (1989).

A Denotational Semantics for Synchronous and Asynchronous Behavior with Multiform Time

(extended abstract)

Marly Roncken

Philips Research Laboratories, Bldg. WAY 4.75

P.O. Box 80000, 5600 JA Eindhoven, The Netherlands

*Rob Gerth**

Eindhoven University of Technology

P.O. Box 513, 5600 MB Eindhoven, The Netherlands

Abstract

We develop a denotational semantics for a concurrent language that allows both synchronous and various degrees of asynchronous behavior. Here, synchrony means that parallel components execute within the same timing regime—e.g., because they share the same clock—whereas asynchrony means that the timing regimes of the components are independent—e.g., because their clocks are unrelated. The semantics allows the timing of components. But time is *multiform* in the sense that different parallel components have different timing regimes. This paper serves as a study to appraise and solve some of the semantic problems that are posed by the task of describing the timed behavior of digital systems. In the course of this study we define a semantics for a language related to a VLSI description language developed at Philip's Research Laboratories.

1 Introduction

The immediate subjects of this paper are

1. a computation model that allows behavior to be timed w.r.t. multiple timing regimcs (e.g., by having multiple clocks) and that forces progress of components where possible, and

2. a programming language that allows both synchrony and asynchrony, synchronized channel communications, and sharing of variables.

*The author is currently working in and partially supported by BRA project P3096: "Formal Methods and Tools for the Development of Distributed and Real-Time Systems (SPEC)"

These ingredients form an important part in the specification of digital systems. This abstract addresses some of the semantic issues that are posed by the computation model and by the language.

The computation model is a necessary one, if one wants to time systems. When no bounds are known on the time at which an action is started after it becomes enabled, then no time bounds can be imposed upon the system as a whole. From a theoretical point of view, the most salient feature of digital systems is the presence of timing regimes, e.g., of clocks that drive the execution in the various components to more or less extend. The most salient, because (quantitative) timing has been the last behavioral aspect of systems to be dealt with formally, and is still the least well understood.

In practice, timing is one of the most troublesome aspects in the design of digital systems [15]. On the circuit level one tends to want *synchronous designs* in which the components are sequenced and timed with respect to a system-wide clock. Such designs tend to be small and fast. But problems arise when integration and size increase, because it takes time to distribute the clock-signal and to distribute other information within a clock-cycle. This not only demonstrates some problems with timing of circuits, but also suggests to introduce components that operate *asynchronously* with respect to each other; and, more generally, to introduce components that are timed w.r.t. separate clocks. On the system level the necessity of the latter is immediately obvious: the devices on, e.g., a system-bus operate asynchronously for all practical purposes. In general, the increase in functional behavior already forces the introduction of more asynchronous components.

Asynchronicity presupposes some kind of synchronization mechanism in order to exchange information. Within a synchronous part, 'communication' is often through writing to and reading from data-stores (i.e., through shared variables).

The language *Asynchronous Modules, AM,* on which these semantic investigations are based, contains all of the above ingredients. AM allows concurrently executing components, that interact through the synchronized exchange of values along channels or through the sharing of variables. Such components can be specified to execute with an arbitrary degree of asynchronicity: the parallel composition of two components allows the (separate) timing regimes of the components to be related. This can be done in such a way as to get complete asynchronicity as well as to get pure synchronicity and everything in between. Components themselves can be sequential or can contain parallel sub components.

Our aim is a so-called *linear* semantics in which a real time computation is modeled by a function that associates collections of observations with every point in time. Ideally, the semantic composition operators should be *local* in the sense that they should be defined pointwise and then be freely extended to functions. Such a semantics is easy for reasoning with and is easy to lift to a specification logic (see e.g. [9]).

This is achieved by introducing observables that record various types of activity and inactivity.

Our research is based on a number of sources. The computation model, known as *maximal parallelism*, originates in [19]. The semantic techniques for dealing with this model were introduced in [13]. They were further developed for purely synchronous languages in [10,5] and, independently, in [14]. Denotational treatment of (standard) interleaving can be found in the seminal [11]. In a linear history setting, it is implicit in [17] and appears explicitly in [4,1].

The rest of the paper is structured as follows. Section 2 introduces the computation model and the language. The observable behavior is explained in Section 3 and formalized in Section 4. Section 5 defines the denotational semantics. Section 6 discusses the results and comments on future work. We finish this section by establishing some notation.

Notation

There is a set of values *Val*, a set of variables *Var*, a set of expressions *Exp*, a set of channels *Chan*and a set of Component variables, *Cvar*, with respectively v, x, e, c and X as meta variables. Let $Var(e)$ be the set of variables appearing in the expression e. We use $\mathcal{A}$ for $Var \cup Chan$, with a as meta variable. The set of states Σ is $Var \mapsto Val$, with meta variable σ. There is an evaluation function, $\mathcal{E}: Exp \mapsto \Sigma \mapsto Val$, for expressions.

Any function $f: Dom \mapsto Ran$ is pointwise extended to $f: \mathcal{P}(Dom) \mapsto \mathcal{P}(Ran)$ by $f(D) = \bigcup\{f(d) \mid d \in D\}$ for $D \subseteq Dom$. For $c \in Ran$ and $d \in Dom$, $f[c/d]$ denotes the function that is like f, except that $f[c/d](d) = c$. Function composition, $f \circ g$, is defined by $f \circ g(x) = f(g(x))$.

If A is a set, then A^* is the set of finite sequences over A, A^ω is the set of infinite sequences over A, and $A^\dagger = A^* \cup A^\omega$.

There is some time domain $\mathcal{T} \cup \{\infty\}$ where $\infty \notin \mathcal{T}$, with metavariables t, $t_0, \ldots$. It has a commutative and associative operation $+$ for addition, and a linear ordering $<$ with respectively 0 and ∞ as minimal and maximal elements. The $+$ and $<$ satisfy: $\forall t_0, t_1 \;\; t_0 < t_1 \rightarrow \exists t \;\; t_1 = t_0 + t$ and $\forall t \;\; t + \infty = \infty$.

2 The language Asynchronous Modules (AM)

Our computational model is one in which the number of actions executed is maximal at every time instance.

We stress that maximalizing activity is done *locally*. I.e., non-deterministic choices within a component are *not* resolved so as to maximalize activity globally. This contrasts with the original model in [19], which we feel is computationally less relevant—at least for our applications.

We now give the syntax of AM and the informal meaning of the language constructs. Let e range over expressions, b over boolean expressions, x over variables, A over sets of channels and variables, C over clock relations (as described below) and X over component variables.

In general, execution of a statement (i.e., component) requires access to resources, i.e., variables or channels, of various types. A component can have read or write access to a resource or can claim a resource. Claiming a resource means that the components reserves the resource for its own use only. Variables in AM are single write and multiple read. So, more than one component can have read access to a variable but, write access excludes any kind of access by other components. This means that having write access to a variable is the same as claiming the variable. Channel access can be acquired by at most two components at a time. One of them has read access; the other write has access. Acquiring read access to a channel has to occur simultaneously with acquiring write access to it (by another component). If a component has claimed a channel, this means that any communication along that channel should involve this component. Note that a component can be suspended forever if it cannot acquire the necessary resources. However, maximal progress implies that a component progresses as soon as it has acquired the necessary access to resources and, in case of a communication, as soon as it obtains a communication partner that has appropriate access to the channel used.

We first describe the atomic statements or components:

$x := e$ Execution suspends until write access to x and read access to the variables in e is obtained. Immediately after the resource have been obtained the assignment takes place.

$c!e$ A send statement first must acquire read access to the variables in $Var(e)$ and write access to channel c. Then the value of e is send along the channel to the communication partner (having acquired the read access).

$c?x$ A receive statement must first get write access to x and read access to c. Then it receives a value from c and assigns it to x.

b Execution of a (boolean) guard needs read access to the variables in $Var(b)$. Once acquired, b is evaluated and the resources are released. If b evaluates to *false* this repeats itself. If b evaluates to *true* the guard terminates (i.e., is passed). So b acts as a busy wait and allows components to synchronize on the values of variables.

If S_0 and S_1 are statements then the following compound statements can be constructed:

$S_0; S_1$ Standard sequential composition.

$S_0 [] S_1$ In a choice, both components start requesting the necessary resources. When a component is ready to execute it can be chosen to start executing. However, a component can never be chosen over the other one if the other one acquires its resources first.

$S_0 \|_C S_1$ This is the parallel execution of S_0 and S_1. Since components execute in different timing regimes, parallel composition allows such regimes to be related by a *timing relation*, $C \subseteq T \times T$, thus producing new timing regimes in which $S_0 [] S_1$ executes. A timing relation specifies the way(s) in which the timing regime of S_1 can be defined in terms of the other one. This is done using *retiming functions*, R which are compatible with C.

2–1 Definition. *A retiming function $R: \mathcal{T} \mapsto \mathcal{T}$ is compatible with C, $R \subseteq C$, if R is surjective and monotonic and if $\{(t, t') \mid f(t) = t'\} \subseteq C$ holds.*

For example, if $C = \{(t, 2t) \mid t \in \mathcal{T}\}$ then this expresses that S_0 executes twice as fast as S_0; if $C = id$ then both components run with the same speed; and if $C = \mathcal{T} \times \mathcal{T}$ then S_0 and S_1 execute completely asynchronous since any retiming function can be used to relate the timing regimes.

$\langle S \rangle_A$ A claim statement starts by claiming all the resources in A. Once these are acquired, S starts executing and when S terminates the resources are released again.

$S \backslash_A$ The hide statement simply hides the channels and variables in A.

X Component variables are needed to define recursive components.

$\mu X.S$ Recursive programs are defined using the μ-calculus. For example, $\mu X.S; X$ describes an endless loop with S as loop body.

3 Observable Behavior

The first task in defining a syntax-directed semantics is to decide what should be observable so that the syntactic structure of a component may direct the construction of its semantics. This calls for a classification of the interactions between a component and its environment.

We distinguish the following interactions:

- access to variables
- communications along channels
- timing

Shared variables may be read and written by more than one component. Hence, their values should be observable. Writing a variable requires exclusive access, in contrast with reading a variable which many components may do simultaneously. This means that reading and writing a variable are separate observables.

A communication along a channel c consists of two synchronized events:

- sending a value (of some expression e) along c ($c!e$)
- receiving the value v from c in a variable x ($c?x$)

Because communication involves two components, these events must be observable. We model the evaluation of e as a read event, and the receipt of v in x as a write event.

Variables and Channels are *claimable*. A claim on a variable x excludes any accesses but those of the claimant. A claim on a channel excludes any communications not involving the claimant. A channel can be claimed either for sending or for receiving or for both. Claiming a channel for either of these activities as well as claiming a variable are observable events. Since claiming a variable and having exclusive access to it have the same effect, we need no separate observable for write access.

In general, simultaneous access to resources—i.e., to channels or variables—is possible for only a limited number of components. Actions in other components that need these resources must be postponed. Maximal progress implies that a computation cannot postpone execution indefinitely unless the resources that it needs never become available. Hence, we need to observe both the requests for access and the kind of access that is needed for all the resources that are involved in the action.

To guarantee maximal progress, we have to know whether a component is executing or not.

As usual, sequential composition requires the observability of termination.

Note that observables describe aspects of a component's execution at a single point in time only. Hence, an execution of a component will be modeled by a function that associates collections of observables with every time instance.

4 Observable Behavior formalized

4–1 DEFINITION (Observables).

- The domain of observables, $\mathcal{O}$, is

$$
\begin{aligned}
\{\langle \sigma, rvar, rchan, wchan, rclaim, wclaim, req, \alpha, \tau \rangle \mid \\
& \sigma \in \Sigma \\
\wedge\ & rvar \in \mathcal{P}(Var) \\
\wedge\ & rchan \in \mathcal{P}(Chan \times Val) \\
\wedge\ & wchan \in \mathcal{P}(Chan \times Val) \\
\wedge\ & rclaim \in \mathcal{P}(Chan) \\
\wedge\ & wclaim \in \mathcal{P}(\mathcal{A}) \\
\wedge\ & req \in \mathcal{P}(\{\langle rreq, wreq \rangle \mid rreq \in \mathcal{P}(\mathcal{A}) \wedge wreq \in \mathcal{P}(\mathcal{A}) \wedge \\
& \qquad \langle rreq, wreq \rangle \neq \langle \emptyset, \emptyset \rangle\}) \\
\wedge\ & \alpha \in Bool \\
\wedge\ & \tau \in Bool \\
\}
\end{aligned}
$$

- Elements of $Chan \times Var$ are called *channel messages*.
- The fields have the following meaning:
  - σ: state
  - $rvar$: variables read
  - $rchan$: channel messages received
  - $wchan$: channel messages sent
  - $rclaim$: channels claimed for receiving

- *wclaim*: channels claimed for sending and variables claimed
- *rreq*: variables and channels requested for simultaneous reading or receiving
- *wreq*: variables and channels requested for simultaneous writing or sending
- *req*: the sets of resources and access types needed by an action
- α: indicates activity
- τ: indicates termination

The observable behavior of a single real-time computation is modeled by a function $f: \mathcal{T} \mapsto \mathcal{O}$. We use $f(t).\sigma$ to denote the state at time t, and likewise for the other fields. Such functions obey certain well-formedness restrictions, which are given below. The set of all such well-formed functions will be denoted by $\mathcal{F}$, with f, $f_0, \ldots$ and g, $g_0, \ldots$ as metavariables. Henceforth, the elements of $\mathcal{F}$ are simply called *behaviors*.

4–2 DEFINITION (Behaviors).

- For notational convenience, we define two predicates to identify empty fields. Let $f: \mathcal{T} \mapsto \mathcal{O}$, $t \in \mathcal{T}$ and *FIELDS* a set of fields (; i.e., $FIELDS \subseteq \{\sigma, rvar, rchan, wchan, rclaim, wclaim, req, \alpha, \tau\}$).

$$Empty(f, t, FIELDS) \Leftrightarrow \forall\, field \in FIELDS \setminus \{\sigma, \alpha, \tau\} \;\; f(t).field = \emptyset$$

$$Empty\_except(f, t, FIELDS) \Leftrightarrow \forall\, field \notin FIELDS \cup \{\sigma, \alpha, \tau\} \;\; f(t).field = \emptyset$$

- $f: \mathcal{T} \mapsto \mathcal{O}$ is a *behavior* if and only if f satisfies the following well-formedness restrictions for any $t_1 \in \mathcal{T}$:
  - *Finite variability:*

$$\forall\, field \;\; \forall\, t_0 < t_1 \rightarrow |\{f(t).field \mid t_0 \leq t \leq t_1\}| < \aleph_0$$

  - *Stability while reading:*

$$\forall\, t_0 < t_1 \, \forall\, x \;\; x \in \bigcap\{f(t).rchan \mid t_0 \leq t \leq t_1\} \rightarrow f(t_1).\sigma(x) = f(t_0).\sigma(x)$$

  - *Single write events:*

$$f(t_1).rvar \cap f(t_1).wclaim = \emptyset$$

  - *Matching 1-1 communications:*

$$\forall\, c \;\; |(f(t_1).rchan \cup f(t_1).wchan) \cap (\{c\} \times Val)| \leq 1$$

  - *Termination is final:*

$$f(t_1).\tau \rightarrow (\neg f(t_1).\alpha \wedge Empty\_except(f, t_1, \emptyset) \wedge \forall\, t \in \mathcal{T} \;\; t_0 \leq t \rightarrow f(t) = f(t_1))$$

- To express equality of two behaviors, f and g, w.r.t. a set of fields $FIELDS$, we use:

$$Equal(f, g, FIELDS) \Leftrightarrow \forall t \in \mathcal{T}\ \forall\, field \in FIELDS \quad f(t).field = g(t).field$$

$$Equal\_except(f, g, FIELDS) \Leftrightarrow \forall t \in \mathcal{T}\ \forall\, field \notin FIELDS \quad f(t).field = g(t).field$$

5 Denotational semantics

The denotational domain is $\mathcal{P}(\mathcal{F})$, with $\supseteq$ as the ordering relation. This is a cpo with $\mathcal{F}$ as least element.

Because the language contains recursion, we need environment functions Env: $Cvar \mapsto \mathcal{P}(F)$ to give meaning to component variables. We use the metavariable η to range over Env. The semantic function $\mathcal{D}$: $Stat \mapsto Env \mapsto \mathcal{P}(\mathcal{F})$ is defined in the subsequent sections.

In the definition of $\mathcal{D}$, we make frequent use of a catenation operation $.\hat{}.: (\mathcal{P}(\mathcal{F}) \times \mathcal{P}(\mathcal{F})) \mapsto \mathcal{P}(\mathcal{F})$, which is the pointwise extension of $.\hat{}.$ on behaviors as defined below.

5–1 Definition (Catenation of behaviors).

- Let $f, g \in \mathcal{F}$ and $t_0 = min(\{\infty\} \cup \{t \in \mathcal{T} \mid f(t).\tau\})$. Then

$$\begin{aligned} f\hat{}g(t) &= f(t), && \text{if } t < t_0 \\ &= g(t - t_0), && \text{otherwise} \end{aligned}$$

In general, we will use the notation fg instead of $f\hat{}g$.

5.1 Denotational semantics of atomic statements

The behavior of an atomic statement comprises three successive phases: the first phase to request the resources that are needed; the second one for execution; and the third one to adjust the observable state. We define semantic functions to describe each of the three phases: $Request(\cdot)$, $Execute(\cdot)$, and $Adjust(\cdot)$.

5–2 Definition.

- Let $REQ \subseteq \mathcal{P}(\mathcal{A}) \times \mathcal{P}(\mathcal{A})$. $Request$ describes the possible request phases for the resources in REQ. During this phase, there is no activity and, hence, no other observations can be made.

$$\begin{aligned} Request(REQ) = \{f \in \mathcal{F} \mid\ & \exists t_0\ (t_0 \neq \infty \rightarrow f(t_0).\tau) \wedge \\ & \forall t < t_0\ \ f(t).req = REQ \wedge \\ & \quad Empty\_except(f, t, \{req\}) \wedge \\ & \quad \neg f(t).\alpha \wedge \neg f(t).\tau \\ \} & \end{aligned}$$

- The collection of all requests:

$$Request = \bigcup\{Request(REQ) \mid REQ \subseteq \mathcal{P}(\mathcal{A}) \times \mathcal{P}(\mathcal{A})\}$$

- Let $T_0 \subseteq \mathcal{T}$, $RVAR \subseteq Var$, $RCHAN \subseteq Chan \times Val$, $WCHAN \subseteq Chan \times Exp$, and $WCLAIM \subseteq \mathcal{A}$. *Execute* describes the possible execute phases with duration in T_0. The other parameters specify the resources and access types that are claimed, together with the values send along the channels.

$$\begin{aligned}
&Execute(T_0, RVAR, RCHAN, WCHAN, RCLAIM, WCLAIM) = \\
&\quad \bigcup\{f \in \mathcal{F} \mid \ \exists\, t_0 \in T_0 \ \ f(t_0).\tau \wedge \forall\, t < t_0 \\
&\qquad\qquad f(t).rvar = RVAR \wedge f(t).rchan = RCHAN \wedge \\
&\qquad\qquad f(t).wchan = \{(c, \mathcal{E}(e)(f(0).\sigma) \mid (c,e) \in WCHAN\} \wedge \\
&\qquad\qquad f(t).rclaim = RCLAIM \wedge f(t).wclaim = WCLAIM \wedge \\
&\qquad\qquad Empty(f, t, \{req\}) \wedge f(t).\alpha \wedge \neg f(t).\tau \\
&\qquad \}
\end{aligned}$$

- Let $EXP \subseteq \mathcal{P}(Exp)$. *Adjust* updates the state so as to describe the effect of the previous execution phase. Each set in EXP gives a set of expressions whose values should be made equal (as an effect of the execution).

$$\begin{aligned}
Adjust(EXP) \;=\; &\{f \in \mathcal{F} \mid f(0).\tau \wedge \forall\, E \in EXP \ \forall\, e_0 \in E \ \forall\, e_1 \in E \\
&\mathcal{E}(e_0)(f(0).\sigma) = \mathcal{E}(e_1)(f(0).\sigma)\}
\end{aligned}$$

There is a function $\Delta\colon Stat \mapsto \mathcal{P}(\mathcal{T})$ that defines the durations of the atomic statements. To avoid infinite computations in zero time, we assume that $\Delta(S) > 0$ for any atomic S.

5.1.1 Semantic denotations of atomic statements

Assignment statements The three phases of behavior show clearly in the denotational semantics of $x := e$. It starts with continuous requests to read the variables of e and to write x. When access is gained to all these variables simultaneously, execution is started. Execution terminates in a state where x has the value of e. Because of the stability restriction on variables being read (see Definition 4–1), the value of e does not change during the execution. Note that execution may be postponed forever. Only when x and $Var(e)$ are claimed, as in $\langle S\rangle_{Var(e)\cup\{x\}}$, or hidden, as in $S\backslash_{Var(e)\cup\{x\}}$, it is required that execution starts as soon as these variables are available.

$$\begin{aligned}
\mathcal{D}(x := e)\eta \;=\; &Request(\{\langle Var(e), \{x\}\rangle\}) \\
&\ {}^\frown Execute(\Delta(x := e), Var(e), \emptyset, \emptyset, \emptyset, \{x\}) \\
&\quad {}^\frown Adjust(\{\{e, x\}\})
\end{aligned}$$

Send statements Because execution of $c!e$ does not change any variables, it is not necessary to include an adjustment phase. Similar to an assignment statement, execution may be postponed forever. Only when claiming or hiding c and $Var(e)$, it is required that communication takes place as soon as both a communication partner and $Var(e)$ are available.

$$\begin{aligned}\mathcal{D}(c!e)\eta \;=\; & \textit{Request}(\{\langle Var(e), \{c\}\rangle\}) \\ & {}^\frown\textit{Execute}(\Delta(c!e), Var(e), \emptyset, \{(c,e)\}, \emptyset, \emptyset)\end{aligned}$$

Receive statements The synchronizing $c!e$ statement for $c?x$ may come from a parallel component with a different timing regime. Thus, the denotational semantics of $c?x$ anticipates any duration for the communication. Likewise, any v is anticipated as value received via c. At parallel composition we require that durations and channel messages match. Again, the communication may be postponed forever. The reasons are similar to the ones for send statements.

$$\begin{aligned}\mathcal{D}(c?x)\eta \;=\; \bigcup_{v\in Val} & \textit{Request}(\{\langle\{c\}, \{x\}\rangle\}) \\ & {}^\frown\textit{Execute}(\mathcal{T}, \emptyset, \{(c,v)\}, \emptyset, \{c\}, \{x\}) \\ & {}^\frown\textit{Adjust}(\{\{v, x\}\})\end{aligned}$$

Boolean guards Note the repeated pattern of the three phases in the denotational semantics of b: first requests are issued to read the variables of b, then b is evaluated and the state is adjusted. This is repeated for as long as b evaluates to *false*. If b ever evaluates to *true*, the repetition stops and the guard is passed. As is the case for the other atomic statements, termination of a request phase depends on the environment.

$$\begin{aligned}\mathcal{D}(b)\eta \;=\; & (\textit{Request}(\{\langle Var(b), \emptyset\rangle\}) \\ & \quad {}^\frown\textit{Execute}(\Delta(b), Var(b), \emptyset, \emptyset, \emptyset, \emptyset) \\ & \quad {}^\frown\textit{Adjust}(\{\{\textit{false}, b\}\}) \\ &)^\dagger \\ & \quad {}^\frown\textit{Request}(\{\langle Var(b), \emptyset\rangle\}) \\ & \quad {}^\frown\textit{Execute}(\Delta(b), Var(b), \emptyset, \emptyset, \emptyset, \emptyset) \\ & \quad {}^\frown\textit{Adjust}(\{\{\textit{true}, b\}\})\end{aligned}$$

5–3 EXAMPLE.

- $\mathcal{D}(\textit{true})\eta = \textit{Execute}(\Delta(\textit{true}), \emptyset, \emptyset, \emptyset, \emptyset, \emptyset)$
- $\mathcal{D}(\textit{false})\eta = (\textit{Execute}(\Delta(\textit{false}), \emptyset, \emptyset, \emptyset, \emptyset, \emptyset))^\omega$

5.2 Denotational semantics of compound statements

In the denotational semantics of choice and parallel composition, we use a pointwise union operation $.\,\dot\cup\,. : (\mathcal{F} \times \mathcal{F}) \mapsto \mathcal{F}$ as defined below.

5–4 DEFINITION (pointwise union).

- Let $f, g \in \mathcal{F}$, and $t \in \mathcal{T}$.

$$\begin{aligned} f \uplus g(t).\sigma &= f(t).\sigma, \quad \text{if } \neg f(t).\tau \\ &= g(t).\sigma, \quad \text{otherwise} \\ f \uplus g(t).\alpha &= f(t).\alpha \vee f(t).\alpha \\ f \uplus g(t).\tau &= f(t).\tau \wedge f(t).\tau \end{aligned}$$

and for any other field:

$$f \uplus g(t).\mathit{field} = f(t).\mathit{field} \cup g(t).\mathit{field}$$

The following facts hold:

5–5 THEOREM.

- *.$\uplus$. is commutative and associative on the sets D_ϕ for any function $\phi: \mathcal{T} \mapsto \Sigma$, where*

$$D_\phi = \{f: \mathcal{T} \mapsto \mathcal{O} \mid \forall t \in \mathcal{T} \;\; \neg f(t).\tau \rightarrow f(t).\sigma = \phi(t)\}$$

- *Let $f, g \in \mathcal{F}$, then $f \uplus g \in \mathcal{F}$, if the following conditions are satisfied for every $t \in \mathcal{T}$:*
  - single write events:

$$\begin{aligned} (f(t).\mathit{rvar} \cup f(t).\mathit{wclaim}) \cap g(t).\mathit{wclaim} \cap \mathit{Var} &= \emptyset \quad \text{and} \\ (g(t).\mathit{rvar} \cup g(t).\mathit{wclaim}) \cap f(t).\mathit{wclaim} \cap \mathit{Var} &= \emptyset \end{aligned}$$

  - 1-1 communications:

$$(f(t).\mathit{rchan} \cap g(t).\mathit{rchan}) \cup (f(t).\mathit{wchan} \cap g(t).\mathit{wchan}) = \emptyset$$

  - matching communications:

$$\forall c \;\; |(f(t).\mathit{rchan} \cup g(t).\mathit{rchan}) \cap (f(t).\mathit{wchan} \cup g(t).\mathit{wchan}) \cap \{c\} \times \mathit{Val}| \leq 1$$

We use the predicate *Consistent* on $\mathcal{F} \times \mathcal{F}$ to express that two behaviors are contained in a domain D_ϕ and satisfy the conditions in the above theorem.

In the denotational semantics of claiming and of hiding, we use an auxiliary function *Maximize*: $\mathcal{P}(\mathcal{A}) \mapsto \mathcal{P}(F) \mapsto \mathcal{P}(F)$ to delete behaviors that do not model maximal progress. Its definition is given below:

5–6 DEFINITION. Let $A \subseteq \mathcal{A}$, $F \subseteq \mathcal{F}$, $f \in \mathcal{F}$, and $t \in \mathcal{T}$. The resources in A are available to the component in the sense that its environment does not use them.

- Let $\langle \mathit{RREQ}, \mathit{WREQ} \rangle \in \mathcal{P}(\mathcal{A}) \times \mathcal{P}(\mathcal{A})$. The predicate ***Submaximal*** expresses that an action that needs access to resources in A, as indicated by the record $\langle \mathit{RREQ}, \mathit{WREQ} \rangle$, can be executed unless some other event in the component prevents this access.

$$\begin{aligned} &\mathit{Submaximal}(\langle \mathit{RREQ}, \mathit{WREQ} \rangle, A, f, t) \Leftrightarrow \\ &\qquad \mathit{RREQ} \subseteq (A \cap \mathit{Var}) \setminus f(t).\mathit{wclaim} \cup (A \cap \mathit{Chan}) \setminus f(t).\mathit{rclaim} \wedge \\ &\qquad \mathit{WREQ} \subseteq (A \cap \mathit{Var}) \setminus (f(t).\mathit{rvar} \cup f(t).\mathit{wclaim}) \cup \\ &\qquad\qquad (A \cap \mathit{Chan}) \setminus f(t).\mathit{wclaim} \end{aligned}$$

- The predicate *Maximal* expresses that every event postponed by the component at a certain time indeed requires access to resources in A that is impossible to get at that time (because of the component's activity).

$$
\begin{aligned}
&\mathit{Maximal}(A, f, t) \Leftrightarrow \\
&\qquad \neg \exists \langle RREQ_0, WREQ_0\rangle \in f(t).req \ \exists \langle RREQ_1, WREQ_1\rangle \in f(t).req \\
&\qquad\quad RREQ_0 \cap Chan = WREQ_1 \cap Chan \wedge \\
&\qquad\quad \mathit{Submaximal}(\langle RREQ_0, WREQ_0\rangle, A, f, t) \wedge \\
&\qquad\quad \mathit{Submaximal}(\langle RREQ_1, WREQ_1\rangle, A, f, t)
\end{aligned}
$$

- The function *Maximize* deletes all behaviors that at some time instance are in conflict with maximal progress.

$$\mathit{Maximize}(A)(F) \quad = \quad \{f \in F \mid \forall t \in \mathcal{T} \ \mathit{Maximal}(A, f, t)\}$$

5.2.1 Semantic denotations of compound statements

Sequential statements As one would expect:

$$\mathcal{D}(S_0; S_1)\eta \quad = \quad (\mathcal{D}(S_0)\eta)^\frown(\mathcal{D}(S_1)\eta)$$

5–7 THEOREM.

- $\mathcal{D}(S_0; (S_1; S_2)) = \mathcal{D}((S_0; S_1); S_2)$

PROOF. $.^\frown.$ is associative. □

Choice statements The behavior of the choice between two alternatives starts with a request phase (requesting for both alternatives). An alternative that acquires its resources later than the other is never executed. So, the execute phase describes executions of the other alternative only. When resources are claimed or hidden, it is required that the request phase does not last longer than necessary.

$$
\begin{aligned}
&\mathcal{D}(S_0 \ [] \ S_1)\eta \quad = \\
&\qquad \{fg \mid \ \exists f_0 g_0 \in \mathcal{D}(S_0)\eta \ \exists f_1 g_1 \in \mathcal{D}(S_1)\eta \ \ f = f_0 \uplus f_1 \wedge \\
&\qquad\qquad\qquad g \in \{g_0, g_1\} \wedge \{f_0, f_1\} \subseteq \mathit{Request} \wedge \mathit{Equal}(f_0, f_1, \{\sigma, \tau\}) \wedge g(0).\alpha \\
&\qquad \}
\end{aligned}
$$

5–8 THEOREM.

- $\mathcal{D}(S_0 \ [] \ S_1) = \mathcal{D}(S_1 \ [] \ S_0)$
- $\mathcal{D}(S_0 \ [] \ (S_1 \ [] \ S_2)) = \mathcal{D}((S_0 \ [] \ S_1) \ [] \ S_2)$

PROOF. The main burden of proof is carried by Theorem 5–5. □

Parallel statements The semantic counterpart of parallel composition is defined below.

5–9 DEFINITION (Parallel composition of behaviors). From the timing relation C specified in the parallel composition of S_0 and S_1, we extract retiming functions R for the calibration of a timing regime of S_1 to one of S_0.

- Let $f, g \in \mathcal{F}$, and $C \subseteq \mathcal{T} \times \mathcal{T}$.

$$f \parallel_C g \;=\; \{f \uplus (g \circ R) \mid \mathit{Consistent}(f,g) \wedge R \subseteq C\}$$

- For sets of behaviors, we take the pointwise extension $. \parallel_C .: (\mathcal{P}(\mathcal{F}) \times \mathcal{P}(\mathcal{F})) \mapsto \mathcal{P}(\mathcal{F})$.

So:

$$\mathcal{D}(S_0 \parallel_C S_1)\eta \;=\; (\mathcal{D}(S_0)\eta) \parallel_C (\mathcal{D}(S_1)\eta)$$

5–10 THEOREM. $\cdot \parallel_{id} \cdot$ and $\cdot \parallel_{\mathcal{T}\times\mathcal{T}} \cdot$ *are commutative and associative.*

PROOF. For $C = id$ we have $f \uplus (g \circ R) = f \uplus g$ for any $R \subseteq C$. For $C = \mathcal{T} \times \mathcal{T}$ we have that $R \subseteq C \Leftrightarrow R^{-1} \subseteq C$. □

Claiming To model the effect of claiming, we use an auxiliary function $\mathit{Claim}: \mathcal{P}(\mathcal{A}) \mapsto \mathcal{P}(\mathcal{F}) \mapsto \mathcal{P}(\mathcal{F})$.

5–11 DEFINITION.

- Let $A \subseteq \mathcal{A}$ be the set of claimed resources and let $F \subseteq \mathcal{F}$. The function *Claim* adds the read and write claims for the resources in A to the behaviors in F.
  We just add the write claims for the variables in A. Getting access to a channel in A still depends on the presence of a communication partner. Such communication partners cannot communicate anymore with any other component. So, the fields *rclaim* and *wclaim* are updated respectively with the channels requested for reading and those requested for writing.

$$\begin{aligned}
\mathit{Claim}(A)(F) \;=\;& \\
& \{g \mid \exists\, f \in F \;\; \mathit{Equal_except}(f, g, \{\mathit{rclaim}, \mathit{wclaim}\}) \wedge \\
& \quad g(t).\mathit{rclaim} = f(t).\mathit{rclaim} \cup \\
& \qquad (A \cap \mathit{Chan} \cap \\
& \qquad\quad (\{c \mid \neg\exists v\ (c,v) \in f(t).\mathit{rchan} \cup f(t).\mathit{wchan}\} \cup \\
& \qquad\qquad f(t).\mathit{rreq})) \wedge \\
& \quad g(t).\mathit{wclaim} = f(t).\mathit{wclaim} \cup (A \cap \mathit{Var}) \cup \\
& \qquad (A \cap \mathit{Chan} \cap \\
& \qquad\quad (\{c \mid \neg\exists v\ (c,v) \in f(t).\mathit{rchan} \cup f(t).\mathit{wchan}\} \cup \\
& \qquad\qquad f(t).\mathit{wreq}))
\end{aligned}$$

Executing $\langle S\rangle_A$ requires exclusive access to the resources in A. Execution does not start until such access is gained; hence the request phase at the beginning. Since the resources in A are now available, any execution should now be maximal for A; hence the application of *Maximize*.

$$\begin{aligned}\mathcal{D}(\langle S\rangle_A)\eta &= \mathit{Request}(\{\langle A \cap \mathit{Chan}, A\rangle\}) \\ &\quad\frown(\mathit{Maximize}(A) \circ \mathit{Claim}(A)\ (\mathcal{D}(S)\eta))\end{aligned}$$

5–12 EXAMPLE.

- $\mathcal{D}(\langle x := e\rangle_{\{x\}}) = \mathcal{D}(x := e)$

Hiding Here, too, we need auxiliary functions.

5–13 DEFINITION. Let $A \subseteq \mathcal{A}$ and $F \subseteq \mathcal{F}$.

- The function *Hide* simply removes all observable involving resources in A, since the use of these resources has become hidden.

$$\begin{aligned}&\mathit{Hide}(A)(F) = \\ &\quad\{g \mid \exists\, f \in F\ \ \mathit{Equal}(f, g, \{\alpha, \tau\}) \wedge \\ &\qquad \forall\, t \in \mathcal{T}\ \ \forall\, x \in \mathit{Var} \setminus A\ \ f.\sigma(x) = g.\sigma(x) \wedge \\ &\qquad\ \ \forall\, \mathit{field} \in \{\mathit{rvar}, \mathit{rclaim}, \mathit{wclaim}\}\ \ g(t).\mathit{field} = f(t).\mathit{field} \setminus A \wedge \\ &\qquad\ \ \forall\, \mathit{field} \in \{\mathit{rchan}, \mathit{wchan}\}\ \ g(t).\mathit{field} = f(t).\mathit{field} \setminus (A \times \mathit{Val}) \wedge \\ &\qquad\ \ g(t).\mathit{req} = \{\langle \mathit{RREQ} \setminus A, \mathit{WREQ} \setminus A\rangle \mid \\ &\qquad\qquad\qquad \langle \mathit{RREQ}, \mathit{WREQ}\rangle \in f(t).\mathit{req} \setminus (A \times A)\} \\ &\quad\}\end{aligned}$$

- The predicate *Match* describes those behaviors in which every communication along a channel in A occurs within the component.

$$\mathit{Match}(A)(F) = \{f \in F \mid \forall\, t \in \mathcal{T}\ \ f(t).\mathit{rchan} \cap A = f(t).\mathit{wchan} \cap A\}$$

Then:

$$\mathcal{D}(S\backslash_A)\eta = \mathit{Hide}(A) \circ \mathit{Maximize}(A) \circ \mathit{Match}(A)\ (\mathcal{D}(S)\eta)$$

Recursive statements Because $\mathcal{D}$ is monotonic, we can define the denotational semantics of a recursive statement as a least fixpoint.

$$\begin{aligned}\mathcal{D}(X)\eta &= \eta(X) \\ \mathcal{D}(\mu X.S)\eta &= \mu\Phi.\mathcal{D}(S)(\eta[\Phi/X])\end{aligned}$$

6 Conclusion and future work

This paper describes a denotational, linear semantics for Asynchronous Modules with an execution model that forces progress within components to be maximal. The language is of interest in itself, since it generalizes an existing language for describing delay-insensitive circuits [2]. In that language, parallel components execute asynchronously and interact via synchronized communications along channels. It serves also as a vehicle to study some of the semantic issues met in specification languages for digital systems: synchronous and asynchronous behavior of various degree; synchronization and mutual exclusion of resources; and multiform time. The paper shows that a judicious choice of observations obtains a continuous, denotational and linear semantics that enables a straightforward description of these aspects.

As such, this paper forms a solid basis to develop a specification language for digital systems with a clean, easy to understand semantics. Among other things, the language and the semantic models should be able to describe more detailed constraints on the use of resources. Two other obvious research directions can be envisaged. One direction is the development of a broader specification framework, using a specification logic, such as temporal logic, that allows *descriptive* specifications of components which are subsequently reified into fully prescriptive specifications. A second direction is to investigate how our specifications can be (semi-) automatically compiled into VLSI-circuits. For purely asynchronous designs such a framework has been suggested in [3,2,18].

Acknowledgment

We were fortunate to be able to use Jozef Hooman's methodology for defining a denotational semantics. Without it, the semantics would have been less clean.

References

[1] BARRINGER, H., KUIPER, R., PNUELI, A. (1984), Now You May Compose Temporal Logic Specifications, *in* "Proceedings 16th Annual Symposium on Theory of Computing (STOC)", pp. 51–64, ACM.

[2] VAN BERKEL, C., SAEIJS, R. (1988), Compilation of Communicating Processes into Delay-Insensitive Circuits, *in* "Proceedings of the IEEE International Conference on Computer Design: VLSI in Computers and Processors", IEEE.

[3] EBERGEN, J. (1987), Translating Programs into Delay-Insensitive Circuits, Ph.D. thesis, Eindhoven University of Technology.

[4] GERTH, R. (1984), Transition Logic *in* "Proceedings 16th ACM Annual Symposium on the Theory of Computing (STOC)", pp. 39–51, ACM.

[5] GERTH, R., BOUCHER, A. (1987), A Timed Failures Model for Communicating Processes, *in* Th. Ottmann ed., "Proceedings 14th International Conference on Automata, Languages and Programming (ICALP)", LNCS **267**, pp. 95–114, Springer Verlag, New York.

[6] GERTH, R., DE ROEVER, W.P., RONCKEN, M. (1982), Procedures and Concurrency: A Study in Proof, *in* M. Dezani-Ciancaglini, M. Montenari eds., "Proceedings 5th International Symposium on Programming Languages (ISOP)", LNCS **137**, pp. 132-164, Springer Verlag, New York.

[7] GERTH, R., DE ROEVER, W.P. (1984), A Proof Systems for Concurrent Ada Programs, *Science of Computer Programming* **4**, pp. 159-204.

[8] GERTH, R., DE ROEVER, W.P. (1986), Proving Monitors Revisited: a first step towards verifying object oriented systems, *Fundamenta Informaticae* **IX**, pp. 371-400.

[9] HOOMAN, J. (1987), A Compositional Proof Theory for Real-Time Distributed Message Passing, *in* J.W. de Bakker, A.J. Nijman, P.C. Treleaven eds., "PARLE, Parallel Architectures and Languages Europe Volume II", LNCS **259**, pp. 315-332, Springer Verlag, New York.

[10] HUIZING, C., GERTH, R., DE ROEVER, W.P. (1987), Full Abstraction for a Real-Time Denotational Semantics for an OCCAM-like Language, *in* "Proceedings ACM Symposium on Principles of Programming Languages (POPL)", pp. 223–237, ACM.

[11] HENNESSY, M., PLOTKIN, G. (1979), Full Abstraction for a Simple Parallel Programming Language, *in* J. Bečvář ed., "Proceedings Mathematical Foundations of Computer Science (MFCS)", LNCS **74**, pp. 108–120, Springer Verlag, New York.

[12] KLOP, J.W., (1987), Term Rewriting Systems: A Tutorial, Bulletin of the EATCS **32**, (June 1987), pp. 143-182.

[13] KOYMANS, R., SHYAMASUNDAR, R.K., DE ROEVER, W.P., GERTH, R., ARUM-KUMAR, S. (1985), Compositional Semantics for Real-Time Distributed Computing, *in* R. Parikh ed., "Proceedings Logic of Programs", LNCS **193**, pp. 167–190, Springer Verlag, New York. Appeared in *Information and Computation*, Vol. **79**, pp. 210–256, 1988.

[14] G.M. REED, A.W. ROSCOE, (1986), A Timed Model for Communicating Sequential Processes, *in* L. Kott ed., "Proceedings 13th International Conference on Automata, Languages and Programming (ICALP)", LNCS **226**, pp. 314–323, Springer Verlag, New York. Appeared in *Theoretical Computer Science*, Vol. **58**, pp. 249–261, 1988.

[15] SEITZ, C., (1980), System Timing, *in*: MEAD, C., CONWAY, L. **Introduction to VLSI Systems**, pp. 218–262, Addison-Wesley.

[16] VAN DE SNEPSCHEUT, J. (1985), **Trace Theory and VLSI Design**, LNCS **200**, Springer Verlag, New York.

[17] SOUNDARARAJAN, N. (1984), A Proof Technique for Parallel Programs, *Theoretical Computer Science*, Vol. **31**, pp. 13–29.

[18] SAEIJS, R., VAN BERKEL, C. (1988), The Design of the VLSI Image-Generator ZaP, *in* "Proceedings of the IEEE International Conference on Computer Design: VLSI in Computers and Processors", IEEE.

[19] SALWICKI, A., MÜLDNER T. (1981), On the Algorithmic Properties of Concurrent Programs, *in* E. Engeler ed., "Proceedings Logic of Programs", LNCS **125**, pp. 169–197, Springer Verlag, New York.

From Failure to Success: Comparing a Denotational and a Declarative Semantics for Horn Clause Logic *

F.S. de Boer
Department of Computer Science, Technical University Eindhoven,
P.O. Box 513, 5600 MB Eindhoven, The Netherlands

J.N. Kok
Department of Computer Science, University of Utrecht,
P.O. Box 80089, 3508 TB Utrecht, The Netherlands

C. Palamidessi
Dipartimento di Informatica, Università di Pisa,
Corso Italia, 40, 56125 Pisa, Italy

J.J.M.M. Rutten
Centre for Mathematics and Computer Science,
Kruislaan 413, 1098 SJ Amsterdam, The Netherlands

Abstract

The main purpose of the paper is to relate different models for Horn Clause Logic: operational, denotational, declarative. We study their relationship by contrasting models based on interleaving, on the one hand, to models based on maximal parallelism, on the other. We make use of complete metric spaces as an important mathematical tool, both in defining and in comparing the various models.

Key words and phrases: operational semantics, denotational semantics, declarative semantics, parallelism, logic languages, correctness, complete metric spaces, partial orders.
1985 Mathematics Subject Classification: 68Q55, 68Q10.
1987 Computing Reviews Categories: D.1.3, D.3.1, F.1.2, F.3.2.

*Part of this work was carried out in the context of ESPRIT Basic Research Action (3020) Integration. The research of C. Palamidessi was partially supported by the Dutch REX (Research and Education in Concurrent Systems) project.

1 Introduction

The most basic example of a (parallel) logic programming language is Horn Clause Logic (HCL). An HCL program is a finite set of definite clauses of the form $H \leftarrow \bar{B}$, where H is an atom and $\bar{B}$ is a finite sequence of atoms. We shall introduce three different types of models for HCL: *operational*, *denotational*, and *declarative*. The first and the latter were already introduced elsewhere (see below). In addition to the definition of two denotational models for HCL, the contribution of this paper consists of a systematic comparison of the different models. In particular, we shall establish a precise relationship between the denotational and the declarative models. Although we have been recently investigating various models for more advanced parallel logic languages like GHC and Parlog [4, 5], which contain constructs like the commit operator and annotations for communication, it is necessary to understand the precise relationship of these models first at the basic level of HCL.

1.1 The operational models

We shall consider two operational models, which are both based on a transition system (in the so-called SOS style [10]). The first one, called $\mathcal{O}_{\mathrm{FI}}$ (FI for fair interleaving), corresponds to the standard (sequential) operational semantics of HCL based on SLD resolution (like in [15, 12]); it uses a fair derivation rule (reduction from left to right) in order to model also failure behavior. From $\mathcal{O}_{\mathrm{FI}}$ we can deduce the three sets that are classically used to describe the operational behavior of an HCL program: the success set, the finite failure set, and the infinite failure set.

The second operational semantics, $\mathcal{O}_{\mathrm{MP}}$, models maximal parallelism; the derivation rule used here amounts to executing in parallel one resolution step for each atom in a goal. (In this way, fairness is automatically ensured.) Then a goal, consisting of several atoms, can do one step by composing all local substitutions of the individual atoms in parallel by means of a parallel composition operator $\hat{o}$ for substitutions (introduced in [13]). It has two effects: it tests whether these substitutions are mutually compatible and, if so, it takes the union of all the bindings. This model is of interest because it could serve as a basis for a parallel implementation of HCL based languages; furthermore, it can be seen as a starting point for the formalization of additional features such as atomic unification (Cf. [14]). Technically, $\mathcal{O}_{\mathrm{MP}}$ will play a role (or, more precisely, the denotational model corresponding to it) as an intermediate in establishing the correspondence between $\mathcal{O}_{\mathrm{FI}}$ and the declarative model, to be presented in a minute.

For both operational models, we shall introduce corresponding denotational models. Their main characteristic is compositionality: the meaning of the conjunction of two goals will be computed by composing the meanings of the separate goals. (Note that we do not study compositionality with respect to the union of programs; this we consider to be a separate issue.)

1.2 The denotational models

In order to be compositional, the denotational models are considerably more complicated than their operational counterparts. This is mainly due to the difficulty of describing failure behavior in a compositional manner. The denotational model corresponding to $\mathcal{O}_{\text{FI}}$ will be called $\mathcal{D}_{\text{FI}}$. In order to allow for the definition of an operator for parallel composition, corresponding to the conjunction of goals, the codomain of this model (also called its semantic universe) will be more complicated than the operational one. Both for $\mathcal{O}_{\text{FI}}$ and $\mathcal{O}_{\text{MP}}$ it suffices to consider sets of sequences (or words) of substitutions. Here, we need sets of sequences (or vectors) of sequences (or words) of *pairs* of substitutions. We shall prove the correctness of $\mathcal{D}_{\text{FI}}$ with respect to $\mathcal{O}_{\text{FI}}$ by showing that the latter equals the composition of an abstraction operation with the former.

Next a second denotational model, called $\mathcal{D}_{\text{MP}}$, is introduced, which equals the operational semantics $\mathcal{O}_{\text{MP}}$. Its semantic universe is the same as the one of $\mathcal{O}_{\text{MP}}$, which is simpler than that of $\mathcal{D}_{\text{FI}}$. The semantic operator for the parallel composition (conjunction) of two goals is the operator $\hat{o}$ described above, but now extended to sets of sequences of substitutions.

1.3 The declarative model

The third type of model we describe is the declarative semantics. We recall the definition of the declarative semantics $\mathcal{D}ec$ as introduced in [9]. The term *declarative* means that the program is seen as a set of first order formulas and that the semantics is intended in the model-theoretic sense, i.e., characterizing the set of logical consequences of the program. This semantics is obtained as the least fixed-point of a continuous transformation T on the *interpretations* of the program, the so-called *immediate consequence operator*. An important distinction between the denotational models above and the declarative semantics is that the latter describes the success set only, whereas the denotational semantics additionally model (finite and infinite) failure. The first declarative semantics for HCL was proposed by van Emden and Kowalski in [15] (see also [12]). In their approach, interpretations are sets of ground atoms and the least fixed-point, which is equivalent to the least Herbrand model of the program, characterizes the validity of the ground atoms only. The construction in [9] extends this approach in that interpretations may also contain non-ground atoms. Therefore $\mathcal{D}ec$ can also express the validity of so-called generic atoms, i.e., atoms of the form $p(\bar{x})$.

1.4 The mathematical tools

We work mainly in the framework of *complete metric spaces*, in which we follow the tradition initiated by De Bakker and Zucker in [3]. The metric approach is particularly useful in those situations where (sets of) sets of sequences occur, since these can be supplied with a standard metric. This is the case in the operational and (all but one) denotational models, since they describe in addition to success behavior also (finite and infinite) failure behavior, for which the use of sequences seems natural. The metric structure of our semantic universa is exploited in two ways: first, it enables us to introduce both our models and our semantic operators as the (by Banach's theorem) unique fixed-points of so-called contractions. Secondly, this uniqueness implies that in order to prove the equality of two models, it is sufficient to show that they are both a fixed-point of the same contraction. It is in particular this second point that distinguishes between the metric and the more usual partial order (or lattice) approach: a continuous operator on a complete partial order has a (least) fixed-point but may have more than one. Therefore it is there more involved to prove such equalities. (Cf. [6].) We shall use ordered structures in those cases where we want to describe only success behavior, such as the declarative semantics.

1.5 Comparing the models

After having introduced all these models, we shall make a precise and complete comparison. The two operational models are related to the corresponding two denotational models, as just mentioned. The main result of the paper consists in establishing a connection between the first denotational model, $\mathcal{D}_{\mathrm{FI}}$, and the declarative model $\mathcal{D}ec$. This is done in two steps.

First we shall relate $\mathcal{D}_{\mathrm{FI}}$ and $\mathcal{D}_{\mathrm{MP}}$. To this end, an intermediate denotational model $\mathcal{I}$ is introduced, to which both are then related. Secondly, and this is the more difficult part, $\mathcal{D}_{\mathrm{MP}}$ and $\mathcal{D}ec$ are compared. Again an intermediate denotational semantics, called $\mathcal{D}_{\mathrm{CS}}$ (CS for computed substitutions) is introduced. It is essentially a model for maximal parallelism, like $\mathcal{D}_{\mathrm{MP}}$, but does not deliver sets of *sequences* of substitutions, but sets of single substitutions only. As a consequence, it only models success behavior. The relationship between $\mathcal{D}_{\mathrm{MP}}$ and $\mathcal{D}_{\mathrm{CS}}$ is fairly easy; the only technical problem is that the first model is defined as the fixed-point of a contraction on a complete metric space, whereas the latter is given as the least fixed-point of a continuous function on a complete lattice. Finally, $\mathcal{D}_{\mathrm{CS}}$ and $\mathcal{D}ec$ are related. Although their connection is intuitively obvious, it takes some (technical) effort to make this precise.

At the end of our paper, we mention some consequences that can be deduced from the various relations between the different models. The most important of these is that we can easily establish a proof of the soundness and completeness of the declarative semantics with respect to the success set (which was derived from $\mathcal{O}_{\mathrm{FI}}$). In this way, we find a fairly transparent alternative to the equivalence proof given in [9], the latter being quite complicated. The main problem is the contrast between the bottom-up and (maximally) parallel nature of the declarative semantics and the top-down and interleaving nature of the operational semantics. The intermediate models that we have introduced above allow for a decomposition of this proof into several steps, and thus give some insight into the contrasting concepts involved.

2 Mathematical preliminaries

We assume the following notions to be known: complete metric space, continuous function on a metric space, compact subset of a metric space. (The reader might consult, e.g., [7].) We shall also use the following notions from order theory: complete partial order (CPO), complete lattice, continuous function on a CPO.

Let (M_1, d_1) and (M_2, d_2) be two complete metric spaces. A function $f : M_1 \rightarrow M_2$ is called *non-expansive* if for all $x, y \in M_1$

$$d_2(f(x), f(y)) \leq d_1(x, y)$$

It is called *contracting* (or a *contraction*) if there exists $\epsilon \in [0, 1)$ such that for all $x, y \in M_1$

$$d_2(f(x), f(y)) \leq \epsilon \cdot d_1(x, y)$$

Non-expansive and contracting functions are continuous. The following fact is known as Banach's Theorem: let (M, d) be a complete metric space and $f : M \rightarrow M$ a contraction. Then f has a unique fixed point, that is, there exists a unique $x \in M$ such that $f(x) = x$.

The set $M_1 \rightarrow M_2$ is the set of all functions from M_1 to M_2. It can be turned into a complete metric space by taking as a metric

$$d(f_1, f_2) = \sup_{x \in M_1}\{d_2(f_1(x), f_2(x))\}$$

(All our metrics will have $[0, 1]$ as their range.) Let

$$\mathcal{P}_{nco}(M) = \{X : X \subseteq M \wedge X \text{ is non-empty and compact } \}$$

We can turn $\mathcal{P}_{nco}(M)$ into a complete metric space by defining a metric d_H, called the *Hausdorff distance* induced by d (the metric on M), as follows: For every $X, Y \in \mathcal{P}_{nco}(M)$

$$d_H(X, Y) = max\{\sup_{x \in X}\{d(x, Y)\}, \sup_{y \in Y}\{d(y, X)\}\}$$

where $d(x, Z) = \inf_{z \in Z}\{d(x, z)\}$ for every $Z \subset M$, $x \in M$.

We shall often use the following notation: we write $(x, y \in)\ X$ when introducing a set X with typical elements x and y.

A typical example of a complete metric space that we shall often use is the set $(w_1, w_2 \in)\ A^\infty = A^* \cup A^\omega$ of all finite and infinite words over an alphabet A, supplied with a metric d given by

$$d(w_1, w_2) = 2^{-\sup\{k:\ w_1(k) = w_2(k)\}}$$

where $w(k)$ denotes the prefix of the word w of length k. We denote the usual concatenation of two words by $w_1 \cdot w_2$.

3 The language HCL

We only give an informal introduction to the language HCL. For further details we refer to [12, 1].

The sets *Term* of terms, $(A, B, H \in)$ *Atom* of atomic formulas (or atoms), and $(\vartheta, \sigma, \gamma \in)$ *Subst* of substitutions are defined as usual. Elementary atoms (*EAtom*) are of the form $p(\bar{x})$, where p is a predicate and $\bar{x}$ is a tuple of distinct variables. A definite clause is a construct of the form $H \leftarrow B_1, \ldots, B_n$ $(n \geq 0)$, where H and each B_i is an atom; H is called the head and $B_1, \ldots, B_n$ (also denoted by $\bar{B}$) the body of this clause. An HCL program W is a finite set of definite clauses. A goal statement (or goal) is a construct of the form $\leftarrow A_1, \ldots, A_n$ $(n \geq 0)$, where each A_i is an atom. If $n > 0$ we denote $\leftarrow A_1, \ldots, A_n$ also by $\leftarrow \bar{A}$. If $n = 0$ we have the so-called empty goal, and we write $\Box$. The set of all goals is denoted by *Goal*.

We have the usual notion of *most general unifier* of two atoms A and H, denoted by $mgu(A, H)$. For the composition of two substitutions we write $\vartheta_1\vartheta_2$. For technical convenience, we shall throughout this paper consider only idempotent substitutions, i.e., satisfying $\vartheta\vartheta = \vartheta$ (see [13] for some discussion on this point). The set of variables occurring in the atom A is indicated by $Var(A)$. For an atom A and a substitution ϑ we write $\vartheta_{|A}$ for the restriction of ϑ to $Var(A)$. The empty substitution is denoted by ϵ.

The classical operational semantics of HCL programs is based on the notion of refutation. Let $G = \leftarrow A_1, \ldots, A_m$ be a goal and let $H \leftarrow B_1, \ldots, B_n$ be a (properly renamed variant of a) clause in the program W. Assume that A_i and H are unifiable with most general unifier ϑ. Then the goal

$$\leftarrow (A_1, \ldots, A_{i-1}, B_1, \ldots, B_n, A_{i+1}, \ldots, A_m)\vartheta$$

is derivable from G by one resolution step. A repeated application of such a resolution step is called a derivation. A derivation is successful (and called a refutation) if it ends with the empty goal $\square$; it is failing if no further reductions are possible while the empty goal has not been reached; and it is infinite otherwise. A selection rule is a function that gives for each goal the atom to be reduced. A derivation according to a certain selection rule is called an SLD-derivation. A selection rule is fair if and only if all the atoms in all the possible goals generated in SLD-derivations are eventually selected. Classically, the (operational) semantics of an HCL program is defined by three sets:

- the success set ($\mathcal{O}_{\text{SS}}$), containing all the atoms that have a refutation, instantiated by the last substitution (the so-called computed answer substitution).
- the finite failure set ($\mathcal{O}_{\text{FFS}}$), containing all the atoms for which all the fair SLD-derivations are failing (see [2]).
- The infinite failure set ($\mathcal{O}_{\text{IFS}}$), containing all atoms, for which there are no successful derivations and there is at least one fair infinite derivation.

The notion of success set given above is not completely satisfactory for characterizing the operational behavior of a logic program. In the present paper, we use a different notion of success set: we take the one introduced in [8, 9], which contains all the elementary atoms that have a refutation, instantiated by the computed answer substitution (see the next section and that on the declarative semantics).

4 Operational semantics

We present two operational semantics for HCL, which will both be based on a labelled transition system (in the style of [10]). The first one models interleaving and uses a breath-first selection rule, which is fair. The second operational semantics, in which all the atoms occurring in a goal are reduced at the same time, describes maximal parallelism. Throughout the rest of this paper, we assume the program W to be fixed.

4.1 Interleaving

First we introduce a labelled transition system for fair interleaving, on which our first operational semantics will be based.

Definition 4.1 *Let* $(Goal, Subst, \rightarrow)$ *be the labelled transition system, of which the transition relation* $\rightarrow \subseteq Goal \times Subst \times Goal$ *is defined as the smallest relation satisfying the following axiom:*

$$\leftarrow A, \bar{A} \xrightarrow{\vartheta} \leftarrow \bar{A}\vartheta, \bar{B}\vartheta$$

(As usual, we write $\leftarrow \bar{A} \stackrel{\vartheta}{\longrightarrow} \leftarrow \bar{B}$ *rather than* $(\leftarrow \bar{A}, \vartheta, \leftarrow \bar{B}) \in \longrightarrow$*.) Here* $\vartheta = mgu(A, H)$ *and* $H \leftarrow \bar{B}$ *is a clause of* W*. We assume this clause to be renamed such that* A*,* $\bar{A}$ *and* H *have no variables in common.*

Note that in the above axiom, a breath-first selection rule is used. In this way, fairness is automatically ensured. This left-to-right strategy does not impose any restrictions; we still get all possible fair behaviors. This can be proved by making use of the so-called switching (or square) lemma (see [12]). Another feature of the above transition system is the fact that the computed substitution (above the arrow) is applied to the goal at the right of the arrow. This ensures that all subsequently computed substitutions will be consistent with (i.e., extensions of) the current one.

Based on this transition system we define an operational semantics $\mathcal{O}_{\mathrm{FI}} : Goal \rightarrow P_{\mathrm{ST}}$, which associates with a goal a set of sequences of substitutions. The semantic universe $(X, Y \in)\ P_{\mathrm{ST}}$ (ST is an abbreviation for streams) is given by

$$P_{\mathrm{ST}} = \mathcal{P}_{\mathrm{nco}}(Subst_{\delta}^{\mathrm{st}})$$

where $Subst_{\delta}^{\mathrm{st}}$, the set of finite, infinite and deadlocking sequences (or words, or streams), is defined by

$$(v, w, z \in)\ Subst_{\delta}^{\mathrm{st}} = Subst^{*} \cup Subst^{\omega} \cup Subst^{*} \cdot \delta$$

As a metric on P_{ST} we take the Hausdorff metric induced by the standard metric on sequences (see the preliminaries). The empty sequence is denoted by λ and the concatenation of two sequences w_1 and w_2 by $w_1 \cdot w_2$. To denote failure we have added to the set of substitutions a special element δ. We postulate for any substitution ϑ that $\vartheta\delta$, the composition of ϑ and δ, equals δ; for any sequence of substitutions v we have that $\delta \cdot v$, the concatenation of δ and v, is equal to δ. Each sequence represents a particular computation that corresponds to a specific choice of clauses. The elements of such a sequence represent the partial results of the computation. Finite sequences not ending in δ (elements of $Subst^{+}$) correspond to successfully terminating computations (refutations). Sequences ending in δ (in $Subst^{*} \cdot \delta$) represent failing computations. Infinite sequences (in $Subst^{\omega}$) are associated with infinitely failing computations.

Definition 4.2 *Let* $\mathcal{O}_{\mathrm{FI}}$ *be the unique fixed point of the contracting operator* $\Phi_{\mathrm{FI}} : (Goal \rightarrow P_{\mathrm{ST}}) \rightarrow (Goal \rightarrow P_{\mathrm{ST}})$*, which is given by*

$$\begin{aligned}
\Phi_{\mathrm{FI}}(F)[\![\Box]\!] &= \{\epsilon\} \\
\Phi_{\mathrm{FI}}(F)[\![\leftarrow \bar{A}]\!] &= \bigcup\{\vartheta \cdot (\vartheta \leadsto_{\mathrm{FI}} F[\![\bar{A}']\!]) : \leftarrow \bar{A} \stackrel{\vartheta}{\longrightarrow} \leftarrow \bar{A}'\} \cup \{\delta : \leftarrow \bar{A} \not\longrightarrow\}
\end{aligned}$$

Here $\leadsto_{\mathrm{FI}}$*:* $Subst \times P_{\mathrm{ST}} \rightarrow P_{\mathrm{ST}}$ *is defined by* $\vartheta \leadsto_{\mathrm{FI}} X = \{\vartheta \leadsto_{\mathrm{FI}} x : x \in X\}$*, with*

$$\vartheta \leadsto_{\mathrm{FI}} \lambda = \lambda$$

$$\vartheta \leadsto_{\mathrm{FI}} (\sigma \cdot z) = (\vartheta\sigma) \cdot (\vartheta \leadsto_{\mathrm{FI}} z)$$

The contractivity of Φ_{FI} in the above definition is straightforward. The compactness of $\Phi_{\mathrm{FI}}(F)[\![\leftarrow \bar{A}]\!]$ follows from the fact that only finitely many transitions are possible from $\leftarrow \bar{A}$.

The definition of $\mathcal{O}_{\mathrm{FI}}[\![\Box]\!]$ is obvious. For a non-empty goal $\leftarrow \bar{A}$ we have that $\mathcal{O}_{\mathrm{FI}}[\![\leftarrow \bar{A}]\!]$ equals $\{\delta\}$ if there are no transitions possible from $\leftarrow \bar{A}$ (indicated by $\leftarrow \bar{A} \not\longrightarrow$). Otherwise, $\mathcal{O}_{\mathrm{FI}}[\![\leftarrow \bar{A}]\!]$ contains all sequences that start with ϑ and continue with a sequence stemming from $\mathcal{O}_{\mathrm{FI}}[\![\leftarrow \bar{A}']\!]$, in which every element is composed with ϑ. The latter is caused by the application of $\vartheta \leadsto_{\mathrm{FI}}$ to $\mathcal{O}_{\mathrm{FI}}[\![\leftarrow \bar{A}']\!]$, which is added because we want to collect the total effect of all intermediate substitutions.

The definition has been presented in a fixed-point format, because this will ease the comparison of $\mathcal{O}_{\mathrm{FI}}$ with other models still to come. We could, however, have given a more direct definition based on transition sequences. A second remark concerns the use of the somewhat abstract operation $\vartheta \leadsto_{\mathrm{FI}}$. This could have been avoided as well by using a different type of transition system, in which a configuration $<\leftarrow \bar{A}, \sigma>$ would consist of both a goal and a substitution. The latter could then be used to store all the bindings found sofar. The axiom corresponding to the one above would be

$$< (\leftarrow A, \bar{A}),\ \sigma > \longrightarrow < (\leftarrow \bar{A}, \bar{B}), \sigma\vartheta >$$

with $\bar{B}$ and ϑ as above.

The following counter example shows that $\mathcal{O}_{\mathrm{FI}}$ is *not* compositional. Consider the following program

$$\{p(x) \leftarrow s_1(x),\ p(x) \leftarrow s_2(x),\ q(x) \leftarrow s_3(x)$$

$$s_1(a) \leftarrow,\ s_2(b) \leftarrow,\ s_3(a) \leftarrow,\ s_3(b) \leftarrow,\ r(a) \leftarrow\}$$

It is easy to see that with respect to this program $\mathcal{O}_{\mathrm{FI}}[\![\leftarrow p(x)]\!] = \mathcal{O}_{\mathrm{FI}}[\![\leftarrow q(x)]\!]$. But, on the other hand, we have $\{x/a\}\delta \in \mathcal{O}_{\mathrm{FI}}[\![\leftarrow r(x), p(x)]\!] \setminus \mathcal{O}_{\mathrm{FI}}[\![\leftarrow r(x), q(x)]\!]$.

4.2 Success, finite failure and infinite failure sets

From the operational semantics $\mathcal{O}_{\mathrm{FI}}$ we can derive the success set, the finite failure set, and the infinite failure set in the following way:

$$\begin{array}{lcl} \mathcal{O}_{\mathrm{SS}} & = & \{p(\bar{x})\vartheta : p(\bar{x}) \in EAtom \wedge \vartheta \in last(\mathcal{O}_{\mathrm{FI}}[\![\leftarrow p(\bar{x})]\!] \cap Subst^{+})\} \\ \mathcal{O}_{\mathrm{FFS}} & = & \{A : \mathcal{O}_{\mathrm{FI}}[\![\leftarrow A]\!] \subseteq Subst^{*} \cdot \delta\} \\ \mathcal{O}_{\mathrm{IFS}} & = & \{A : \mathcal{O}_{\mathrm{FI}}[\![\leftarrow A]\!] \cap Subst^{*} = \emptyset \wedge \mathcal{O}_{\mathrm{FI}}[\![\leftarrow A]\!] \cap Subst^{\omega} \neq \emptyset\} \end{array}$$

In the first set, the function *last* takes from a set of sequences the last elements (not equal to δ). Those elements represent the computed answer substitution for successful refutations. The notion of success set we consider here is introduced in [9, 8] and extends the standard one given in [12, 15]. (See also the section on the declarative semantics for some more discussion.) The second set, $\mathcal{O}_{\mathrm{FFS}}$, contains those atoms that give rise to only failing computations, i.e., sequences of substitutions that end in δ. The last set, $\mathcal{O}_{\mathrm{IFS}}$, contains the so-called infinitely failing atoms; those give rise to no successful computations and at least one fair infinite one.

4.3 Maximal parallelism

The next execution model we consider for our language is called maximally parallel. Each step in the execution of a goal consists conceptually of two stages: first, all atoms present in the goal perform one step independently. Secondly, the substitutions resulting from these local computations are composed in order to obtain the global outcome of the computation. For this composition we introduce a new operator on substitutions called *parallel composition.* (Sometimes it is called *reconciliation* operator; Cf. [11].) It is defined as follows.

Definition 4.3 *We define the parallel composition of two substitutions ϑ and σ, denoted by $\vartheta \hat{\circ} \sigma$, by*

$$\vartheta \hat{\circ} \sigma = \begin{cases} mgu(S(\vartheta) \cup S(\sigma)) & \text{if it exists} \\ \delta & \text{otherwise} \end{cases}$$

where $S(\vartheta) = \{< x, t >: x/t \in \vartheta\}$. Furthermore we define $\vartheta \hat{\circ} \delta = \delta \hat{\circ} \vartheta = \delta$. (Note that the notion of mgu is extended to sets of pairs of terms.)

This operator tests whether the two substitutions are compatible and, if this is the case, yields the minimal substitution containing the same information (bindings) as these substitutions. Otherwise it yiels δ. It is straightforward to show that $\hat{\circ}$ is commutative, associative, and idempotent (modulo the renaming of variables).

The proof of the correspondence of the interleaving and the maximally parallel semantics will make use of the following property of this operator.

Lemma 4.4 *For all substitutions ϑ_1 and ϑ_2*

$$\vartheta_1 \hat{\circ} \vartheta_2 = \vartheta_1 mgu(S(\vartheta_2)\vartheta_1)$$

where $S(\vartheta_2)\vartheta_1 = \{< x\vartheta_1, t\vartheta_1 >: < x, t > \in S(\vartheta_2)\}$.

For the proof of this lemma and additional discussion of $\hat{\circ}$ we refer to [13]. The definition of $\hat{\circ}$ is illustrated by the following example.

Example 4.5 *Let $\vartheta_1 = \{x/f(y,a),\ z/g(b)\}$ and $\vartheta_2 = \{x/f(b,w),\ z/g(y)\}$. Then*

$$\begin{aligned} \vartheta_1 \hat{\circ} \vartheta_2 &= mgu\{< x, f(y,a) >, < z, g(b) >, < x, f(b,w) >, < z, g(y) >\} \\ &= \{x/f(b,a),\ z/g(b),\ y/b,\ w/a\} \end{aligned}$$

If we take ϑ_1 as before and $\vartheta_2 = \{x/f(a,w),\ z/g(y)\}$ we have

$$\begin{aligned} \vartheta_1 \hat{\circ} \vartheta_2 &= mgu\{< x, f(y,a) >, < z, g(b) >, < x, f(a,w) >, < z, g(y) >\} \\ &= \delta \end{aligned}$$

Next we introduce a transition relation for maximal parallelism. It is specified by the following axiom and rule.

Definition 4.6 *We define*

1.

$$\leftarrow A \xrightarrow{\vartheta} \leftarrow \bar{B}$$

where $\vartheta = mgu(A, H)$ and $H \leftarrow \bar{B}$ is an (appropriately renamed) clause of W.

2.

$$\frac{\leftarrow \bar{A} \xrightarrow{\vartheta} \leftarrow \bar{A}', \; \leftarrow \bar{B} \xrightarrow{\sigma} \leftarrow \bar{B}'}{\leftarrow \bar{A}, \bar{B} \xrightarrow{\vartheta \,\hat{\circ}\, \sigma} \leftarrow \bar{A}', \bar{B}'}$$

Note that in the conclusion of the rule above, we can have that $\vartheta \,\hat{\circ}\, \sigma$ equals δ. This means that the two substitutions are not compatible.

Definition 4.7 *The operational semantics $\mathcal{O}_{\mathrm{MP}}$ is defined as the fixed point of the contraction $\Phi_{\mathrm{MP}} : (Goal \to P_{\mathrm{ST}}) \to (Goal \to P_{\mathrm{ST}})$, given by*

$$\begin{aligned} \Phi_{\mathrm{MP}}(F)[\![\Box]\!] &= \{\epsilon\} \\ \Phi_{\mathrm{MP}}(F)[\![\leftarrow \bar{A}]\!] &= \bigcup\{\vartheta \cdot (\vartheta \rightsquigarrow_{\mathrm{MP}} F[\![\leftarrow \bar{A}']\!]) : \leftarrow \bar{A} \xrightarrow{\vartheta} \leftarrow \bar{A}'\} \cup \{\delta : \leftarrow \bar{A} \not\longrightarrow\} \end{aligned}$$

Here $\rightsquigarrow_{\mathrm{MP}}$: $Subst \times P_{\mathrm{ST}} \to P_{\mathrm{ST}}$ is defined by $\vartheta \rightsquigarrow_{\mathrm{MP}} X = \{\vartheta \rightsquigarrow_{\mathrm{MP}} x : x \in X\}$, with

$$\begin{aligned} \vartheta \rightsquigarrow_{\mathrm{MP}} \lambda &= \lambda \\ \vartheta \rightsquigarrow_{\mathrm{MP}} \sigma \cdot z &= \begin{cases} \delta & \textit{if } \vartheta \,\hat{\circ}\, \sigma = \delta \\ \vartheta \,\hat{\circ}\, \sigma \cdot (\vartheta \rightsquigarrow_{\mathrm{MP}} z) & \textit{otherwise} \end{cases} \end{aligned}$$

The definition of $\mathcal{O}_{\mathrm{MP}}$ is very similar to that of $\mathcal{O}_{\mathrm{FI}}$. Two differences should be noticed here. First, the transition relation that is used is different from the one in the definition of $\mathcal{O}_{\mathrm{FI}}$; secondly, the definition of the function $\vartheta \rightsquigarrow_{\mathrm{MP}}$ differs from the fuction $\vartheta \rightsquigarrow_{\mathrm{FI}}$. It composes ϑ *in parallel* with the elements of $\mathcal{O}_{\mathrm{MP}}[\![\leftarrow \bar{A}']\!]$, as opposed to $\vartheta \rightsquigarrow_{\mathrm{FI}}$, which uses ordinary composition. Here we use the parallel composition, because in the transition system above, the substitution above the arrow is not applied to the atom at its right-hand side. Therefore, the next computation step will not take this substitution into account and the next substitution that is computed has to be reconciled with the previous one.

5 Denotational semantics for interleaving

In this section, we develop a denotational semantics $\mathcal{D}_{\mathrm{FI}}$ for the operational interleaving semantics $\mathcal{O}_{\mathrm{FI}}$. We start by introducing the complete metric space P_{FI}, which is defined by

$$P_{\mathrm{FI}} = \mathcal{P}_{\mathrm{nco}}(((Subst \times Subst_\delta)^+)^\infty)$$

with a metric on P_{FI} similar to the one on P_{ST}. It consists of sets of (finite and infinite) sequences of finite sequences of pairs of substitutions. Such a sequence (called a vector) we denote by $< v_1, \ldots, v_n, \ldots >$, where each v_i is a finite sequence of pairs of substitutions. We shall use the following prefixing operator, which composes a vector containing one pair of substitutions, $< (\vartheta_1, \vartheta_2) >$ and a vector $< v_1, v_2, \ldots >$, and is defined by

$$< (\vartheta_1, \vartheta_2) > \cdot < v_1, v_2, \ldots > = < (\vartheta_1, \vartheta_2), v_1, v_2, \ldots >$$

We use *pairs* of substitutions to represent the basic (unification) steps in the computation. The first substitution of a pair is called the input substitution and can be seen as an assumption on the behavior of the environment or, in other words, the computation that has taken place sofar. The second one, called the output substitution, denotes the result of this computation step. As we shall see below, it will be the substitution resulting from a unification. Failure of such a unification is denoted by δ. (An alternative would have been to use functions from substitutions to substitutions. This would yield a semantics that is less abstract, i.e., more discriminating.)

Next we explain why we use vectors (instead of just sequences of pairs of substitutions). When we define a compositional semantics we introduce a semantic merge operator $\|_{\mathrm{FI}}$. Operationally, a goal is executed by performing from left to right one step of each atom in the goal. The operator $\|_{\mathrm{FI}}$ is defined such that it mimics this strategy. If we had sequences of pairs of substitutions in our basic domain we would not be able to do this: we would not know how many processes (atoms) contributed to this goal. Vectors have this kind of information. The intuition is that the n-th element of a vector represents the n-th left to right swap of the goal. Hence the operator $\|_{\mathrm{FI}}$ combines two vecors by concatenating their elements, i.e., their sequences of substitutions, component-wise.

Definition 5.1 *We define* $\|_{\mathrm{FI}}$: $P_{\mathrm{FI}} \times P_{\mathrm{FI}} \to P_{\mathrm{FI}}$, *for every* $X, Y \in P_{\mathrm{FI}}$, *by*

$$X \|_{\mathrm{FI}} Y = \bigcup \{x \|_{\mathrm{FI}} y : x \in X, y \in Y\}$$

where

$$< v_1, v_2, \ldots >\|_{\mathrm{FI}}< w_1, w_2, \ldots >=< v_1 \cdot w_1, v_2 \cdot w_2, \ldots >$$

$$< v_1, \ldots, v_n >\|_{\mathrm{FI}}< w_1, w_2, \ldots >=< v_1 \cdot w_1, \ldots, v_n \cdot w_n, w_{n+1}, \ldots >$$

Now we are ready to give the definition of the denotational semantics $\mathcal{D}_{\mathrm{FI}}$.

Definition 5.2 *We define* $\mathcal{D}_{\mathrm{FI}} : Goal \to P_{\mathrm{FI}}$:

$$\begin{array}{lcl} \mathcal{D}_{\mathrm{FI}}[\![\Box]\!] & = & \{\lambda\} \\ \mathcal{D}_{\mathrm{FI}}[\![\leftarrow A]\!] & = & \{< (\vartheta, \vartheta mgu(A\vartheta, H)) > \cdot \mathcal{D}_{\mathrm{FI}}[\![\leftarrow \bar{B}]\!] : \vartheta \in Subst,\ H \leftarrow \bar{B} \in W\} \\ & & \cup \{< (\vartheta, \delta) >: \forall H \leftarrow \bar{B} \in W[mgu(A\vartheta, H) \textit{ does not exist }]\} \\ \mathcal{D}_{\mathrm{FI}}[\![\leftarrow \bar{A}_1, \bar{A}_2]\!] & = & \mathcal{D}_{\mathrm{FI}}[\![\leftarrow \bar{A}_1]\!] \|_{\mathrm{FI}} \mathcal{D}_{\mathrm{FI}}[\![\leftarrow \bar{A}_2]\!] \end{array}$$

This recursive definition can be justified with the use of contractions in the standard way. (See Definition 6.2 for an example.)

In section 8, the correctness of $\mathcal{D}_{\mathrm{FI}}$ with respect to $\mathcal{O}_{\mathrm{FI}}$ will be proved.

6 Denotational semantics for maximal parallelism

We next introduce a denotational variant, named $\mathcal{D}_{\mathrm{MP}}$, of the operational model $\mathcal{O}_{\mathrm{MP}}$ for maximal parallelism. Unlike the case of fair interleaving, we need not introduce a new semantic universe; we can again take P_{ST}. Recall that P_{ST} is defined as

$$P_{\mathrm{ST}} = \mathcal{P}_{\mathrm{nco}}(Subst_{\delta}^{\mathrm{st}})$$

Before we introduce the model $\mathcal{D}_{\mathrm{MP}}$, we first extend the parallel composition operator $\hat{\circ}$ to a parallel operator $\|_{\mathrm{MP}}$ defined on sets of sequences of substitutions.

Definition 6.1 *We define* $\|_{\mathrm{MP}}$: $P_{\mathrm{ST}} \times P_{\mathrm{ST}} \to P_{\mathrm{ST}}$ *by, for all* X *and* Y *in* P_{ST},

$$X \|_{\mathrm{MP}} Y = \bigcup\{x \|_{\mathrm{MP}} y : x \in X, y \in Y\}$$

Here $x \|_{\mathrm{MP}} y$ *is defined by the following cases.*

$$(\sigma_1 \cdot z_1) \|_{\mathrm{MP}} (\sigma_2 \cdot z_2) = \begin{cases} \delta & \text{if } \sigma_1 \hat{\circ} \sigma_2 = \delta \\ (\sigma_1 \hat{\circ} \sigma_2) \cdot (z_1 \|_{\mathrm{MP}} z_2) & \text{otherwise} \end{cases}$$

$$\sigma_1 \|_{\mathrm{MP}} (\sigma_2 \cdot z) = (\sigma_2 \cdot z) \|_{\mathrm{MP}} \sigma_1 = \begin{cases} \delta & \text{if } \sigma_1 \hat{\circ} \sigma_2 = \delta \\ (\sigma_1 \hat{\circ} \sigma_2) \cdot (\sigma_1 \|_{\mathrm{MP}} z) & \text{otherwise} \end{cases}$$

Note that $\|_{\mathrm{MP}}$ is recursively defined. Formally, we can introduce it as the unique fixed point of a suitably defined contraction.

Now we can introduce the semantics $\mathcal{D}_{\mathrm{MP}}$. It turns out to be equal to $\mathcal{O}_{\mathrm{MP}}$, which will be proved in section 8.

Definition 6.2 *Let the function* $\mathcal{D}_{\mathrm{MP}} : Goal \to P_{\mathrm{ST}}$ *be the unique fixed point of the contraction* $\Psi_{\mathrm{MP}} : (Goal \to P_{\mathrm{ST}}) \to (Goal \to P_{\mathrm{ST}})$, *given by*

$$\Psi_{\mathrm{MP}}(F)[\![\Box]\!] = \{\epsilon\}$$

$$\Psi_{\mathrm{MP}}(F)[\![\leftarrow A]\!] = \bigcup\{mgu(A,H) \rightsquigarrow_{\mathrm{MP}} F(\leftarrow \bar{B}) : H \leftarrow \bar{B} \in W\} \cup \{\delta : \forall H \leftarrow \bar{B} \in W \; mgu(A,H) \text{ does not exist}\}$$

$$\Psi_{\mathrm{MP}}(F)[\![\leftarrow \bar{A}_1, \bar{A}_2]\!] = \Psi_{\mathrm{MP}}(F)[\![\leftarrow \bar{A}_1]\!] \|_{\mathrm{MP}} \Psi_{\mathrm{MP}}(F)[\![\leftarrow \bar{A}_2]\!]$$

It is not difficult to show that Ψ_{MP} in the above definition is contracting; a proof would make use of the fact that $\|_{\mathrm{MP}}$ is non-expansive, an observation that on its turn is rather straightforward.

7 Declarative semantics

In this section, we recall the definition of the declarative semantics $\mathcal{D}ec$ introduced in [9]. The term *declarative* means that the program is seen as a set of first order formulas and that the semantics is intended in the model-theoretic sense, i.e., characterizing the set of logical consequences of the program. This semantics is obtained as the least fixed-point of a continuous transformation T on the *interpretations* of the program. Such a transformation is called *immediate consequence operator* because for an interpretation I, the set $T(I)$ contains all the (atomic) consequences obtained from the (atomic) formulas that are true in I by a one step inference from the program. The first declarative semantics for HCL was proposed by van Emden and Kowalski in [15]. In their approach, interpretations are sets of ground atoms and the least fixed-point, shown equivalent to the least Herbrand model of the program, characterizes the validity of the ground atoms only. The construction in [9] extends this approach in that interpretations contain also non ground atoms and therefore the least fixed-point allows to express validity for so-called generic atoms.

Next we give the construction of [9] in more detail. We refer to that paper for the proofs of the results we mention here. For Theorem 7.7 a proof will be presented in section 9.

Definition 7.1 *The partially ordered set of (extended) interpretations, with typical element I, is defined as $(P_{\mathrm{Dec}}, \subseteq)$, where $P_{\mathrm{Dec}} = \mathcal{P}(Atom)$.*

Proposition 7.2 *$(P_{\mathrm{Dec}}, \subseteq)$ is a complete lattice.*

Definition 7.3 *The (extended) immediate consequence operator $T : P_{\mathrm{Dec}} \rightarrow P_{\mathrm{Dec}}$, is defined by*

$$T(I) = \{H\, mgu(\bar{B}, \bar{B}') : \; H \leftarrow \bar{B} \in W, \bar{B}' \in I\}$$

Proposition 7.4 *The operator T is continuous.*

Since T is continuous, its least fixed-point $lfp(T)$ exists; moreover, $lfp(T) = \bigcup_{n \geq 0} T^n(\emptyset)$, where $T^n(I)$ is defined by

$$T^0(I) = I, \;\; T^{n+1}(I) = T(T^n(I))$$

The declarative semantics is defined as follows.

Definition 7.5 $\mathcal{D}ec = lfp(T)$

The next theorem gives the relation between the model-theoretic semantics of W and $\mathcal{D}ec$.

Theorem 7.6 *For every atom A,*

$$W \models A \;\; (\text{i.e., } A \text{ is a logical consequence of } W) \;\; \text{iff}$$

$$\exists A' \in \mathcal{D}ec\; \exists \vartheta \in Subst\; [A'\vartheta = A].$$

Finally, the following result expresses the relation between $\mathcal{D}ec$ and the success set.

Theorem 7.7 $\mathcal{D}ec \; = \; \mathcal{O}_{\mathrm{SS}}$

8 The relations between the models

8.1 The relations between the denotational and the operational models

8.1.1 Relating $\mathcal{O}_{\mathrm{FI}}$ and $\mathcal{D}_{\mathrm{FI}}$

We start with the relation between $\mathcal{O}_{\mathrm{FI}}$ and $\mathcal{D}_{\mathrm{FI}}$, the operational and denotational semantics based on interleaving. They will be connected by the following abstraction operator.

Definition 8.1 *The operator $\beta_{\mathrm{FI}} : Subst_\delta \rightarrow P_{\mathrm{FI}} \rightarrow P_{\mathrm{ST}}$ is defined by $\beta_{\mathrm{FI}}(\delta)(X) = \{\lambda\}$, and for $\vartheta \neq \delta$, by*

$$\begin{array}{lcl} \beta_{\mathrm{FI}}(\vartheta)(\{\lambda\}) & = & \{\lambda\} \\ \beta_{\mathrm{FI}}(\vartheta)(X) & = & \bigcup\{\vartheta_1 \cdot \beta_{\mathrm{FI}}(\vartheta_1)(X_{(\vartheta,\vartheta_1)}) : \; X_{(\vartheta,\vartheta_1)} \neq \emptyset\} \end{array}$$

Here $X_{(\vartheta,\vartheta_1)}$ is defined by $X_{(\vartheta,\vartheta_1)} = \{< v_1, v_2, \ldots >:< (\vartheta, \vartheta_1) \cdot v_1, v_2, \ldots > \in X\}$.

(The well-definedness of β_{FI} can be established in the by now familiar way: it can be given as the fixed-point of a contraction.) The abstraction operator β_{FI} first selects from the set X the *connected* sequences, that is, those sequences such that the output substitution of a pair equals the input substitution of the following pair. From such a connected sequence it takes all the output substitutions.

We have the following theorem relating $\mathcal{O}_{\mathrm{FI}}$ and $\mathcal{D}_{\mathrm{FI}}$. (Recall that ϵ is the empty substitution.)

Theorem 8.2 *For every goal* $\leftarrow \bar{A}$ *we have* $\beta_{\mathrm{FI}}(\epsilon) \circ \mathcal{D}_{\mathrm{FI}}[\![\leftarrow \bar{A}]\!] = \mathcal{O}_{\mathrm{FI}}[\![\leftarrow \bar{A}]\!]$.

Proof We prove $\beta_{\mathrm{FI}}(\epsilon) \circ \mathcal{D}_{\mathrm{FI}} = \mathcal{O}_{\mathrm{FI}}$ by showing that $\beta_{\mathrm{FI}}(\epsilon) \circ \mathcal{D}_{\mathrm{FI}}$ is a fixed-point of the contraction Φ_{FI}. Then the equality follows from Banach's theorem. We ommit the deadlock case, which can be taken care of straightforwardly.

$\Phi_{\mathrm{FI}}(\beta_{\mathrm{FI}}(\epsilon) \circ \mathcal{D}_{\mathrm{FI}})[\![\leftarrow A, \bar{A}]\!] =$

$\bigcup\{\vartheta \cdot (\vartheta \leadsto_{\mathrm{FI}} (\beta_{\mathrm{FI}}(\epsilon) \circ \mathcal{D}_{\mathrm{FI}}[\![\leftarrow \bar{A}\vartheta, \bar{B}\vartheta]\!])) : H \leftarrow \bar{B} \in W \text{ and } \vartheta = mgu(A, H)\} =$

(remark 1)

$\bigcup\{\vartheta \cdot (\beta_{\mathrm{FI}}(\vartheta) \circ \mathcal{D}_{\mathrm{FI}}[\![\leftarrow \bar{A}, \bar{B}]\!]) : H \leftarrow \bar{B} \in W \text{ and } \vartheta = mgu(A, H)\} =$

$\beta_{\mathrm{FI}}(\epsilon)(\bigcup\{< (\epsilon, \vartheta) > \cdot (\mathcal{D}_{\mathrm{FI}}[\![\leftarrow \bar{A}]\!] \parallel_{\mathrm{FI}} \mathcal{D}_{\mathrm{FI}}[\![\leftarrow \bar{B}]\!]) :$

$H \leftarrow \bar{B} \in W \text{ and } \vartheta = mgu(A, H)\}) =$

(remark 2)

$\beta_{\mathrm{FI}}(\epsilon)(\bigcup\{< (\epsilon, \vartheta) > \cdot \mathcal{D}_{\mathrm{FI}}[\![\leftarrow \bar{B}]\!] \parallel_{\mathrm{FI}} \mathcal{D}_{\mathrm{FI}}[\![\leftarrow \bar{A}]\!] :$

$H \leftarrow \bar{B} \in W \text{ and } \vartheta = mgu(A, H)\}) =$

$\beta_{\mathrm{FI}}(\epsilon)(\bigcup\{< (\epsilon, \vartheta) > \cdot \mathcal{D}_{\mathrm{FI}}[\![\leftarrow \bar{B}]\!] :$

$H \leftarrow \bar{B} \in W \text{ and } \vartheta = mgu(A, H)\} \parallel_{\mathrm{FI}} \mathcal{D}_{\mathrm{FI}}[\![\leftarrow \bar{A}]\!]) =$

$\beta_{\mathrm{FI}}(\epsilon)(\mathcal{D}_{\mathrm{FI}}[\![\leftarrow A]\!] \parallel_{\mathrm{FI}} \mathcal{D}_{\mathrm{FI}}[\![\leftarrow \bar{A}]\!]) =$

$\beta_{\mathrm{FI}}(\epsilon) \circ \mathcal{D}_{\mathrm{FI}}[\![\leftarrow A, \bar{A}]\!]$

Remark 1 The identity $\vartheta \leadsto_{\mathrm{FI}} \beta_{\mathrm{FI}}(\epsilon) \circ \mathcal{D}_{\mathrm{FI}}[\![\leftarrow \bar{A}\vartheta, \bar{B}\vartheta]\!] = \beta_{\mathrm{FI}}(\vartheta) \circ \mathcal{D}_{\mathrm{FI}}[\![\leftarrow \bar{A}, \bar{B}]\!]$ is justified by the following observations. Let $< v_1, \ldots > \in \mathcal{D}_{\mathrm{FI}}[\![\leftarrow \bar{A}, \bar{B}]\!]$ be a connected sequence with its first pair of the form (ϑ, ϑ'), for some ϑ'. It follows that $v_1 =< (\vartheta, \vartheta\vartheta_1), \ldots, (\vartheta\vartheta_1 \ldots \vartheta_{n-1}, \vartheta\vartheta_1 \ldots \vartheta_n) >$, with $\vartheta_i = mgu(A_i\vartheta\vartheta_1 \ldots \vartheta_{i-1}, H_i)$, for some $H_i \leftarrow \bar{B}_i$. Here we have $A_1, \ldots A_n = \bar{A}, \bar{B}$. So for $v_1' =< (\epsilon, \vartheta_1), \ldots, (\vartheta_1 \ldots \vartheta_{n-1}, \vartheta_1 \ldots \vartheta_n) >$ there exists a sequence $< v_1', \ldots > \in \mathcal{D}_{\mathrm{FI}}[\![\leftarrow \bar{A}\vartheta, \bar{B}\vartheta]\!]$. Now each pair occurring in $< v_2, \ldots > \in \mathcal{D}_{\mathrm{FI}}[\![\leftarrow \bar{B}_1, \ldots, \bar{B}_n]\!]$ is of the form $(\vartheta\vartheta', \vartheta\vartheta'\vartheta'')$, where $\vartheta'' = mgu(B\vartheta\vartheta', H)$, for some atoms B and H. But due to the renaming mechanism, which we implictly assume, we have that ϑ does not affect the variables of B. So we have that $\vartheta'' = mgu(B\vartheta', H)$ implying that we can eliminate ϑ from the sequence $< v_2, \ldots >$. This argument could be formalized by the introduction of an explicit renaming mechanism.

Remark 2 We show that $\beta_{FI}(\epsilon)(<(\epsilon,\vartheta)> \cdot (X \parallel_{FI} Y)) = \beta_{FI}(\epsilon)(<(\epsilon,\vartheta)> \cdot Y \parallel_{FI} X)$. (For convenience, we write $< v_n >_n$ for $< v_1, v_2, \ldots >$.)

$$\beta_{FI}(\epsilon)(<(\epsilon,\vartheta)> \cdot (X \parallel_{FI} Y)) =$$

$$\beta_{FI}(\epsilon)(\{<(\epsilon,\vartheta)> \cdot (< w_n >_n \parallel_{FI} < v_n >_n) :$$

$$< w_n >_n \in X,\ < v_n >_n \in Y\}) =$$

(from Definition 5.1 and Definition 8.1)

$$\beta_{FI}(\epsilon)(\{<(\epsilon,\vartheta)w_1, v_1w_2, \ldots >: < w_n >_n \in X,\ < v_n >_n \in Y\}) =$$

$$\beta_{FI}(\epsilon)(\{<(\epsilon,\vartheta), v_1, \ldots > \parallel_{FI} < w_1, \ldots >: < w_n >_n \in X,\ < v_n >_n \in Y\}) =$$

$$\beta_{FI}(\epsilon)(<(\epsilon,\vartheta)> \cdot Y \parallel_{FI} X)$$

8.1.2 Relating $\mathcal{O}_{MP}$ and $\mathcal{D}_{MP}$

Next we prove the identity of the operational model $\mathcal{O}_{MP}$ and the denotational model $\mathcal{D}_{MP}$ for maximal parallelism.

Theorem 8.3 $\mathcal{O}_{MP} = \mathcal{D}_{MP}$

Proof Similarly to the proof of Theorem 8.2, it can be shown that $\mathcal{D}_{MP}$ is a fixed-point of the contraction Φ_{MP}, from which the theorem follows.

8.2 Relating $\mathcal{D}_{FI}$ and $\mathcal{D}_{MP}$

In order to relate $\mathcal{D}_{FI}$ and $\mathcal{D}_{MP}$, we introduce an intermediate semantics $\mathcal{I} : Goal \rightarrow P_I$, with $P_I = \mathcal{P}_{nco}((Subst_\delta{}^+)^\infty)$, as the fixed-point of the contraction $\Psi : (Goal \rightarrow P_I) \rightarrow (Goal \rightarrow P_I)$ defined as follows.

Definition 8.4 *We define*

$$\begin{array}{lcl} \Psi(F)[\![\Box]\!] & = & \{\epsilon\} \\ \Psi(F)[\![\leftarrow A]\!] & = & \left\{ \begin{array}{l} \bigcup\{< mgu(A,H) > \cdot F(\bar{B}) :\ H \leftarrow \bar{B} \in W\} \\ \bigcup\{\delta : \forall H \leftarrow \bar{B} \in W\ mgu(A,H) \ does\ not\ exist\} \end{array} \right. \\ \Psi(F)[\![\leftarrow \bar{A}_1, \bar{A}_2]\!] & = & \Psi(F)[\![\leftarrow \bar{A}_1]\!] \parallel \Psi(F)[\![\leftarrow \bar{A}_2]\!] \end{array}$$

Here $\parallel$ *is defined in a similar way as* $\parallel_{FI}$.

Now $\mathcal{D}_{FI}$ and $\mathcal{I}$ are related by the following abstraction operator.

Definition 8.5 *We define* $\alpha : P_{FI} \rightarrow P_I$ *by*

$$\alpha(X) = \{< \vartheta_1 \cdots \vartheta_k, \vartheta_{k+1} \cdots \vartheta_l, \cdots >: < (\epsilon,\vartheta_1) \cdots (\epsilon,\vartheta_k), (\epsilon,\vartheta_{k+1}) \cdots (\epsilon,\vartheta_l), \cdots > \in X\}$$

(We have omitted the case that X *contains finite sequences.)*

This abstraction operator selects from each set those sequences that make no assumptions on the environment, i.e., of which all pairs have ϵ (the empty substitution) as the first element.

Theorem 8.6 $\mathcal{I} = \alpha \circ \mathcal{D}_{\mathrm{FI}}$

Proof It can be shown that $\alpha \circ \mathcal{D}_{\mathrm{FI}}$ is a fixed-point of Ψ.

We continue the equivalence proof of $\mathcal{D}_{\mathrm{FI}}$ and $\mathcal{D}_{\mathrm{MP}}$ by relating $\mathcal{I}$ and $\mathcal{D}_{\mathrm{MP}}$. For this purpose we again need an abstraction operator.

Definition 8.7 *We define* $\alpha_{\mathrm{MP}} : P_{\mathrm{I}} \rightarrow P_{\mathrm{ST}}$ *by* $\alpha_{\mathrm{MP}}(< s_1, s_2, \ldots >) = (\hat{\circ}\, s_1) \cdot (\hat{\circ}\,(s_1 \cdot s_2)) \cdots$, *where* $s_i \in \mathit{Subst}_\delta{}^+$ *and* $\hat{\circ}\, \vartheta_1 \cdots \vartheta_n = \vartheta_1 \,\hat{\circ}\, \cdots \,\hat{\circ}\, \vartheta_n$.

This operator takes for each word $\vartheta_1 \cdots \vartheta_n \in \mathit{Subst}_\delta{}^+$ the parallel composition, thus turning it into one maximally parallel step. Further, it passes through the result of previous steps to the next one to be considered. This mimics the behavior of the $\leadsto_{\mathrm{MP}}$ operator in the definition of $\mathcal{D}_{\mathrm{MP}}$. Now we can establish the following theorem.

Theorem 8.8 $\mathcal{D}_{\mathrm{MP}} = \alpha_{\mathrm{MP}} \circ \mathcal{I}$

Proof Again it can easily be shown that $\alpha_{\mathrm{MP}} \circ \mathcal{I}$ is a fixed-point of Ψ_{MP}.

Combining the two above theorems yields the following corollary.

Corollary 8.9 $\mathcal{D}_{\mathrm{MP}} = \alpha_{\mathrm{MP}} \circ \alpha \circ \mathcal{D}_{\mathrm{FI}}$

8.3 Relating $\mathcal{D}_{\mathrm{MP}}$ and $\mathcal{D}ec$: an intermediate model $\mathcal{D}_{\mathrm{CS}}$

We introduce an intermediate denotational semantics $\mathcal{D}_{\mathrm{CS}}$ (CS is an abbreviation for computed substitutions), to which both $\mathcal{D}_{\mathrm{MP}}$ and $\mathcal{D}ec$ will be related. It can be seen as a denotational variant of $\mathcal{D}ec$, which yields for every goal the set of computed answer substitutions; since it delivers a set of substitutions, rather than a set of sequences of substitutions, it models only success behavior. Like $\mathcal{D}_{\mathrm{MP}}$ it is a model for maximal parallelism. Formally, $\mathcal{D}_{\mathrm{CS}}$ is introduced as the least fixed-point of a continuous function on a complete lattice, which we introduce next.

Definition 8.10 *The set* P_{CS}*, with typical element* F *is given by* $P_{\mathrm{CS}} = \mathit{Goal} \rightarrow \mathcal{P}(\mathit{Subst})$.

The set $\mathcal{P}(\mathit{Subst})$ of sets of substitutions, is a complete lattice with respect to set inclusion. Thus P_{CS} is also a complete lattice, when supplied with the inclusion relation induced by the one on $\mathcal{P}(\mathit{Subst})$: $f_1 \subseteq f_2$ iff $\forall \leftarrow \bar{A}[f_1(\leftarrow \bar{A}) \subseteq f_2(\leftarrow \bar{A})]$. Since we do not need to consider sequences, a lattice structure, rather than a metric one, suffices as a domain for $\mathcal{D}_{\mathrm{CS}}$.

The least upper bound of a set $\mathcal{F} \subseteq P_{\mathrm{CS}}$, denoted by $\bigcup_{F \in \mathcal{F}}$, is defined by

$$(\bigcup_{F \in \mathcal{F}})[\![\leftarrow \bar{A}]\!] = \bigcup_{F \in \mathcal{F}} F[\![\leftarrow \bar{A}]\!]$$

Before giving the definition of $\mathcal{D}_{CS}$ we first extend the definition of $\hat{\circ}$, the operator for the parallel composition of substitutions, to sets of substitutions. We put, for $X, Y \in \mathcal{P}(Subst)$,

$$X \hat{\circ} Y = \{\vartheta \hat{\circ} \sigma : \vartheta \in X, \sigma \in Y, \vartheta \hat{\circ} \sigma \neq \delta\}$$

The following lemma states that it is continuous, a fact that we shall need in the definition below.

Lemma 8.11 *Let* $\{X_m\}_{m\geq 0}, \{Y_n\}_{n\geq 0}$ *be chains in* $\mathcal{P}(Subst)$ $(\forall k\ [X_k \subseteq X_{k+1} \wedge Y_k \subseteq Y_{k+1}])$. *Then* $\bigcup_{k\geq 0}(X_k \hat{\circ} Y_k) = (\bigcup_{m\geq 0} X_m) \hat{\circ} (\bigcup_{n\geq 0} Y_n)$.

Next we introduce $\mathcal{D}_{CS} : Goal \rightarrow \mathcal{P}(Subst)$.

Definition 8.12 *Let* $\mathcal{D}_{CS} : Goal \rightarrow \mathcal{P}(Subst)$ *be the least fixed-point of the continuous (with respect to the lattice structure on* P_{CS}*) operator* $\Psi_{CS} : (Goal \rightarrow \mathcal{P}(Subst)) \rightarrow (Goal \rightarrow \mathcal{P}(Subst))$, *given by*

$$\begin{aligned}
\Psi_{CS}(F)[\![\Box]\!] &= \{\epsilon\} \\
\Psi_{CS}(F)[\![\leftarrow A]\!] &= \bigcup\{(mgu(A,H) \hat{\circ} F(\leftarrow \bar{B}))|_{Var(A)} : H \leftarrow \bar{B} \in W\} \\
\Psi_{CS}(F)[\![\leftarrow \bar{A}_1, \bar{A}_2]\!] &= \Psi_{CS}(F)[\![\leftarrow \bar{A}_1]\!] \hat{\circ} \Psi_{CS}(F)[\![\leftarrow \bar{A}_2]\!]
\end{aligned}$$

The continuity of Ψ_{CS} is a direct consequence of Lemma 8.11.

8.4 Relating $\mathcal{D}_{MP}$ and $\mathcal{D}_{CS}$

The relation between the models $\mathcal{D}_{MP}$ and $\mathcal{D}_{CS}$ is described by the abstraction operator

$\alpha_{CS} : P_{ST} \rightarrow \mathcal{P}(Subst)$ defined by $\alpha_{CS}(X) = last(X \cap Subst^+)$

(The function *last* used above yields for a set of finite sequences the set of their last elements.) We have the following theorem.

Theorem 8.13 $\mathcal{D}_{CS} = \alpha_{CS} \circ \mathcal{D}_{MP}$

The theorem is immediate from the following two lemmas, which can be proved by induction on n. Let the functions $\perp$ and f_{ϵ^ω} be defined by $\perp(\leftarrow \bar{A}) = \emptyset$ and $f_{\epsilon^\omega}(\leftarrow \bar{A}) = \{\epsilon^\omega\}$, for all $\leftarrow \bar{A}$.

Lemma 8.14 *For all* n*:* $\Psi^n_{CS}(\perp) = (\alpha_{CS} \circ \Psi^n_{MP})(f_{\epsilon^\omega})$

Lemma 8.15 *For all* n *and* $\leftarrow \bar{B}$*:* $(\alpha_{CS} \circ \Psi^n_{MP})(f_{\epsilon^\omega})(\leftarrow \bar{B}) \subseteq (\alpha_{CS} \circ \Psi^{n+1}_{MP})(f_{\epsilon^\omega})(\leftarrow \bar{B})$

Proof of Theorem 8.13: For any $\leftarrow \bar{B}$ we have

$$\begin{aligned}
(\alpha_{CS} \circ \mathcal{D}_{MP})(\leftarrow \bar{B}) &= \alpha_{CS}(\lim_{n\rightarrow\infty} \Psi^n_{MP}(f_{\epsilon^\omega})(\leftarrow \bar{B})) \\
&= (\text{Lemma 8.15})\ \alpha_{CS}(\bigcup_n \Psi^n_{MP}(f_{\epsilon^\omega})(\leftarrow \bar{B})) \\
&= \bigcup_n \alpha_{CS}(\Psi^n_{MP}(f_{\epsilon^\omega})(\leftarrow \bar{B})) \\
&= (\text{Lemma 8.14})\ \bigcup_n \Psi^n_{CS}(\perp)(\leftarrow \bar{B}) \\
&= \mathcal{D}_{CS}(\leftarrow \bar{B}).
\end{aligned}$$

□

8.5 Relating $\mathcal{D}_{CS}$ and $\mathcal{D}ec$

Next we shall compare the denotational semantics modeling the computed answer substitutions, on the one hand, and the declarative semantics, on the other. The relation will be given by defining two *uniform* functions, ν and μ and by showing that $\mathcal{D}ec = \nu(\mathcal{D}_{CS})$ and $\mathcal{D}_{CS} = \mu(\mathcal{D}ec)$. Here uniform means that these two functions do not depend upon the specific program W.

The sketch of the proof is the following: first we consider a sub-domain P of the domain of Ψ_{CS} such that μ and ν make T and Ψ_{CS} to commute on this domain, namely: $\Psi_{CS}(\mu(I)) = \mu(T(I))$, and $\nu(\Psi_{CS}(F)) = T(\nu(F))$ for all $F \in P$. Then we show that ν allows to *simulate* step by step the fixed-point construction of Ψ_{CS} by T and vice-versa, namely: for each $n \geq 0, T^n(\emptyset) = \nu(\Psi^n_{CS}(F_0))$ and $\Psi^n_{CS}(F_0) = \mu(T^n(\emptyset))$ (where F_0 is the minimal element of P). Finally, by continuity of ν and μ, we can commute also the least upper bounds of these chains, so that $lfp(T) = \bigcup_{n\geq 0} T^n(\emptyset) = \nu(\bigcup_{n\geq 0} \Psi^n_{CS}(F_0)) = \nu(lfp(\Psi_{CS}))$ and $lfp(\Psi_{CS}) = \bigcup_{n\geq 0} \Psi^n_{CS}(F_0) = \mu(\bigcup_{n\geq 0} T^n(\emptyset)) = \mu(lfp(T))$.

We use the following notation: $Var(\bar{A})$ is the set of variables occurring in $\bar{A}$. $Dom(\vartheta)$ (the domain of ϑ) is the set $\{x : x\vartheta \neq x\}$. $Cod(\vartheta)$ (the codomain of ϑ) is the set $\bigcup_{x\in Dom(\vartheta)} Var(x\vartheta)$. If X is a set of substitutions and A is an atom, then X_A is the set $\{\vartheta_A : \vartheta \in X\}$, where ϑ_A is any renaming of ϑ with respect to A, i.e., such that $\forall x[\, Var(x\vartheta_A) \cap Var(A) = \emptyset]$.

Definition 8.16 *P is the subset of $P_{CS} = Goal \to \mathcal{P}(Subst)$ of all elements F that satisfy the following properties.*

R1 $F[\![\Box]\!] = \{\epsilon\}$

R2 $\forall\vartheta\ [Dom(\vartheta) \subseteq \bar{x} \Rightarrow (\vartheta\, \hat{\circ}\, F[\![\leftarrow p(\bar{x})]\!]_{p(\bar{x})\vartheta})_{|p(\bar{x})\vartheta} = F[\![\leftarrow p(\bar{x})\vartheta]\!]]$

R3 $F[\![\leftarrow \bar{A}_1, \bar{A}_2]\!] = F[\![\leftarrow \bar{A}_1]\!]\ \hat{\circ}\ F[\![\leftarrow \bar{A}_2]\!]$

R4 $\forall\bar{A}\ \forall\vartheta \in F[\![\leftarrow \bar{A}]\!]\ [Dom(\vartheta) \subseteq Var(\bar{A})]$

The motivation of these restrictions is of a technical nature: the set P will turn out to be isomorphic to the set P_{Dec}. The isomorphism pair, $< \nu, \mu >$, will be defined later. **R3** requires the information given by F about generic goals to be obtainable by the information about *atomic* goals. This correspond to the compositional nature of interpretations in P_{Dec}: the meaning of a conjunction is declaratively defined in terms of its conjuncts. **R2** also reflects a kind of compositionality: the possibility to obtain the information about an instantiated atom from the uninstantiated one. **R1** and **R4** impose a sort of *minimality* on the information associated to a goal.

The set P is a complete partial order with respect to the ordering it inherits from P_{CS}. This we prove next.

Proposition 8.17 *$(P, \subseteq)$ is a complete partial order; the least upper bound of a chain $(F_n)_n$ is given by $(\bigcup_n F_n$. In other words, $(P, \subseteq)$ is a sub CPO of $(P_{CS}, \subseteq)$.*

Proof We have to show that for any chain $(F_n)_n$ in P, $\bigcup_n F_n$ preserves the properties **R1-R4**. **R1**, **R2** and **R4** are obvious. **R3** follows by lemma 8.11. $\Box$

Definition 8.18

- *The function* $\nu : P \to P_{\mathrm{Dec}}$ *is defined by*

$$\nu(F) = \{p(\bar{x})\vartheta : \vartheta \in F[\![\leftarrow p(\bar{x})]\!] \wedge p(\bar{x}) \in EAtom\}$$

- *The function* $\mu : P_{\mathrm{Dec}} \to P$ *is defined by*

$$\begin{array}{lcl} \mu(I)[\![\Box]\!] & = & \{\epsilon\} \\ \mu(I)[\![\leftarrow A]\!] & = & \{mgu(A, A')_{|A} : A' \in I \wedge Var(\bar{A}') \cap Var(\bar{A}) = \emptyset\} \\ \mu(I)[\![\leftarrow \bar{A}_1, \bar{A}_2]\!] & = & \mu(I)[\![\leftarrow \bar{A}_1]\!] \,\hat{\circ}\, \mu(I)[\![\leftarrow \bar{A}_2]\!] \end{array}$$

Remark 8.19 *The function* μ *is well defined, i.e.,* $\forall I \in P_{\mathrm{Dec}}\ [\mu(I) \in P]$.

Proof R1, R3 and **R4** are trivial, and **R2** is an immediate consequence of the following lemma.

Lemma 8.20 *Let* ϑ *be an idempotent substitution, and assume* $Dom(\vartheta) \subseteq \bar{x}$. *Let* A *be an atom such that* $Var(A) \cap \{\bar{x}\} = \emptyset$ *and* $Var(A) \cap Var(\{\bar{x}\vartheta\}) = \emptyset$. *Then*

$$(\vartheta \,\hat{\circ}\, mgu(p(\bar{x}), A))_{|p(\bar{x})\vartheta} = mgu(p(\bar{x})\vartheta, A)_{|p(\bar{x})\vartheta}.$$

Proof The proof uses some elementary properties of idempotent substitutions (see [13]).

The following facts can be readily established.

Proposition 8.21 *The functions* ν *and* μ *are continuous.*

Proposition 8.22 P *is closed with respect to* Ψ_{CS}, *i.e.,* $\forall F \in P\ [\Psi_{\mathrm{CS}}(F) \in P]$.

The following result shows that μ and ν commute the functions Ψ_{CS} and T on P.

Lemma 8.23

1. *If* $F \in P$ *then* $\nu(\Psi_{\mathrm{CS}}(F)) = T(\nu(F))$
2. *If* $I \in P_{\mathrm{Dec}}$ *then* $\Psi_{\mathrm{CS}}(\mu(I)) = \mu(T(I))$

The functions ν and μ allow to simulate, step by step, the fixed-point construction of $\mathcal{D}_{\mathrm{CS}}$ in $\mathcal{D}ec$, and vice-versa. There is only one difficulty: the fixed-point construction of Ψ_{CS} starts from the minimal element of P_{CS}, that is the function $F_\perp$ such that for every $\bar{A}$, $F_\perp[\![\leftarrow \bar{A}]\!] = \emptyset$. Unfortunately, $F_\perp$ is not the minimal element of P, in fact $F_\perp \notin P$. The minimal element of P is the function F_0 such that

$$F_0[\![\leftarrow \bar{A}]\!] = \begin{cases} \{\epsilon\} & \text{iff } \leftarrow \bar{A} = \Box \\ \emptyset & \text{otherwise} \end{cases}$$

However, the fixed-point of Ψ_{CS} can be also obtained by starting from F_0, as the following remark shows.

Remark 8.24 *We have* $F_0 = \mu(\emptyset)$ *and* $F_0 = \Psi_{\mathrm{CS}}(F_\perp)$.

Lemma 8.25

1. $\forall n \geq 0\ [T^n(\nu(F_0)) = \nu(\Psi^n_{CS}(F_0))]$
2. $\forall n \geq 0\ [\Psi^n_{CS}(\mu(\emptyset)) = \mu(T^n(\emptyset))]$.

Proof By induction on n.

Finally, we show the correspondence between $\mathcal{D}_{CS}$ and $\mathcal{D}ec$

Theorem 8.26

1. $\mathcal{D}ec = \nu(\mathcal{D}_{CS})$ 2. $\mathcal{D}_{CS} = \mu(\mathcal{D}ec)$

Proof

$$
\begin{aligned}
1.\ \mathcal{D}ec &= lfp(T) \\
&= \bigcup_{n\geq 0} T^n(\emptyset) \\
&= \bigcup_{n\geq 0} T^n(\nu(F_0)) \text{ (by Remark 8.24, part 1)} \\
&= \bigcup_{n\geq 0} \nu(\Psi^n_{CS}(F_0)) \text{ (by Lemma 8.25, part 1)} \\
&= \nu(\bigcup_{n\geq 0}(\Psi^n_{CS}(F_0)) \text{ (by continuity of } \nu) \\
&= \nu(lfp(\Psi_{CS})) \text{ (by Remark 8.24, part 2)} \\
&= \nu(\mathcal{D}_{CS}).
\end{aligned}
$$

2. Similar to the previous one. □

9 Collecting the results

After the long and exhausting previous section, the reader might be comforted by a schematic overview of the relationships that were established. We have the following equalities.

$$
\begin{aligned}
\mathcal{O}_{FI} &= \beta_{FI} \circ \mathcal{D}_{FI} \\
\mathcal{I} &= \alpha \circ \mathcal{D}_{FI} \\
\mathcal{O}_{MP} &= \mathcal{D}_{MP} = \alpha_{MP} \circ \mathcal{I} \\
\mathcal{D}_{CS} &= \alpha_{CS} \circ \mathcal{D}_{MP} \\
\mathcal{D}_{CS} &= \mu(\mathcal{D}ec) \\
\mathcal{D}ec &= \nu(\mathcal{D}_{CS})
\end{aligned}
$$

In Figure 1, these equalities are graphically represented. Moreover, it contains some arrows between $\mathcal{O}_{FI}$ and the sets $\mathcal{O}_{SS}$, $\mathcal{O}_{FFS}$ and $\mathcal{O}_{IFS}$, indicating that the definition of these sets is based on that of $\mathcal{O}_{FI}$.

Combining some of the equalities above, we find

$$\mathcal{D}ec = \nu(\alpha_{CS} \circ \alpha_{MP} \circ \alpha \circ \mathcal{D}_{FI}),$$

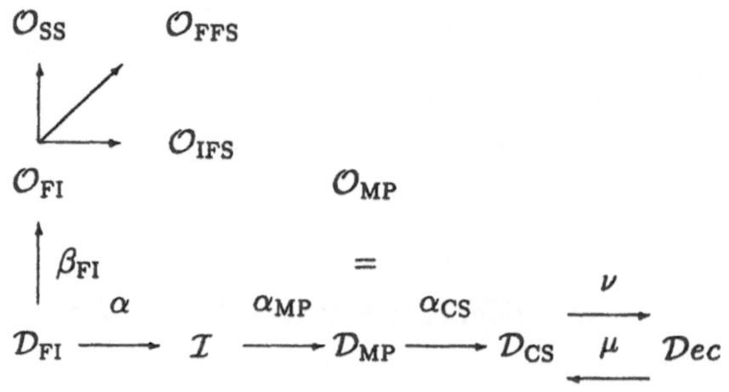

a maybe somewhat complicated but precise relationship between the declarative semantics $\mathcal{D}ec$ and the denotational semantics $\mathcal{D}_{FI}$. From this the following theorem, which establishes the soundness and completeness of the declarative semantics, is fairly immediate. Thus an alternative is given for the quite complicated proof that is given in [9]. The fact that here the relationship between $\mathcal{D}ec$ and $\mathcal{D}_{FI}$ and, hence, between $\mathcal{D}ec$ and $\mathcal{O}_{SS}$ has been decomposed into several steps makes the proof below more transparent.

Theorem 9.1 $A \in \mathcal{O}_{SS} \Leftrightarrow A \in \mathcal{D}ec$

Proof

$A \in \mathcal{O}_{SS}$

$\Leftrightarrow$ (definition $\mathcal{O}_{SS}$) $\exists p(\bar{x})\exists\vartheta_1 \cdots \vartheta_n \in \mathcal{O}_{FI}[\![\leftarrow p(\bar{x})]\!] : \; A = p(\bar{x})\vartheta_n$

$\Leftrightarrow$ ($\mathcal{O}_{FI} = \beta_{FI} \circ \mathcal{D}_{FI}$) $\exists p(\bar{x})\exists s_1, \ldots, s_k \in \mathcal{D}_{FI}[\![\leftarrow p(\bar{x})]\!] :$

$s_1 \cdots s_k =< (\epsilon, \vartheta_1), (\vartheta_1, \vartheta_2), (\vartheta_2, \vartheta_3), \cdots, (\vartheta_{n-1}, \vartheta_n) > \wedge\, A = p(\bar{x})\vartheta_n$

$\Leftrightarrow$ (using $\vartheta mgu(A\vartheta, H) = \vartheta \,\hat{\circ}\, mgu(A, H)$, a direct consequence of Lemma 4.4)

$\exists p(\bar{x})\exists s_1, \ldots, s_k \in \mathcal{D}_{FI}[\![\leftarrow p(\bar{x})]\!] :$

$s_1 \cdots s_k =< (\epsilon, \vartheta_1), (\epsilon, \vartheta_2), \cdots, (\epsilon, \vartheta_n) > \wedge\, A = p(\bar{x})(\vartheta_1 \,\hat{\circ}\, \cdots \,\hat{\circ}\, \vartheta_n)$

$\Leftrightarrow$ ($\mathcal{I} = \alpha \circ \mathcal{D}_{FI}$)

$\exists p(\bar{x})\exists < v_1, \ldots, v_k > \in \mathcal{I}[\![\leftarrow p(\bar{x})]\!] : \; v_1 \cdots v_k = \vartheta_1 \cdots \vartheta_n \wedge A = p(\bar{x})(\vartheta_1 \,\hat{\circ}\, \cdots \,\hat{\circ}\, \vartheta_n)$

$\Leftrightarrow$ ($\mathcal{D}_{MP} = \alpha_{MP} \circ \mathcal{I}$) $\exists p(\bar{x})\exists\vartheta_1 \cdots \vartheta_n \in \mathcal{D}_{MP}[\![\leftarrow p(\bar{x})]\!] : \; A = p(\bar{x})\vartheta_n$

$\Leftrightarrow$ ($\mathcal{D}_{CS} = \alpha_{CS} \circ \mathcal{D}_{MP}$) $\exists p(\bar{x})\exists\vartheta \in \mathcal{D}_{CS}[\![\leftarrow p(\bar{x})]\!] : \; A = p(\bar{x})\vartheta$

$\Leftrightarrow \; A \in \mathcal{D}ec$

□

We deduce from the equalities above a second fact, which says that $\mathcal{O}_{\rm SS}$, $\mathcal{O}_{\rm FFS}$ and $\mathcal{O}_{\rm IFS}$ can be characterized in terms of $\mathcal{O}_{\rm MP}$ ($= \mathcal{D}_{\rm MP}$), instead of $\mathcal{O}_{\rm FI}$. In other words, for the semantics of an HCL program, it does not matter whether we consider an interleaving or a maximally parallel model. Although this might seem not very surprising, it is not completely straightforward, since $\mathcal{O}_{\rm MP}$ and $\mathcal{O}_{\rm FI}$ have a different deadlock behavior: the former delivers deadlock for more goals than the latter. (See the counter example at the end of section 4.1.)

Theorem 9.2 *We have the following equalities.*

$$\begin{aligned} \mathcal{O}_{\rm SS} &= \{p(\bar{x})\vartheta : p(\bar{x}) \in EAtom \wedge \vartheta \in last(\mathcal{O}_{\rm MP}[\![\leftarrow p(\bar{x})]\!] \cap Subst^{+})\} \\ \mathcal{O}_{\rm FFS} &= \{A : \mathcal{O}_{\rm MP}[\![\leftarrow A]\!] \subseteq Subst^{*} \cdot \delta\} \\ \mathcal{O}_{\rm IFS} &= \{A : \mathcal{O}_{\rm MP}[\![\leftarrow A]\!] \cap Subst^{*} = \emptyset \wedge \mathcal{O}_{\rm MP}[\![\leftarrow A]\!] \cap Subst^{\omega} \neq \emptyset\} \end{aligned}$$

Proof Similar to that of the previous theorem.

Acknowledgements

We thank Jean-Marie Jacquet, Peter Knijnenburg and Erik de Vink for their detailed comments on a draft of this paper.

References

[1] K.R. Apt. Introduction to logic programming. Technical Report CS-R8741, Centre for Mathematics and Computer Science, Amsterdam, 1987. To appear as a chapter in J. van Leeuwen, editor, Handbook of Theoretical Computer Science, North-Holland.

[2] K.R. Apt and M.H. van Emden. Contributions to the theory of logic programming. *Journal of the ACM*, 29(3):841–862, 1982.

[3] J.W. de Bakker and J.I. Zucker. Processes and the denotational semantics of concurrency. *Information and Control*, 54:70–120, 1982.

[4] F.S. de Boer, J.N. Kok, C. Palamidessi, and J.J.M.M. Rutten. Control flow versus logic: a denotational and a declarative model for guarded horn clauses. In A. Kreczmar and G. Mirkowska, editors, *Proceedings Mathematical Foundations of Computer Science (MFCS 89)*, volume 379 of *Lecture Notes in Computer Science*, pages 165–177, 1989.

[5] F.S. de Boer, J.N. Kok, C. Palamidessi, and J.J.M.M. Rutten. Semantic models for a version of parlog. In G. Levi and M. Martelli, editors, *Proceedings International Conference on Logic Programming (ICLP 89)*, pages 621–636. MIT Press, 1989. To appear in Theoretical Computer Science.

[6] E.P. de Vink. Concurrency semantics applied to logic programming. Technical report, Vrije Universiteit, Amsterdam, 1990.

[7] R. Engelking. *General Topology.* Polish Scientific Publishers, 1977.

[8] M. Falaschi, G. Levi, C. Palamidessi, and M. Martelli. A new declarative semantics for logic languages. In *Proceedings Conference and Symposium on Logic Programming*, pages 993–1005. MIT press, 1988.

[9] M. Falaschi, G. Levi, C. Palamidessi, and M. Martelli. Declarative modeling of the operational behaviour of logic languages. *Theoretical Computer Science*, 69(3):289–318, 1989.

[10] M. Hennessy and G.D. Plotkin. Full abstraction for a simple parallel programming language. In J. Becvar, editor, *Proceedings Mathematical Foundations of Computer Science (MFCS 79)*, volume 74 of *Lecture Notes in Computer Science*, pages 108–120. Springer Verlag, 1979.

[11] J.-M. Jacquet. *Conclog: A methodological approach to concurrent logic programming.* PhD thesis, Facultes Universitaires Notre Dame de la Paix, Namur, 1989.

[12] J.W. Lloyd. *Foundations of Logic Programming.* Springer Verlag, 1987. Second edition.

[13] C. Palamidessi. Algebraic properties of idempotent substitutions. Technical Report TR-32/89, Dipartimento di Informatica, University of Pisa, Pisa, 1989. To appear in the Proceedings of the 17th International Colloquium on Automata, Languages and Programming, Warwick, England, 1990.

[14] E.Y. Shapiro. A subset of concurrent prolog and its interpreter. Technical Report TR-003, ICOT, 1983.

[15] M.H. van Emden and R.A. Kowalski. The semantics of predicate logic as a programming language. *Journal of the ACM*, 23(4):733–742, 1976.

Negations of Transactions and Their Use in the Specification of Dynamic and Deontic Integrity Constraints

F.P.M. Dignum

Free University Amsterdam†

J.-J.Ch. Meyer

Free University Amsterdam/University of Nijmegen

ABSTRACT

We introduce the negations of transactions in the sense of non-performance as an ingredient of a specification language for integrity constraints. We investigate their (non-trivial) semantics in two stages: firstly a uniform semantics in terms of uninterpreted events, secondly a non-uniform semantics in terms of state (world) transforming functions. In particular we show the use of negated transactions in deontic integrity constraints.

1. Introduction

Recently it has been realized in the data- and knowledge base community, in particular that subgroup of researchers that occupy themselves with conceptual modelling, that integrity constraints often possess a *deontic* flavour. I.e. they often describe a *desirable* situation (or way of proceeding in a dynamic context) rather than an actual or *necessary* one (cf. [5,6,7,9,17,18,19]). To do justice to this status quo of the constraints to be imposed, it is not sufficient to just state the desirable situation or effect as if it were necessarily true and unescapable.

For instance, in a library knowledge base (KB), when it is an obligation (requirement or constraint) for a lender of a book to return it within 3 weeks, it is completely wrong to specify that a lender *will* return it within 3 weeks. The KB simply has no influence on the behaviour of lenders. At best it can put penalties upon the non-fulfilment of their obligations.

In order to give an adequate treatment of deontically flavoured integrity

† Current address: University of Swaziland, P/B Kwaluseni, Swaziland.

constraints [5,6] and [18] use a deontic logic based on dynamic logic. In [5] and [6], this deontic extension of dynamic logic functions as the logical interpretation of a conceptual modelling language (CPL). In this language all the integrity constraints (including the deontic and dynamic ones) can be described on a conceptual level.

The framework that is described in the above publications deals with three deontic modalities:

Prohibition: $F(\alpha)$ meaning that α is forbidden
Permission: $P(\alpha)$ meaning that α is permitted and
Obligation: $O(\alpha)$ meaning that α is obliged

where α stands for an action.

Roughly, actions are either primitive or composite, in the sense that they consist of the simultaneous or the non-deterministic performance of (sub)actions. Actions should, however, be distinguished from transactions. In transactions the sequential composition of (trans)actions is allowed.

The F and P modalities can be defined, in dynamic logic, in a straightforward manner. The F modality can be defined using the idea that an action is forbidden iff its performance leads to an illegal state, in which we can observe that something illegal has taken place. The P modality can then be defined as the negation of F.

The modality O of obligation, however, is less trivial. In the view of [18] and [5] the obligation to perform α is treated as the prohibition to NOT perform α, or rather to perform not-α. Here we encounter the problem to associate a meaning (semantics) to the action "not-α". In [9], Khosla shrinks from interpreting $O(\alpha)$ as $F(\text{not-}\alpha)$ for exactly this reason, viz. "difficulties in interpreting negative actions". In [5] and [18], however, a semantics is given for not-α, where α is an action as described above.

In this paper, we want to advance this line of work even further. While in [5,18] not-α and thus $O(\alpha) \equiv F(\text{not-}\alpha)$, is only defined for actions, we shall extend this semantics to *transactions* (i.e. sequential compositions of (trans)actions) in the present paper.

Although our work on negations of transactions is motivated mainly from the viewpoint of deontic constraints for transactions, we believe that negated transactions also have a more general use. It is sometimes useful in a specification to use negated (trans)actions. This may seem a little unorthodox. Specifications, usually, contain only positive information about the performance of actions. This is understandable, because in programs and algorithms only positive (trans)actions are used. We claim that in specifications of more complex and flexible systems (e.g. specifications of systems in which also the role of the users is specified) the expressibility of the consequences of the non-performance of (trans)actions is convenient as well, if not necessary.

This is also related to the issue of open vs. closed specification. The latter type of specification specifies the behaviour of a system under a closed world assumption (cf. [15]). I.e., what is not stated will not occur. An open specification only states that what is specified is *guaranteed* to occur, among other things. Under an open specification of actions it becomes relevant to specify e.g. *a* and not-*b* and not-*c*. In the closed specification of *a* one would only specify *a*, because the non-performance of *b* and *c* would be assumed implicitly.

The version of dynamic logic that is used in this paper is based on [8,11,12,18]. However, some parts have been changed and/or extended. Therefore, we will first give an overview of the syntax and semantics of the dynamic logic as it is used in this paper in the section 2, indicating the points where it differs from the other forms. Then in section 3 we connect the actions to the worlds in which the actions are performed. In section 4 we describe how the actions can be parameterized in order to cope with predicates rather than with propositions. Finally, in section 5 we describe the logical language L_{dyn} of dynamic assertions. After this introduction of dynamic and deontic logic, some examples of its use in the specification of integrity constraints are shown in section 6. Finally, in section 7, some conclusions are drawn.

2. Actions, transactions and their semantics

We will now introduce the language of action and transaction expressions and their formal semantics.

We start with a set of events $\mathcal{A}$, with typical elements a,b,c.... Furthermore, we introduce one special event δ, which is not an element of $\mathcal{A}$, and which models failure.† Together they constitute the set of elementary events. This set is to be regarded as the set of basic semantical entities. In our language we may write underlined versions of elements of $\mathcal{A}$, e.g. $\underline{a}$ with $a \in \mathcal{A}$. These underlined versions of events denote the atomic actions of the language. The meaning of these atomic actions will be the performance of a complex of (sets of) events, which include at least the event involved (i.e. *a* in the example). The set of all transaction expressions $\mathcal{Tract}$ can now be determined by the following BNF for its elements (α):

$$\alpha ::- \underline{a} \mid \alpha_1 \underline{\cup} \alpha_2 \mid \alpha_1 \& \alpha_2 \mid \alpha_1 ; \alpha_2 \mid \overline{\alpha} \mid \textbf{any} \mid \textbf{fail}$$

The meaning of $\alpha_1 \underline{\cup} \alpha_2$ is a choice between α_1 and α_2. $\alpha_1 \& \alpha_2$ stands for the parallel execution of α_1 and α_2, $\alpha_1;\alpha_2$ stands for the execution of α_1 followed by the execution of α_2. $\overline{\alpha}$ stands for the negation (or non-execution) of action α. As might be expected, the semantics of these negations of actions will be rather complex. The **any** action is a universal or "don't care which" action. Finally, the

† This event does not occur in other versions of dynamic logic in the literature. It is, however, comparable with the deadlock in process algebra.

fail action is the action that always fails. After this action the system stops and nothing can be done any more.

It is important to note the difference between the syntactical atomic actions and the semantical events. The meaning of an atomic action $\underline{a}$ involves the execution of the corresponding semantical event a possibly together with other events. The meaning of $\underline{a}$ only specifies the performance of the corresponding semantical a, but one is free to perform any other set of events simultaneously with a.

Actually our semantics consists of two parts. First we interpret our (trans)actions in terms of (sets of sequences of sets of) events. These events are left uninterpreted. This is what is called a *uniform* semantics in the literature on the semantics of concurrency (e.g. [1]). Next, in section 3, we shall interpret these denotations in terms of events further as state (or world) transforming functions. This yields a so-called non-uniform semantics.

The first part of this approach, which we shall discuss in this section, is also closely related to process algebras in the realm of concurrency research. In fact, one could consider it as an extension of basic process algebra in the sense of [3] with a simple SCCS-like form of concurrency (cf. [14]) and, most importantly, a "non-performance" operator (negation). This is combined with full distributivity of sequential composition over non-deterministic choice (resulting in a so-called linear time semantics [1]). We should also mention that the "&" operator is interpreted in a manner akin to what is called "step" semantics in that part of concurrency research where one tries to capture the nature of "true" concurrency rather than concurrency simulated by interleaving [13].

We will now start with the uniform semantics of actions in the following. It is based on the formal semantics as described in [11,12], but extended by the use of the failing event δ.

We give the semantics of transactions by sets of sequences of what are called *synchronicity* sets. These synchronicity sets denote sets of events that are executed simultaneously. Sequences of these entities are used to model sequential composition. Sets of these sequences are needed to model the non-determinism in our approach arising from the choice operator and the open specification.

The following definitions formally describe the synchronicity sets and how they can be combined to form sets of sequences of synchronicity sets.

Definition 1: (i) The set $\{\delta\}$ is a synchronicity set (s-set).

(ii) Every non-empty(!) subset of $\mathcal{A}$ is an s-set.

End Definition

Notation: We use $S, S_1, S_2, \ldots, S', \ldots$ for s-sets. In concrete cases we write such a set using square brackets. Thus to distinguish them from the sets modelling non-determinism and choices. So, the s-set consisting of the event δ is written as $[\delta]$ and the s-set consisting of the events a and b is written as $\begin{bmatrix} a \\ b \end{bmatrix}$. The powerset of s-sets will be denoted by $\mathcal{P}^+(\mathcal{A})$, where the '+' indicates that the s-sets are non-empty.

Definition 1 prevents the simultaneous execution of the special event δ with other events, because it is not in $\mathcal{A}$. This is needed because it is, of course, not possible to perform an event and at the same time have a deadlock.

To denote the subsequent execution of actions, we use sequences of s-sets. These sequences can be finite or infinite, although in practice they will usually be finite. They are very close to what are called "traces" or "streams" in the semantics of concurrent programming [4,10,16]. The definition of a sequence of s-sets is given as follows:

Definition 2:
A synchronicity sequence (s-sequence) is a finite or infinite sequence $S_1 S_2 \ldots S_n \ldots$ of s-sets S_i; ϵ stands for the empty sequence.
Only the last s-set of a synchronicity sequence may be $[\delta]$.
We refer to the number of s-sets in an s-sequence t as the *length* or *duration* of t, denoted by $dur(t)$; $dur(\epsilon)=0$. (Note that it is also possible that $dur(t)=\infty$)
End Definition
Notation: We use $t, t_1, t_2, \ldots, t', \ldots$ to denote s-sequences.

In the process of defining sequences of s-sets, obviously it must be possible to concatenate these sequences. This is possible by using the "$\circ$" operator, which is defined in the following definition.

Definition 3:
Let $t=S_1 \ldots S_n$ and $t'=S'_1 \ldots S'_m \ldots$ be two s-sequences (t' possibly infinite), then

$$t \circ t' = \begin{cases} S_1 \ldots S_n & \text{if } S_n = [\delta] \\ S_1 \ldots S_n S'_1 \ldots S'_m \ldots & \text{if } S_n \neq [\delta] \end{cases}$$

If t is an infinite s-sequence, $t \circ t' = t$ for any s-sequence t'; $t \circ \epsilon = \epsilon \circ t = t$.
End Definition
Note: $[\delta] \circ t = [\delta]$.

Since the language of actions contains a choice operator ($\underline{\cup}$), introducing non-determinism, we have to consider sets of s-sequences as the semantics of an action. Moreover, non-determinism is introduced by the use of the open specification of actions as we have seen in the intended semantics of $\underline{a}$. Each s-sequence in such a set stands for a possible choice of a sequence of synchronicity sets.
Notation: We use $T, T_1, T_2, \ldots, T', \ldots$ to denote sets of s-sequences.

These sets of s-sequences can also be concatenated. For this purpose the definition of "$\circ$" is extended in the following way:

Definition 4: Let T and T' be sets of s-sequences. Then $T \circ T'$ is defined as the set of s-sequences $\{t \circ t' \mid t \in T, t' \in T'\}$.

End Definition

Note that $T \circ \{\epsilon\} = \{\epsilon\} \circ T = T$ and that $\{[\delta]\} \circ T = \{[\delta]\}$ and $T \circ \{[\delta]\} = \{t \circ [\delta] \mid t \in T\}$. We also define the length of sets of s-sequences.

Definition 5:

The *length* or *duration* of a set of s-sequences T, denoted by $dur(T)$ is defined as follows:

$$dur(T) = \max\{dur(t) \mid t \in T\}$$

End Definition

The denotations of transactions will be the sets of s-sequences as they are defined above.

Note: the semantics of actions will be sets T of s-sequences with length 1, i.e. $dur(T)=1$.

We will now formally define the semantic domain of the transactions with its operators.†

Definition 6:

The domain $\mathscr{C}$ for our model for transactions from $\mathscr{Tract}$ is the collection of sets T consisting of s-sequences.

End Definition

To give the denotation for all transactions in $\mathscr{Tract}$ we define the semantical counterparts of the syntactical operators $\underline{\cup}$, & and $^{-}$ of the language $\mathscr{Tract}$. (Concatenation will, of course, be the semantical counterpart of ";".)

Before we give the definition of these operators, we will give some definitions that will help in the definition of these operators. The first definition is of a function *pref* that gives all the prefixes of a given s-sequence.

Definition 7: $pref(t) = \{t' \mid t' \circ t'' = t\}$

Note that ϵ is an element of the *pref* of any s-sequence.

For example,

$$pref([a] \circ [b] \circ \begin{bmatrix} c \\ d \end{bmatrix}) = \{\epsilon, [a], [a] \circ [b], [a] \circ [b] \circ \begin{bmatrix} c \\ d \end{bmatrix}\}$$

The next function defines the longest common prefix of two s-sequences.

Let $t = S_1 \ldots S_n \ldots$ and $t' = S'_1 \ldots S'_m \ldots$. Then $maxpref(t,t')$ is the longest s-sequence t'' such that $t'' \in pref(t)$ and $t'' \in pref(t')$. (Note that if $S_1 \neq S'_1$, $maxpref(t,t') = \epsilon$.)

† We will not extend the definition of s-sequences with relevant and irrelevant parts as is done in [11]. As a consequence thereof, the definitions of the operators on s-sequences are different, although the intuitive meaning of the operators will be the same.

End Definition

Finally, we define an operator on sets of s-sequences, which deletes s-sequences ending in $[\delta]$ if there is another sequence that is the same but with $[\delta]$ replaced by another s-sequence.

Definition 9:

Let T be a set of s-sequences then

$$T^{\delta} = T \setminus \{t \mid t = t' \circ [\delta] \wedge \exists t'' \in T \colon t'' \neq t \wedge t' \in pref(t'')\}$$

End Definition

This operator is closely related to what is called "*failure removal*" in [2]. The idea is that failure is avoided when possible, i.e. when there is a non-failing alternative. Such an interpretation of nondeterminism, where a 'good' alternative is preferred to a 'bad' one, is sometimes called *angelic* nondeterminism (cf. [4]).

Having defined these functions, we can now define the semantical operators on $\mathscr{C}$.

Definition 10:

(a) The definition of $\cap\!\!\!\cdot$ on s-sequences is given by:

For s-sequences t and t':

$$t \cap\!\!\!\cdot\, t' = \begin{cases} t & \text{if } maxpref(t,t') = t' \\ t' & \text{if } maxpref(t,t') = t \\ maxpref(t,t') \circ [\delta] & \text{otherwise} \end{cases}$$

(b) The definition of $\cap\!\!\!\cdot$ on sets of s-sequences in $\mathscr{C}$ is given by:

For $T, T' \in \mathscr{C}$:

$$T \cap\!\!\!\cdot\, T' = (\bigcup\{ t \cap\!\!\!\cdot\, t' \mid t \in T,\ t' \in T'\})^{\delta}$$

End Definition

Note that the "$\cap\!\!\!\cdot$" operator is very similar to the "$\cap$" operator in set-theory. The difference is in the case that we have two s-sequences that are not equal but one is a prefix of the other. In that case the longest sequence is put in the intersection. The underlying reason for this (seemingly awkward) definition of the intersection of two (sets of) s-sequences is that this intersection will later on serve as the semantical counterpart of the simultaneous execution of two transactions. The length of the resulting transaction has to be equal to the length of the longest of the two transactions. Definition 10 accomplishes this goal by putting also s-sequences in the intersection of which only a prefix is present in the other set. The interpretation of simultaneous execution also accounts for the third clause in Definition 10: If neither one of the s-sequences is a prefix of the other, e.g. $t = [a][b]$ and $t' = [a][c]$, we take their maximal common prefix after which we register a conflict between the two sequences, since the rest of the sequences cannot be executed simultaneously. (In the example we obtain $[a][\delta]$, since after a we cannot execute both *only a* and *only c*.)

A more elaborate example:

$$\{\begin{bmatrix} a \\ b \end{bmatrix}\} \mathbin{\dot{\cap}} \{[b]\circ[a], [b]\circ\begin{bmatrix} a \\ b \end{bmatrix}, \begin{bmatrix} a \\ b \end{bmatrix}\circ[a], \begin{bmatrix} a \\ b \end{bmatrix}\circ\begin{bmatrix} a \\ b \end{bmatrix}\} =$$

$$(\{\begin{bmatrix} a \\ b \end{bmatrix} \mathbin{\dot{\cap}} [b]\circ[a]\} \cup \{\begin{bmatrix} a \\ b \end{bmatrix} \mathbin{\dot{\cap}} [b]\circ\begin{bmatrix} a \\ b \end{bmatrix}\} \cup$$

$$\{\begin{bmatrix} a \\ b \end{bmatrix} \mathbin{\dot{\cap}} \begin{bmatrix} a \\ b \end{bmatrix}\circ[a]\} \cup \{\begin{bmatrix} a \\ b \end{bmatrix} \mathbin{\dot{\cap}} \begin{bmatrix} a \\ b \end{bmatrix}\circ\begin{bmatrix} a \\ b \end{bmatrix}\})^{\delta} =$$

$$\{[\delta], [\delta], \begin{bmatrix} a \\ b \end{bmatrix}\circ[a], \begin{bmatrix} a \\ b \end{bmatrix}\circ\begin{bmatrix} a \\ b \end{bmatrix}\}^{\delta} =$$

$$\{\begin{bmatrix} a \\ b \end{bmatrix}\circ[a], \begin{bmatrix} a \\ b \end{bmatrix}\circ\begin{bmatrix} a \\ b \end{bmatrix}\}$$

Note: $\begin{bmatrix} a \\ b \end{bmatrix} \mathbin{\dot{\cap}} [a] = [\delta]$. This is caused by the fact that it is not possible to perform both a and b (denoted by the first s-set) and simultaneously perform only a and NOT b (denoted by the second s-set).

Definition 11:

The definition of $\dot{\cup}$ on sets of s-sequences in $\mathscr{C}$ is given by:
For $T, T' \in \mathscr{C}$:

$$T \mathbin{\dot{\cup}} T' = ((T \cup T') \setminus (\bigcup \{t \mathbin{\dot{\cap}} t' \mid t \in T, t' \in T' \text{ and } t \neq t'\}))^{\delta}$$

End Definition

Here $(T \cup T') \setminus (\bigcup \{t \mathbin{\dot{\cap}} t' \mid t \in T, t' \in T' \text{ and } t \neq t'\})$ stands for the set-theoretic complement of $\bigcup \{t \mathbin{\dot{\cap}} t' \mid t \in T, t' \in T' \text{ and } t \neq t'\}$ with respect to $T \cup T'$.

The "$\dot{\cup}$" operator acts as a kind of union. That is, it yields the set-theoretic union of two sets of s-sequences but subtracts a kind of intersection of the two sets. This intersection is not the set-theoretic intersection, but consists of a part of the intersection as defined above. This part consists of the elements that are not elements of the intersection in a set-theoretic sense. In other words, "$\dot{\cup}$" takes the usual union but in the case of two s-sequences of which one is a proper prefix of the other, it deletes the longest (i.e., takes only the shortest). The "$\dot{\cup}$" will be the semantical counterpart of the choice operator. The length of a transaction resulting from the choice between two transactions will never be longer than the shortest of the two. Definition 11 establishes this property, as can be seen from the following example.

Examples:

(1) $\{[a]\} \mathbin{\dot{\cup}} \{[a]\} = \{[a]\} \setminus \emptyset = \{[a]\}$

$$(2)\ \{[a], \begin{bmatrix} a \\ b \end{bmatrix}\} \Cup \{[a]\circ[b], [a]\circ\begin{bmatrix} a \\ b \end{bmatrix}, \begin{bmatrix} a \\ b \end{bmatrix}\circ[b], \begin{bmatrix} a \\ b \end{bmatrix}\circ\begin{bmatrix} a \\ b \end{bmatrix}\} =$$

$$(\{[a], \begin{bmatrix} a \\ b \end{bmatrix}, [a]\circ[b], [a]\circ\begin{bmatrix} a \\ b \end{bmatrix}, \begin{bmatrix} a \\ b \end{bmatrix}\circ[b], \begin{bmatrix} a \\ b \end{bmatrix}\circ\begin{bmatrix} a \\ b \end{bmatrix}\} \setminus$$

$$\{[\delta],[a]\circ[b], [a]\circ\begin{bmatrix} a \\ b \end{bmatrix}, \begin{bmatrix} a \\ b \end{bmatrix}\circ[b], \begin{bmatrix} a \\ b \end{bmatrix}\circ\begin{bmatrix} a \\ b \end{bmatrix}\})^{\delta} =$$

$$\{[a], \begin{bmatrix} a \\ b \end{bmatrix}\}$$

Definition 12:

The definition of "$\tilde{\ }$" is given as follows:

(a) For an s-set S,

$$\tilde{S} = \begin{cases} \mathcal{P}^+(\mathcal{A})\setminus\{S\} & \text{if } S \neq [\delta] \\ \mathcal{P}^+(\mathcal{A}) & \text{if } S = [\delta] \end{cases}$$

(b) for a non-empty s-sequence $t = S_1 \ldots S_m \ldots$

$$\tilde{t} = \bigcup_{n \leq dur(t)} S_1 \circ \ldots \circ S_{n-1} \circ \tilde{S}_n$$

(c) For a non-empty set $T \in \mathcal{C}$

$$\tilde{T} = \Cap\{\tilde{t} \mid t \in T\}$$

End Definition

Note that the above definition implies that $\mathcal{P}^+(\mathcal{A})^{\sim} = [\delta]$.

The idea behind this definition is the following: For an s-set $S \neq [\delta]$ the negation yields just the set-theoretic complement of $\{S\}$ with respect to $\mathcal{P}^+(\mathcal{A})$. For instance, if $\mathcal{A} = \{a,b\}$, and $S = [a]$, $\tilde{S} = [a]^{\sim} = \mathcal{P}^+(\mathcal{A}) \setminus \{[a]\} = \{[a],[b], \begin{bmatrix} a \\ b \end{bmatrix}\}\setminus\{[a]\} = \{[b], \begin{bmatrix} a \\ b \end{bmatrix}\}$. This captures the simple idea that from all possible s-sets the s-set S is *not* chosen. If $S = [\delta]$, i.e. failure, $\tilde{S} = [\delta]^{\sim} = \mathcal{P}^+(\mathcal{A})$, indicating that if one does not fail, any s-set is possible. The negation of an s-sequence $t = S_1 \ldots S_m \ldots$ consists of the possibilities to non-perform the sequence t: such a possibility must have a point where a difference occurs as compared to t. For instance, if $\mathcal{A} = \{a,b\}$ again, $([a][b])^{\sim} = \{[b], \begin{bmatrix} a \\ b \end{bmatrix}, [a][a], [a]\begin{bmatrix} a \\ b \end{bmatrix}\}$: either the first s-set is different from $[a]$ or the first s-set is $[a]$ but then the second one must differ from $[b]$. Note that in the definition it is allowed to have an infinite s-sequence t ($dur(t) = \infty$). For the negation of a set T of s-sequences we consider all negations $\tilde{t}$ of s-sequences t in T (which are all *sets*!), and take the $\Cap$-intersection of these, in particular only the longest s-sequences of pairs which are prefix-related.

The definition of "$\tilde{\ }$" is further illustrated by the following example: we assume again that $\mathcal{A}$ consists of only two events a and b. So $\mathcal{P}^+(\mathcal{A}) = \{ [a], [b], \begin{bmatrix} a \\ b \end{bmatrix} \}$. Now

$$\{ [a], \begin{bmatrix} a \\ b \end{bmatrix} \}^- = [a]^- \Cap \begin{bmatrix} a \\ b \end{bmatrix}^- =$$

$$\{ [b], \begin{bmatrix} a \\ b \end{bmatrix} \} \Cap \{ [a], [b] \} = \{ \epsilon \circ [\delta], [b] \}^\delta =$$

$$\{ [b] \}$$

With these definitions, we can now define the semantics of transaction expressions from $\mathcal{Tract}$.

Definition 13:

The semantic function $[\![\,]\!] \in \mathcal{Tract} \to \mathcal{C}$ is given by:†

$$[\![\underline{a}]\!] = \{ S \in \mathcal{P}^+(A) \mid a \in S \}$$
$$[\![\beta_1 ; \beta_2]\!] = [\![\beta_1]\!] \circ [\![\beta_2]\!]$$
$$[\![\beta_1 \underline{\cup} \beta_2]\!] = [\![\beta_1]\!] \Cup [\![\beta_2]\!]$$
$$[\![\beta_1 \& \beta_2]\!] = [\![\beta_1]\!] \Cap [\![\beta_2]\!]$$
$$[\![\bar{\alpha}]\!] = [\![\alpha]\!]^-$$
$$[\![\mathbf{fail}]\!] = \{[\delta]\}$$
$$[\![\mathbf{any}]\!] = \mathcal{P}^+(\mathcal{A})$$

End Definition

In the semantics as defined above, the semantics of the negation of the atomic action $\underline{a}$ consists of the set of all s-sets that do not contain the event a, i.e. $[\![\bar{\underline{a}}]\!] = \{ S \in \mathcal{P}^+(A) \mid a \notin S \}$. This can be seen in the following, where for simplicity we assume again that $\mathcal{A}$ consists of only two events a and b.

$$[\![\bar{\underline{a}}]\!] = [\![\underline{a}]\!]^- = \{ [a], \begin{bmatrix} a \\ b \end{bmatrix} \}^- = \{ [b] \} \quad \text{(see example above)}$$

So, in this example, the semantics of $\bar{\underline{a}}$ comprises the possibility to perform only b and NOT the possibility of a simultaneous performance $\begin{bmatrix} a \\ b \end{bmatrix}$.

The following definitions are needed to be able to refer to the duration of transactions and equality of transactions in terms of the duration and equality in the semantics of the transactions.

Definition 14:

Let β be a transaction in $\mathcal{Tract}$. The *duration* of β is defined as $dur(\beta) = dur([\![\beta]\!])$.

---

† In [11], negations of transactions are considered as well. Apart from some omissions in that semantics added in [12], the main difference with our present approach is that in the semantics of [11] $[\![\mathbf{fail}]\!] = \varnothing$ instead of $[\delta]$. This implies $[\![\beta;\mathbf{fail}]\!] = [\![\mathbf{fail}]\!]$ and consequently also $[\![\mathbf{any}^n]\!] = [\![\mathbf{any}]\!]$ for any $n \in \mathbb{N}$, which is highly undesirable for our present purposes.

Definition 15: We put $\beta_1 =_{\mathscr{C}} \beta_2$ iff $[\![\beta_1]\!]=[\![\beta_2]\!]$.

We can now state the following proposition concerning transactions and their relations:

Proposition

(i) $(\mathscr{C}, \underline{\cup}, \&, \bar{\ }, \mathbf{fail})$ is a boolean algebra.

(ii) $\mathscr{C}$ satisfies the following properties regarding ";" :

(1) $\beta_1 \underline{\cup} (\beta_1;\beta_2) =_{\mathscr{C}} \beta_1$

(2) $\overline{\beta_1;\beta_2} =_{\mathscr{C}} \overline{\beta_1} \underline{\cup} (\beta_1;\overline{\beta_2})$

(3) $\beta_1 \& (\beta_2;\beta_3) =_{\mathscr{C}} (\beta_1 \& \beta_2);\beta_3$, if $dur(\beta_1)=dur(\beta_2)$

(4) $(\beta_1;\beta_2) \& (\beta_3;\beta_4) =_{\mathscr{C}} (\beta_1 \& \beta_3);(\beta_2 \& \beta_4)$, if $dur(\beta_1)=dur(\beta_3)$

(5) $(\beta;\beta_1) \underline{\cup} (\beta;\beta_2) =_{\mathscr{C}} \beta;(\beta_1 \underline{\cup} \beta_2)$

(6) $(\beta_1;\beta) \underline{\cup} (\beta_2;\beta) =_{\mathscr{C}} (\beta_1 \underline{\cup} \beta_2);\beta$, if $dur(\beta_1)=dur(\beta_2)$

(iii) $\mathscr{C}$ satisfies the following property concerning the special actions:

$\overline{\mathbf{fail}} =_{\mathscr{C}} \mathbf{any}$

End Proposition

In the following we define a normal form for transactions. This form is needed for some axioms on the postconditions of transactions. These axioms will only hold if the transactions are in normal form.

Definition 16:

A transaction $\beta \in \mathscr{T}\!ract$ is said to be in *normal form* (or a *normal transaction*) if the following holds:

> Every subexpression of β of the form $\beta_1 \underline{\cup} \beta_2$ or $\beta_1 \& \beta_2$ has the property that $\bigcup\{t_1 \sqcap t_2 \mid t_1 \in [\![\beta_1]\!], t_2 \in [\![\beta_2]\!] \text{ and } t_1 \neq t_2\} = \emptyset$, i.e. $[\![\beta_1]\!]$ and $[\![\beta_2]\!]$ have no intersection consisting of s-sequences that do not occur in both sets.

End Definition

The subclass of $\mathscr{T}\!ract$ consisting of actions in normal form will be denoted by $\mathscr{T}\!ract_0$.

The normal form excludes mainly transaction expressions that are a union of two transactions of which one is a prefix of the other. The simplest example hereof is: $\underline{a} \underline{\cup} (\underline{a};\underline{b})$.

Fortunately, the following theorem holds for the transaction model $\mathscr{C}$:

Theorem: For any transaction $\beta \in \mathscr{T}\!ract$ there exists a transaction $\beta' \in \mathscr{T}\!ract_0$ such that $\beta =_{\mathscr{C}} \beta'$.

Note: If $\alpha_1 \underline{\cup} \alpha_2$ is in normal form then $[\![\alpha_1 \underline{\cup} \alpha_2]\!]=[\![\alpha_1]\!] \cup [\![\alpha_2]\!]$. Also, if $\alpha_1 \& \alpha_2$ is in normal form then $[\![\alpha_1 \& \alpha_2]\!]=[\![\alpha_1]\!] \cap [\![\alpha_2]\!]$.

3. Transactions and worlds

We have to relate the transactions of $\mathcal{T}ract$ to worlds in which they are performed. Intuitively, the execution of a transaction in a world yields (a collection of) world(s) which one gets after having performed the transaction entirely. This will result in a so-called non-uniform semantics in the sense of [1].

First we introduce a function ϱ. For a given set of worlds W this function is an element of $\mathcal{P}^+(\mathcal{A})\cup[\delta]\to(W\to\mathcal{P}_1(W))$. Here $\mathcal{P}_1(W)$ stands for the sets of elements of W that consists of at most one element (i.e. the singletons and the empty set). The function determines the behaviour of each set of events that are executed simultaneously. By this set-up we assume that each s-set has deterministic behaviour. (This restriction is not really essential, technically speaking, but it is rather plausible.) The function ϱ is not further specified here, except for its behaviour when the s-set is $[\delta]$, which is defined in the following definition, stipulating that the failing s-set has no successor worlds.
Taking the function ϱ as a basis the rest of the definition gives the behaviour of s-sequences and sets of s-sequences in terms of this function.

Definition 17:
(a) $\varrho([\delta])(w) = \varnothing$

(b) The function $R(T)\in\mathcal{P}^+(W)\to\mathcal{P}^+(W)$ is defined inductively by:

$$R(S)(W_0) = \bigcup_{w\in W_0}\{\varrho(S)(w)\} \text{ for } S\in\mathcal{P}^+(\mathcal{A})\cup[\delta] \text{ and } W_0\subset W$$

$$R(t_1\circ t_2)(W_0) = R(t_2)(R(t_1)(W_0)) \quad (t_1 \text{ and } t_2 \text{ are s-sequences})$$

$$R(T)(W_0) = \bigcup_{t\in T} R(t)(W_0)$$

End Definition
The semantics of transactions in a certain world can now be given by the function $[\![\cdot]\!]_R$ which is defined as follows:

Definition 18:
The function $[\![\cdot]\!]_R: \mathcal{T}ract\to(W\to\mathcal{P}^+(W))$ is defined by:

$$[\![\beta]\!]_R(w) = R([\![\beta]\!])(\{w\}).$$

End Definition

We will at this moment expand the information contained in the worlds. They will not give only information about the truth values of the static predicates and constraints. The worlds will also contain some information about which actions have been performed. The *history* of a world is described by recording by which action this world has been reached.

Formally, the history of a world is denoted by a (set of) special propositional variables. For each event a there exists a propositional variable D_a. The constraints on the truth values of these special variables are given in the following definition.

Definition 19:

$$w \models D_a \text{ iff } \exists S \in \mathcal{P}^+(\mathcal{A}): a \in S \wedge \exists w': \varrho(S)(w') = w$$

End Definition

The definition stipulates that the history of a world is completely determined by the set of events through which the world is reached.

4. Parameterized transactions

In the previous sections we described transactions without parameters. In practice transactions will, however, contain parameters. In this section, we will describe how these parameters are introduced in transactions.

The parameterized atomic actions consist of an action predicate and a number of arguments. The number of arguments that a certain action predicate possesses, is called the arity of the action predicate. In the same way it is done with static predicates, we use a valuation function to map the variables into constants.

Formally, we define the parameterized actions as follows:

$\mathcal{AP}$ is the set of action predicates, with typical elements $p,q,r,\ldots$. There is a function *arity* that maps each action predicate into an integer, which is the number of arguments of that action predicate. As in first-order logic, we assume the existence of an infinite number of variables $(x_1, x_2, \ldots)$ and at least one but at most a finite number of constants $(c_1, c_2, \ldots)$. The set of parameterized action expressions $\mathcal{ParAct}$ is now defined inductively as follows:

Definition 20:

(a) A *term* is either a variable or a constant.

(b) If p is an action predicate with arity n and $t_1,\ldots,t_n$ are terms then $\underline{p}(t_1,\ldots,t_n)$ is an atomic parameterized action.

(c) $\mathcal{ParTract}$ is defined as follows:

- (i) Every atomic parameterized action is an element of $\mathcal{ParTract}$.
- (ii) **any** and **fail** are elements of $\mathcal{ParTract}$.
- (iii) If $\alpha_1, \alpha_2 \in \mathcal{ParTract}$ then $\alpha_1 \underline{\cup} \alpha_2$, $\alpha_1 \& \alpha_2$, $\overline{\alpha_1}$ and $\alpha_1 ; \alpha_2$ are also elements of $\mathcal{ParTract}$

End Definition

Note: we now use the variables α, α',...,α_1,... to vary over parameterized actions and the variables β, β',...,β_1,... to vary over parameterized transactions.

Notation: For notational convenience we will write the negation of the atomic action $\overline{p(t_1,...,t_n)}$ as $\overline{p}(t_1,...,t_n)$, instead of the (more correct) notation $\underline{p}(t_1,...,t_n)$.

Definition 21:

The set $\mathcal{A}$ of events is now redefined as follows:

Let $p \in \mathcal{AP}$ and *arity* $(p)=n$ then $p(t_1,...,t_n) \in \mathcal{A}$ iff $\forall t_i$: t_i is a constant.

The set of (proper) transaction expressions $\mathcal{Tract}$ is now redefined as the set of parameterized transactions such that all the arguments of the action predicates are constants.

End Definition

Of course, it holds that two atomic actions are different if either the action predicate is different or if one of the arguments is different.

Let I, g be given functions that interpret constants and evaluate variables, respectively. We next define a valuation function h working on terms and parameterized transactions.

Definition 22:

(a) If t is a term then:

$$h(t) = \begin{cases} I(t) & \text{if } t \text{ is a constant} \\ g(t) & \text{if } t \text{ is a variable} \end{cases}$$

(b) If $\underline{p}(t_1,...,t_n)$ is an atomic parameterized action, then

$$h(\underline{p}(t_1,...,t_n)) = \underline{p}(h(t_1),...,h(t_n))$$

(c) If $\beta_1, \beta_2 \in \mathcal{ParTract}$ then

$$h(\beta_1 \underline{\cup} \beta_2) = h(\beta_1) \underline{\cup} h(\beta_2)$$
$$h(\beta_1 \& \beta_2) = h(\beta_1) \& h(\beta_2)$$
$$h(\overline{\beta_1}) = \overline{h(\beta_1)}$$
$$h(\beta_1 ; \beta_2) = h(\beta_1) ; h(\beta_2)$$

End Definition

Note that if the arity of an action predicate p is zero then $h(\underline{p})=\underline{p}$.

This means that e.g. h(**any**)=**any**.

The notion of normal transactions is now extended to that of normal parameterized transactions with the following definition.

Definition 23:

A parameterized transaction $\beta \in \mathcal{ParTract}$ is said to be in *normal form* (or a *normal parameterized transaction*) if it holds that for all valuation functions h: $h(\beta) \in \mathcal{Tract}_0$.

End Definition

The subclass of $\mathcal{ParTract}$ consisting of the normal parameterized transactions will be denoted by $\mathcal{ParTract}_0$.

The semantics of parameterized transactions can now be given in terms of the function $[\![\cdot]\!]_{R,h}$ which is defined as follows:

Definition 24:

The function $[\![\cdot]\!]_{R,h}: \mathcal{ParTract} \rightarrow (W \rightarrow \mathcal{P}^+(W))$ is defined by:

$$[\![\beta]\!]_{R,h}(w) = R([\![h(\beta)]\!])(\{w\}).$$

End Definition

To record the history of a world, we now do not use special propositional variables, but we use special predicates. For each parameterized atomic action $(p(t_1,\ldots,t_n))$ we define a corresponding predicate D_p with the same arity as the corresponding action.

The truth value of this predicate is determined in the following way:

Definition 25:

$w \models_h D_p(t_1,\ldots,t_n)$ iff $\exists S \in \mathcal{P}^+(\mathcal{A}): p(h(t_1),\ldots,h(t_n)) \in S \wedge \exists w': \varrho(S)(w') = w$

End Definition

In the above definition we use "$\models_h$" to indicate the valuation of a formula (in a world) with respect to the valuation function h.

5. Dynamic and deontic assertions

Given the semantics of the actions as defined in the previous sections, we can now define the logical language L_{dyn} that makes use of these actions. The language is a variant of what is called PDL (Propositional Dynamic Logic) in the literature [11,12] and is similar to the one defined in [18].

Definition 26:

The language L_{dyn} of dynamic expressions, with typical elements Φ and Ψ, is given by the BNF:

$$\Phi ::= \phi \mid \Phi_1 \wedge \Phi_2 \mid \Phi_1 \vee \Phi_2 \mid \neg\Psi \mid \forall x \Psi \mid [\beta]\Psi \mid DONE{:}\alpha \mid PERF{:}\alpha$$

where ϕ is a formula from first-order logic.

End Definition

We will not give the formal semantics for all formulas from L_{dyn}, but only for the "dynamic" parts. (The rest is usual, as is the defintion of validity.) Before we give these semantics, we say a few words about the *DONE* predicate. *DONE*:α expresses the fact that α has just been performed. As a consequence it holds in the worlds that are reached by performing α. It may be clear that the truth value of this operator depends on the special predicates of a world that describe its history. Note that the *DONE* operator is only defined for actions and not for transactions. This is due to the fact that to our knowledge it is not possible to give a meaningful and consistent definition for the *DONE* operator for transactions. See [12] for an attempt of this definition.

We will now give the semantics for the dynamic parts of L_{dyn}:

Definition 27:

(a) $w \models_h [\beta]\Psi$ iff $\forall w' \in [\![\beta]\!]_{R,h}(w)$: $w' \models_h \Psi$

(b) $w \models_h DONE{:}\underline{p}(t_1,\dots,t_n)$ iff $\exists S \in [\![\underline{p}(h(t_1),\dots,h(t_n))]\!]$:
$\forall p'(s_1,\dots,s_k) \in S$: $w \models_h D_{p'}(s_1,\dots,s_k)$ and
$\forall p'(s_1,\dots,s_k) \notin S$: $w \not\models_h D_{p'}(s_1,\dots,s_k)$

End Definition

The following are valid assertions in L_{dyn}:

Proposition

(1) $[\beta](\Phi_1 \rightarrow \Phi_2) \rightarrow ([\beta]\Phi_1 \rightarrow [\beta]\Phi_2)$

(2) $[\beta_1;\beta_2]\Phi \leftrightarrow [\beta_1]([\beta_2]\Phi)$

(3) $[\beta_1 \underline{\cup} \beta_2]\Phi \leftrightarrow [\beta_1]\Phi \wedge [\beta_2]\Phi$

(4) $[\beta_1 \& \beta_2]\Phi \leftarrow [\beta_1]\Phi \vee [\beta_2]\Phi$

(5) $[\alpha_1 \& \alpha_2]\Phi \leftrightarrow [\alpha_1](DONE{:}\alpha_2 \rightarrow \Phi)$

(6) $[\alpha_1]\Phi \rightarrow [\alpha_2](DONE{:}\alpha_1 \rightarrow \Phi)$

(7) $[\mathbf{fail}]\Phi \leftrightarrow$ true

(8) $DONE{:}\mathbf{any} \leftrightarrow$ true

(9) $[\alpha]DONE{:}\alpha$

Remarks:

1. Some of the above axioms only hold if the events are in normal form. E.g. axiom 3. We have that $\underline{a} =_{\mathscr{E}} \underline{a} \underline{\cup} (\underline{a};\underline{b})$. However, $[\underline{a} \underline{\cup} (\underline{a};\underline{b})]\Phi \leftrightarrow [\underline{a}]\Phi \not\leftrightarrow [\underline{a}]\Phi \wedge [\underline{a};\underline{b}]\Phi$.
2. As to the issue of the *completeness* of the above assertions viewed as a logical system we note that the proof in [13] may be adapted to render a complete dynamic logic with respect to *actions*. With respect to *transactions* in general, however, this question remains open..

With the language as introduced above, together with a special propositional variable *Violation* to indicate a state in which a violation has taken place, we can now express formally when an action is forbidden, permitted or obliged. To express these notions we use the following abbreviations:

Definition 28:

$F(\beta)$ is an abbreviation for $[\beta]Violation$
$P(\beta)$ is an abbreviation for $\neg[\beta]Violation$
$O(\beta)$ is an abbreviation for $[\overline{\beta}]Violation$

End Definition

We have of course that $F(\alpha) = O(\overline{\alpha})$ and $P(\alpha) = \neg F(\alpha)$.

Note: The obligation of an action in this theory means the *immediate* obligation to perform the action, NOT that the action should *eventually* be performed. It is possible to loosen this definition of obligation in a way that it can be used to model deadlines. I.e. a certain action should be performed before a certain time (has passed). How this can be done in a simple way is described in [18]. In this paper we will not introduce this temporal aspect, but suffice to indicate that it is possible to do so.

We give the following theorem on the relations between the deontic operators and the operators that connect actions.

Proposition

$$
\begin{array}{l}
P(\beta_1 \underline{\cup} \beta_2) \leftrightarrow P(\beta_1) \vee P(\beta_2) \\
F(\beta_1 \underline{\cup} \beta_2) \leftrightarrow F(\beta_1) \wedge F(\beta_2) \\
O(\alpha_1 \underline{\cup} \alpha_2) \leftarrow O(\alpha_1) \vee O(\alpha_2) \\
P(\beta_1 \& \beta_2) \rightarrow P(\beta_1) \wedge P(\beta_2) \\
F(\beta_1 \& \beta_2) \leftarrow F(\beta_1) \vee F(\beta_2) \\
O(\alpha_1 \& \alpha_2) \leftrightarrow O(\alpha_1) \wedge O(\alpha_2) \\
P(\beta_1 ; \beta_2) \leftrightarrow \neg [\beta_1] F(\beta_2) \\
F(\beta_1 ; \beta_2) \leftrightarrow [\beta_1] F(\beta_2) \\
O(\beta_1 ; \beta_2) \leftrightarrow O(\beta_1) \wedge [\beta_1] O(\beta_2)
\end{array}
$$

With the dynamic logic as introduced in this section it is now possible to specify the dynamic features of the knowledge base. Examples of how this can be done are given in [18]. In the next section we will only show some examples that show the importance of the possibility to specify the negation of actions as well as transactions.

6. Specification of dynamic and deontic integrity constraints

Because $O(\alpha)$ is an abbreviation of $[\overline{\alpha}]$*Violation* it is obvious that the specification of the negation of (trans)actions is especially important for the specification of obligations. The importance of the use of this deontic notion for the specification of integrity constraints is already indicated in [18]. One of the main advantages of the use of deontic constraints is that it is also possible to specify what has to happen when the constraints are violated. The following example shows how this can lead to a chain of triggered obligations. These all have the following form:

$$O(\alpha_i) \rightarrow [\overline{\alpha_i}] O(\alpha_j)$$

This schema indicates that if an action is obliged and not performed then a new obligation is created. This schema can be used indefinitely, creating new obligations every time an obliged action is not performed.

Usually, however, this sequence of new obligations is ended by the fact that the

non-performance of a certain action triggers a (system)action. After this action is performed the system is (usually) in a state where *violation* is not true. If the action would not be performed, the system would get into an inconsistent state.
The schema of this trigger is expressed in L_{dyn} as follows:

$$O(\alpha_i) \rightarrow [\overline{\alpha_i}][\overline{\alpha_j}]false$$

The following is an example of a sequence of new obligations:

> If a person borrows a book he has to return it.
> If a person does not return it he has to pay a fine.
> If a person does not pay the fine he is expelled.

With the expulsion of the person, the system comes back to a state which does not violate the constraints any more.
The description of the above example in L_{dyn} is as follows:
$\forall p \forall b(person(p) \wedge book(b) \rightarrow [borrow(p,b)]O(return(p,b)));$
$\forall p \forall b(person(p) \wedge book(b) \wedge O(return(p,b)) \rightarrow [\overline{return}(p,b)] \exists f(fine(f) \wedge O(pay(p,f))));$
$\forall p \forall f(person(p) \wedge fine(f) \wedge O(pay(p,f)) \rightarrow [\overline{pay}(p,f)][\overline{expel}(p)]false).$

The example above involves only actions. It is also possible to give an example involving transactions (which was our original motivation to consider negations of transactions):

> An undergraduate student with a speciality in information systems has to take exams in elementary logic, introductory database systems,
> applied logic, advanced database systems (in this order, let's say);
> a student in theoretical computer science has to take exams in elementary logic, formal languages, applied logic and semantics of programming languages.

This example is easily formalised as:

$$i \supset O(el;ids;al;ads)$$
$$t \supset O(el;fl;al;spl),$$

using self-evident abbreviations for the actions of taking the various exams and the kinds of students.

In the approach we have taken, negations of (trans)actions appear (albeit somewhat hidden) in obligations: $O\alpha \equiv [\overline{\alpha}]V$. Here we have that the performance of a negated action leads to a state where V holds. Of course, one could also imagine that in a specification formulas of the form $[\overline{\alpha}]\phi$ with $\phi \neq V$ would be useful. One may think of another special variable, signalling some special situation. Or ϕ might, for instance, specify that some other actions need to be done. In fact, we saw already an example of this when considering action triggers, where the non-returning of a book resulted in a state in which an obligation to pay a fine was imposed.

Here also variations using *trans*actions may be devised. For example, let us consider a specification of the famous "publish or perish" paradigm.

> If a researcher does not write and subsequently publish his paper (every year), he will perish.

This is modelled in L_{dyn} as follows:

$$\forall p\, \exists a(\, researcher(p) \wedge article(a) \rightarrow [\overline{write(p,a);publish(a)}]perished(p)\,)$$

7. Conclusions

In this paper we have proposed negations of transactions as a specification tool for dynamic and deontic integrity constraints. Since the semantics of negated transactions is by no means obvious, we have investigated this thoroughly with means adapted from the semantics of concurrent programming languages including the use of stream-like objects and a failing event δ. We have shown in particular how to use negated transactions for the formalisation of deontic constraints, but we strongly believe that their use goes beyond this and may play an important role in open specifications of transactions.

REFERENCES

1. J.W. de Bakker, J.N. Kok, J.-J.Ch. Meyer, E.-R. Olderog and J.I. Zucker, "Contrasting Themes in the Semantics of Imperative Concurrency" in Current Trends in Concurrency: Overviews and Tutorials, (eds.) J.W. de Bakker, W.P. de Roever and G. Rozenberg, LNCS 224, Springer, Berlin (1986), pp.51-121.
2. J.W. de Bakker, J.-J. Ch. Meyer, E.-R. Olderog and J.I. Zucker, Transition Systems, Metric Spaces and Ready Sets in the Semantics of Uniform Concurrency, Journal of Comp. Syst. Sci. 36(2) (1988), pp. 158-224.
3. J.A. Bergstra and J.W. Klop, "Process Algebra for Synchronous Communication", Information and Control 60(1/3) (1984), pp.109-137.
4. M. Broy, "A Theory for Nondeterminism, Parallelism, Communication and Concurrency", Theoretical Computer Science 45 (1986), pp.1-62.
5. F. Dignum, "A Language for Modelling Knowledge Bases", Ph.D. thesis, Vrije Universiteit, Amsterdam (1989).
6. F. Dignum and R.P. van de Riet, "Knowledge Base Modelling, Based on Linguistics and Founded in Logic", Data & Knowledge Engineering, (to appear).
7. J. Fiadeiro and T. Maibaum, "Temporal Reasoning over Deontic Specifications", Technical Report, Imperial College, London (1989).

8. D. Harel, "Dynamic Logic" in Handbook of Philosophical Logic (Vol.2), (eds.) D. Gabbay, F. Guenther, Reidel, Dordrecht (1984).

9. S. Khosla, "System Specification: A Deontic Approach", Ph.D. thesis, Imperial College, London (1988).

10. J.-J.Ch. Meyer and E.P. de Vink, "Step Semantics for "True" Concurrency with Recursion", Distributed Computing 3 (1989), pp.130-145.

11. J.-J.Ch. Meyer, "Merging Regular Processes by Means of Fixed Point Theory", Theoretical Computer Science 145 (1986), pp.193-260.

12. J.-J.Ch. Meyer, "A Different Approach to Deontic Logic: Deontic Logic Viewed as a Variant of Dynamic Logic", Notre Dame Journal of Formal Logic (29) (1988), pp.109-136.

13. J.-J.Ch. Meyer, "Using Programming Concepts in Deontic Reasoning" in Semantics and Contextual Expression, (eds.) R. Bartsch, J. van Benthem, P. van Emde Boas, Foris, Dordrecht, (to appear).

14. R. Milner, Calculi for Synchrony and Asynchrony, Theoretical Computer Science 25(3) (1983), pp. 267-310.

15. R. Reiter, "On Closed World Databases" in Logic and Databases, (eds.) H. Gallaire and J. Minker, Plenum Press, New York (1978), pp.55-76.

16. M. Rem, "Trace Theory and Systolic Computations", in Proc. PARLE: Parallel Architectures and Languages Europe, Vol.1, (eds.) J.W. de Bakker, A.J. Nijman and P.C. Treleaven, LCNS 258, Springer, Berlin (1987), pp.14-33.

17. H. Weigand, "Linguistically Motivated Principles of Knowledge Base Systems", Ph.D. Thesis, Vrije Universiteit, Amsterdam (1989).

18. R. Wieringa, J.-J.Ch. Meyer and H. Weigand, "Specifying Dynamic and Deontic Integrity Constraints in Knowledge Bases", Data & Knowledge Engineering 4(4), (1989).

19. R. Wieringa, H. Weigand, J.-J.Ch. Meyer and F. Dignum, "The Inheritance of Dynamic and Deontic Integrity Constraints", IR-199, Vrije Universiteit, Amsterdam (1989).

Experimenting with Process Equivalence

*Bard Bloom**
Department of Computer Science,
Cornell University,Ithaca, NY 14853, USA
bard@cs.cornell.edu

Albert R. Meyer†
Laboratory for Computer Science
MIT Cambridge Ma. 02139, USA
meyer@theory.lcs.mit.edu

Abstract

Following paradigms originated by Hennessy, Hoare, and Milner, distinctions between concurrent processes based on observable outcomes of computational experiments are examined. Variations in experimental protocols yield several distinct experimental equivalences. The experimental scenario thus offers a uniform setting in which to compare notions of process equivalence. We identify one equivalence, called *ready simulation*, as offering a better motivated and equally elegant alternative to the widely accepted notion of bisimulation.

1 Introduction

Numerous efforts to develop a theory of discrete concurrent processes begin with the notion of a state machine, generally infinite and nondeterministic [13, 16, 10, 3, 5, 9, 19, 4, 11]. The state diagram of such a machine may, without loss of generality, be unwound into a *synchronization tree*, namely, a rooted, unordered tree whose edges are labeled with symbols denoting basic *actions* or events. Milner's CCS [16], [18] and Hoare's CSP [13], [14] are notable theories of this kind.

These theories further agree that synchronization trees are an *over*specification of process behavior, and certain distinct trees must be regarded as equivalent processes. The main theoretical difference among the theories is in which trees are identified.

In CSP [14], two processes are identified if they are equivalent with respect to a certain class of experiments. A process is thought of as a black box, with one

*Supported by an NSF Fellowship, also NSF Grant No. 8511190-DCR and ONR grant No. N00014-83-K-0125.
†Supported by NSF Grant No. 8511190-DCR and by ONR grant No. N00014-83-K-0125.

button for each action that it can potentially take. The experimenter presses buttons on the box. If the process can actually take that action, the machine will change state; if it cannot, the button refuses to allow itself to be pressed. Two processes are identified if they can perform the same sequences of actions and refusals.

De Nicola and Hennessy [10] consider observing complete sequences of actions only—not refusals—but their basic experiment on a process P is to observe it connected up with any other system C of processes—technically, to place it in some context $C[P]$—and then observe the action sequences of $C[P]$. The De Nicola-Hennessy context-experiment equivalence and the CSP action/refusal experiment equivalence esentially coincide.

CCS is based on a much finer equivalance relation on synchronization trees called ***bisimulation*** [18]. Although Milner's original definition of bisimulation was not given in terms of button-pushing experiments on black boxes, he does offer a justification in these terms in [17]. In these experiments, the experimenter is given the ability to perform repeated subexperiments from any state, allowing the exploration of the alternatives available in a given state. This may be phrased in several ways; for example, one might permit the experimenter to ***save*** states and later ***restore*** the process to any saved state. These must be the only operations on states, *e.g.*, the experimenter cannot test states for equality. An alternative formulation is that the experimenter is equipped with a ***duplicator***, allowing the creation of identical copies of the process in any state. The experimenter may perform experiments on the copies, and combine the results.

In this paper we restrict ourselves to the technically simpler case of "synchronous" systems of processes. Formally, this means we do not introduce the concept of an invisible "hidden" or τ-action. We expect similar results to apply in the asynchronous case, but have not investigated this as yet.

In general, an experiment on P should consist of placing P in a context, $C[P]$, and performing experiments on $C[P]$. However, it will turn out that the use of contexts expressible in CCS—or indeed in a very generous class of extensions of CCS—does not change any of the experimental equivalences which we consider, and so it suffices simply to perform experiments on isolated processes. In other words, all the experimental equivalences are in fact congruences.

In the next section, we offer what we consider to be the most natural formalization of the kind of experiment described informally above, which we call ***duplicator*** experiments. (See [2] for an extensive algebraic analysis of a variety of testing scenarios.) In contrast to Milner's scenario, we establish:

Proposition 1.1 *The relation of equivalence with respect to duplicator experiments is a strictly coarser relation than bisimulation.*

In fact, one of the main results of this paper is a remarkable confirmation of an argument we made earlier in [7], namely, that *GSOS Congruence*—the relation

know when he has made enough duplicates to explore all possible alternative behaviors of the duplicated process. Milner uses the metaphor of "weather conditions"; these determine which nondeterministic choice the process will make. Following Abramsky [1], we refer to this as a *global-testing duplicator*, which allows the experimenter to be sure that he has in fact explored all possible process behaviors.

However, allowing the experimenter unrestricted use of global-testing outcomes still disagrees with Milner's scenario:

Theorem 1.4 *Two processes are equivalent with respect to global-testing experiments iff they are* isomorphic *as unordered labeled trees. In particular, equivalence with respect to global-testing experiments is strictly finer than bisimulation.*

To arrive at bisimulation in the "weather" setting, Milner implicitly places a restriction on the experimenter: he is forbidden to *count* the number of kinds of weather available. The experimenter can collect results of experiments on duplicate processes only by asking whether *all* or *some* experiments succeed, not how many. Call these *modal* global-testing experiments; we can now rephrase Milner's result:

Theorem 1.5 *[17] Two processes are bisimilar iff they agree on all* modal *global-testing duplicator experiments.*

We find it hard to provide a physical justification or operational rationale for this modal restriction on the use of experimental outcomes.

2 Experiments on Machines

The idea of "button-pushing" experiments on processes has been highlighted by Hoare as an explanation of CSP semantics. A process is presented as a black box with buttons labeled with the visible atomic actions, and no other controls. If process P can perform action a, then it is possible to press the a-button and then the machine will change state. If P cannot perform a, then the a-button is locked; the experimenter can press the button, discover that the machine cannot perform an a, and then continue experimenting on P itself.

A number of variants of simple button-pushing experiments have been considered [21, 19]. Perhaps the most detailed kind of simple button-pushing is a *lighted-button experiment*. In this scenario, the black box resembles certain soft-drink machines: its buttons have lights inside them, and the light on the a-button is lit when that button is disabled. In other words, the experimenter can see at every stage which actions are possible and which are not, without changing the state of the machine. Formally, a lighted button experiment is a sequence $S_0a_0S_1 \ldots a_nS_{n+1}$ alternating between sets S_i of actions and actions $a_i \notin S_i$; it succeeds when S_0 is the set of initially disabled actions, S_1 is the set of disabled actions after a_1 is pressed, and so on.

Definition 2.1 *Two processes are* equivalent *with respect to a class of experiments iff they can succeed on precisely the same experiments of that class.*

Both CSP equivalence and Phillips' somewhat finer *refusal testing* equivalence [19] can be characterized as equivalences based on slight restrictions of lighted button experiments.

Note that a process may be able both to succeed and to fail on the same experiment, depending on which nondeterministic choices the process makes. For example, the process $ab + ac$ can pass the experiment $\{b, c\}a\{a, c\}$ if it takes its first a-action alternative or fail if it takes its second alternative. On the other hand, the process $a(b + c)$ cannot pass this experiment, since it cannot refuse c after doing a. Thus $ab + cd$ and $a(b + c)$ are not lighted-button experiment equivalent, and indeed the simple kind of experiment which distinguishes them establishes that they are not CSP equivalent.

Lighted-button experiments actually make more distinctions than CSP, but do not yet represent the full experimental scenario we wish to examine. For example, is easy to check that:

Lemma 2.2 *The processes $abc + abd$ and $a(bc + bd)$ are equivalent with respect to all lighted button experiments.*

Nevertheless, there is a simple experiment distinguishing these processes. We imagine equipping the experimenter with a *duplicator*, allowing him to copy the machine at any time, and perform independent experiments on the copies. Equivalently, we allow him to save and restore states of the machine. For example, we might think of implementing such experiments in software using an operating system fork.

The typical sort of *duplicator*-experiment looks something like the following:

1. Press the a-button on P, and call the resulting machine P_a. Fail if the a-button cannot be pushed.
2. Make two copies of P_a, call them P_{a1} and P_{a2}. This step cannot fail.
3. Press the b-button and then the c-button of P_{a1}. Fail if either cannot be pushed.
4. Press the b-button and then the c-button of P_{a2}. Fail if either the b-button cannot be pushed, or the c-button can be pushed.
5. Succeed if none of the previous steps have failed.

The process $a(bc + bd)$ can pass this test, but the process $abc + abd$ cannot. So duplication increases the power of a lighted-button experimenter. In fact,

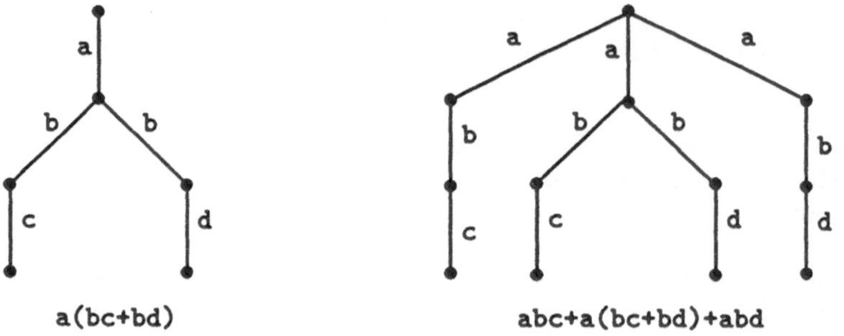

Figure 1: Ready Similar but not Bisimilar

equivalence with respect to duplicator experiments is precisely ready simulation; this is a corollary to Theorem 2.7.

It is well-known that understanding bisimulation in general seems to require exploring the behavior of all the children of a process. We present an excessively powerful form of duplicator experiment, called ***wild duplicator experiments***, in which the experimenter is allowed to make any quantity (not necessarily finite) of copies of the process at each stage, and perform separate experiments on the copies. In particular, it is possible for the experimenter to see all the children of a process. We will show that this form of duplicator still only observes ready simulation.

We will allow infinite numbers of tests, and arbitrary Boolean combinations of the results. We do not restrict infinities to be countable. The infinities allow the results of this section apply to arbitrarily branching processes, and *a fortiori* to finitely branching processes.

However, even wild duplicator experiments still do not explain bisimulation. It is easy to exhibit ready simulations between the nonbisimilar processes $a(bc + bd)$ and $abc + a(bc + bd) + abd$ of Figure 1, and so by Theorem 1.3 they cannot be distinguished by duplicator experiments.

Let $\mathbf{B}$ be the set $\{\mathrm{tt}, \mathrm{ff}\}$ of Booleans; we use tt for success and ff for failure of experiments.

Definition 2.3 *A* wild duplicator experiment *is an ordered tree, possibly countably deep and arbitrarily wide, with node labels and branching as follows. Each node ν is labeled either* choose, $a \in$ Act, *or* $B : \mathbf{B}^\kappa \to \mathbf{B}$, *where κ is a cardinal ≥ 0, such that*

1. *If ν is labeled a, then ν has exactly two children ν_+ and ν_-.*

2. If ν is labeled $B : \mathbf{B}^\kappa \to \mathbf{B}$, then ν has κ children, where κ is any ordinal ≥ 0. If $\kappa = 0$ then ν is a leaf node.

3. If ν is labeled choose *then ν may have any positive cardinality of children.*

The intent is that nodes ν labeled with actions a involve pushing the a-button on the process. If the button can be pushed, then the experimenter proceeds with ν_+ on the resultant process; otherwise, the experimenter performs ν_- on the unchanged original process. Nodes labeled with κ-ary Boolean functions instruct the experimenter to make κ copies of the process, perform the appropriate experiment on each copy, and combine the results with B. Nodes labeled choose allow the experimenter to choose one of the children and perform that experiment.

A simple duplication is modelled by a Boolean node. For example, consider an experiment which makes two copies of the process, runs tests E_1 and E_2 on them, and succeeds iff both tests succeed; this is formalized by a node labelled by the binary **and** function, with children given by the formalizations of E_1 and E_2. The wild duplicator, which produces some unknown number of children, is a choice node with one child for the experiment to be performed on each number of children. For example, if the experiment is "Wild-duplicate P, and perform E on each copy, succeeding iff each copy succeeds," then the formalization starts with a single choose node with countably many children, the nth of which is an n-fold **and** node.

We write root(E) for the root node of the tree E.

Definition 2.4 *We define $P \Uparrow E$ (resp. $P \Downarrow E$), pronounced "P can pass (resp. fail) E", iff there is some partial function ζ from the nodes of E to pairs of truth values and processes, such that $\zeta(\text{root}(E)) = \langle \text{tt}, P \rangle$, (resp. $\langle \text{ff}, P \rangle$) and whenever $\zeta(\nu) = \langle b, R \rangle$ we have:*

- *If ν is labeled a, then either*
  - *There is some R' such that $R \xrightarrow{a} R'$ and $\zeta(\nu_+) = \langle b, R' \rangle$; or*
  - *$R \stackrel{a}{\not\to}$, and $\zeta(\nu_-) = \langle b, R \rangle$.*
- *ν is labeled by $B : \mathbf{B}^\kappa \to \mathbf{B}$, and there is some κ-length vector $\vec{b}$ of Booleans such that $B(\vec{b}) = b$ and the αth child ν_α of ν has $\zeta(\nu_\alpha) = \langle b_\alpha, R \rangle$.*
- *ν is labeled* choose*, has κ children ν_α, and there is some $\beta < \kappa$ such that $\zeta(\nu_\beta) = \langle b, P \rangle$.*

We say that ζ demonstrates that $P \Uparrow E$ (resp. $P \Downarrow E$).

Intuitively, ζ assigns to each node a process and the success or failure of the experiment given by that node on that process; the consistency conditions chart the progress of the experiment. It is possible that both $P \Uparrow E$ and $P \Downarrow E$; consider the wild duplicator experiment which succeeds precisely when the duplicator produces a prime number of copies. It is also possible to define experiments which can report both success and failure from the same sequence of actions of the process; *e.g.*, the experiment which consists of infinitely often duplicating the process and never actually letting it perform an action.

We define $P \leq_{\mathsf{Wild}} Q$ as for all experiments E, whenever $P \Uparrow E$ then $Q \Uparrow E$. For each experiment E there is an experiment $\neg E$ such that $P \Uparrow \neg E$ iff $P \Downarrow E$ and vice versa; take $\neg E$ to be the experiment E with an extra root node labeled by the negation function. Thus, we lose no generality by considering only successes.

We will need to construct demonstrations ζ; the following lemma makes the construction easier.

Definition 2.5 *The function f is a* consistent choice function *for $P \sqsubseteq P'$ if f is a function from the descendants of P to those of P', such that $f(P) = P'$ and for all $Q \xrightarrow{a} R$ descendants of P, the following holds:*

$$\begin{array}{ccc} Q & \sqsubseteq & f(Q) \\ \downarrow a & & \downarrow a \\ R & \sqsubseteq & f(R) \end{array}$$

Lemma 2.6 *Suppose that P and P' are arbitrarily-branching trees such that $P \sqsubseteq P'$. Then there is a consistent choice function for $P \sqsubseteq P'$.*

Proof:

We may non-constructively build such a function f by the Axiom of Choice.[2] Let $\leq$ be a well-ordering of the descendants of P'. Define a sequence of partial functions f_i, taking the ith level of P (counting the root as level 1) to that of P', as follows. Let $f_1(P) = P'$. Suppose that R is on the nth level of P, and $R \xrightarrow{a} S$. Let $f_{n+1}(S)$ be S', the $\leq$-first descendant of $f_n(R)$ such that $S \sqsubseteq S'$; there is at least one such S' by the fact that $R \sqsubseteq f(R)$. Let $f(T) = f_n(T)$ where T is on the nth level of P. It is easy to see that f is a consistent choice function for $P \sqsubseteq P'$. □

Theorem 2.7 *For all (arbitrarily branching) processes P and Q, $P \leq_{\mathsf{Wild}} Q$ iff $P \sqsubseteq Q$*

Proof:

[2]Note that if P and P' are finitely branching trees, this may be done without the Axiom of Choice.

We first show that $\leq_{\mathsf{Wild}}$ is a ready simulation relation, and hence $P \leq_{\mathsf{Wild}} Q$ implies $P \sqsubseteq Q$. Suppose that $P \leq_{\mathsf{Wild}} Q$ and $P \xrightarrow{a} P'$; we must show $Q \xrightarrow{a} Q'$ for some Q' such that $P' \leq_{\mathsf{Wild}} Q'$. Suppose that there were no such Q'. Then for each a-child Q'_α, we have $P' \not\leq_{\mathsf{Wild}} Q'_\alpha$; thus, there is some experiment E_α such that $P' \pitchfork E_\alpha$ but not $Q'_\alpha \pitchfork E_\alpha$. Let E' be the experiment which takes the conjunction of all the E_α. Then $P' \pitchfork E'$, but no Q_α can pass E'. Let E be the experiment which starts by pushing the a button, and then running E'; P can pass E, but Q cannot. This violates the hypothesis that $P \leq_{\mathsf{Wild}} Q$.

For the other clause of ready simulation, suppose that $P \leq_{\mathsf{Wild}} Q$ and $P \not\xrightarrow{a}$. Then P can pass the experiment which pushes the a button, failing if it can be pushed and succeeding if it cannot. Q must pass this experiment as well; hence $Q \not\xrightarrow{a}$.

For the converse, suppose that $P \sqsubseteq Q$ and $P \pitchfork E$. Let ζ be any function demonstrating that $P \pitchfork E$. We will construct a function ζ' demonstrating that $Q \pitchfork E$. Let f be a consistent choice function for $P \sqsubseteq Q$. Define

$$\zeta'(\nu) = \begin{cases} \langle b, f(R)\rangle & \zeta(\nu) = \langle b, R\rangle \text{ and } R \in \text{descendants}(P) \\ \langle b, R\rangle & \zeta(\nu) = \langle b, R\rangle \text{ and } R \notin \text{descendants}(P) \\ \text{undefined} & \text{otherwise} \end{cases}$$

It is straightforward to check that ζ' demonstrates that $Q \pitchfork E$. □

It is worth noting that simple duplicator experiments (with binary Boolean operations and no choice nodes) suffice to capture ready simulation of finitely-branching processes; see [6] for more details.

3 Global Testing Experiments

For any process P, let $\mathrm{Succ}_a(P) = \left\{P' : P \xrightarrow{a} P'\right\}$. In our setting, this set of successor processes of P will always be finite. Notice that a duplicator, by making $|\mathrm{Succ}_a(P)|$ copies of P and pressing an a button on each copy, has the possibility of getting the entire set $\mathrm{Succ}_a(P)$ to experiment upon. Milner's experimental explanation of bisimulation reveals that the experimenter must, however, do more than merely have the *possibility* to see all the successors—he must *know* when he has seen them all.

This is formalized in [17], where Milner describes a mechanism for exploring all the alternatives available from a given state, by allowing variation of some "ambient ('weather') conditions" which determine which nondeterministic choice the machine will take. We formulate 'weathers' in terms of a *global-testing duplicator* [1]. The global-testing duplicator is a device with a chamber, a control panel with one button per action, and a chute. The experimenter places the machine in the chamber, and presses a button on the control panel, say the a-button. Out of the chute drops one copy of each a-descendant of the process.

However, global-testing goes too far; global-testing equivalence is strictly finer than bisimulation. The experimenter can simply count the black boxes that come out of the chute, or, in Milner's metaphor, count the number of varieties of weather available. In fact,

Theorem 3.1 *Global-testing duplicator experiment equivalence coincides with isomorphism of unordered trees. In particular, the bisimilar proceses a and $a+a$ are not global-testing duplicator equivalent.*

The test which distinguishes them is: "put the process in the global-testing duplicator. Press the a button. Succeed iff one box comes out the chute."

Actually this simple form of global-testing duplicator does not precisely match Milner's weather scenario: two different forms of weather may drive the process into the same state. Milner's description directly corresponds to the *wild global-testing duplicator*, which may produce *one or more* copies of each descendent of its input. This uncertainty blurs the counting of successor processes, raising the *prima facie* possibility that nonisomorphic process trees might be identified.

The same experiment distinguishes a from $a + a$, although in a slightly different way. Now, a may pass the experiment, although it will no longer pass it in every run; however $a + a$ must fail in every run.

In fact, the wildness does not blur any distinctions at all:

Theorem 3.2 *Wild global-testing duplicator equivalence coincides with unordered tree isomorphism.*

We will first define a partial order $P \preceq Q$ on finite trees. Unlike most comparisons between processes we have considered, $\preceq$ is antisymmetric; $P \preceq Q$ and $Q \preceq P$ will imply $P \equiv Q$ (viz. that P and Q are isomorphic synchronization trees). We will construct experiments $E_{Q,n}$ such that P can pass $E_{Q,n}$ iff $P / n \preceq Q / n$. If P and Q are distinct synchronization trees, then for some n we have $P / n \not\equiv Q / n$, and so either $P / n \not\preceq Q / n$ or $Q / n \not\preceq P / n$. So, $E_{Q,n}$ or $E_{P,n}$ will distinguish P and Q, and the theorem will follow. The necessary mathematics will take up the rest of this section.

First, our partial order on finite trees. The condition $P \preceq Q$ holds if, informally, Q can be obtained by repeated duplication of subtrees of P. Formally, this is defined by induction on the depth of finite trees:

Definition 3.3 $\mathbf{0} \preceq \mathbf{0}$*, and whenever*

$$P = \sum_{a \in \mathsf{Act}} \sum_{i=1}^{p_a} aP_{ai} \quad , \qquad Q = \sum_{a \in \mathsf{Act}} \sum_{i=1}^{q_a} aQ_{aj} \tag{1}$$

we have

1. *For each Q_{aj} there is some P_{ai} such that $P_{ai} \preceq Q_{aj}$.*

2. There is a 1-1 function $f : [1 \ldots p_a] \to [1 \ldots q_a]$ *such that* $P_{aj} \preceq Q_{a,f(j)}$.

That is, each child of Q has a "cousin" which is a child of P, and distinct children of P have distinct cousins in Q. It is easy to show that $\preceq$ is a preorder.

Lemma 3.4 $\preceq$ *is a partial order, and a congruence with respect to* $a(\cdot)$, $+$, *and* $/n$.

Proof: Reflexitivity, transitivity, and congruence are straightforward. By a predictable induction on n, we show that it is antisymmetric; that is, if $P \preceq Q \preceq P$ then P and Q are isomorphic synchronization trees. This is trivial if $P = Q = 0$. Let P and Q be expressed as in (1), fix an action a and let $f : [1 \ldots p_a] \to [1 \ldots q_a]$ and $g : [1 \ldots q_a] \to [1 \ldots p_a]$ be the 1-1 functions showing that $P \preceq Q$ and $Q \preceq P$ respectively. The existence of 1-1 functions shows that $p_a \leq q_a \leq p_a$ and hence $p_a = q_a$. Therefore f and g are also onto, and so fg and gf are permutations. Recall that if h is a permutation of a finite set and i is an element of that set, then the set $\left\{i, h(i), h^{(2)}(i), \ldots\right\}$ is a finite set, called the *orbit* of i under h; as h is 1-1, we must have $h^{(k)}(i) = i$ for some k, called the *period* of i.

Fix i. We have

$$P_{ai} \preceq Q_{a,f(i)} \preceq P_{a,gf(i)} \preceq \cdots \preceq P_{a,(gf)^{(k)}(i)} = P_{a,i}$$

where k is the period of i. By transitivity, we have $Q_{a,f(i)} \preceq P_{a,i}$, and so by induction $P_{a,i} \equiv Q_{a,f(i)}$. With a little bit of work, this establishes a bijection between the children of P and those of Q as desired. □

We now define the experiments $E_{Q,n}$ such that P can pass $E_{Q,n}$ iff $P \,/\, n \preceq Q \,/\, n$. The experiment $E_{Q,0}$ always succeeds. To see if P can pass $E_{Q,n+1}$, wild-duplicate P under each action a, giving $P'_{a1}, \ldots, P'_{a,p'_a}$. If $p'_a \neq q_a$ then the experiment fails. If $p'_a = q_a$ then for each i, see if P'_{ai} passes $E_{Q_{ai},n}$. $E_{Q,n+1}$ succeeds if each $E_{Q_{ai},n}$ succeeds.

Lemma 3.5 *P can pass $E_{Q,n}$ iff $P \,/\, n \preceq Q \,/\, n$.*

Proof: This clearly is true for $n = 0$. For greater n, suppose that P can pass $E_{Q,n}$. Let P and Q be given as in (1). Suppose that the wild global-testing duplicator produced $\left\langle P'_{aj} : a \in \mathsf{Act}, j \in [1 \ldots q_a]\right\rangle$, where each child of P appears in this listing at least once. We have $P \preceq \sum_{a,j} aP'_{aj}$. As each P'_{aj} passes $E_{Q_{aj},n-1}$ we have $P'_{aj} \,/\, (n-1) \preceq Q_{aj} \,/\, (n-1)$ by induction, and hence we have

$$P \,/\, n \preceq \sum_{a,j} aP'_{aj} \,/\, (n-1) \preceq \sum_{a,j} aQ_{aj} \,/\, (n-1) = Q \,/\, n$$

as desired. The other direction is similar. □

Lemma 3.6 *P and Q agree on all wild global-testing duplicator experiments iff $P \equiv Q$.*

Proof: Clearly the result of performing an experiment on a process depends only on its synchronization tree. Conversely, suppose that $P \not\equiv Q$. Then there is some n such that $P/n \not\equiv Q/n$. By antisymmetry, we have $P/n \not\lesssim Q/n$ or $Q/n \not\lesssim P/n$; suppose the former. Then by Lemma 3.5, we know that P cannot pass $E_{Q,n}$ but Q can. Hence P and Q are distinguishable with a wild global-testing experiment. □

4 Modal Logic

Modal logics which arise naturally in process specification are intimately connected to experimental equivalence.

It is possible to give a straightforward logic for ready simulation, which we call *denial logic* (called "limited modal logic" in [7]). Disjunction does not increase the descriptive power of denial logic, because the law $\langle a\rangle(\varphi\vee\psi) = (\langle a\rangle\varphi)\vee(\langle a\rangle\psi)$ is valid. The syntax of *denial logic* is

$$\varphi ::== \text{Can't}(a) \mid \text{tt} \mid \varphi\wedge\varphi \mid \langle a\rangle\varphi$$

and satisfaction is defined as usual:

- $P \models \text{tt}$ always.
- $P \models \varphi\wedge\psi$ iff $P \models \varphi$ and $P \models \psi$.
- $P \models \langle a\rangle\varphi$ iff for some P', $P \xrightarrow{a} P'$ and $P' \models \varphi$.
- $P \models \text{Can't}(a)$ if $P \stackrel{a}{\not\rightarrow}$.

Formulas of denial logic correspond quite naturally to a certain set of "elementary" duplicator experiments. For example, Can't(a) is an experiment which succeeds if the a button cannot be pressed, and $\varphi\wedge\psi$ is an experiment which starts by duplicating the process, and then performing appropriate experiments on the copies. In this way we can show that equivalence with respect to denial logic is identical to equivalence with respect to duplicator experiments.

An even more natural *Hennessy-Milner Logic (HML)* logic is well known to yield to bisimulation [12]. The syntax of HML is

$$\varphi ::= \text{tt} \mid \text{ff} \mid \varphi\wedge\varphi \mid \varphi\vee\varphi \mid \langle a\rangle\varphi \mid [a]\varphi$$

The significant new clause in the definition of satisfaction is $P \models [a]\varphi$ iff for all P' such that $P \xrightarrow{a} P'$, $P' \models \varphi$. Note that the denial formula Can't(a) is expressible in HML as $[a]\text{ff}$, so denial formulas can be seen as a special case of HML formulas.

Now it is straightforward to see how to distinguish non-bisimilar processes using a (modal) global-testing duplicator. Processes P and Q are not bisimilar iff there is some Hennessy-Milner formula φ which distinguishes them, say $P \models \varphi$ and $Q \not\models \varphi$. We can construct an experiment e_φ from φ on which P can succeed, but Q never will. For example, the experiment $e_{\langle a \rangle \varphi}$ starts with pressing the a-button, and then performs e_φ on the resulting machine (or failing if the a-button cannot be pressed). Dually, the experiment $e_{[a]\varphi}$ does an a-button global-test duplication of the machine in the chamber and checks to see that every machine coming out of the chute passes e_φ.

5 Conclusion

Bisimulation can be seen as a *logically* fundamental notion of equivalence of concurrent processes, but we find it hard to justify bisimulation as a *computationally* fundamental notion based on experiments. The natural choices of experimental equivalence we have examined either coarsen or refine bisimulation.

The debate about the proper choice of process equivalence continues to be technically fruitful. Recently, Larsen and Skou [15] have argued that bisimulation can be understood experimentally in the setting of experiments on *probabilistic* processes (*cf.* [8]), and Vaandrager and Groote [11] propose other equivalences finer than ready simulation, but still coarser than bisimulation, based on a relaxed SOS discipline.

We believe the results of this paper strengthen our earlier arguments for ready simulation as the finest reasonable process equivalence, and we are continuing to investigate the theory of processes under ready simulation. For example, we have a finite axiomatization of ready simulation on finite trees and a polynomial-time algorithm for deciding ready simulations of finite-state processes. A major, crucial, development yet to be undertaken is the extension of the theory of ready simulation to handle hidden moves.

6 Acknowledgements

We are grateful to Robin Milner, Kim Larsen, Sorin Istrail, and Miller Maley for several helpful discussions.

References

[1] S. Abramsky. Observation equivalence as a testing equivalence. *Theoretical Computer Sci.*, 53:225–241, 1987.

[2] S. Abramsky and S. Vickers. Quantales, observational logic, and process semantics. Research Report DOC 90/1, Imperial College, London, 1990.

[3] D. Austry and G. Boudol. Algèbre de processus et synchronisation. *Theoretical Computer Sci.*, 30:91–131, 1984.

[4] J. C. M. Baeten and R. J. van Glabbeek. Another look at abstraction in process algebra. In T. Ottman, editor, *Automata, Languages and Programming* 14th *ICALP*, volume 267 of *Lect. Notes in Computer Sci.*, pages 84–94. Springer-Verlag, 1987.

[5] J. A. Bergstra and J. W. Klop. Process algebra for synchronous communication. *Information and Control*, 60:109–137, 1984.

[6] B. Bloom. *Ready Simulation, Bisimulation, and the Semantics of CCS-Like Languages*. PhD thesis, MIT, August 1989.

[7] B. Bloom, S. Istrail, and A. R. Meyer. Bisimulation can't be traced: Preliminary report. In 15th *Symp. Principles of Programming Languages*, pages 229–239. ACM, 1988. Final version in preparation for journal submission.

[8] B. Bloom and A. R. Meyer. A remark on the bisimulation of probabilistic processes. In A. Meyer and M. Taitslin, editors, *Logic at Botik '89, Proceedings*, volume 363 of *Lect. Notes in Computer Sci.*, pages 26–40, July 1989.

[9] R. de Simone. Higher-level synchronising devices in MEIJE-SCCS. *Theoretical Computer Sci.*, 37:245–267, 1985.

[10] R. DeNicola and M. C. Hennessy. Testing equivalences for processes. *Theoretical Computer Sci.*, 34:83–133, 1984.

[11] J. F. Groote and F. Vaandrager. Structured operational semantics and bisimulation as a congruence (extended abstract). In J. G. Ausiello, M. Dezani-Ciancaglini and S. Ronchi Della Rocca, editors, *Automata, Languages, and Programming* 16th *ICALP*, volume 372 of *Lect. Notes in Computer Sci.*, pages 423–438. Springer-Verlag, 1989.

[12] M. C. B. Hennessy and R. Milner. On observing nondeterminism and concurrency. In J. D. Bakker and J. van Leeuwen, editors, *Automata, Languages, and Programming*, volume 85 of *Lect. Notes in Computer Sci.*, pages 299–309. Springer-Verlag, 1980.

[13] C. Hoare. Communicating sequential processes. *Comm. ACM*, 21:666–677, 1978.

[14] C. A. R. Hoare. *Communicating Sequential Processes*. Series in Computer Science. Prentice-Hall, 1985. 256 pp.

[15] K. Larsen and A. Skou. Bisimulation through probabilistic testing (preliminary report). In 16th *Symp. Principles of Programming Languages*, pages 344–352. ACM, Jan. 1989.

[16] R. Milner. *A Calculus of Communicating Systems*, volume 92 of *Lect. Notes in Computer Sci.* Springer-Verlag, 1980.

[17] R. Milner. A modal characterisation of observable machine-behavior. In E. Astesiano and C. Böhm, editors, *CAAP '81. Proceedings*, volume 112 of *Lect. Notes in Computer Sci.* Springer-Verlag, 1981.

[18] R. Milner. Calculi for synchrony and asynchrony. *Theoretical Computer Sci.*, 25:267–310, 1983.

[19] I. Phillips. Refusal testing. In L. Kott, editor,*Automata, Languages and Programming* 13th *ICALP*, volume 226 of *Lect. Notes in Computer Sci.*, pages 304–313. Springer-Verlag, 1986.

[20] G. D. Plotkin. A structural approach to operational semantics. Technical Report DAIMI FN-19, Aarhus Univ., Computer Science Dept., Denmark, 1981.

[21] A. Pnueli. Linear and branching structures in the semantics and logics of reactive systems. In W. Brauer, editor, *Automata, Languages, and Programming*, volume 194 of *Lect. Notes in Computer Sci.*, pages 15–32. Springer-Verlag, 1985.

Iteration Theories of Synchronization Trees

*S. L. Bloom**
Dept. of Comp. Sc., Stevens Institute of Technology
Castle Point, Hoboken, NJ 07030, U.S.A.

Z. Ésik†
Bolyai Institute, A. József University
6721 Szeged, Hungary

D. Taubner‡
Inst. f. Informatik, Techn. Univ. München
Arcisstr. 21, D-8000 München 2, F.R. Germany

Abstract

Synchronization trees are shown to form an iteration theory in a natural way. The class of grove iteration theories is introduced. The regular synchronization trees are shown to be the free theories in the subclass of synchronization theories. Moreover, the bisimulation equivalence classes of regular synchronization trees are shown to be the free synchronization theories satisfying an 'infinite' idempotency law.

Introduction

Synchronization trees were used by Milner in [21] as models of the computation of communicating processes. More accurately, it were the equivalence classes of trees under the relation of bisimularity which were his primary focus. At the end of the introduction of Milner's paper, he conjectured that with a different treatment of variables, his work might fit into the framework of Elgot's *iterative* theories (see [12]).

The current paper shows that Milner's conjecture was essentially correct. A slightly different definition of synchronization tree is used here (reflecting a different treatment of variables), and the structure of these trees is characterized. In fact, both of the structure of the trees themselves and the bisimulation equivalence classes of trees are characterized. The characterizations take the following form: the structure in question is free in a particular variety of *iteration* theories.

Thus, while one might guess that the current paper was inspired by Milner's conjecture, in fact the motivation was somewhat different. In a number of papers, various structures related to the theory of computation have been shown to be iteration theories. It has been conjectured that wherever a repetitive process is involved, an iteration theory can be found. Strong and weak behaviours of flowchart schemes, input-output and stepwise behaviours of algorithms, functors involved in circular data type specifications have all been shown to form iteration theories in natural ways (see [6] and [7]). It was natural to attempt to show that synchronization trees also form iteration theories.

*Partially supported by NSF grant CCR-8620250
†Research supported by Alexander von Humboldt Foundation
‡Present address: Siemens AG, Corporate R & D, Otto-Hahn-Ring 6, D-8000 München 83

A naive attempt to show that synchronization trees form iteration theories would be to use the same ideas as for unfoldings of flowchart schemes (see [13]). It is not surprising that this fails immediately. We had to consider a finer structure on these trees, which makes them into a special kind of 2-category. Thus, while the technical details are not routine, no one should be surprised by the result. Indeed, it is the technical details that form the main point of the current paper. The question answered here is not just whether synchronization trees form an iteration theory, but precisely what kind of iteration theory. We give some more specific information in the rest of this introduction.

One difference between Elgot's iterative theories [12] and iteration theories [4, 5] is that only in iteration theories is the operation $f \mapsto f^\dagger$ always defined. Another is that in iteration theories the properties of iteration are completely captured by means of identities. Otherwise, both types of theories are categories with finite coproducts which are generated by a single object – i.e. each object is a finite copower $X + \ldots + X$ of a single object X. (For simplicity, the objects are then identified with the nonnegative integers.) For any morphism $f : n \to n + p$ in an iteration theory there is a morphism $f^\dagger : n \to p$ which satisfies a number of identities.

For a fixed set A of action symbols, a synchronization tree $t : 1 \to p$ is a rooted, at most countably branching tree whose edges are labeled by elements in $A \cup [p]$, (here $[p]$ denotes $\{1, \ldots, p\}$). If the edge (u, v) is labeled by an element of $[p]$, the vertex v must be a leaf of the tree. A synchronization tree $n \to p$ is just an n-tuple of synchronization trees $1 \to p$. A morphism between two synchronization trees $n \to p$ is an n-tuple of root, successor, and label preserving functions between the underlying set of vertices. The category $ST(A)(n, p)$ of synchronization trees $n \to p$ is shown to be countably cocomplete – i.e. any countable diagram has a colimit. In particular, all ω-diagrams

$$f_0 \xrightarrow{\rho_0} f_1 \xrightarrow{\rho_1} f_2 \cdots$$

have a colimit. An operation of horizontal composition is defined,

$$\begin{array}{rcl} ST(A)(n,p) \times ST(A)(p,q) & \to & ST(A)(n,q) \\ (f_1, \ldots, f_n), g & \mapsto & (f_1 \circ g, \ldots f_n \circ g). \end{array}$$

Here $g = (g_1, \ldots, g_p)$ and for each tree $f_j : 1 \to p$, the tree $f_j \circ g$ is defined as the tree obtained from f_j by replacing each edge of f_j labeled i by a copy of the tree g_i. It is shown that horizontal composition commutes with colimits of ω-diagrams.

The structure of the categories $ST(A)(n,p)$, $n, p \geq 0$, is the same as that of the categories of ω-functors considered in [7]. Here we introduce the concept explicitly: the *ω-continuous 2-theories*. The iterate $f^\dagger : n \to p$ of a synchronization tree $f : n \to n + p$ is then defined as the colimit of an ω-diagram corresponding to the Kleene sequence of approximations.

We work with a skeletal 2-category $ST'(A)$ of $ST(A)$. We show that, equipped with the operation of iteration, $ST'(A)$ is an iteration theory. Further, each hom-set $ST'(A)(n,p)$ has the structure of a commutative monoid (where $f + g$ is the coproduct of f and g) and right composition distributes over finite sums, in particular $(f + g) \circ h = f \circ h + g \circ h$. Such structures are called *grove iteration theories*, following the terminology of [1]. These categories of synchronization trees satisfy three further identities involving the † operation which we use to define the variety of *synchronization theories*.

The regular synchronization trees are those trees in the least sub grove iteration theory of $ST'(A)$ containing the *atomic* trees $a\eta : 1 \to 1, a \in A$ (which consist of a two edge path, the first edge labeled by a, and the second labeled 1). One of the main results shows that the theory of regular synchronization trees is freely generated by the map $a \mapsto a\eta$ in the variety of synchronization theories. The relation of bisimularity on synchronization trees is shown to be an iteration theory congruence on the theories $ST'(A)$ (in effect, this fact was noted by Milner, cf. [21, Proposition 3.2]). The quotient, restricted to regular synchronization trees, is shown to be freely generated in the variety of *ω-idempotent* synchronization theories.

Throughout this extended abstract we omit proofs. They will be provided in the full version.

Section 1: 2-theories and theories

The concept of 2-theory is a combination of Lawvere theories [19] and 2-categories [18, 17]. An equational presentation of 2-theories would be adoptable from [12] and [3].

The set of nonnegative integers is denoted N. For $n \in \mathrm{N}$ we write $[n] = \{1, \ldots, n\}$, so that $[0]$ is another notation for the empty set.

1 Definition A *2-theory* T consists of the following data.

1.1 A set $T(n,p)$ for each pair of nonnegative integers $n, p \in \mathrm{N}$. The elements of $T(n,p)$ are thought of as (horizontal) morphisms $n \to p$. Accordingly we write $f : n \to p$ for $f \in T(n,p)$.

1.2 A set $T(f,g)$ for each pair of morphisms $f, g : n \to p$. Again we write $u : f \to g$ for $u \in T(f,g)$ and call u a (vertical) morphism.

1.3 An operation of horizontal composition defined both for horizontal and vertical morphisms of appropriate source and target. Given $f : n \to p$ and $g : p \to q$, the horizontal composite $f \circ g$ is a morphism $n \to q$. If $f, f' : n \to p$ and $g, g' : p \to q$ are horizontal morphisms, moreover $u : f \to f'$ and $v : g \to g'$ are vertical morphisms, then $u \circ v = f \circ g \to f' \circ g'$ is a vertical morphism.

1.4 An operation of vertical composition defined for vertical morphisms. In more detail, for $u : f \to g$ and $v : g \to h$ with $f, g, h : n \to p$, $u \cdot v$ is a vertical morphism $f \to h$.

1.5 An operation of tupling. A morphism with source 1 is called scalar. For given scalar morphisms $f_i : 1 \to p$, $i \in [n]$, $\langle f_1, \ldots, f_n \rangle$ is a horizontal morphism $n \to p$. If $f_i, g_i : 1 \to p$ are horizontal morphisms for $i \in [n]$, and if $u_i : f_i \to g_i$ are given vertical morphisms, then $\langle u_1, \ldots, u_n \rangle$ is a vertical morphism $\langle f_1, \ldots, f_n \rangle \to \langle g_1, \ldots, g_n \rangle$. When $n = 0$, tupling just selects a constant $0_p : 0 \to p$ for each $p \in \mathrm{N}$.

1.6 Associated with each $f : n \to p$ there is a constant $I(f) : f \to f$, called identity.

1.7 For $i \in [n], n \in \mathrm{N}$, a distinguished morphism $i_n : 1 \to n$.

The above data are subject to a number of axioms that jointly express that the horizontal structure is a category whose objects are the nonnegative integers and whose morphisms are the horizontal morphisms. Composition is horizontal composition with identity morphisms

$$1_n = \langle 1_n, \ldots, n_n \rangle : n \to n.$$

Further each set $T(n,p)$ is itself a category with objects the horizontal morphisms $n \to p$ and morphisms the vertical morphisms $f \to g$ for $f, g : n \to p$. Composition in $T(n,p)$ is vertical composition with identity morphisms $I(f)$. Horizontal composition is also defined for vertical morphisms. The horizontal and vertical stuctures are related by the interchange

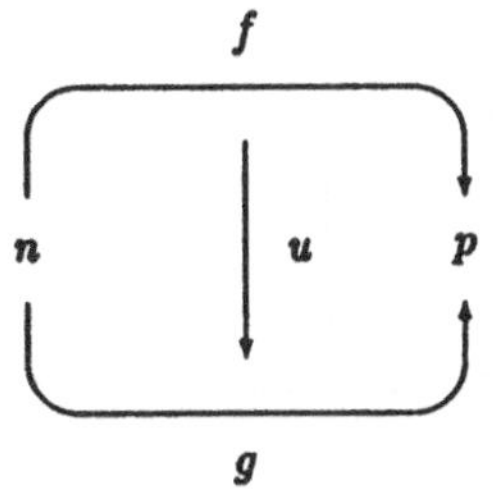

Figure 1: A cell $n \to p$

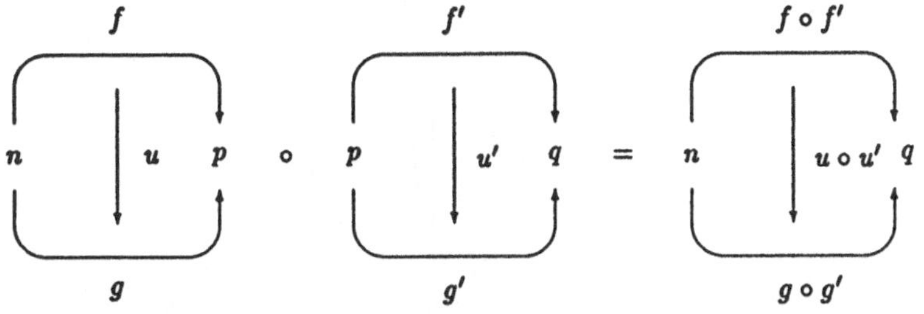

Figure 2: Horizontal composition of cells

rule. Moreover, the morphisms $I(1_n)$ are identity morphisms with respect to the horizontal composition of vertical morphisms, and horizontal composition (and also tupling) preserves vertical identities. It is therefore legitimate to use the notation f for $I(f)$. These conditions jointly mean that 2-theories are 2-categories. The structure of 2-categories is conveniently described by using cells. Accordingly we define a cell $x : n \to p$ in a 2-theory to be a triple

$$x = (f, g, u)$$

consisting of two horizontal morphisms $f, g : n \to p$ and a vertical morphism $u : f \to g$, as in Figure 1. When $f = g$ and u is the identity vertical morphism $f \to f$, the cell is called an identity cell, denoted f.

Given cells $x = (f, g, u) : n \to p$ and $y = (f', g', u') : p \to q$, their horizontal composite $x \circ y$ is the cell $(f \circ f', g \circ g', u \circ u') : n \to q$, see Figure 2.

Cells can be composed vertically, also. Given $x = (f, g, u) : n \to p$ and $y = (g, h, v) : n \to p$, the vertical composition $x \cdot y$ is the cell $(f, h, u \cdot v) : n \to p$, see Figure 3.

Now both cell compositions are associative and have identities, 1_n (horizontal composition), f (vertical composition). Horizontal composition of identity cells is an identity cell.

Let $x_i = (f_i, g_i, u_i) : 1 \to p$ be cells for $i \in [n]$. We may extend the operation of tupling to cells by defining

$$\langle x_1, \ldots, x_n \rangle = (\langle f_1, \ldots, f_n \rangle, \langle g_1, \ldots, g_n \rangle, \langle u_1, \ldots, u_n \rangle) : n \to p.$$

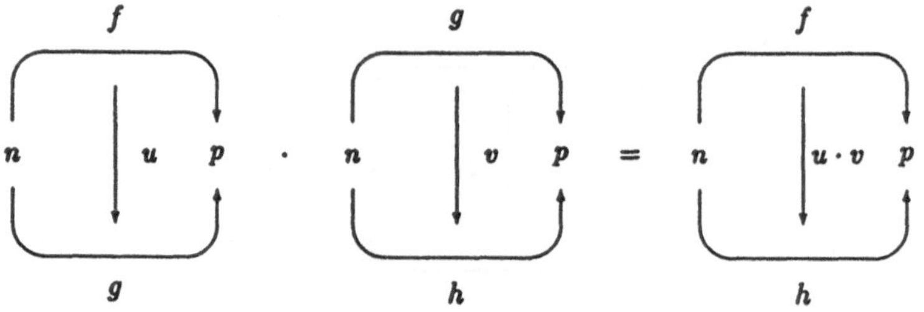

Figure 3: Vertical composition of cells

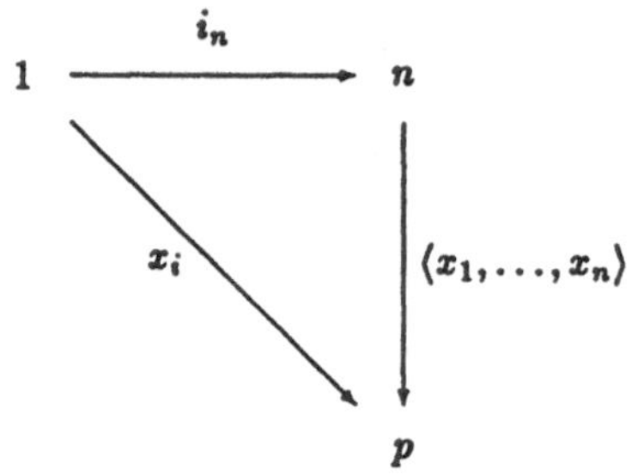

Figure 4: Coproduct diagram for cells

It is now required that if all the x_i's are identity cells then so is their tupling. Additionally it is required that the diagram in Figure 4 is a coproduct diagram for horizontal composition of cells. When $n = 0$ the diagram asserts that 0_p is the unique cell $0 \to p$.

The cells corresponding to the distinguished morphisms i_n of 1.7 may be called distinguished also. Finally it is required that $x = \langle x \rangle$ for all cells $x : 1 \to p$. □

2 Examples

2.1 *Lawvere theories.* A Lawvere theory is a 2-theory T such that each vertical category $T(f, g)$ for $f, g : n \to p$ is discrete, so that each cell is an identity cell. Hence we may drop the vertical structure (together with horizontal composition of vertical morphisms).

2.2 An example of a theory is the theory of all functions $[n] \to [p]$, for $n, p \in \mathrm{N}$. Composition is function composition written from left to right. For $f_i : [1] \to [p]$, $i \in [n]$, the morphism $\langle f_1, \ldots, f_n \rangle$ is defined to be the function $f : [n] \to [p]$ with $if = 1f_i$ for any $i \in [n]$. The distinguished morphism i_n, for $i \in [n]$, is the function $[1] \to [n]$ with value i. We denote this theory by T_0.

2.3 *Functor theories.* Let C be a small category and, for $n \in \mathrm{N}$, denote by C^n the n-fold direct product of C with itself. We define a 2-theory $Th(C)$ of multifunctors over C. A horizontal morphism $n \to p$ is a functor $F : C^p \to C^n$, note the reversal of the arrow. Given functors $F, G : C^p \to C^n$, a vertical morphism in $Th(C)(F, G)$ is a natural

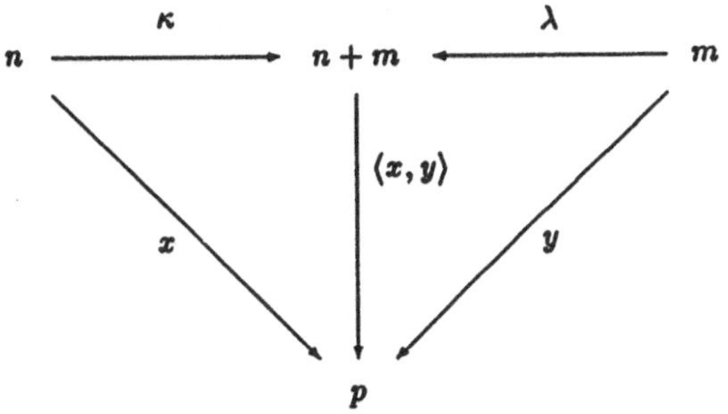

Figure 5: Coproduct diagram defining the operation of pairing

transformation $u : F \to G$. Horizontal composition of functors is functor composition. For natural transformations both compositions have their usual meaning. For a functor F, $I(F)$ is just the identity natural transformation corresponding to F. The distinguished morphism $i_n : 1 \to n$, for $i \in [n]$, is the i-th projection functor $C^n \to C$. This example is in a sense universal.

3 Derived operations A number of derived operations may be defined for theories. Following [12], below we define the operations of pairing and separated sum for cells in 2-theories, henceforth defining these operations both for horizontal and vertical morphisms.

3.1 Pairing. Let $x : n \to p$ and $y : m \to p$ be cells. We define a cell $n + m \to p$ by

$$\langle x, y\rangle = \langle 1_n \circ x, \ldots, n_n \circ x, 1_m \circ y, \ldots, m_m \circ y\rangle.$$

Thus, if

$$x = (\langle f_1, \ldots, f_n\rangle, \langle f'_1, \ldots, f'_n\rangle, \langle u_1, \ldots, u_n\rangle),$$
$$y = (\langle g_1, \ldots, g_m\rangle, \langle g'_1, \ldots, g'_m\rangle, \langle v_1, \ldots, v_m\rangle),$$

then

$$\langle x, y\rangle = (\langle f_1, \ldots, f_n, g_1, \ldots, g_m\rangle, \langle f'_1, \ldots, f'_n, g'_1, \ldots, g'_m\rangle, \langle u_1, \ldots, u_n, v_1, \ldots, v_m\rangle).$$

Our notation for pairing is legitimate as tupling can be expressed by repeated applications of pairing.

3.2 Separated sum. For $x : n \to p$ and $y : m \to q$ we define

$$x \oplus y = \langle x \circ \kappa, y \circ \lambda\rangle : n + m \to p + q$$

with $\kappa = \langle 1_{p+q}, \ldots, p_{p+q}\rangle$ and $\lambda = \langle (p+1)_{p+q}, \ldots, (p+q)_{p+q}\rangle$.

We see that, for $i \in [n]$, $i_{n+m} \circ (x \oplus y) = i_n \circ x$. Similarly, for $i \in [m]$, $(n+i)_{n+m} \circ (x \oplus y) = i_m \circ y$.

3.3 The operations of pairing and separated sum can be conveniently defined by the coproduct property: $\langle x, y\rangle$ and $x \oplus y$ are the unique mediating cells of Figures 5 and 6, respectively. For the definition of the κ's and λ's see 3.2.

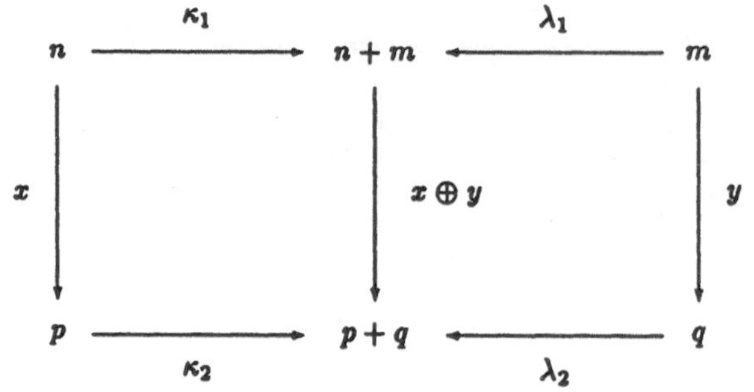

Figure 6: Coproduct diagram defining the operation of separated sum

4 Example 2-theories and 2-theory morphisms form a category. The theory T_0 can be identified as the initial 2-theory (and henceforth also initial theory). Given a 2-theory T, the unique 2-theory morphism $F : T_0 \to T$ can be described as the assignment $fF = \langle (1f)_p, \ldots, (nf)_p \rangle$, for any $f : [n] \to [p]$. (This definition makes sense both for horizontal or vertical morphisms, or for cells.) The morphisms of the form fF constitute the smallest sub 2-theory in T that we call the 2-theory of base morphisms. If f is surjective (injective, bijective, monotonic), then the corresponding base morphism is also said to have this property. If T is a theory, the base morphisms are usually treated as horizontal morphisms.

Base morphisms are usually denoted by small Greek letters and are often given as functions $[n] \to [m]$. It is known that a theory T is either trivial (i.e. each $T(n, m)$ contains at most one morphism), or the subtheory of base morphisms in T is isomorphic to T_0. A similar fact is true for 2-theories.

Section 2: Iteration theories

In [4] and [5] *iteration theories* have been defined as the variety generated by pointed iterative theories, which are basically iterative theories [12] with iteration turned into a totally defined operation.

It seems that iteration theories are a basic underlying structure to many investigations in theoretical computer science, see e.g. [6], [7] and [8] for some new results. Nevertheless the underlying iteration theories are not always made explicit. In this paper we show that synchronization trees form iteration theories, so that iteration theories may provide an algebraic framework for communicating systems.

The following axiomatization of iteration theories was obtained in [14]. A *preiteration theory* is an algebraic theory T equipped with an operation of iteration that takes a morphism $f : n \to n + p$, $n, p \in \mathrm{N}$, into a morphism $f^\dagger : n \to p$. In a preiteration theory, iteration is not required to have any particular properties. A morphism of preiteration theories is a theory morphism which preserves iteration.

1 Theorem A preiteration theory is an iteration theory if and only if it satisfies the following identities.

1.1 *Left zero identity* $\qquad (0_n \oplus f)^\dagger = f, \; f : n \to p$

1.2 *Right zero identity* $(f \oplus 0_q)^\dagger = f^\dagger \oplus 0_q,\ f : n \to n+p$

1.3 *Pairing identity* $\langle f, g\rangle^\dagger = \langle f^\dagger \circ \langle h^\dagger, 1_p\rangle, h^\dagger\rangle$, $f : n \to n+m+p, q : m \to n+m+p$, where $h = g \circ \langle f^\dagger, 1_{m+p}\rangle : m \to m+p$

1.4 *Commutative identity*

$$\langle 1_m \circ \rho \circ f \circ (\rho_1 \oplus 1_p), \ldots, m_m \circ \rho \circ f \circ (\rho_m \oplus 1_p)\rangle^\dagger = \rho \circ (f \circ (\rho \oplus 1_p))^\dagger,$$

where $f : n \to m+p, \rho : m \to n$ is surjective base, and each $\rho_i : m \to m$ is base with $\rho_i \cdot \rho = \rho$. □

For other axiomatizations the reader is referred to [25] and [15]. The operation of iteration is sometimes replaced by the operation of feedback, cf. [9]. As noted in [14], the commutative identity is implied by the following much simpler condition.

1.5 *Weak functorial dagger* $f \circ (\rho \oplus 1_p) = \rho \circ g \Rightarrow f^\dagger = \rho \circ g^\dagger$
where $f : m \to m+p,\quad g : n \to n+p$ and $\rho : m \to n$ is a surjective base morphism.

An iteration theory satisfying 1.5 is called an iteration theory with a weak functorial dagger. In any iteration theory we define $\perp = 1_1^\dagger$ and $\perp_{np} = (1_n \oplus 0_p)^\dagger$. It then follows that $\perp = \perp_{10}$ and that $\perp_{np} = \langle \perp \cdot 0_p, \ldots, \perp \cdot 0_p\rangle$.

2 Definition An *ω-continuous theory* is a strict ordered theory T such that each $T(n,p)$ is an ω-complete poset and composition is ω-continuous, i.e.,

2.1 $(\sup f_k) \circ g = \sup(f_k \circ g)$ and $h \circ (\sup f_k) = \sup(h \circ f_k)$

hold for any ω-chain $f_k : n \to p, k \in \mathrm{N}$, and morphisms $g : p \to q, h : m \to n$. □

Let T be an ω-continuous theory. Given $f : n \to n+p$, the equation in the variable $\xi : n \to p$

$$\xi = f \circ \langle \xi, 1_p\rangle$$

has a least solution, namely

$$f^\dagger = \sup f^{(k)},$$

where the Kleene sequence $f^{(k)}$ is defined as $f^{(0)} = \perp_{np}$, and for $k \geq 0$, $f^{(k+1)} = f \circ \langle f^{(k)}, 1_p\rangle$. It is known, cf. [14], that the preiteration theories obtained by this definition of iteration are iteration theories with weak functorial dagger, in fact they generate the variety of iteration theories. The notation $\perp_{np}$ for the bottom element in $T(n,p)$ is in accordance with the notation introduced for iteration theories, for clearly $(1_n \oplus 0_p)^\dagger = \perp_{np}$.

The following 2-categorial generalization of ω-continuous theories derives from [7]. An ω-category is a category with initial object and ω-colimits.

3 Definition An *ω-continuous 2-theory* is a 2-theory T such that each vertical category $T(n,p)$ is an ω-category and horizontal composition preserves ω-colimits on both sides. Thus, if $v_k : f_k \to f$, $k \in \mathrm{N}$, is a colimit cone to an ω-diagram $u_k : f_k \to f_{k+1}$ in $T(n,p)$, and if $g : p \to q$ and $h : m \to n$ are horizontal morphisms, then

$$v_k \circ g : f_k \circ g \to f \circ g$$

and

$$h \circ v_k : h \circ f_k \to h \circ f$$

are colimit cones to the ω-diagrams $u_k \circ g : f_k \circ g \to f_{k+1} \circ g$ and $h \circ u_k : h \circ f_k \to h \circ f_{k+1}$, respectively. Furthermore it is required that $\perp_{np} \circ f$ is initial in the vertical category $T(n,q)$ whenever $\perp_{np}$ is initial in $T(n,p)$ and f belongs to $T(p,q)$. □

Let us fix an initial object, i.e. a horizontal morphism, $\perp_{np} : n \to p$ for all $n,p \in \mathrm{N}$. Given $f : n \to n+p$, the equation in the variable $\xi : n \to p$

$$\xi \cong f \circ \langle \xi, 1_p \rangle$$

has an initial solution $f^\dagger : n \to p$ which is unique up to isomorphism. In fact, it can be constructed in the very same way as for ω-continuous theories. Let

$$f^{(0)} = \perp_{np},\ f^{(k+1)} = f \circ \langle f^{(k)}, 1_p \rangle,$$

and
$$u^{(0)} = \perp_{np} \to f^{(1)},\ u^{(k+1)} = f \circ \langle u^{(k)}, 1_p \rangle$$

for $k \in \mathrm{N}$, where $u^{(0)}$ is the unique vertical morphism $\perp_{np} \to f^{(1)}$. We define $f^\dagger$ to be the colimit of the diagram $u_k : f^{(k)} \to f^{(k+1)}$, $k \in \mathrm{N}$.

A 2-theory is skeletal if each vertical category $T(n,p)$ is skeletal. The following result is drawn from [7] where the case of ω-continuous 2-theories of ω-functors is treated.

4 Theorem Every skeletal ω-continuous 2-theory gives rise to an iteration theory with weak functorial dagger. The iteration theories so obtained generate the variety of iteration theories. □

In Theorem 4, the vertical structure is needed only to define the operation of iteration, and is otherwise completely ignored. It is possible to define iteration also for cells, and this will be treated elsewhere. The notation $\perp_{np}$ for the initial horizontal morphism in $T(n,p)$ is again in accordance with the notation for iteration theories as $(1_n \oplus 0_p)^\dagger = \perp_{np}$ in any skeletal ω-continuous 2-theory T.

Section 3: Grove iteration theories

In this section we consider iteration theories with an additional constant $1 \to 2$, denoted $+$, which satisfies certain identities. Following [1], any right distributive abelian seminear ring with a left absorbtive zero is called a grove. Therefore the algebraic theories arising in connection with groves will be called grove theories below.

1 Definition Let T be an algebraic theory with additional constants $+ : 1 \to 2$ and $\# : 1 \to 0$. We define an operation of addition. For $f, g : 1 \to p$, $p \in \mathrm{N}$, let

1.1 $$f + g = + \circ \langle f, g \rangle,$$

and for $f, g : n \to p$, $n, p \in \mathrm{N}$, $n \neq 1$, let

1.2 $$f + g = \langle 1_n \circ f + 1_n \circ g, \ldots, n_n \circ f + n_n \circ g \rangle,$$

where it is understood that composition has stronger precedence than addition. We clearly have $+ = 1_2 + 2_2$.

Moreover, for each $n, p \in \mathrm{N}$, we define a morphism $0_{np} : n \to p$ by letting

1.3 $$0_{1p} = \# \circ 0_p$$

and

1.4 $$0_{np} = \langle 0_{1p}, \ldots, 0_{1p} \rangle,$$

for $n \neq 1$, so that $0_{0p} = 0_p$. □

2 Proposition The following equations hold in T.

2.1 $$(f + g) \circ h = f \circ h + g \circ h, \quad f, g : n \to p, \quad h : p \to q$$

2.2 $$0_{np} \circ f = 0_{nq}, \quad f : p \to q$$

2.3 $$i_n \circ (f + g) = i_n \circ f + i_n \circ g, \quad f, g : n \to p, \quad i \in [n]$$

2.4 $$i_n \circ 0_{np} = 0_{1p}, \quad i \in [n].$$ □

The converse of Proposition 2 also holds.

3 Proposition Let T be an algebraic theory with an operation of addition defined on each set $T(n,p)$. Suppose that we are given constants $0_{np} : n \to p$. Define $+ : 1 \to 2$ by $1_2 + 2_2$ and let $\# = 0_{10}$. If the equations 2.1–2.4 hold, then so do the equations 1.1–1.4. In other words addition can be defined in terms of the constant $+ : 1 \to 2$, and the constants 0_{np} are related to $\#$ by the equations 1.3 and 1.4. □

Roughly speaking, a grove theory is an algebraic theory T such that each set $T(n,p)$ is an additive abelian monoid and composition distributes over finite sums on the right. Moreover, it is required that target tupling creates an isomorphism between the n-th direct power of $T(1,p)$ and the monoid $T(n,p)$, for all $n, p \in \mathrm{N}$. An equivalent definition, motivated by the previous propositions, is given below.

4 Definition A *grove theory* is a theory T with additional constants $+ : 1 \to 2$ and $\# : 1 \to 0$ subject to the following conditions:

4.1 $$(1_3 + 2_3) + 3_3 = 1_3 + (2_3 + 3_3)$$

4.2 $$1_2 + 2_2 = 2_2 + 1_2$$

4.3 $$1_1 + 0_{11} = 1_1$$

A morphism of grove theories is a theory morphism that preserves the constants $+$ and $\#$. □

5 Proposition A grove theory satisfies the following identities:

5.1 $$(f + g) + h = f + (g + h), \quad f, g, h : n \to p$$

5.2 $$f + g = g + f, \quad f, g : n \to p$$

5.3 $$f + 0_{np} = f, \quad f : n \to p$$

5.4 $$(f + g) \circ h = f \circ h + g \circ h, \quad f, g : n \to p, \ h : p \to q$$

5.5 $$0_{np} \circ f = 0_{nq}, \quad f : p \to q.$$

We further refine our notations. Let T be a grove theory and $n \in \mathrm{N}$. We define the morphism $n : 1 \to 1$ by

$$n = 1_1 + \ldots + 1_1 \qquad (n\text{-times}).$$

When $n = 0$ we take $0 = 0_{11}$. Thus we have a constant in T for each $n \in \mathrm{N}$.

6 Proposition In a grove theory we have $n \circ (f+g) = n \circ f + n \circ g$ and $n \circ 0_{1p} = 0_{1p}$ for all $f, g : 1 \to p$, $n, p \in \mathbb{N}$. □

We now turn to grove iteration theories.

7 Definition Let T be an iteration theory with an additional constant $+ : 1 \to 2$ and $\# : 1 \to 0$, so that we obtain an operation of addition according to 1.1 and 1.2. We define an operation of Kleene star. For $f : n \to n+p$, f^* is defined as the iterate of $\bar{f}$, where $\bar{f}$ is the sum of $f \cdot (1_n \oplus 0_n \oplus 1_p)$ and $0_n \oplus 1_n \oplus 0_p$, i.e.,

$$f^* = (f \circ (1_n \oplus 0_n \oplus 1_p) + (0_n \oplus 1_n \oplus 0_p))^\dagger : n \to n+p.$$ □

It is known that iteration and Kleene star are equivalent operations in matrix iteration theories, cf. [25], [9] and [8]. This fact holds under weaker assumptions, too.

8 Proposition Suppose that $1_1 + 0_{11} = 1_1$ holds in T. Then iteration can be expressed by Kleene star, namely

$$f^\dagger = f^* \circ \langle 0_{np}, 1_p \rangle$$

for all $f : n \to n+p$. □

Thus, whenever $1_1 + 0_{11} = 1_1$ holds in T, identities involving iteration can be expressed by Kleene star and conversely. It would be interesting to see what form some identities of iteration theories take when expressed by Kleene star. However we do not consider this question here. Instead we provide an identity that will be useful in the sequel.

9 Proposition Let T be an iteration theory with additional constants $+ : 1 \to 2$ and $\# : 1 \to 0$. The following identity holds in T.

9.1 $f \circ \langle f^*, 0_n \oplus 1_p \rangle + (1_n \oplus 0_p) = f^*, \quad f : n \to n+p$ □

Remark By letting $p = 0$ in 9.1 we obtain

$$f \circ f^* + 1_n = f^*,$$

explaining the terminology. □

10 Definition A theory T which is simultaneously a grove theory and an iteration theory is a *grove iteration theory*. Thus, T has constants $+$, $\#$ and an iteration operation $\dagger$. A *synchronization theory* is a grove iteration theory which, in addition, satisfies the following conditions:

10.1 $1^* \circ (1_2 + 2_2) = 1^* \circ 1_2 + 1^* \circ 2_2$

10.2 $1^* = 1^{**}$

10.3 $\# = \bot$

A grove iteration theory morphism is an iteration theory morphism which preserves the constants $+$ and $\#$. A synchronization theory morphism is a grove iteration theory morphism. Condition 10.1 obviously implies $1^* \circ (f+g) = 1^* \circ f + 1^* \circ g$, for all $f, g : 1 \to p$. □

11 Proposition Let T be a grove iteration theory. Then T is a synchronization theory if and only if 10.1, 10.3 and 11.1 hold, where

11.1 $2^* = 1^*$. □

Next we treat an important subclass of synchronization theories.

12 Definition A grove theory is an *idempotent grove theory* if it satisfies the identity

12.1 $1 + 1 = 1.$

Let T be a grove iteration theory. T is an *ω-idempotent grove iteration theory* if the following identity holds in T:

12.2 $1 = 1^*$ □

13 Proposition

(i) The idempotency law 13.1 holds in any idempotent grove theory:

13.1 $f + f = f, \quad f : n \to p.$

(ii) Every ω-idempotent grove iteration theory with $\# = \perp$ is a synchronization theory.

(iii) Every ω-idempotent grove iteration theory is an idempotent grove theory. □

In virtue of Proposition 13, below an ω-idempotent grove iteration theory with $\# = \perp$ will be called *ω-idempotent synchronization theory.*

Section 4: Synchronization trees

Milner [20], [22] introduced synchronization trees to describe the behaviours of communicating processes. The structure of these trees has continued to play a central role in the study of such processes. Winskel [28] imposed two partial orderings on synchronization trees with the property that ω-chains have suprema. This fact is used to solve recursive fixed point equations in a manner that should be quite familiar. However, his treatment fails to be abstract in the sense that apparently isomorphic synchronization trees are treated as distinct objects. It is not known whether it is possible to define a partial order on isomorphism classes of synchronization trees so that recursive equations can be solved by taking suprema of the corresponding Kleene sequence of approximations. In our framework we can formulate the question as follows: does there exist a reasonable ω-continuous theory of synchronization trees? We believe that such a theory does not exist, although we do not discuss our reasons here. Nevertheless we show that there is a natural way to impose the weaker structure of an ω-continuous 2-theory on synchronization trees which does allow the use of Kleene approximations. In order to do this, we need to take into account the morphisms between synchronization trees. Unlike the case for morphisms between the trees Σtr which are unfoldings of flowchart algorithms [13], there may be several morphisms between two synchronization trees. Whereas the trees in Σtr form an ω-continuous theory, in this section we show that the synchronization trees form an ω-continuous 2-theory. Thus we provide an alternate foundation for the study of communicating processes to the metric space methods of [11], [24], [10].

1 Notation We let $PSET$ denote the category whose objects are pointed sets (X, x) consisting of a set X and an element x in X. A morphism $f : (X, x) \to (Y, y)$ is a function $f : X \to Y$ such that $xf = y$. The category $PSET_\omega$ is the full subcategory determined by the collection of objects (X, x) such that X is finite or countable.

Throughout this section A denotes a fixed set of action symbols. We assume that A is disjoint from the set of integers.

2 Definition A *synchronization tree* $t : 1 \to p$, $p \in \mathbf{N}$, over A is a 4-tuple (V, v_0, E, l) consisting of

2.1 an object (V, v_0) in $PSET_\omega$; the elements of V are vertices and the point v_0 is the root;

2.2 a set $E \subseteq V \times V$ of (directed) edges;

2.3 a function $l : E \to A \cup [p]$, the labeling function.

These data must obey the following restrictions. The directed graph (V, v_0, E) is a rooted tree—i.e. there is a unique directed path from v_0 to u for each vertex u. Further, if $(u, v) \in E$ and $l(u, v) \in [p]$ then the vertex v must be a leaf. An edge whose label is in $[p]$ is called an exit edge and the target v of an exit edge (u, v) is called an exit vertex.

If $t = (V, v_0, E, l)$ is a synchronization tree $1 \to p$, we introduce the following notation for subsets of vertices.

$$V_{ex_i} = \{v \in V \mid \exists u \in V : \quad (u, v) \in E \text{ and } l(u, v) = i\}$$

$$V_{ex} = \bigcup (V_{ex_i} \mid i \in [p]), \quad \hat{V} = V - V_{ex}, \quad \overline{V} = V - \{v_0\}$$

Let $t_i = (V_i, v_i, E_i, l_i)$, $i = 1, 2$, be synchronization trees $1 \to p$. A synchronization tree morphism $\varphi : t_1 \to t_2$ is a morphism in $PSET_\omega$ $(V_1, v_1) \to (V_2, v_2)$ such that

φ preserves edges, i.e. if $(u, v) \in E_1$ then $(u\varphi, v\varphi) \in E_2$;

φ preserves the labeling, i.e. $l_1(u, v) = l_2(u\varphi, v\varphi)$, for all edges $(u, v) \in E_1$.

The composite $\varphi \cdot \psi : t_1 \to t_3$ of two synchronization tree morphisms $\varphi : t_1 \to t_2$ and $\psi : t_2 \to t_3$ is the composite in $PSET_\omega$. We call this operation vertical composition. Corresponding to any synchronization tree $t : 1 \to p$ there is an identity morphism $t \to t$ which is the identical mapping on the vertex set of t.

Thus the synchronization trees $1 \to p$ form a category $ST(A)(1, p)$. Two such trees are isomorphic if there is a bijection of their vertices which preserves the root, the edges and the labeling. For $n, p \geq 0$ we let $ST(A)(n, p)$ be the category which is the n-th direct power of $ST(A)(1, p)$. An object in $ST(A)(n, p)$ is an n-tuple $(t_1, \ldots, t_n)$ where each t_i, $i \in [n]$ is an object in $ST(A)(1, p)$. Morphisms in $ST(A)(n, p)$ are n-tuples of morphisms in $ST(A)(1, p)$. An object in $ST(A)(n, p)$ is called a synchronization tree $n \to p$. □

We wish to prove that each category $ST(A)(n, p)$ has all countable colimits. It will be sufficient to prove this only for the case that $n = 1$. In our argument we make use of the underlying $PSET_\omega$ functor

$$U : ST(A)(1, p) \to PSET_\omega$$

$$(V, v, E, l) \mapsto (V, v).$$

3 Proposition U creates coequalizers. □

4 Proposition U creates countable coproducts. □

5 Corollary The functor U creates all countable colimits. □

for all composable $\varphi : t_1 \to t_2$, $\varphi' : t_2 \to t_3$ and $\psi : s_1 \to s_2$, $\psi' : s_2 \to s_3$ with $t_i \in ST(A)(n,p)$ and $s_i \in ST(A)(p,q)$, $i = 1,2,3$.

Synchronization trees thus have the structure of a 2-category. The cells $n \to p$ in this 2-category are triples (t, s, φ) where t and s are in $ST(A)(n,p)$ and $\varphi : t \to s$ is a synchronization tree morphism. As usual, we will write t also for the identity morphism $t \to t$.

Next we indicate why horizontal composition preserves all countable colimits in its first argument and all ω-colimits in its second. Fix a synchronization tree $t : p \to q$. We define two functors R_t and L_t by right and left composition.

$$\begin{aligned} R_t : ST(A)(n,p) &\to ST(A)(n,q) \\ s \xrightarrow{\varphi} s' &\mapsto s \circ t \xrightarrow{\varphi \circ t} s' \circ t \end{aligned}$$

$$\begin{aligned} L_t : ST(A)(q,r) &\to ST(A)(p,r) \\ s \xrightarrow{\varphi} s' &\mapsto t \circ s \xrightarrow{t \circ \varphi} t \circ s'. \end{aligned}$$

10 Proposition R_t preserves countable colimits. □

11 Proposition L_t preserves ω-colimits. □

The trees we have been considering up to now might be called concrete synchronization trees, since isomorphic trees with distinct sets of vertices are distinct. From now on, we will identify all isomorphic concrete synchronization trees, and define a synchronization tree as a suitably selected representative of an isomorphism class of concrete synchronization trees. This is spelled out below.

For each integer $p \in \mathbf{N}$, let $ST'(A)(1,p)$ be a skeletal subcategory of $ST(A)(1,p)$. Further, for $n \in \mathbf{N}$, $n \neq 1$, let $ST'(A)(n,p)$ be the n-th direct power of $ST'(A)(1,p)$. Thus, for each synchronization tree t in $ST(A)(n,p)$ there is a unique synchronization tree $\bar{t}$ in $ST'(A)(n,p)$ isomorphic to t. Let x_t denote a fixed isomorphism $t \to \bar{t}$.

The synchronization trees in $ST'(A)$ posses the structure of a 2-theory. Indeed, the vertical structure is provided by the categorial structures of the component categories $ST'(A)(n,p)$. To define horizontal composition, let $t, t' : n \to p$ and $s, s' : p \to q$ be synchronization trees in $ST'(A)$ with morphisms $\varphi : t \to t'$ and $\psi : s \to s'$. We define the horizontal composite of t by t' in $ST'(A)$ to be the synchronization tree $\overline{t \circ t'}$. Similarly, we define the horizontal composite of φ and ψ in $ST'(A)$ as the morphism

$$x_{tot'}^{-1} \cdot (\varphi \circ \psi) \cdot x_{sos'}.$$

The tupling of synchronization trees $t_i : 1 \to p$, $i \in [n]$, in $ST'(A)$ is just the n-tuple $(t_1, \ldots, t_n)$. Finally, for $i \in [n]$, we define i_n to be the synchronization tree in $ST'(A)(1,n)$ which has one edge labeled i, see Figure 7.

12 Proposition $ST'(A)$ is an ω-continuous 2-theory. □

Figure 7: The synchronization tree i_n

Figure 8: The synchronization tree $+$

Section 5: Axiomatizing synchronization trees

In this section we give an algebraic characterization of regular synchronization trees. We show that these trees form free synchronization theories. Thus the axioms of synchronization theories can be considered as an axiomatization of regular synchronization trees or of the variety generated by all theories of synchronization trees. For this and the next section by a ***synchronization tree*** we shall mean a synchronization tree in a skeletal ω-continuous 2-theory $ST'(A)$. For convenience we may agree that all synchronization trees $1 \to p$ in $ST'(A)$ share the same root which will be henceforth denoted $*$. Therefore a synchronization tree $1 \to p$ will be represented by a triple

$$(V, E, l)$$

where V is the set of non-root vertices, $E \subseteq V_* \times V_*$ is the set of edges, where $V_* = V \cup \{*\}$, and l is the labeling of the edges.

By Section 2, Theorem 4, we may impose an iteration theory structure on $ST'(A)$, the resulting iteration theory is denoted $\mathcal{ST}(A)$. We observe that $\mathcal{ST}(A)$ contains a synchronization tree shown in Figure 8. Denoting this tree by $+$,

$$t_1 + t_2 = + \circ \langle t_1, t_2 \rangle$$

is just the coproduct of synchronization trees $t_1, t_2 : 1 \to p$. In $\mathcal{ST}(A)$ we interpret the constant $\# : 1 \to 0$ as the trivial synchronization tree consisting of one vertex, so that $\# = \perp$.

1 Theorem $\mathcal{ST}(A)$ is a synchronization theory. □

2 Definition Let t be a synchronization tree $1 \to p$ and v a vertex of t. The vertices that are accessible from v by a directed path form the vertex set of a tree $1 \to p$ with root v isomorphic to a synchronization tree t' in $ST'(A)$. We call t' the subtree of t at vertex v. A synchronization tree $1 \to p$ is regular if it has a finite number of subtrees, and it is finite if its vertex set is finite. A synchronization tree $t : n \to p$ is regular (finite respectively) if each $i_n \circ t$ is regular (finite) for $i \in [n]$. □

Figure 9: The synchronization tree $\eta(a)$

It is straightforward to see that regular (finite) synchronization trees are closed under the theory operations and addition, and that the regularity of $t : n \to n + p$ implies that $t^{\dagger} : n \to p$ is regular. We have thus established the following result.

3 Proposition Regular synchronization trees over a set A of action symbols form a sub synchronization theory $\mathcal{RST}(A)$ of $\mathcal{ST}(A)$. Finite synchronization trees form a grove theory $\mathcal{FST}(A)$. □

For any $a \in A$ let $\eta(a)$ denote the tree shown in Figure 9. We may regard η either as a function $A \to \mathcal{RST}(A)$ or $A \to \mathcal{FST}(A)$.

We are now ready to state the main result of the section.

4 Theorem Let T be a synchronization theory and $\psi : A \to T$ a function such that $\psi(a) : 1 \to 1$ for all $a \in A$. There exists a unique synchronization theory morphism $\psi^{\#} : \mathcal{RST}(A) \to T$ with $\eta\psi^{\#} = \psi$. □

The following corollary of Theorem 4 is a reformulation of Proposition 1.2 in [1]. Recall that $\mathcal{FST}(A)$ is the grove theory of finite synchronization trees over A.

5 Theorem Let T be a grove theory and $\psi : A \to T$ a function such that $\psi(a)$ is a morphism $1 \to 1$ for all $a \in A$. There is a unique grove theory morphism $\psi^{\#} : \mathcal{FST}(A) \to T$ with $\eta\psi^{\#} = \psi$.

Section 6: Bisimularity

There are many equivalence notions for behaviours of concurrent systems. One of the best known is the notion of bisimularity. It has been introduced by [23] for finite automata. However, [20, Theorem 5.6] already contains the same idea.

The notion of bisimularity has been called a branching time semantics. It is a finer classification of the behaviour of processes than the so-called linear time semantics or trace semantics, see [26] for a brief overview and further references.

1 Definition Let $f, g : 1 \to p$ be synchronization trees in $\mathcal{ST}(A)$, say $f = (V, E, l)$ and $g = (V', E', l')$. A bisimulation between f and g is a relation

$$R \subseteq V_* \times V'_*$$

subject to the following conditions:

1.1 $*R*$ holds, i.e. the roots are related.

1.2 If $u, v \in V_*$ and $u' \in V'_*$ are vertices with uRu' and $(u,v) \in E$ then there exists $v' \in V'_*$ with vRv', $(u',v') \in E'$ and $l(u,v) = l'(u',v')$.

1.3 Symmetrically, if $u', v' \in V'_*$ and $u \in V_*$ are vertices with uRu' and $(u',v') \in E'$ then there exists $v \in V_*$ with vRv', $(u,v) \in E$ and $l(u,v) = l'(u',v')$. □

2 Definition Let $f, g : 1 \to p$ be synchronization trees in $\mathcal{ST}(A)$. We say that f is bisimular to g if there exists a bisimulation between f and g. Two synchronization trees $f, g : n \to p$ are bisimular, denoted $f \sim g$, if $i_n \circ f$ is bisimular to $i_n \circ g$, for all $i \in [n]$. We call the relation $\sim$ the relation of bisimularity. □

3 Proposition Bisimularity is an iteration theory congruence on $\mathcal{ST}(A)$. In more detail,

3.1 $f \sim f'$ and $g \sim g'$ imply $f \circ g \sim f' \circ g'$ for all $f, f' : n \to p$ and $g, g' : p \to q$ in $\mathcal{ST}(A)$.

3.2 If $f_i \sim g_i$ for $i \in [n]$, where $f_i, g_i : 1 \to p$, then $\langle f_1, \ldots, f_n \rangle \sim \langle g_1, \ldots, g_n \rangle$.

3.3 If $f \sim g$ for $f, g : n \to n + p$ then $f^\dagger \sim g^\dagger$. □

For a proof of Proposition 3 the reader is referred to [21, Proposition 3.2], where a similar statement appears. The operation of composition corresponds to Milner's substitution. We let $\mathcal{BST}(A)$ denote the quotient synchronization theory

$$\mathcal{BST}(A) := \mathcal{ST}(A)/\sim .$$

Similarly, $\mathcal{BRST}(A)$ stands for the synchronization theory $\mathcal{RST}(A)/\sim$. The following fact is immediate.

4 Propositon $\mathcal{BST}(A)$ and $\mathcal{BRST}(A)$ are ω-idempotent synchronization theories. □

Let ψ denote the grove iteration theory morphism $\mathcal{RST}(A) \to \mathcal{BRST}(A)$ that takes a regular synchronization tree to its equivalence class modulo $\sim$. The composition

$$\eta' : A \xrightarrow{\eta} \mathcal{RST}(A) \xrightarrow{\psi} \mathcal{BRST}(A)$$

gives an embedding of A into $\mathcal{BRST}(A)$.

5 Theorem $\mathcal{BRST}(A)$ is freely generated by η' in the class of ω-idempotent synchronization theories. □

The following result derives from the more general Theorem 2.23 of [2] where also the silent action is treated, see also [1, p. 281].

6 Theorem $\mathcal{BFST}(A)$ is freely generated by η' in the class of idempotent grove theories. □

References

[1] D. Benson and J. Tiuryn. Fixed points in free process algebras, part I. *Theoret. Comput. Sci.*, 63:275–294, 1989.

[2] J.A. Bergstra and J.W. Klop. Algebra of communicating processes with abstraction. *Theoret. Comput. Sci.*, 37:77–121, 1985.

[3] S.L. Bloom and C.C. Elgot. The existence and construction of free iterative theories. *J. Comput. Syst. Sci.*, 12:305–318, 1976.

[4] S.L. Bloom, C.C. Elgot, and J.B. Wright. Solutions of the iteration equation and extensions of the scalar iteration operation. *SIAM J. Comput.*, 9:26–45, 1980.

[5] S.L. Bloom, C.C. Elgot, and J.B. Wright. Vector iteration in pointed iterative theories. *SIAM J. Comput.*, 9:525–540, 1980.

[6] S.L. Bloom and Z. Ésik. Varieties of iteration theories. *SIAM J. Comput.*, 17:939–966, 1988.

[7] S.L. Bloom and Z. Ésik. Equational logic of circular data type specification. *Theoret. Comput. Sci.*, 63:303–331, 1989.

[8] S.L. Bloom and Z. Ésik. Matrix and matrical iteration theories. submitted for publication, 1989.

[9] V.E. Cazanescu and Gh. Stefanescu. Feedback, iteration and repetition. Research Report 42, National Institute for Scientific and Technical Creation, Bucharest, 1988.

[10] J.W. de Bakker, J.N. Kok, J.-J.Ch. Meyer, E.-R. Olderog, and J.I. Zucker. Contrasting themes in the semantics of imperative concurrency. In J.W. de Bakker, W.-P. de Roever, and G. Rozenberg, editors, *Current trends in concurrency*, volume 224 of *Lect. Notes Comput. Sci.*, pages 51–121, Springer, Berlin, 1986.

[11] J.W. de Bakker and J.I. Zucker. Processes and the denotational semantics of concurrency. *Information and Control*, 54:70–120, 1982.

[12] C.C. Elgot. Monadic computation and iterative algebraic theories. In H.E. Rose and J.C. Shepherdson, editors, *Logic Colloquium '73, Studies in Logic and the Foundations of Mathematics*, pages 175–230, North-Holland, Amsterdam, 1975.

[13] C.C. Elgot, S.L. Bloom, and R. Tindell. On the algebraic structure of rooted trees. *J. Comput. Sys. Sci.*, 16:362–399, 1978.

[14] Z. Ésik. Identities in iterative and rational algebraic theories. *Comput. Ling. and Comput. Lang.*, 14:183–207, 1980.

[15] Z. Ésik. A note on the axiomatization of iteration theories. to appear in *Acta Cybernetica*, 1990.

[16] J.A. Goguen, J.W. Thatcher, E.G. Wagner, and J.B. Wright. Initial algebra semantics and continuous algebras. *JACM*, 24:68–95, 1977.

[17] J.W. Gray. Formal category theory, adjointness for 2-categories. *Lect. Notes Math. (Springer, Berlin)*, 391, 1974.

[18] G.M. Kelly and R. Street. Review of the elements of 2-categories. *Lect. Notes Math. (Springer, Berlin)*, 420:76–103, 1974.

[19] F.W. Lawvere. Functorial semantics of algebraic theories. *Proc. Nat. Acad. Sci.*, 50(5):869–872, 1963.

[20] R. Milner. *A calculus of communicating systems*, volume 92 of *Lect. Notes Comput. Sci.* Springer, Berlin, 1980.

[21] R. Milner. A complete inference system for a class of regular behaviours. *J. Comput. Sys. Sci.*, 28:439–466, 1984.

[22] R. Milner. *Communication and Concurrency.* Prentice Hall, Englewood Cliffs, 1989.

[23] D. Park. Concurrency and automata on infinite sequences. In P. Deussen, editor, *Theoretical Computer Science*, volume 104 of *Lect. Notes Comput. Sci.*, pages 167–183, Springer, Berlin, 1981.

[24] W.C. Rounds. On the relationships between Scott domains, synchronization trees, and metric spaces. Comp. Research Lab. Report CRL-TR-25-83, University of Michigan, 1983.

[25] Gh. Stefanescu. On flowchart theories, Part I: The deterministic case. *J. Comput. Sys. Sci.*, 35:163–191, 1986.

[26] D. Taubner. *Finite Representations of CCS and TCSP Programs by Automata and Petri Nets*, volume 369 of *Lect. Notes Comput. Sci.* Springer, Berlin, 1989.

[27] E. Wagner. Algebraic theories, data types and control constructs. *Fund. Inform.*, 9:343–370, 1986.

[28] G. Winskel. Synchronization trees. *Theoret. Comput. Sci.*, 34:33–82, 1984.

Towards a Theory of Parallel Algorithms on Concrete Data Structures

*Stephen Brookes**
Carnegie Mellon University
School of Computer Science
Pittsburgh, PA 15213, USA

*Shai Geva**
Carnegie Mellon University
School of Computer Science
Pittsburgh, PA 15213, USA

Abstract

Berry and Curien, building on Kahn and Plotkin's theory of Concrete Data Structures and sequential functions, have defined a sequential exponentiation of Concrete Data Structures. Their construction gives rise to an appealing intensional model of sequential computation. We propose to develop a similar intensional model of *concurrent computation* by formulating an appropriate notion of *parallel algorithm* and generalizing their construction to obtain a *parallel exponentiation.* The introduction of parallelism into this setting raises many interesting issues, which we begin to investigate in this paper. We hope that our ideas will yield insights into the mathematical treatment of parallel programming.

We present here our notion of parallel algorithm and our parallel exponentiation of Concrete Data Structures. We motivate carefully the ideas behind our construction, and we explain how it can be viewed as a natural generalization of the Berry-Curien construction. We introduce application and currying operations suitable for our parallel setting. We show how a new ordering on algorithms, which we call *intensional strictness*, arises naturally as the ordering with respect to which application is well behaved. Finally, we indicate some directions for further research on issues raised by our model.

***This research was sponsored by the Defense Advanced Research Projects Agency (DOD) and monitored by the Avionics Laboratory, Air Force Wright Aeronautical Laboratories, Aeronautical Systems Division (AFSC), United States Air Force, Wright-Patterson AFB, OHIO 45433-6543, under Contract F33615-87-C-1499, ARPA Order No. 4976, Amendment 20.**

The views and conclusions contained in this document are those of the authors and should not be interpreted as representing the official policies, either expressed or implied, of the Defense Advanced Research Projects Agency or the U.S. government.

1 INTRODUCTION

The search for a satisfactory syntactic and semantic account of sequential computation has led to a considerable body of research. In the classic paper [9], Plotkin showed that under its standard interpretation the programming language PCF is inherently sequential, and that its standard continuous functions semantic model is not fully abstract because the model contains inherently parallel functions (such as parallel-or) that cannot be defined in PCF. This model is, however, fully abstract for a parallel version of PCF obtained by including a parallel conditional. A substantial body of work has been directed at obtaining a truly sequential model for the original PCF with a suitably restricted notion of function [4].

Kahn and Plotkin [8] defined *concrete data structures* (CDSs), together with their order-theoretic counterparts, *concrete domains*, which made possible a suitable definition of *sequentiality* of functions. Berry [1] introduced the notion of *stability*, a property of functions intermediate between sequentiality and continuity. However, Berry and Curien [2, 5] showed that the category of concrete domains fails to be cartesian closed when the morphisms in the category are taken to be the continuous functions, or the stable functions, or the sequential functions. Consequently, neither stability nor sequentiality produces a sufficiently restricted notion of function to serve satisfactorily as the basis for a definition of exponentiation for concrete domains. Berry [1] also introduced the *stable ordering* on stable functions and showed that it possesses some natural and interesting properties. These investigations pointed out that other orderings than the usual extensional ordering on functions might be necessary in achieving a satisfactory semantic treatment; moreover, they paved the way for the development of an intensional model, since extensional models based even on restricted notions of function were shown to be inadequate.

Berry and Curien were able to define an exponentiation for concrete data structures, by replacing functions by *sequential algorithms*. For *deterministic* CDSs (DCDSs), the resulting category of DCDSs and sequential algorithms turns out to be cartesian closed. Furthermore, a notation for elements of DCDSs is a basis for a functional language CDS0 [3], which is given a semantic model with several interesting properties: the semantics is fully abstract with respect to a notion of observability that is sensitive to computation strategy and extends uniformly to higher-order DCDSs; the model is intensional rather than extensional; the sequential algorithms may be viewed as the sequential functions paired with computation strategies. The operational semantics is essentially based on an extension of Kahn-MacQueen's coroutine mechanism [7], employing lazy evaluation.

We report here a generalization of Berry and Curien's sequential exponentiation construction that incorporates *deterministic concurrency* into the framework. We believe that there are fundamental insights into the semantic treatment of parallelism to be gained by doing this. We have made the decision to restrict our attention so far to deterministic computation, thereby allowing us to retain an essentially functional semantics. We will, of course, allow non-determinism in the scheduling of computations; indeed, one of our objectives is to improve on the original construction so as to avoid unnecessary scheduling constraints.

In section 2 we summarize the key background material on DCDSs and their product and sequential exponentiation, as well as the definitions of stable and sequential functions. The section is based on the development in [5].

In section 3 we present our notions of parallel algorithms and parallel exponentiation for deterministic concrete data structures. We explain carefully how our construction arises in generalizing the Berry-Curien concepts. The key idea is to replace the "valof" command of a sequential exponentiation with a "query" command that spawns parallel sub-computations; the formal treatment leads naturally to the use of a powerdomain construction. We also present currying and uncurrying operations for parallel algorithms.

In section 4 we formalize what it means to *execute* a parallel algorithm by defining a suitable *application* operation. We show that our notion of parallel application is intuitively right by discussing several natural example algorithms and their applicative behavior. We show that application for parallel algorithms, unlike its sequential counterpart, is not continuous with respect to set inclusion; this is not a defect of our model or of our definition of application, but rather shows that set inclusion is not fine enough to serve as the underlying order on parallel algorithms. We identify the causes of this failing and introduce the appropriate ordering, which we call the *intensional strictness* order. Informally, an algorithm a' is above another algorithm a in this order if a' needs less information, at an earlier stage of the computation, to achieve at least the same output as a. We regard intensional strictness as the natural generalization to the intensional setting of the standard ordering on continuous functions.

Finally, we point out some limitations of our model and outline how we intend to overcome them in future work. We discuss a number of very interesting topics for further investigation.

2 BACKGROUND

2.1 Concrete Data Structures

A *concrete data structure*, or *CDS*, $(\mathrm{C}, \mathrm{V}, \mathrm{E}, \vdash)$ consists of a set C of *cells*, a set V of *values*, a set $\mathrm{E} \subseteq \mathrm{C} \times \mathrm{V}$ of *events*, and an *enabling* relation $\vdash$ between finite sets of events and cells. We denote events as pairs (c, v). We also use an alternative notation $c = v$ in examples and discussions.

For a CDS $M = (\mathrm{C}_M, \mathrm{V}_M, \mathrm{E}_M, \vdash_M)$, $x, y \subseteq \mathrm{E}_M$, and $c \in \mathrm{C}_M$, if $y \vdash_M c$ we say that y is an *enabling* of c. If, moreover, $y \subseteq x$ we say that y is an enabling of c in x and write $y \vdash_x c$. If $\emptyset \vdash_M c$ we say that c is *initial*. We define $\mathrm{F}(y)$, the cells *filled in* y, to be the collection of cells in the events of y. $\mathrm{E}(y)$, the cells *enabled in* y, is the collection of cells that have an enabling in y. $\mathrm{A}(y)$, the cells *accessible in* y, is the collection of cells which are enabled in y but are not filled.

For $c, c' \in \mathrm{C}_M$, we say that c *immediately precedes* c', denoted $c \ll_M c'$, iff there is an enabling $y \vdash_M c'$ such that $c \in \mathrm{F}(y)$. If, moreover, $y \subseteq x$ we say that c immediately precedes c' in x, denoted $c \ll_x c'$. Taking the reflexive and transitive closure of $\ll_M$, we say that c *precedes* c' iff $c \ll_M^* c'$, and analogously $\ll_x^*$ defines precedence in x. M is *well founded* iff $\ll_M$ is well founded.

For M a well founded CDS let $\mathcal{E}(M)$ be the collection of sets of events of M.

$y \in \mathcal{E}(M)$ is *functional*[1] iff any cell is filled in y with at most one value; let $\mathcal{F}(M)$ be the collection of functional sets of events. If $\mathrm{F}(y) \subseteq \mathrm{E}(y)$ we say that y is *safe*[2], and y is a *state* of M iff it is functional and safe; let $\mathcal{D}(M)$ be the collection of states of M. We add a subscript to indicate finiteness, *e.g.*, $\mathcal{D}_{fin}(M)$ for the finite states. The posets $(\mathcal{F}(M), \subseteq)$, $(\mathcal{F}_{fin}(M), \subseteq)$, $(\mathcal{D}(M), \subseteq)$ and $(\mathcal{D}_{fin}(M), \subseteq)$ are all consistently complete. $(\mathcal{D}(M), \subseteq)$ is in fact a concrete domain[3].

A well founded CDS is *stable* iff for any state x and cell c enabled in x, c has a unique enabling in x. A CDS is a *deterministic* CDS (DCDS) iff it is well founded and stable. We work here with DCDSs, although some of the development could be carried out more generally.

Example 2.1 The empty DCDS **Null** has no cells, values, events, or enablings; its only state is the empty state $\emptyset$.

The DCDS **Bool** has a single, initial, cell $\mathtt{b}$, which may be filled with either of the values $\mathtt{tt}$ or $\mathtt{ff}$; its states are $\emptyset$, $\{\mathtt{b} = \mathtt{tt}\}$ and $\{\mathtt{b} = \mathtt{ff}\}$, and $(\mathcal{D}(\mathbf{Bool}), \subseteq)$ is isomorphic to the conventional flat boolean cpo.

The DCDS **Nat** has a single, initial, cell $\mathtt{n}$, which may be filled with a natural number; its states are $\emptyset$ and $\{\mathtt{n} = k\}$ for $k \in \mathbb{N}$, so that $(\mathcal{D}(\mathbf{Nat}), \subseteq)$ is isomorphic to the conventional flat natural numbers cpo. •

2.2 Product of DCDSs

If c is a cell of a DCDS M and i is a tag or label, we write $c.i$ for the labelled cell (c, i). We extend the notation to sets of cells and of events, so that, for $C \subseteq \mathrm{C}_M$ and $y \in \mathcal{E}(M)$, $C.i = \{c.i \mid c \in C\}$ and $y.i = \{(c.i, v) \mid (c, v) \in y\}$.

The product of the DCDSs M_1 and M_2, $M_1 \times M_2$, is a DCDS obtained by taking a "disjoint union" of all cells, values, events and enablings of M_1 and M_2, in which all cells are labelled by 1 or 2 to indicate where the cell, event or enabling originated: $\mathrm{C}_{M_1 \times M_2} = \mathrm{C}_{M_1}.1 \cup \mathrm{C}_{M_2}.2$; $\mathrm{V}_{M_1 \times M_2} = \mathrm{V}_{M_1} \cup \mathrm{V}_{M_2}$; $\mathrm{E}_{M_1 \times M_2} = \mathrm{E}_{M_1}.1 \cup \mathrm{E}_{M_2}.2$; and for $i = 1, 2$, $y.i \vdash_{M_1 \times M_2} c.i$ iff $y \vdash_{M_i} c$.

Pairs of sets of events are denoted $\langle z_1, z_2 \rangle = z_1.1 \cup z_2.2$. The projection functions satisfy $\mathrm{fst}(\langle z_1, z_2 \rangle) = z_1$ and $\mathrm{snd}(\langle z_1, z_2 \rangle) = z_2$. We use $\bar{x}$, $\bar{y}$, etc. to denote pairs.

Example 2.2 The DCDS **Bool** × **Bool** has two initial cells, $\mathtt{b.1}$ and $\mathtt{b.2}$, each of which may be filled with a value of $\mathtt{tt}$ or $\mathtt{ff}$. It has 9 states, one of which is $\{\mathtt{b.1} = \mathtt{tt}, \mathtt{b.2} = \mathtt{ff}\}$, alternatively denoted by $\langle \{\mathtt{b} = \mathtt{tt}\}, \{\mathtt{b} = \mathtt{ff}\} \rangle$. •

2.3 Stable and Sequential Functions

A continuous function $f : \mathcal{D}(M) \rightarrow \mathcal{D}(M')$ is *stable* if for any $x \in \mathcal{D}(M)$ and $x' \in \mathcal{D}(M')$ below $f(x)$ there exists a least state $M(f, x, x') \in \mathcal{D}(M)$ below x on which f attains or surpasses x', *i.e.*, for any $z \subseteq x$, $x' \subseteq f(z)$ iff $M(f, x, x') \subseteq z$.

[1] Berry and Curien use the term *consistent* instead of functional.

[2] We simplify the definition of safety by assuming a well founded CDS. The definition in [5] requires that each cell filled in y have a linear deduction in y (w.r.t the enabling relation). This is then shown equivalent to having a tree-like proof in y, and, for a well founded CDS, to having an enabling in y.

[3] When suitable countability requirements are imposed. See [8] and [5, section 2.2] for the representation theorem relating concrete domains and states of CDSs ordered by inclusion.

A continuous function $f : \mathcal{D}(M) \to \mathcal{D}(M')$ is *sequential at* $x \in \mathcal{D}(M)$ if, for all $c' \in \mathrm{A}(f(x))$, one of the following holds:

(1) Either $\mathrm{A}(x) = \emptyset$, and thus x has no super-state;[4]

(2) Or there exists some $c \in \mathrm{A}(x)$ that must be filled in any y that increases x such that c' is filled in $f(y)$, that is–

$$\exists c \in \mathrm{A}(x) \,.\, \forall y \in \mathcal{D}(M) \,.\, x \subseteq y \;\&\; c' \in \mathrm{F}(f(y)) \Rightarrow c \in \mathrm{F}(y).$$

A cell $c \in \mathrm{A}(x)$ satisfying (2) is called a *sequentiality index* of f at x for c'.

$f : \mathcal{D}(M) \to \mathcal{D}(M')$ is *sequential* if it is continuous and it is sequential at every $x \in \mathcal{D}(M)$.

A sequential function is stable. The converse, however, does not hold.

Example 2.3 The doubly-strict-or function $sor : \mathcal{D}(\mathbf{Bool} \times \mathbf{Bool}) \to \mathcal{D}(\mathbf{Bool})$ is both stable and sequential. Both $\mathtt{b.1}$ and $\mathtt{b.2}$ are sequentiality indices at $\emptyset$ for $\mathtt{b}$.

The parallel-or function $por : \mathcal{D}(\mathbf{Bool} \times \mathbf{Bool}) \to \mathcal{D}(\mathbf{Bool})$ is the least monotone function satisfying:

$$\begin{array}{lcl}
por(\langle \quad \emptyset \quad ,\{\mathtt{b}=\mathtt{tt}\}\rangle) & = & \{\mathtt{b}=\mathtt{tt}\} \\
por(\langle \{\mathtt{b}=\mathtt{tt}\}, \quad \emptyset \quad \rangle) & = & \{\mathtt{b}=\mathtt{tt}\} \\
por(\langle \{\mathtt{b}=\mathtt{ff}\},\{\mathtt{b}=\mathtt{ff}\}\rangle) & = & \{\mathtt{b}=\mathtt{ff}\}.
\end{array}$$

The por function is neither stable nor sequential — it has no sequentiality index at $\emptyset$ for $\mathtt{b}$; and there is no unique minimal state of $\mathbf{Bool} \times \mathbf{Bool}$ below $\langle \{\mathtt{b}=\mathtt{tt}\}, \{\mathtt{b}=\mathtt{tt}\}\rangle$ for which por attains $\{\mathtt{b}=\mathtt{tt}\}$.

Let $gf : \mathcal{D}((\mathbf{Bool} \times \mathbf{Bool}) \times \mathbf{Bool}) \to \mathcal{D}(\mathbf{Bool})$ be the least monotone function satisfying:

$$\begin{array}{lcl}
gf(\langle\langle \{\mathtt{b}=\mathtt{tt}\},\{\mathtt{b}=\mathtt{ff}\}\rangle, \quad \emptyset \quad \rangle) & = & \{\mathtt{b}=\mathtt{tt}\} \\
gf(\langle\langle \quad \emptyset \quad ,\{\mathtt{b}=\mathtt{tt}\}\rangle,\{\mathtt{b}=\mathtt{ff}\}\rangle) & = & \{\mathtt{b}=\mathtt{tt}\} \\
gf(\langle\langle \{\mathtt{b}=\mathtt{ff}\}, \quad \emptyset \quad \rangle,\{\mathtt{b}=\mathtt{tt}\}\rangle) & = & \{\mathtt{b}=\mathtt{tt}\} \\
gf(\langle\langle \{\mathtt{b}=\mathtt{ff}\},\{\mathtt{b}=\mathtt{ff}\}\rangle,\{\mathtt{b}=\mathtt{ff}\}\rangle) & = & \{\mathtt{b}=\mathtt{ff}\}.
\end{array}$$

This is a variant of "Gustave's function" (attributed to Berry [1] by Huet [6]). The gf function is stable, but not sequential — it has no sequentiality index at $\emptyset$ for $\mathtt{b}$. •

2.4 Sequential Exponentiation of DCDSs

For DCDSs M and M', the *sequential exponentiation* $M \to_{seq} M'$ is the DCDS $(\mathrm{C}, \mathrm{V}, \mathrm{E}, \vdash)$ defined as follows:

$$\mathrm{C} = \mathcal{D}_{fin}(M) \times \mathrm{C}_{M'}$$

---

[4]The definition in [5] uses (1′) instead:

(1′) c' is not filled in $f(y)$ for any y above x, that is– $\forall y \in \mathcal{D}(M) \,.\, x \subseteq y \Rightarrow c' \notin \mathrm{F}(f(y))$.

The overall definitions (1, 2) and (1′, 2) are equivalent, but we prefer to use (1), since it is disjoint from (2).

We denote a cell $(x, c') \in \mathrm{C}$ as xc'.

$$\begin{aligned} \mathrm{V} = \ & \{\mathbf{valof}\ c \mid c \in \mathrm{C}_M\} \\ & \cup\{\mathbf{output}\ v' \mid v' \in \mathrm{V}_{M'}\} \end{aligned}$$

$$\begin{aligned} \mathrm{E} = \ & \{(xc', \mathbf{valof}\ c) \in \mathrm{C} \times \mathrm{V} \mid c \in \mathrm{A}(x)\} \\ & \cup\{(xc', \mathbf{output}\ v') \in \mathrm{C} \times \mathrm{V} \mid (c', v') \in \mathrm{E}_{M'}\} \end{aligned}$$

$$(xc', \mathbf{valof}\ c) \vdash yc' \ \text{ iff } \ y = x \cup \{(c, v)\} \text{ for some } v \in \mathrm{V}_M$$

$$\{(x_j c'_j, \mathbf{output}\ v'_j)\}_{j=1}^{l} \vdash xc' \ \text{ iff } \ \{(c'_j, v'_j)\}_{j=1}^{l} \vdash_{M'} c' \text{ and } x = \cup_{j=1}^{l} x_j$$

We call a state of $M \rightarrow_{seq} M'$ a *sequential algorithm*.

Operationally, computation is demand driven: an external observer's information about the result of applying an algorithm to an input state may be gradually increased by filling the cells of the result state, with each demand for the value of a cell spawning a new computation. A cell of the exponentiation consists of a finite current state x, describing the information currently known about the input, and a request for computation of a value for a cell c' in the output. The events of an algorithm associate with such a cell xc' a command, either an **output** v' command that terminates the computation and determines that (c', v') is in the output, or a **valof** c command that attempts to increase the current state x at c. This c, naturally enough, is a sequentiality index (of the algorithm's input-output function) at x, so that the choice of c among all sequentiality indices at x (if not unique) determines the computation strategy. Once the sub-computation terminates (if it does), with a value v for c in the input, the main computation resumes with the enabled cell $(x \cup \{(c, v)\})c'$, until a value is output for c'. The sub-computation of c proceeds in the same manner: hence the overall coroutine flavor.

For $a \in \mathcal{D}(M \rightarrow_{seq} M')$ and $x \in \mathcal{D}(M)$, the *sequential application* of a to x, denoted $a \cdot_{seq} x$, is given by $a \cdot_{seq} x = \{(c', v') \mid \exists y.\ (yc', \mathbf{output}\ v') \in a \ \&\ y \subseteq x\}$. The *input-output function* of a is the function $\lambda x.a \cdot_{seq} x : \mathcal{D}(M) \rightarrow \mathcal{D}(M')$.

Sequential exponentiation preserves well foundedness and stability, and sequential application is well defined. The input-output function of a sequential algorithm $a \in \mathcal{D}(M \rightarrow_{seq} M')$ is a sequential function from $(\mathcal{D}(M), \subseteq)$ to $(\mathcal{D}(M'), \subseteq)$. The category of DCDS and sequential algorithms is cartesian closed.

Example 2.4 There are two sequential algorithms that compute the doubly-strict-or function: `lsor`, which first evaluates the "left" input cell `b.1` and then evaluates `b.2`; and `rsor`, which first evaluates the "right" input cell. There is a unique sequential algorithm `lor` computing the left-strict-or function. •

The sequential algorithms from M to M', may be viewed as the sequential functions from $\mathcal{D}(M)$ to $\mathcal{D}(M')$, paired with computation strategies. Under the extensional quotient (*i.e.*, taking only the function component) the set inclusion ordering on algorithms corresponds to the stable ordering of sequential functions [5, proposition 2.5.6].

3 PARALLEL EXPONENTIATION OF DCDS

We would now like to generalize the sequential exponentiation so as to be able to express algorithms for non-sequential functions, such as *por*, while retaining as far as possible suitable analogues to the other properties of sequential exponentiation. Why, then, are sequential algorithms sequential? From an operational viewpoint, the reason is that a valof command may only start one sub-computation, and only after it returns may the main computation proceed. If the sub-computation does not terminate then the whole computation does not terminate.

A natural first step towards a generalization, then, would be to allow a valof command to start a number of sub-computations, with the understanding that not all of them have to terminate before the main computation may resume. In addition to naming a set of input cells for each of which a sub-computation is to be started, one needs to specify sufficient conditions for resumption of the main computation. Such a condition, which we will call a ***branch***, will naturally be phrased in terms of the results of one or more of the sub-computations: that is, a branch will be a functional set of events. The valof command is hence generalized into what we will call a *query* command, that proposes a set of alternative branches; a sub-computation is started for each of the input cells mentioned in the query, and the main computation is resumed when at least one of the branches is satisfied. A branch is satisfied when all of its events are satisfied, and an event (c, v) is satisfied when a sub-computation for the cell c terminates with the value v.

For a parallel-or algorithm, for example, the branches of the query issued when nothing is known about the input should be $\{\mathtt{b.1} = \mathtt{tt}\}$, $\{\mathtt{b.2} = \mathtt{tt}\}$ and $\{\mathtt{b.1} = \mathtt{ff}, \mathtt{b.2} = \mathtt{ff}\}$. A query with these branches would cause sub-computations to be started for the input cells b.1 and b.2, with the branches spelling out the conditions for resumption of the main computation.

We will impose the restriction that a query contain no superfluous branches in that satisfaction of one branch will not imply satisfaction of another branch in the same query. Such branches do not make sense operationally, and their presence may impair full abstraction. Technically this translates into a requirement that no two branches of a query be related by set inclusion; we call this property *trimness*, and we will encapsulate it later in the notion of a *trim powerdomain*. Queries will be drawn from the trim powerdomain of functional sets of events.

For the above query for a parallel-or algorithm, any additional branch would violate trimness. The branch $\{\mathtt{b.1} = \mathtt{tt}, \mathtt{b.2} = \mathtt{ff}\}$, for example, is rendered superfluous by the branch $\{\mathtt{b.1} = \mathtt{tt}\}$.

We also impose another intuitively natural restriction on queries: that the empty branch is not allowed, since a query containing the empty branch need not be issued at all (it is trivially satisfied).

It may be that several consistent[5] branches of the same query are satisfied simultaneously. If each such branch enables a distinct cell, then we could associate with it a distinct command, and thus obtain a non-deterministic relational semantics[6]. We choose, however, to limit ourselves to a deterministic, functional semantics. We do this by having each *equivalence class* of branches of a query enable

[5] Consistency of branches is taken to mean consistency in $(\mathcal{F}_{fin}(M), \subseteq)$ for the appropriate M. That is, two branches are consistent iff their union is functional.

[6] Assuming that the selection of the branch taken is non-deterministic.

a cell, with *equivalence* defined to be the transitive closure of the (restriction to the query of the) consistency relation. Transitivity is needed to ensure that no matter which two consistent branches satisfy the input, they will be bundled together for the purpose of enabling a common cell. The conglomeration of equivalent branches makes it impossible (for the algorithm, or any external observer of its behavior) to determine which specific branch was taken by a query, and thus we achieve a deterministic functional semantics. We believe that this is a crucial aspect, since if an algorithm, or computational agent, can distinguish between consistent possibilities which are satisfied by the environment, then it may reflect non-determinism in scheduling by the environment as non-deterministic behavior on its part. We would argue that it is necessary to equate all such equivalent possibilities in order to get a properly deterministic notion of behavior.

Therefore, in contrast to the sequential case, the information currently known about the input state can no longer be given as a single state x; instead, we need to use a *set* of states (or a *class*, as we will call it); the information content of this class is that the input state is a superset of some state in the class. Analogously to queries, and for the same reasons, we require that classes belong to a *trim powerdomain* of states. The exponentiation cells will consist of a class and a request cell.

Continuing with our tentative construction of a parallel-or algorithm, the branches $\{\texttt{b.1} = \texttt{tt}\}$ and $\{\texttt{b.2} = \texttt{tt}\}$ are consistent. The determinism constraint requires that they enable the same cell (whose class consists of the two states $\{\texttt{b.1} = \texttt{tt}\}$ and $\{\texttt{b.2} = \texttt{tt}\}$).

Up to this point it might seem that we are going to build the DCDS $M \rightarrow M'$ by means of classes of states of M and queries whose branches are functional sets of events of M; for the parallel-or algorithm of type **Bool** $\times$ **Bool** $\rightarrow$ **Bool** this is adequate. However, this example is not really general enough, as is readily seen when considering what kind of state information is needed in cells and queries to build an algorithm that returns an algorithm as its result. Consider, for instance, the *curried* parallel-or algorithm, whose type is **Bool** $\rightarrow$ (**Bool** $\rightarrow$ **Bool**). For a fully general treatment we must allow each branch of a query to combine two features: a request for computation(s) of input cell(s), with conditions for satisfaction, as described above; and a (possibly vacuous) "residual" that can be used to build the algorithm's result in case the input state satisfies the conditions. Again consider the curried parallel-or algorithm. Starting with no information about the input, this algorithm needs to issue a query with three branches; one branch has input condition $\{\texttt{b} = \texttt{ff}\}$ and a residual $\{\texttt{b} = \texttt{ff}\}$; a second branch has input condition $\{\texttt{b} = \texttt{tt}\}$ and a vacuous residual; and the third branch has a vacuous input condition but has a residual of $\{\texttt{b} = \texttt{tt}\}$. In contrast, the uncurried parallel-or issues a query with three branches, each of which has a vacuous residual.

The way we choose to formalize these ideas is to associate with every DCDS M a *representation* DCDS rep(M) and a *base* DCDS base(M). Intuitively, rep(M) is a product DCDS with a component for each successive argument type to which an algorithm of type M could be applied; and base(M) is the "ground" or "basic" type of the result obtained by repeatedly applying an algorithm of type M. In constructing $M \rightarrow M'$, branches of queries will be functional sets of events of $M \times \text{rep}(M')$, so that a residual (the rep(M') component) will "make sense" in building a result of type M'; the M component embodies the "input condition" of the branch. Similarly, the classes used in constructing $M \rightarrow M'$ will be sets of states of $M \times \text{rep}(M')$. We form the cells of $M \to M'$ by pairing such classes with cells of base(M'), which represent the demands for computation of a result at base type.

By taking advantage of the use of a representation we will in fact be able to define currying and uncurrying operations on algorithms that simply move elements of a branch or of a class from the input part to the residual and vice versa.

Our query command will now turn out to be a generalization of both the valof and the output commands of the sequential exponentiation; operationally, a query only starts sub-computations for cells in the input parts of its branches (cells of M) and the residuals may contribute to query events in the output algorithm – as determined by the application of the algorithm to an input state. Again this is illustrated by the curried parallel-or algorithm. Its query may, obviously, only start one sub-computation, corresponding to the single cell of its argument; when the algorithm is applied to the input state $\{\mathtt{b} = \mathtt{ff}\}$, the corresponding residual (also $\{\mathtt{b} = \mathtt{ff}\}$) will become (part of) a query of the result algorithm. We defer further discussion of application until later.

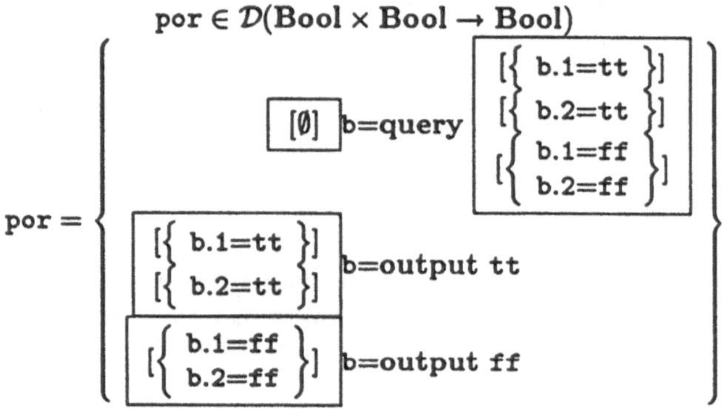

Figure 1: The parallel-or algorithm

Example 3.1 Figure 1 presents the parallel-or algorithm. The full definitions are given later, but an example at this point may help to illustrate the above considerations.

We use the following notation to display algorithms. Vertical stacking is used to list elements of sets, *e.g.*, the events of a state. An event (c, v) is denoted by $c = v$. Juxtaposition is used for cells of the exponentiation, *e.g.* pc. Classes and queries are framed in boxes, rather than curly braces. The elements of classes and queries – states or functional sets of events of the representation DCDS – are enclosed in square brackets. We use a shorthand notation for pairs, denoting $\emptyset \in \mathcal{E}(\text{Null})$ as $[]$, and denoting $\langle y_0, [y_1, \ldots, y_d]\rangle$ as $[y_0, y_1, \ldots, y_d]$ for $d \geq 0$. In this particular example, for instance, the branch $\langle\{\mathtt{b.2} = \mathtt{tt}\}, \emptyset\rangle$ of por is abbreviated as $[\{\mathtt{b.2} = \mathtt{tt}\}]$; the notation allows us to treat vacuous residuals implicitly. •

3.1 Queries and Classes

Definition 3.2 The *trim powerdomain* over a poset $(D, \leq)$, denoted by $(\mathcal{P}_t(D), \sqsubseteq)$, is defined by:

- $\mathcal{P}_t(D)$ is the collection of all the non-empty subsets p of D such that no two elements of p are related by $\leq$, that is, if $x_1, x_2 \in p$ and $x_1 \leq x_2$ then $x_1 = x_2$.
- $p_1 \sqsubseteq p_2$ iff $\forall x_2 \in p_2 \,.\, \exists x_1 \in p_1 \,.\, x_1 \leq x_2$.

•

The $\sqsubseteq$ relation is the Smyth preorder on $\mathcal{P}(D)$, and is a partial order on $\mathcal{P}_t(D)$. The trim powerdomain is essentially identical to the Smyth powerdomain [10], but rather than dealing directly with $\sqsubseteq$-equivalence classes of $\mathcal{P}(D)$ we take canonical representatives, chosen for their trimness. Define, for $p \subseteq D$, trim(p) to be the (possibly empty) set of $\leq$-minimal elements of p:

$$\forall p \subseteq D \,.\, \mathrm{trim}(p) = \{x \in p \mid \forall x' \in p \,.\, x' \leq x \Rightarrow x' = x\}.$$

We are mainly interested in the trim powerdomains formed over the well founded and consistently complete posets $(\mathcal{F}_{fin}(M), \subseteq)$ and $(\mathcal{D}_{fin}(M), \subseteq)$, from which we draw queries and classes, respectively. Each of these trim powerdomains is consistently complete. To motivate the ordering for our powerdomain construction, recall our earlier remark that a class is interpreted as the assertion that the input state is a superset of some member of the class, and interpret each class as a disjunction of conjunctions, so that the information about the input state may be increased by reducing the number of disjuncts and/or increasing the number of conjuncts in one or more of the disjuncts.

Proposition 3.3 *If $P \subseteq \mathcal{P}_t(D)$ is consistent, and $(D, \leq)$ is consistently complete and well founded, then*

$$\sqcup P = \mathrm{trim}(\{\vee X \mid X \subseteq \cup P \ \&\ \Uparrow_D X \ \&\ (\forall p \in P \,.\, p \cap X \neq \emptyset)\}).$$

Here we write $\Uparrow_D X$ to indicate that X is consistent in D. Thus, in particular, the lub of a consistent set P of queries or of states is obtained (by trimming) from the set of all unions of consistent cross-sections of P.

We extend the notions of a cell being filled, enabled and accessible in a state to queries (and to sets of states, similarly):

Definition 3.4 For M a CDS and $q \in \mathcal{P}_t(\mathcal{E}(M))$, a cell is *filled* in q iff it is filled in any of q's elements; $\mathrm{F}(q) = \cup_{y \in q} \mathrm{F}(y)$. A cell is *enabled* in q iff it is enabled in all of q's elements; $\mathrm{E}(q) = \cap_{y \in q} \mathrm{E}(y)$. A cell is *accessible* in q iff it is enabled in q, and is not filled in q; $\mathrm{A}(q) = \mathrm{E}(q) \setminus \mathrm{F}(q)$. Equivalently, a cell is accessible in q iff it is accessible in all of q's elements; $\mathrm{A}(q) = \cap_{y \in q} \mathrm{A}(y)$. •

Let $q \in \mathcal{P}_t(\mathcal{F}_{fin}(M))$. Two elements (or branches) y_1, y_2 of q are consistent iff $y_1 \cup y_2 \in \mathcal{F}_{fin}(M)$. We say that y_1 and y_2 are *equivalent* in q (written $y_1 \approx_q y_2$) iff there is a finite sequence of elements of q leading from y_1 to y_2, such that each successive pair is consistent. This clearly determines an equivalence relation on the branches in q. We denote by $[y]_q$ the equivalence class of y in q.

Proposition 3.5 *If $p \in \mathcal{P}_t(\mathcal{D}_{fin}(M))$, $q \in \mathcal{P}_t(\mathcal{F}_{fin}(M))$, $\mathrm{F}(q) \subseteq \mathrm{A}(p)$, and $y \in q$, then $p \sqcup [y]_q \in \mathcal{P}_t(\mathcal{D}_{fin}(M))$ and is equal to $\{x \cup y' \mid x \in p, y' \in [y]_q\}$.*

3.2 Representation and Base

We use a simple algebra of DCDS names. We assume a given collection of *atomic* DCDSs that contains at least **Null**, and we concern ourselves with the binary operators $\times$ (product) and $\rightarrow$ (exponentiation). We assume that atomic DCDSs mentioned earlier and the product of DCDSs are interpreted as given above. We say that a DCDS M is an *exponentiation* if its outermost constructor is $\rightarrow$, and M is *basic* otherwise.

Definition 3.6 We define two maps, rep and base, from DCDSs to DCDSs. If a DCDS M is basic we let $\mathrm{rep}(M) = \mathbf{Null}$ and $\mathrm{base}(M) = M$. For an exponentiation $M \rightarrow M'$, we let

$$\begin{aligned} \mathrm{rep}(M \rightarrow M') &= M \times \mathrm{rep}(M') \\ \mathrm{base}(M \rightarrow M') &= \mathrm{base}(M'). \end{aligned}$$

•

Note that this formal definition matches the informal remarks made earlier about the role of these two maps. We let both $\times$ and $\rightarrow$ associate to the *right* so that the representation of an exponentiation will correspond to its argument structure; for instance, if M_0 is basic, the DCDS $M_k \rightarrow \cdots \rightarrow M_1 \rightarrow M_0$ has $M_k \times \cdots \times M_1 \times \mathbf{Null}$ for its representation and M_0 for its base. Note that $\mathrm{base}(M)$ is always basic.

3.3 Parallel Exponentiation

Definition 3.7 Let M and M' be DCDSs. We define their *parallel exponentiation* $M \rightarrow M'$, to be the CDS $(\mathrm{C}, \mathrm{V}, \mathrm{E}, \vdash)$, defined as follows. We let $M_\times$ abbreviate $\mathrm{rep}(M \rightarrow M')$ and let M_0 abbreviate $\mathrm{base}(M \rightarrow M')$.

$$\mathrm{C} = \mathcal{P}_t(\mathcal{D}_{fin}(M_\times)) \times \mathrm{C}_{M_0}$$

We denote a cell (p, c) of C as pc.

$$\begin{aligned} \mathrm{V} = \ & \{\mathbf{query}\ q \mid q \in \mathcal{P}_t(\mathcal{F}_{fin}(M_\times))\ \&\ \emptyset \notin q\} \\ & \cup \{\mathbf{output}\ v \mid v \in \mathrm{V}_{M_0}\} \end{aligned}$$

$$\begin{aligned} \mathrm{E} = \ & \{(pc, \mathbf{query}\ q) \in \mathrm{C} \times \mathrm{V} \mid \mathrm{F}(q) \subseteq \mathrm{A}(p)\} \\ & \cup \{(pc, \mathbf{output}\ v) \in \mathrm{C} \times \mathrm{V} \mid (c, v) \in \mathrm{E}_{M_0}\} \end{aligned}$$

$$(pc, \mathbf{query}\ q) \vdash p'c \ \text{ iff } \ \exists \bar{y} \in q \,.\, p' = p \sqcup [\bar{y}]_q$$

$$\{(p_j c_j, \mathbf{output}\ v_j)\}_{j=1}^{l} \vdash pc \ \text{ iff } \ \{(c_j, v_j)\}_{j=1}^{l} \vdash_{M_0} c \text{ and } p = \sqcup_{j=1}^{l} p_j.$$

Note: If $(pc, \mathbf{query}\ q) \vdash_x p'c$ and $\bar{y}$ is a branch of q such that $p' = p \sqcup [\bar{y}]_q$ we may write $(pc, \mathbf{query}\ q) \vdash_{x,\bar{y}} p'c$ to indicate the branch explicitly.

We call a state of $M \rightarrow M'$ a *parallel algorithm*, or just an *algorithm*. •

An initial cell of $M \rightarrow M'$ has a vacuous output enabling (with $l = 0$), and is of the form $\{\emptyset\}c$, with c an initial cell of M_0.

Example 3.8 We have already seen the parallel-or algorithm. There is a unique algorithm **gf** computing the non-sequential function *gf*. In its (initial and only) query, all pairs of branches are inconsistent. A variant for which this is no longer the case is based on the function $gf' : \mathcal{D}((\textbf{Bool} \times \textbf{Bool}) \times \textbf{Bool}) \to \mathcal{D}(\textbf{Bool})$, defined to be the least monotone function satisfying:

$$
\begin{aligned}
gf'(\langle\langle\{\mathtt{b}=\mathtt{tt}\},\{\mathtt{b}=\mathtt{ff}\}\rangle, \quad \emptyset \quad\rangle) &= \{\mathtt{b}=\mathtt{tt}\}\\
gf'(\langle\langle \quad \emptyset \quad ,\{\mathtt{b}=\mathtt{tt}\}\rangle,\{\mathtt{b}=\mathtt{ff}\}\rangle) &= \{\mathtt{b}=\mathtt{tt}\}\\
gf'(\langle\langle\{\mathtt{b}=\mathtt{ff}\}, \quad \emptyset \quad\rangle,\{\mathtt{b}=\mathtt{tt}\}\rangle) &= \{\mathtt{b}=\mathtt{tt}\}\\
gf'(\langle\langle\{\mathtt{b}=\mathtt{ff}\},\{\mathtt{b}=\mathtt{tt}\}\rangle, \quad \emptyset \quad\rangle) &= \{\mathtt{b}=\mathtt{tt}\}\\
gf'(\langle\langle \quad \emptyset \quad ,\{\mathtt{b}=\mathtt{ff}\}\rangle,\{\mathtt{b}=\mathtt{tt}\}\rangle) &= \{\mathtt{b}=\mathtt{tt}\}\\
gf'(\langle\langle\{\mathtt{b}=\mathtt{tt}\}, \quad \emptyset \quad\rangle,\{\mathtt{b}=\mathtt{ff}\}\rangle) &= \{\mathtt{b}=\mathtt{tt}\}\\
gf'(\langle\langle\{\mathtt{b}=\mathtt{ff}\},\{\mathtt{b}=\mathtt{ff}\}\rangle,\{\mathtt{b}=\mathtt{ff}\}\rangle) &= \{\mathtt{b}=\mathtt{ff}\}.
\end{aligned}
$$

Again this function is not sequential, but (unlike *gf*) it is also not stable: there is no unique minimal state below $\langle\langle\{\mathtt{b}=\mathtt{tt}\},\{\mathtt{b}=\mathtt{ff}\}\rangle,\{\mathtt{b}=\mathtt{ff}\}\rangle$ for which gf' attains $\{\mathtt{b}=\mathtt{tt}\}$. There is again a unique algorithm $\mathbf{gf'}$ for this function; but (unlike **gf**) its query contains distinct consistent branches. This observation is not accidental: roughly, an algorithm computes a stable function iff none of its queries has a consistent pair of branches. The $\mathbf{gf'}$ algorithm also demonstrates branches which are equivalent, but not consistent. •

An algorithm $a \in \mathcal{D}(M \to M')$ determines a directed graph, which we call the *precedence graph* of a, with enabled cells as nodes, and the immediate precedence relation $pc \lll_{M\to M'} p'c'$ giving a directed edge from pc to $p'c'$, if they are enabled in a. If $M \to M'$ is well founded the graph is acyclic, hence a *precedence DAG*. By functionality of a, each filled cell is associated with a unique event.

The Tree Lemma states that the subgraph of a precedence graph induced by taking only query enablings is a *forest*, in which the roots pc, $p'c'$ of distinct trees are inconsistent (either $c \neq c'$ or p and p' are inconsistent). This generalizes to our setting a corresponding result of Berry and Curien [5, proposition 2.5.3]. It enables us to prove that parallel exponentiation is well defined:

Theorem 3.9 *For any DCDSs M and M', $M \to M'$ is a DCDS.*

3.4 Currying

Definition 3.10 Let M_1, M_2 and M' be DCDSs. Let M_u and M_c be the DCDSs

$$M_u = M_1 \times M_2 \to M' \qquad \text{and} \qquad M_c = M_1 \to M_2 \to M'$$

so that $\mathrm{rep}(M_u) = (M_1 \times M_2) \times \mathrm{rep}(M')$ and $\mathrm{rep}(M_c) = M_1 \times (M_2 \times \mathrm{rep}(M'))$. Define $\mathrm{curry} : \mathcal{E}(\mathrm{rep}(M_u)) \to \mathcal{E}(\mathrm{rep}(M_c))$ and $\mathrm{uncurry} : \mathcal{E}(\mathrm{rep}(M_c)) \to \mathcal{E}(\mathrm{rep}(M_u))$ by

$$
\begin{aligned}
\forall \langle\langle y_1, y_2\rangle, \bar{y}'\rangle \in \mathcal{E}(\mathrm{rep}(M_u))\,. \qquad \mathrm{curry}(\langle\langle y_1, y_2\rangle, \bar{y}'\rangle) &= \langle y_1, \langle y_2, \bar{y}'\rangle\rangle\,,\\
\forall \langle y_1, \langle y_2, \bar{y}'\rangle\rangle \in \mathcal{E}(\mathrm{rep}(M_c))\,. \qquad \mathrm{uncurry}(\langle y_1, \langle y_2, \bar{y}'\rangle\rangle) &= \langle\langle y_1, y_2\rangle, \bar{y}'\rangle\,.
\end{aligned}
$$

Extend curry to queries $q \in \mathcal{P}_t(\mathcal{F}(\mathrm{rep}(M_u)))$ and algorithms $a \in \mathcal{D}(M_u)$ as follows, and extend uncurry similarly:

$$\mathrm{curry}(q) = \{\mathrm{curry}(\bar{y}) \mid \bar{y} \in q\}$$

$$\text{curry}(a) = \{(\text{curry}(p)c, \textbf{query}\ \text{curry}(q)) \mid (pc, \textbf{query}\ q) \in a\} \cup \{(\text{curry}(p)c, \textbf{output}\ v) \mid (pc, \textbf{output}\ v) \in a\}$$

•

Proposition 3.11 *The maps* curry *and* uncurry *are well defined, that is, they produce states of* M_c*,* M_u*, when applied to states of* M_u*,* M_c*, respectively. Moreover,* curry *is an isomorphism from* $\mathcal{D}(M_u)$ *to* $\mathcal{D}(M_c)$*, and* uncurry *is its inverse. The two maps preserve enablings.*

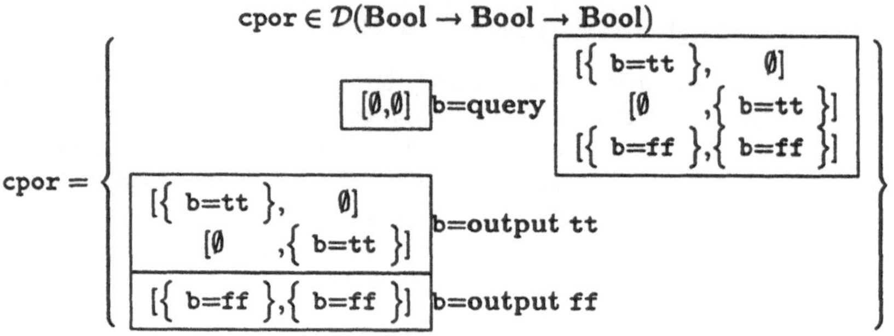

Figure 2: The curried parallel-or algorithm, cpor = curry(por)

Note that currying the parallel-or function *por* to *cpor* reduces parallelism, in an as yet informal sense, as reflected by a comparison of the por and cpor algorithms. por's query initiates two parallel sub-computations, while cpor's query initiates a single sub-computation. Even though cpor does not compute in parallel, the *cpor* function is not sequential (as defined above), since it is not even monotone with respect to set inclusion– contrast $cpor(\emptyset)$ and $cpor(\{\mathtt{b} = \mathtt{tt}\})$. This observation is a premonition of problems we will encounter with application.

4 APPLICATION AND THE INTENSIONAL STRICTNESS ORDER

4.1 Projection

Recall that for a sequential algorithm a of $M \rightarrow_{seq} M'$ and a state x of M, Berry and Curien defined the application of a to x by

$$a \cdot_{seq} x = \{(c', v') \mid \exists y.\ (yc', \textbf{output}\ v') \in a\ \&\ y \subseteq x\}.$$

One might read this as saying that the events (c', v') of $a \cdot_{seq} x$ are obtained by "projection" from events $(yc', \textbf{output}\ v')$ of a whose state component y is below x, and thus may be an accurate partial description of the input x.

We start with a technical definition of a generalized projection fitted to our parallel setting. This is an operation that projects those residuals corresponding to fully-satisfied input conditions.

Definition 4.1 For $x \in \mathcal{D}(M)$, and $q \in \mathcal{P}_t(\mathcal{E}(\text{rep}(M \to M')))$, define the *projection* by x of q, denoted $\pi_x(q)$, to be

$$\pi_x(q) = \text{trim}(\{\text{snd}(\bar{z}) \mid \bar{z} \in q \ \& \ \text{fst}(\bar{z}) \subseteq x\}).$$

$\pi_x(q)$ is either empty, or a member of $\mathcal{P}_t(\mathcal{E}(\text{rep}(M')))$. Extend π_x to $V_{M \to M'}$ by setting:

$$\begin{aligned} \pi_x(\text{query } q) &= \text{query } \pi_x(q), \\ \pi_x(\text{output } v) &= \text{output } v. \end{aligned}$$

•

Proposition 4.2 *For any $x \in \mathcal{D}(M)$ and $Q \subseteq \mathcal{P}_t(\mathcal{E}_{fin}(\text{rep}(M \to M')))$, if $\sqcup Q$ exists then $\sqcup\{\pi_x(q) \mid q \in Q\} = \pi_x(\sqcup Q)$. The left hand side is to be taken as the empty set in case it is not well defined, that is, when $\pi_x(q) = \emptyset$ for some $q \in Q$.*

The above proposition, which states that projection is continuous, is also true for the trim powerdomain over functional sets of events, and over states.

4.2 Guidelines for Defining Application

Consider the application of an algorithm $a \in \mathcal{D}(M \to M')$ to $x \in \mathcal{D}(M)$. If M' is an exponentiation itself, then the result should be an algorithm $a' \in \mathcal{D}(M')$. Intuitively speaking, there ought to be an operational correspondence between the events of a and the events of a', in the rough sense that for each event $(pc, u) \in a$ there are some events of a' which are responsible for a' exhibiting the same behavior that (pc, u) entails when the argument to a is known to be x. For now, assume that each event of a has at most one corresponding event of a' — call this the *uniqueness* assumption.

Example 4.3 Application of the curried parallel-or algorithm cpor to $\{b = \text{ff}\}$ should, intuitively, produce the identity algorithm on **Bool**. There is a clear one-to-one correspondence between the events of the algorithms, and the uniqueness assumption holds.

$$\text{cpor} \cdot \left\{ b = \text{ff} \right\} = \left\{ \begin{array}{l} \boxed{[\emptyset]} \ b = \text{query} \ \boxed{\begin{array}{l} [\{ \ b = \text{tt} \ \}] \\ [\{ \ b = \text{ff} \ \}] \end{array}} \\ \boxed{[\{ \ b = \text{tt} \ \}]} \ b = \text{output tt} \\ \boxed{[\{ \ b = \text{ff} \ \}]} \ b = \text{output ff} \end{array} \right\}$$

•

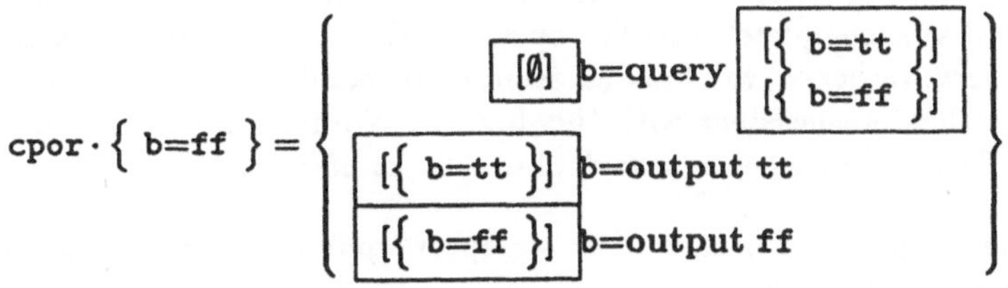

Consider an output event $(pc, \text{output } v) \in a$. When a is applied to x, a particular $\bar{x} \in p$ may be a (partial) description of a's input only if its input component $\text{fst}(\bar{x})$ is contained in x. For such an $\bar{x}$ there must then be a corresponding output event $(p'c, \text{output } v) \in a'$ with the residual $\text{snd}(\bar{x})$ in p'. By the uniqueness assumption, this implies that $p' = \pi_x(p)$ — and this is, in fact, the motivation behind the definition of projection.

If no $\bar{x} \in p$ has $\mathrm{fst}(\bar{x}) \subseteq x$, then the output event $(pc, \mathbf{output}\ v)$ will not take place at all when a is applied to x. Therefore there need not be a corresponding event in a'. We will identify this case by $p' = \pi_x(p) = \emptyset$, which is not a valid class.

For a query event $(pc, \mathbf{query}\ q) \in a$ there should be a corresponding query event $(p'c, \mathbf{query}\ q')$ in a'. As for output events, using the uniqueness assumption, we should have $p' = \pi_x(p)$. Similarly, q' need only contain the residual $\mathrm{snd}(\bar{y})$ for the branches $\bar{y} \in q$ for which the input condition $\mathrm{fst}(\bar{y})$ is satisfied by x: no other branch of q will ever be satisfied by x. We have then $q' = \pi_x(q)$ — independently of the uniqueness assumption.

As with output events, if $p' = \pi_x(p) = \emptyset$ then no element of p is a true description of the input state, when a is applied to x, and there need be no corresponding event in a'. Quite similarly, if $\mathrm{fst}(\bar{y}) \not\subseteq x$ for all branches $\bar{y}$ of q, then no branch of the query can be satisfied when a is applied to x, and there need not be a corresponding event in a'. This case is identified by $q' = \pi_x(q) = \emptyset$, which is not a valid query. In both cases, no event of a following from $(pc, \mathbf{query}\ q)$ can be executed either, when applying a to x.

Example 4.4 Consider the application of cpor to $\emptyset$. The resulting algorithm will not have or need an event with an **output ff** command, and, in fact, projection of that event of cpor produces an invalid empty class.

$$\mathtt{cpor} \cdot \emptyset = \left\{ \begin{array}{l} \qquad\qquad \boxed{[\emptyset]}\ \mathtt{b{=}query}\ \boxed{[\{\ \mathtt{b{=}tt}\ \}]} \\ \boxed{[\{\ \mathtt{b{=}tt}\ \}]}\ \mathtt{b{=}output\ tt} \end{array} \right\}$$

•

A third case of a query event in a that need not have a corresponding query event in a' arises when some branch $\bar{y} \in q$ is *completely* satisfied by x, that is, the input condition is satisfied ($\mathrm{fst}(\bar{y}) \subseteq x$) and the residual is vacuous ($\mathrm{snd}(\bar{y}) = \emptyset$). It is then the case that $\emptyset \in q' = \pi_x(q)$, and again q' is not a valid query.

In this third case, in contrast to the previous two, some event *following* $(pc, \mathbf{query}\ q)$ may have a corresponding event in a'; but $(pc, \mathbf{query}\ q)$ itself has no corresponding event in a' because a when applied to x may "jump to conclusions" without waiting for any additional arguments. That is, it will act according to the branch that is completely satisfied by x, and there is no need to issue any corresponding query; rather, a' will have an event corresponding to some subsequently enabled event that is consistent with this branch. We refer to this phenomenon, involving the loss or "abstracting away" of events, as ***abstraction***.

Example 4.5 Abstraction occurs when we apply cpor to $\{\mathtt{b} = \mathtt{tt}\}$, obtaining a non-strict constant algorithm:

$$\mathtt{cpor} \cdot \{\ \mathtt{b{=}tt}\ \} = \left\{\ \boxed{[\emptyset]}\ \mathtt{b{=}output\ tt}\ \right\}$$

•

So far we have outlined application in terms of our projection operator. Indeed, $\pi_x(a) = \{(\pi_x(p)c, \pi_x(u)) \in \dot{\mathrm{E}}_{M'} \mid (pc, u) \in a\}$ is a fairly natural generalization of the Berry-Curien formulation of $a \cdot_{seq} x$. It yields a useful approximation of application

— for all examples mentioned so far in this section it yields precisely what we would intend application to produce. But it cannot serve as the definition of application since, in general, $\pi_x(a)$ is not a state. The reason is that *splitting* of equivalence classes may occur: equivalent but inconsistent branches in a query q need not remain equivalent when q is projected by x. Each equivalence class of q will be mapped into one or more equivalence classes of $\pi_x(q)$, so that if $(\pi_x(p)c, \mathbf{query}\ \pi_x(q)) \vdash_{M'} p'c$ then there exists p_1 such that $(pc, \mathbf{query}\ q) \vdash_{M \to M'} p_1c$ and $p' \subseteq \pi_x(p_1)$.

Example 4.6 Let $\mathbf{cgf'} = \mathsf{curry}(\mathsf{curry}(\mathbf{gf'}))$.

$$\mathbf{cgf'} \cdot \emptyset = \left\{ \begin{array}{l} \boxed{[\emptyset,\emptyset]}\ \mathtt{b}{=}\mathbf{query} \boxed{\begin{array}{l} [\{\ \mathtt{b=tt}\ \},\{\ \mathtt{b=ff}\ \}] \\ [\{\ \mathtt{b=ff}\ \},\{\ \mathtt{b=tt}\ \}] \end{array}} \\ \boxed{[\{\ \mathtt{b=tt}\ \},\{\ \mathtt{b=ff}\ \}]}\ \mathtt{b}{=}\mathbf{output}\ \mathtt{tt} \\ \boxed{[\{\ \mathtt{b=ff}\ \},\{\ \mathtt{b=tt}\ \}]}\ \mathtt{b}{=}\mathbf{output}\ \mathtt{tt} \end{array} \right\}$$

Contrast this with $\pi_\emptyset(\mathbf{cgf'})$, which is not safe. Splitting occurs because the two branches which are projected, though not consistent, are equivalent in the original query by means of branches which are not projected. There is no longer, after projection, an equivalence chain *in the query* relating these two branches. •

In order to handle splitting correctly we now have to abandon the uniqueness assumption. The definition of application can no longer be local, but must rather be an inductive definition, proceeding by the above intuitions, with safety built into the definition, so that we reconstruct the correct classes.

The above discussion assumes that $a \cdot x$ is an algorithm. If M' is not an exponentiation, then one would obtain a trivial algorithm a' of a "unary exponentiation" $\to M'$ that is constructed as an exponentiation out of a representation **Null** and a base M'. Such an a' will have no query events, since the only possible branch is the empty branch; therefore it is isomorphic to a state of M' by the isomorphism which maps the event $(\{\emptyset\}c, \mathbf{output}\ v)$ to (c, v). We will omit explicit mention of this isomorphism.

4.3 Application

We build $a \cdot x$ by induction on its enabling layers[7]; we define $(a \cdot x)_{n+1}$ so that it will turn out to be the maximal sub-state of $a \cdot x$ such that $\mathrm{F}((a \cdot x)_{n+1}) \subseteq \mathrm{E}((a \cdot x)_n)$. The sequence thus obtained is increasing, and $a \cdot x$ is its limit.

Definition 4.7 For $a \in \mathcal{D}(M \to M')$, $x \in \mathcal{D}(M)$, define the *application* of a to x, denoted by $a \cdot x$, to be $\bigcup_{n \geq 0}(a \cdot x)_n$, where the sequence $\{(a \cdot x)_n\}_{n \geq 0}$ is inductively defined as follows:

- $(a \cdot x)_0 = \emptyset$.
- $(a \cdot x)_{n+1} = \{(p'c, \pi_x(u)) \in \mathrm{E}_{M'} \mid (pc, u) \in a \ \&\ p' \subseteq \pi_x(p) \ \&\ p'c \in \mathrm{E}(a \cdot x)_n\}$.

•

[7] The induction may be formulated on the height of the proof for a cell in $a \cdot x$.

Note especially the requirement that events of $a \cdot x$ belong to $\mathrm{E}_{M'}$. This requirement filters out the undesired by-products of π_x, identified above as arising when projection produces an empty class, an empty query, or a query with an empty branch – all invalid.

Proposition 4.8 *Application is well defined, that is, for* $a \in \mathcal{D}(M \to M')$ *and* $x \in \mathcal{D}(M)$, $a \cdot x \in \mathcal{D}(M')$.

We define the input-output function of a parallel algorithm $a \in \mathcal{D}(M \to M')$ to be $\lambda x.a \cdot x : \mathcal{D}(M) \to \mathcal{D}(M')$.

4.4 Ordering Algorithms

Application as defined is monotone and continuous in its first argument with respect to set inclusion, but not even monotone in its second argument[8]. This is due to two phenomena: *amplification* and *abstraction* of queries.

Contrast $a \cdot x$ and $a \cdot x'$, for an algorithm a and $x \subseteq x'$. Increasing the argument from x to x' may increase the set of branches of a query q of a whose input conditions are satisfied.

- If the event of a with query q has corresponding query events in both $a \cdot x$ and $a \cdot x'$, with $\pi_{x'}(q) \sqsubseteq \pi_x(q)$, then we say that the query $\pi_x(q)$ is amplified into the query $\pi_{x'}(q)$. The query event in $a \cdot x$ may not belong to $a \cdot x'$, but an amplified version of it does.

- If, however, the event of a with query q has a corresponding event in $a \cdot x$, but none in $a \cdot x'$, because $\emptyset \in \pi_{x'}(q)$ (rendering it an invalid query), then the query event in $a \cdot x$ has no corresponding event in $a \cdot x'$, and we say that the query $\pi_x(q)$ is abstracted.

Example 4.9 For instance, $\mathtt{cpor} \cdot \emptyset \not\subseteq \mathtt{cpor} \cdot \{\mathtt{b} = \mathtt{ff}\}$, owing to amplification; and $\mathtt{cpor} \cdot \emptyset \not\subseteq \mathtt{cpor} \cdot \{\mathtt{b} = \mathtt{tt}\}$, owing to abstraction. •

These counter-examples cannot be resolved by redefining application, since they are intuitively correct and serve as guidelines that any definition of application must obey. The desire for monotonicity and continuity of application therefore motivates a finer order on states; we define a pre-order $\leq^i$ based on the existence of a morphism between algorithms that preserves the enabling DAG up to amplification and abstraction.

Definition 4.10 The *intensional strictness* pre-order $\leq^i_M$ on $\mathcal{D}(M)$ is defined by induction on M as follows.

For an atomic DCDS M let $\leq^i_M$ be set inclusion.

For $M_1 \times M_2$ let $\langle x_1, x_2 \rangle \leq^i_{M_1 \times M_2} \langle x'_1, x'_2 \rangle$ iff $x_1 \leq^i_{M_1} x'_1$ and $x_2 \leq^i_{M_2} x'_2$.

For $M \to M'$, if $x, x' \in \mathcal{D}(M \to M')$ let $x \leq^i_{M \to M'} x'$ iff there exists a function $f : \mathrm{E}(x) \to \mathrm{E}(x')$ such that the following hold:

[8] Application is monotone and continuous in both arguments with respect to set inclusion when its results are states of a basic DCDS. The same is true of ground application, repeated application until the result is basic.

(1) If $f(pc) = p'c'$ then $c = c'$.

(2) If $(pc, \textbf{output } v) \in x$ then $(f(pc), \textbf{output } v) \in x'$.

(3) If $\{(p_j c_j, \textbf{output } v_j)\}_{j=1}^{l} \vdash_x pc$ then $\{(f(p_j c_j), \textbf{output } v_j)\}_{j=1}^{l} \vdash_{x'} f(pc)$. Note that, by taking $l = 0$, f must map initial cells into initial cells.

(4) If $(pc, \textbf{query } q) \in x$ then one of the following holds:

(AMP) There exists q' such that $(f(pc), \textbf{query } q') \in x'$, and if $(pc, \textbf{query } q) \vdash_{x,\bar{y}} p_1 c$ then for some $\bar{y}' \subseteq \bar{y}$, $(f(pc), \textbf{query } q') \vdash_{x',\bar{y}'} f(p_1 c)$. Consequently $q' \sqsubseteq q$.
If this is the case we say that f amplifies $(pc, \textbf{query } q)$.

(ABS) If $(pc, \textbf{query } q) \vdash_x p_1 c$ then $f(p_1 c) = f(pc)$.
If this is the case we say that f abstracts $(pc, \textbf{query } q)$.

In other words, f preserves basic cells, output commands and output enablings, and may either amplify a query or abstract it. Roughly speaking, x' is less strict than x in the sense that it may require less information about the inputs, and may ask for it at an earlier point of the computation, in order to produce at least the same results as x. •

Example 4.11 Note that our previous counter-examples to monotonicity, in example 4.9, now become examples of algorithms related by $\leq^i$. We also have $\texttt{gf} \leq^i \texttt{gf}'$, by amplification. The order also makes sense for parallel algorithms that compute sequentially (and may thus be expressed using the Berry–Curien sequential exponentiation). For instance, `lsor` is intensionally stricter than `lor`, by abstraction. The same relation holds for their curried versions. •

Proposition 4.12 *$\leq^i$ contains the set inclusion relation, and is a pre-order. It is a partial order on output-closed algorithms, i.e. algorithms in which any branch of a query eventually leads to an output event.*

Note that $\leq^i$ is not anti-symmetric in general. Intuitively, this is because queries that do not have an output event following them may be abstracted and re-introduced at will, thus generating distinct but $\leq^i$-equivalent algorithms.

Example 4.13 Take $\leq^i_{\textbf{Bool}\to\textbf{Bool}}$. We have

$$\emptyset \leq^i \left\{ \boxed{\emptyset}\,\texttt{b=query} \boxed{[\{\ \texttt{b=tt}\ \}]} \right\} \leq^i \emptyset$$

by, respectively, inclusion and abstraction. •

We point out some of the properties of $\leq^i$, and show to what extent it achieves its stated goals for application. But first, in order to be able precisely to state the results, we first need to define the *first-order* DCDSs to be those Ms generated by the following grammar, where A is atomic:

$$M ::= P \mid P \to M \qquad P ::= A \mid P \times P.$$

Note that algorithms of first-order type may return algorithms as results but do not take algorithms as arguments. Thus, for instance, **Bool** $\rightarrow$ **Bool** $\rightarrow$ **Bool** is a first-order DCDS but (**Bool** $\rightarrow$ **Bool**) $\rightarrow$ **Bool** is not. All examples of algorithms discussed in this paper so far have been of first-order type. We use the term higher-order to refer to general types in the DCDS algebra, with no restrictions.

The first-order DCDSs are those DCDSs for which the set inclusion ordering on the representation coincides with the intensional strictness ordering[9]. This enables us to show that by adopting the intensional strictness order we have achieved a satisfactory model of first-order parallel exponentiation.

Proposition 4.14 *For $M \rightarrow M'$ a first-order DCDS, application is monotone (with respect to $\leq^i$) in of both its arguments.*

Corollary 4.15 *For a first-order DCDS, $\leq^i$ is contained in $\leq^e$, the input-output approximation order, defined to be set inclusion on basic DCDSs and defined on $M \rightarrow M'$ by $a \leq^e a'$ iff $\forall x \in \mathcal{D}(M)\ .\ a \cdot x \leq^e a' \cdot x$.*

Proposition 4.16 *For M a first-order DCDS, $(\mathcal{D}(M), \leq^i_M)$ is directed complete, i.e., every $\leq^i$-directed subset of $\mathcal{D}(M)$ has a least upper bound.*

An element of a pre-order is *finite* iff, whenever it is below a least upper bound of a directed set it must be below some element of that set.

Proposition 4.17 *For a first-order DCDS M, $a \in \mathcal{D}(M)$ is finite iff a is a finite set of events, and all of its queries are finitely branching. For every algorithm a, its finite approximations form a directed set with a as a least upper bound.*

Proposition 4.18 *For $M \rightarrow M'$ a first-order DCDS, application is continuous (with respect to $\leq^i$) in both of its arguments.*

Our proofs do not extend to the higher-order case, where intensional strictness on the representation departs from set inclusion. At fault is not the definition of intensional strictness, nor the definition of application, but rather the construction of the exponentiation. In the next section we will outline the problem and our solution to it, which extends the properties given here to the general case. Nevertheless, we would like to point out that the achievement of a first-order model of parallel algorithms is noteworthy in its own right, since the class of first-order parallel algorithms is already significantly different from the class of sequential algorithms (it contains, for example, a parallel-or algorithm), and is closed under currying and uncurrying.

---

[9]Strictly speaking, the definition of $\leq^i$ should have been given simultaneously with a revised construction of the exponentiation that employs $\leq^i_{\text{rep}(M)}$ *in lieu* of set inclusion on $\mathcal{D}(\text{rep}(M))$. This is not necessary for our limited purposes here, since for first-order DCDSs the two coincide, so that first-order exponentiation remains unchanged; for instance, currying remains an isomorphism. The same remark is true for the order used in the definition of application.

5 FUTURE RESEARCH DIRECTIONS

We have tried to stay close in spirit to the foundational work of Berry and Curien. Since set inclusion was the underlying order of the Berry–Curien model and that model is sequential, it is not surprising that we have been forced to depart from their approach in adopting a new underlying order. It is interesting to look back and determine to what extent the phenomena of abstraction and amplification, upon which our ordering is based, occur in the Berry-Curien model. Sequential algorithms correspond to parallel algorithms with trivial parallelism: each query involves a single cell. Amplification in the sequential setting is reduced to set inclusion. Abstraction is not. Our intensional strictness pre-order induces a pre-order on the Berry-Curien model, still (strictly) finer than set inclusion and (strictly) coarser than input-output approximation.

We regard queries as generalized sequentiality indices, perhaps better called *computation indices*, since they are applicable to the parallel setting. We can characterize the class of parallel algorithms which have a stable input-output function, in Berry's sense, in terms of their computation indices. We intend to investigate the new notions of stability and sequentiality obtained by employing intensional strictness as the underlying order on states rather than set inclusion. We conjecture that (in line with remarks made earlier) the curried parallel-or *cpor* will turn out to be sequential in this new sense, while the uncurried *por* remains parallel.

The intensional strictness order seems to be a natural outcome of our definition of application, which in turn seems quite natural and intuitive. This new ordering, however, only makes application well behaved for first-order DCDSs. A reason for its failure to do so at higher-order is that addition of query events to an algorithm no longer constitutes an increase in the information content of the algorithm; therefore a higher-order algorithm is not able to build an internal representation of its algorithmic argument. A modification is now needed to the way in which the internal representation is built. We do this by changing the *values* of $M \rightarrow M'$ to be trees whose internal nodes correspond to queries, and whose leaves correspond to output events. We will report on the properties of this model in a future paper.

A major objective of our research is to obtain a cartesian closed category suitable for modelling parallelism. We have adopted the Berry-Curien cartesian product; we have shown that parallel exponentiation of DCDSs makes sense, and we have given appropriate and natural application and currying operations. We are currently working out the details of a suitable composition for parallel algorithms.

We intend to establish a "parallel analogue" to the Berry-Curien characterization of sequential algorithms. Their result [5, proposition 2.5.6] showed that the sequential algorithms, ordered by set inclusion, correspond to the sequential functions under the stable ordering. A sequential algorithm may thus be viewed as a sequential function paired with a (sequential) computation strategy. Our analogue will establish that the parallel algorithms, ordered by intensional strictness, correspond to the continuous functions under the usual extensional ordering; and a parallel algorithm may be viewed as a continuous function paired with a (parallel) computation strategy. This would be further evidence in favor of the naturalness of our model.

REFERENCES

[1] Berry G. Stable models of typed λ-calculi. In: Proc. 5th Coll. on Automata, Languages and Programming. Springer, Berlin, New York, 1978, pp 72–89 (Lecture notes in computer science no. 62)

[2] Berry G, Curien P-L. Sequential algorithms on concrete data structures. Theor Comput Sci 1982; 20:265–321

[3] Berry G, Curien P-L. Theory and practice of sequential algorithms: the kernel of the applicative language CDS0. In: Nivat, Reynolds (eds) Algebraic Methods in Semantics. Cambridge University Press, 1985, pp 35–87

[4] Berry G, Curien P-L, Lévy J-J. Full abstraction for sequential languages: the state of the art. In: Nivat, Reynolds (eds) Algebraic Methods in Semantics. Cambridge University Press, 1985, pp 89–132

[5] Curien P-L. Categorical Combinators, Sequential Algorithms and Functional Programming. Pitman, London, 1986 (Research notes in theoretical computer science)

[6] Huet G. Formal structures for computation and deduction. Class notes for course at CMU, 1986

[7] Kahn G, MacQueen DB. Coroutines and networks of parallel processes. In: Information Processing 1977. North Holland, 1977, pp 993–998

[8] Kahn G, Plotkin G. Domaines concrets. Rapport 336, IRIA-LABORIA, 1978

[9] Plotkin G. LCF considered as a programming language. Theor Comput Sci 1977; 5(3):223–255

[10] Smyth MB. Power domains. J Comput Syst Sci 1978; 16(1):23–36

Causal Automata I: Confluence $\equiv$ {AND, OR} Causality

Jeremy Gunawardena
Hewlett-Packard Laboratories, Information Systems Centre,
Filton Road, Stoke Gifford, Bristol BS12 6QZ.

Abstract

In this paper we introduce causal automata, a formalism for reasoning about reactive systems. In contrast to other formalisms in common use, causal automata permit complex causal relationships to be specified in a straightforward manner while having at the same time a simple and intuitive operational behaviour. Our main result, which follows on from earlier work in [4,5], uses causal automata to give a characterisation of Milner's notion of confluence.

1 INTRODUCTION

In this paper we introduce causal automata, a formalism for reasoning about reactive systems, [7], and we use it to shed some light on Milner's notion of confluence in CCS, [10, Chapter 10], [11, Chapter 11]. We devote this introductory section to giving an informal overview of the rest of the paper.

1.1 Determinism and Confluence

It is convenient to use the neutral terminology of reactive systems to describe the basic objects of study. A plethora of mathematical formalisms have been suggested for reasoning about such systems, [13], a situation which we shall exacerbate by suggesting yet another one! Reactive systems engage in sequences of actions. These may be hidden, as in the τ action of CCS, or be observable by the environment. A sequence of observable actions is referred to as a trace. We shall be exclusively concerned with finite reactive systems and the word finite should be taken as read throughout this paper.

Milner's introduction of confluence was motivated by his work on determinism. (We use the word determinism in preference to Milner's *determinacy.*) There seems to be some confusion about the exact meaning of this word. For us it will always mean that the past determines the present. This corresponds to the dictionary definition of determinism[1] and is the one adopted by Milner for CCS, [11, Chapter 11, Definition 3] (weak determinacy), and by Vaandrager, [15, §3.6],

[1]The philosophical doctrine that all events $\cdots$ are fully determined by preceding events. (Collins Dictionary of the English Language, Second Edition, 1986.)

for event structures. Note that it differs from the one used by Aceto *et al* in [1, Definition 3.3].

More precisely, a reactive system is deterministic if, after executing a given trace t, it always engages in the same observable actions. The CCS process $\tau.a.NIL + \tau.b.NIL$ is hence non-deterministic, since to begin with (ie: after executing the empty trace), it may sometimes be prepared to offer a and sometimes not. One frequently encounters the assertion that the process $a.b.NIL + b.a.NIL$ "exhibits sequential non-determinism". As far as we are concerned, this process is perfectly deterministic; it merely offers an initial choice between the actions a and b.

Deterministic systems are interesting for two main reasons. They occur widely in real-life and they are particularly easy to reason about: their behaviour is determined by trace-level information. This "folk theorem" has to be stated differently depending on the formalism which is used. Milner shows, [11, Chapter 11, Proposition 5], that two deterministic CCS processes are observationally equivalent if, and only if, they have the same set of traces. Vaandrager shows, [15, §5.1], that two deterministic event structures are isomorphic if, and only if, they have the same set of step sequences.

The problem with determinism in CCS is that it lacks compositionality. If we place two deterministic CCS processes in parallel, the result need not be deterministic, as the example of $a.b.NIL|a.c.NIL$ shows. Similarly for most of the other algebraic operators in CCS. This is a serious difficulty, because compositionality is a key feature of algebraic formalisms like CCS. Milner's answer to this is to introduce the stronger property of confluence. Confluent processes are necessarily deterministic but not all deterministic processes are confluent. Confluence does exhibit some compositionality: Milner shows that certain operations in CCS, in particular a form of restricted parallel composition, do preserve confluence, [11, Chapter 11, Proposition 17]. This provides a method for building up confluent, and hence deterministic, processes. Rem and others have considered a similar notion, conservatism, in CSP, [14].

In earlier papers, [4,5], we studied the processes, called purely parallel, which could be built up by using these confluence-preserving operations. This was undertaken quite independently of Milner's work and for quite different reasons. We were interested in unravelling the causal relationships between observable actions in a CCS process. Purely parallel processes turned out to be the simplest and most natural setting for our methods. Our main result was to exhibit a one-to-one correspondence between equivalence classes of purely parallel processes, under observational equivalence, and finite deterministic pomsets, [5, Theorem 3]. In more detail, the result shows that the causal relationships between observable actions in a purely parallel process can be expressed using only a partially ordered set. Moreover, this can be done in a manner consistent with interleaving semantics; it is not necessary to invoke "true concurrency". Conversely, every finite deterministic partially ordered set corresponds to some purely parallel process.

Unfortunately, not all confluent processes are purely parallel, even up to observational equivalence. Indeed, we used the result above to show that the specific process

$$C = (a.x.NIL|b.x.NIL|\overline{x}.c.NIL)\backslash\{x,\overline{x}\}$$

is confluent but cannot be observationally equivalent to a purely parallel process, [4, §7]. What is the precise relationship between confluence and pure parallelism? Are most confluent processes purely parallel? What needs to be added to the language of pure parallelism in order to construct all confluent processes? These questions are the starting point of the present paper.

1.2 Causal Automata

It is instructive to follow the philosophy of [4] and to work out the causal relationships between the observable actions in the process C above. The actions a and b are causally independent and can appear in any order in the traces of C. However, c is causally dependent either on a or on b, where "or" is used in the logical sense of inclusive or. This makes it clear why C is not equivalent to a purely parallel process: partially ordered sets on their own are incapable of expressing OR causality.

The idea of OR causality seems a very natural one. However, none of the formalisms used for specifying reactive systems seem to provide a convenient way to express it. Indeed the example above is isomorphic to one given by Winskel, [16, page 7], as an illustration of instability in event structures. Most authors, [1,2,3,15,16], have studied stable event structures and have found instability to be either unnecessary or undesirable.

In this paper we would like to take causality more seriously by introducing causal automata, a formalism in which causal relationships like OR causality can be easily expressed.

Definition 1.1 *A causal automaton consists of a finite set, E, of events and a function, $\rho : E \to BE$, from E to the free Boolean algebra, BE, generated by E.*

We shall only require very basic information about Boolean algebras; a convenient reference is [9, Chapter 1].

Causal automata are conveniently specified in tabular form, as shown below. The first column gives the events e while the second gives $\rho(e)$.

$$C1 = \begin{array}{|ll|}\hline a & \mathsf{T} \\ b & \mathsf{T} \\ c & a \vee b \\ \hline\end{array} \qquad C2 = \begin{array}{|ll|}\hline a & \neg b \\ b & \neg a \\ \hline\end{array} \qquad C3 = \begin{array}{|ll|}\hline e_1 & e_3 \Rightarrow e_4 \\ e_2 & e_1 \\ e_3 & e_1 \Rightarrow e_2 \\ e_4 & e_3 \\ \hline\end{array}$$

The Boolean expression $\rho(e)$ represents the causal "guard" which must become TRUE before the event e can occur. Initially, no events have occurred. This is expressed by setting each of the generators $e \in E$ to FALSE. The expressions $\rho(e)$ then simplify to some truth value. Those events for which $\rho(e)$ becomes TRUE are said to be enabled and may occur. The others, for which $\rho(e)$ evaluates to FALSE, cannot yet do so.

If an event e occurs, then it is removed from the set E of events. However, the causal guards of the remaining events may still contain e. We may express the fact that e has occurred by setting e to TRUE, thereby removing the generator e from the values of the function ρ. It should now be clear that we have constructed a new causal automaton F where $F = E - \{e\}$ and $\rho_F(x) = \rho_E(x)[e \to \mathsf{T}]$ for each $x \in F$. E has engaged in the event e and evolved into the automaton F.

The example $C1$ represents the same behaviour as the CCS process C described above. Setting each of a, b and c to FALSE, we see that only a and b are enabled. If either of these occur, then c will become enabled in the resulting automaton, since $(\mathsf{T} \vee p) \equiv \mathsf{T}$.

The behaviour of $C3$ is rather different. If we set each of the events e_1, e_2, e_3 and e_4 to FALSE then e_1 and e_3 become enabled since $(\mathsf{F} \Rightarrow \mathsf{F}) \equiv \mathsf{T}$. Either of these events may occur. If e_1 occurs then $C3$ evolves into the automaton

$$D = \boxed{\begin{array}{cc} e_2 & \mathsf{T} \\ e_3 & e_2 \\ e_4 & e_3 \end{array}}$$

since $(\mathsf{T} \Rightarrow e_2) \equiv e_2$. The further behaviour of automaton D is straightforward: the events e_2, e_3 and e_4 are offered in that order. If, on the other hand, $C3$ were to engage in e_3 initially then the events e_4, e_1 and e_2, in that order, will be offered subsequently. Although the event e_3 is enabled in $C3$ it becomes disabled in D and remains so until e_2 has been offered.

Example $C2$ uses NOT causality. If both a and b are set to FALSE then both events are seen to be enabled and either may occur. However, if a occurs this has the effect of permanently disabling b and vice-versa. There is a close similarity between NOT causality and conflict in event structures.

Causal automata are similar to event structures in that both are based on an underlying set of events. However they differ in the fuel which drives their behaviour. Event structures use a mixture of consistency and enablement, [16, Definition 1.1.1], while causal automata run on pure causality. The two formalisms may be compared by looking at the families of configurations which they give rise to, where by configuration we mean, intuitively, *"a set of events which have occurred by some stage in a process"*, [16, §1.1]. Event structures give rise to domain-like families, [12, Theorem 9] and [16, Theorem 1.1.16]; a fundamental feature of the event structure world-view. However, causal automata give rise to more general families of configurations. We hope to give a more precise account of this in a subsequent paper, [6].

The events in a causal automaton do not correspond directly to actions but rather to occurrences of actions. It is customary to use a labelling function, $\ell : E \to \mathcal{A}$, to associate an action with each event. This need not be injective; different events may give rise to the same action. As a general rule, the Latin letters $a, b, c, e_1, \cdots$ will denote events, while Greek letters $\alpha, \beta, \cdots$ will denote actions. In tabular descriptions of causal automata a third column will be used to indicate the labels of events, as shown below.

$$C4 = \begin{array}{|llr|} e_1 & e_3 \Rightarrow e_4 & \alpha \\ e_2 & e_1 & \beta \\ e_3 & e_1 \Rightarrow e_2 & \alpha \\ e_4 & e_3 & \gamma \end{array}$$

If this third column is omitted then the labelling function is deemed to be the identity and actions are identical with events.

1.3 AND, OR Causality

Our intention in this paper is not to give a systematic treatment of causal automata. Instead, we feel it is best to show first that they are genuinely useful. Returning to the problem of confluence, we remarked above that purely parallel processes only require AND causality, while example C uses OR causality. This suggests that we investigate automata which only use AND and OR causality. More precisely, we shall say that the automaton E is a $\{\wedge, \vee\}$-automaton if each $\rho(e)$ can be written in terms of the generators of E using only the operations $\wedge$ and $\vee$, and possibly also the constant T. $C1$ above is a $\{\wedge, \vee\}$-automaton while $C2$ and $C3$ are not. The main result of this paper is the following causal characterisation of confluence.

Theorem 1.1 *If E is a deterministic $\{\wedge, \vee\}$-automaton then the set of action traces of E is a confluent trace set. Conversely, every confluent trace set is the set of action traces of some deterministic $\{\wedge, \vee\}$-automaton.*

A deterministic automaton will be defined precisely in §2, but the discussion given at the start of this Introduction should make it fairly clear what form the definition will take. A confluent trace set is the set of traces of some confluent process; once again a precise definition will be given later. Theorem 1.1 makes it clear how confluence differs from pure parallelism. It differs twice as much! Confluence has an entirely independent and orthogonal dimension of variability measured by OR causality. We do not yet understand how to build arbitrary confluent processes in CCS, but we do, at least, have a clue as to what to look for. We need to identify mechanisms in CCS which yield OR causality. We might also wish to know about other, more general forms of causal relationship. This leads us in the direction of a pure causal semantics for CCS, a topic which we hope to address in subsequent work.

It may be felt that Theorem 1.1 has too much of the flavour of formal language theory. It says in effect that a confluent trace set is one which is accepted by a suitable automaton. The use of the word automaton probably reinforces this. We feel this restricted viewpoint is justified because of the deterministic nature of the problem.

The result above is best possible, in the sense that there are causal automata, which are not $\{\wedge, \vee\}$-automata, which nonetheless have confluent sets of action traces. Example $C5$ below

$$C5 = \boxed{\begin{array}{ll} a & b \Rightarrow c \\ b & a \\ c & b \end{array}} \qquad C6 = \boxed{\begin{array}{ll} a & \top \\ b & a \\ c & b \end{array}} \qquad C7 = \boxed{\begin{array}{ll} a & c \\ b & a \\ c & b \end{array}}$$

has action traces $\{\varepsilon, a, ab, abc\}$, which is certainly confluent. This is an interesting example: the causal guard for the event a is expressed in terms of events which cannot in fact occur until after a. In other words, $C5$ is causally implausible. The operational behaviour of this automaton would be more sensibly described by automaton $C6$, which is indeed a $\{\wedge, \vee\}$-automaton. To some extent this is part of the general question of identifying a suitable notion of equivalence between automata. Unlike event structures, causal automata may contain junk: example $C7$ does precisely nothing. However, one might ask more specifically whether there is a simplest ("most sensible") causal interpretation of a given operational behaviour. This is an interesting problem but it falls outside the scope of the present paper.

1.4 Summary

The proof of Theorem 1.1 falls into two distinct parts. The heart of the argument is in §3 where the result is proved first for event traces. The labelling, and the property of determinism, are not relevant at this point. An important result in §3 is Lemma 3.1 which identifies the crucial characteristic property of $\{\mathsf{AND}, \mathsf{OR}\}$ causality. In §4 these initial results are used to prove the first part of the theorem. It is here that the assumption of determinism becomes essential. §5 contains the proof of the second part of Theorem 1.1. The details in §4 and §5 have a different flavour to those in §3 and largely concern the properties of strings and of labellings rather than of $\{\mathsf{AND}, \mathsf{OR}\}$ causality. §2 contains the initial definitions and some preparatory material on traces and confluence.

2 Causal automata

This section covers the initial definitions and Lemmas needed for the proof of Theorem 1.1. We begin by recalling the definition given in the Introduction.

Definition 2.1 *A causal automaton is a triple* (E, ρ, ℓ) *where*

- E *is a finite set of events;*
- $\rho : E \to BE$ *is a function to the free Boolean algebra,* BE*, generated by* E*;*
- $\ell : E \to \mathcal{A}$ *is a labelling function to some set* $\mathcal{A}$ *of actions.*

We shall refer to an automaton by its set, E, of events and where necessary use subscripts, ρ_E and ℓ_E, to make it clear which causal automaton is being referred to.

Definition 2.2 *If S is some set of Boolean operations then E is an S-automaton if $\forall e \in E$, $\rho(e)$ can be expressed using only operations from the set S together with the constant* T.

A valuation, v, of a set E is a function $v : E \to \{\mathsf{T}, \mathsf{F}\}$ which assigns a truth value to each element of E. Note that any valuation on E lifts uniquely to a function, $BE \to \{\mathsf{T}, \mathsf{F}\}$, which is also denoted v. It is convenient to think of valuations as characteristic functions and to identify v with the subset of elements $\{e \in E \mid v(e) = \mathsf{T}\}$. With this identification, $v_1 \subseteq v_2$ indicates that if $v_1(e) = \mathsf{T}$, then $v_2(e) = \mathsf{T}$. Let v_F be the valuation which corresponds to the empty subset of E so that $v_\mathsf{F}(e) = \mathsf{F}$ for all $e \in E$.

Definition 2.3 *If (E, ρ, ℓ) is a causal automaton, the event $e \in E$ is enabled if $v_\mathsf{F}(\rho(e)) = \mathsf{T}$.*

The idea of enabled events permits the definition of an operational semantics for causal automata. As is now customary, this semantics takes the form of a labelled transition system.

Definition 2.4 *If E_1, E_2 are causal automata and $e \in E_1$ is an event, then $E_1 \xrightarrow{e} E_2$ if, and only if,*

- *e is enabled in E_1;*
- *$E_2 = E_1 - \{e\}$;*
- *$\forall x \in E_2 \;\; \rho_{E_2}(x) = \rho_{E_1}(x)[e \to \mathsf{T}]$ (substitute T for e in $\rho_{E_1}(x)$);*
- *$\forall x \in E_2 \;\; \ell_{E_2}(x) = \ell_{E_1}(x)$.*

If $\alpha \in \mathcal{A}$ is an action, then $E_1 \xrightarrow{\alpha} E_2$ if, and only if, $E_1 \xrightarrow{e} E_2$ for some event e with $\ell(e) = \alpha$.

If S is any set, then S^* denotes the set of strings over S. The empty string is denoted by ε and concatenation of $s, t \in S^*$ is by juxtaposition, st, or - when clarity dictates - $s.t$. The event and action relations defined above extend in the usual way to relations over strings of events or strings of actions. If E, F are causal automata and $s = e_1 e_2 \cdots e_n \in E^*$ is a string of events, then $E \stackrel{s}{\Longrightarrow} F$ if there are causal automata $E_0, \cdots, E_n$ such that

$$E = E_0 \xrightarrow{e_1} E_1 \xrightarrow{e_2} \cdots \xrightarrow{e_n} E_n = F.$$

It is always true that $E \stackrel{\varepsilon}{\Longrightarrow} E$. If $E \stackrel{s}{\Longrightarrow} F$ for some $s \in E^*$ then s is said to be an event trace of E. The set of all event traces is $traces_\mathsf{E}(E)$.

Similar definitions hold for strings of actions. If E is a causal automaton over the labels $\mathcal{A}$, then $\sigma \in \mathcal{A}^*$ is an action trace of E if for some event trace $s = e_1 \cdots e_n$ we have $\sigma = \ell(e_1) \cdots \ell(e_n)$. If also $E \stackrel{s}{\Longrightarrow} F$ then we use the notation $E \stackrel{\sigma}{\Longrightarrow} F$ for the corresponding action trace. The set of action traces is $traces_\mathsf{A}(E)$. In general we shall use Latin letters $s, t, \cdots$ for event traces and Greek letters $\sigma, \tau, \cdots$ for action traces.

An event trace, in contrast to an action trace, is always a pure string: each event appears at most once in the string. Event traces hence give rise to subsets of events or to valuations. If $s \in traces_{\mathsf{E}}(E)$, let v_s denote the valuation corresponding to the subset of events in s.

$$v_s(e) = \begin{cases} \mathsf{T} & \text{if } e \text{ appears in } s \\ \mathsf{F} & \text{otherwise.} \end{cases}$$

Lemma 2.1 *Suppose that $E \stackrel{s}{\Longrightarrow} F$ for some event trace s of E. The event $a \in F$ is enabled in F if, and only if, $v_s(\rho_E(a)) = \mathsf{T}$ in E.*

Proof: If v_{F} denotes the all-FALSE valuation on F, it is clear from the operational semantics that $v_{\mathsf{F}}(\rho_F(a)) = v_s(\rho_E(a))$. The result follows.

QED

Recall that a trace set, T, over some alphabet A is a subset $T \subseteq A^*$ such that $\varepsilon \in T$ and if $s.t \in T$ then $s \in T$. It is clear that both $traces_{\mathsf{E}}(E)$ and $traces_{\mathsf{A}}(E)$ are trace sets. If T is a trace set and $s \in T$, then T/s denotes "*T after s*", in the sense of [8, §1.8.3].

$$T/s = \{t \mid s.t \in T\}.$$

This construct is undefined if $s \notin T$. Note that $T/\varepsilon = T$ and that $T/s_1s_2 = (T/s_1)/s_2$.

Lemma 2.2 *If E is a causal automaton and $E \stackrel{s}{\Longrightarrow} F$ for some event trace s of E then $traces_{\mathsf{E}}(F) = traces_{\mathsf{E}}(E)/s$.*

Proof: It is clear that $traces_{\mathsf{E}}(F) \subseteq traces_{\mathsf{E}}(E)/s$. For the other direction suppose that $t \in traces_{\mathsf{E}}(E)/s$ so that $st \in traces_{\mathsf{E}}(E)$. Then by definition, $E \stackrel{s}{\Longrightarrow} E_1 \stackrel{t}{\Longrightarrow} E_2$. Comparing E_1 and F, we see that they have both been obtained from E by removing the same set of events; namely, those events which appear in the string s. Similarly, the causality functions of both automata are obtained from that of E by replacing the same generators with T. Finally, the labelling functions are clearly identical. So $E_1 = F$ and $t \in traces_{\mathsf{E}}(F)$ as required.

QED

Of particular interest to us are confluent trace sets. These are, in effect, the trace sets of confluent CCS processes but we shall adopt a more intrinsic definition. We need the following operation on strings. If r and s are strings, the excess of r over s, [10, page 155], denoted r/s, is defined recursively by the rules below.

$$\begin{aligned} \varepsilon/s &= \varepsilon \\ (ar)/s &= \begin{cases} a(r/s) & \text{if } a \text{ does not appear in } s \\ r/(s/a) & \text{otherwise.} \end{cases} \end{aligned}$$

The operation "/" is being used in two different senses here depending on whether the left operand is a trace or a trace set. No confusion should result.

The excess operation has many properties, [10, page 155]. The following are particularly useful.

$$\begin{aligned} s/t &= s \quad \text{if } s \text{ and } t \text{ have no elements in common} \\ s/t_1t_2 &= (s/t_1)/t_2 \\ s_1s_2/t &= (s_1/t).(s_2/(t/s_1)) \end{aligned}$$

Following the precedent of [10], we leave the proofs as exercises for the reader.

Definition 2.5 *A trace set T is said to be confluent if for any $r, s \in T$, $r(s/r)$ is also in T.*

For example $C1$ in the Introduction, $traces_{\mathsf{E}}(C1)$ consists of all the strings in $\{a, b, c\}^*$ which do not start with event c. It is not difficult to show, [4, §7], that this set is confluent. On the other hand, $traces_{\mathsf{E}}(C3)$ is not confluent since e_1 and e_3 are both action traces of $C3$ but $e_1e_3 = e_1(e_3/e_1)$ is not.

In reasoning about the excess operation, it is useful to be able to count the number of occurrences of a particular element in the string. Multisets provide a convenient language for this.

Definition 2.6 *A multiset, f, over the set A is a function, $f : A \to \mathbf{N}$, from A to the natural numbers $\mathbf{N}$. The set of multisets over A is denoted $A^{\mathbf{N}}$.*

A string $s \in A$ gives rise to a multiset, $[s]$, over A as shown below.

$$\begin{aligned} [\varepsilon](a) &= 0 \ \forall a \in A \\ [bs](a) &= \begin{cases} [s](a) + 1 & \text{if } b = a \\ [s](a) & \text{otherwise.} \end{cases} \end{aligned}$$

A multiset $f \in A^{\mathbf{N}}$ is a set if $f(a) = 0$ or 1 for all $a \in A$. Note that a string $s \in A^*$ is pure if, and only if $[s]$ is a set. Furthermore, s and t are permutations of each other if, and only if, $[s] = [t]$. It is convenient to regard elements of A as strings of length 1, so that if $a \in A$ then $[a]$ is the multiset having the value 1 at a and 0 everywhere else. The usual operations and relations on numbers ($+$, $-$, $\leq$, $\cdots$) lift pointwise to operations on multisets.

The following result collects together some elementary properties of strings which will be used later. It makes clear in what sense the operation s/t is one of "excess".

Lemma 2.3 *If $s, t \in A^*$ are traces and $a, b \in A$ then*

1. $[st] = [s] + [t]$
2. $[t/b] = \begin{cases} [t] & \textit{if } [t](b) = 0 \\ [t] - [b] & \textit{otherwise} \end{cases}$
3. $[s/t](a) = \begin{cases} [s](a) - [t](a) & \textit{if } [s](a) > [t](a) \\ 0 & \textit{otherwise} \end{cases}$
4. $[s(t/s)] = [t(s/t)]$

Proof: *1.* By induction over the length of s. If $s = \varepsilon$ the result holds immediately. Suppose that $s = bs_1$ and the result holds for s_1. Choose $a \in A$. If $a = b$ then by the definition of the bracket function $[bs_1t](a) = [s_1t](a) + 1$ while $[bs_1](a) = [s_1](a) + 1$. By the inductive hypothesis $[s_1t](a) = [s_1](a) + [t](a)$. Hence, $[st](a) = [s](a) + [t](a)$. If $a \neq b$ then $[bs_1t](a) = [s_1t](a)$ and $[bs_1](a) = [s_1](a)$ and the result follows similarly. This proves *1.*

2. First suppose that b does not appear in t. In other words that $[t](b) = 0$. Then t and b have no element in common and by a remark made above, $t/b = t$. Hence, $[t/b] = [t]$ as required. Now suppose that b does appear in t. Then we can write t in the form ubv where we may suppose that b does not appear in u. Note that u may be the empty string. It follows that $t/b = ubv/b = (u/b).(bv/(b/u))$. But b and u have no elements in common and so $u/b = u$ and $b/u = b$. Hence $t/b = u.(bv/b) = u.v$. So we have $[t/b] = [u] + [v]$ while $[t] = [u] + [b] + [v]$. It follows that $[t/b] = [t] - [b]$ as required. This proves *2*.

3. We proceed by induction over the length of t. If $t = \varepsilon$ then $s/t = s$ for any s and the result is easily seen to hold. If $t = b$ where $b \in A$ then the result follows from part *2*. This starts the induction off. Now assume that $t = t_1t_2$ and the result holds for t_1 and t_2 separately, with any s as the left hand argument.

Suppose first that $[s](a) > [t](a)$. Then since $[t] = [t_1] + [t_2]$ by part *1*, we must have $[s](a) > [t_1](a)$. Therefore, by the inductive hypothesis for t_1, $[s/t_1](a) = [s](a) - [t_1](a)$. Furthermore, $[s/t_1](a) > [t_2](a)$. Hence by the inductive hypothesis for t_2,

$$[(s/t_1)/t_2](a) = [s/t_1](a) - [t_2](a) = [s](a) - [t_1](a) - [t_2](a) = [s](a) - [t](a).$$

The required result follows since $s/t = (s/t_1)/t_2$.

Now suppose that $[s](a) \leq [t](a)$. If $[s](a) \leq [t_1](a)$, then by the inductive hypothesis for t_1, $[s/t_1](a) = 0$ and clearly $[s/t_1](a) \leq [t_2](a)$. Hence by the inductive hypothesis for t_2, $[s/t](a) = 0$ as required. If on the other hand, $[s](a) > [t_1](a)$ then by the inductive hypothesis for t_1, $[s/t_1](a) = [s](a) - [t_1](a)$. But, $[s/t_1](a) \not> [t_2](a)$ for otherwise $[s](a) > [t](a)$. So by the inductive hypothesis for t_2, $[(s/t_1)/t_2](a) = 0$ and so $[s/t](a) = 0$ as required.

4. Choose $a \in A$ and suppose that $[s](a) > [t](a)$. Then, by part *3*, $[s(t/s)](a) = [s](a) + 0$ while $[t(s/t)](a) = [t](a) + [s](a) - [t](a) = [s](a)$. Hence $[s(t/s)](a) = [t(s/t)](a)$. By symmetry of s and t the result follows.

QED

We can now prove some elementary properties of confluent trace sets.

Lemma 2.4 *Suppose that T is a confluent trace set. The following statements are true.*

1. *If $t \in T$, then T/t is also confluent.*
2. *If $p, q \in T$ and $[p] = [q]$ then $T/p = T/q$.*

Proof: *1.* Choose $r, s \in T/t$. Then $tr, ts \in T$ and since T is confluent $tr(ts/tr) \in T$. But $ts/tr = (ts/t)/r = ((t/t).(s/(t/t)))/r = s/r$ since, by Lemma 2.3(3), $t/t = \varepsilon$. It follows that $r(s/r) \in T/t$ and hence T/t is confluent.

2. If $[p] = [q]$ then it follows from Lemma 2.3(3) that $p/q = q/p = \varepsilon$. If $u \in T/p$ then $pu \in T$ and since T is confluent, $q(pu/q)$ is also in T. But, $pu/q = (p/q)(u/(q/p)) = u$. Hence $qu \in T$ and $u \in T/q$. So $T/p \subseteq T/q$ and by symmetry, $T/p = T/q$ as required.

QED

This completes the preparatory material. In the next section we begin the proof of the main results.

3 AND, OR causality

We begin this section with a simple observation about Boolean expressions built up using only AND and OR.

Lemma 3.1 *Suppose that $\rho \in BE$ is an element of the free Boolean algebra over E other than* F. *ρ can be expressed using only the operations* T, $\wedge$ *and* $\vee$ *if, and only if, for any valuations v_1, v_2 such that $v_1 \subseteq v_2$ and $v_1(\rho) = \mathsf{T}$, it follows that $v_2(\rho) = \mathsf{T}$.*

Proof: Suppose that ρ is expressed using only the operations T, $\wedge$ and $\vee$ and suppose given a pair of valuations such that $v_1 \subseteq v_2$ and $v_1(\rho) = \mathsf{T}$. We have to prove that $v_2(\rho) = \mathsf{T}$. The proof is by structural induction over the form of the expression for ρ. If $\rho = \mathsf{T}$, or if ρ consists of a single generator, the result is clearly true. This starts the induction off. More generally, it is either the case that $\rho = \rho_1 \wedge \rho_2$ or $\rho = \rho_1 \vee \rho_2$ where ρ_1 and ρ_2 are expressions of the same form for which the result may be assumed, inductively, to hold.

In the former case it is evident that $v_1(\rho_1) = v_1(\rho_2) = \mathsf{T}$. By the inductive hypothesis $v_2(\rho_1) = v_2(\rho_2) = \mathsf{T}$ and so $v_2(\rho) = \mathsf{T}$. In the latter case, one at least of $v_1(\rho_1)$ and $v_1(\rho_2)$ must be T. Suppose, WLOG, that $v_1(\rho_1) = \mathsf{T}$. By the inductive hypothesis $v_2(\rho_1) = \mathsf{T}$ and so $v_2(\rho) = \mathsf{T}$. This completes the first part.

Now suppose that $\rho \in BE$ satisfies the valuation property in the statement of the Lemma. Define a valuation w to be minimal with respect to ρ if $w(\rho) = \mathsf{T}$ but $v(\rho) = \mathsf{F}$ for any $v \subset w$. Since $\rho \neq \mathsf{F}$, minimal valuations must exist.

It may happen that v_F is a minimal valuation for ρ. If v is any valuation, then $v(\rho) = \mathsf{T}$ since $v_\mathsf{F} \subseteq v$. Hence $\rho = \mathsf{T}$ and there is nothing to prove.

So assume that v_F is not a minimal valuation for ρ. Note that any minimal valuation w must then have some $e \in E$ such that $w(e) = \mathsf{T}$. Let $\{w_1, w_2, \cdots, w_n\}$ be the set of minimal valuations of ρ and let e vary over elements of E. Define

$$\sigma = \bigvee_{1 \leq i \leq n} \Big(\bigwedge_{w_i(e)=\mathsf{T}} (e) \Big)$$

which is well defined by the preceding remark. σ is expressed in terms of the generators of BE using only the operations $\wedge$ and $\vee$. We claim that $\rho = \sigma$ in BE. It suffices to show that $v(\rho) = v(\sigma)$ for any valuation v.

Suppose given a valuation v. If $v(\rho) = \mathsf{T}$ then there must exist a (not necessarily unique) minimal valuation w_j of ρ such that $w_j \subseteq v$. But if $e \in E$ and $w_j(e) = \mathsf{T}$, then clearly $v(e) = \mathsf{T}$. Hence, $v(\bigwedge_{w_j(e)=\mathsf{T}}(e)) = \mathsf{T}$ and so $v(\sigma) = \mathsf{T}$.

Now suppose that $v(\sigma) = \mathsf{T}$. Then for some $1 \leq j \leq n$, $v(\bigwedge_{w_j(e)=\mathsf{T}}(e)) = \mathsf{T}$. Hence, for each $e \in E$ such that $w_j(e) = \mathsf{T}$ we must have $v(e) = \mathsf{T}$. In other words, $w_j \subseteq v$. But, $w_j(\rho) = \mathsf{T}$ and so, by the valuation property, $v(\rho) = \mathsf{T}$. It follows that $\rho = \sigma$ in BE. This completes the proof.

QED

We have spelt out this proof in some detail because the valuation behaviour is the only property of $\{\wedge, \vee\}$-causality which is subsequently used. It is therefore important to know that this property characterises $\{\wedge, \vee\}$-causality.

Proposition 3.1 *If E is a $\{\wedge, \vee\}$-automaton then $traces_{\mathsf{E}}(E)$ is a confluent trace set.*

Proof: Choose $s, t \in traces_{\mathsf{E}}(E)$. We have to show that $t(s/t) \in traces_{\mathsf{E}}(E)$. The proof is by induction on the length of s. If $s = \varepsilon$ then $t(s/t) = t$ and there is nothing to prove. So suppose that $s = s_1 a$ and assume that $t(s_1/t)$ has been shown to be an event trace of E. We then have $s/t = (s_1/t).(a/(t/s_1))$. If a appears in t/s_1 then $a/(t/s_1) = \varepsilon$ and $s/t = s_1/t$. By the inductive hypothesis $t(s_1/t) \in traces_{\mathsf{E}}(E)$ and there is nothing more to do.

So assume that a does not appear in t/s_1 in which case $s/t = (s_1/t).a$. Since event traces are pure, it is clear that $[s_1](a) = 0$. By Lemma 2.3(3), $[t](a) = 0$ for otherwise a would appear in t/s_1. Furthermore, again by Lemma 2.3(3), $[s_1/t] \leq [s_1]$ and so $[s_1/t](a) = 0$. It follows that a does not appear in the trace $t(s_1/t)$.

By the inductive hypothesis, there is an automaton F such that $E \stackrel{t(s_1/t)}{\Longrightarrow} F$. Evidently, $a \in F$. All we have to do is to show that a is actually enabled in F. By Lemma 2.1, this amounts to showing that $v_{t(s_1/t)}(\rho_E(a)) = \mathsf{T}$.

Since s_1 is also an event trace, there is an automaton G such that $E \stackrel{s_1}{\Longrightarrow} G$. By Lemma 2.2, we know that $a \in traces_{\mathsf{E}}(G)$ and must hence be enabled in G. By Lemma 2.1, $v_{s_1}(\rho_E(a)) = \mathsf{T}$.

But now, from Lemma 2.3(4), $[s_1] \leq [t(s_1/t)]$. The events which appear in each of these traces are precisely those which have the value T in the corresponding valuations. Hence, $v_{s_1} \subseteq v_{t(s_1/t)}$ and the required result follows immediately from Lemma 3.1.

QED

The next result is a partial converse to Proposition 3.1. Since an arbitrary confluent trace set may contain non-pure strings, it is clear that some restriction is necessary for a converse to be true. We shall say that a trace set is pure if every string in the set is pure; the event traces of any causal automaton then always form a pure trace set. Since we are not at present interested in action traces, the labellings on our causal automata are irrelevant and we shall assume that they are always the identity function.

Proposition 3.2 *If T is a pure confluent trace set then there exists a $\{\wedge, \vee\}$-automaton, E, such that $traces_{\mathsf{E}}(E) = T$.*

Proof: It is convenient for the proof to enlarge the conclusions of the Proposition. Suppose that A is the set of all elements which appear in the strings of T, so that $T \subseteq A^*$ and A is the smallest set with this property. What we shall prove is that if T is pure and confluent then there is a $\{\wedge, \vee\}$-automaton, of the specific form (A, ρ), such that $traces_{\mathsf{E}}(A) = T$.

The proof is by induction over the size of the trace set T. If $T = \emptyset$ then the empty causal automaton has both the right form and the right traces. This starts off the induction. Now choose T, a non-empty pure confluent trace set and suppose that all pure confluent trace sets of strictly smaller size have been shown to fulfil the conclusion stated in the previous paragraph. Let $e_1, e_2, \cdots, e_n$ be all the events which appear initially on some string of T. In other words, $e_i \in T$ for $1 \le i \le n$ and if $t \in T$ and $t \ne \varepsilon$ then $t = e_i s$ for some i. By Lemma 2.4(1), T/e_i is a confluent trace set which is clearly pure and of strictly smaller size to T. By the inductive hypothesis there exists a $\{\wedge, \vee\}$-automaton A_i such that $traces_{\mathsf{E}}(A_i) = T/e_i$. We shall use ρ_i to denote the causality function for the i'th automaton, $\rho_i : A_i \to BA_i$.

Let $f_1, f_2, \cdots, f_m$ be the elements other than $e_1, e_2, \cdots, e_n$ which appear in strings of T and, as above, let

$$A = \{e_1, e_2, \cdots, e_n, f_1, f_2, \cdots, f_m\}.$$

We need to construct a causal automaton on this specific set of events.

It is clear by the purity of T that the event e_i does not appear on any string in T/e_i. However, by confluence of T, it is easy to see that every other event in A must appear in some string of T/e_i. It follows from the expanded inductive hypothesis that $A_i = A - \{e_i\}$. In particular, $\rho_i(f_j)$ is defined for each $1 \le i \le n$ and $1 \le j \le m$ and we may take it that $\rho_i(f_j) \in BA$. This allows us to define the following $\{\wedge, \vee\}$-automaton (A, ρ) of the required form.

$$\begin{array}{lcll} \rho(e_i) & = & \mathsf{T} & 1 \le i \le n \\ \rho(f_j) & = & \bigvee_{1 \le i \le n}(e_i \wedge \rho_i(f_j)) & 1 \le j \le m. \end{array}$$

We claim that $traces_{\mathsf{E}}(A) = T$.

The first point to note is that the enabled events of A are precisely e_1, e_2, $\cdots$, e_n, for clearly $v_{\mathsf{F}}(\rho(f_j)) = \mathsf{F}$ for any $1 \le j \le m$. Hence there are causal automata B_i, for $1 \le i \le n$, such that $A \xrightarrow{e_i} B_i$. Moreover, it is clear that B_i and A_i have the same sets of events, namely $A - \{e_i\}$. We would be done if it were true that $B_i = A_i$ as causal automata. It is important to realise that this need not be the case. However, what we shall show is that $traces_{\mathsf{E}}(B_i) = traces_{\mathsf{E}}(A_i)$. It follows easily from Lemma 2.2 that this is sufficient to show $traces_{\mathsf{E}}(A) = T$. The remainder of the proof is hence concerned with showing that $traces_{\mathsf{E}}(B_i) = traces_{\mathsf{E}}(A_i)$. Since the proof is the same for each index i it will be convenient and no less general to do the case $i = 1$. This will cut down on the number of indices which appear in the text.

We shall start be showing $traces_{\mathsf{E}}(A_1) \subseteq traces_{\mathsf{E}}(B_1)$. The proof is by induction on the length of strings in $traces_{\mathsf{E}}(A_1)$. It is clear that $\varepsilon \in traces_{\mathsf{E}}(B_1)$ which starts off the induction. So suppose that $t \in traces_{\mathsf{E}}(A_1)$ is a non-empty string and that all strings in $traces_{\mathsf{E}}(A_1)$ of strictly smaller length have been shown to be in $traces_{\mathsf{E}}(B_1)$. We can write $t = se$ where $e \in A_1$ is an event and $s \in traces_{\mathsf{E}}(A_1)$ is a string of strictly smaller length than t. By the inductive hypothesis $s \in traces_{\mathsf{E}}(B_1)$ and $e_1 s \in traces_{\mathsf{E}}(A)$. If e is one of the e_i, it will be permanently enabled and clearly $se \in traces_{\mathsf{E}}(B_1)$ and there is nothing to prove. So assume that e is one of the f_j. From the description of the automaton A given above, it is easy to see that

$$v_{e_1 s}(\rho(e)) = v_s(\rho_1(e)) \vee (\cdots)$$

where the exact nature of the omitted elements is not relevant.

Now by assumption, $se \in traces_{\mathsf{E}}(A_1)$, and so by Lemma 2.1, $v_s(\rho_1(e)) = \mathsf{T}$. It follows immediately that $v_{e_1 s}(\rho(e)) = \mathsf{T}$. Hence by Lemma 2.1 $e_1 se \in traces_{\mathsf{E}}(A)$ and so by Lemma 2.2, $t = se \in traces_{\mathsf{E}}(B_1)$. If follows by induction that $traces_{\mathsf{E}}(A_1) \subseteq traces_{\mathsf{E}}(B_1)$.

It remains to prove the opposite inclusion, $traces_{\mathsf{E}}(B_1) \subseteq traces_{\mathsf{E}}(A_1)$. As before the proof is by induction on the length of strings. Suppose that $t \in traces_{\mathsf{E}}(B_1)$ is a non-empty string and all strings of strictly smaller length in $traces_{\mathsf{E}}(B_1)$ have been shown to be in $traces_{\mathsf{E}}(A_1)$. We may write $t = se$ where $e \in B_1$ and $s \in traces_{\mathsf{E}}(B_1)$ is a string of strictly smaller length to which the inductive hypothesis applies. Hence $s \in traces_{\mathsf{E}}(A_1)$. Suppose first that e is one of the e_i. Because T is confluent, $e \in T/e_1$ and hence e must be enabled in A_1. By Lemma 3.1, it must be the case that $\rho_1(e) = \mathsf{T}$. Therefore e is permanently enabled in A_1 and clearly $se \in traces_{\mathsf{E}}(A_1)$.

Now suppose that e is one of the f_j. Because $se \in traces_{\mathsf{E}}(B_1)$, we know from Lemma 2.1 that $v_{e_1 s}(\rho(e)) = \mathsf{T}$ in BA. Note that the Boolean expression $\rho_i(e) \in BA_i$ does not involve the generator e_i. Furthermore, if e_i appears in s then by purity we may write $(e_1 s)/e_i = e_1(s/e_i)$. This allows us to simplify the expression for $\rho(e)$ as shown below.

$$v_{e_1 s}(\rho(e)) = v_s(\rho_1(e)) \;\vee\; \left(\bigvee_{[s](e_i)=1} v_{e_1(s/e_i)}(\rho_i(e)) \right).$$

Hence, either $v_s(\rho_1(e)) = \mathsf{T}$ or there must be some k, with $[s](e_k) = 1$, such that $v_{e_1(s/e_k)}(\rho_k(e)) = \mathsf{T}$ in A_k.

If the former then, by Lemma 2.1, $se \in traces_{\mathsf{E}}(A_1)$ and we are done. So suppose the latter. Since $e_1 s$ and e_k are both in T, and T is confluent, it follows that $e_k((e_1 s)/e_k) = e_k e_1(s/e_k) \in T$. Hence, $e_1(s/e_k) \in T/e_k$ and so by Lemma 2.1 applied to A_k we see that $e_1(s/e_k)e \in T/e_k$. It follows that $e_k e_1(s/e_k)e \in T$ which we may rewrite as saying that $e \in T/(e_k e_1(s/e_k))$.

Note that $e_1 s(e_k/(e_1 s)) = e_1 s$, since e_k appears in s, and so by Lemma 2.3(4), $[e_1 s] = [e_k e_1(s/e_k)]$. Since T is confluent, Lemma 2.4(2) tells us that $e \in T/(e_1 s)$. In other words, $se \in T/e_1$. Hence $t \in traces_{\mathsf{E}}(A_1)$ as required. It follows by induction that $traces_{\mathsf{E}}(B_1) \subseteq traces_{\mathsf{E}}(A_1)$.

We have shown that for each $1 \le i \le n$, $T/e_i = traces_{\mathsf{E}}(B_i)$ and it follows as remarked above that $T = traces_{\mathsf{E}}(A)$. Since A is a $\{\wedge, \vee\}$-automaton on the correct set of events, the Proposition follows by induction.

QED

4 Deterministic automata

We now consider how to extend the results above to action traces. The first point to note is that Proposition 3.1 is false, as stated, if action traces are used in place of event traces. Consider the following $\{\wedge, \vee\}$-automaton.

$$C5 = \begin{array}{|ccc|} \hline a & \top & \alpha \\ b & a & \beta \\ c & \top & \alpha \\ d & c & \gamma \\ \hline \end{array}$$

It is easy to see that $\alpha\beta$ and $\alpha\gamma$ are action traces of $C5$. But $\alpha\gamma/\alpha\beta = \gamma$ and the string $\alpha\beta\gamma = \alpha\beta(\alpha\gamma/\alpha\beta)$ is not an action trace of $C5$. Hence $traces_{\mathsf{A}}(C5)$ is not confluent.

The missing ingredient is determinism. The following definition accords exactly with the informal one given at the start of the Introduction.

Definition 4.1 *A causal automaton E is said to be deterministic if, whenever $E \stackrel{s}{\Longrightarrow} F$ for some event trace s of E, then all enabled events in F have distinct labels.*

The labelling function ℓ of an automaton A gives rise to a function on traces, $\ell^* : traces_{\mathsf{E}}(E) \to traces_{\mathsf{A}}(E)$. This is always a surjection: every action trace arises from some underlying event trace. It is not in general a bijection. Note further that ℓ^* always commutes with juxtaposition: $\ell^*(st) = \ell^*(s)\ell^*(t)$.

Lemma 4.1 *If E is a deterministic $\{\wedge, \vee\}$-automaton then ℓ^* commutes with excess. That is, if $s, t \in traces_{\mathsf{E}}(E)$ then $\ell^*(s/t) = \ell^*(s)/\ell^*(t)$.*

Proof: The proof is by induction on the length of the second argument t. If $t = \varepsilon$ then $s/\varepsilon = s$ and $\ell^*(t) = \varepsilon$ so clearly $\ell^*(s/t) = \ell^*(s) = \ell^*(s)/\ell^*(t)$.

Now suppose that $t = a$ where a is an event in E and let $\ell(a) = \alpha$. There are two cases according as $[s](a) = 0$ or $[s](a) > 0$. Suppose the first, so that a does not appear in s.

We claim that then α does not appear in $\ell^*(s)$. Suppose on the contrary that it does and write $\ell^*(s) = \mu.\alpha.\nu$ where $[\mu](\alpha) = 0$. We can similarly write $s = m.e.n$ where $\ell^*(m) = \mu$, $\ell(e) = \alpha$ and $\ell^*(n) = \nu$. It is clear that a does not appear in m for otherwise α would necessarily appear in μ. Since $me \in traces_{\mathsf{E}}(E)$ it follows from Lemma 2.1 that $v_m(\rho(e)) = \mathsf{T}$. Also $v_{\mathsf{F}}(\rho(a)) = \mathsf{T}$ since a is enabled in E. But $v_{\mathsf{F}} \subseteq v_m$ and so, by Lemma 3.1, $v_m(\rho(a)) = \mathsf{T}$. Hence, by Lemma 2.1 again, if $E \stackrel{m}{\Longrightarrow} F$ then both a and e are enabled in F. But $\ell(a) = \ell(e) = \alpha$ which contradicts the fact that E is deterministic. This shows that α does not appear in $\ell^*(s)$. It follows from Lemma 2.3(2) that both $s/a = s$ and $\ell^*(s)/\ell^*(a) = \ell^*(s)$. Hence, $\ell^*(s/a) = \ell^*(s)/\ell^*(a)$ as required.

Now suppose that a does appear in s. We may write $s = m.a.n$ where $[m](a) = 0$. Then $\ell^*(s) = \ell^*(m).\alpha.\ell^*(n)$ and by the preceding paragraph $[\ell^*(m)](\alpha) = 0$. It is then easy to see that $s/a = mn$ and, by a similar argument, that $\ell^*(s)/\alpha = \ell^*(m)\ell^*(n)$. It follows that $\ell^*(s/a) = \ell^*(s)/\ell^*(a)$ as required.

This argument suffices to start off the induction. Suppose now that we have $t \in traces_{\mathsf{E}}(E)$ of length greater than 1 and that the result has been shown to hold (for arbitrary first argument) for all event traces of length strictly less than t. We can write $t = t_1t_2$ where both t_1 and t_2 have length strictly less than t. Then $\ell^*(s/(t_1t_2)) = \ell^*((s/t_1)/t_2) = \ell^*(s/t_1)/\ell^*(t_2)$ by the inductive hypothesis applied to t_2. Proceeding further, by the inductive hypothesis applied to t_1, $\ell^*(s/t_1) = \ell^*(s)/\ell^*(t_1)$. Hence, $\ell^*(s/t) = (\ell^*(s)/\ell^*(t_1))/\ell^*(t_2) = \ell^*(s)/(\ell^*(t_1)\ell^*(t_2)) = \ell^*(s)/\ell^*(t)$ as required. The result follows by induction.

QED

It is now a simple matter to prove the first part of Theorem 1.1.

Theorem 4.1 *If E is a deterministic $\{\wedge, \vee\}$-automaton then $traces_{\mathsf{A}}(E)$ is a confluent trace set.*

Proof: Choose action traces $\mu, \nu \in traces_{\mathsf{A}}(E)$. Let $m, n \in traces_{\mathsf{E}}(E)$ be event traces such that $\ell^*(m) = \mu$ and $\ell^*(n) = \nu$. By Proposition 3.1, $traces_{\mathsf{E}}(E)$ is confluent and so certainly $m(n/m) \in traces_{\mathsf{E}}(E)$. Hence $\ell^*(m(n/m))$ is an action trace. But now Lemma 4.1 shows that $\ell^*(m(n/m)) = \mu(\nu/\mu)$. So $\mu(\nu/\mu) \in traces_{\mathsf{A}}(E)$ and $traces_{\mathsf{A}}(E)$ is confluent. This completes the proof.

QED

5 Numbered traces

An arbitrary confluent set is not in general pure. In this section we present a method for constructing a pure trace set from any given trace set. The main result is that this method preserves confluence. This allows us to use Proposition 3.2 to prove the second part of Theorem 1.1. Let $\mathbf{N}^+$ denote the positive natural numbers.

Definition 5.1 *Given a set A, the numbering function, $\mu : A^* \times A^* \to (A \times \mathbf{N}^+)^*$ is given inductively by the equations*

$$\begin{aligned}\mu(r, \varepsilon) &= \varepsilon \\ \mu(r, sa) &= \mu(r, s).(a, [r](a) + [s](a) + 1)\,.\end{aligned}$$

We shall use the short-hand: $\mu_r(s) = \mu(r, s)$ and $\mu(s) = \mu_\varepsilon(s)$. It is easy to see that if $[p] = [q]$ then $\mu_p = \mu_q$, so that μ factors over $A^{\mathbf{N}} \times A^*$. As an example of a numbered string, if $t = aabacaccb$, then $\mu(t)$ is

$$(a,1)(a,2)(b,1)(a,3)(c,1)(a,4)(c,2)(c,3)(b,2).$$

The effect of the first argument is to translate the numbering: if $r = bcbecc$ then $\mu_r(t)$ is

$$(a,1)(a,2)(b,3)(a,3)(c,4)(a,4)(c,5)(c,6)(b,4).$$

Unlike t, both these strings are pure. The numbering function satisfies many interesting identities and the next result collects together those which are of immediate benefit to us. To avoid unnecessary complication, we have chosen not to state these in their most general form.

Lemma 5.1 *Let A be a set and $r, s \in A^*$ be strings over A. The following statements are true.*

1. $[\mu(s)](a,k) = \begin{cases} 0 & \text{if } k > [s](a) \\ 1 & \text{otherwise} \end{cases}$

2. $\mu(rs) = \mu(r)\mu_r(s)$.

3. $\mu_s(r/s) = \mu(r)/\mu(s)$.

4. $\mu(r(s/r)) = \mu(r)(\mu(s)/\mu(r))$.

Proof: *1.* By induction on the length of s. If $s = \varepsilon$ then from the definition $\mu(s) = \varepsilon$. Hence $[\mu(s)](a,k) = 0$. Since $k > 0$ by convention, certainly $k > [s](a)$ and so the result is true. Now suppose that $s \in A^*$ is non-empty and the result has been shown to hold for all strings of length strictly less than s. We can write $s = tb$ where $b \in A$ and the inductive hypothesis applies to t. Then, by definition, $\mu(s) = \mu(t).(b, [t](b) + 1)$.

Consider the two cases separately. If $k > [s](a)$ then certainly $k > [t](a)$ and so by the inductive hypothesis $[\mu(t)](a,k) = 0$. Hence $[\mu(s)](a,k) = [(b, [t](b) + 1)](a,k)$. If $a \neq b$ then this is certainly zero. If $a = b$ then still $k > [s](a) = [t](a) + 1$. Hence $[\mu(s)](a,k) = 0$ as required.

Now suppose $k \leq [s](a)$. If also $k \leq [t](a)$ then by the inductive hypothesis $[\mu(t)](a,k) = 1$. Since $(b, [t](b) + 1) \neq (a,k)$ it follows that $[\mu(s)](a,k) = 1$ as required. If, on the other hand, $k > [t](a)$ then again by the inductive hypothesis $[\mu(t)](a,k) = 0$. However, $[s](a) = [t](a) + [b](a)$, so it must be the case that $a = b$ and $k = [s](a)$. But then $(b, [t](b) + 1) = (a,k)$ and so $[\mu(s)](a,k) = 1$ as required.

2. By induction on the length of s. If $s = \varepsilon$ then the result is easily seen to hold. So suppose that s is a non-empty string and that the result has been shown to hold for all strings of strictly smaller length and arbitrary r. We may write $s = ta$ where $a \in A$ and the inductive hypothesis applies to t. Then, $\mu(rs) = \mu((rt)a) = \mu(r)\mu_r(t)(a, [rt](a) + 1)$. On the other hand, by definition, $\mu_r(ta) = \mu_r(t).(a, [r](a) + [t](a) + 1)$. It follows from Lemma 2.3(1) that $\mu(r.s) = \mu(r).\mu_r(s)$.

3. By induction on the length of r. If $r = \varepsilon$ then the result is easily seen to hold. So suppose that r is a non-empty string and that the result holds for all strings of length strictly less than r and arbitrary s. We may write $r = ta$ where $a \in A$ and the inductive hypothesis applies to t. Since $ta/s = (t/s)(a/(s/t))$, it is easy to see from Lemma 2.3(3) that

$$ta/s = \begin{cases} (t/s)a & \text{if } [s](a) \leq [t](a) \\ (t/s) & \text{otherwise} \end{cases}$$

We shall consider each of these cases separately. First suppose that $[s](a) \leq [t](a)$. Then,

$$\mu_s(ta/s) = \mu_s((t/s)a) = (\mu(t)/\mu(s))(a, [s](a) + [t/s](a) + 1).$$

On the other hand,

$$\mu(ta)/\mu(s) = \mu(t)(a, [t](a) + 1)/\mu(s)$$

But, by part *1*, $[\mu(s)](a, [t](a) + 1) = 0$ since $[t](a) + 1 > [s](a)$. Similarly, $[\mu(t)](a, [t](a) + 1) = 0$ since $[t](a) + 1 > [t](a)$. Hence, $[\mu(s)](a, [t](a) + 1) \leq$

$[\mu(t)](a, [t](a)+1)$. So by the previous paragraph, applied to numbered strings, we see that $\mu(ta)/\mu(s) = (\mu(t)/\mu(s))(a, [t](a)+1)$. Finally, by Lemma 2.3(3), $[t/s](a) = [t](a) - [s](a)$. So $\mu_s(r/s) = \mu(r)/\mu(s)$ as required.

Now suppose that $[s](a) > [t](a)$. Then $\mu_s(ta/s) = \mu_s(t/s) = \mu(t)/\mu(s)$. Also $\mu(ta)/\mu(s) = (\mu(t)(a, [t](a)+1))/\mu(s)$. But now, by part *1*, $[\mu(s)](a, [t](a)+1) = 1$ since $[t](a)+1 \leq [s](a)$ and similarly $[\mu(t)](a, [t](a)+1) = 0$. Hence, $[\mu(s)](a, [t](a)+1) > [\mu(t)](a, [t](a)+1)$ and, as remarked above, this shows that $(\mu(t)(a, [t](a)+1))/\mu(s) = \mu(t)/\mu(s)$. Hence $\mu_s(r/s) = \mu(r)/\mu(s)$ as required.

4. By parts *2* and *3*, $\mu(r(s/r)) = \mu(r)\mu_r(s/r) = \mu(r)(\mu(s)/\mu(r))$.

QED

Let $\pi : A \times \mathrm{N}^+ \rightarrow A$ be projection on to the first component of a numbered pair: $\pi(a, k) = a$. This extends in the usual way to a function on strings: $\pi^* : (A \times \mathrm{N}^+)^* \rightarrow A^*$. It is easy to see from the definition of the numbering function that

$$\pi^*(\mu_r(s)) = s$$

and this has some simple consequences.

Lemma 5.2 *Let A be a set and $s, t \in A^*$ be strings. The following statements are true.*

1. *If $\mu(s) = \mu(t)$ then $s = t$.*
2. *If $\mu(t) = \mu(s)(a, k)$ then $t = sa$ and $k = [t](a)$.*

Proof: *1*. $s = \pi^*(\mu(s)) = \pi^*(\mu(t)) = t$.

2. t cannot be empty since (a, k) appears in $\mu(t)$, so we can write $t = ub$ where $b \in A$. Hence $\mu(t) = \mu(u)(b, [u](b)+1)$. Comparing this with $\mu(s)(a, k)$ we see that $\mu(u) = \mu(s)$ and $(b, [u](b)+1) = (a, k)$. It follows from part *1* that $u = s$. Also, $b = a$ and $k = [s](a)+1$. Hence $t = sa$, and it is clear that $[t](a) = k$, as required.

QED

We can now prove the result which we have been working towards.

Theorem 5.1 *If T is a confluent trace set, there exists a deterministic $\{\wedge, \vee\}$-automaton, E, such that $traces_{\mathsf{A}}(E) = T$.*

Proof: Let A be the set of elements which appear in the traces of T and let $\mu(T) \subseteq (A \times \mathrm{N}^+)^*$ be the corresponding set of numbered traces: $\mu(T) = \{\mu(t)$ such that $t \in T\}$. It follows from Lemma 5.1(1) that $\mu(T)$ is pure and from Lemma 5.1(4) that $\mu(T)$ is confluent. Hence, by Proposition 3.2, there exists a $\{\wedge, \vee\}$-automaton E such that $traces_{\mathsf{E}}(E) = \mu(T)$.

In the construction of E the labelling function was not relevant and was taken to be the identity. We are at liberty to provide an alternative. It is clear that $E \subseteq A \times \mathrm{N}^+$ so we can take $\ell_E = \pi|_E$, the restriction to E of the projection function defined above. If $\mu(t) \in traces_{\mathsf{E}}(E)$ then $\ell_E^*(\mu(t)) = \pi^*(\mu(t)) = t$. It follows that $traces_{\mathsf{A}}(E) = T$.

It remains to show that E is deterministic under this labelling. Suppose not and assume that $E \overset{\mu(s)}{\Longrightarrow} F$ and F contains two enabled events with the same label. These events must have the form (a, k_1) and (a, k_2) where $k_1 \neq k_2$. Moreover, since they are both enabled, $\mu(s)(a, k_1)$ and $\mu(s)(a, k_2)$ must both be event traces of E. It follows from Lemma 5.2(2) that $k_1 = [s](a) + 1 = k_2$. This contradiction shows that E must be deterministic. The result follows.

QED

This completes the proof of Theorem 1.1.

6 Conclusion

We have introduced causal automata, a new formalism for describing (finite) reactive systems and have shown how they can be used to characterise and shed light upon Milner's notion of confluence in CCS. We believe that the formalism has the virtues of simplicity and generality and that its operational behaviour is particularly easy to understand (at least at a superficial level). A more systematic study should appear in a sequel to the present paper, [6], where we hope to discuss several of the issues which were raised in the Introduction.

ACKNOWLEDGEMENTS

The work described here was undertaken as part of project VESPA at Hewlett-Packard's Information Systems Centre in Bristol, England. I am grateful to Claudio Condini and Miranda Mowbray for spotting various *faux pas*. Thanks are also due to Matthew Hennessy and Gérard Boudol for much-needed encouragement while some of the ideas were being developed. Any indiscretions that remain are due solely to my own efforts.

References

[1] Aceto L, De Nicola R, Fantechi A. Testing Equivalences for Event Structures. In: Proceedings Advanced School, Rome. Springer LNCS 280.

[2] Boudol G, Castellani I. Permutation of Transitions: an Event Structure Semantics for CCS. INRIA Research Report No 798. February 1988.

[3] Degano P, De Nicola R, Montanari U. Partial Orderings Descriptions and Observations of Nondeterministic Concurrent Processes. In: Proceedings REX Workshop. Springer LNCS 354, 1989.

[4] Gunawardena J. Purely Parallel Processes. Technical Memo HPL-ISC-TM-89-002, Hewlett-Packard Laboratories, Information Systems Centre, March 1989.

[5] Gunawardena J. Deducing Causal Relationships in CCS. In: Veni Madhavan CE (ed). Foundations of Software Technology and Theoretical Computer Science. Proceedings, 1989. Springer LNCS 405, 1989. Also Technical Memo HPL-ISC-TM-89-077, Hewlett-Packard Laboratories, Information Systems Centre, May 1989.

[6] Gunawardena J. Boolean Algebras for Concurrency. In preparation. Expanded version of a talk given at the 2nd Workshop on Concurrency and Compositionality, San Miniato, Italy, 28 February - 3 March, 1990.

[7] Harel D, Pnueli A. On the Development of Reactive Systems. In: Apt KR (ed). Logics and Models of Concurrent Systems. Springer, 1985.

[8] Hoare CAR. Communicating Sequential Processes. International Series in Computer Science. Prentice-Hall, 1985.

[9] Johnstone PT. Notes on Logic and Set Theory. Cambridge Mathematical Textbooks. Cambridge Univeristy Press, 1987.

[10] Milner R. A Calculus of Communicating Systems. Springer LNCS 92, 1980.

[11] Milner R. Communication and Concurrency. International Series in Computer Science. Prentice-Hall, 1989.

[12] Nielsen M, Plotkin G, Winskel G. Petri Nets, Event Structures and Domains. Theoretical Computer Science, 1981;13: 85-108.

[13] Olderog E-R, Goltz U, van Glabbeek R (eds). Combining Compositionality and Concurrency. GMD Report 320, Gesellschaft Für Mathematik und Datenverarbeitung, Bonn. June 1988.

[14] Rem M. Trace Theory and Systolic Computations. In: de Bakker JW, Nijman AJ, Treleaven PC (eds). PARLE, Parallel Architectures and Languages Europe. Proceedings, Volume I. Springer LNCS 258, 1987.

[15] Vaandrager FW. Determinism $\rightarrow$ (Event structure isomorphism = Step sequence equivalence). CWI Report CS-R8839. Amsterdam, October 1988.

[16] Winskel G. Event Structures. In: Brauer W, Reisig W, Rozenberg G (eds). Advances in Petri Nets. Springer LNCS 255.

A Simple Generalization of Kahn's Principle to Indeterminate Dataflow Networks

(Extended Abstract)

*Eugene W. Stark**
Department of Computer Science
State University of New York at Stony Brook
Stony Brook, NY 11794 USA
(stark@sbcs.sunysb.edu)

Abstract

Kahn's principle states that if each process in a dataflow network computes a continuous input/output function, then so does the entire network. Moreover, in that case the function computed by the network is the least fixed point of a continuous functional determined by the structure of the network and the functions computed by the individual processes. Previous attempts to generalize this principle in a straightforward way to "indeterminate" networks, in which processes need not compute functions, have been either too complex or have failed to give results consistent with operational semantics. In this paper, we give a simple, direct generalization of Kahn's fixed-point principle to a large class of indeterminate dataflow networks, and we sketch a proof that results obtained by the generalized principle are in agreement with a natural operational semantics.

1 Introduction

Dataflow networks are a parallel programming paradigm in which a collection of concurrently and asynchronously executing sequential processes communicate by transmitting sequences or "streams" of "tokens" containing data values over unidirectional FIFO communication channels. Kahn [13, 14] envisioned a simple programming language built on this paradigm, in which the communication primitives available to processes are sufficiently restrictive that only functional processes can be programmed. That is, each process may be viewed as computing a function from the complete history of values received on its input channels to the complete history of values emitted on its output channels. Kahn argued that such processes compute functions that are in fact continuous with respect to a suitable complete partial order (cpo) structure on the sets of input and output histories. Moreover, a network of such processes also computes a continuous function, which can be characterized as the least fixed point of a continuous functional associated with the network. This

*Research supported in part by NSF Grants CCR-8702247 and CCR-8902215.

elegant idea has been called "the Kahn principle," and it has been shown [9, 19, 30] to give results in agreement with a natural "token-pushing" operational semantics.

In practical programming applications of the dataflow idea, the restriction to functional processes is somewhat limiting, because there are useful programs one wants to write that do not describe processes with functional input/output behavior. An example of a class of such processes are the *merge* processes, which shuffle together values arriving on two input channels onto a single output channel. A variety of such processes can be defined, corresponding to various conditions under which arriving inputs are guaranteed to be eventually transmitted to the output [22, 33]. They do not have functional behaviors, because in general there are many possible output interleavings for a single pair of input sequences. We use the term *indeterminate* to refer to dataflow networks in which processes need not have functional behaviors.

There have been many attempts to generalize Kahn's theory to a class of indeterminate networks. The obvious idea of generalizing functions to relations fails to give results consistent with token-pushing semantics. This fact was first noticed by Keller [15], and subsequently became known as the "Brock/Ackerman anomaly," after Brock and Ackerman [7] demonstrated convincingly by some clever examples that no denotational semantics based on set-theoretic input/output relations can give results consistent with token-pushing semantics. Subsequently, a rather large literature has developed on this subject. A variety of sophisticated approaches, such as powerdomains [1, 8], categories [3], "scenarios" [6, 7], sets of "linear traces" [4, 11, 16, 21], "pomsets" [10], multilinear algebra [20], and other ideas [17, 23, 24, 28, 31, 29] have been tried, but up until now none of these approaches has resulted in a truly simple and natural generalization of Kahn's principle that also maintains a clear connection with operational semantics.

In the remainder of this extended abstract, we present a very simple and straightforward generalization of Kahn's principle, and sketch a proof that it gives results in agreement with operational semantics. Complete details of the proof will appear elsewhere, in the full version of the paper [34].

2 Kahn's Fixed-Point Principle

To give a precise statement of the Kahn principle, we must first formalize the notion of the input/output relation of a dataflow network. We begin by postulating a countably infinite set $\mathcal{V}$, whose elements represent the possible *data values* that can be communicated between processes. For convenience, we suppose that $\mathcal{V}$ contains at least all the natural numbers. Let $\mathcal{V}^\infty$ be the set of all finite and infinite sequences of elements of $\mathcal{V}$, partially ordered by the *prefix relation* $\sqsubseteq$. We use ϵ to denote the empty sequence, which is the least element of $\mathcal{V}^\infty$. If X is a finite or countably infinite set (of *channels*), then an *X-history* is a function from X to $\mathcal{V}^\infty$. We think of such a function as representing the complete history of values communicated on the channels in X during some computation of a dataflow network. Let HX denote the set of all X-histories, then HX is also partially ordered, with $x \sqsubseteq x'$ iff $x(c) \sqsubseteq x'(c)$ for all $c \in X$. The poset HX has the structure of a *Scott domain* (an ω-algebraic, consistently complete cpo [26]). The least element $\perp$ is the identically ϵ function. The *finite elements* (or *compact elements*, or *isolated elements*) of HX are exactly those histories x with $x(c)$ finite for all channels $c \in X$, and with $x(c) = \epsilon$

for all but finitely many $c \in X$. It is also important for us that HX is *finitary*, which means that each finite element can have at most a finite set of elements below it.

Functions on channel sets induce corresponding functions on channel histories. Formally, if X and Y are sets of channels, then a function $\phi : Y \to X$ induces a function $H\phi : HX \to HY$ satisfying $H\phi(x)(c) = x(\phi(c))$ for all $c \in Y$. The function $H\phi$ is obviously continuous; in fact the mapping H is a contravariant functor from the category of at most countable sets and functions to the category of Scott domains and continuous maps. Moreover, this functor maps the empty set to the one-point domain, and maps coproducts of sets (disjoint union) to products of domains; that is, we have a natural isomorphism $H(X+Y) \simeq HX \times HY$.

In Section 5, we shall continue with this formal development, defining an operational model for dataflow networks in which both a network and its constituent processes are represented as a certain kind of automata having fixed sets of input and output channels. Computation of a dataflow network may be regarded as a token-pushing game played on a graph whose nodes are automata, and whose arcs indicate when an output channel c of one automaton A is connected to an input channel d of another automaton B (we admit the possibility that $A = B$). As execution progresses, the automata change state and tokens containing data values move around on the graph. Communication between automata occurs when a token containing a data value is simultaneously output on channel c by process A and input on channel d by process B. This synchronized communication model looks at first glance to be different from the usual formulations of operational semantics for dataflow networks, in which communication channels are regarded as FIFO buffers distinct from processes. Instead of following the usual approach, we find it more convenient and economical to imagine each process as having, for each of its input channels, a component of its internal state that serves as an input buffer for that channel. We do not actually impose any direct structural requirements on the states of an automaton, but instead merely axiomatize the essential properties of the transition relation that are consequences of this structure. Among other things, the axioms imply that an automaton is always prepared to accept arbitrary input on an input channel (the buffer is never full), and the production of output in a step can depend only on input received in a previous step. In this way, we obtain the effect of a buffered communication model without the notational inconvenience.

Once a formal definition of "token-pushing semantics" has been given, it becomes possible to define the input/output relation of a network. In particular, the input/output relation of a network with input channels X and output channels Y is a subset of $HX \times HY$, whose elements are pairs $\langle x, y\rangle$ representing the history of input and output that could occur in one particular network computation. We are not interested in including in the input/output relation pairs $\langle x, y\rangle$ corresponding to all possible computations, but rather only in those pairs obtained from *completed* computations. Intuitively, a computation of a network is completed if each component process that is capable of performing some non-input step eventually does so. We need this condition to rule out uninteresting computations in which a process fails to process data in its input buffer simply because that process is never scheduled to execute a step. Having defined the input/output relation of a network, we may then classify networks as *determinate* or *indeterminate* according to whether or not their input/output relations are functional (*i.e.* are graphs of functions from

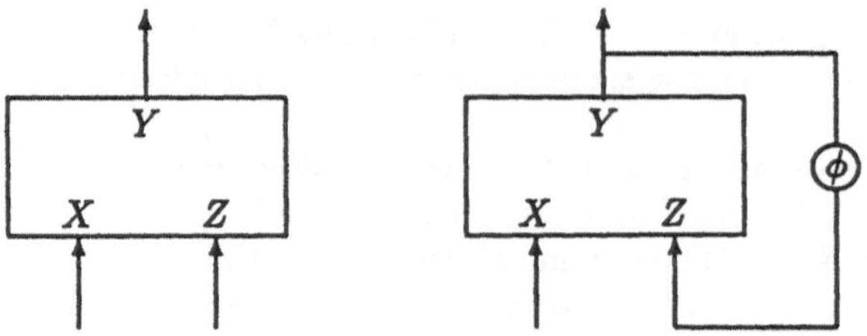

Figure 1: An Open-Loop Network and One with Feedback

HX to HY) or nonfunctional. In [19] it is shown that, for a formal operational model of dataflow networks defined along these lines, if the input/output relation of a network is functional, then in fact it is the graph of a continuous function from HX to HY.

Kahn's principle concerns determinate networks. In its simplest form, the principle gives a relationship between the function computed by a determinate network with a feedback loop and the corresponding "open-loop" network. The principle may be stated as follows:

The Kahn Principle

Suppose a network computes the continuous function $f : HX \times HZ \to HY$. Let $\phi : Z \to Y$ be an injective function, which we regard as designating, for each channel in Z, a corresponding channel in Y to which it is to be connected in a feedback loop (see Figure 1). Define the *feedback functional*

$$\Phi : [HX \to HY] \to [HX \to HY]$$

by

$$\Phi(g)(x) = f(x, H\phi(g(x))).$$

Then Φ is continuous, and the function computed by the closed-loop network is the least fixed-point $\mu\Phi$ of Φ.

3 A Generalization of Kahn's Principle

To motivate the generalized version of Kahn's principle, we reconsider the original version stated above, with a few changes in notation. First of all, instead of representing the behavior of a network with input channels X and output channels Y by a continuous function $f : HX \to HY$, let us use instead the function $p : HX \to [HY \to HY]$ defined by $p(x)(y) = f(x) \sqcap y$. Here $f(x) \sqcap y$ denotes the greatest lower bound of $f(x)$ and y, which always exists due to the fact that HY is a consistently complete cpo, and is continuous because HX and HY are algebraic. Observe that no information is lost in replacing f by p, because $f(x) = \bigsqcup\{y : y = p(x)(y)\}$. Note also that for each $x \in X$ the function $p(x) : HY \to HY$ has the following properties:

1. $p(x) \circ p(x) = p(x)$.

2. $p(x) \sqsubseteq \mathrm{id}_{HY}$.

That is, $p(x)$ is a *projection* on the domain HY [12]. In the sequel, we use $\mathcal{P}(D)$ to denote the set of all projections on the domain D. It can be shown that $\mathcal{P}(D)$, partially ordered by $\sqsubseteq$, is a domain; in fact it is a complete lattice.

Now, let us redefine the feedback functional to be compatible with the new notation. If $p : HX \times HZ \to \mathcal{P}(HY)$ represents the open-loop behavior of a network, and $\phi : Z \to Y$ is an injective function, then the corresponding feedback functional

$$\Psi : [HX \to [HY \to HY]] \to [HX \to [HY \to HY]]$$

is defined by

$$\Psi qxy = p\langle x, H\phi(qxy)\rangle y.$$

Here, and in the rest of the paper, we omit unnecessary parentheses under the convention that application associates to the left, and we use angle brackets to indicate tupling of arguments. It is immediate from the above definition that Ψ is continuous. Moreover, the least fixed point $\mu\Psi$ of Ψ determines the least fixed point $\mu\Phi$ of Φ in the same way as p determines f.

Proposition 3.1 $\mu\Phi x = \bigsqcup\{y : y = \mu\Psi xy\}$.

We thus see that Kahn's principle generalizes in a straightforward way to the new representation of network behaviors. However, the new representation has an important advantage over the old one: it is general enough to permit the specification of some nonfunctional behaviors. We observed above that if $f : HX \to HY$ is continuous, and $p : HX \to \mathcal{P}(HY)$ is defined by $pxy = fx \sqcap y$, then $fx = \bigsqcup\{y : y = pxy\}$; that is to say, fx is the maximal fixed point of the projection $px \in \mathcal{P}(HY)$. Instead of just considering functions $p : HX \to \mathcal{P}(HY)$ of the form $fx \sqcap y$, we may consider the whole class of continuous functions $p : HX \to \mathcal{P}(HY)$. For an arbitrary such function p, the set of fixed points of px need not be directed, hence it may contain many maximal elements. Given $x \in HX$, we regard each maximal fixed point y of px as a possible output on input x, and in this way we may think of the function p as describing an indeterminate network whose input/output relation is the set of all $\langle x, y\rangle$ such that y is a maximal fixed point of px.

As a simple example of an indeterminate behavior, consider a network with no input channels ($X = \emptyset$, hence $HX \simeq \{\bot\}$) and one output channel ($Y = \{*\}$, hence $HY \simeq \mathcal{V}^{\infty}$), which simply emits an arbitrary infinite sequence of values on its output channel. Such a network is described by the function $p : HX \to \mathcal{P}(HY)$ satisfying $pxy = y$. It is clear that any maximal element y of HY is a maximal fixed point of $p\bot$, hence determines a pair $\langle \bot, y\rangle$ in the input/output relation of the network. This kind of "oracle" network can be used in the construction of a variety of other indeterminate behaviors. For example, it can be shown that a network that implements a kind of merging operation called *infinity-fair merge* [22, 33] can be constructed using functional components and an oracle that outputs an infinite sequence of natural numbers.

Although the generalizations we have made so far permit us to describe some indeterminate networks, we can get a larger and more interesting class by making one further generalization. The additional generalization is to replace the single map $p : HX \to \mathcal{P}(HY)$ by two maps: $p : HX \to \mathcal{P}(D)$ and $l : D \to HY$, where D is an arbitrary finitary domain. We therefore arrive at the following general definition of an indeterminate behavior:

An (X, Y)-*behavior* is a triple (D, p, l), where D is a finitary domain, and $p : HX \to \mathcal{P}(D)$ and $l : D \to HY$ are continuous functions.

The *input/output relation* corresponding to an (X, Y)-behavior (D, p, l) is the set of all $\langle x, ld \rangle \in HX \times HY$ such that d is a maximal fixed point of the projection px.

As an example of the kind of indeterminate networks that can be described as behaviors (D, p, l), we consider *angelic merge*. A network that performs angelic merge has two input channels ($X = \{a, b\}$) and one output channel ($Y = \{c\}$), and operates by merging together the sequences of data values on its two input channels into a single output sequence. It is required to satisfy the following liveness condition: In any completed computation, if only a finite number of values arrive on one of the inputs, then eventually all the values from the *other* input will be transmitted to the output.

To describe angelic merge as an (X, Y)-behavior, we first define $\sigma : \{a, b\}^\infty \times HY \to HX$ to be the continuous function that on argument $\langle w, y \rangle$, splits the sequence of values y into two result sequences, where the ith value in y goes to the result sequence for channel a, if a is the ith value in the sequence w, otherwise to the result sequence for channel b. Angelic merge may then be defined to be the behavior $(\{a, b\}^\infty \times HY, p, l)$, where

- $l : \{a, b\}^\infty \times HY \to HY$ is defined by $l\langle w, y \rangle = y$.
- $p : HX \to \mathcal{P}(\{a, b\}^\infty \times HY)$ satisfies the following condition: for each $x \in HX$, $w \in \{a, b\}^\infty$, and $y \in HY$, $px\langle w, y \rangle$ is the greatest $\langle w', y' \rangle \sqsubseteq \langle w, y \rangle$ such that $\sigma\langle w', y' \rangle \sqsubseteq x$.

Many interesting indeterminate networks can be constructed using angelic merge and functional components. However, it should be pointed out that there is yet a more powerful kind of merging operation that cannot be described as a behavior (D, p, l). This is the *fair merge*, which shuffles two input sequences together onto a single output sequence in such a way that every value in both input channels eventually appears in the output channel. The results of this paper do not apply to indeterminate networks having this powerful merging capability.

We now state our generalized version of Kahn's principle.

The Generalized Kahn Principle

Suppose (D, p, l) is an $(X \times Z, Y)$-behavior that corresponds to the open-loop network shown in Figure 1. Let $\phi : Z \to Y$ be an injective function that assigns to each input channel in Z a corresponding output channel in Y. Define the *feedback functional* corresponding to (D, p, l) and ϕ to be the map:

$$\Phi : [HX \to [D \to D]] \to [HX \to [D \to D]]$$

defined by:

$$\Phi qxd = p\langle x, H\phi(l(qxd)) \rangle d.$$

Then Φ is continuous, and $(D, \mu\Phi, l)$ is the behavior corresponding to the closed-loop network.

4 Resolution of the Anomalies

In this section, we briefly examine the way in which Keller/Brock/Ackerman-type "anomalies" are avoided by our semantics for networks. We consider a particularly simple example of such an anomaly, due to J. Russell [25]. Suppose P is a process, having one input channel and one output channel, that obeys the following intuitive algorithm: Nondeterministically choose either: (1) read an input value, then output 0 followed by 1, or (2) output 0, read an input value, then output 0. Let Q be a similar process that has the additional possibility: (3) output 0, read an input value, then output 1. The input/output relation of P consists of all pairs of histories of the form $\langle \bot, 0\rangle$, $\langle vx, 01\rangle$, or $\langle vx, 00\rangle$, where v is an arbitrary value in $\mathcal{V}$, and x an arbitrary sequence of elements of $\mathcal{V}$. The input/output relation of Q is identical to that of P.

Even though P and Q have identical input/output relations, a difference between the two processes can be detected by placing them in a feedback loop. If $P_{\circlearrowleft\phi}$ denotes the network consisting of P with its output fed back to its input, and similarly for $Q_{\circlearrowleft\phi}$, then under token-pushing semantics the set of possible outputs of $P_{\circlearrowleft\phi}$ is $\{\bot, 00\}$, whereas the set of possible outputs of $Q_{\circlearrowleft\phi}$ is $\{\bot, 00, 01\}$. This demonstrates that no semantics for indeterminate networks, in which processes and networks are represented by their input/output relations, can support a definition of the feedback operation that gives results in agreement with token-pushing semantics.

Let us now see how the difficulty is resolved using our definition of behavior. Let $X = \{a\}$ and $Y = \{b\}$, and let $\{1,2\}_\bot$ denote the flat domain generated by $\{1,2\}$. Then the process P can be represented as the (X,Y)-behavior $(\{1,2\}_\bot \times HY, p, l)$, where $l\langle w, y\rangle = y$ and

$$p : HX \to [\{1,2\}_\bot \times HY \to \{1,2\}_\bot \times HY]$$

is defined as follows:

$$\begin{aligned} px\langle \bot, y\rangle &= \langle \bot, \bot\rangle \\ px\langle 1, y\rangle &= \begin{cases} \langle 1, \bot\rangle, & \text{if } x = \bot \\ \langle 1, 01 \sqcap y\rangle, & \text{otherwise.} \end{cases} \\ px\langle 2, y\rangle &= \begin{cases} \langle 2, 0 \sqcap y\rangle, & \text{if } x = \bot \\ \langle 2, 00 \sqcap y\rangle, & \text{otherwise.} \end{cases} \end{aligned}$$

Similarly, the process Q can be represented by the (X,Y)-behavior $(\{1,2,3\}_\bot \times HY, q, l)$, where

$$q : HX \to [\{1,2,3\}_\bot \times HY \to \{1,2,3\}_\bot \times HY]$$

is defined by:

$$\begin{aligned} qx\langle \bot, y\rangle &= \langle \bot, \bot\rangle \\ qx\langle 1, y\rangle &= px\langle 1, y\rangle \\ qx\langle 2, y\rangle &= px\langle 2, y\rangle \\ qx\langle 3, y\rangle &= \begin{cases} \langle 3, 0 \sqcap y\rangle, & \text{if } x = \bot \\ \langle 3, 01 \sqcap y\rangle, & \text{otherwise.} \end{cases} \end{aligned}$$

Let $\phi : X \to Y$ be the map taking a to b. Applying the generalized Kahn principle, the behavior of $P_{\circlearrowleft\phi}$ is the $(\emptyset, Y)$-behavior $(\{1,2\}_\perp \times HY, p_{\circlearrowleft\phi}, l)$, where

$$p_{\circlearrowleft\phi} : \{\perp\} \to [\{1,2\}_\perp \times HY \to \{1,2\}_\perp \times HY]$$

is defined by:

$$p\perp\langle w,y\rangle = \begin{cases} \langle\perp,\perp\rangle, & \text{if } w = \perp \\ \langle 1,\perp\rangle, & \text{if } w = 1 \\ \langle 2, 00 \sqcap y\rangle, & \text{if } w = 2. \end{cases}$$

The maximal fixed points of $p_{\circlearrowleft\phi}$ are $\{\langle 1,\perp\rangle, \langle 2,00\rangle\}$, hence the input/output relation of $P_{\circlearrowleft\phi}$ is $\{\langle\perp,\perp\rangle, \langle\perp,00\rangle\}$.

The behavior of $Q_{\circlearrowleft\phi}$ is the $(\emptyset, Y)$-behavior $(\{1,2,3\}_\perp \times HY, q_{\circlearrowleft\phi}, l)$, where

$$q_{\circlearrowleft\phi} : \{\perp\} \to [\{1,2,3\}_\perp \times HY \to \{1,2,3\}_\perp \times HY]$$

is defined by:

$$q\perp\langle w,y\rangle = \begin{cases} \langle\perp,\perp\rangle, & \text{if } w = \perp \\ \langle 1,\perp\rangle, & \text{if } w = 1 \\ \langle 2, 00 \sqcap y\rangle, & \text{if } w = 2 \\ \langle 3, 01 \sqcap y\rangle, & \text{if } w = 3. \end{cases}$$

The maximal fixed points of $q_{\circlearrowleft\phi}$ are $\{\langle 1,\perp\rangle, \langle 2,00\rangle, \langle 3,01\rangle\}$, hence the input/output relation of $Q_{\circlearrowleft\phi}$ is $\{\langle\perp,\perp\rangle, \langle\perp,00\rangle, \langle\perp,01\rangle\}$.

Evidently, the input/output relations of $P_{\circlearrowleft\phi}$ and $Q_{\circlearrowleft\phi}$, obtained by the generalized Kahn principle, are in agreement with token-pushing semantics.

5 Operational Semantics

In this section, we define an operational semantics for indeterminate dataflow networks. In this semantics a network is represented as a certain kind of automaton, called a *monotone automaton* [22, 33]. The construction of larger networks from component automata is modeled by certain operations on automata. In fact, assuming the existence of sufficiently many "basic" determinate automata (in particular, the existence of an automaton that computes function $H\phi : HX \to HY$ for each function $\phi : Y \to X$), then any finite network can be constructed using basic automata and just three network-building operations: *parallel composition*, *hiding*, and *feedback*. Parallel composition corresponds to simply placing two automata side-by-side in a network, without any communication. Hiding makes some of the output channels of an automaton into "internal" channels, which are not available for external communication. Feedback is the operation depicted in Figure 1. Hiding and parallel composition pose no particular semantic difficulties in the framework we have set up here, and we shall not discuss them further. The focus of our attention will instead be on the feedback operation.

5.1 Monotone Automata

A *monotone automaton* (henceforth simply "automaton") is a tuple

$$A = (X, W, Y, Q, \imath, T)$$

where

- X, W, and Y are pairwise disjoint sets of *channels*, which we assume are at most countable. The elements of X, Y, and W are called *input channels*, *output channels*, and *internal channels*, respectively. Let $E = (X+Y+W)\times\mathcal{V}$, then the elements of E are called *actions* of A. If $e = \langle c, v\rangle$ is an action of A, then we write $\text{chan}(e)$ for the channel component c and $\text{val}(e)$ for the value component v, of e. An action e is an *input action* or a *non-input action*, according to whether $\text{chan}(e) \in X$ or $\text{chan}(e) \notin X$.
- Q is a set of *states*, and $\text{I} \in Q$ is a distinguished *initial state*.
- $T : Q \times E \to Q$ is a partial *transition function*.

These data are required to satisfy the following conditions:

(Commutativity) For all states q and actions e, e', if $\text{chan}(e) \neq \text{chan}(e')$, $r = T(q,e)$, and $r' = T(q,e')$, then there exists a state s such that $s = T(r',e) = T(r,e')$.

(Receptivity) For all states q and input actions e, there exists a state r such that $r = T(q,e)$.

These automata are closely related to the input/output automata defined by Lynch and Tuttle [19], and also to the automata that have been studied by Bednarczyk [5], Kwiatkowska [18], and Shields [27].

A *transition* of A is a triple $q \xrightarrow{e} r$, where $r = T(q,e)$. We write $t : q \xrightarrow{e} r$, or just $q \xrightarrow{e} r$, to assert the existence of a transition $t = q \xrightarrow{e} r$ of A. Intuitively, a transition $q \xrightarrow{e} r$ represents a potential computation step of A in which action e occurs and the state changes from q to r. We say that action $e \in E$ is *enabled* in state q if there exists a transition $q \xrightarrow{e} r$ in T.

The receptivity condition in the definition of an automaton can be viewed as an abstract statement of the unboundedness of the buffers associated with input channels. The commutativity property can be thought of as saying that actions for different ports are concurrent, hence affect different components of the state. Together, the commutativity and receptivity imply the following *monotonicity* property: if non-input action e is enabled in state q, and e' is an arbitrary input action with $r = T(q,e')$, then e is enabled in state r as well. One can think of this condition as saying that it is possible to test for the *presence* of inputs in an input buffer, but not for their *absence*.

As an example of how we can model a dataflow process as an automaton, consider the case of the angelic merge process already discussed. Recall that $X = \{a,b\}$ and $Y = \{c\}$. Let $W = \{d\}$. We then represent the merge process as an automaton

$$A = (\{a,b\},\{d\},\{c\},\mathcal{V}^* \times \mathcal{V}^* \times \mathcal{V}^*, \langle\epsilon,\epsilon,\epsilon\rangle, T),$$

where there is a transition

$$\langle x_1, x_2, y\rangle \xrightarrow{e} \langle x_1', x_2', y'\rangle$$

iff one of the following conditions holds:

1. $e = \langle a, v\rangle$, $x_1' = x_1 v$, $x_2' = x_2$, and $y' = y$.

2. $e = \langle b, v\rangle$, $x_1' = x_1$, $x_2' = x_2 v$, and $y' = y$.

3. $e = \langle d, 1\rangle$, $vx_1' = x_1$, $x_2' = x_2$, and $y' = yv$.

4. $e = \langle d, 2\rangle$, $x_1' = x_1$, $vx_2' = x_2$, and $y' = yv$.

5. $e = \langle c, v\rangle$, $x_1' = x_1$, $x_2' = x_2$, and $vy' = y$.

It is straightforward to check that A satisfies the conditions for an automaton. In cases (3) and (4), the actions $\langle d, 1\rangle$ and $\langle d, 2\rangle$ are in E by our assumption that $\mathcal{V}$ contains all the natural numbers. (It is actually not important that the numbers 1 and 2 be used here; they could be replaced by any two distinct elements of $\mathcal{V}$.)

Intuitively, the state of A contains two "input buffers" and one "output buffer." Transitions of type (1) and (2) correspond to arriving input values being placed at the end of the appropriate input buffer. Transitions of type (3) and (4) are internal transitions that correspond to the indeterminate selection of input in one input buffer or the other to be moved to the output buffer. Transitions of type (5) correspond to the transmission of output from the output buffer. Similar constructions can be used to model many other kinds of dataflow processes.

5.2 Computations of Automata

Suppose $A = (X, W, Y, Q, \text{I}, T)$ is an automaton. A *finite computation sequence* for A is a finite sequence γ of transitions of A of the form:

$$q_0 \xrightarrow{e_1} q_1 \xrightarrow{e_2} \ldots \xrightarrow{e_n} q_n.$$

An *infinite computation sequence* is an infinite sequence of transitions:

$$q_0 \xrightarrow{e_1} q_1 \xrightarrow{e_2} \ldots.$$

Each computation sequence γ of A determines a corresponding *channel history* $\mathcal{H}(\gamma) \in H(X+W+Y)$, where for each channel $c \in X+W+Y$, the sequence $\mathcal{H}(\gamma)(c)$ is the subsequence of all $\text{val}(e_i)$ for those actions e_i with $\text{chan}(e_i) = c$. In view of the natural isomorphism $H(X+W+Y) \simeq HX \times HW \times HY$, we may think of the history $\mathcal{H}(\gamma)$ of a computation sequence γ as a triple $\langle x, w, y\rangle \in HX \times HW \times HY$, and it will generally be convenient to do so. Let $\mathcal{H}(A) \subseteq HX \times HW \times HY$ denote the set of all histories of initial computation sequences γ of A.

To state properly the next results, we need some concepts from domain theory. If D is a domain, then a *subdomain* of D is a subset U of D, which is a domain under the restriction of the ordering on D, such that the inclusion of U in D is continuous. A subdomain U is *normal* if for all $d \in D$, the set $\{u \in U : u \sqsubseteq d\}$ is directed. Suppose U is a subdomain of D, and let $m : U \to D$ be the inclusion map. If U is a normal subdomain of D, then we may define a map $e : D \to U$ by: $ed = \bigsqcup\{u \in U : u \sqsubseteq d\}$. It is then easy to see that $e \circ m = \text{id}_U$ and $m \circ e \sqsubseteq \text{id}_D$. Then $(m \circ e) \circ (m \circ e) = m \circ (e \circ m) \circ e = m \circ e$, so the map $m \circ e : D \to D$ is a projection, and $U = \{d \in D : d = m(ed)\}$. Thus, normal subdomains determine projections. Conversely, if $p : D \to D$ is a projection on a finitary domain D, then $U = p(D) = \{d \in D : d = pd\}$ is a normal subdomain of D. Hence there is a correspondence between projections on D and normal subdomains of D. In fact, the following is easily shown:

Proposition 5.1 *For any finitary*[1] *domain D, the set of all normal subdomains of D, partially ordered by inclusion, is a complete lattice that is isomorphic to the set of projections on D, partially ordered by $\sqsubseteq$. Moreover, if $\{D_i : i \in I\}$ is a collection of normal subdomains of D which is directed under inclusion order, then its supremum in the lattice of normal subdomains is given by:*

$$(\bigcup\{D_i : i \in I\})^c,$$

where $(\ )^c$ denotes closure under directed suprema.

An *interval* in a domain D is a pair $[d, d']$ of elements of D such that $d \sqsubseteq d'$. An interval $[d, d']$ is *prime* if there exists no $d'' \in D$ such that $d \sqsubset d'' \sqsubseteq d'$. The result below, proved in [29, 32], gives a great deal of information about the structure of the set $\mathcal{H}(A)$.

Proposition 5.2 *Suppose $A = (X, W, Y, Q, \iota, T)$ is an automaton. Then the set $\mathcal{H}(A)$, partially ordered by $\sqsubseteq$, is a normal subdomain of $HX \times HW \times HY$. Moreover, the inclusion of $\mathcal{H}(A)$ in $HX \times HW \times HY$ preserves prime intervals.*

From this, we can derive the following result, which is the basis for extracting behaviors from automata.

Proposition 5.3 *Suppose $A = (X, W, Y, Q, \iota, T)$ is an automaton. Then the map taking x to the set*

$$U(x) = \{\langle w, y\rangle : \langle x, w, y\rangle \in \mathcal{H}(A)\},$$

is a continuous function from HX to the lattice of normal subdomains of $HW \times HY$.

5.3 Behaviors of Automata

There is a simple way to obtain an (X, Y)-behavior from an automaton $A = (X, W, Y, Q, \iota, T)$. Specifically, let $D = HW \times HY$, and define functions

$$p : HX \to [D \to D] \qquad\qquad l : D \to HY$$

as follows:

$$\begin{aligned} px\langle w, y\rangle &= \bigsqcup\{\langle w', y'\rangle \sqsubseteq \langle w, y\rangle : \langle x, w', y'\rangle \in \mathcal{H}(A)\}. \\ l\langle w, y\rangle &= y. \end{aligned}$$

The definition of p makes sense because by Proposition 5.3, the set on the right-hand side is directed.

Proposition 5.4 *Suppose $A = (X, W, Y, Q, \iota, T)$ is an automaton and D, p, l are defined as above. Then (D, p, l) is an (X, Y)-behavior.*

[1]The author thanks Carl Gunter for pointing out that for a projection p on an arbitrary domain D, it is not necessarily the case that $p(D)$ is algebraic. However, in case D is finitary, then $p(d)$ is a finite element of $p(D)$ whenever d is a finite element of D, and this is sufficient for algebraicity.

Recall that we defined the input/output relation of an (X, Y)-behavior (D, p, l) to be the set of all $\langle x, ld \rangle$ such that d is a maximal fixed point of px. A few words are in order here about why this makes sense if (D, p, l) is the behavior of an automaton $A = (X, W, Y, Q, \text{I}, T)$. For such a behavior, a history $d \in D$ is a maximal fixed point of the projection px iff the history $\langle x, d \rangle$ is maximal among all histories of the form $\langle x, d' \rangle \in \mathcal{H}(A)$. In [22], it was shown that for monotone automata that are obtained by composing a collection of "sequential" component automata into networks, a history $\langle x, d \rangle$ is maximal among all histories of the form $\langle x, d' \rangle \in \mathcal{H}(A)$ iff $\langle x, d \rangle$ is the history of a "completed" or "fair" computation sequence. Since we wish all and only the completed computation sequences to contribute pairs to the input/output relation, we regard the coincidence of completedness and maximality as the justification for our definition of the input/output relation associated with a behavior. Of course, it might be that there are automata that are not representable as a network of sequential components, and whose input/output relations thus do not necessarily have any relationship to any concrete, intuitive notion of completed or fair computation sequences. However, we do not regard this potential extra generality of our model as any cause for alarm.

5.4 Automata from Behaviors

For certain (X, Y)-behaviors (D, p, l), it is possible to construct an automaton having (D, p, l) as its behavior up to isomorphism of the domain D. In particular, suppose (D, p, l) is an (X, Y)-behavior that satisfies the following assumptions:

1. $D \simeq HW \times HY$ for some set W.
2. For all $x \in HX$, the inclusion of the normal subdomain
$$\{\langle w, y \rangle \in HW \times HY : \langle w, y \rangle = px\langle w, y \rangle\}$$
in $HW \times HY$ preserves prime intervals.

Then, define Q to be the set of all finite elements of $HX \times HW \times HY$, and let $\text{I} = \langle \bot, \bot, \bot \rangle$. If $q \in Q$ and $e = \langle c, v \rangle \in (X + W + Y) \times \mathcal{V}$, then let $q; e \in Q$ denote the history such that $(q; e)c = (qc)v$ and $(q; e)c' = qc'$ for $c' \neq c$. Let $r = T(q, e)$ iff $r = q; e$ and one of the following holds:

1. $\text{chan}(e) \in X$.
2. $\text{chan}(e) \in Y + W$, and if $r = \langle x, w, y \rangle$ then $\langle w, y \rangle = px\langle w, y \rangle$.

It is straightforward to check that $A = (X, W, Y, Q, \text{I}, T)$ is an automaton, and that (D, p, l) is its behavior up to isomorphism. Assumption (2) above implies that for all $x \in HX$, every maximal fixed point $\langle w, y \rangle$ of px is reachable from $\langle \bot, \bot \rangle$ by a sequence of prime intervals. This fact is used to prove that for each state $q = \langle x, w, y \rangle$, if $\langle w, y \rangle$ is not a maximal fixed point of px, then there exists some non-input action e that is enabled in state q.

5.5 The Feedback Operation

We now formalize the feedback operation depicted schematically in Figure 1 as a construction on automata. Suppose

$$A = (X + Z, W, Y, Q, \text{I}, T)$$

is an automaton, and let $\phi : Z \to Y$ be an injection. Then the *feedback of A by ϕ* is the automaton

$$A_{\circlearrowleft\phi} = (X, W, Y, Q, \text{I}, T_{\circlearrowleft\phi})$$

where $r = T_{\circlearrowleft\phi}(q, e)$ iff one of the following conditions holds:

1. $\text{chan}(e) \notin \phi(Z)$ and $r = T(q, e)$.
2. $e = \langle\phi(c), v\rangle$ for some $c \in Z$ (which is then unique by the injectiveness of ϕ) and if $e' = \langle c, v\rangle$, then there exists a state s with $s = T(q, e)$ and $r = T(s, e')$.

It is easy to check that $A_{\circlearrowleft\phi}$ satisfies the conditions for an automaton.

The intuition behind this construction is as follows: The automaton $A_{\circlearrowleft\phi}$ behaves exactly as A does in the case of actions e with $\text{chan}(e) \notin \phi(Z)$. Such actions correspond either to inputs on channels in X or outputs on channels in Y that are not to be fed back to channels in Z. However, if $e = \langle\phi(c), v\rangle$ for some $c \in Z$, then e corresponds to the production of an output value v that is immediately reapplied as feedback input on channel c.

6 Correctness of the Generalized Kahn Principle

Suppose $A = (X + Z, W, Y, Q, \text{I}, T)$ is an automaton, and $\phi : Z \to Y$ is an injection. Let $A_{\circlearrowleft\phi}$ be the feedback of A by ϕ. Let (D, p, l) be the behavior of A, and let $(D_{\circlearrowleft\phi}, p_{\circlearrowleft\phi}, l_{\circlearrowleft\phi})$ be the behavior of $A_{\circlearrowleft\phi}$. Note that $D = D_{\circlearrowleft\phi} = HW \times HY$, and both l and $l_{\circlearrowleft\phi}$ take $\langle w, y\rangle$ to y.

The feedback functional corresponding to (D, p, l) and ϕ is the map:

$$\Phi : [HX \to [D \to D]] \to [HX \to [D \to D]]$$

defined by:

$$\Phi qxd = p\langle x, H\phi(l(qxd))\rangle d.$$

It is obvious from the definition that Φ is continuous. The generalized Kahn principle then states that $p_{\circlearrowleft\phi} = \mu\Phi$.

Recall that the fundamental fixed-point theorem (see, *e.g.* [26]) in the theory of complete partial orders states that if a functional $\Phi : B \to B$ is continuous, then $\mu\Phi = \bigsqcup_i \Phi^i 0$, where 0 denotes the least element of B, and the *iterates* Φ^i of Φ are defined inductively by: $\Phi^0 = \text{id}$, $\Phi^{i+1} = \Phi \circ \Phi^i$. Now, for all $x \in HX$, $z \in HZ$, and $i \geq 0$, define

$$\begin{aligned}
p_i &= \Phi^i 0 \\
D(x, z) &= \{\langle w, y\rangle : \langle w, y\rangle = p\langle x, z\rangle\langle w, y\rangle\} = \{\langle w, y\rangle : \langle x, z, w, y\rangle \in \mathcal{H}(A)\} \\
D_{\circlearrowleft\phi}(x) &= \{\langle w, y\rangle : \langle w, y\rangle = p_{\circlearrowleft\phi} x\langle w, y\rangle\} = \{\langle w, y\rangle : \langle x, w, y\rangle \in \mathcal{H}(A_{\circlearrowleft\phi})\}. \\
D_i(x) &= \{\langle w, y\rangle : \langle w, y\rangle = p_i x\langle w, y\rangle\}.
\end{aligned}$$

Intuitively, $D(x, z)$ is the set of non-input portions of histories of initial computation sequences of A on input $\langle x, z\rangle$, and $D_{\circlearrowleft\phi}(x)$ is the set of non-input portions of histories of initial computation sequences of $A_{\circlearrowleft\phi}$ on input x. The sets $D_i(x)$ may be thought of as approximations to $D_{\circlearrowleft\phi}(x)$ in which feedback of output to input is limited to at most i cycles.

Proposition 6.1

1. *For all $x \in HX$ and all $i \geq 0$, the map $p_i x : D \to D$ is a projection, hence $D_i(x)$ is a normal subdomain of D.*

2. *For all $x \in HX$, the map $\mu\Phi x : D \to D$ is a projection.*

The next result establishes the basic approximation relationship between the domains $D_i(x)$ and the domain $D_{\circlearrowleft\phi}(x)$. Its proof requires an analysis of the relationship between the set of finite initial computation sequences of A and those of $A_{\circlearrowleft\phi}$.

Proposition 6.2 *Suppose $\langle x, w, y\rangle \in HX \times HW \times HY$ is finite. Then $\langle w, y\rangle \in D_{\circlearrowleft\phi}(x)$ iff $\langle w, y\rangle \in D_n(x)$ for some n.*

We use the preceding result and the algebraicity of HX to obtain the following:

Proposition 6.3 $D_{\circlearrowleft\phi}(x) = (\bigcup_i D_i(x))^c$.

Finally, we have the main theorem.

Theorem 1 *$p_{\circlearrowleft\phi} = \mu\Phi$, hence the generalized Kahn principle is correct.*

Proof – First note that for all $x \in HX$ we have $\mu\Phi x = \bigsqcup_i p_i x$. Also, for all $x \in HX$, the projection $p_{\circlearrowleft\phi}x$ is the projection corresponding to the normal subdomain $D_{\circlearrowleft\phi}(x)$ of $HW \times HY$, under the isomorphism between the lattice of normal subdomains of $HW \times HY$ and the lattice of projections on $HW \times HY$. Similarly, $p_i x$ is the projection corresponding to the normal subdomain $D_i(x)$. By the previous proposition, $D_{\circlearrowleft\phi}(x) = (\bigcup_i D_i(x))^c$. But $(\bigcup_i D_i(x))^c$ is the least normal subdomain containing all the $D_i(x)$, hence is the normal subdomain corresponding to the projection $\bigsqcup_i p_i x = \mu\Phi$. ∎

7 Conclusion

We have stated a generalized version of Kahn's fixed-point principle for a class of indeterminate networks, and we have sketched a proof that it gives results in accordance with token-pushing operational semantics. Our generalized Kahn Principle is simple to state, and parallels Kahn's original fixed-point principle in a pleasant way. The class of dataflow networks to which it applies includes at least all networks that can be constructed from functional processes and angelic merge, but not to networks built using fair merge or an equivalent primitive such as "poll" [22]. Although our generalized Kahn Principle is easily stated, the proof that it agrees with token-pushing semantics seems to require a rather detailed analysis of a particular operational model, using results the author has been accumulating over the past several years. It remains to be seen whether a simpler proof can be given. Other interesting possibilities for future work are to extend the result to recursively defined networks, and to look at possibilities for treating fair merge.

Abramsky [2] has recently proposed a generalized Kahn Principle that can be viewed as a "pointwise" extension of Kahn's result to those networks whose behaviors can be represented as sets of continuous functions. In Abramsky's work, a network with input channels X and output channels Y would be represented as a set of functions from HX to HY. A precise relationship can be drawn between the generalized Kahn Principle of the present paper and a pointwise version like that of Abramsky. Suppose $B = (D, p, l)$ is an $(X + Z, Y)$-behavior with the following special form: $D \simeq (HX \times HZ) \times D'$, and up to this isomorphism we have $p\langle x, z\rangle(\langle x', z'\rangle, d') = \langle\langle x \sqcap x', z \sqcap z'\rangle, d'\rangle$. Such a behavior models a network in which all indeterminacy arises from the choices made by an "oracle" (represented by D') that operates independently of the network input. These behaviors were called "semi-determinate" in [33]. We may associate with such a semi-determinate behavior the set $F(B)$ of all functions $f_{d'} : HX \times HZ \to HY$ satisfying $f_{d'}\langle x, z\rangle = l(p\langle x, z\rangle(\langle x, z\rangle, d')) = l(\langle\langle x, z\rangle, d'\rangle)$, where d is a maximal element of D'. Notice that the special form of B ensures that the set $F(B)$ contains enough information to recover the input/output relation $R(B)$ of B, because $R(B) = \{\langle\langle x, z\rangle, f\langle x, z\rangle\rangle : f \in F(B)\}$. Now, if $B_{\circlearrowleft\phi}$ is the (X, Y)-behavior obtained by applying our generalized Kahn Principle to B, and if $f_{\circlearrowleft\phi} : HX \to HY$ denotes the result of applying the original Kahn Principle to a function $f : HX \times HZ \to HY$, then $F(B_{\circlearrowleft\phi}) = \{f_{\circlearrowleft\phi} : f \in F(B)\}$.

The comments of the previous paragraph apply only to semi-determinate behaviors. All networks built using functional processes and infinity-fair merge are semi-determinate, however it can be shown [33] that angelic merge is not semi-determinate. Thus, when viewed in this way, it would appear that our generalized Kahn principle applies to a larger class of networks than does the pointwise version of Abramsky. However, B. A. Trakhtenbrot and A. Rabinovich [private communication] have recently reminded the author that there is another way to associate a set of functions with a behavior, and that is to assign to each $(X \times Z, Y)$-behavior $B = (D, p, l)$ the set $G(B)$ of all functions $g_d : HX \times HZ \to D \times HY$ satisfying $g_d\langle x, z\rangle = \langle p\langle x, z\rangle d, l(p\langle x, z\rangle d)\rangle$, where d is an arbitrary element of D. If B is not semi-determinate, then we cannot discard the D component of the codomains of the functions g_d, since to do so would mean that the set $G(B)$ would no longer contain sufficient information to recover the input/output relation of B.[2] As in the previous paragraph, we have that $G(B_{\circlearrowleft\phi}) = \{g_{\circlearrowleft\phi} : g \in G(B)\}$, so from this standpoint it appears that the "set of functions" model and the "pointwise lifted Kahn Principle" is just as good as the behavior model and generalized Kahn Principle presented here. At present, we have to accept this conclusion, since the only argument we can advance in favor of the behavior model over the set of functions model is the somewhat vague assertion that the former contains a bit more useful algebraic structure. Our generalized Kahn Principle serves to reduce the problem of reasoning about indeterminate networks to that of reasoning about continuous functions, whereas the pointwise version requires reasoning about sets of continuous functions.

[2] If however, as in the work of Trakhtenbrot and Rabinovich to date, one does not insist that only "completed" computation sequences contribute to the input/output relation, then it is no problem to throw away the domain D.

In conclusion, we note that, because of the presence of the domain D, neither of the two models is sufficiently abstract, and therefore further investigation is required to reach the goal of a highly structured, fully abstract model of indeterminate dataflow networks.

References

[1] S. Abramsky. Experiments, powerdomains, and fully abstract models for applicative multiprogramming. In *Foundations of Computation Theory*, pages 1–13, Springer-Verlag. Volume 158 of *Lecture Notes in Computer Science*, 1983.

[2] S. Abramsky. A generalized Kahn principle for abstract asynchronous networks. In *Mathematical Foundations of Program Semantics*, Springer Verlag, 1990. (to appear).

[3] S. Abramsky. On the semantic foundations for applicative multiprogramming. In *ICALP 83*, Springer Verlag, 1983.

[4] R. J. Back and N. Mannila. A refinement of Kahn's semantics to handle non-determinism and communication. In *Proc. ACM Symposium on Principles of Distributed Computing*, pages 111–120, 1982.

[5] M. Bednarczyk. *Categories of Asynchronous Systems*. PhD thesis, University of Sussex, October 1987.

[6] J. D. Brock. *A Formal Model of Non-Determinate Dataflow Computation*. PhD thesis, Massachusetts Institute of Technology, 1983. Available as MIT/LCS/TR-309.

[7] J. D. Brock and W. B. Ackerman. Scenarios: a model of non-determinate computation. In *Formalization of Programming Concepts*, pages 252–259, Springer-Verlag. Volume 107 of *Lecture Notes in Computer Science*, 1981.

[8] M. Broy. Fixed point theory for communication and concurrency. In D. Bjørner, editor, *Formal Description of Programming Concepts II*, pages 125–148, North-Holland. 1983.

[9] A. A. Faustini. An operational semantics for pure dataflow. In *Automata, Languages, and Programming, 9th Colloquium*, pages 212–224, Springer-Verlag. Volume 140 of *Lecture Notes in Computer Science*, 1982.

[10] H. Gaifman and V. Pratt. Partial order models of concurrency and the computation of functions. In *Symposium on Logic in Computer Science*, pages 72–85, Ithaca, NY, June 1987.

[11] B. Jonsson. *Compositional Verification of Distributed Systems*. PhD thesis, Uppsala University, Uppsala, Sweden, 1987.

[12] A. Jung. *Cartesian Closed Categories of Domains*. PhD thesis, University of Darmstadt, 1988.

[13] G. Kahn. The semantics of a simple language for parallel programming. In J. L. Rosenfeld, editor, *Information Processing 74*, pages 471–475, North-Holland, 1974.

[14] G. Kahn and D. B. MacQueen. Coroutines and networks of parallel processes. In B. Gilchrist, editor, *Information Processing 77*, pages 993–998, North-Holland, 1977.

[15] R. M. Keller. Denotational models for parallel programs with indeterminate operators. In E. J. Neuhold, editor, *Formal Description of Programming Concepts*, pages 337–366, North-Holland. 1978.

[16] R. M. Keller and P. Panangaden. Semantics of networks containing indeterminate operators. In S. D. Brookes, A. W. Roscoe, and G. Winskel, editors, *Seminar on Concurrency*, pages 479–496, Springer-Verlag. Volume 197 of *Lecture Notes in Computer Science*, 1984.

[17] J. N. Kok. A fully abstract semantics for data flow nets. pages 351–368, Springer-Verlag. Volume 259 of *Lecture Notes in Computer Science*, 1987.

[18] M. Kwiatkowska. *Fairness for Non-Interleaving Concurrency*. PhD thesis, University of Leicester, May 1989.

[19] N. A. Lynch and E. W. Stark. A proof of the Kahn principle for input/output automata. *Information and Computation*, 82(1):81–92, July 1989.

[20] M. G. Main and D. B. Benson. Functional behavior of nondeterministic and concurrent programs. *Information and Control*, 62:144–189, 1984.

[21] J. Misra. Equational reasoning about nondeterministic processes (preliminary version). In *ACM Symposium on Principles of Distributed Computing*, pages 29–44, 1989.

[22] P. Panangaden and E. W. Stark. Computations, residuals, and the power of indeterminacy. In T. Lepisto and A. Salomaa, editors, *Automata, Languages, and Programming*, pages 439–454, Springer-Verlag. Volume 317 of *Lecture Notes in Computer Science*, 1988.

[23] D. M. R. Park. The "fairness problem" and nondeterministic computing networks. In *Proceedings, 4th Advanced Course on Theoretical Computer Science*, pages 133–161, Mathematisch Centrum, 1982.

[24] A. Rabinovich and B. A. Trakhtenbrot. Nets and data flow interpreters. In *Logic in Computer Science*, IEEE, 1989.

[25] J. Russell. Full abstraction for nondeterministic dataflow networks. June 1989. Unpublished manuscript, Cornell University.

[26] D. A. Schmidt. *Denotational Semantics: A Methodology for Language Development*. Allyn and Bacon, 1986.

[27] M. W. Shields. Deterministic asynchronous automata. In E. J. Neuhold and G. Chroust, editors, *Formal Methods in Programming*, pages 317–345, North-Holland. 1985.

[28] J. Staples and V. L. Nguyen. A fixpoint semantics for nondeterministic data flow. *Journal of the ACM*, 32(2):411–444, April 1985.

[29] E. W. Stark. Compositional relational semantics for indeterminate dataflow networks. In *Category Theory and Computer Science*, pages 52–74, Springer-Verlag. Volume 389 of *Lecture Notes in Computer Science*, Manchester, U. K., 1989.

[30] E. W. Stark. Concurrent transition system semantics of process networks. In *Fourteenth ACM Symposium on Principles of Programming Languages*, pages 199–210, January 1987.

[31] E. W. Stark. Concurrent transition systems. *Theoretical Computer Science*, 64:221–269, 1989.

[32] E. W. Stark. Connections between a concrete and abstract model of concurrent systems. In *Fifth Conference on the Mathematical Foundations of Programming Semantics*, Springer-Verlag. *Lecture Notes in Computer Science*, New Orleans, LA, 1990. (to appear).

[33] E. W. Stark. On the relations computed by a class of concurrent automata. In *Seventeenth Annual ACM Symposium on Principles of Programming Languages*, pages 329–340, January 1990.

[34] E. W. Stark. *A Simple Generalization of Kahn's Principle to Indeterminate Dataflow Networks.* Technical Report TR-89-29, SUNY at Stony Brook Computer Science Dept., 1989.

Defining Fair Merge as a Colimit: Towards a Fixed-Point Theory for Indeterminate Dataflow

David B. Benson*
Computer Science Department
Washington State University
Pullman, Washington, 99164-1210 USA

Prakash Panangaden†
James R. Russell‡
Department of Computer Science
Cornell University
Ithaca, NY 14853 USA

Abstract

We define the action of the indeterminate dataflow primitive, fair merge, on infinite inputs as a limit. Fair merge is known to embody unbounded indeterminacy and is hence not continuous. Recent results about the expressiveness of indeterminate primitives shows that it is not even monotone in a suitable sense. Given this it is rather surprising that one can give a limiting description of fair merge. The key idea is to define fair merge in terms of the limit of a sequence of "tests". The approach is suggested by an algebraic theory of distributed computing based on the notion of a bimonoid or bialgebra.

1 Introduction

In this paper we show how the troublesome but important fair merge construct can be defined through a limiting process *without using timing or other operational information.* This offers hope that one could develop an elegant, abstract fixed-point theory for dataflow networks having fair merge as a component. Our ideas are based on a duality between fair merge and another indeterminate primitive called *spray.* These ideas represent an interaction between an algebraic theory of distributed computing [7] and an analysis of approximation between the results on indeterminate computations. They represent an interesting interplay between some traditional ideas from denotational semantics and new ideas about the role of tensor structure in concurrency [7, 6, 9, 10, 11, 15].

In the functional programming setting fair merge was introduced by programmers as an abstraction of a fair resource allocator. It is hard to pin down who should get credit for inventing it, but it was talked about over a decade ago [14] and has made its way into introductory texts [2]. It is easy to imagine implementing a fair

*Research supported by NSF Grant CCR-8801886.

†Research supported in part by NSF Grant CCR-8818979. Present address: School of Computer Science, McGill University, Montreal, PQ, CANADA.

‡Research supported in part by an NSF predoctoral fellowship and by an IBM fellowship.

merge, provided one has the ability to branch on availability of data. It thus seems surprising that it should lead to such problems when one considers formal semantics. Brock and Ackerman [8] have shown that one cannot develop a compositional semantics for it just using input-output relations. Recently Jonsson [12] has shown that a semantics based on traces is compositional and fully abstract for dataflow networks with fair merge. This indicates that one must have some timing information in the semantics. Park has proposed using explicit timing information as part of the semantics for fair merge [21], an idea that was pursued by one of us [17]. While one can give a reasonable fixed-point semantics using hiatons, the semantics is not fully abstract [13] and is clumsy to use in practice.

Recent discoveries about the expressive power of fair merge [18, 20] show that fair merge embodies a particularly "vicious" form of indeterminacy, more than unbounded indeterminacy, and is not even "monotone" in a certain sense. It had long been known that when one has unbounded indeterminacy there are continuity problems; if one has infinite output streams then even bounded indeterminacy produces continuity problems as was first pointed out by Abramsky. The recent book by Stoughton contains a discussion of these examples [27].

Recent category-theoretic [3] and other techniques [5, 22] have been successful in defining a fixed-point semantics for systems that embody unbounded indeterminacy, but these do not handle the interaction of dataflow and the type of indeterminacy present in fair merge. From an intuitive point of view, what makes fair merge nasty is that arrival of input can disable an enabled output. It is this that manifests itself as a monotonicity failure. In view of this it is rather surprising that the fair merge of infinite sequences can be described through a limiting process.

The merges that are commonly considered are *fair merge*, *angelic merge* and *infinity-fair merge* [21]. All of these are dataflow processes with a pair of input channels and a single output channel. Given a pair of input streams each of the merges produces some interleaving of the input values (or *tokens*). A fair merge is guaranteed to output any token that appears on its input channels. An angelic merge will output every token on an input channel if the *other* channel has only finitely many tokens. Thus it will be indistinguishable from fair merge on finite input streams; to indulge in a vulgar anthropomorphism, it is "bottom avoiding." Angelic merge corresponds to what one would get if one wrote a naive recursive program using Macarthy's *amb*. It is not possible to use amb to program a fair merge [19]. The infinity-fair merge produces a fair merge if both its input streams are infinite; if either one is finite it will produce only finite output. All three of these merges embody unbounded indeterminacy. The expressiveness results alluded to show that fair merge cannot be implemented with any combination of determinate primitives and angelic merges and likewise angelic merge cannot be implemented with any combination of determinate primitives and infinity-fair merge.

Infinity-fair merge is "oraclizable"; that is, one can view it as being implemented by a network of purely determinate primitives and an input-free process that emits an arbitrary sequence of positive integers. Recently Abramsky [4] has extended Kahn's principle to networks that feature only oraclizable indeterminacy. Russell [23] has shown that the semantics of such networks can be described by a *set* of functions in a fully abstract way, and that the generalized Kahn principle amounts to using each possible functional behaviour in the ordinary Kahn principle. He has also shown that the oraclizable networks are a proper subset of the

Egli-Milner monotone networks. One of the consequences of the expressiveness theorems [18, 20], or rather of their proofs, is that fair merge and angelic merge are not Egli-Milner monotone. Thus, these ideas are not likely to lead to a fixed-point semantics for networks involving fair merge. It should be remarked that prior to the appearance of [20] some authors were unaware of these distinctions or the fact that fair merge could not be viewed as an oraclizable primitive.

The one earlier attempt that we have seen that defines fair merge through a limiting process is due to Smyth [24]. In his paper, a *finitary relation*, R, is defined as a relation satisfying the following two properties

1. If $\vec{x_1} \sqsubseteq \vec{x_2} \ldots \vec{x_n} \ldots$ and the $\vec{x_i}$ are all in R, then $\sqcup \vec{x_i}$ is in R.
2. If $\vec{x}$ is in R then there is a series of *finite* tuples $\vec{x_1} \sqsubseteq \vec{x_2} \ldots \vec{x_n} \ldots$, all in R, such that $\sqcup \vec{x_i}$ is $\vec{x}$.

It is easy to see that fair merge is finitary. This construction is more or less the same as the one that we describe at the end of section 3 as the ad-hoc inductive construction. He evidently did not pursue this or publish the original report. Our approach is not based on Smyth's but takes a "dual" view. We show how to regard fair merge as the limit of a sequence of *tests*. We did make several attempts to express a construction like Smyth's in terms of categorical concepts, but it appears not to fit in in any simple way.

The key to developing an abstract formulation that is applicable to networks containing fair merge is to combine a suitably abstract presentation of timing information, perhaps using an abstract "scheduler" as advocated by Olderog and Apt [16], with a "continuous" description of fair merge. This paper shows how the latter can be done. It remains to combine these ideas into their final form.

2 Algebraic Background

Benson has given an algebraic presentation of certain common operations that arise in a variety of models of distributed computing [7]. This section is a quick summary of that work with an emphasis on the role of merge or shuffle and spray and the duality between them. We will not give explicit verifications of routine statements as all of them will be obvious to experts.

Two operations that arise in the analysis of dataflow computations are *concatenation* and *shuffle*. Concatenation arises when one considers computations of determinate processes since one can incrementally construct the computations using Kahn's principle. In the indeterminate case shuffle arises naturally in the analysis of merging. Each of these operations has a dual, *cut* and *spray* respectively, and the pairs shuffle, cut and spray, concatenation form an algebraic structure called a *bimonoid*; i.e. a structure that is both a monoid and a comonoid. In discussions of Hopf algebras [1, 28], such structures (with modules over rings rather than over semirings) are called *bialgebras*. We will use the terms interchangeably in this paper.

We will consider sequences and strings over some fixed alphabet, Σ; in this section they will all be finite strings. As is well known, the set of strings over Σ has the structure of a free monoid with concatenation as the multiplication. We can view certain collections of sets of strings as a module over a semiring. Let I be the semiring $\{0,1\}$ with boolean "and" as the multiplication and boolean "or" as the addition. We can think of 0 as the empty set of strings and 1 as the set containing the empty string. Now an I-module is a monoid with a right action by I satisfying the usual equations for a ring-module and, in addition, the equation $0 \cdot x = x \cdot 0 = 0$, since this does not follow from the usual equations for a semiring-module. The free I-module generated by Σ^* is isomorphic to the set of finite subsets of Σ^*; we write this as $\Sigma^* - I$. In this paper it suffices to have this particular concrete picture of I-modules but the theory developed by Benson [7] applies more generally.

The collection $\mathbf{I-mod}$ of I-modules and linear maps forms a symmetric monoidal category; in this setting "linear map" simply means homomorphism of I-modules. One can view the usual concatenation monoid as an internal monoid in $\mathbf{I-mod}$. The internal monoid is the triple $\langle \Sigma^* - I, \cdot, \eta \rangle$, where $\cdot$ is the pointwise extension of ordinary concatenation and η is the unit map of the monoid, taking 1 to the set containing the empty string and 0 to the empty set. There is another interesting internal monoid in $\mathbf{I-mod}$ that is related to nondeterminism. Let shuffle represent the relation of interleaving. Thus shuffle$(x, y; z)$ says that z is a possible interleaving of the sequences x and y. We write $\sigma(\langle x, y \rangle)$ for the set of sequences that result from forming all possible interleavings of x and y. In this monoid also the empty string is the identity for shuffle. The signature of this shuffle monoid is $\langle \Sigma^* - I, \sigma, \eta \rangle$.

There are also interesting internal comonoids in $\mathbf{I-mod}$. The two that we consider are the *cut* comonoid and the *spray* comonoid. Let Γ represent the comultiplication operation "breaking a string into two pieces in all possible ways." More precisely, if x is a string in Σ^*

$$\Gamma(x) = \{\langle y, z \rangle | y \cdot z = x\}.$$

The action of Γ is extended pointwise to sets of strings. The counit structure map ϵ is generated by its action on strings. It takes the empty string to 1 in I and all other strings to 0. This extends to mapping any set of strings containing the empty string to 1 in I and all other sets to 0. The triple $\langle \Sigma^* - I, \Gamma, \epsilon \rangle$ is then a comonoid in $\mathbf{I-mod}$. As before, there is another comonoid structure on $\Sigma^* - I$ related to nondeterminism. This is defined by the spray relation. The comultiplication operation is χ; on strings it is defined by

$$\chi(x) = \{\langle y, z \rangle | x \in \sigma(\langle y, z \rangle)\}.$$

We write spray$(x; y, z)$ to mean that $\langle y, z \rangle \in \chi(x)$. Using the same counit structure map we get a comonoid $\langle \Sigma^* - I, \chi, \epsilon \rangle$.

The monoid and the comonoid structures are closely related. First we recall that $\mathbf{I-mod}$, like any symmetric monoidal category, has tensor structure and, hence, comes with canonical construction for a tensor products of internal monoids and comonoids. Suppose that $\langle B, \mu, \eta \rangle$ is a monoid in $\mathbf{I-mod}$ and that $\langle B, \nu, \epsilon \rangle$ is a comonoid in $\mathbf{I-mod}$. We have that $\mu; \nu$ is a map from $B \otimes B$ to $B \otimes B$ and $\mu \otimes \mu$ is a map from $B \otimes B \otimes B \otimes B$ to $B \otimes B$. Thus we get the possibility of a commuting diagram which would make μ a comonoid homomorphism from $B \otimes B$ to B. When μ and η are comonoid homomorphisms or, equivalently, when ν and ϵ are monoid homomorphisms, we have a *bimonoid* or *bialgebra*.

The two important bialgebras, for our purposes, are the shuffle-cut bialgebra and the spray-concatenation bialgebra. It is relatively straightforward to check that these are bialgebras. This makes the study of indeterminate dataflow based on merger processes less ad hoc. The important point is that shuffle pairs with only one comonoid, namely the cut comonoid, to form a bimonoid in a natural way. Similarly for spray and concatenation.

From the point of view of developing the fixed-point definitions of fair merge in the next section we write down the important equations that follow from the bialgebra structure and from the basic duality between shuffle and spray. The first important equation is

$$\mathsf{spray}(x; y, z) \Leftrightarrow \mathsf{shuffle}(y, z; x) \tag{1}$$

one can check operationally that this applies for unfair spray and fair merge even in the limit. It is the key to the construction described in the next section. The next two equations help explain why the right limiting construction works smoothly but a left limiting one does not. Define a function truncate that removes the last symbol of a string and extend it pointwise to sets of strings. We have the following equation

$$\mathsf{truncate}(\sigma(\langle x, y\rangle)) = \sigma(\langle \mathsf{truncate}(x), y\rangle \bigcup \sigma(\langle x, \mathsf{truncate}(y)\rangle \tag{2}$$

or, more abstractly,

$$\sigma; \mathsf{truncate} = (\mathsf{truncate} \otimes 1) \oplus (1 \otimes \mathsf{truncate}); \sigma. \tag{3}$$

These equations say that truncate is a homomorphism of the shuffle monoid; this is essentially a restatement of the fact that shuffle and cut form a bialgebra. Note that the process of extending a string with an additional token does not have this pleasant interaction with shuffle; the new token need not appear as the last token of the shuffled string. Intuitively, this suggests that it would be difficult to define fair merge incrementally from its finite approximants but that the "dual" construction might go through smoothly. The process of adding a symbol, say a, from Σ to the end of a string does not interact well with shuffling but it does interact well with spray. The equation, in concrete form, is

$$\chi(x \cdot a) = \{\langle y \cdot a, z\rangle | \langle y, z\rangle \in \chi(x)\} \bigcup \{\langle y, z \cdot a\rangle | \langle y, z\rangle \in \chi(x)\}. \tag{4}$$

3 Fixed Point Definitions of Fair Merge

In this section we describe how fair merge can be defined through a limiting process. We give a concrete presentation of this construction that is based on the algebraic theory of the last section. The algebraic theory provides the proper analysis of the finite case, while describing the limiting process involves rigourously capturing the proper notion of approximation.

We always consider an underlying complete partial order of finite or infinite sequences over some fixed alphabet. The ordering is the prefix ordering and the least element is the empty sequence. We write $\sqsubseteq$ for the prefix ordering on sequences. The construction that we present uses equation 1 between the spray relation and the shuffle relation. Note that spray is a simple process, there are no fairness assumptions and it has only bounded indeterminacy, while the fair merge that we are trying to define has a very subtle limiting behaviour. In order to avoid clumsy phrases we write "string" for a finite or denumerable sequence of symbols from Σ.

A fair shuffle of two finite sequences is easy to define. Suppose that x and y are infinite sequences. We wish to define the set of all possible fair merges of x and y by a limit process. Let x_n and y_n be the n-length finite approximants to x and y. We define the following collection of sets of sequences.

$$M_0 = \{s | s \text{ is a sequence}\}$$
$$M_k = \{s | \exists p, q. x_k \sqsubseteq p \wedge y_k \sqsubseteq q \wedge \mathsf{spray}(s; p, q)\}.$$

Intuitively, M_k is the set of all sequences that could, when sprayed, start with x_k and y_k. Note that $M_{k+1} \subseteq M_k$. We now have the following basic fact:

Fact 1 *The fair merge of x and y is $\bigcap_i M_i$.*

Proof: Consider any sequence z in $FM(x, y)$; this can be written as $x^1y^1x^2y^2\ldots$ where the x^i and y^i are finite nonempty segments of x and y respectively, satisfying $x^1x^2\ldots = x$ and $y^1y^2\ldots = y$. Any such sequence will clearly be in all the M_i. Suppose that z is a sequence in all the M_i. Any token in z will eventually be sprayed and hence will eventually be in one of x_i or y_i for some i, thus z consists exclusively of tokens that came from x or y. Furthermore, the tokens in z appear in the same relative order as they do in x or y because of the spraying requirement. Finally any token in x and y must appear in z because it must be possible to spray z so that it produces any given prefix of x and y. ∎

In the case that one of the inputs, say x, is finite we modify the definition of M_k above to be

$$M_k = \{s | \exists q. y_k \sqsubseteq q \wedge \mathsf{spray}(s; x, q)\}.$$

The same argument goes through.

This construction can be defined as a colimit in a category. Define a category $\mathcal{C}$ with objects sets of sequences and arrows defined as follows. Let A and B be objects of $\mathcal{C}$. An arrow from A to B is a binary relation, $R \subseteq A \times B$ satisfying

1. $aRb \Rightarrow a \sqsubseteq b$,
2. $\forall b \in B. \exists a \in A. aRb$.

Note that if there is an arrow from A to B, then A is less than B in the "upper" preorder, the preorder used to define the Smyth powerdomain [25]. Clearly if $B \subseteq A$ then there is an arrow from A to B. The sequence of sets M_i, above, with the obvious inclusion relations forms an ω diagram in this category and the intersection, $\bigcap_i M_i$, is the colimiting object.

Note that the construction described uses the correspondence between shuffle and spray; it embodies the intuition that the spray is a "tester" for a fair merge. The approximation between the M_i is very hard to express directly in terms of the underlying sequences. Is there a "direct" inductive construction of fair merge from the finite shuffles? It turns out that there is.

We can also define fair merge using the following ad hoc "inductive" construction. Let x and y be as before, infinite sequences. We construct a series of approximating sets as follows.

$S_0 = \{s | s \text{ is the empty sequence}\}$
$S_k = \sigma(x_k, y_k)$

The sets S_i are related as follows. Define a relation, r, between two sets A and B to be a subset of $A \times B$ satisfying

1. $\forall a \in A \forall b \in B. arb \Rightarrow a \sqsubseteq b$.

2. $\forall a \in A \exists b \in B. arb$.

The first condition just says that the approximation between individual sequences is the usual prefix ordering, the second condition says that when there is an arrow from A to B then A is less than B in the preorder used to define the lower powerdomain.

Consider the sequence of sets S_i as defined above. Now consider the set of sequences of strings of the form $\langle s_{k_0}, s_{k_1}, s_{k_2}, \ldots \rangle$ where $k_0 \leq k_1 \leq k_2 \ldots$ and $\forall i \in \{k_0, k_1 \ldots\}. s_i \in S_i$ and finally $\forall i, j \in \{k_0, k_1, k_2 \ldots\}$ we have $i \leq j \Rightarrow s_i \sqsubseteq s_j$. Each such sequence of strings forms a chain in the cpo of strings and, hence, has a lub. The collection of all such lubs is exactly the fair merge of a and b. Unfortunately, this is *not* a colimit in the category of sets of sequences and Hoare relations. This is because in a sequence like $\langle s_{k_0}, s_{k_1}, s_{k_2}, \ldots \rangle$ the indices need not be consecutive and thus it must be possible to skip some of the objects in the sequence S_i. Arrow composition is not general enough to describe this. The first construction that we have defined is the more pleasant one as it does correspond to a colimit in a simple way.

Angelic Merge

Angelic merge has the curious property of being exactly like fair merge in the case that both its input streams are finite and of being exactly like unfair merge in the case that both its input streams are infinite. Since the behaviour of unfair merge is easy to describe, even in the limit, the interesting case for angelic merge is when one input is finite and the other is infinite. Let x be the finite input stream and y be the infinite input stream. Let $AM(x, y)$ represent the set of sequences that result from calculating the angelic merge of x and y and correspondingly $FM(x, y)$ for fair merge. Then angelic merge can be constructed as a limit by observing that

$$AM(x, y) = \bigcup_{x' \sqsubseteq x} FM(x', y)$$

and using the above construction for fair merge.

An angelic merge can also be constructed by taking the *maximal* elements of an unfair merge. It is not clear to us how one can view this as a limiting construction.

In fact angelic merge can be defined as a limit in a suitable category of *graded* modules. The following is a very brief sketch of this. Let truncate denote the truncate linear function defined above. We define T as follows

$$T = (\mathsf{truncate} \otimes 1) + (1 \otimes \mathsf{truncate})$$

and σ denotes the shuffle function. Each X_i denotes the finite powerset over all strings of length i relative to some fixed alphabet. Let $Y_n = \Sigma_{i,j|i+j=n}(Xi \otimes Xj)$.

Note that these definitions of X_n, Y_n place us in the graded setting, i.e., we can work in the category of graded objects and graded linear maps. We have the following commuting diagram which extends to the left.

```
       T         T         T
... ---> Y2 ---> Y1 ---> Y0
 |        |        |
 |        |        | (all vertical arrows are shuffles)
 |        |        |
 v        v        v
... ---> X2 ---> X1 ---> X0
       t         t         t
```

The (left) limit of this diagram gives angelic merge. The reason is that the left limit of the top row has arrows in the cone which chop pairs of (finite and infinite) sequences to the length given by the grading. That is, if L is the left limiting object of the top row, and $l_n : L \to Y_n$ is the arrow of the cone to Y_n, l_n truncates every pair of sequences to the total length n.

4 Conclusions

In this paper we have shown how one can express the fair merge of infinite strings as a colimit in a suitable category. Given the continuity and monotonicity problems associated with fair merge, this is rather unexpected. It indicates that one can use finitary arguments in reasoning about fair merge. The most pressing remaining problem is to define a compositional fixed-point semantics for networks that contain fair merges. Given the full abstraction results, it is clear that we need to encode the information in traces inductively. Recently E. W. Stark has given a very interesting fixed-point principle for networks containing angelic merge [26].

Acknowledgements

We have benefited from helpful discussions with Roberto di Cosmo and Edmund Robinson. This research was supported in part by NSF grant CCR-8801886 to Washington State University, by NSF grant CCR-8818979 to Cornell University, an NSERC grant to Queen's University and by IBM and NSF predoctoral fellowships to Jim Russell.

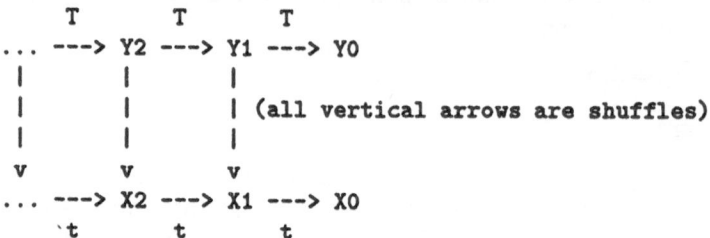

References

1. Abe, E. *Hopf Algebras*. Cambridge University Press, 1977
2. Abelson, H. and Sussman, G. *The Structure and Interpretation of Computer Programs*. McGraw-Hill, 1985
3. Abramsky, S. On semantic foundations for applicative multiprogramming. In J. Diaz, editor, *Automata, Languages and Programming*, 10th Coll., Lecture Notes in Computer Science 154, pp 1-14, Springer-Verlag, New York, 1983
4. Abramsky, S. A generalized Kahn's principle. In *Mathematical Foundations of Programming Language Semantics*, 5th Workshop, to appear. (Conference held in March 1989)
5. Apt, KR. and Plotkin, DG. Countable nondeterminism and random assignment. *JACM* 33(4):724-767, 1986
6. Benson, DB. The shuffle bialgebra. In *Mathematical Foundations of Programming Language Semantics*, 3rd Workshop Lecture Notes in Computer Science 298, pp 616-637, Springer-Verlag, 1988
7. Benson, DB. Bialgebras: Some foundations for distributed and concurrent computation. *Fund. Inform.*, December 1989. In press, available as Technical Report CS-88-186, Washington State University
8. Brock, JD. and Ackerman, WB. Scenarios: A model of non-determinate computation. In J.Diaz and I.Ramos, editors, *Formalization of Programming Concepts*, Lecture Notes in Computer Science 107, pp 252-259, Springer-Verlag, 1981
9. Degano, P. Meseguer, J. and Montanari, U. Axiomatizing net computations and processes. In *Proceedings of the Fourth IEEE Symposium on Logic in Computer Science*, pp 175-185, 1989
10. Girard, J-Y. Linear logic. *Theor. Comp. Sci.*, 50:1-102, 1987
11. Gunter, C. and Gehlot, V. Nets as tensor theories. Technical Report MS-CIS-89-68, University of Pennsylvania, 1989
12. Jonsson, B. Fully abstract trace semantics for dataflow networks. In *Proceedings of the Sixteenth Annual ACM Symposium on Principles of Programming Languages*, ACM Press, 1989
13. Jonsson, B. and Kok, J. Comparing dataflow models, Manuscript, 1988
14. Keller, RM. Denotational models for parallel programs with indeterminate operators. In E.J.Neuhold editor, *Formal Description of Programming Concepts*, pp 337-366. North-Holland, 1978
15. Main, MG. and Benson, DB. Functional behavior of nondeterministic and concurrent programs. *Inform. and Control*, 62:144-189, 1984
16. Olderog, E.-R. and Apt, KR. Fairness in parallel programs: The transformational approach. *Transaction on Programming Languages and Systems*, 10(3):420-455, 1988

17. Panangaden. P. Abstract interpretation and indeterminacy. In S.D.Brookes, A.W.Roscoe and G.Winskel editors, *Proceedings of the 1984 CMU Seminar on Concurrency*, Lecture Notes in Computer Science 197, pp 497-511, Springer-Verlag, 1985
18. Panangaden, P. and Shanbhogue, V. On the expressive power of indeterminate primitives. Technical Report 87-891, Cornell University, Computer Science Department, November 1987
19. Panangaden, P. and Shanbhogue, V. McCarthy's amb cannot implement fair merge. In K.V.Nori and S.Kumar editors, *Foundations of Software Technology and Theoretical Computer Science*, Lecture Notes in Computer Science 338, pp 348-363, Springer-Verlag, 1988
20. Panangaden, P. and Stark, EW. Computations, residuals and the power of indeterminacy. In T.Lepisto and A.salomaa editors, *Automata Languages and Programming*, Lecture Notes in Computer Science 317, pp 348-363, Springer-Verlag, 1988
21. Park, DMR. The "fairness problem" and non-deterministic computing networks. In *Proceedings, 4th Advanced Course on Theoretical Computer Science*, pp 133-161, Mathematisch Centrum, 1982
22. Plotkin, GD. A powerdomain for countable nondeterminism. In M.Nielsen and E.M.Schmidt editors, *Automata, Languages and Programming*. Lecture Notes in Computer Science 140, Springer-Verlag, 1982
23. Russell, JR. On oracleizable networks and Kahn's principle. In *Proceedings of the Seventeenth Annual ACM Symposium on Principles of Programming Languages*, ACM Press, 1990
24. Smyth, M. Finitary relations and fair merge. Technical Report 107/82, Edinburgh University
25. Smyth, MB. Powerdomains. *J. Comp. System Sci.*, 16:23-36, 1978
26. Stark, EW. A simple generalization of Kahn's principle to indeterminate dataflow networks. In M.Z.Kwiatkowska, M.W.Shields and R.M.Thomas editors, *Semantics for Concurrency*. Springer-Verlag, 1990. Available as SUNY Stonybrook Technical Report 89-29
27. Stoughton, A. *Fully Abstract Models of Programming Languages*. Research Notes in Theoretical Computer Science. John Wiley and Sons, 1988. Edinburgh PhD dissertation
28. Sweedler, M. *Hopf Algebras*. W.A. Benjamin 1969

High-Level Nets For Dynamic Dining Philosophers Systems

Greg Findlow and Jonathan Billington
Telecom Australia Research Laboratories
P.O. Box 249, Clayton, Victoria 3168, Australia

Abstract

Four dynamic extensions of the dining philosophers system are described, in which philosophers may now join and leave the dining party. Many-Sorted Predicate-Transition Nets (MPrT-Nets) are given for the third and fourth models. For the net of the fourth model, boundedness, absence of deadlocks, and fairness are proved.

1 INTRODUCTION

The provision of information and communication services is of vital importance to modern economies. This implies the need to create and maintain the necessary infrastructures to support these services. Important characteristics of these infrastructures are that they are geographically distributed, loosely coupled, highly concurrent and dynamically changing (e.g. nodes in networks are constantly being commissioned and decommissioned).

In order to provide services that are robust, reliable and maintainable, it is useful to be able to write specifications for systems that can be analysed and refined before being implemented and set in concrete. This implies the use of a formal (i.e. mathematically based) specification language.

Predicate-Transition nets (PrT-nets) [5, 4] have been used for the specification of concurrent systems for several years. Many-Sorted Predicate-Transition Nets (MPrT-Nets) [1] extend PrT-nets to include a many-sorted structure while retaining the graphical syntax. A case study is presented to illustrate the feasibility of using MPrT-Nets for the specification and analysis of dynamically changing systems. The example chosen is that of the dynamically changing dining philosophers [6]. In [6], the impression is given that it is difficult to represent dynamically changing systems using Petri nets. Perhaps this was because the authors of [6] felt that it required the underlying structure of the net (the sets of places, transitions, and arcs) to be dynamically changing. This is not the case, as is illustrated here. In Petri nets, the dynamics of systems are represented by the creation and destruction of tokens, rather than changing the graph structure as illustrated in [6] for graph grammars.

We provide a complete specification of the dynamically changing dining philosophers system with as few restrictions as possible. The specification allows there to be an arbitrary (but finite) number of philosophers, who can concurrently join the dining party at any position at the table or concurrently leave. (The concurrency is interleaving rather than true.) There are many ways of specifying such a system and some of these ways are investigated here. Two of the models are specified formally. (Formal specifications of the others may be found in [3].) One of these models is of interest because at any instant it could be considered to be the same as the static system. This model is deadlock-free, but does not prevent starvation. Another model is specified that simulates a waiter serving the philosophers, and it is proved to be bounded, deadlock-free and starvation-free.

In Section 2 we introduce the dining philosophers system and the notion of a dynamic extension of this system. Section 3 describes four models of dynamic systems. A MPrT-Net is given for the third model in Section 4. The fourth of the models, which is the only one which addresses the need for some sort of organisation of the philosophers' eating, is given as a MPrT-Net in Section 5. Section 6 proves that the net of the fourth model is bounded, and that the net is fair when the concept of 'fairness' as defined for finite state programs in [7] is applied.

2 THE DINING PHILOSOPHERS

The (static) dining philosophers problem (see [2]) is as follows: a fixed number of philosophers are seated at a round table. Between each pair of neighbouring philosophers is one fork. In order to eat, a philosopher must pick up two forks—one from each side of him. We would like to describe a suitable mode of behaviour for the philosophers. Here 'suitable' means that the philosophers should avoid situations where none of them can eat, such as all philosophers simultaneously picking up their left forks and then looking for right forks which have already been taken. [8] gives a solution which avoids such deadlocks by forcing philosophers to commence eating by picking up two forks simultaneously.

The dynamic dining philosophers problem [6] is an extension of this where the philosophers at the table may come and go. Variants of such a system can be derived, depending on the selection of rules determining the behaviour of the philosophers, the management of the forks, etc. For instance, the order in which the philosophers eat can be controlled by a round robin scheduler or similar device, or may be left uncontrolled.

3 MODELS OF THE DYNAMIC SYSTEM

Model 1 *(Fixed seats model)* There are a fixed number of philosophers, and a fixed number of seats at the table (the two numbers need not be related). There is a fork on the table between each pair of seats. A philosopher coming to the table chooses a vacant seat at which to sit. A philosopher who is at the table may start eating by picking up the two forks either side of him, provided they are available. When he stops eating, he replaces the two forks on each side of him. A philosopher may leave the table at any time when he is not eating.

Model 2 *(Expanding table model)* This model was developed so that there are no gaps at the table, i.e. it should expand or contract to seat whatever number of philosophers is present. The expanding/contracting table now makes it convenient to have each philosopher bring a fork to the table when he arrives, and take one

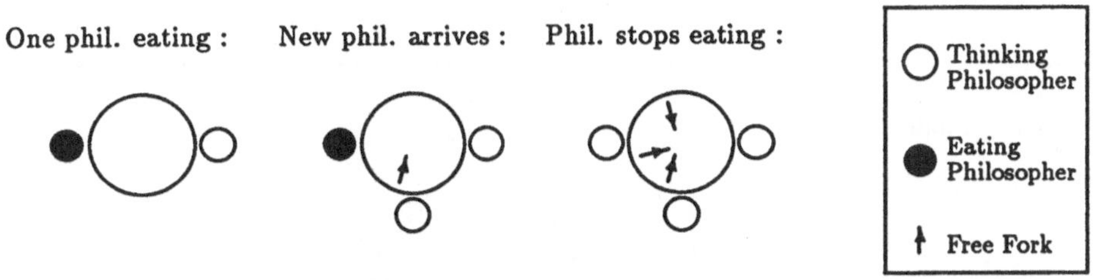

Figure 1: Fork accumulation in the second model

when he leaves. (This feature is retained in all subsequent models). An arriving philosopher chooses a left neighbour, sits immediately on the right of his choice (so that there are no free forks between the two philosophers), and places his fork between himself and his chosen left neighbour. This model has the undesirable characteristic that forks may accumulate between philosophers, and consequently there may be no forks between other philosophers. (The latter is really the more serious problem, since if two adjacent thinking philosophers have no forks between them, then neither will be able to eat until some other philosopher chooses to sit between them.) Figure 1 illustrates how forks may accumulate : if the chosen left neighbour of an incoming philosopher happens to be eating, and later stops, there will be two forks between these two philosophers. In this model, a philosopher at the table may start eating whenever he has at least one fork on each side of him, although there may be more. A philosopher may stop eating at any time; he simply puts his two forks down, one on each side of him. A philosopher who wishes to leave the table may do so as long as he is thinking and there is at least one fork beside him (on his left or right) available to take.

Model 3 *(Second expanding table model)* This model avoids the accumulation of forks, characteristic of the previous model, by requiring an incoming philosopher to place his fork on the table, when he arrives, in such a way that the state of the table will then be identical to a state of a table in a static dining philosophers system. This means that he may arrive in one of four ways (depending on the states of his neighbours, and how he sits down between them and places his fork on the table), as illustrated in Figure 2. For example, in the second arrival mode shown, the chosen right neighbour of the incoming philosopher is eating. His left neighbour must be thinking, and there are no forks between the new arrival's chosen neighbours, assuming that immediately before the new arrival, the state of the table was identical to a state of the static system. In this case, the new philosopher is required to place his fork between himself and his left neighbour. (An alternative way of describing how a philosopher must arrive is to say that he must sit on the immediate right or left of a thinking philosopher, i.e. with no forks between himself and that philosopher, and then place his fork on the table between himself and the thinking philosopher.) Apart from this change, this model closely resembles the previous one. A MPrT-Net for this model is described in Section 4.

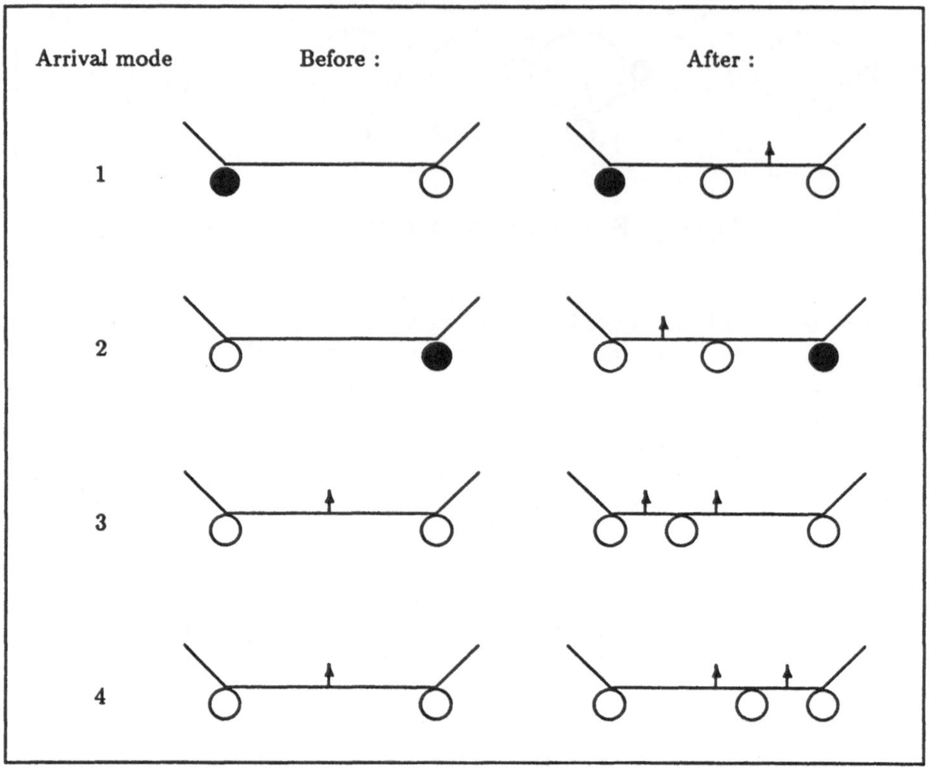

Figure 2: Arrival modes for philosophers in the third model (only the portion of the table where the new philosopher arrives is shown in each picture). The same key as is in Figure 1 applies.

Model 4 *(Fair queueing model)* The above models are not fair. It is possible to have firing sequences in which some philosophers, although present at the table, never eat, or never eat after a certain point, while other philosophers eat infinitely many times. This model is fair. The previous model is extended by including a queue of philosophers waiting to eat. The queue is managed as follows. An arriving philosopher joins at the end of the queue. A philosopher may begin eating as long as he is at the head of the queue and has access to two forks. (One may visualise a waiter serving only the next philosopher waiting to eat, and only doing so when that philosopher has two forks available.) A philosopher who finishes eating rejoins at the end of the queue. A thinking philosopher who leaves the table is removed from wherever he is in the queue. The other new feature in this model is that a philosopher is required to eat at least once before he may leave the table, in order to eliminate the possibility of executions of the system in which philosophers come and go without eating, effectively doing nothing but providing extra forks at the table (which is not really desirable as it would seem to make it too easy for other philosophers to eat). More importantly, we cannot achieve starvation-freeness without such a rule. A MPrT-Net for this model is given in Section 5.

4 A NET FOR MODEL 3

Figure 3 is a MPrT-Net for model 3. The philosophers are elements of a finite set Q, having at least two elements (for eating to occur there must be two philosophers and two forks at the table). Each philosopher at the table is in one of two states—eating (E) or thinking (T). The rôles of the places and transitions in this net are as follows:

- Place P_1 contains a token $\varphi \in Q$ for each philosopher φ who is not at the table. Initially all philosophers are away from the table.
- Place P_2 contains the token EMPTY at only those times when the table is unoccupied. (This place is affected only when a philosopher arrives at the unoccupied table, and when a philosopher departs leaving the table unoccupied). Initially the table is not occupied so that P_2 contains the token EMPTY.
- Place P_3 contains all necessary information about the philosophers seated at the table, i.e. the seating arrangement, whether each one is thinking or eating, and (implicitly) where all the forks are. Each token in this place is of the form $(s_1, \varphi, \psi, s_2)$, representing philosopher φ in state s_1 seated on the left of philosopher $\psi \in Q$ in state s_2. P_3 is initially empty.
- Transition t_1 allows a philosopher to arrive at an unoccupied table. He will then be the left neighbour of himself.
- Transition t_2 covers the more 'normal' arrival where the incoming philosopher chooses an existing pair of adjacently seated philosophers and sits between them.

Declarations :

$Q = \{q_1, \ldots, q_N\}$: Set of $N \geq 2$ philosophers
$S = \{\mathrm{E,T}\}$: Set of states for philosophers
$A = \{\mathrm{EMPTY}\}$: Set containing table emptiness information
Variables $a, b, c : Q$; $r, s : S$
$M_0(P_1) = q_1 + \ldots + q_N$; $M_0(P_2) = \mathrm{EMPTY}$; $M_0(P_3) = \emptyset$

Graph :

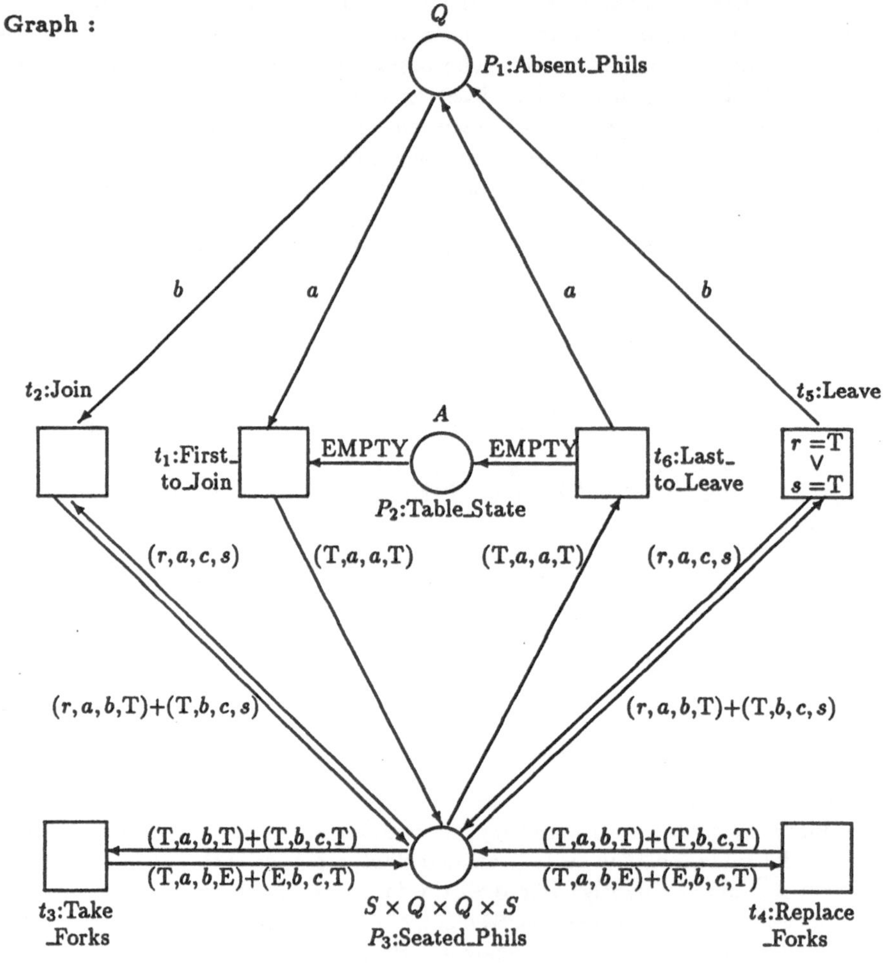

Figure 3: A MPrT-Net for the dynamic system without fairness

- The occurrence of transition t_3 describes the event of a philosopher starting to eat. A thinking philosopher, whose left and right neighbours are also both thinking, picks up the two available forks and starts to eat.

- The occurrence of transition t_4 causes an eating philosopher to put down his two forks and revert to thinking.

- Transition t_5 covers a 'normal' departure in which a philosopher picks up a fork from either side of him (providing at least one of his neighbours is thinking) and departs, leaving the table still occupied.

- Transition t_6 is included so that a philosopher who is the sole occupant of the table may take his fork and leave.

It is worth noting that by including in the net information about which philosophers are eating, but no explicit indication of where all the forks are, we are able to abstract the forks out of the problem (one of the consequences of this is that different transitions are not needed to cover the different 'arrival modes' shown in Figure 2). It is however, quite straightforward to obtain the distribution of forks at the table from the tokens in place P_3 : for each token of the form (T,φ, ψ,T), there is a fork on the table between the two thinking philosophers φ and ψ, and for each token of the form (E,θ,...), philosopher θ is using two forks to eat.

Later in this paper we will use place-invariants to verify that the net given in the following section for the fourth dynamic dining philosophers model represents the behaviour of philosophers as specified by that model. It is straightforward to do this for the net discussed in this section, although such a verification is not included in this paper due to lack of space. It may be found in [3], however.

Before proceeding to the fair net in the next section, we give a simple example of an execution of the net for the third model in which a philosopher at the table 'starves'. This will confirm the need for a refined version of the third model, and associated net. The execution proceeds as follows :

Let A (Aristotle) and S (Socrates) be two elements of the set of philosophers Q.

1. From the initial marking, t_1 fires with $a =$ A, depositing in place P_3 a single token (T,A,A,T).

2. t_2 then fires with $b =$ S, $a = c =$ A, and $r = s =$ T. This replaces the single token in P_3 by a pair of tokens (T,A,S,T) and (T,S,A,T).

3. From this marking, t_3 fires with a,b, and c taking the same values as in step 2. (Socrates starts eating.)

4. t_4 then fires in the only enabled way ($a = c =$ A; $b =$ S) so that Socrates stops eating.

5. Steps 3 and 4 then repeat *ad infinitum*, causing Socrates to eat infinitely many times, while Aristotle starves.

5 A FAIR NET FOR MODEL 4

The MPrT-Net corresponding to the fourth of the models described in Section 3 is given in Figure 4. There are two major differences between this net and the net of Figure 3. Firstly, there are now three places containing the information regarding the philosophers at the table—one place containing pairs of adjacent philosophers, one containing the states of all the philosophers at the table, and a place containing the queue of philosophers waiting to eat. The other major change is that the two transitions covering philosopher arrivals in the previous net have been 'folded' into a single transition, as have been the two transitions covering departures. (This has been done to limit the size of the net in Figure 4). Again the philosophers are elements of a finite set Q having at least two elements—this is particularly important in this model to avoid an almost immediate deadlock, because of the rule that a philosopher must eat before leaving the table. One might ask whether the 'eat-before-leaving' rule is really necessary—it will turn out to be essential when we come to the proof of fairness in the next section. (Without such a rule a philosopher may be infinitely often present at the table, but never eat; this will be prohibited by our definition of fairness.) The rôles of the five places and four transitions of the net given in Figure 4 are now described in detail:

- Place P_1 contains a token $\varphi \in Q$ for each philosopher φ who is not at the table. Initially all philosophers are away from the table.
- Place P_2 contains a token 0 or 1, depending on whether the table is empty or occupied respectively. Initially this place contains the token 0.
- Place P_3 contains a token for each adjacent pair of philosophers seated at the table, indicating their relative position. P_3 is initially empty. Each token in this place is of the form (φ, ψ), representing philosopher φ seated on the left of philosopher ψ.
- Place P_4 contains a token (φ, s, x) for each philosopher φ at the table, where s is the state of the philosopher (E or T), and x is 1 if φ has already eaten since arriving at the table, 0 otherwise. P_4 is initially empty.
- Place P_5 contains a single token representing a queue of philosophers waiting to eat, and is initially marked by the empty word λ over the set of philosophers, representing an empty queue.
- Transition t_1 has two classes of occurrence colours, depending on whether x (the input token from place P_2) is 0 or 1. This transition allows a philosopher to arrive at the unoccupied table ($x = 0$), and also covers the more 'normal' arrival ($x = 1$) where the incoming philosopher chooses an existing pair of adjacently seated philosophers and sits between them. On arrival the philosopher is placed at the tail of the queue, his relative position at the table is recorded in P_3, and his state (his name, that he is thinking, and that he has not yet eaten) is recorded in P_4.
- Transition t_2 also has two classes of occurrence colours. The first class covers a 'normal' departure ($a = b$) in which a philosopher picks up a fork from either

Declarations :

$Q = \{q_1, \ldots, q_N\}$: Set of $N \geq 2$ philosophers
$S = \{\mathrm{E,T}\}$: Set of states for philosophers
$A = \{0,1\}$: Set of 'answers'
Q^* : Set of words over Q, including the empty word: λ
Variables $a, b, c : Q$; $x, y, z : A$; $v, w : Q^*$
Function '$\cdot$' : $Q^* \times Q^* \rightarrow Q^*$: word concatenation operator
Function $[\,]$: $Bool \rightarrow \{0,1\}$ where $[false] = 0$ and $[true] = 1$
Function $\triangleleft$: $Q \times Q^* \rightarrow Bool$ where $a \triangleleft w = true$ iff a is a letter in the word w
$M_0(P_1) = q_1 + \ldots + q_N$; $M_0(P_2) = 0$; $M_0(P_3) = \emptyset$; $M_0(P_4) = \emptyset$; $M_0(P_5) = \lambda$

Graph :

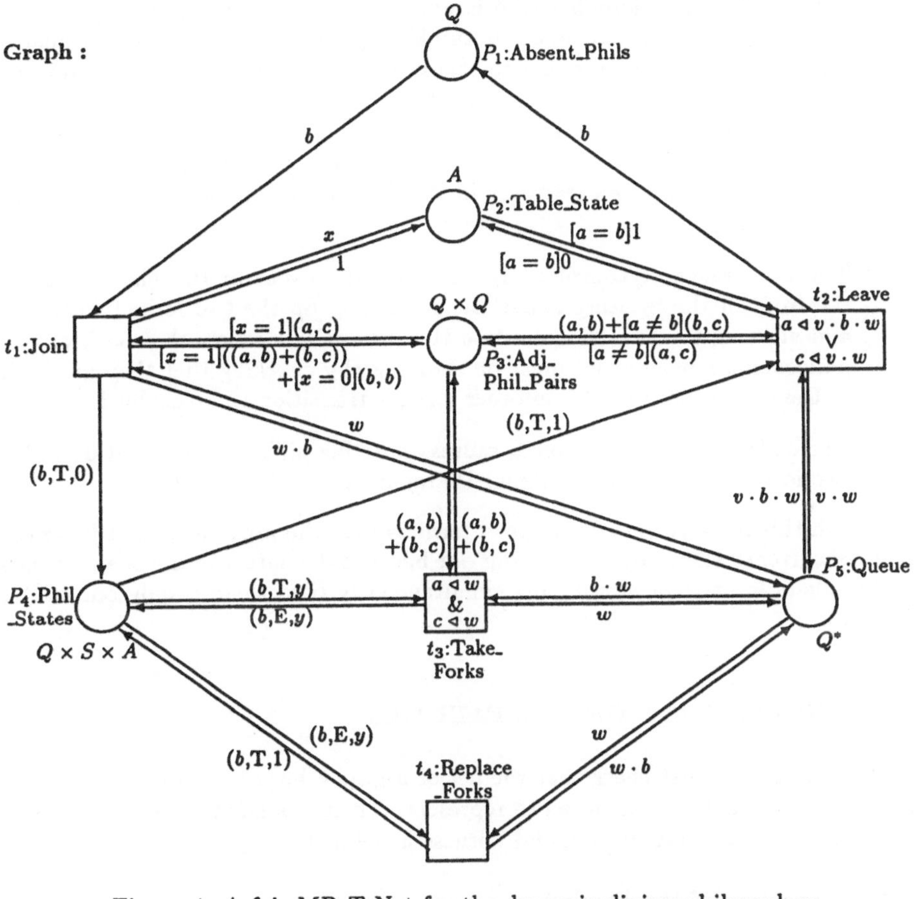

Figure 4: A fair MPrT-Net for the dynamic dining philosophers

side of him (providing at least one of his neighbours is thinking) and departs, leaving the table still occupied. In this case the departing philosopher appears in two tokens in place P_3; these two tokens are removed and replaced by a single token, describing how the two neighbours of the departing philosopher now become neighbours of each other. The other class of occurrence colours of this transition describes those departures in which the philosopher who leaves the table leaves it unoccupied. In this case, there is a single token in place P_3, thus the only alteration to the marking of that place is the removal of that token. In each case, the philosopher leaving the table must be thinking and must have eaten at least once since his last arrival. The philosopher can leave from any position in the queue. The transition features a guard which ensures that a philosopher who is not alone at the table may only leave if at least one of his neighbours is thinking (so that there is a fork available for the departing philosopher to take). It was found to be easier to do this by checking that at least one of the departing philosopher's neighbours was in the queue of (thinking) philosophers waiting to eat, rather than looking at the tokens recording the states of the departing philosopher's neighbours. (The latter requires an extra arc in the net, not to mention complicated arc inscriptions).

- The occurrence of transition t_3 describes the event of the philosopher at the front of the 'waiting-to-eat' queue picking up the two forks beside him and starting to eat. The guard on this transition ensures that both of this philosopher's neighbours must be thinking (by checking that they are both in the queue token in P_5), in order for this transition to be enabled.

- The occurrence of transition t_4 causes an eating philosopher to put down his two forks and revert to thinking. He rejoins the end of the queue.

Although this net has the advantage of fairness over the previous one, it lacks the true concurrency shown by the previous one because the nature of the queue forbids philosophers to start or stop eating simultaneously (i.e. there is only one waiter serving).

6 VERIFICATION OF THE FAIR NET

In this section, we first check that the net of Figure 4 has some of the basic properties of the model it is supposed to represent. Then, boundedness of the net and absence of deadlock are proved, and fairness is defined and proved.

6.1 Properties of the Model

We begin this subsection by giving a matrix (Figure 5) showing the initial marking, and the overall effect of each transition, for the fair net. Because the matrix shows only the overall effect of each transition, it contains less information than the net; however it does contain all the information we will need for what follows. This matrix shall be used below in confirming that the net matches the fourth model of the dynamic dining philosophers. In the given matrix, transitions t_1 and t_2 have

	$t_1^{(x=0)}$	$t_1^{(x=1)}$	$t_2^{(a=b)}$	$t_2^{(a\neq b)}$	t_3	t_4	M_0
P_1	$-b$	$-b$	$+b$	$+b$			$q_1 + \ldots + q_N$
P_2	$-0+1$		$-1+0$				0
P_3	$+(b,b)$	$-(a,c)+(a,b)+(b,c)$	$-(b,b)$	$-(a,b)-(b,c)+(a,c)$			$\emptyset$
P_4	$+(b,\mathrm{T},0)$	$+(b,\mathrm{T},0)$	$-(b,\mathrm{T},1)$	$-(b,\mathrm{T},1)$	$-(b,\mathrm{T},y)+(b,\mathrm{E},y)$	$-(b,\mathrm{E},y)+(b,\mathrm{T},1)$	$\emptyset$
P_5	$-w+w\cdot b$	$-w+w\cdot b$	$-v\cdot b\cdot w+v\cdot w$	$-v\cdot b\cdot w+v\cdot w$	$-b\cdot w+w$	$-w+w\cdot b$	λ

Figure 5: A matrix derived from the fair net

been 'unfolded' into their two classes of occurrence colours (as discussed in Section 5) for convenience. Hence the matrix has a column for each of six transitions. The column vector corresponding to one of these transitions t will be denoted by $\underline{t}$.

The following lemmas confirm that the net of Figure 4 has the major properties of the model it claims to represent. For the proofs we use place-invariants as in [9] (although a little less formally, as no algebraic specification is explicitly given). For our purposes, a place invariant i will be a vector associating with each place of the net a term over a variable y, such that $\underline{t}.i$ always gives an empty multiset, whenever t is any one of the (six) transitions of the matrix in Figure 5. (The important result for such invariants is that $M.i = M_0.i$, for any $M \in [M_0\rangle$.) The product '.' used here is defined as follows:

- For a multiset A and a term B over the variable y, $A.B$ is the result of substituting A for y in B.
- For any (reachable) marking $M = (A_1, A_2, A_3, A_4, A_5)^T$ (of the fair net) and a vector $I = (B_1, B_2, B_3, B_4, B_5)^T$ of terms over y, $M.I$ is the multiset obtained by adding the five multisets $A_j.B_j$, j=1 to 5, i.e. the sum of the termwise products.

The other notation used in the following lemmas is D_{MS}, for the set of multisets over a set D.

Lemma 1 *Every philosopher $\varphi \in Q$ is either away from the table (there is one token corresponding to the philosopher φ in P_1) or at the table (there is one token of the form $(\varphi,\ldots)$ in P_4).*

Proof : We use the invariant $i_1 = (y, \emptyset, \emptyset, proj(y), \emptyset)^T$ where $proj : (Q \times S \times A)_{MS} \rightarrow Q_{MS}$ is the linear extension to multisets of the projection mapping $(\varphi,\ldots)$ to the single element multiset φ.

Checking that i_1 is in fact a place invariant involves verifying that $\underline{t}.i = \emptyset$ holds for each of the six transitions of the matrix in Figure 5. We will not go through this procedure in full, but instead give an example of how it is done by looking just at the first of the six transitions. We have, for $t = t_1^{(x=0)}$,

$$\begin{aligned} \underline{t}.i_1 &= (-b).y + (b,T,0).proj(y) \\ &= -b + proj(b,T,0) \\ &= -b + b \\ &= \emptyset \end{aligned}$$

In the following lemmas such checking of place invariants is not shown.

Now, for any reachable marking $M \in [M_0\rangle$, we have

$$\begin{aligned} M(P_1) + proj(M(P_4)) &= M(P_1).y + M(P_4).proj(y) \\ &= M.i_1 \\ &= M_0.i_1 \\ &= (q_1 + \ldots + q_N).y + \emptyset.proj(y) \\ &= q_1 + \ldots + q_N \end{aligned}$$

□

Lemma 2 *Every philosopher at the table (i.e. represented by a token in P_4, and not appearing as a token in P_1) appears as the first component of exactly one (ordered pair) token in P_3 (i.e. is seated on the left of somebody). Furthermore, each philosopher not at the table (i.e. in place P_1) does not appear as the first component of any such token.*

Proof : We need to show that for each reachable marking $M \in [M_0\rangle$, $M(P_1) + pr_1(M(P_3)) = Q$, where $pr_1 : (Q \times Q)_{MS} \rightarrow Q_{MS}$ is the linear extension to multisets of the projection which maps each ordered pair of philosophers to the multiset over Q consisting solely of the first element of the pair.

We use the invariant $i_2 = (y, \emptyset, pr_1(y), \emptyset, \emptyset)^T$. Let $M \in [M_0\rangle$ be arbitrary. We have

$$\begin{aligned} M(P_1) + pr_1(M(P_3)) &= M(P_1).y + M(P_3).pr_1(y) \\ &= M.i_2 \\ &= M_0.i_2 \\ &= q_1 + \ldots + q_N \end{aligned}$$

□

Lemma 3 *Every philosopher at the table (i.e. represented by a token in P_4, and not appearing as a token in P_1) appears as the second component of exactly one (ordered pair) token in P_3 (i.e. is seated on the right of somebody). Furthermore, each philosopher not at the table (i.e. in place P_1) does not appear as the second component of any such token.*

Proof : The proof is entirely similar to the proof of Lemma 2. □

Lemma 4 *For every token of the form $(\varphi, T, ..)$ in P_4, φ is a letter in the word token in P_5 (i.e. every thinking philosopher at the table is in the queue).*

Proof : To obtain an invariant with which this lemma may be proved, we first define a function $mset : Q^* \rightarrow Q_{MS}$ which converts each word over Q to the multiset of its letters. We also define $think : (Q \times S \times A)_{MS} \rightarrow Q_{MS}$ as the linear extension to multisets of the function with action $(\varphi,\mathrm{T},..) \mapsto \varphi$, $(\varphi,\mathrm{E},..) \mapsto \emptyset$.

With the above definitions, the lemma says that for each reachable marking M, $think(M(P_4)){=}mset(M(P_5))$. These definitions also give us the invariant :

$$i_4 = (\emptyset, \emptyset, \emptyset, think(y), -mset(y))$$

For each reachable M, we then have

$$\begin{aligned} think(M(P_4)) - mset(M(P_5)) &= M(P_4).think(y) + M(P_5).(-mset(y)) \\ &= M.i_4 \\ &= M_0.i_4 \\ &= \emptyset \end{aligned}$$

The desired result follows immediately. □

Lemma 5 *There is always exactly one (queue) token in P_5.*

Proof : This is clear since every transition in the matrix of Figure 5 removes one token from and adds one token to place P_5. □

Lemma 6 *The tokens in place P_3 properly represent a group of philosophers seated at one round table, i.e. they may be arranged into a sequence of the form (a_1, a_2), (a_2, a_3),...,(a_j, a_1) (where $j \leq N$), in which the a_i's are distinct.*

Proof *(Sketch)*: By induction over reachable markings : the Lemma is clearly true in the initial marking since P_3 is then empty; the first transition to fire must be t_1 in a colour with $x = 0$ (nothing else is enabled), and when this happens the Lemma is true with $j = 1$. By inspection of the net, the firing of any transition after this first arrival preserves the truth of the Lemma (Lemmas 2 and 3 ensure that the a_i's remain distinct because a philosopher already in a token in P_3 is not in P_1, and thus not able to arrive again). □

Lemma 7 *There is a token of the form (b, b) in P_3 iff there is only one token in this place (i.e. a philosopher is his own (left and right) neighbours iff he is alone at the table).*

Proof : This lemma follows immediately from the previous one. □

Lemma 8 *P_2 contains the token 1 iff P_3 is marked by a nonempty multiset (i.e. iff the table is occupied).*

Proof : Firstly note the (obvious) fact that P_2 always contains exactly one token, either 0 or 1. Now, by inspection of the matrix of Figure 5, the marking of P_2 is changed exactly when a token of the form (b, b) is added to or removed from P_3. By Lemma 7, such an action changes the 'status' of P_3 (whether this place is empty or not). The fact that initially P_2 is marked by 0, while P_3 is empty, completes the proof by establishing the truth of the Lemma in the initial marking. □

6.2 Boundedness

Proposition 1 *The net in Figure 4 is bounded by the total number of philosophers, N.*

Proof: Let $|M(P_i)|$ denote the number of tokens in place P_i in any given reachable marking M. By Lemma 5 we must have $|M(P_5)| = 1$, and it is also clear that $|M(P_2)| = 1$ in any reachable marking. Hence these two places are clearly bounded by 1.

By Lemma 1, we have $|M(P_1)| + |M(P_4)| = N$, hence places P_1 and P_4 are each bounded by N. Finally, since (by Lemma 2) $|M(P_1)| + |M(P_3)| = N$, place P_3 is also bounded by N.

We have now shown that each place is bounded by N (or better), in other words that the net is bounded by N. □

6.3 Absence of Deadlock

Proposition 2 *The net in Figure 4 cannot deadlock. That is, at least one transition is enabled in every reachable marking.*

Proof: Consider any reachable marking $M \in [M_0\rangle$. Firstly, suppose that place P_1 is not empty in M. Then t_1 must be enabled in some occurrence colour, since:

- If place P_2 contains the token 0, then t_1 is enabled in a colour with $x = 0$.
- If place P_2 contains the token 1 then by Lemma 8 there is at least one philosopher pair in place P_3, and hence t_1 is enabled in a colour with $x = 1$.

Now suppose that place P_1 *is* empty in M, in which case there are $N \geq 2$ tokens in each of places P_3 and P_4 (by Lemmas 1 and 2). Then there is still at least one enabled transition:

- If there is a token of the form (..,E,..) in P_4, then t_4 is enabled.
- Otherwise, all N tokens in P_4 are of the form (..,T,..), and the queue token in P_5 is an N-letter word containing each element of Q once (by Lemma 4). Let φ be the first letter of the word token in P_5 (so that this token is of the form $b \cdot w$ with $b = \varphi$). Since φ appears in a token (φ,T,..) in P_4, by Lemma 2 there is a token (φ, θ) (for some $\theta \in Q$) in P_3. By Lemma 3, there is also a token (ψ, φ) in P_4 (for some $\psi \in Q$). Furthermore, by Lemma 7 we must have $\psi \neq \varphi \neq \theta$ since there are N tokens in P_3. It follows that the tokens (ψ, φ) and (φ, θ) are distinct. (We note this because transition t_3—which we shall soon show is enabled—requires *two* tokens to be in P_3.) By assumption, P_4 contains a token of the form (..,T,..) for every philosopher in Q, so in particular the philosophers ψ and θ each appear in such a token. By Lemma 4, ψ and θ are both letters in the word token in P_5, so since they are distinct from φ, the guard on t_3 is satisfied. We have now shown that sufficient tokens are in place to enable t_3 (with a, b, c taking the values ψ, φ, θ respectively).

Since $M \in [M_0\rangle$ was arbitrary, at least one transition is enabled in any reachable marking. □

6.4 Fairness

Before we prove fairness of the net, we must define what the concept of fairness should mean in the dynamic dining philosophers system. The definition which will be given shortly is based on a concept of fairness for finite state programs given in [7]. Intuitively, fairness of the net should be related to how often the various philosophers actually eat, i.e. transition t_3 is the one of interest. Keeping this in mind, the definition given in [7] adapted to the dining philosophers would tell us that a particular execution of the net is fair if every philosopher who is infinitely often enabled to start eating actually starts eating infinitely often. The following definitions make this concept precise.

Let $\Gamma = M_0[t_{i_0}\rangle M_1[t_{i_1}\rangle M_2 \ldots$ be an execution of the net (by Proposition 2 we may take Γ to be infinite), where associated with each fired transition t_{i_k} is an occurrence colour α_k.

Definition 1 *For each philosopher $\varphi \in Q$, a φ-*occurrence colour *of a transition t is an occurrence colour of t in which the variable b is assigned the value φ. (We shall consider an occurrence colour of a transition to be simply an assignment to the variables appearing in arcs surrounding that transition which validates the transition guard.)*

Definition 2 *A transition t is said to be φ-*enabled *if it is enabled for some φ-occurrence colour.*

Definition 3 *A φ-*firing *of a transition t is a firing of t in a φ-occurrence colour.*

Definition 4 *Γ is* fair *if for each $\varphi \in Q$, either t_3 is never φ-enabled after some marking M_j, or else t_3 undergoes infinitely many φ-firings in Γ.*

Definition 5 *The net is* fair *if every execution Γ is fair.*

Proposition 3 *The net in Figure 4 is fair.*

Proof *(Sketch)*: Let $\varphi \in Q$ be a philosopher, and let Γ be an arbitrary execution of the net, as above. We must show that Γ is fair. It suffices to show that whenever t_3 becomes φ-enabled, then either a φ-firing of this transition occurs within a finite number of steps of the execution, or else t_3 somehow becomes continuously disabled.

Now suppose that t_3 is φ-enabled at some stage of the execution Γ. (In what follows, we will talk only about what happens after this point in Γ; thus a phrase such as "t_3 never fires" will mean that t_3 never fires after the given stage in Γ.) Since t_3 is φ-enabled at the given stage of the execution, the following tokens (and others) must be in place:

- a token of the form (φ,T,y) in place P_4
- a queue token of the form $\varphi.w$ in place P_5

We consider two cases, corresponding to the two possible values of y.

Case 1 **The philosopher φ has not yet eaten ($y = 0$) :** We show that in this case, t_3 must φ-fire within a finite number of steps. The proof is by contradiction— we assume that in fact t_3 never φ-fires, and then show that we eventually (within a finite number of steps) reach a point where no other transition firing is enabled, and hence the (infinite) execution stops.

Since, by assumption, t_3 never φ-fires, there can never be a token of the form (φ,E,..) in P_4 (by the proof of Lemma 1, the token (φ,T,..) in P_4 must be the only token involving φ in this place). Thus t_4 can never become φ-enabled, which in turn means that there can never be a token (φ,T,1) in P_4. Consequently t_2 is never φ-enabled. This shows that φ remains permanently in the queue token in place P_5 (by Lemma 5 we may talk about *the* token in this place). Furthermore, since philosophers may only be added onto the end of the queue (by transitions t_1 and t_4), φ must remain at the *front* of the queue. Thus t_3 may not become ψ-enabled for any other philosopher $\psi \neq \varphi$. So the fact that t_3 never φ-fires implies that in fact this transition never fires in any occurrence colour (since every occurrence colour of t_3 is a ψ-occurrence colour for some $\psi \in Q$).

Suppose that m is the number of tokens in place P_4, in which case (by the proof of Lemma 1) there will be $N - m$ tokens in place P_1. Furthermore, let k be the number of tokens of the form (..,E,..) ('eating tokens') in place P_4, so that there are $m - k$ tokens of the form (..,T,..) ('thinking tokens') in this place. (Here we must have $0 \leq k < m \leq N$).

Since t_3 never fires, no 'eating' tokens may be created in place P_4. Now, every firing of t_4 decreases the number of eating tokens in this place by 1, hence t_4 may fire at most k times, and then never again (because there are only k eating tokens in P_4 at the given stage of the execution).

Now note that since P_4 contains $m - k$ thinking tokens, this place certainly contains no more than $m-k$ tokens of the particular form (..,T,1), and also that t_4 (which may fire only k times) is the only transition which creates tokens of the form (..,T,1). From this we conclude that since t_2 removes one token of this particular form each time it fires, it can fire at most $m - k$ times using the tokens already in place P_4, and at most k times using tokens created by t_4 after the given stage of the execution. Thus t_2 may fire at most m times, and then never again.

A similar argument shows that t_1 may fire no more than N times.

We have now shown that if t_3 never φ-fires after the given stage (and hence never fires again in any occurrence colour, by the result at the end of the second paragraph of this case), then each other transition may fire only finitely many times before it becomes disabled. But this means that within a finite number of steps, the execution reaches a point after which *no* transition ever fires again. This contradicts the fact that Γ is infinite.

Hence the original assumption is false, i.e. t_3 must φ-fire within a finite number of steps.

Case 2 **The philosopher φ has already eaten ($y = 1$)** : This case differs from Case 1 because t_2 is φ-enabled (i.e. φ may leave the table as he has already eaten, and is not forced to remain at the front of the queue as in the previous case). If, in the execution Γ, t_3 fires before t_2 fires (i.e. before φ leaves the table), then the firing must be a φ-firing (because φ is at the head of the queue, and this situation may only be changed by a φ-firing of t_2 or t_3), and there is no problem. If φ does leave the table before t_3 fires, then one of two things must happen in Γ.

The first possibility is that t_1 never φ-fires after this point (φ never returns to the table) in which case t_3 is never again φ-enabled, and so Γ is fair.

The second possibility is that t_1 does φ-fire, in which case φ returns to the table, but this time is represented by a token (φ,T,0) (indicating that he has not eaten since his return. If it so happens that he never again becomes enabled to start eating (see the end of Remark 2 below) then the definition of fairness maintains that the execution Γ is fair; if t_3 does become φ-enabled, then Case 1 above ensures that he will start eating within a finite number of steps, and again Γ is fair. □

It is possible to make the above proof more formal, by the use of firing count vectors, i.e. vectors which associate with each transition of the net the number of times that transition fires in some given finite execution of the net. A version of the above proof formalized in this manner may be found in [3].

Remark 1: The above proof does not use the fact that a φ-enabling of t_3 requires both neighbours of φ to be in the queue, so we have in fact proved that within a finite number of steps of reaching the head of the queue, φ will have *gained access to two forks* and *started eating* (unless he leaves the table and does not return).

Remark 2: We note here without proof that the given fair net has a slightly better property than the fairness concept adapted from finite state programs. It has been designed so that the only way in which a philosopher may become permanently disabled from starting to eat in an execution is if he leaves the table and never returns. This means that a philosopher at the front of the eating queue *will* eventually have access to two forks, and will then be enabled to start eating. (Proving this merely requires some repetition of the arguments used in Case 1 of Proposition 2 above). According to the definition of fairness used here, this behaviour is not necessary to have a fair system, however such behaviour is an added bonus to fairness because it ensures that the queue must keep moving. Hence in Case 2 of the above proof, the philosopher who leaves the table and then returns *will* eventually reach the front of the queue again, and thus will also be able to start eating again.

The concepts of deviation bound, fairness bound, synchronic lead, and synchronic distance defined by Silva in [10] were considered in relation to the net given here, but were found to be unsuitable for use because of the number of adaptions that would have to be made in order to satisfactorily describe the properties of interest in our net (for example, restricting our attention to transition t_3, and allowing one philosopher to eat an unlimited number of times while another one does not eat at all, on the condition that the latter philosopher is away from the table). It is felt that the definitions and notations of [10] would be of much greater use in a static dining philosophers system with fairness, where the complication of philosophers joining and leaving the dining party is absent.

7 FURTHER MODIFICATIONS OF THE SYSTEM

It may be that we wish to represent, in a form similar to the dynamic dining philosophers, a system in which there is a minimum and/or maximum number of entities (philosophers) allowed to be present at the table (or whatever that may represent). We now describe a way of ensuring that an (arbitrary) minimum or maximum number of philosophers allowed at the table is respected in the fourth model, by describing suitable modifications of the net of Figure 4.

Suppose the minimum number of philosophers allowed at the table is m. Firstly, modify the initial marking so that this minimum is respected. Now, include in the net a new place P_{excess}, which will contain a 'black dot' token for every 'excess' philosopher (above the minimum number allowed) at the table. P_{excess} should have an arc from t_1, and an arc going to t_2 (each of weight 1). This will cause t_2 to become disabled if P_{excess} is empty, i.e. prevent anyone from leaving when there are exactly m philosophers present, i.e. no excess ones.

The procedure is similar if we desire a maximum n to be respected (although if there is not also a minimum then the initial marking need not be changed, except to mark the new place). We include a place P_{spare} which will contain a black dot token for every 'spare seat' that could be introduced at the table without exceeding the maximum n. This place would have an arc coming in from t_2, and an arc going out to t_1. (Leaving philosophers create more 'spare room', entering philosophers decrease the space available.) The initial marking of P_{spare} should be $n - |M(P_4)|$. The main rôle of P_{spare}, similarly to P_{excess}, is that it disables a transition when empty, namely t_1 cannot fire, so no new philosophers can arrive if n philosophers are already present and there is no spare space (the table cannot expand any further).

The procedures described above are intended to be very general—if we wanted to enforce the particularly 'nice' minimum value 1, we could do so without introducing a new place. Simply, we would modify transitions t_1 to eliminate the class of occurence colours with $x = 0$, and t_2 to eliminate the class of occurrenc colours with $a = b$. (The initial marking would also be suitably adjusted, and place P_2 could be removed altogether.)

8 CONCLUSION

Various models of a dynamic dining philosophers system have been examined. A MPrT-Net for the most refined of the unfair models has been described. A MPrT-Net representing a fair model in which philosophers are enabled to start eating in an order determined by a queue has also been given. This latter net has the desired properties—it is bounded, deadlock-free, and starvation-free. The loss of concurrency associated with the introduction of fairness in the latter net suggests that a more sophisticated approach is needed if fairness and concurrency are to be combined.

ACKNOWLEDGEMENTS

Mr. Paul King of the Key Centre for Software Technology, Department of Computer Science, University of Queensland, challenged us to specify the dynamically changing dining philosophers system with nets. We are grateful for his stimulus and comments. We also acknowledge the helpful comments, arguments, and suggestions given by Geoff Wheeler during the work on this paper.

The permission of the Executive General Manager, Telecom Australia Research Laboratories, to present this paper is hereby acknowledged.

REFERENCES

[1] Billington J. Many-Sorted High-Level Nets. In: Proceedings of the Third International Workshop on Petri Nets and Performance Models, Kyoto, Japan, 11–13 December 1989, IEEE CS Press, Washington , D.C., USA, 1989

[2] Dijkstra EW. Hierarchical Ordering of Sequential Processes. Acta Informatica 1, 1971, pp 115–138

[3] Findlow G. An Investigation of Dynamically Changing Systems Using High-Level Nets. Draft Telecom Australia Research Laboratories Report

[4] Genrich HJ. Predicate/Transition Nets. In: Brauer, Reisig, Rozenberg (eds) Petri Nets: Central Models and their Properties. Advances in Petri Nets 1986, Part 1: Proceedings of an Advanced Course, Bad Honnef, September 1986. Springer-Verlag, Berlin, February 1987, pp 207–247 (Lecture notes in computer science no. 254)

[5] Genrich HJ, Lautenbach K. System modelling with high-level Petri nets. Theoretical Computer Science 1981; 13: 109–136, 1981

[6] Kaplan SM, Goering SK, Campbell RH. Specifying Concurrent Systems with Δ-Grammars. In: Fifth International Workshop on Software Specification and Design. IEEE, Pittsburgh, May 1989, pp 20–27

[7] Lichtenstein O, Pnueli A. Checking That Finite State Concurrent Programs Satisfy Their Linear Specification. In: Proc. 12th Annual ACM Symp. on Principles of Programming Languages, New Orleans, 1985, pp 97–107

[8] Peterson JL. Petri Net Theory and the Modeling of Systems. Prentice Hall, Englewood Cliffs, N.J., 1981

[9] Reisig W. Petri Nets and Abstract Data Types. To appear in: Theoretical Computer Science

[10] Silva M. Towards a Synchrony Theory for P/T Nets. In: Voss, Genrich, Rozenberg (eds) Concurrency and Nets. Springer-Verlag, Berlin, 1987

FORMALIZING THE BEHAVIOUR OF PARALLEL OBJECT-BASED SYSTEMS BY PETRI NETS

Joost Engelfriet
George Leih[1)]
Grzegorz Rozenberg

Department of Computer Science, Leiden University,
P.O.Box 9512, 2300 RA Leiden, The Netherlands

Abstract

Parallel object-based systems are modelled by POTs, where a POT is a Petri net with an additional structure imposed on its places (POT abbreviates Parallel Object-based Transition system). In a POT, parallelism, objects, references, communication, and creation are handled explicitly. Some basic properties of object-based systems are formalized as properties of POTs, viz. properties concerning reference passing and handshaking. Non-interleaving observations of (runs of) a POT are investigated, in particular when the POT satisfies the above properties.

1 INTRODUCTION

In this paper we propose a model for parallel systems that are "object-based" (following the classification of [18] "object-oriented" systems are object-based systems with "classes" and "inheritance"). The model, called Parallel Object-based Transition system (for short POT), is a Petri net with an additional structure imposed on its places. Using a Petri net allows one to specify the non-interleaving behaviour of a system, while the additional structure facilitates the modelling of specific object-based features.

1) The work of this author was conducted as part of the PRISMA project, a joint effort with Philips Research, partially supported by the Dutch "stimuleringsprojectteam informaticaonderzoek" (SPIN).

In an object-based system the task to be performed is divided into several subtasks, each of which is performed by a certain component (called object) of the system. As new subtasks are initiated, new objects may be created. All objects act in principle autonomously, and in parallel. Each object has its own local memory, in which it stores its private data (such as integers, booleans, and in particular references to other objects). Since these memories may not be shared, objects can exchange information only by communicating with each other. Communication partners are often selected through the use of references.

Now, in the underlying Petri net of a POT each place models an object in a certain state (of its local memory), and the additional structure of the place indicates the identity of the object and the set of references stored in its local memory.

In Section 2 we discuss the Petri nets that will be used for POTs. POTs themselves are introduced in Section 3. Section 4 shows, through examples, that POTs are suited to model parallel systems and languages with objects, references, and creation. Some fundamental properties of object-based systems, concerning reference passing and communication based on handshaking, are formalized in Section 5. A notion of an observation of (a run of) a POT is introduced in Section 6, and the observations of POTs with the above properties are investigated in Sections 6 and 7.

2 PETRI NETS

We will model parallel object-based systems by (possibly infinite) safe place-transition nets, to which some additional structure is added (in fact, Elementary Net systems ([16,17]) are also suited; the only reason for not considering this model is that it has a firing rule which prevents transitions with a "loop", as t_4 in Figure 1, to occur). In this section the definitions of such nets and their behaviour are recalled; we assume the reader to be familiar with P/T nets (see, e.g., [4,15]). For a set S, $\mathcal{P}_{fin}(S)$ is the set of all finite subsets of S, and |S| denotes the cardinality of S.

A *place-transition net* (for short *P/T net*) is a triple N = (Pl,Tr,Init), where Pl is the set of *places*, Tr is the set of *transitions*, and Init: Pl $\longrightarrow \mathbb{N}$ is the *initial marking*. Each transition

$t \in Tr$ is of the form $t = (pre,post)$, with $pre,post \in (\mathcal{P}_{fin}(Pl) - \{\emptyset\})$; thus, we consider simple transitions only. We use pre(t) and post(t) to denote the components of t; for $p \in Pl$, $pre(p) = \{t \in Tr \mid p \in post(t)\}$ and $post(t) = \{t \in Tr \mid p \in pre(t)\}$.

For a net N = (Pl,Tr,Init), a *marking* of N is a function $M: Pl \to \mathbb{N}$. Let M and M′ be markings of N, and $t \in Tr$. Then t is called a *step* from M to M′ if $M(p) \geq 1$, for all $p \in pre(t)$, and $M'(p) = M(p) - |pre(t) \cap \{p\}| + |post(t) \cap \{p\}|$, for all $p \in Pl$. A sequence $s = M_0,t_1,M_1,t_2,\ldots,t_n,M_n$, with $n \geq 0$, is called a *firing sequence* of N if $M_0 = Init$ and t_i is a step from M_{i-1} to M_i, for all $1 \leq i \leq n$. A marking M of N is *reachable* if there exists a firing sequence of N in which M appears. A marking M of N such that $M(p) \in \{0,1\}$, for all $p \in Pl$, will be called *safe*. Such a marking will be identified with the set $\{p \in Pl \mid M(p) = 1\}$; this should not lead to confusion. N is called *safe* if all its reachable markings are safe. We will be interested in safe nets only.

The non-interleaving behaviour of P/T nets is usually defined using occurrence nets (also called causal nets), defined next (see, e.g., [3,4,9]). An occurrence net is meant to formalize a run of some net.

We use the following notation and terminology. Let N = (Pl,Tr,Init) be a net, and let $x,y \in Pl \cup Tr$. We say that x *precedes* y in N if there exist $n \geq 1$ and $x_0,\ldots,x_n \in Pl \cup Tr$ such that $x = x_0$, $y = x_n$, and $x_i \in pre(x_{i+1})$, for all $0 \leq i \leq n-1$. N is called *acyclic* if no element in $Pl \cup Tr$ precedes itself, and it is called *finitely preceded* if no element in $Pl \cup Tr$ is preceded by infinitely many others.

An *occurrence net* is an acyclic, finitely preceded net N = (Pl,Tr,Init) such that, for all $p \in Pl$, $|pre(p)| \leq 1$ and $|post(p)| \leq 1$, and $Init = \{p \in Pl \mid pre(p) = \emptyset\}$. It is well known that occurrence nets are safe.

We next define the non-interleaving behaviour of a safe P/T net N = (Pl,Tr,Init), using the notion of a process. A *process of* N is a pair (N′,h), where N′ = (Pl′,Tr′,Init′) is an occurrence net and $h: Pl' \to Pl$ is such that the restriction of h to Init′ is a bijection $Init' \to Init$ and, for every $t' \in Tr'$, there is a $t \in Tr$ such that the restriction of h to pre(t′) is a bijection $pre(t') \to pre(t)$ and the restriction of h to post(t′) is a bijection $post(t') \to post(t)$. The set of processes of N forms its (non-interleaving) behaviour.

3 POTS

Parallelism, objects, communication, references, and creation are the main features of parallel object-based systems. It is well known that Petri nets can model parallelism and communication; in this section we show how the other three features can be modelled by augmenting a Petri net with two functions 'obj' and 'ref'. Let N = (Pl,Tr,Init) be a safe P/T net.

The *object function* 'obj' assigns to each place an element of Ob (the infinite set of *objects*, which is fixed for the whole paper). The idea is that, for an object $b \in Ob$, the places in $obj^{-1}(b)$ represent b's potential local states. Obviously, since an object can only be in one state at a time, 'obj' should be injective on the reachable markings. This is realized by requiring that 'obj' is injective on the initial marking, and by requiring that, for all $t \in Tr$ and $b \in Ob$, there is a (unique) $p \in pre(t)$ with $obj(p) = b$ if and only if there is a (unique) $q \in post(t)$ with $obj(q) = b$; intuitively, p represents b's state before t took place, and q represents b's state afterwards. Note that this implies that obj(Init) = obj(M), for each reachable marking M.

Creation is modelled by considering an object to be *unborn* (= not yet created) as long as it is represented by a place in Init (and *alive* if it is represented by a place not in Init). Whenever $t \in Tr$ and $p \in pre(t)$ are such that $p \in Init$, obj(p) is said to be *created* in t; if $p \notin Init$, obj(p) is said to be *communicating* in t. Obviously, in order to assure that no object is created twice, it has to be required that $pre(p) = \emptyset$ for all $p \in Init$; note that the requirement that 'obj' is injective on Init is also crucial in this respect.

The *reference function* 'ref' assigns to each place a finite subset of Ob. Intuitively, if $b \in ref(p)$ for some $p \in Pl$, then obj(p) refers to b when it is in state p. Since objects represented by a place in Init are unborn, we take Pl - Init as domain for 'ref'.

Definition. A *parallel object-based transition system* (for short POT) is a triple S = (N,obj,ref), where N = (Pl,Tr,Init) is a safe P/T net, $obj: Pl \rightarrow Ob$ is the *object function*, and $ref: (Pl - Init) \rightarrow \mathcal{P}_{fin}(Ob)$ is the *reference function*, such that

1. $Init \subseteq \{p \in Pl \mid pre(p) = \emptyset\}$,

2. obj is injective on Init, and
3. $|obj^{-1}(b) \cap pre(t)| = |obj^{-1}(b) \cap post(t)| \leq 1$, for every $t \in Tr$ and $b \in Ob$.

For a POT S = (N,obj,ref) with N = (Pl,Tr,Init), we use N_S, obj_S, ref_S, Pl_S, Tr_S, and $Init_S$ to denote the different components of S. Note that to ensure that N is safe, it actually suffices to require that Init is safe (the special transitions of a POT preserve safeness).

A POT S such that N_S is an occurrence net is called a (*object-based*) *computation*. COMP denotes the set of all computations. A pair (R,h) is called a *process of* POT S if R ∈ COMP and h are such that (N_R,h) is a process of N_S and, for all $p \in Pl_R$, $obj_R(p) = obj_S(h(p))$, and $ref_R(p) = ref_S(h(p))$. The set of all processes of S forms its (non-interleaving) behaviour. In this paper we are mainly interested in computations; note that each element of COMP appears in the behaviour of some POT (viz. in its own behaviour).

4 EXAMPLES

We will now illustrate the definition of a POT by considering some examples. Figure 1 gives a graphical representation of a (finite) POT.

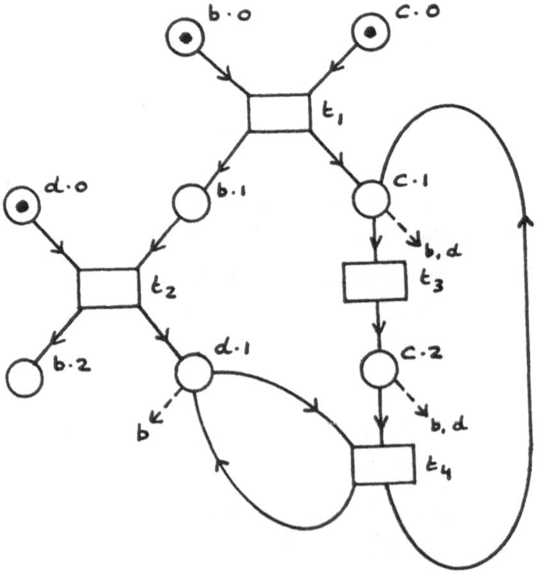

Figure 1

It is the POT S = ((Pl,Tr,Init),obj,ref), defined by Pl = {x·i | x ∈ {b,c}, 0 ≤ i ≤ 2} ∪ {d·0, d·1}, Init = {b·0, c·0, d·0}, obj(x·i) = x for all x·i ∈ Pl, ref(c·1) = ref(c·2) = {b,d}, ref(d·1) = {b}, and ref(b·1) = ref(b·2) = ∅. Moreover, Tr = $\{t_1,t_2,t_3,t_4\}$ with pre(t_1) = {b·0, c·0}, post(t_1) = {b·1, c·1}, pre(t_2) = {b·1, d·0}, post(t_2) = {b·2, d·1}, pre(t_3) = {c·1}, post(t_3) = {c·2}, pre(t_4) = {d·1, c·2}, and post(t_4) = {d·1, c·1}. The P/T net is drawn as usual, and the references of a place are indicated by dashed arrows. The object function is encoded in the identity of the places. In the initial marking objects b, c, and d (∈ Ob) are unborn. In t_1 objects b and c are created, whereas d is created in t_2 (by object b). Transition t_3 is an "internal" event of object c; note that t_2 and t_3 are concurrent. The only communication that can take place is between objects c and d in t_4. Note that d does not know its communication partner (i.e., c ∉ ref(d·1)), but c does (d ∈ ref(c·2)). Note also that c already refers to d (viz. in c·1) when d is not yet created. In the next section we discuss how to deal with situations like this.

Figure 2 shows an (infinite) computation; it is not in the behaviour of the POT of Figure 1. The labels of the transitions should be disregarded for the moment. Using the drawing conventions as explained above, the reader can easily recover the formal definition of this computation. Note that there are infinitely many objects that are never created.

It is well known that Petri nets can be used to formalize the operational non-interleaving semantics of programming languages with parallelism (see, e.g., [6,8,12,13]). We now consider a very simple toy programming language in which object creation, parallelism, and communication play a central role (we will later add references), and we show that POTs can be used to give such a semantics for this language. Let α and β be two *actions*. The set Stat of *statements* (typically s) and the set Prog of *programs* (typically p) are defined as follows.

$$s ::= \quad \alpha \mid \beta \mid \underline{\text{do}}\ s_1; \ldots ;s_n\ \underline{\text{od}} \mid \underline{\text{new}}(p) \qquad (n \geq 1)$$
$$p ::= \quad s_1; \ldots ;s_n;\ \underline{\text{end}} \mid \underline{\text{end}} \qquad (n \geq 1)$$

Each program $\bar{p}$ is initiated by creating an object that starts executing $\bar{p}$. In a statement of the form new(p), a new object is created, which

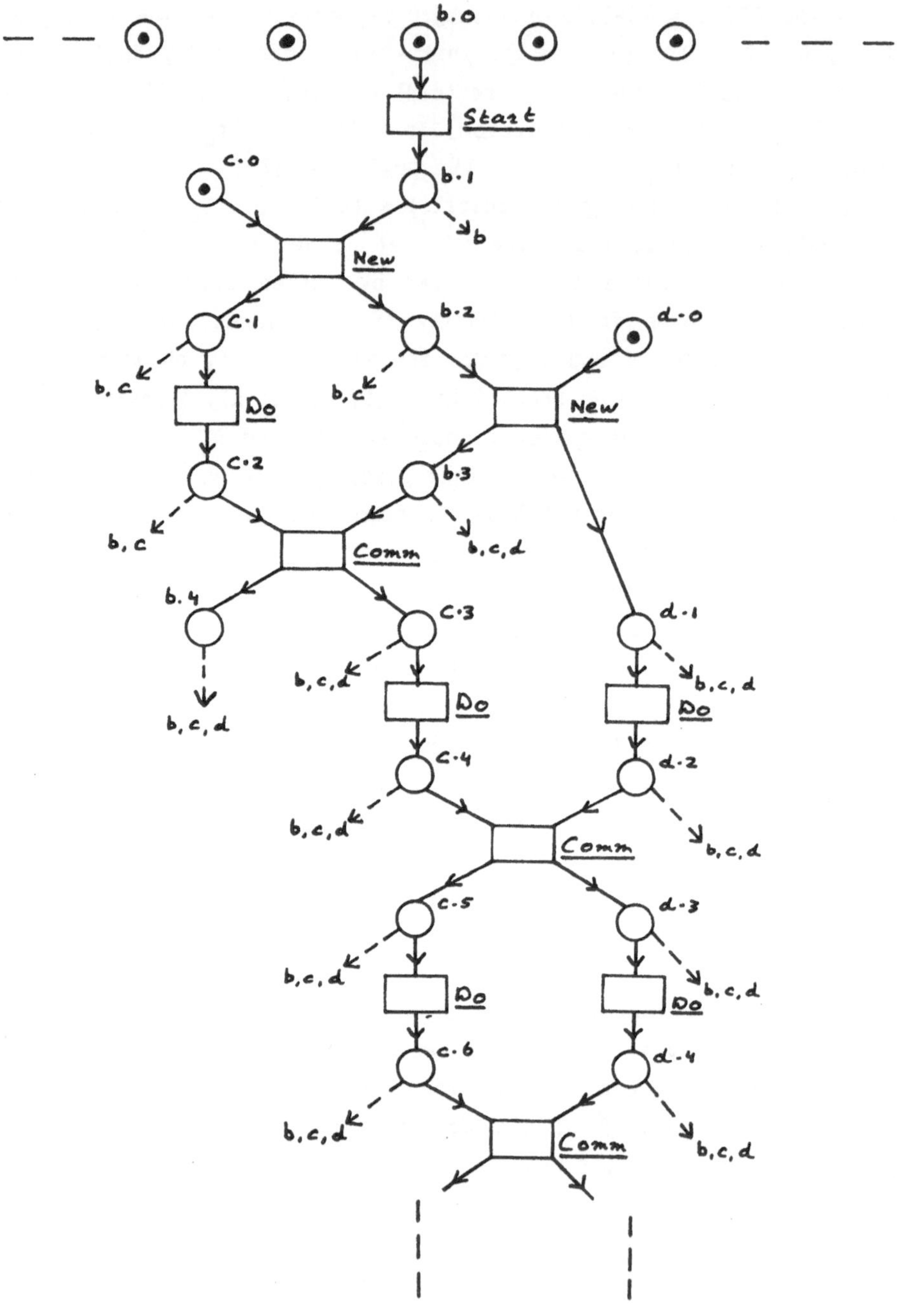
b.0
Start
c.0
b.1
b
New
c.1
b.2
d.0
b, c
Do
b, c
New
c.2
b.3
b, c
Comm
b, c, d
b.4
c.3
d.1
b, c, d
Do
b, c, d
Do
b, c, d
c.4
d.2
b, c, d
Comm
b, c, d
c.5
d.3
b, c, d
Do
Do
b, c, d
c.6
d.4
b, c, d
Comm
b, c, d

Figure 2

performs p in parallel with all other existing objects. An object performing action α has to communicate with another object performing β, and the other way around; thus, these objects have to wait for each other, they "shake hands". The do-statement repeats a sequence of statements arbitrarily many times.

We formalize the non-interleaving behaviour of our toy programs by associating with each program $\bar{p} \in$ Prog an infinite POT $S(\bar{p})$ = ((Pl,Tr,Init),obj,ref), as follows. Let Pl = Ob × (Prog ∪ {u}), where u stands for unborn, let Init = Ob × {u}, let obj(b,x) = b, for all (b,x) ∈ Pl, and let ref(b,p) = ∅. Tr is defined by the following axioms (cf. [14]), where a transition (pre,post) is written as pre ⟶ post. All meta-variables, except for b_{fix} which is an arbitrary but fixed element of Ob, are universally quantified, and $b_1 \neq b_2$.

Start $\{(b_{fix},u)\} \longrightarrow \{(b_{fix},\bar{p})\}$.

Comm $\{(b_1,\alpha;p_1),\ (b_2,\beta;p_2)\} \longrightarrow \{(b_1,p_1),\ (b_2,p_2)\}$.

Do $\{(b,\underline{do}\ s_1;\ldots;s_n\ \underline{od};p)\} \longrightarrow \{(b,s_1;\ldots;s_n;\underline{do}\ s_1;\ldots;s_n\ \underline{od};p)\}$
and
$\{(b,\underline{do}\ s_1;\ldots;s_n\ \underline{od};p)\} \longrightarrow \{(b,p)\}$.

New $\{(b_1,\underline{new}(p_2);p_1),\ (b_2,u)\} \longrightarrow \{(b_1,p_1),\ (b_2,p_2)\}$.

It is easily checked that $S(\bar{p})$ is a POT. We already know that objects cannot be created twice in POTs; since b_2 ranges over the infinite set Ob in axiom New, there is always a fresh name available if an object has to be created.

As an example, consider the program $\bar{p}$ = new(do α od; end); new(do β od; end); β; end. Then Figure 2, with all references removed, contains a picture of one of the infinite computations of $S(\bar{p})$. Each transition is labeled by the axiom that defines it. We have used b for b_{fix}. Note that c and d are arbitrary objects. Note also that, in other computations of $S(\bar{p})$, c could have communicated with d arbitrarily often before communicating with b.

From this example it can be seen that POTs can be used to formalize the operational semantics of languages with object-based features; only references are not yet present. Reference passing can be added to the above language, or rather to its semantics, in the following (unnatural, but easy and didactically useful) way. We assume that during communication objects exchange all references they have, that a newly created object inherits all references of its creator, and that its creator refers to it. Moreover, we assume that each object refers to itself. Finally, we require that objects may only communicate if they refer to each other.

Instead of using places of the form (b,p) $\in$ Ob $\times$ Prog, we now use places of the form (b,p,σ), where $\sigma \in \mathcal{P}_{fin}(Ob)$ is the current set of references of object b; hence, ref((b,p,σ)) = σ. The axioms above can now be adapted as follows.

<u>Start'</u> $\{(b_{fix},\omega)\} \longrightarrow \{(b_{fix},\bar{p},\{b_{fix}\})\}$.

<u>Comm'</u> $\{(b_1,\alpha;p_1,\sigma_1),\ (b_2,\beta;p_2,\sigma_2)\} \longrightarrow$
$\{(b_1,p_1,\sigma_1 \cup \sigma_2),\ (b_2,p_2,\sigma_1 \cup \sigma_2)\}$,
provided $b_1 \in \sigma_2$ and $b_2 \in \sigma_1$.

<u>Do'</u> $\{(b,\underline{do}\ s_1;\ldots;s_n\ \underline{od};p,\sigma)\} \longrightarrow \{(b,s_1;\ldots;s_n;\underline{do}\ s_1;\ldots s_n\ \underline{od};p,\sigma)\}$
and
$\{(b,\underline{do}\ s_1;\ldots;s_n\ \underline{od};p,\sigma)\} \longrightarrow \{(b,p,\sigma)\}$.

<u>New'</u> $\{(b_1,\underline{new}(p_2);p_1,\sigma),\ (b_2,\omega)\} \longrightarrow$
$\{(b_1,p_1,\sigma \cup \{b_2\}),\ (b_2,p_2,\sigma \cup \{b_2\})\}$.

This time Figure 2, including the references, contains the unique infinite computation of the POT associated to the example program we considered above: since c·2 does not refer to object d, c has to communicate with b first to obtain d's address.

We would like to remark that, in [7], POTs are used to give a non-interleaving operational semantics of a toy version of the programming language POOL-T (see [2]). As a matter of fact we hope to give such a semantics for full POOL-T.

5 DESIRABLE PROPERTIES OF POTS

In a "real" object-based language an object may not communicate with another object at will: it is always required that communicating objects refer to each other, or that one of them (the "sender") refers to the other (the "receiver"), or something like that. In the language presented in the previous section (without the references), objects are allowed to communicate with arbitrary objects; this unnatural situation was corrected by introducing references, and by requiring that two objects may only communicate if they refer to each other (as in CSP, see [11]). Such a requirement on communication, which we call handshaking, can be formulated as follows.

Definition. Let S be a POT. S has the *handshaking property* if, for every $t \in Tr_S$ and for all distinct $p,q \in (pre(t) - Init)$, $obj_S(p) \in ref_S(q)$.

Since, in the sequel, we are mainly concerned with computations, it suffices to have a notation only for the set of all computations with the handshaking property: this set is denoted HANDSHAKE. Notice that HANDSHAKE is precisely the set of all computations of all POTs with the handshaking property. The computation in Figure 1 does not have the handshaking property (since $c \notin ref(d \cdot 1)$), the one in Figure 2 does. In fact, all POTs and computations associated with the programs of the previous section (with references added) have the handshaking property, due to the demands in Comm'.

We next formulate a property of POTs which is even more fundamental than the handshaking property. Reconsider the POT in Figure 1. In this computation object c refers to object d after transition t_1, whereas d is not present in $pre(t_1)$ (in fact, d is still unborn). This is a situation one would not expect in object-based systems: objects can exchange information only during communication. This means that each new reference an object obtains in a communication transition t must have been either a reference of one of the communication partners of t, or one of the objects involved in t. This demand on the proper transfer of references is now formalized. For a set of places $X \subseteq Pl_S$ in a POT S, $ref_S(X) = \cup \{ref_S(p) \mid p \in (X - Init_S)\}$.

Definition. Let S be a POT. S has the *reference passing property* if, for each $t \in Tr_S$, $ref_S(post(t)) \subseteq ref_S(pre(t)) \cup obj_S(pre(t))$.

The set of all computations with the reference passing property is denoted REFPAS. This is also the set of all computations of POTs having the reference passing property, as can be seen easily. The POT in Figure 1 does not have the reference passing property ($ref(post(t_1)) = \{b,d\} \not\subseteq ref(pre(t_1)) \cup obj(pre(t_1)) = \emptyset \cup \{b,c\}$), the computation in Figure 2 does have this property. In fact, all POTs and computations associated with one of the programs of the previous section have the reference passing property (even with = instead of ⊆).

In our opinion a POT describes a "real" object-based system only if it satisfies some demands concerning reference passing and concerning communication. Hence, it is quite natural to consider the computations in HANDSHAKE ∩ REFPAS, where both of the component properties are intuitively appealing and still rather simple. We would like to observe here that the above statement is especially meaningful in systems with object creation. In fact, if there would be finitely many objects which were all present right from the start, one could, to trivialize the matter, assume that everybody knows everybody; then the handshaking property would of course be satisfied, and there would be no need for passing references (as in CSP, see [11]).

Since it will be very handy in the sequel, we now give alternative definitions, using a uniform notation, of the handshaking and reference passing property for computations.

Let, for each R ∈ COMP, the function $handshake_R$: $(Pl_R - Init_R) \rightarrow \mathcal{P}_{fin}(Ob)$ be defined by $handshake_R(p) = \{obj(q) \mid q \in pre(post(p)), q \neq p, q \notin Init\}$, for all $p \in (Pl_R - Init_R)$. It is obvious that R ∈ HANDSHAKE iff $handshake_R \subseteq ref_R$[2]. Let, moreover, the function $refpas_R$: $(Pl_R - Init_R) \rightarrow \mathcal{P}_{fin}(Ob)$ be defined by $refpas_R(p) = \{b \in Ob \mid \exists q \in pre(pre(p))$ such that $obj_R(q) = b$ or $b \in ref_R(q)\}$, for all $p \in (Pl_R - Init_R)$. Then it is easily seen that R ∈ REFPAS iff $ref_R \subseteq refpas_R$. Thus, R ∈ HANDSHAKE ∩ REFPAS iff $handshake_R \subseteq ref_R \subseteq refpas_R$.

6 OBSERVATIONS

In the rest of this paper we discuss the view an observer may have of a computation. We will assume that the observer recognizes the different objects, and that he can see all transitions and their causalities. Thus, the observer is concurrent himself. The only thing an observer cannot see in a computation is the contents of the local memories of the objects, since these are private (an object is a black box). Consequently, when observing a computation R he sees $(N_R, obj_R, empty_R)$, where $empty_R$ is the function defined by $empty_R(p) = \emptyset$, for all $p \in (Pl_R - Init_R)$.

---

[2] For functions f,g: $A \rightarrow \mathcal{P}(B)$, we use the following notation. $f \subseteq g$ if $f(a) \subseteq g(a)$ for all $a \in A$. $(f \cup g)(a) = f(a) \cup g(a)$, for all $a \in A$.

However, when the observer knows a certain property of R, i.e., when a set $P \subseteq$ COMP is given with $R \in P$, the observer may be able to infer partial knowledge about ref_R. For instance, if P = HANDSHAKE and $R \in P$, he may infer that each place p refers to the objects in $handshake_R(p)$, since $handshake_R(p) \subseteq ref_R(p)$. Thus, he concludes that $(N_R, obj_R, handshake_R)$ is an approximation of R. In general, he may infer any (N_R, obj_R, ref) such that $ref(p) \subseteq ref_R(p)$, for all $p \in Pl_R - Init_R$. This is the intuition behind the following definition.

Definition. Let R be a computation. A computation R′ is an *observation of* R if $N_{R'} = N_R$, $obj_{R'} = obj_R$, and $ref_{R'} \subseteq ref_R$.

Thus, an observation is obtained from a computation by simply removing some of the references. The set of all observations of R is denoted obs(R). For a set $P \subseteq$ COMP, $obs(P) = \cup\{obs(R) \mid R \in P\}$.

The main result of this section is a simple characterization of the set obs(HANDSHAKE ∩ REFPAS), based on the existence of certain paths in the observation. As a corollary we obtain a polynomial time (even nondeterministic logarithmic space) algorithm to determine whether or not a given finite observation is an observation of a computation in HANDSHAKE ∩ REFPAS (note that the straightforward algorithm to solve this problem, trying out all possible additions of references, would require exponential time). We first investigate two easier cases, of which one (viz. REFPAS) is nontrivial.

It is obvious that each $R \in$ COMP is the observation of some handshaking computation, viz. of $(N_R, obj_R, ref_R \cup handshake_R)$, and thus obs(HANDSHAKE) = COMP.

To investigate obs(REFPAS), we first consider Figure 2 a bit closer. Recall that it is a reference passing computation. One might say that the reference c of d.2 has been "passed" from a place representing c to d·2 via the sequence c·0, b·2, d·1, d·2. In general, if place p refers to object c in a reference passing computation R, then there is an $n \geq 1$ and a sequence of places $p_0, \ldots, p_n$ such that

1. $p_n = p$, $obj_R(p_0) = c$, and $p_i \in pre(pre(p_{i+1}))$, for all $0 \leq i \leq n-1$, and

2. $c \in ref_R(p_i)$ for all $1 \leq i \leq n$.

A sequence satisfying 1 (in any computation R) will be called a *potential passing line of* c *to* p *in* R (if 2 also holds, then c is passed via this line to p; if 2 does not hold, then c could have been passed via this line). These considerations can also be formulated using the function $born_R$: $(Pl_R - Init_R) \rightarrow \mathcal{P}_{fin}(Ob)$, which is defined by $born_R(p) = \{c \in Ob \mid$ there exists a potential passing line of c to p in R$\}$, for all $p \in (Pl_R - Init_R)$. Now $ref_R \subseteq born_R$ for all reference passing computations R.

If, in an observation R′ of R, it has been concluded that p refers to c, then obviously the sequence $p_0,\ldots,p_n$ satisfying 1 also exists in R′. Thus, (because $born_{R'} = born_R$) this means that $ref_{R'} \subseteq born_{R'}$ also holds for observations R′ of reference passing computations.

Conversely, if observation R is such that $ref_R \subseteq born_R$ then there exists for each place p and $b \in ref_R(p)$ a sequence $p_0,\ldots,p_n$ satisfying 1 above. If b is added to $ref_R(p_i)$ for all $1 \leq i \leq n$, then also demand 2 is satisfied. If this is done for all p and $b \in ref_R(p)$, then we obtain a computation with the reference passing property of which R is an observation. This shows the following theorem.

Theorem. *Let* $R \in$ COMP. *Then* $R \in$ obs(REFPAS) *iff* $ref_R \subseteq born_R$.

Since $born_R$ can be determined in polynomial time (even in nondeterministic logarithmic space), we get as a corollary that it is polynomially decidable, for finite $R \in$ COMP, whether or not $R \in$ obs(REFPAS).

Now we proceed to formulate an analogous theorem for obs(HANDSHAKE ∩ REFPAS). Notice that R is an observation of some R′ ∈ HANDSHAKE ∩ REFPAS if and only if $R'' = (N_R, obj_R, ref_R \cup handshake_R)$ is an observation of some reference passing computation: the if-direction follows because R", and thus all computations of which R" is an observation, has the handshaking property, and the only-if direction follows because R" is an observation of R′ ($handshake_R = handshake_{R'} \subseteq ref_{R'}$). Using the previous theorem, we can now directly derive the following result.

Theorem. *Let* $R \in$ COMP. *Then*
$R \in$ obs(HANDSHAKE ∩ REFPAS) *iff* $ref_R \cup handshake_R \subseteq born_R$.

Again it is easily seen that, for finite R, it is polynomially decidable whether or not $R \in$ obs(HANDSHAKE ∩ REFPAS).

7 DERIVING REFERENCES

In this section we define the "best" observation in a given set obs(R) with respect to a given property $P \subseteq COMP$, where $R \in P$. Then we give a simple characterization of this "best" observation in the case that P is the set of all computations with the handshaking and the reference passing property. Again, our characterization yields a polynomial time algorithm which, without using ref_R, determines the best observation in this case.

An observer can make no distinction between two computations R and R′ in P with $N_R = N_{R'}$ and $obj_R = obj_{R'}$: they are both observed in the same way. Thus, if an observer concludes that b has to be a reference of place p in his observation, then b must have been a reference of p both in R and in R′. More precisely, an observer of a computation R in P may conclude that b is a reference of $p \in Pl_R$ iff b is a reference of p in each computation $R' \in P$ with $N_{R'} = N_R$ and $obj_{R'} = obj_R$. This can be formalized as follows.

Definition. Let $P \subseteq COMP$ and $R \in P$.

1. The function $derive_{R,P}$: $(Pl_R - Init_R) \rightarrow \mathcal{P}_{fin}(Ob)$ is defined by $derive_{R,P}(p) = \{b \in Ob \mid b \in ref_{R'}(p)$ for all $R' \in P$ with $N_{R'} = N_R$ and $obj_{R'} = obj_R\}$, for all $p \in (Pl_R - Init_R)$.
2. The *best observation of* R *using* P is best-obs(R,P) = $(N_R, obj_R, derive_{R,P})$.

Note that $derive_{R,P}$ does not depend on the reference function of R, i.e., $derive_{R,P} = derive_{R',P}$ for all $R' \in P$ with $N_{R'} = N_R$ and $obj_{R'} = obj_R$. This is precisely what one would expect: since an observer of R cannot see ref_R, R and R′ have the same best observation. Notice, moreover, that $derive_{R,P} \subseteq ref_R$; hence, the best observation is indeed in obs(R). Finally, note that the term "best" is justified: if one would add one more reference b to a place p, then there would be a computation R′ in P in which b is not a reference of p, whereas R′ could well have been the computation that is observed.

Now we are going to characterize $derive_{R,P}$ for P = HANDSHAKE ∩ REFPAS. Again we consider separately the cases HANDSHAKE and REFPAS, which turn out to be rather easy: best-obs(R,HANDSHAKE) = $(N_R, obj_R, handshake_R)$, for all $R \in$ HANDSHAKE, and best-obs(R,REFPAS) =

$(N_R, obj_R, empty_R)$, for all $R \in$ REFPAS. In fact, since the obtained observation has the handshaking (reference passing, resp.) property itself, one cannot possibly add more references.

The case HANDSHAKE $\cap$ REFPAS is more difficult; one cannot simply add the functions $handshake_R$ and $empty_R$, which is shown as follows. Consider the computation R in Figure 2, and assume that the fact that $R \in$ HANDSHAKE $\cap$ REFPAS is given. Using the handshaking property it can be concluded that d·2 refers to c. Moreover, since there is just one potential passing line of c to d·2 in R (viz. c·0, b·2, d·1, d·2), b·2 and d·1 must have referred to c too. Similarly, c.4 has to refer to d because c and d communicate, and consequently also c·3 and b·3 must have referred to d. The fact that b is a reference of c·5 (which, by the way, cannot be concluded from our two properties) is not enough to conclude that b is also a reference of c·3 and c·4, since b might have been passed as well via d·1 and d·2.

These considerations lead to the following definition. Let P = HANDSHAKE $\cap$ REFPAS and $R \in P$, and let the function $extra_R$: $(Pl_R - Init_R) \rightarrow \mathcal{P}_{fin}(Ob)$ be defined as follows. Let $p \in (Pl_R - Init_R)$. Then $extra_R(p) = \{b \in (Ob - \{obj_R(p)\}) \mid \exists q \in Pl_R\colon b \in handshake_R(q)$, and all potential passing lines of b to q in R contain p$\}$. It should be clear that $extra_R$ contains references that can be derived from our two properties. In the following theorem, which is proved in [7], we state that no more references can be derived.

Theorem. *Let* $R \in$ HANDSHAKE $\cap$ REFPAS. *Then*
best-obs(R,HANDSHAKE $\cap$ REFPAS) = $(N_R, obj_R, handshake_R \cup extra_R)$.

Note that $extra_R$ depends on $handshake_R$, but not on ref_R. Thus, an observer can use the above characterization to determine the best observation of a computation in HANDSHAKE $\cap$ REFPAS that he is observing (of course without knowing ref_R). He can in fact determine it in polynomial time (if R is finite), because $extra_R$ can be computed in polynomial time (and the same holds for $handshake_R$).

With this characterization, we can now determine the best observation of the computation in Figure 2, if P = HANDSHAKE $\cap$ REFPAS is given. It can be derived that b is a reference of c·1 and c·2, that c is a reference of b·2, b·3, and d.i for all $i \geq 1$, and that d is a reference of b·3 and c·i for all $i \geq 3$. No other references can be determined.

CONCLUSION

We conclude by discussing two additional topics.

In [7], on which this paper is based, we give a definition of a POT that can also handle object destruction. For the results in the present paper we do not need destruction, while [7] contains some results which rely on destruction. The problem of "dangling references", for instance, is rather simple for the POTs of this paper: one can show that, for $R \in COMP$, each reachable marking M of R has the property that $ref_R(M) \subseteq obj_R(M - Init_R)$ if and only if $ref_R \subseteq born_R$. In particular, this means that if R has the reference passing property, then it is impossible to reach a situation in which a place refers to a non-existing (i.e., unborn) object (this even holds for arbitrary POTs). One can imagine that the dangling references problem becomes more intricate for POTs with destruction.

We noted already that there are other natural demands on communication and reference passing that one can consider. For instance, one might investigate POTs S for which Pl_S contains two disjoint subsets SEND and RECEIVE, such that for each transition $t \in Tr_S$ in which objects communicate there is a $p \in SEND$ and a $q \in RECEIVE$ with $pre(t) = \{p,q\}$ and $obj_S(q) \in ref_S(p)$. Thus, in each transition, just two objects may communicate, of which one is the sender and the other is the receiver. The reference passing property should now be adapted in such a way that the sender cannot obtain new references in such a transition. As another example, we have modelled actor systems ([1,5,10]) as POTs, see [7]; actor systems use asynchronous messages for communication.

REFERENCES

1. G.A.Agha. Actors: a model of concurrent computation in distributed systems. PhD thesis, M.I.T. Press, 1986.
2. P.America. Definition of the programming language POOL-T. ESPRIT-Project 415, Doc.no.91, Philips Research Labs., Eindhoven, The

Netherlands, 1985.

3. E.Best, R.Devillers. Sequential and concurrent behaviour in Petri net theory. Theor Comput Sci 55, 1987, pp 87-136.
4. E.Best, C.Fernández C. Nonsequential processes. Springer, Berlin Heidelberg New York, 1988 (EATCS monographs of Theor Comput Sci vol 13, eds W.Brauer, G.Rozenberg, A.Salomaa).
5. W.D.Clinger. Foundations of actor semantics. PhD thesis, Technical Report 633, M.I.T. AI Lab, 1981.
6. P.Degano, R.DeNicola, U.Montanari. A distributed operational semantics for CCS based on Condition/Event systems. Acta Informatica 26, 1988, pp 59-92.
7. J.Engelfriet, G.Leih, G.Rozenberg. Parallel object-based systems and Petri nets--Part 1 and 2. Reports 90-04 and 90-05, University of Leiden, The Netherlands, 1990.
8. U.Golzl. On representing CCS programs by finite Petri nets. In: M.P.Chytil, L.Janiga, V.Koubek (eds), Proceedings, Math Found of Comput Sci, Springer, Berlin Heidelberg New York, 1988, pp 339-350 (Lecture notes in computer science no 324).
9. U.Goltz, W.Reisig. The non-sequential behaviour of Petri nets. Information and Control 57, 1983, pp 125-147.
10. C.Hewitt. Viewing control structures as patterns of passing messages. Journal of Artificial Intelligence 8, 1977, pp 323-364.
11. C.A.R. Hoare. Communicating sequential processes. Comm of the ACM 21, 1978, pp 666-677.
12. M.Nielsen. CCS--and its relationship to net theory. In: W.Brauer, W.Reisig, G.Rozenberg (eds), Petri nets: applications and relationships to other models of concurrency, Springer, Berlin Heidelberg New York, 1987, pp 393-415 (Lecture notes in computer science 255).
13. E-R.Olderog. Operational Petri net semantics for CCSP. In: G.Rozenberg (ed), Advances in Petri nets, Springer, Berlin Heidelberg New York, 1987, pp 196-223 (Lecture notes in computer science 266).
14. G.D.Plotkin. A structural approach to operational semantics. DAIMI Report FN-19, Aarhus University, Denmark, 1981.
15. W.Reisig. Petri nets: an introduction. Springer, Berlin Heidelberg New York, 1985 (EATCS monographs of Theor Comput Sci vol 4, eds W.Brauer, G.Rozenberg, A.Salomaa).

16. G.Rozenberg. Behaviour of Elementary Net Systems. In: W.Brauer, W.Reisig, G.Rozenberg (eds), Petri nets: central models and their properties, Springer, Berlin Heidelberg New York, 1987, pp 60-94 (Lecture notes in computer science 254).

17. P.S.Thiagarajan. Elementary Net Systems. In: W.Brauer, W.Reisig, G.Rozenberg (eds), Petri nets: central models and their properties, Springer, Berlin Heidelberg New York, 1987, pp 26-59 (Lecture notes in computer science 254).

18. P.Wegner. Learning the language. Byte vol 14, no 3, March 1989, pp 245-253.

High Level Distributed Transition Systems

Nisse Husberg*

Digital Systems Laboratory, Department of Computer Science,
Helsinki University of Technology, SF-02150 Esbo, FINLAND

Abstract

A high level distributed transition system is defined as a diagram which is the basis of a heterogeneous algebraic theory seen as a category. The support structure can be defined as another heterogeneous algebraic theory. The behaviour is a diagram in the same category. This approach is close to both Petri net theory and the initial algebra semantics of programming languages.

1 Introduction

Petri nets have been used for a long time to model parallel and distributed systems. In practice only the *higher level nets* are useful because the more elementary nets often generate "football fields" when modelling real systems. The higher level nets are rather intuitive concepts, however, and use primitive mathematical tools.

One good candidate for a more efficient formalism is category theory. The use of category theory is advantageous in models of parallel and distributed systems because it is easy to build strongly *hierarchical* categorial constructs which provides tools for *abstraction*. Another reason is that *composition* is one of the basic concepts in category theory. The concept of *universality* is very important especially in defining the behaviour of concurrent systems because it states that universal constructs "always exist and are unique". Category theory should be seen as a collection of mathematical *tools* for defining models of distributed systems and proving properties. In itself it does not give new results but compared to traditional formalisms it makes it easier to work with the system models.

Category theory has been used in several approaches to concurrent systems [23], [1], [17], [25]. In this paper a new approach is presented in which the concurrent system (a distributed transition system) not only is an object in a category but itself is a special category (or rather the basis of a category). Also *high level* features can be described in a natural way. There is not one specific "high level system" but rather a collection of behaviourally equivalent systems where structural complexity is transformed to denotational complexity and vice versa. Thus it is possible to choose a suitable tradeoff for each application.

*Supported by a grant from the Finnish Academy of Science

The modelling was originally done for Petri nets in form of Elementary Net systems [12] and extended to Place/Transition systems and distributed transition systems [13], but it is very natural to incorporate high level features - instead of *free* categories the quotient categories are used which are obtained by applying a congruence to the free categories. As before Petri nets can be seen as special cases.

In modelling parallel and distributed systems the properties of the categorial *product* are the most essential. Note that the products used here have *projections* in contrast to the *tensor products* used by [17]. This is essential because algebraic theories are used and the projections can intuitively be considered as special operators "gathering arguments" and "distributing results" of a transition (a proper operator). Without projections there would be no target tuples which have a most important function in this model. In Meseguer's and Montanari's approach this is handled by special operators *added* to the monoid, but in a heterogeneous algebraic theory all these special operators are "built in".

Algebraic theories are special categories with products, which are abstractions of algebras. Here the more general heterogeneous (or many-sorted) algebraic theory is used. The homogeneous (or one-sorted) algebraic theory is simply a special case. It was first used in [15] and later extensively by the ADJ group [8].

Heterogeneous algebraic theories are well known in computer science for applications in abstract data types and semantics of programming languages [9], [3]. Thus this approach can be seen as an extension of the categorial semantics to concurrency.

2 Mathematical tools

The heterogeneous algebraic theories used here are virtually the same as the many-sorted algebraic theories used in [5] and [22] - for formal definitions see [11] and [12]. They are based on *products* and dual to those algebraic theories based on coproducts normally used in the ADJ group papers like [8]. In general the term "heterogeneous" is synonymous to "many-sorted" throughout the paper.

The definitions of category and other basic concepts in category theory can be found in [8] and [19] or in any textbook on category theory. The class of objects of a category $\underline{K}$ is denoted $Ob_{\underline{K}}$ and the class of morphisms $Mor_{\underline{K}}$. A morphism f from A to B, i.e. $f \in Mor_{\underline{K}}(A, B)$, is usually denoted $f : A \rightarrow B$, where A is the *source* and B the *target*. Note the order of composition ($fg : A \rightarrow C$, if $f : A \rightarrow B$ and $g : B \rightarrow C$).

2.1 Products and multisets

A product in category theory is an *object* together with *projections* (special morphisms from the product object to other objects from which the product is formed) and *mediating morphisms* from certain other products. All these constructs play an important rôle when modelling concurrent systems in an algebraic theory.

Definition 1 (Product object) A *product* is an *object* A^I (or $\Pi_{i \in I} A_i$) with *morphisms* p_i^I: $A^I \rightarrow A_i$ for $i \in I$ such that for each object $Y \in Ob_{\underline{K}}$ and for *any* family of morphisms (f_i: $Y \rightarrow A_i | i \in I$) there is *exactly one* morphism h: $Y \rightarrow A^I$ such that $f_i = hp_i^I$ for all $i \in I$ (the universal property).

Usually the *mediating morphism* h is denoted (h_i) or $(h_1, \ldots, h_n)$ if I is a finite set. The morphism h is also called *universal arrow* or *target tuple*. Here the name *target tuple* is preferred because in the heterogeneous (or many-sorted) case the *sorts* of the elements in the tuple must be the same as the sorts in the product which is the target of the morphism h.

The morphisms p_i^I are called *projections*. A *finite* product has a finite index set I. The *identity* for a product A^I is the I-tuple of projections $(p_i | i \in I)$, where $p_i\colon A^I \to A_i$.

If $I = \phi$ (the empty set) then for each object $Y \in Ob_{\underline{K}}$ there must be exactly one morphism from Y into the *empty product* $E = A^{\phi}$, i.e. the *empty target tuple* $()\colon Y \to E$. Thus E is a *terminal object* [19,p.31].

In heterogeneous algebraic theories the objects are *sort strings* u: $[n] \to S$. These strings are *products* and often denoted $u = s_{i_1} s_{i_2} \ldots s_{i_n}$ where $i_j \in I$ and $I = [n]$. The projections are then denoted p_j^u for $j = 1 \ldots n$ and the *empty string* is named λ.

Certain target tuples behave exactly like projections. If w = abc and u = ab then there is a target tuple $p_u^w = (p_1^w, p_2^w)\colon w \to u$, which "picks the ab-tuple out of the abc-tuple". This means that composition of any morphism $t = (t_1, t_2, t_3)\colon v \to w$ with p_u^w will give the morphism $t' = (t_1, t_2)\colon v \to u$, where $t_1\colon v \to a$, $t_2\colon v \to b$, and $t_3\colon v \to c$. Here target tuples of projections only are also called projections. A *subproduct* can be defined using this general concept of projections.

Definition 2 (Subproduct) In a heterogeneous algebraic theory based on the sort set S an object u: $[n] \to S$ is a *subproduct* of another object w: $[p] \to S$ iff there is a projection $p_u^w\colon w \to u$ and $n \leq p$.

If the products are strings, then a substring is a subproduct but not vice versa, because "ca" is a subproduct of "abc" although it is not a substring.

All products of the same family of objects are *isomorphic* which in category theory means that they are essentially the same as most constructs in category theory are unique up to isomorphism. Thus it is possible to talk about *the* product instead of *a* product of a family of objects. It is sometimes useful to forget the order in the sort strings and talk about the *underlying family* of objects of the sort string. Then the definitions of many properties will be very close to the traditional ones, e.g. for transition systems and Petri nets (see Section 3).

Definition 3 (Family of elements) A *family* of elements over a set S is a mapping $F\colon I \to S$, where I is an index set.

The underlying family of objects can be used to construct a *multiset*, that is, a set with several occurrences of the same element. A multiset is often defined as a function $M\colon S \to \mathbf{N}$, where $\mathbf{N}$ is the set of natural numbers, as in [20] and [23]. In [18], however, this is called a *multinumber* and a multiset (I, ϱ) is seen as a "normal" set I with an equivalence relation ϱ on I. Monro considers the elements in the equivalence classes to be different but of the same *sort* - a view that is very suitable in heterogeneous algebraic theories. The multinumber is very close to Monro's multiset and can easily be determined from the multiset.

Here Monro's approach is used with a small difference in the notation. Monro says that elements of I which are in the same equivalence class are *of the same sort* but does not define the set of sorts explicitely. Here the sort of an equivalence class is *named* in S and the multiset is a mapping $\mathcal{M}$: I $\rightarrow$ S: i $\mapsto$ s=j$\mathcal{M}$ iff (i,j) $\in \varrho$. The only important thing with the set I is that it contains the right number of elements.

Let the index set I of a family of elements be the disjoint union of sets $[n_1]$, $[n_2]$, ... , with n_i indicating the number of elements of sort s_i. The corresponding multiset (or multinumber according to Monro) would be the mapping M : S $\rightarrow$ N : $s_i \mapsto [n_i]$.

If I = [n] = {1, 2, ... , n}, where n indicates the total number of elements, then a family can be interpreted as a *string* F : [n] $\rightarrow$ S. The *index* $1 \leq i \leq n$ is mapped to the i*th* element in the string.

Thus families $(s_i)_{i \in I}$ are isomorphic to the objects of the heterogeneous algebraic theories based on the sort set S because its objects are all sort strings w: [n] $\rightarrow$ S over the set S [11]. The only difference is really that the elements in the strings are ordered. A family represents the *isomorphism class of products* constructed from this family of objects.

A *morphism* between families F: I $\rightarrow$ S and G: J $\rightarrow$ T is a pair f = (f_I, f_S) of mappings f_I: I $\rightarrow$ J and f_S: S $\rightarrow$ T such that $(if_I)G = (iF)F_S$ for all i $\in$ I.

Proposition 1 (Underlying family of objects) The *underlying family of objects* F : I $\rightarrow$ S of a string (product) w : [n] $\rightarrow$ S in an algebraic theory based on S is isomorphic to each permutation of the string w.

Proof. Define I as the set of all projections $p_i^w : w \rightarrow s_i$. Then I is isomorphic with [n] and the family F: I $\rightarrow$ S isomorphic with w : [n] $\rightarrow$ S. Because all products from the same family of objects are isomorphic, F is also isomorphic to each permutation of the string w.

□

For the construction above, let UF(w) denote the underlying family of objects for a product w in the heterogeneous algebraic theory.

The *subproduct* can also be defined using the underlying family of objects. The family F will be a *subfamily* of G iff there is a morphism f = (f_I, f_S): F $\rightarrow$ G which is an *inclusion*, i.e. f_S must be an inclusion as it is essential that the sorts are the same, but it is enough for f_I to be an injection. An object u is a subproduct of an object w if UF(u) is a subfamily of UF(w).

2.2 Operators

The most important morphisms in a heterogeneous algebraic theory are the (proper) *operators*. The traditional definition of an operator must be generalized a bit when modelling concurrent systems. Definition 4 below can be found in [6], but it was not really used and the other ADJ papers have a single sort as target.

Given some operator symbol set Σ and sort set S, a *parallel* (heterogeneous) operator is defined as follows:

Definition 4 (Parallel operator) A *(parallel) operator* $\sigma_{w,u}$ is a typed operator symbol $(\sigma,(w,u)) \in R$, where $\sigma \in \Sigma$, $(w,u) \in S^* \times S^+$ and R is a type relation R: $\Sigma \times (S^* \times S^+)$.

R can be divided into (w,u)-indexed subsets (operator sets) which are denoted $\Sigma_{w,u} = \{\sigma \mid \sigma_{w,u} \in R\}$. Sometimes Σ is used (ambigiously) to denote the union of all operator sets $\Sigma_{w,u}$. Usually the pair $S\Sigma = (S,\Sigma)$ is called a (sorted) *signature* [7].

The parallel operator $\sigma_{w,u}$ has *type* (w,u), *arity* w, and *sort* u. No operator can have sort $u = \lambda$, but $w = \lambda$ is perfectly possible ($\lambda \in S^*$) and defines a *constant* (operator) of sort u. If u = s, where $s \in S$, then the operator is the normal *single-sorted* operator used in most ADJ papers like [9].

As the concept of operator soon will be extended to all morphisms in a heterogeneous algebraic theory, the operator in Definition 4 will be called a *proper* operator to distinguish it from the projections and target tuples.

An S-sorted heterogeneous algebraic theory $\underline{T}_{S\Sigma}$ based on Σ is usually constructed from the string category $\underline{St}S$ by adding the proper operators from Σ to the morphism sets with the right source and target and requiring that composition and "target tupling" are defined for these too. The objects of both categories are *products* of sorts from the sort set S, i.e. they are *strings* w of elements from S (see Definition 6).

In the S-sorted heterogeneous algebraic theories *all morphisms* can be seen as (general) operators, not only the proper operators but also projections and derived operators [11], [8], [22]:

Definition 5 (General operator) A (general) *operator* is a morphism $\sigma_{w,u}$: w $\rightarrow$ u in an S-sorted heterogeneous algebraic theory $\underline{T}_{S\Sigma}$.

Thus a proper operator and a single-sorted operator are special cases of the general operator. Similar constructions were presented in [6] and in [25]. Zamfir used a special "constructor" (or "higher order operation") $\|$ to define her parallel operator. In the algebraic theory context used here (with *products* as objects, not coproducts) the parallel operator is a *primitive*.

Proposition 2 (Operator equivalence) In an S-sorted heterogeneous algebraic theory the general operator $\sigma_{w,u} = (\sigma_{w,s_1}, \sigma_{w,s_2}, \ldots, \sigma_{w,s_n}) : w \rightarrow u$ is equivalent to the target tuple of operators $\sigma_{w,s_i}: w \rightarrow s_i$, where s_i is in the string u.

Proof. Given a general operator $\sigma_{w,u}$: w $\rightarrow$ u, it will be equivalent to the target tuple of single-sorted operators defined by composition $\sigma_{w,s_i} = \sigma_{w,u}p_i^u$ for all i such that s_i is in the string u. On the other hand, if there are operators σ_{w,s_i} for i in some index set I, then there is a product (string) in the algebraic theory $u = s_i^I$ and a target tuple $(\sigma_{w,s_i})^u$ by the universal property of the product. This tuple is a general operator by Definition 5.

□

In a heterogeneous algebraic theory $\underline{T}$, if there are three operators (morphisms) σ_1, σ_2, σ_3 from object w to objects s_3, s_4, s_5 then there must be a general operator $\sigma = (\sigma_1,\sigma_2,\sigma_3)$ from w to the product $u = s_3s_4s_5$ (Figure 1). Of course the composition $\sigma p_i^u = \sigma_i$.

The projections are special operators which take one component out of a tuple and could intuitively be seen as "distributing" the results from applying a proper operator. On the other hand the definition of a product $w = s_1 \ldots s_n$ requires that there must be a target tuple h: Y $\rightarrow$ w from any object Y which has morphisms f_i: Y $\rightarrow$ s_i to the objects in the product (Definition 1) such that $f_i = hp_i^w$. Thus it is

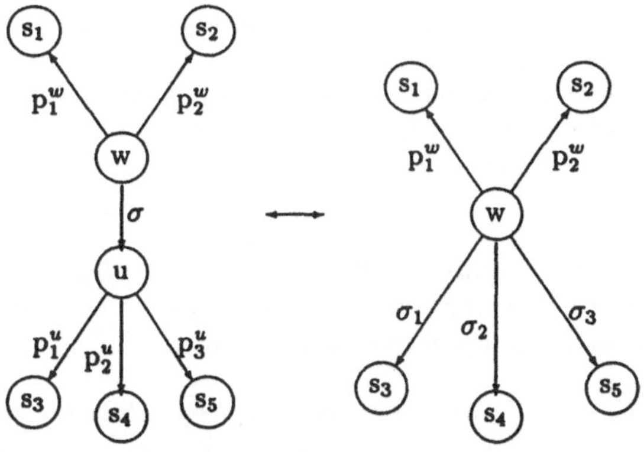

Figure 1: The general operator σ

also possible to intuitively see the projections as operators "gathering arguments" to a proper operator.

A certain general operator is often needed, that is, a tuple of operators where all but one are identities, i.e. projections $p_1^{s_i}$ for all s_i in w which are *not* in the source of the proper operator σ. This operator, the *extended* operator (σ), can be composed with a target tuple which consists of "too many" arguments. It simply uses only those arguments needed and composes the rest with identities.

Proposition 3 (Extended operator) For each operator σ: w $\rightarrow$ u and product w′ which has w as its subproduct there is an *extended operator* (σ): w′ $\rightarrow$ u′ which is a target tuple of σ and identities.

Proof. If w is a subproduct of w′ then for w′ there is an isomorphic product w″ = wv. Any target tuple t: x $\rightarrow$ w′ determines another target tuple t′: x $\rightarrow$ w″ which has the same elements, that is, t′ is the composition of t with the isomorphism from w′ to w″. The elements of t will not be changed, only reordered, because this isomorphism is a target tuple of projections only [11]. There must be projections from w″ to w and v, $p_w^{w''}$: w″ $\rightarrow$ w and $p_v^{w''}$: w″ $\rightarrow$ v, respectively. Then the composition of $p_w^{w''}$ and σ is a morphism σ': w″ $\rightarrow$ u. Consider the product uv. It has projections p_u^{uv}: uv $\rightarrow$ u and p_v^{uv}: uv $\rightarrow$ v. By the universal property of the product there must be a target tuple (σ', p_v^v): w″ $\rightarrow$ uv. Let u′ be isomorphic to uv. Then there is an isomorphism (projection) $p_{u'}^{uv}$: uv $\rightarrow$ u′.

The composition $p_{w''}^{w'}(\sigma', p_v^v)p_{u'}^{uv}$: w′ $\rightarrow$ u′ is the extended operator (σ).

□

This means that an operator is completely local, but its effect can always be included in any global "state" - if this global state contains the local one. Because σ is a parallel operator, it can consist of several other operators.

2.3 Algebraic theories

An explicit construction of a heterogeneous algebraic theory is not included in this paper, only the functorial definition based on the string category StS, which has objects which are strings over a sort set S and morphisms which are projections or target tuples of projections only.

The string category is very interesting although it has a simple structure (detailed construction in [11], [8]). Here it is important to note that the strings are *products*. This means that the morphisms are projections and target tuples of projections only.

Definition 6 (S-sorted heterogeneous algebraic theory) Let $\underline{StS}$ be an S-sorted string category. An *S-sorted heterogeneous algebraic theory* is a functor T: $\underline{StS} \rightarrow \underline{T}_{S\Sigma}$ which is *bijective* on objects and which *preserves finite products.*

If S is the sort set and $\Sigma = \{\Sigma_{w,u}\}$ is the set of proper operators the algebraic theory $\underline{T}_{S\Sigma}$ has objects $Ob_{\underline{T}_{S\Sigma}} = Ob_{\underline{STS}} = S^*$ (the set of all strings over the set S including the empty string λ) and morphisms which are *projections, proper operators* $\sigma_{w,u}$: w $\rightarrow$ u, *target tuples* and *compositions.*

Usually the algebraic theory is identified with the target category $\underline{T}_{S\Sigma}$. Here it is sufficient to consider a heterogeneous algebraic theory which is constructed from the string category $\underline{StS}$ by adding proper operators Σ to the appropriate morphism sets of $\underline{StS}$ and including all target tuples and compositions. These constructions are discussed in detail in [11] (for the homogeneous or one-sorted case see [19]).

The heterogeneous algebraic theories are objects in a category $\underline{Th}$ where the morphisms are *theory morphisms* [3]:

Definition 7 (Theory morphism) Let $\underline{T}$ and $\underline{T}'$ be heterogeneous algebraic theories with sort sets S and S', respectively. Then a *theory morphism* (f,F): $\underline{T} \rightarrow \underline{T}'$ consists of a sort mapping f: S $\rightarrow$ S' and an (S*×S*)-indexed family ($F_{u,v}$: $Mor_{\underline{T}}(u,v) \rightarrow Mor_{\underline{T}'}(uf,vf)$, for u,v $\in$ S*) of mappings which preserve composition, identities, and projections, that is,

1. if f: u $\rightarrow$ v $\in Mor_{\underline{T}}(u,v)$ and g: v $\rightarrow$ w $\in Mor_{\underline{T}}(v,w)$ then
   $(fF_{u,v} o gF_{v,w}) = (fog)F_{u,w}$
2. $p_i^u F_{u,iu} = p_{iuf}^{uf}$ for u = $s_1 \ldots s_n$: [n] $\rightarrow$ S and i = 1, ... ,n.

Note that the preservation of projections implies the preservation of identities because the identities of an algebraic theory are projections.

3 High Level Distributed Transition Systems

A transition system consists of *states* and *transitions* between these states. In a graphical representation (a *diagram*) the states could be represented by nodes and the transitions by arrows between nodes. If the arrows have labels the system is called a *labelled* transition system. Here this more general form is used, defined as a *distributed* transition system close to [20].

The traditional transition systems are on a rather low level and can generate very large descriptions. It is, however, not very difficult to "fold" similar parts together and *transform the structural complexity into a descriptional complexity.* From a categorial point of view it means that the *free* constructions are replaced by quotients defined by congruences. In practice these congruences are determined by a set of equations expressing equivalences between the morphisms of the heterogeneous algebraic theory.

If the structure is "folded" so that similar substructures are identified, the new labelling obviously must contain all the information that was expressed in the original structure. This could be seen as a *transformation* of an elementary distributed transition system into another (high level) distributed transition system so that *the behaviour is preserved.* The behaviour could be defined as a diagram in a category with markings as objects. Thus this behaviour diagram must remain unchanged or with some trivial changes like renaming.

The elementary distributed transition system consists of a diagram and simple sets of labels for the nodes and the arrows, but high level distributed transition systems can have rather complex labelling and a set of equations between morphisms. The idea is to keep the diagram of the high level distributed transition system as the basis of one algebraic theory TS but to see the *support* structure [4] as a heterogeneous algebraic theory of its own (a category ST).

The relationship between the diagram and the support structure can be defined by a function BS: TS → ST, assigning sorts from S to the places B. There are functors (inclusions) from both these categories to the combined algebraic theory HTS, which is a complete model of the high level distributed transition system, such that the diagram in Figure 2 commutes.

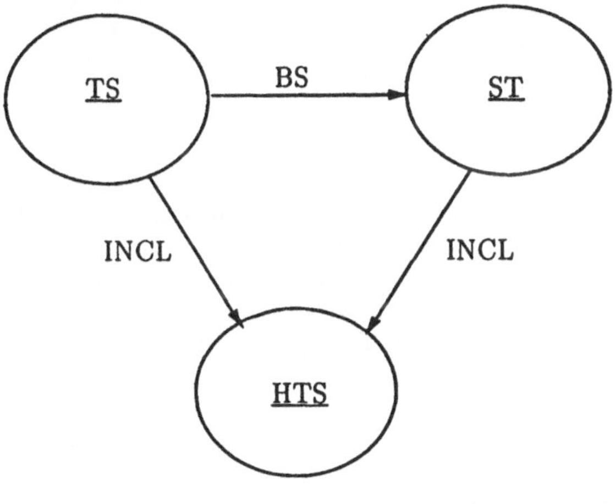

Figure 2: High level distributed transition system.

3.1 Folding elementary systems

In an elementary system a place intuitively can be interpreted as a proposition, a certain property holds for a certain individual. In a high level system a place can be interpreted as a predicate, a certain property holds for some individuals of a certain sort (here only the more general heterogeneous or many-sorted case is considered). The difference in the formal system is that each individual has "its own sort" in the elementary case while this is not necessary in the high level case.

The well-known problem with the dining philosophers can be used as an example [21]. In Figure 3(a) there is a simple transition system (or an EN system) which describes the situation when there are three philosophers and three forks. Ti means that "philosopher i is thinking", Ei that "philosopher i is eating" and Gi that "fork i is available". Thus for three philosophers nine places (sorts) are needed. It is clear that the same structure is repeated many times in this formalism.

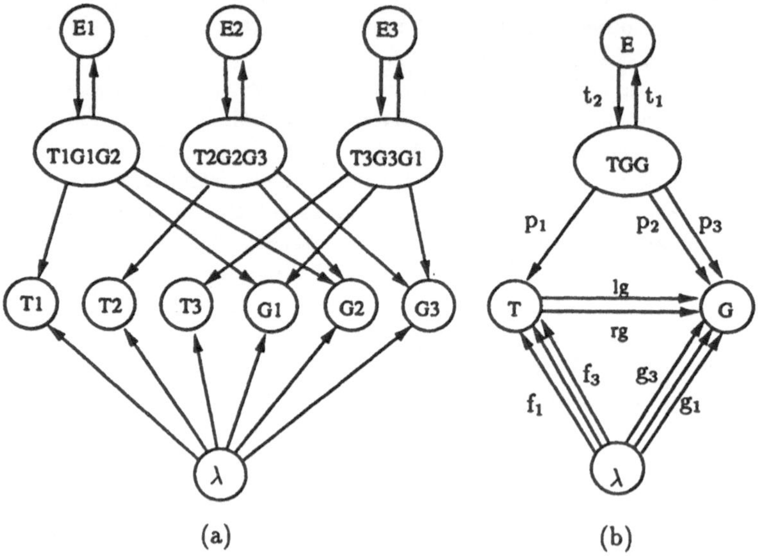

Figure 3: Dining philosophers as a (a) low level and (b) high level transition system.

Another transition system in Figure 3(b) describes the same problem, but the system has a simpler graph. There are, however, some restrictions on the behaviour of the system. In the general case with n philosophers these could be seen as equations:

$f_i lg = g_i$,

$f_i rg = g_{i+1}$ for i = 1,...,n-1 and,

$f_n rg = g_1$.

Note that arrows lg and rg are not needed in the elementary case because the structure determines which forks each philosopher must take. To be sure that the transitions t_1 and t_2 do not generate completely new philosophers or forks it might be necessary to require that the composition of t_1 and t_2 is an identity for the target tuples consisting of f_i, $(f_i)lg$, and $(f_i)rg$, i.e. $(f_i,(f_i)lg,(f_i)rg)t_1t_2 = (f_i,(f_i)lg,(f_i)rg)$ for all i = 1,...,n.

The behaviour of the high level system is a diagram consisting of products of places (sorts) and tuples of transitions between them, as for the elementary case. There are, however, also some differences. Because each individual has its own sort in the elementary case, it is possible to define a *marking* as a product, e.g. c_{in} = T1T2T3G1G2G3 in Figure 3(a). This is not possible in the high level case because TT could mean that philosophers f_1 and f_2 are thinking but also f_2 and f_3 or f_1 and f_3.

Thus *a marking is a morphism* in the high level case. Of course this definition can be used for elementary systems too because each product has exactly one target tuple, for example $(f_1,f_2,f_3,g_1,g_2,g_3)$: $\lambda \rightarrow$ T1T2T3G1G2G3. This is the natural way to think of a marking and it is adopted from now on. It is also easy to express that "there is a token in E" as a morphism $(f_i,(f_i)lg,(f_i)rg)$: $\lambda \rightarrow$ E.

In the algebraic theory there are also target tuples like (f_1,g_2,g_2) but the composition of this target tuple with t_1 is *not* in the model because $(f_1)lg \neq g_2$. Thus the new arrows lg,rg: T $\rightarrow$ G pick the interesting morphisms out of the morphism sets of the algebraic theory. For algebraic nets [21] lg and rg are partial functions because only homogeneous algebra is used. The heterogeneous approach is much more natural because rg and lg has nothing to do with any other places than T and G.

In this model lg and rg *can* be interpreted as (total) functions but the point in category theory is that lg and rg are *just arrows*. The only important thing is that the composition of f_i with lg must be equal to gi etc. It is no sense in trying to interpret these arrows within the heterogeneous algebraic theory. An interpretation must be a relation to another category, e.g. a functor to Set (the category of sets and total mappings between the sets). In fact, in category theory an algebra is defined as a product-preserving functor from an algebraic theory to Set.

This level of abstraction gives the possibility to interpret the same high level distributed transition systems in many ways - as long as the structure remains unchanged. The "interpreted" system must still have the property that composition of the interpreted f_i with interpreted lg must be equal to the interpreted gi.

To make the model still more general, the support structure could be separated from the transition system, that is, the behaviour of the remaining transition system would be rather abstract - there would be no individuals. For example, in the case of the philosophers, the abstract transition system would be the same but there would be a different support structure for different numbers of philosophers. This is a very natural division, no programmer would make a different program for each case - instead the number of philosophers would be given as a parameter to the program.

3.2 Formal Definitions

Transition systems were independently developed by Lien and Keller in 1972 [16], [14]. There are many different modern definitions but here a definition is used which is close to [16] and [20]. The difference is that Reisig uses labelled transitions and multisets, while Lien's transitions were unlabelled and he used a state that is a "sum" with coefficients (which can be seen as a multiset).

The definition used here is almost the same as the definition of *distributed transition systems* in [20] but instead of multisets, products are used. If the product is identified with its underlying family of objects (see Definition 1), which usually is possible because the products of a family are isomorphic, the definitions could be considered equivalent as it is possible to determine the corresponding multiset from this family and vice versa.

The use of strings will make the transition systems more concrete because there are several (isomorphic) products for the same family of objects, i.e. all permutations of the string. In category theory it does not make much difference because the level of abstraction is so high that isomorphic constructs are practically the same. In some cases, e.g. for nets with individual tokens, it could even be advantageous as the ordering of the places in a string makes it possible to discriminate between several occurrences of the same element.

Definition 8 (Transition system) An elementary distributed *transition system* is a quadruple TS=(B,T,R), where B is a finite set of *places*, the (labelled) *transition relation* $R \subseteq C\times T\times C$ is a set of transitions with labels in the set T and the set of *states* $C \subseteq B^*$ (strings in B).

The definition of a category requires that the transition system must have the property that, for transitions (c_1,t_1,c_1') and (c_2,t_2,c_2'), if $c_1=c_2$, $t_1=t_2$, and $c_1'=c_2'$ then they are the same transition. This is equivalent to the basic requirement for a category that all morphisms from A to B must be different for all pairs of objects (A,B) in the category.

A transition system is *nondeterministic* in general. It is possible to have two transitions (c,t,c_1) and (c,t,c_2) with $c_1 \neq c_2$, that is, an action t can end up in state c_1 or in state c_2. Another type of nondeterminism arises when there are two transitions (c,t_1,c_1) and (c,t_2,c_2). Then in general there is a nondeterministic choice between transition t_1, transition t_2 and the parallel transition (t_1,t_2) in state c. If *conflict* is not allowed then the parallel transition (t_1,t_2) is not allowed.

A distinction should be made between the labels in T (sometimes called *actions*) and transitions which are triples (c,t,c′), i.e. source and target are included. Several transitions can have the same label, e.g. (c,t,c′) and (c,t,c″). Thus the statement "firing an action x" is in general ambiguous but the statement "firing a transition y" is not (in a categorial framework).

Petri nets are special cases of transition systems. In [10] C/E-systems, P/T-nets and nets with individual tokens are interpreted as "abstract nets", i.e. as distributed transition systems. In [20] also PrT-nets are considered from this point of view. In this approach, however, a high level net will *not* be an elementary transition system although it could be unfolded to one.

It is possible to define a high level distributed transition system as one single heterogeneous algebraic theory, but here it is defined using two other algebraic theories, an elementary transition system <u>TS</u> (with no initial marking) and a support structure <u>ST</u>. The equations E, describing the restrictions on the high level system, and the initial marking M_{in} must be given in the combined category <u>HTS</u>. The equations are pairs of morphisms in the algebraic theory.

Definition 9 (High level distributed transition system) A *high level distributed transition system* HTS = (TS,SΣ,E,M_{in}), where TS = (B,T,R) is an elementary transition system and SΣ = (S,Σ) is a signature, is a heterogeneous algebraic theory based on the signature S′Σ′ with sort set $S' = B \cup S$ and family of operators $\Sigma' = R \cup \Sigma$ and satisfying the morphism equations E. Its *initial marking* is a morphism M_{in}: $\lambda \rightarrow w$, where w is an object in the algebraic theory.

The *underlying elementary transition system* TS = (B,T,R), without initial marking, determines an algebraic theory <u>TS</u> and the signature SΣ another algebraic theory $\underline{ST}$, the ***support structure***, so that BS: $\underline{TS} \rightarrow \underline{ST}$ is a function assigning sorts in S to places in B. Sometimes TS=(B,T,R) is called the ***structure*** or the ***graph*** and $S\Sigma$ the ***support*** of the high level distributed transition system.

The elementary transition system is the special case with $S' = B$, $\Sigma' = R$, and $E = \phi$. In this case the initial marking (morphism) $M_{in}: \lambda \rightarrow w$ can be identified with its target w.

Most properties of elementary transition systems can be defined as special cases of high level distributed transition systems.

3.3 A Category of Transition Systems

Definition 8 of a transition system makes it easy to define a heterogeneous algebraic theory *based* on the transition system. The set B of places is taken as the sort set S in Definition 6 of an S-sorted algebraic theory and the transitions (c,t,c′) in R are taken as proper operators $\sigma_{w,u}$, where $\sigma = t$, $c = w$ and $c' = u$. As R is a relation it is possible that for some transition label $t \in T$ there are several morphisms $t: c \rightarrow c'$ and $t: c'' \rightarrow c^*$. Then in a category it is necessary to use the "disjointifying trick" and consider all morphisms t to be *indexed* by their source and target.

Here the transition system is defined without an initial state c_{in}, but it can be added if needed. A product can be seen as a *state* in elementary transition systems because the morphism $M_{in}: \lambda \rightarrow w$ will be unique in this case (there is only one "individual" for each sort).

Proposition 4 (TS-based algebraic theory) For each elementary transition system $TS = (B,T,R)$ there is a *heterogeneous algebraic theory* $\underline{TS}$ *based on the transition system* consisting of all possible states and transition sequences.

Proof. Given a transition system TS it is always possible to construct a heterogeneous algebraic theory by taking the set B of places and constructing the string category $\underline{St}$B with objects in $C = B^*$, all strings (products) over B. This is the initial B-sorted heterogeneous algebraic theory [11].

The initial algebraic theory $\underline{St}$B is then extended by adding the transitions in R to the morphism sets of $\underline{St}$B so that $(c,t,c') \in R$ will be a morphism $t \in Mor_{\underline{St}B}(c,c')$ and requiring that the extended construct also is an algebraic theory, i.e. that composition and target tupling are defined for all morphisms and objects.

□

The composition and target tupling of algebraic theories give rise to morphisms modelling sequences of steps (also parallel) between states. Note that these steps are *completely unrestricted* (the algebraic theory is *free*). For certain transition systems, e.g. Petri nets which are Elementary Net Systems, some restrictions must be added, e.g. transitions must be *independent* and no transition target sort may appear in the target of the marking [12].

The states in C are *products* in $\underline{St}$B, but all products of the same family of elements $(b_i | i \in I)$ are isomorphic. In the string category $\underline{St}$B it means that all objects (strings), which are permutations of each other, are isomorphic. Thus it is possible to concentrate on the family of objects forming the product rather than some specific product when defining properties of transition systems.

A category of distributed transition systems (or, strictly, heterogeneous algebraic theories based on distributed transition systems) would be a subcategory of

Th with a special kind of morphisms, let us call them dts-morphisms. The natural candidates for dts-morphisms are theory morphisms which preserve the dynamics.

Exactly what "preserving the dynamics" means depends on the "firing rules". One obvious condition is that composition and products should be preserved because composition and target tupling model the dynamics in this approach. That is already satisfied in Definition 7. If there are no restrictions at all on the dynamics then dts-morphisms will be the same as theory morphisms.

Another obvious condition is that the initial marking should be preserved (if there is one), that is, $M_{in}(f,F) \subseteq M'_{in}$ or possibly $M_{in}(f,F) = M'_{in}$ (using the notations from Section 3.2).

Compared to the net morphism in [23] and [24] a theory morphism which preserves initial markings is more restricted. Winskel's η-mapping is a *partial* mapping between events while a theory morphism is a total mapping (called *synchronous* in [23]). It seems that the theory morphism should be more general. Especially the sort mapping f: $S \rightarrow S'$ is very restrictive.

3.4 Behaviour of Transition Systems

The support structure is a normal heterogeneous algebraic theory based upon a set S of *sorts* and a S-sorted family of operators $\Sigma = \cup\, \Sigma_{w,u}$ (a *signature* $S\Sigma$). In Figure 3 this structure is very simple, but for the railway system in [4] it is quite interesting (Figure 4). The transition system itself is trivial - it is a morphism t: VU $\rightarrow$ VU, where VU is the product of V and U in Figure 5.

The graph is different from the corresponding graphs for a PrT-net and a coloured net in Figure 4 because the transition boxes are split into "input" and "output" parts in this approach and there is not much idea in presenting these as different places (products) because they happen to be the same in this example. Of course it is also possible to write the PrT-net and coloured net in a form with one place and one transition only, but that would make the annotations too complex. Thus the optimal tradeoff between structural and denotational complexity in general is different in this approach.

The coloured net is presented in a form using many sorts like in [2]. The main difference between PrT-nets and coloured nets on one hand and the high level distributed transition systems on the other is that the labels of transitions and arcs are transformed into equations between morphisms. In Figure 5 the places have the same labels (U and V) as in Figure 4. In this special case the arcs CUR and NXT both happen to correspond to projection p_1: VU $\rightarrow$ V in Figure 5 (Nxt and Prv both correspond to p_2: VU $\rightarrow$ U), because the target of the transition t is the same as the source, i.e. VU, but this is *not* the case in general.

The information in the arc labels (functions) can be found in the support structure and in the equations. Thus the operator (p_1+1) denotes the modulo 7 addition and (p_1-1) the modulo 7 subtraction (Figure 5), where p_1 is the projection from sort S to sort S, i.e. the identity. Projections are acting as variables in algebraic theories [11] and the composition of arrow (constant operator) $4_{\lambda,S}$ with (p_1+1) is substitution of $4_{\lambda,S}$ for p_1, i.e. 4+1, where the parenthesis is a metasymbol. The support structure is not free because in this case it must obey equations 0+1 = 1, 1+1 = 2, ... , 6+1 = 0.

In the same way a composition of a morphism i: $\lambda \rightarrow$ S with the support

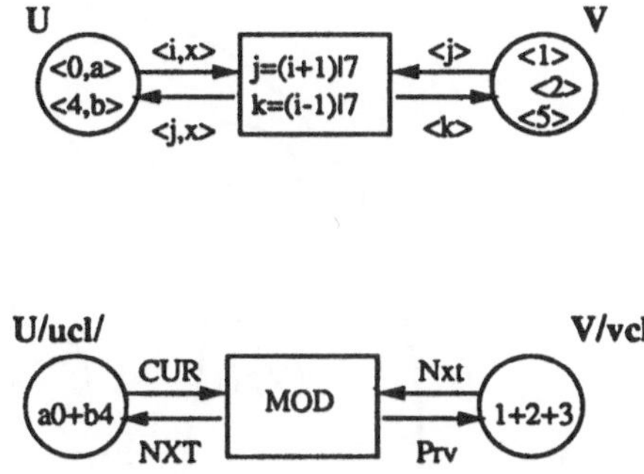

sorts T = {a,b} and S = {0,..,6}
colours **ucl** = MOD = T × S and vcl = S

CUR: $T \times S \rightarrow T \times S$: $(x,i) \mapsto (x,i)$;
NXT: $T \times S \rightarrow T \times S$: $(x,i) \mapsto (x,(i+1)|7)$;
Nxt: $T \times S \rightarrow S$: $(x,i) \mapsto (i+1)|7$;
Prv: $T \times S \rightarrow S$: $(x,i) \mapsto (i-1)|7$.

Figure 4: Railway system as a PrT-net and a coloured net.

structure operator (Vp_1): $S \rightarrow V$ is a morphism Vi: $\lambda \rightarrow V$. Because an algebraic theory has products, there are target tuples (j,a), (j,b): $\lambda \rightarrow ST$, where j: $\lambda \rightarrow S$ and a,b: $\lambda \rightarrow T$. The composition of these target tuples with operator (Up_1p_2) gives morphisms Uja,Ujb: $\lambda \rightarrow U$, because morphism j must be substituted for projection p_1 and morphism a or b for p_2. Then there must be target tuples (Vi,Uja),(Vi,Ujb): $\lambda \rightarrow VU$ in the algebraic theory.

A marking of the high level distributed transition system in Figure 5 corresponding to the marking in Figure 4 would be a morphism (V1,V2,V5,U0a,U4b): $\lambda \rightarrow$ VVVUU. The behaviour of the railway system will now be modelled by compositions of this initial marking with transitions (extended operators) like (id_V,id_V,t_V,id_U,t_U): VVVUU $\rightarrow$ VVVUU, where $id_V = p_1^V$ and $id_U = p_1^U$ and t = (t_V,t_U) (see Proposition 2).

The transition t: VU $\rightarrow$ VU in Figure 5 must have the following property: (Vi+1,Uix)t = (Vi-1,Ui+1x) for all i $\in Mor_{\underline{ST}}(\lambda,S$ and all x $\in Mor_{\underline{ST}}(\lambda,T)$.

The transition t can be closed by requiring that it acts as an identity for all other arguments than (Vi+1,Uix). The addition and subtraction operators are those modulo 7 operators defined above. Applying the the extended operator (t) to the initial marking, i.e. taking the composition of (V1,V2,V5,U0a,U4b) and (id_V,id_V,t_V,id_U,t_U) would give a new marking (V1,V2,V3,U0a,U5b): $\lambda \rightarrow$ VVVUU. In this case the markings (morphisms) belong to the same morphism set, but it is not generally true.

Consider a high level distributed transition system (TS,SΣ,E,M_{in}) with graph

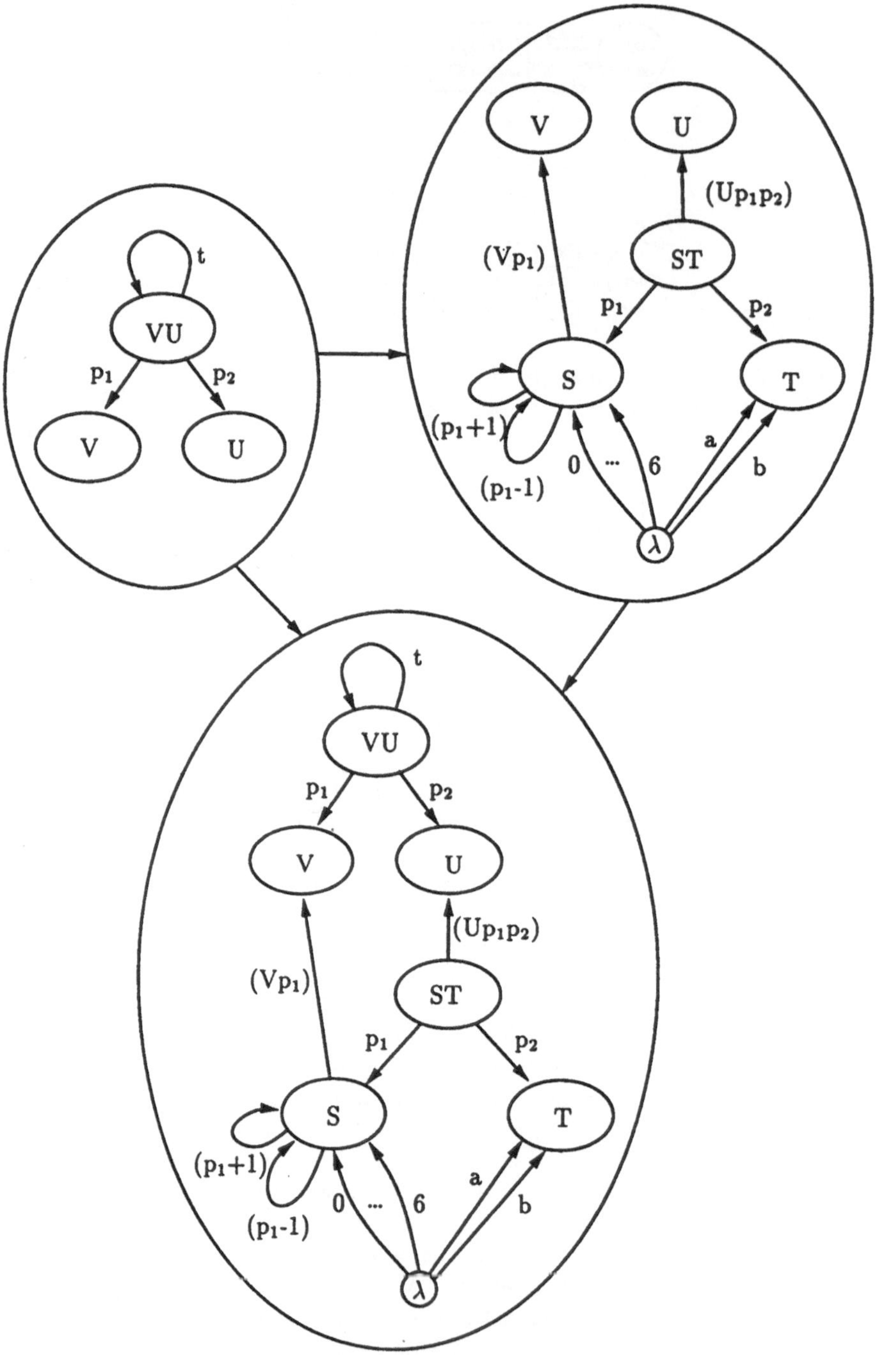

Figure 5: Railway system as a high level distributed transition system.

TS=(B,T,R) and support $S\Sigma$. It has a marking M: $\lambda \rightarrow$ w, which is a *constant* operator because the source is λ. Here it will be defined as a target tuple of single-sorted constants k: $\lambda \rightarrow$ s, where s $\in$ S. Thus the marking is a tuple of *individuals* in sorts w = $s_1,...,s_n$. It is possible to have several individuals of the same sort and it is also possible to distinguish between them because the tuple is ordered.

Intuitively, a transition is changing the marking of a system. In category theory this dynamics is modelled by the *composition of morphisms.*

Definition 10 (Marking) A *marking* in a high level distributed transition system is a morphism M: $\lambda \rightarrow$ w which is a target tuple $(k_1,...,k_n)$ of constants k_i: $\lambda \rightarrow s_i$ for all s_i in w = $s_1,...,s_n$.

It is in general not possible to define the composition of a marking M: $\lambda \rightarrow$ w and a transition (an operator) σ: v $\rightarrow$ u because w $\neq$v. Thus the concept of *submarking* is needed. This is important also because a *global* marking can be divided into *local* markings this way.

Proposition 5 (Submarking) A (global) marking M: $\lambda \rightarrow$ w can always be divided into (local) *submarkings* M = $(M^{u_1},...,M^{u_k})$, where all u_i are subproducts of w.

Proof. If u_i is a subproduct of w then there is a projection (target tuple of projections) $p^w_{u_i}$: w $\rightarrow u_i$. The marking M: $\lambda \rightarrow$ w is a w-tuple and can be written $(k_1,...,k_n)$, where k_i: $\lambda \rightarrow s_i$. The submarking is the composition $Mp^w_{u_i} = (k_j)^{u_i} = M^{u_i}$, which is always defined.

□

A special case of a submarking is an *elementary marking* M: $\lambda \rightarrow$ s, where s $\in$ S is a single sort. The identity for λ, the *empty marking* $p^\lambda_\lambda = M_\lambda$: $\lambda \rightarrow \lambda$ is a submarking of every marking M: $\lambda \rightarrow$ w, because λ is a subproduct of every product w. The projection is the empty tuple of projections. In concurrent situations it is important to state that two markings have no common submarkings, i.e. they are *independent.*

Definition 11 (Independent markings) Two markings M_1: $\lambda \rightarrow w_1$ and M_2: $\lambda \rightarrow w_2$ in a high level distributed transition system are *independent* if they have no common elementary submarkings, i.e. if $M'_1 \neq M'_2$ for all submarkings M'_1: $\lambda \rightarrow s_1$ of M_1 and M'_2: $\lambda \rightarrow s_2$ of M'_2.

Now it is possible to give the *general* definition for an *enabled* transition. Note that this definition only uses the *local* marking.

Definition 12 (Enabled transition) A transition (c_1,t,c_2) in a transition system is *enabled* (or fireable) in a marking M: $\lambda \rightarrow$ c iff M has a *submarking* M_1: $\lambda \rightarrow c_1$.

This is a very general definition and for most classes of Petri nets the enabling rule must be restricted, for example if the capacity of the places is limited. Thus the enabled steps of a more restricted class of transition systems are a subset of the set of morphisms from a certain state.

In a distributed transition system in general several transitions can be enabled "at the same time". This does not mean that they are *concurrent*, e.g. if there is a *conflict.*

Definition 13 (Conflict) There is a *conflict* in a high level distributed transition system if for some pair of transitions (c_1,t_1,c_1'), $(c_2,t_2,c_2') \in R$ there is a marking $M: \lambda \to w$ such that both transitions are enabled with submarkings $M_1: \lambda \to c_1$ and $M_2: \lambda \to c_2$ (of M), but M_1 and M_2 are *not independent.*

Intuitively, the dependency of the transitions means that they cannot both be fired although they are enabled. Firing one of them produces a new marking such that the other is no more enabled. If firing a third transition in the same system either creates or ends a conflict, then there is *confusion* in the system.

If there is no conflict, all the enabled transitions can be fired concurrently. The procedure of going through all possible compositions of the initial marking and the extended operators (transitions) t gives a behaviour diagram of the high level distributed transition system. It is a kind of interleaving semantics with parallel steps which are target tuples which can contain several transitions. The projections in the target tuple are identities on places in B, that is, they indicate that a local state is not changed.

An enabled transition can be "fired", i.e. the composition of the submarking with the transition (operator) determines a new marking. This new marking can be defined using the *extended* operator in Proposition 3.

Definition 14 (Firing a transition) When a transition (c_1,t,c_2) in a transition system is enabled in a marking $M: \lambda \to w$ and is *fired*, the new marking will be $M': \lambda \to w'$, which is a composition of M and the extended operator $(t): w \to w'$.

The firing rule is *local* and does not tell what to do if there is a conflict. It is very easy to extend Definition 14 to a concurrent rule if there is no conflict. Then the extended operator simply contains several transitions.

Because transitions are relations in $B^* \times T \times B^*$ it is possible to have transitions with an empty preset or an empty postset. It is not possible in a category, however, to have a morphism without source or without target.

The *empty product* λ is an object in any heterogeneous algebraic theory and it will work correctly when defining the behaviour of the system. If a transition t has λ as source it will always be enabled because $M_\lambda: \lambda \to \lambda$ is a submarking of every marking $M: \lambda \to w$. If λ is the target, firing the transition (c,t,λ) will only remove the submarking M^c because the new local marking will be the empty marking M_λ which is the identity on λ.

Thus the empty product is a very special object. As a source it is always "enabled" and as a target is is always "empty".

If a transition (c_1,t,c_2) is enabled in a marking M and the new marking obtained by firing t is M', then M' is *reachable* from M. And in general:

Definition 15 (Reachability) A marking M_n is *reachable* from a marking M_1 in a transition system TS=(B,T,R) iff there is a composition of extended operators (transitions) $(t_1),(t_2), \ldots ,(t_{n-1})$ such that each $t_i \in R$ is enabled for $i = 1,2, \ldots$, n-1 and M_n is obtained by firing (t_{n-1}).

The *set of reachable markings* of a transition system is the set $\{M \mid M$ is reachable from $M_{in}\}$.

Definition 16 (Liveness) A transition t in a high level distributed transition system is *live* for a marking M iff there is a marking M' such that M' is reachable from M and t is enabled in M.

3.5 Properties of Transition Systems

The following definitions are made for categorial high level distributed transition systems, but are in many cases generalisations of the corresponding Petri net concept and very close to "normal" definitions [16]. For a high level distributed transition system the definitions concerning structural properties are given for the underlying elementary transition system TS=(B,T,R), i.e. the algebraic theory $\underline{TS}$. Transitions are thus proper operators (morphisms) t: c $\rightarrow$ c′ in this category and the (local) states c,c′ are strings over the set B.

Definition 17 (Pre- and postset) For a transition t = (c,t,c′) the *preset* $^\bullet$t is the underlying family UF(c) and the *postset* t$^\bullet$ is UF(c′). For a place b $\in$ B the *preset* $^\bullet$b = {t | (c,t,c′) $\in$ R and b $\subseteq$ c′ } and the *postset* b$^\bullet$ = {t | (c,t,c′) $\in$ R and b $\subseteq$ c }.

The source of a transition is (almost) equal to its preset and the target (almost) equal to the postset. The only difference is that the source and target are products and thus ordered.

Definition 18 (Pure) A transition system is *pure* if there are no *self-loops*, i.e. UF(c) $\cap$ UF(c′) = ϕ for all transitions (c,t,c′) $\in$ R

This requirement is stronger than banning endomorphisms, i.e. morphisms that have the same object as source and target. Source and target must have no projections to the same object.

Definition 19 (Simple) A transition system is *simple* iff there is at most one transition (c,t,c′) in every morphism set $Mor_{\underline{TS}}$(c,c′) for all c,c′ $\in$ C, i.e. if (c,t,c′) $\in$ R and (c,t′,c′) $\in$ R then t = t′.

There might be several morphisms in $Mor_{\underline{TS}}$(c,c′) but only one should be a proper transition, i.e. derived operators are not taken into account.

Definition 20 (Isolated places and transitions) A place b $\in$ B is *isolated* iff $^\bullet$b $\cup$ b$^\bullet$ = ϕ. A transition (c,t,c′) $\in$ R is isolated iff c = c′ = λ.

Note that a transition *must* have a source and a target in a category. Here the *empty product* λ of sorts is used in the cases where the preset or the postset is empty.

4 Conclusions

The categorial model of high level distributed transition systems is a generalisation of Petri nets and in many respects it is easy to see the common properties. In the high level model there are, however, more differences than in the Elementary Net System [12] and Place/Transition System [13] models although these are special cases of the high level definition. Thus it might be necessary to change the definitions when more experience with this new model is obtained.

The most important difference to Predicat/Transition nets and coloured nets is *in the annotation of places (objects) and transitions (arrows)*. In category theory it is natural to express restrictions as equivalences between morphisms and compositions of morphisms. For example predicates annotating transitions must be expressed in a new way. There is not yet an algorithm for this, but it would be nice to have a automatic procedure of changing a high level Petri net into a categorial high level distributed transition system and vice versa.

In Petri net theory there is much work done to make nets practically applicable and efficient. Therefore this model is as close as possible to traditional Petri nets so that the results obtained can be transferred without problems.

References

1. Bednarczyk MA. Categories of Asynchronous Systems. PhD thesis, University of Sussex, October 1987
2. Billington J. Many-Sorted High Level Nets. In: Proc. 3rd Workshop on Petri Nets and Performance Models, Kyoto 11-13 December 1989. IEEE CS Press, Washington, 1989, pp 166–179
3. Bloom SL, Wagner EG. Many-Sorted Theories and their Algebras with Some Applications to Data Types. In: Nivat M, Reynolds JC (eds) Algebraic Methods in Semantics. Cambridge University Press, 1985, pp 133–168
4. Genrich HJ. Predicate/Transition Nets. In: Brauer W, Reisig W, Rozenberg G (eds) Advances in Petri Nets 1986, Part I, Bad Honnef. Springer-Verlag, Berlin, 1986, pp 207–247 (Lecture notes in computer science vol. 254)
5. Goguen JA. Correctness and Equivalence of Data Types. In: Int. Symp. of Mathematical Systems Theory, Udine 1975. Springer-Verlag, Berlin, 1976, pp 352–358 (Lecture notes in economics and mathematical systems vol. 131)
6. Goguen JA. Abstract Errors for Abstract Data Types. In: Neuhold EJ (ed) Formal Descriptions of Programming Concepts. North-Holland, 1978, pp 491–522
7. Goguen JA, Burstall R. Some Fundamental Properties of Algebraic Theories: A Tool for Semantics of Computation. D.A.I. Research Report No. 53, July 1978
8. Goguen JA, Thatcher JW, Wagner EG, Wright JB. An Introduction to Categories, Algebraic Theories and Algebras. IBM Report RC-5369, Yorktown Heights, New York, 1975
9. Goguen JA, Thatcher JW, Wagner EG, Wright JB. Initial Algebra Semantics and Continous Algebras. J. Assoc. Comput. Mach. 1977; 24: 68–95
10. Goltz U. Considering Nets as Distributed Transition Systems. Petri Net Newsletter June 1985; 21: 10–19
11. Husberg N. Categorial Heterogeneous Algebraic Models of Programming Languages. DAIMI PB-163, Computer Science Department, Aarhus University, 1983
12. Husberg N. Petri Nets in Algebraic Theories - a Category Theory Approach. Technical Report No.B5, Digital Systems Laboratory, Helsinki University of Technology, June 1988
13. Husberg N. A Category of Distributed Transition Systems. Research Report No.A10, Digital Systems Laboratory, Helsinki University of Technology, May 1989

14. Keller RM. Formal Verification of Parallel Programs. Comm. Assoc. Comput. Mach. July 1976; 19: 371–384

15. Lawvere FW. Functional semantics of algebraic theories. Proc. Nat. Acad. Sci. 1963; 50: 869–872

16. Lien YE. A Note on Transition Systems. Information Sciences 1976; 10: 347–362

17. Meseguer J, Montanari U. Petri Nets Are Monoids: A New Algebraic Foundation for Net Theory. In: Proc. Symp. on Logic in Computer Science, Edinburgh 5-8 July 1988. IEEE CS Press, Washington, 1988, pp 155–164

18. Monro GP. The Concept of Multiset. Zeitschr. f. math. Logik und Grundlagen d. Math. 1987; 33: 171–178

19. Pareigis B. Categories and Functors. Academic Press, New York, 1970

20. Reisig W. Das Verhalten verteilter Systeme. GMD-Bericht Nr. 170, Bonn, 1987

21. Reisig W, Vautherin J. An Algebraic Approach to High Level Petri Nets. In: Proc. 8th Workshop on Application and Theory of Petri Nets, Zaragoza, Spain 24-26 June 1987. 1987, pp 51–72

22. Wagner EG. Algebraic theories, Data Types, and Control Constructs. Fundamenta Informaticae 1986; IX: 343–370

23. Winskel G. Petri Nets, Algebras and Morphisms. Technical Report 79, Computer Laboratory, University of Cambridge, 1985

24. Winskel G. A Category of Labelled Petri Nets and Compositional Proof System. In: Proc. Symp. on Logic in Computer Science, Edinburgh 5-8 July 1988. IEEE CS Press, Washington, 1988, pp 142–154

25. Zamfir-Bleyberg M. Petri Nets: An Initial Semantics Approach (part I). Report TR-CS-88-1, Kansas State University, 1988

A Compositional Axiomatisation of Safety and Liveness Properties for Statecharts

J. J. M. Hooman *

Department of Mathematics and Computing Science

Eindhoven University of Technology, 5600 MB Eindhoven, The Netherlands

S. Ramesh †

Department of Computer Science and Engineering

Indian Institute of Technology, Bombay 400 076, India

W. P. de Roever ‡

Department of Mathematics and Computing Science

Eindhoven University of Technology, 5600 MB Eindhoven, The Netherlands

Abstract

Statecharts is a behavioral specification language proposed for specifying large real-time, event driven, reactive systems. It is a graphical language based on state-transition diagrams for finite state machines extended with many features like hierarchy, concurrency, broadcast communication and time-out. By generating external events symbolically, Statecharts can be executed, thereby turning it into a programming language for real-time concurrency (as well as enabling rapid prototyping). As such it is amenable to compositional program verification. We supply Statecharts with a compositional proof system for both safety and liveness properties which we prove to be sound and (relatively) complete. Especially, we focus on extending compositional techniques for proving safety properties to liveness, without immediately adopting temporal logic, since that formalism, elegant as it is, introduces some difficulties with a compositional treatment of sequentiality and looping.

1 Introduction

This paper concerns formal specification and verification of real-time reactive systems. Real-time reactive systems usually run forever, interact continuously with their environment, and have critical time requirements. Typical examples are telecommunication networks and avionic systems. Formal specification of real-time reactive systems is an important area of research judging by the sheer number of proposed specification languages such as Statecharts [10,11], Esterel [1], Lustre [2] and Signal [8]. All these specification languages are based on operational descriptions that

*This research was supported by Esprit Project 937 (DESCARTES) and Esprit-BRA project 3096 (SPEC).

†The work described here was done while this author was at the Eindhoven University of Technology, partially supported by the Netherlands National Facility for Informatics (NFI).

‡Present address: Institut für Informatik und Praktische Mathematik II, Christian-Albrechts-Universität Kiel, 2300 Kiel 1, Fed. Rep. Germany.

characterize how a system evolves. Such behavioral specifications, although useful for system implementors and rapid prototyping, are error-prone. The aim of this paper is to complement behavioral specifications with more abstract property-based specifications. More precisely, we give a logical specification language and develop a sound and relatively complete axiomatic system to verify a behavioral specification with respect to a property-based specification.

Our aim is to develop a *compositional* axiomatic system, i.e., a specification of a statechart should be derived *purely* from specifications of its constituents without referring to the derivation of the latter specifications. Such a system requires syntactic operators for building large statecharts from smaller ones. Our compositional axiomatisation is based on a syntax for Statecharts which has been proposed in [12]. Statecharts are related to our logical specification language by formulae of the form S **sat** φ, meaning that statechart S satisfies assertion φ. Assertions are written in a first-order typed language which is strong enough to express real-time safety properties and liveness properties. Real-time safety properties are properties that can be falsified in finite time, such as, "event e is generated within 5 steps". A typical example of a liveness property is: "eventually event e is generated".

There exist in the literature many axiomatic systems (see [3,4,14,24,28,15,32, 19], to mention a few) for deducing properties of real-time or reactive systems. All these systems deal with CSP-like languages [13,21] which do not possess many features of Statecharts, such as interrupts and broadcast communication. Often 'sat'-based formalisms are used for specifications [4,14,24,32,19]. Some of the works [3, 14,15,32] deal with safety properties while others [4,24,28,19] derive both safety and liveness properties. For expressing liveness properties the latter works make use of temporal logic, and compositionality is achieved in [4,24,19] by using chop operators or greatest fixed point operators in the assertion language. In this paper such operators are avoided by making explicit reference to time and using the availability of unbounded time. As Lamport already observed in [22], this simplifies the step from real-time safety to liveness.

To analyse the correctness of a statechart several tools have been implemented, mostly based on finite state methods. The full Statecharts language, however, allows the use of variables, and hence completely automated verification is impossible. Furthermore, the limits of automated finite state verification begin to be reached (see, e.g., [27]). Our result obtains added significance due to the partly mechanizable nature of compositional proof systems, as examplified in [26].

In [32, 30] it has been shown how the kind of sat-system as developed here can be turned into a (compositional) generalized Hoare system based on pre- and post-conditions on computation histories, and into trace-invariant systems in which concurrency is characterized by a communication interface. The remaining prevalent styles of compositional specification and proof systems, viz. the assumption-commitment paradigm for distributed computation (tracing back to early work of Misra & Chandy [23]) as well as the rely-guarantee paradigm (tracing back to early work of C. Jones [20]), can be canonically converted into trace-invariant proof systems as indicated in [31]. Once it is determined by future research which adaptation of these three specification styles—generalized Hoare Logic, trace-invariant, assumption-commitment—is most natural to reason about Statecharts, our proof system can be lifted to suit that style using the canonical proof transformation techniques developed by Zwiers et al, cited above. This provides added motivation to our aim to develop first a compositional proof system for Statecharts which is as simple as possible.

To prove soundness and (relative) completeness of our proof system, we have defined a denotational, and hence compositional, semantics for Statecharts. An early operational, non-compositional, semantics for Statecharts can be found in [16]. In [12] a compositional semantic model with minimal amount of non-observable entities (i.e. a fully abstract semantics) has been presented. The denotations of this semantics are prefix-closed sets of linear histories; infinite computations are represented by all their finite prefixes. Our semantics is derived from this model, but since it has to serve as a basis for our formalism expressing liveness properties, several changes have been made. Instead of using prefix closed sets, our histories represent complete (possibly infinite) computations. Furthermore, in [12] the least fixed point is used to describe a looping construct whereas we use the greatest fixed point for also obtaining infinite computations.

This paper is structured as follows. In Section 2 we introduce Statecharts by giving syntax, informal meaning, and semantic model. Section 3 contains the details of our sat-formalism and the assertion language. The proof system, given in Section 4, consists of an axiom for basic statecharts and a rule for each of the syntactic operators. Soundness and relative completeness of the system has been established, and the proof of relative completeness is sketched in Section 5. The full denotational semantics and a proof of soundness and completeness can be found in [18].

2 Statecharts

The behavioral specification language considered here is Statecharts [10]. Realizing the intuitive and pictorial appeal of state-transition diagrams for finite state machines, Statecharts has been designed on the basis of such diagrams. But it is free from the limitations of state machines, such as sequentiality, unstructuredness and exponential growth of states when describing concurrency. Indeed, Statecharts are double exponentially more succinct than state machines, as has been shown in [6]. Quoting [11],

Statecharts=state-transition diagrams+depth+orthogonality+broadcast

Depth is achieved in Statecharts by allowing super states containing substates or even complete statecharts. When such a super state is exited all the computations inside are terminated. Super states may consist of orthogonal sub-statecharts which are executed in parallel. Orthogonal components interact with each other and with their environment by means of events which are broadcast throughout the whole system. External events or events generated in one component can cause new events in another component which, in turn, can cause more events. Thus a single event can give rise to a whole chain of events all of which are assumed to take place simultaneously; this assumption is essentially Berry's synchrony hypothesis [1] according to which a system is infinitely faster than its environment. It facilitates the specification task by abstracting from internal reaction times.

The synchrony hypothesis might introduce causal paradoxes like an event causing itself. In Esterel [1] causal paradoxes are syntactically disallowed whereas in Statecharts causal relationships are respected and paradoxes are removed semantically. Real-time is incorporated in Statecharts by having an implicit clock, by allowing transitions to be triggered by time-outs relative to this clock and by requiring that if a transition can be taken then it should be taken immediately.

The next sections contain a brief introduction into Statecharts. In Section 2.1 we give a general overview about the structure of Statecharts. Section 2.2 contains a formal syntax. Details about the semantic model are described in Section 2.3. More information can be found in [10,11]. An introduction from a theoretical point of view is given in [17], with special emphasis on an abstract notion of time in Statecharts.

2.1 General overview

A statechart can be considered as a tree of states, with the root state as the initial state. The leaves of the tree are basic states, like the states in a finite state machine. Other states are <u>super states</u> containing their sons (in the tree) as substates. There are two types of super states: AND-states and OR-states. For instance, the statechart in Figure 1 has root state A and leaves F, G, H, I, J and K. A is an OR-state, with substates B and C. B is an AND-state (indicated by the dashed line) with D and E as its substates, called <u>orthogonal</u> components, whereas C is an OR-state having I, J and K as its substates. States are entered/exited either <u>explicitly</u> by taking a transition or <u>implicitly</u> because certain other states are entered/exited. Entering an AND-state (OR-state resp.) results in entering *all* (*exactly one* resp.) of its substates implicitly. In Figure 1: entering AND-state B results in entering both D and E, entering OR-state C results in entering exactly one of its substates I, J and K. Similarly, entering an orthogonal component of an AND-state results in implicitly entering all other components of this AND-state. When entering a super state the particular substate(s) that should be entered is (are) marked by a <u>default transition</u>, drawn as a transition with no source state, e.g. the default transition inside C pointing to I.[1] When the transition from I to H is taken, H is entered explicitly and B, D, E, F are entered implicitly. Note that with a forked transition such as the one from K, more than one orthogonal component can be entered explicitly. Transitions between orthogonal components are not allowed (e.g. no transitions between F and H). When a state is exited all its substates are exited implicitly. Exiting an orthogonal component implies an implicit exit of all its

[1]Unlike [10], we attach a default transition to every super state; so also to AND-states.

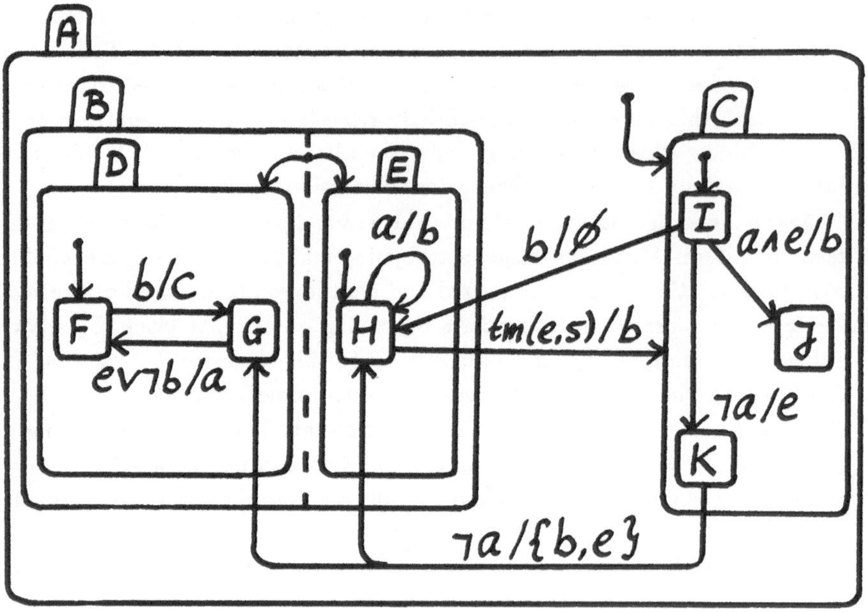

Figure 1:

orthogonal partners. So the transition from H to C leads to an implicit exit of D (and its substate F or G).

Transitions have labels of the form *'event part/action part'*.[2] The event part is a boolean expression involving atomic events a, b, e ,... - signals without measurable duration. These events can be generated by the outside world as an input to the statechart as well as by the statechart itself. The event expression specifies when the transition is enabled. The action part is a set of atomic events that are generated when the transition is taken (a singleton is denoted by its element).

Execution in orthogonal components proceeds concurrently, and events generated in one component are broadcast throughout the system, possibly triggering new transitions in other components. This will in general lead to a whole chain of transitions that, by the synchrony hypothesis, take place simultaneously in a single (time) step. The set of transitions taken in a step is a *maximal* set in which there is at most one transition per orthogonal component and there exists a causal relationship between transitions: each transition is enabled by either external events or events generated by other transitions. The general idea is that staying in a state takes some time, whereas taking a transition is instantaneous.
In our example, the system can be in the states A, B, D, E, F and H simultaneously. When a is generated externally in this configuration the transition from (and to) state H will generate b, causing a transition from F to G which generates c.

[2]For the sake of simplicity we do not consider the general syntax of labels given in [16]. There, a label includes an additional condition part, variable assignments are allowed in action parts and there are special events to signal entry and exit of a state. Our axiomatic system can be easily extended to the general case.

A transitions with event part a is taken when a is generated somewhere in the system. The meaning of $a \wedge b$ (resp. $a \vee b$) is: a transition with this event part is taken in a step if both a and b (resp. a or b) are generated somewhere in the system in this step. λ is a special event that occurs (by definition) in every step. $tm(e,n)$ denotes a *time-out* event that is generated at a particular step if event e happened n time steps earlier. A transition with event part $\neg a$ is taken in a step if a is not generated at all during this step.[3] In our syntax, negations are immediately succeeded by atomic events, time-outs or λ.

2.2 Syntax of Statecharts

Using the syntax given in this section, complete statecharts can be obtained by means of intermediate objects that may have transitions without either source or target states (see, e.g., the basic element in Figure 2). Henceforth, we use the word "statechart" for both these intermediate objects and complete statecharts.
The primitive objects of our syntax are:

- Basic Statecharts $[I, O, N]$, where N is a state name, I a set of incoming transitions and O a set of outgoing transitions. Only the outgoing transitions are labeled with an event/action pair (see Figure 2).

We have the following operators (let B be a basic statechart, S, S_1, S_2 be statecharts, T, T_1, T_2 be transition names, and a the name of an atomic event):

- Statification $Stat(B, S, T)$; makes (the state of) B a super state with S inside it and the incoming transition T of S as its default (see Figure 3).

- Or-construct $Or(S_1, S_2)$; leads to a statechart that becomes an OR-state after statification.

- And-construct $And(S_1, S_2)$; yields an AND-state after statification.

In the constructs, above both constituents should not have joint incoming or joint outgoing transitions with the same name, except for the AND-construct where joint incoming transitions are allowed.

- Connect $Connect(S, T_1, T_2)$; results in a statechart identical to S except that outgoing transition T_1 and incoming transition T_2 of S are connected to form a single complete transition (see Figure 4).

- Hide-Closure $HiCl(S, a)$; hides any generation of a by S (Hiding) and makes S insensitive to any a generated by the environment (Closure).

After the informal introduction into the syntax of Statecharts above, we give the formal syntax. First we define the labels that can be associated with the transitions of any statechart and the event expressions used in these labels.

[3]There are several possible interpretations of $\neg a$, here we take the approach from [25].

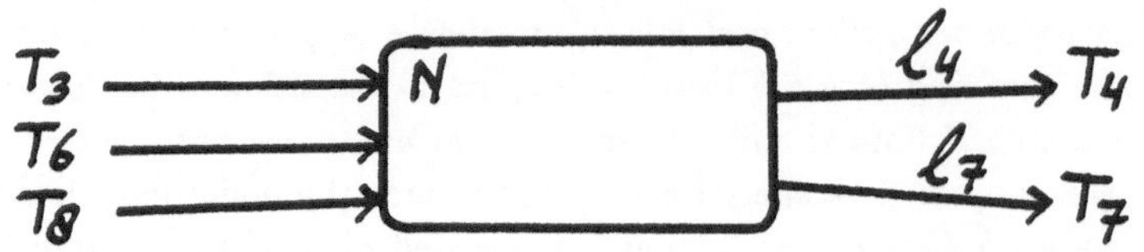

Figure 2: Basic Statechart $[I, O, N]$, with $I = \{T_3, T_6, T_8\}$ and $O = \{T_4, T_7\}$

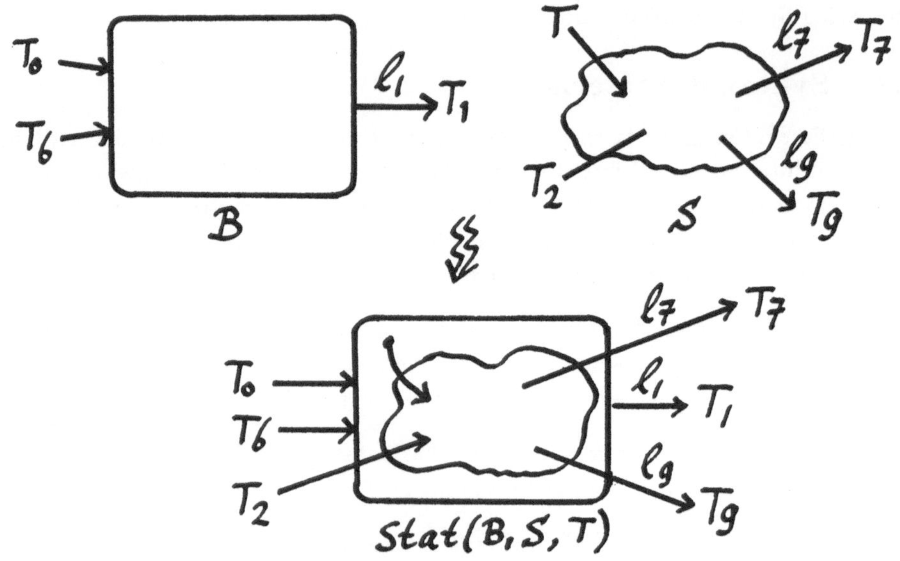

Figure 3: Statification

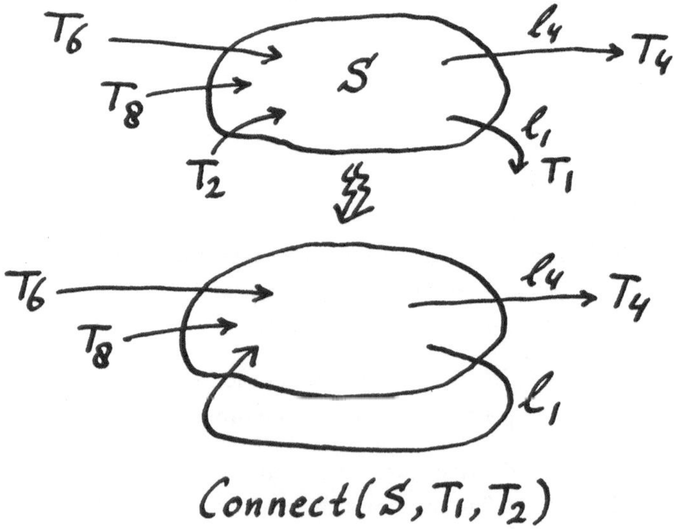

Figure 4: Connection

2.2.1 Events

Let E_e be a set of elementary/atomic events. $\mathbb{N}$ denotes the set of natural numbers. The set of composite events Exp is defined inductively as the least set satisfying:

- $\lambda \in Exp$, $\neg\lambda \in Exp$.
- if $e \in E_e$ then $e \in Exp$, $\neg e \in Exp$.
- if $e \in Exp$, $n \in \mathbb{N} - \{0\}$ then $tm(e,n) \in Exp$, $\neg tm(e,n) \in Exp$.
- if $e_1, e_2 \in Exp$ then $e_1 \vee e_2 \in Exp$, $e_1 \wedge e_2 \in Exp$.

2.2.2 Transition Labels

The set Lab of all symbols that can label the transitions of a statechart is defined by:

$$Lab = \{E/A \mid E \in Exp, A \subseteq E_e,\ A \text{ is finite}\}$$

If A is a singleton set, we often use the event itself; i.e. E/a is an abbreviation for $E/\{a\}$.[4]

2.2.3 Formal Syntax of Statecharts

Let Σ be the set of all states (or more precisely state names) and $\mathcal{T}_I$ and $\mathcal{T}_O$ be the set of all (names of) incoming and outgoing transitions of any statechart such that $\mathcal{T}_I \cap \mathcal{T}_O = \emptyset$. Also let $L : \mathcal{T}_O \to Lab$ denote the labeling function that labels all the outgoing transitions. The set of statecharts is defined by the following BNF-grammar, where $a \in E_e$, $I \subseteq \mathcal{T}_I$, $O \subseteq \mathcal{T}_O$, I and O are finite, $\{T, T_2\} \subseteq \mathcal{T}_I$, $T_1 \in \mathcal{T}_O$, $N \in \Sigma$.

$$\begin{aligned}
S &::= Disj \mid Conj \\
Disj &::= Prim \mid \mathbf{Or}(Disj,Disj) \mid \mathbf{Connect}(Disj, \mathbf{T_1}, \mathbf{T_2}) \\
Conj &::= \mathbf{And}(Default,Default) \mid \mathbf{And}(Default,Conj) \\
Prim &::= Basic \mid Default \mid \mathbf{HiCl}(S, \mathbf{a}) \\
Default &::= \mathbf{Stat}(Basic,S,\mathbf{T}) \\
Basic &::= [\mathbf{I}, \mathbf{O}, \mathbf{N}]
\end{aligned}$$

2.2.4 Syntactic Restrictions

There are certain syntactic conditions to be satisfied by any statechart. In order to describe these conditions, we define two functions IN and OUT; for a given statechart S, $IN(S)$ and $OUT(S)$ are the sets of incoming and outgoing transitions of S, respectively.

[4] In the original syntax of labels as given in [16], the action A is of the form $a_1, \cdots, a_n$ whereas we take A to be the set containing these events.

	IN	OUT
$[I,O,N]$	I	O
$Stat(B,S,T)$	$(IN(B) \cup IN(S)) - \{T\}$	$OUT(B) \cup OUT(S)$
$Connect(S,T_1,T_2)$	$IN(S) - \{T_2\}$	$OUT(S) - \{T_1\}$
$Or(S_1,S_2)$	$IN(S_1) \cup IN(S_2)$	$OUT(S_1) \cup OUT(S_2)$
$And(S_1,S_2)$	$IN(S_1) \cup IN(S_2)$	$OUT(S_1) \cup OUT(S_2)$
$HiCl(S,a)$	$IN(S)$	$OUT(S)$

Then we have the following syntactic restrictions:

- For $Connect(S,T_1,T_2)$: $T_1 \in OUT(S)$ and $T_2 \in IN(S)$.
- For $Stat(B,S,T)$: $T \in IN(S)$, $IN(B) \cap IN(S) = \emptyset$, and $OUT(B) \cap OUT(S) = \emptyset$.
- For $Or(S_1,S_2)$: $IN(S_1) \cap IN(S_2) = \emptyset$ and $OUT(S_1) \cap OUT(S_2) = \emptyset$.
- For $And(S_1,S_2)$: $OUT(S_1) \cap OUT(S_2) = \emptyset$.

Remarks:

1. In $And(S_1,S_2)$, the intersection of $IN(S_1)$ and $IN(S_2)$ need not be empty. Incoming transitions with identical names are 'merged'.
2. The *Concat* operation given in [12] has not been provided in our syntax. It can be considered as a derived operation:
   $Concat(S_1,S_2,T_1,T_2) \equiv Connect(Or(S_1,S_2),T_1,T_2)$.

2.3 Semantic Model of Statecharts

As mentioned in the introduction, the semantic model associates with a statechart the set of all (maximal) computation histories representing complete computations. It has been shown in [12] that, besides denotations for events generated at each computation step (the observables) and denotations for entry and exit, the following two additional denotations are necessary and sufficient to obtain a compositional semantics: (1) a set of all events assumed to be generated by the whole system (i.e. statechart together with its environment) at each step and (2) a causality relation between generated events. More precisely, a computation history h of a statechart S is of the form $h = (\hat{s}, i, f, o, s)$ where

- $\hat{s} \in \mathbb{N}$ models the start step ($\mathbb{N}$ denotes the set of natural numbers).
- i is an incoming transition or $\star$ to model an implicit entry.
- $f : \mathbb{N} \to \{(F,C,<) | F \subseteq C$ and $<$ a total order on $C\}$ records for every step n a triple $(F,C,<)$, where
  - F is a subset of the events generated by S. Considering the chain of transitions in step n, F contains the events that are generated by S, for the first time in this chain.

- C is the set of events generated by the total system (i.e. S and its environment) in step n.
- $<$ denotes the causal relationship between events generated by the whole system . If a causes b then $a < b$. If there is no causal relation, then the semantics of S will contain two histories; one with $a < b$ and another with $b < a$.

- o is an outgoing transition or $\star$ for an implicit exit, or $\perp$ when there is no exit.
- $s \in I\!N \cup \{\infty\}$ denotes the exit step (we require $\hat{s} < s$ and $s = \infty \leftrightarrow o = \perp$).

For a function f as above, the fields of $f(n)$ are selected by $f^F(n)$, $f^C(n)$ and $f^<(n)$. Figure 5 explains why F is not equal to the set of *all* events generated by S. If a

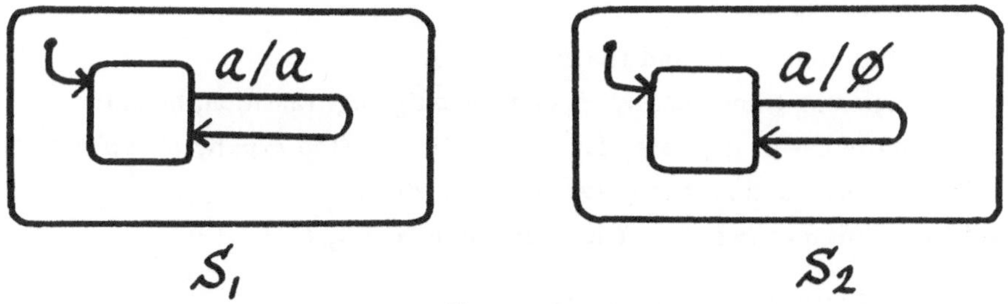

Figure 5:

occurs externally, then S_1 generates a at every step, whereas S_2 does not generate a. This difference can not be sensed, however, by other statecharts, because in both cases a is already generated in the system. In order to get the same semantics for S_1 and S_2, both should have an empty F-set to denote that both are not responsible for the first generation of a.

The semantic function $\mathcal{M}$ assigns to every statechart S a set $\mathcal{M}(S)$ of histories. It is a, so called, ***a priori*** semantics that anticipates an arbitrary environment. The most interesting case is the Connect-construct. Execution of $Connect(S, T_1, T_2)$ consists of first (a) entering S via a transition other than T_2 and then (b) taking transitions as specified by S and possibly exiting S either via a transition other than T_1 or via T_1, reentering S via T_2 and repeating (b). Given two sets of histories D_1, D_2, we define $CONC(D_1, D_2, T_1, T_2)$ (informally) as the set of (i) histories of D_1 that do not exit via T_1, and (ii) histories that consist of a history from D_1 exiting via T_1 followed by a history of D_2 entering via T_2.[5]
Then $\mathcal{M}(Connect(S, T_1, T_2))$ can be obtained by removing the histories with a T_2 entry from the largest set satisfying $D = CONC(\mathcal{M}(S), D, T_1, T_2)$, i.e., the greatest fixed point $\nu_X.CONC(\mathcal{M}(S), X, T_1, T_2))$. (Note that such a set D will not contain histories that exit via T_1.) In order to have such a fixed point definition (see e.g. [5]), our semantic domain is turned into a complete lattice by using the subset ordering

[5]$CONC$ stands for concatenation.

between sets of histories, and $CONC$ is shown to be monotonic in its second argument. This leads to $\mathcal{M}(Connect(S,T_1,T_2)) = del_{T_2}(\nu_X.CONC(\mathcal{M}(S),X,T_1,T_2))$, where $del_{T_2}(D) = \{h \in D \mid h = (\hat{s},i,f,o,s) \wedge i \neq T_2\}$.
Since $CONC$ is anti-continuous, this greatest fixed point can be obtained by an iteration: let D_0 be the set of all histories and $D_{k+1} = CONC(\mathcal{M}(S),D_k,T_1,T_2))$, then $\nu_X.CONC(\mathcal{M}(S),X,T_1,T_2) = del_{T_2}(\bigcap_{k\in N} D_k)$.

3 Assertion Language and Specifications

As already mentioned in the introduction, we will use formulas S **sat** φ to express properties of a statechart S. In this section we describe the first-order language used for assertion φ. φ contains two kinds of variables: reserved variables and logical variables. The reserved symbols are: st, in, F, occ, $<$, out, es. With these symbols we can express:

- The start step, by st, and the exit step, by es.
- The incoming transition, by in, and the outgoing transition, by out.
- The set of events generated for the first time in step exp, by $F(exp)$.
- That event a occurs in step exp, by $occ(a,exp)$.
- That event a causes event b in step exp, by $a <_{exp} b$.

We use three types of logical variables:

- Logical $\mathbb{N}$-variables, ranging over the natural numbers.
  Typical symbols are k, n, m, v, ...
- Logical transition variables, ranging over transition names.
  Typical symbols are t, t_1, ...
- Logical F-variables, ranging over functions from $\mathbb{N}$ to sets of events.
  Typical symbols are f, f_1, ...

In addition, the assertion language includes first-order arithmetic. Quantification is allowed over logical $\mathbb{N}$-variables only, and the usual logical connectives like $\neg$, $\vee$, $\wedge$ and $\rightarrow$ are used.

The interpretation of an assertion requires a computation history (of a statechart), which assigns values to reserved variables, and a logical variable environment that assigns values to logical variables. Given an assertion φ, a history $h = (\hat{s},i,f,o,s)$ and a logical variable environment γ, its interpretation, denoted by $[\![\varphi]\!]\gamma h$, is defined as follows (assume exp denotes an expression yielding a natural number—if it yields ∞ we take a default value):

- $[\![st]\!]\gamma h = \hat{s}$,
- $[\![in]\!]\gamma h = i$,
- $[\![F(exp)]\!]\gamma h = f^F([\![exp]\!]\gamma h)$,
- $[\![occ(a,exp)]\!]\gamma h = true$ iff $a \in f^C([\![exp]\!]\gamma h)$,
- $[\![a <_{exp} b]\!]\gamma h = true$ iff $(a,b) \in f^<([\![exp]\!]\gamma h)$,

- $[\![out]\!]\gamma h = o$,
- $[\![es]\!]\gamma h = s$
- $[\![v]\!]\gamma h = \gamma(v)$, $\quad [\![t]\!]\gamma h = \gamma(t)$, $\quad [\![f]\!]\gamma h = \gamma(f)$.

We leave the first-order model, relative to which validity is defined, implicit: it is the standard model of arithmetic throughout this paper.

An assertion φ is (universally) valid, notation $\models \varphi$, iff for all γ and for all h: $[\![\varphi]\!]\gamma h$. Specifications S **sat** φ are interpreted as usual: S **sat** φ is valid, notation $\models S$ **sat** φ, iff for all γ and for all $h \in \mathcal{M}(S)$: $[\![\varphi]\!]\gamma h$.

Using our assertion language, we can express all real-time safety properties (i.e. what can be falsified in finite time), such as:
"event e is generated within 5 steps" $\equiv \exists n < 5 : occ(e, st + n)$ and
"never exit" $\equiv es = \infty$.
But also liveness properties can be expressed, for instance;
"eventually event e is generated" $\equiv \exists n : occ(e, n)$,
"eventually exit" $\equiv es \neq \infty$, and
"event e is generated infinitely often" $\equiv \forall k\, \exists n \geq k : occ(e, n)$.

4 Proof System for Statecharts

The proof system consists of an axiom for basic statecharts, a proof rule for each of the operators mentioned earlier, and a consequence rule. Most of the rules require (implications between) assertions in their premises. In order to derive these assertions without having to formulate an axiomatisation for assertions, we add a relative completeness axiom by which all valid assertions are derivable.

Basic Statechart

Any computation of a basic statechart $[I, O, N]$ enters state N either implicitly (denoted by $\star$) or via a transition in I, and starts waiting to exit N. Then there are three possible situations: either it waits forever, not being able to take any of the outgoing transitions, or it exits the statechart at a certain step either implicitly (denoted by $\star$), or explicitly by taking an outgoing transition in O. Let $WAIT(O, v)$ denote an assertion that is true when a computation waits at step v. $FIRE(O, v)$ describes the condition for taking a transition $t \in O$ at step v. Then the axiom for basic statecharts is formulated as follows:

$$\begin{aligned}[I, O, N] \ \ \mathbf{sat} \ \ & in \in (I \cup \{\star\}) \wedge \forall v, st < v < es : WAIT(O, v) \wedge \\ & [(out = \perp \wedge es = \infty) \vee (out = \star \wedge F(es) = \emptyset) \vee FIRE(O, es)]\end{aligned}$$

Let the label of an outgoing transition $t \in O$ be given by E_t/A_t.
$WAIT(O, v)$ is true when a computation waits at step v. During waiting no event

is generated by the basic statechart and no transition in O can be taken. Hence:

$$WAIT(O,v) \equiv F(v) = \emptyset \wedge \bigwedge_{t \in O} \neg occ(E_t, v)$$

where $occ(E_t, v)$ is the natural extension of occ for complex event expressions E_t, e.g.

$$\begin{array}{rclrcl} occ(\lambda, v) & \equiv & true & occ(e_1 \vee e_2, v) & \equiv & occ(e_1, v) \vee occ(e_2, v) \\ occ(\neg e, v) & \equiv & \neg occ(e, v) & occ(e_1 \wedge e_2, v) & \equiv & occ(e_1, v) \wedge occ(e_2, v) \end{array}$$

$$occ(tm(e,n),v) \equiv \begin{cases} occ(e, v-n) \wedge \forall v', v-n < v' < v : \neg occ(e, v') & \text{if } v \geq n \\ false & \text{if } v < n \end{cases}$$

$FIRE(O, v)$ describes the condition for taking a transition $t \in O$ at step v. Then $occ(E_t, v)$ must hold and all the events in A_t are generated. Furthermore, certain causal relations exist between newly generated events and the events that triggered the transition. These relations are represented by assertion $soc(E_t, a, v)$, defined below, for $a \in A_t$. Consequently,

$FIRE(O, v) \equiv$

$$\bigvee_{t \in O} [out = t \wedge occ(E_t, v) \wedge F(v) \subseteq A_t \wedge \bigwedge_{a \in A_t} (occ(a, v) \wedge [a \in F(v) \rightarrow soc(E_t, a, v)])]$$

Assertion $soc(E_t, a, v)$ provides the necessary causal relation between a and the events in E_t. For instance, if $E_t = b$ then we need $b <_v a$, whereas if $E_t = \neg b$ then no relation should exist between b and a, since b does not occur at step v. We define soc by

$$\begin{array}{rcl} soc(\lambda, a, v) & \equiv & true \\ soc(b, a, v) & \equiv & \begin{cases} b <_v a & \text{if } b \not\equiv a \\ false & \text{if } b \equiv a \end{cases} \\ soc(\neg e, a, v) & \equiv & \neg occ(e, v) \\ soc(tm(e,n), a, v) & \equiv & occ(tm(e,n), v) \\ soc(e_1 \vee e_2, a, v) & \equiv & soc(e_1, a, v) \vee soc(e_2, a, v) \\ soc(e_1 \wedge e_2, a, v) & \equiv & soc(e_1, a, v) \wedge soc(e_2, a, v) \end{array}$$

Or-construct

Any history describing a computation of $Or(S_1, S_2)$ is a history from the semantics of either S_1 or S_2. Hence the rule for the Or construct is simply given by

$$\frac{S_1 \textbf{ sat } \varphi_1,\ S_2 \textbf{ sat } \varphi_2}{Or(S_1, S_2) \textbf{ sat } \varphi_1 \vee \varphi_2}$$

Connection

In order to give a rule for the $Connect(S, T_1, T_2)$ construct, we first define, similar to the semantics, the concatenation of two assertions φ_1 and φ_2 with respect to T_1 and T_2:

$$conc(\varphi_1, \varphi_2, T_1, T_2) \equiv$$
$$(\varphi_1 \wedge out \neq T_1) \vee (\varphi_1[f_1/F, T_1/out, v/es] \wedge \varphi_2[v/st, T_2/in, f_2/F] \wedge F = f_1 \uplus f_2)$$

where v, f_1, f_2 are fresh logical variables and $(f_1 \uplus f_2)(n) = f_1(n) \cup f_2(n)$. Corresponding to the greatest fixed point $\bigcap_{k \in N} D_k$ in the semantics, we use $\forall n : \varphi(n)$ with $\varphi(n)$ such that D_k satisfies $\varphi(k) \equiv \varphi[k/n]$. In particular $\varphi(0)$ is valid, representing arbitrary behaviour by allowing all histories. Furthermore, assuming $\models S$ **sat** $\hat{\varphi}$, we have $\models conc(\hat{\varphi}, \varphi(n), T_1, T_2) \rightarrow \varphi(n+1)$. In general, $\varphi(n)$ represents the behaviour of a sequence of n copies of S which are connected via T_1 and T_2 with arbitrary behaviour after an T_1-exit of the last copy. This leads to the following rule:

$$\frac{S \text{ sat } \hat{\varphi} \text{ , } \varphi(0) \text{ , } conc(\hat{\varphi}, \varphi(n), T_1, T_2) \rightarrow \varphi(n+1)}{Connect(S, T_1, T_2) \text{ sat } in \neq T_2 \wedge \forall n : \varphi(n)}$$

with n a logical $I\!N$-variable not occurring free in $\hat{\varphi}$.

And-construct

Assume $\models S_j$ **sat** φ_j for $j = 1, 2$. Since the semantics of any statechart contains histories with all possible values for start step, exit step, C- and $<$-components, for any history h from the semantics of $And(S_1, S_2)$ there are histories from the semantics of S_1 and S_2 that have the same values for these components. Hence, by substituting logical variables for the other components, this history h will satisfy $\varphi_1[t_1^i/in, f_1/F, t_1^o/out] \wedge \varphi_2[t_2^i/in, f_2/F, t_2^o/out]$ for certain values of the logical variables $t_1^i, f_1, t_1^o, t_2^i, f_2, t_2^o$. These remaining components are related as follows:

- Entry of $And(S_1, S_2)$ is done either (i) implicitly (notation $\star$), by entering both S_1 and S_2 implicitly, or (ii) via a joint transition of S_1 and S_2, or (iii) via a transition of S_1 that is not a transition of S_2; then S_2 is entered implicitly. Similarly for S_1 and S_2 interchanged.
- At every computation step the F-set of $And(S_1, S_2)$ is the union of the F-sets of S_1 and S_2.
- $And(S_1, S_2)$ exits either (i) both S_1 and S_2 implicitly (denoted by $\star$), or: (ii) via a transition of S_1 (S_2 resp.); then S_2 (S_1 resp.) is exited implicitly, or: (iii) neither S_1 nor S_2 (denoted by $\perp$).

These considerations lead to the following definitions
$and\_in \equiv (in = t_1^i = t_2^i) \vee (in = t_1^i \wedge t_2^i = \star) \vee (in = t_2^i \wedge t_1^i = \star)$,
$and\_out \equiv (out = t_1^o \neq \perp \wedge t_2^o = \star) \vee (out = t_2^o \neq \perp \wedge t_1^o = \star) \vee (out = t_1^o = t_2^o = \perp)$,
and the following rule:

$$\frac{\begin{array}{l} S_1 \textbf{ sat } \varphi_1,\ S_2 \textbf{ sat } \varphi_2 \\ \varphi_1[t_1^i/in, f_1/F, t_1^o/out] \wedge \varphi_2[t_2^i/in, f_2/F, t_2^o/out] \wedge \mathit{and\_in} \wedge \mathit{and\_out} \wedge F = f_1 \uplus f_2 \\ \hfill \rightarrow \varphi \end{array}}{\mathit{And}(S_1, S_2) \textbf{ sat } \varphi}$$

with t_1^i, t_2^i, t_1^o, t_2^o fresh logical transition variables, and f_1, f_2 fresh logical F-variables.

Statification

The $Stat(B, S, T)$ construct is similar to the *And* construct, except for the way of entering: (i) entering B (via a transition or implicitly) implies entering S via default T, and (ii) entering S via a transition (different from T) leads to an implicit entry of B. Hence define
$\mathit{stat\_in} \equiv (in = t_1^i \wedge t_2^i = T) \vee (in \neq \star \wedge in \neq T \wedge in = t_2^i \wedge t_1^i = \star)$,
$\mathit{stat\_out} \equiv (out = t_1^o \neq \perp \wedge t_2^o = \star) \vee (out = t_2^o \neq \perp \wedge t_1^o = \star) \vee (out = t_1^o = t_2^o = \perp)$.
Then the rule for Statification can be formulated as follows:

$$\frac{\begin{array}{l} B \textbf{ sat } \varphi_1,\ S \textbf{ sat } \varphi_2 \\ \varphi_1[t_1^i/in, f_1/F, t_1^o/out] \wedge \varphi_2[t_2^i/in, f_2/F, t_2^o/out] \wedge \mathit{stat\_in} \wedge \mathit{stat\_out} \wedge F = f_1 \uplus f_2 \\ \hfill \rightarrow \varphi \end{array}}{\mathit{Stat}(B, S, T) \textbf{ sat } \varphi}$$

with t_1^i, t_2^i, t_1^o, t_2^o fresh logical transition variables, and f_1, f_2 fresh logical F-variables.

Hide-Closure

Assume $\models S$ **sat** φ. To obtain a specification φ' for $HiCl(S, a)$, the histories satisfying φ are restricted to those where S is responsible for every occurrence of a (i.e. $occ(a, n)$ implies $a \in F(n)$ for every step n). Next a is hidden: it is removed from F (represented in the rule by a substitution in φ') and by the requirement that φ' should not refer to a. This leads to the following rule:

$$\frac{S \textbf{ sat } \varphi\ ,\ \varphi \wedge (\forall n : occ(a, n) \rightarrow a \in F(n)) \rightarrow \varphi'[F \dot{-} \{a\}/F]}{HiCl(S, a) \textbf{ sat } \varphi'}$$

provided a does not occur in φ'. $F \dot{-} \{a\}$ is a function defined by
$(F \dot{-} \{a\})(n) = F(n) - \{a\}$.

Consequence

Finally we have the usual consequence rule by which an assertion can be weakened:

$$\frac{S \textbf{ sat } \varphi,\ \varphi \rightarrow \varphi'}{S \textbf{ sat } \varphi'}$$

Relative Completeness Axiom

Observe that the application of most of the rules above requires the proof of (implications between) assertions. Since we aim at a complete proof system for Statecharts (i.e. a proof system in which every valid specification is also provable), this would imply that we also have to give a complete axiomatisation for assertions. This, however, is impossible by Gödels incompleteness theorem for arithmetic. Hence the best we can achieve is a *relatively* complete proof system, which is complete relative to the proof of assertions. In the next section we show that, indeed, every valid formula S **sat** φ can be derived provided all valid assertions are provable. This is modelled by the following *relative completeness axiom*:

φ iff $\models \varphi$

5 Soundness and Completeness of the Proof System

Let $\vdash S$ **sat** φ denote that S **sat** φ is derivable using the axiomatic system given in the previous section. Then soundness and completeness are defined in the usual way (see e.g. [5]): The proof system is sound if $\vdash S$ **sat** φ implies $\models S$ **sat** φ, and relatively complete if $\models S$ **sat** φ implies $\vdash S$ **sat** φ. Since our interpretation includes the standard model of first-order arithmetic, our notion of completeness is in fact *arithmetical completeness* in the sense of [9].

Soundness has been proved in [18] along the lines of our informal explanation given in the previous section. Relative completeness of the system is proved in [18] using the notion of characteristic assertion. An assertion φ is a characteristic assertion of a statechart S if a history satisfies φ (for all logical environments γ) iff it is a computation history of S.

Theorem 5.1 (Expressibility) *For any statechart S there exists a characteristic assertion of S.*

Using this Theorem we can prove:

Theorem 5.2 (Derivability) *For any statechart S: $\vdash S$ **sat** φ for a characteristic assertion φ of S.*

Then completeness follows easily: assume $\models S$ **sat** φ'. From Theorem 5.2: $\vdash S$ **sat** φ, for some characteristic assertion φ for S. Hence a history satisfying φ is a history from the semantics of S, and hence satisfies φ'. Thus $\models \varphi \rightarrow \varphi'$ which leads by the relative completeness axiom (which expresses that all valid assertions are derivable) to $\vdash \varphi \rightarrow \varphi'$. Using the consequence rule we obtain $\vdash S$ **sat** φ'.

We shall now provide a rough sketch of the proof of Theorems 5.1 and 5.2. In principle, we follow a standard way of proving expressibility (Theorem 5.1): first code the denotations from the semantics into the natural numbers and show that the semantics of every language construct is recursively enumerable. Next use the fact

that recursively enumerable sets are arithmetical, i.e. expressible by a formula in first-order arithmetic [29]. Often it is not possible to code the denotations directly (e.g. due to an infinite number of variables), but then it can be shown that the semantics is determined by a finite part of these denotations (e.g. the finite set of variables in the program). In our framework we have a similar problem, due to the f-component of histories:
a) this function f has an infinite domain (viz. $I\!N$), and
b) the C-component of $f(n)$ can be infinite.

To cope with a), we consider approximations of histories: Given a history h and a natural number k, we define the kth approximation of h, denoted by $h\downarrow k$. Informally, $h\downarrow k$ is the set of all histories coinciding with h from 0 up to k steps and assuming arbitrary values at other points. The kth-approximation of a set of histories D, notation $D\downarrow k$, is given by $D\downarrow k = \bigcup_{h\in D} h\downarrow k$. Then we have the following lemma:

Lemma 5.3 *For any statechart S, the sequence $\mathcal{M}(S)\downarrow k$, for $k = 0, 1, \cdots$, is a non-increasing (in the subset ordering) sequence of sets that converges to $\mathcal{M}(S)$, i.e. $\mathcal{M}(S) = \bigcap_{k\in N} \mathcal{M}(S)\downarrow k$.*

Note that convergence is achieved thanks to the absence of any fairness constraints in Statecharts. (Fairness constraints require higher ordinals transcending ω [7].) Although histories in $\mathcal{M}(S)\downarrow k$ have an infinite f-component, they are arbitrary after k. Hence $\mathcal{M}(S)\downarrow k$ is characterized by so-called k-histories which have an f-component that is restricted to $\{0, .., k\}$.

To deal with b), observe that the C-components are arbitrary outside $Events(S)$, that is, the *finite* set of events occurring (syntactically) in S. Hence $\mathcal{M}(S)\downarrow k$ is determined by k-histories which have C-components contained in $Events(S)$. Now these restricted k-histories can be coded into the natural numbers (by Gödel numbering), yielding a set of codes $\mathcal{M}^c(S)\downarrow(k, Events(S))$. Next we prove the main lemma:

Lemma 5.4 *For every statechart S,*
$\{(l, k) \mid l \in \mathcal{M}^c(S)\downarrow(k, Events(S)), k \in I\!N, l \in I\!N\}$ *is a recursively enumerable set.*

Since our assertion language includes first-order arithmetic, recursion theory (see e.g. [29]) leads to the following lemma.

Lemma 5.5 *For every statechart S, there exists an assertion $\psi(n, m)$ with free variables n and m such that $\models \psi[k/n, l/m]$ iff $l \in \mathcal{M}^c(S)\downarrow(k, Events(S))$.*

Since the coding of the restricted k-histories is also expressible in our assertion language and $\mathcal{M}(S)\downarrow k$ is characterized by these k-histories, we obtain the following lemma:

Lemma 5.6 *For every statechart S there exists an assertion φ with a free variable n such that for all $k \in I\!N$: $\varphi[k/n]$ characterizes the set $\mathcal{M}(S)\downarrow k$.*

Expressibility is a direct consequence of Lemma 5.3 and 5.6: if φ is an assertion satisfying the condition of Lemma 5.6 then the assertion $\forall n : \varphi(n)$ characterizes $\bigcap_{k\in N} \mathcal{M}(S){\downarrow}k$ which is identical to $\mathcal{M}(S)$ because of Lemma 5.3.

The proof of Theorem 5.2 is relatively easier and given by induction on the structure of S. The proof for the base case follows from the fact that the basic statechart axiom directly yields a characteristic assertion. For the inductive case, assume that S is composed using an operator (say) *op* from one or two substatecharts whose characteristic specifications are derivable. Then the proof is complete once we show that a characteristic assertion of S (given by Theorem 5.1) satisfies the premises of the rule for *op*. Except for the case $op \equiv Connect$, the proof is straightforward and almost the converse of the soundness proof. The proof for $S \equiv Connect(S', T_1, T_2)$ is slightly more complicated because, assuming S' sat $\hat{\varphi}$, the *Connect* rule requires an assertion φ with a free variable n that satisfies: $\models \varphi(0)$ and $\models conc(\hat{\varphi}, \varphi(n), T_1, T_2) \rightarrow \varphi(n+1)$. Let D_k be defined as in the semantics of *Connect*: D_0 is the set of all histories and $D_{k+1} = CONC(\mathcal{M}(S'), D_k, T_1, T_2))$. Similar to the proof of Lemma 5.6 we show that there exists a first-order assertion φ with a free variable n s.t. for all k: $\varphi[k/n]$ characterizes D_k. Then it is easy to prove that this φ satisfies the required conditions.

6 Conclusion and Future Work

The present paper offers a compositional proof system for both safety and liveness properties which is as simple as we can imagine for Statecharts. As a consequence, one can object that we merely axiomatize the semantics. The techniques given in [32,30,31], however, illustrate that such a simple formalism can be lifted to a more sophisticated formalism, e.g., based on assumption-commitment or rely-guarantee pairs. Determining which formalism is most elegant for Statecharts is left to future research.

One of the main aims in the present work has been to investigate how the elegant compositional verification techniques for safety properties from Zwiers [32] could be extended to liveness properties. In discussing this extension with Amir Pnueli, the issue has been raised as to the exact relationship between proving liveness properties by means of higher ordinals, and proving liveness on the basis of natural numbers (using that these are able to code the precise computations). This suggests an interesting topic for future research.

References

[1] Berry B, Cosserat L. The synchronous programming language Esterel and its mathematical semantics. Proceedings CMU Seminar on Concurrency, pages 389–349. LNCS 197, Springer-Verlag, 1985.

[2] Bergerand J-L, Caspi P, Halbwachs N. Outline of a real-time data flow language. Proceedings IEEE Real-Time Systems Symposium, 1985.

[3] Bernstein A, Harter (Jr) PK. Proving real-time properties of programs with temporal logic. Proceedings 8th Annual ACM Symposium on Operating System Principles, pages 1–11, 1981.

[4] Barringer H, Kuiper R, Pnueli A. Now you may compose temporal logic specifications. Proceedings 16th Annual ACM Symposium on Theory of Computing, pages 51–63, 1984.

[5] de Bakker J. Mathematical Theory of Program Correctness. Prentice-Hall, 1980.

[6] Drusinsky D, Harel D. On the power of cooperative concurrency. Proceedings of Concurrency 88, pages 74–103. LNCS 335, Springer-Verlag, 1988.

[7] Francez N. Fairness. Springer-Verlag, 1986.

[8] le Guernic P, Benveniste A. Real-time, synchronous, data-flow programming: The language Signal and its mathematical semantics. Technical Report 620, INRIA, Rennes, 1986.

[9] Harel D. First Order Dynamic Logic. LNCS 68, Springer-Verlag, 1979.

[10] Harel D. Statecharts: A visual formalism for complex systems. Science of Computer Programming, 8(3):231–374, 1987.

[11] Harel D. On visual formalisms. Communications of the ACM, 31:514 – 530, 1988.

[12] Huizing C, Gerth R, de Roever WP. Modelling Statecharts behaviour in a fully abstract way. Proceedings 13th Colloquium on Trees in Algebra and Programming, pages 271–394. LNCS 299, Springer-Verlag, 1988.

[13] Hoare CAR. Communicating Sequential Processes. Communications of the ACM, 21(8):666–677, 1978.

[14] Hoare CAR. Communicating Sequential Processes. Prentice-Hall, 1985.

[15] Hooman J. A compositional proof theory for real-time distributed message passing. Parallel Architectures and Languages Europe, pages 315–332. LNCS 259, Springer-Verlag, 1987.

[16] Harel D, Pnueli A, Pruzan-Schmidt J, Sherman R. On the formal semantics of Statecharts. Proceedings IEEE Symposium on Logic in Computer Science, pages 54–64, 1987.

[17] Huizing C, de Roever WP. Everything you always wanted to know about Statecharts but were afraid to ask. Technical Report TIR 90.3, Eindhoven University of Technology, The Netherlands, 1990.

[18] Hooman J, Ramesh S, de Roever WP. A compositional axiomatisation of Statecharts: Soundness and completeness. Technical Report TIR 89.2, Eindhoven University of Technology, The Netherlands, 1989.

[19] Hooman J, Widom J. A temporal-logic based compositional proof system for real-time message passing. Parallel Architectures and Languages Europe, volume II, pages 424–341. LNCS 366, Springer-Verlag, 1989.

[20] Jones CB. Tentative steps towards a development method for interfering programs. ACM Transactions on Programming Languages and Systems, 5(4):596–619, 1983.

[21] Koymans R, Shyamasundar RK, de Roever WP, Gerth R, Arun-Kumar S. Compositional semantics for real-time distributed computing. Information and Computation, 79(3):210–356, 1988.

[22] Lamport L. What Good is Temporal Logic, pages 657–668. Information Processing, R.E. Manson (ed). North Holland, 1983.

[23] Misra J, Chandy KM. Proofs of networks of processes. IEEE Transactions on Software Engineering, 7(7):417–326, 1981.

[24] Nguyen V, Demers A, Gries D, Owicki S. A model and temporal proof system for networks of processes. Distributed Computing, 1(1):7–35, 1986.

[25] Shalev M. On the Operational Semantics of Statecharts. M.Sc. thesis, The Weizmann Institute of Science, Rehovot, Israel, 1988.

[26] Staunstrup J, Garland S, Guttag J. Compositional verification of VLSI circuits. Proceedings Workshop On Automatic Verification Methods For Finite State Systems. pages 349-364, LNCS 407, Springer-Verlag, 1989.

[27] Sifakis J (editor). Proceedings Workshop On Automatic Verification Methods For Finite State Systems. LNCS 407, Springer-Verlag, 1989.

[28] Shankar AU, Lam SS. Time-dependent distributed systems: proving safety, liveness and real-time properties. Distributed Computing, 2:61–79, 1987.

[29] Weihrauch K. Computability, volume 9 of EATCS Monographs on Theoretical Computer Science. Springer-Verlag, 1987.

[30] Zwiers J, de Roever WP. Predicates are predicate transformers: a unified compositional theory for concurrency. Proceedings 8th ACM Symposium on Principles of Distributed Computing, 1989.

[31] Zwiers J, de Roever WP, van Emde Boas P. Compositionality and concurrent networks: soundness and completeness of a proofsystem. Technical Report 57, University of Nijmegen, The Netherlands, 1984.

[32] Zwiers J. Compositionality, Concurrency and Partial Correctness. LNCS 321, Springer-Verlag, 1989.

Defining Conditional Independence Using Collapses

Shmuel Katz Doron Peled
Department of Computer Science
The Technion
Haifa 32000, Israel

Abstract

Trace semantics is extended to allow conditional commutativity among operations. Conditional commutativity is obtained by identifying the context (the set of global states) in which operations are commutative using special predicates. These will allow collapsing execution histories into equivalence classes of conditional traces. Using this approach, it is possible that the execution of two operations will be dependent in one context and independent in another. The predicates allow defining a family of possible semantic definitions for each language, where each is an extension of previous standard definitions. Examples are shown when such a semantics is desired. As an example of an application, a proof method for total correctness is introduced.

1 Introduction

The interaction among atomic operations of a concurrent program is an issue essential to implementation [1] and verification [16, 25, 31]. Implementation is often concerned with the restriction that two operations accessing a mutual memory location (either read or write), cannot be executed in parallel when at least one access is a write [6]. However, this demand can be sometimes relaxed [8]. The effect of two independent concurrent operations is typically commutative. Verification of concurrent programs can benefit from the commutativity among operations by reducing the set of program states which are considered, arranging commutable operations in some convenient order.

Partial order semantics as seen in theories such as traces [20, 21] or interleaving sets [15] gives an appropriate treatment for the independence (commutativity) among operations. However, such formulations have the disadvantage of dealing with a fixed independence relation [16, 25] which cannot fully cover commutativity situations. Trace semantics is extended in this paper to allow conditional dependency (independence) among operations. That is, instead of using a fixed dependency relation among program operations, a set of predicates is used that identify when executions of pairs of operations are considered independent.

Conditional commutativity can be conceived as a direct extension of trace semantics or of interleaving sets. In addition to being useful for verification, it has semantic justification of its own since the execution of two operations might produce two causally dependent events in one occurrence and independent events in another. Some interesting cases are:

- if two operations refer to indexed memory elements such as arrays or pointer expressions. For example, the transitions $\langle x := A[i] \rangle$ and $\langle A[j] := y \rangle$ would be considered dependent iff $i = j$,
- if operations on communication channels are considered. Putting an element on a communication channel and removing an element from the channel are (directly) dependent iff they concern the same element [10],
- if the truth of an enabling condition is unchanged by an operation. The transitions $\langle \mathit{await}\ p - c < N \rangle$ and $\langle c := c + 1 \rangle$ achieve the same result in either order when $p - c < N$ is already *true*, because incrementing c keeps this condition *true*.

Many definitions for semantics and verification methods suggest adding more structure to the set of interleaving sequences generated by program executions. These methods exploit some observations about the nature of concurrent programs:

Locality Some tasks or subtasks in different processes may execute independently without inter-communication. After identifying this independence, there is no reason to consider all the possible interleavings of events of these tasks.

Sequentiality Some tasks, constructed from sets of program segments belonging to different processes, can be identified such that the program behaves as if the involved processes collaborate to perform one task, then they (perhaps with some processes joined or retired) commence the second task, and so forth. Once conditions for this behavior are identified, there is no reason to consider states where one process is involved in one task and the other is involved in another.

In both cases, some of the global states are identified as "not interesting" (although they occur in some execution sequences) and special proof methods are devised to handle them. We will mention a few:

- Several works [2, 27, 19, 4, 5] allow defining different granularities of atomic operations. That is, recognizing that various intermediate states of some program segments (which are considered as a single atomic operation) are not interesting for the correctness of the program. This obviously reduces the number of states one has to consider.
- Sequentiality is reflected by the definition of *communication closed layers* [11]. Segments of different processes are identified to execute together a common task. The program is decomposed into a set of layers (this decomposition is orthogonal to the decomposition into processes) such that there is no interaction (communication) among different layers. Then, the program behaves as if

the tasks are executed according to some predefined order. Identifying layers can be done using the proof rules of [12]. Using layers for verification is done in [30].

- Reducing the state space of a concurrent program by considering a representative subset of interleavings is suggested in [15, 31, 14, 11]. It is observed that under some conditions of independence among program operations, it is possible to recognize classes of execution sequences that are indistinguishable up to permuting independent operations. For properties which cannot distinguish between sequences of such a class it is possible to use proof rules such as [16, 25]. This obviously can handle locality, because a sequence in which local independent tasks appear entirely one after the other (in any order) is a representative for all the interleavings in which these tasks are merged. As proved in [17], sequentiality can also be captured, choosing representative sequences that commence each layer at the same time.

We propose a semantics which allows exploiting both locality and sequentiality of a concurrent program. This work also provides a semantic framework for the works of [16, 31, 14, 11] which suggest using a reduced state space of global states. Moreover, since the semantics suggested here extends the definition of independence among program operations, a proof method which extends those works is also facilitated. We will show how this can be done. In Section 2, the semantics of conditional traces is introduced. In Section 3, the semantic approach is further described and demonstrated. As an application, it is shown how verification for total correctness can be done within the proposed semantics. Finally, Section 4 discusses when the semantics is most beneficial.

2 Conditional Traces

The semantics presented in this paper is defined within the framework of traces. However, it may be defined similarly with respect to partial orders among events, where interpreted slices (left closed subsets of events) represent the possible global states of the program (as in [15]). This would give a model known as interleaving sets. Translations between these two models often exist, although they do have some different assumptions in their construction, concerning infinite executions and fairness. Infinite conditional traces can also be defined as an extension of infinite traces [18], and evidently most other partial order semantics could be treated similarly. The programs considered will be given as collections of transitions, although of course it is possible to express the ideas directly in terms of a higher level language.

2.1 Collapses

Traces, as presented in [20, 21] are equivalence classes of strings of program operations T where each string can be viewed as an interleaved history of an execution. The strings in a single class are indistinguishable in the sense that concurrently executable operations are interleaved in either order. Traces are used to represent partial order semantics. Pairs of operations which can execute concurrently are represented as a symmetric and irreflexive relation $I \subseteq T \times T$ called the *independence.* Note that this relation is over operations, and not events (occurrences of operations), and is assumed to be given for each semantic model. We use α, α_i, α', $\beta \ldots$ for typical operations. Strings of operations are denoted by v, w, x, $y, \ldots$ The empty string is denoted by ϵ.

A program Pr is a triple $\langle T,\ \bar{y},\ \Theta\rangle$ where T is a finite set of *operations* or *transitions*, $\bar{y}$ is a finite set of variables, and Θ is a predicate called the *initial condition.* Each operation $\alpha \in T$ is associated with a pair $\langle en_\alpha,\ f_\alpha\rangle$ where en_α is a predicate (the *enabling condition*) and f_α (the *transformation*) is a tuple of $|\,\bar{y}\,|$ terms over some fixed first order language. The predicates Θ and en_α for each $\alpha \in T$ contain no free occurrences other than the variables of $\bar{y}$. The same holds for the variables used in the terms f_α.

The intuitive meaning of en_α and f_α is as follows: A (global) state of a program is an assignment function, associating to each of the program variables a value from its domain. In order that an operation α executes from a global state ρ, ρ must satisfy en_α. When α executes, the new program state is $f_\alpha(\rho)$.

An operation α can be written as the guarded command $\langle en_\alpha(\bar{y}) \longrightarrow \bar{y} := f_\alpha(\bar{y})\rangle$. The condition before the arrow controls when the operation may execute and the effect of the operation is to simultaneously assign the $|\bar{y}|$ expressions $f_\alpha(\bar{y})$ into the set of of variables $\bar{y}$ respectively. Notice that in some cases, it is convenient to use partial functions for f_α. For example, when $\alpha = \langle x \neq 0 \longrightarrow y := z\ div\ x\rangle$, the term $z\ div\ x$ is defined only for a non-zero x. We can always complete f_α into a total function which returns some arbitrary values when $\neg en_\alpha$ holds.

Since a typical operation changes only a subset of the program variables, we will consider only the part of the assignment which is not the identity. Thus, we write $\langle cond \longrightarrow x := y\rangle$ instead of $\langle cond \longrightarrow (x,\ y,\ z \ldots) := (y,\ y,\ z \ldots)\rangle$. For CSP-like [13] programs and shared memory programs (with *await*), a transformation into a set of operations appears in [22]. Petri–nets [26] can be represented as operations as shown in [25]. The notation $\varphi[f_\alpha(\bar{y})/\bar{y}]$ means the result of substituting in φ for each $1 < i \leq |\,\bar{y}\,|$, the ith term of $f_\alpha(\bar{y})$ instead of each of the free occurrences of $y_i \in \bar{y}$. The predicate transformer $wp_\alpha(\varphi) = en_\alpha(\bar{y}) \wedge \varphi[f_\alpha(\bar{y})/\bar{y}]$ is called the *weakest precondition* [9]. For a predicate φ, $wp_\alpha(\varphi)$ returns the predicate that is satisfied exactly by states from which α can execute and produce a state satisfying φ.

We now will redefine histories, traces and the independence conditions.

Definition 2.1 *A* history *of a program Pr is a pair $s = \langle\sigma,\ v\rangle$ where σ is an interpretation of $\bar{y}$ (that is, an assignment) called the* initial state *of s, and $v \in T^*$. Let $n =|\,v\,|$, $v = \alpha_1\alpha_2 \ldots \alpha_n$. We require that $\sigma \models \Theta$ (σ satisfies Θ). Furthermore, there exists a sequence of interpretations $\sigma_0,\ \sigma_1,\ \ldots,\ \sigma_n$ with $\sigma_0 = \sigma$ such that:*

1. *For each $1 \leq i \leq n$, $\sigma_{i-1} \models en_{\alpha_i}$.*
2. *For each $1 \leq i' \leq n$, $\sigma_i = f_{\alpha_i}(\sigma_{i-1})$.*

For each history $s = \langle \sigma, v \rangle$, let the nth interpretation in the above sequence, namely $\sigma_{|v|}$ (which is a function of s) be denoted by fin_s. This is called the *final interpretation* of s. We use s, s', s_i, r,... for histories. It is obvious from the definition that for a history $s = \langle \sigma, v \rangle$, if w is a prefix of v, then $s' = \langle \sigma, w \rangle$ is also a history.

Definition 2.2 *A collapse of Pr is a set of predicates $\mathcal{I} = \{\Delta_{\alpha,\beta} \mid \alpha, \beta \in T, \alpha \neq \beta\}$ such that $\Delta_{\alpha,\beta} = \Delta_{\beta,\alpha}$ satisfying:*

1. $\forall \bar{y}\, \Delta_{\alpha,\beta} \wedge en_\alpha(\bar{y}) \wedge en_\beta(\bar{y}) \rightarrow f_\alpha(f_\beta(\bar{y})) = f_\beta(f_\alpha(\bar{y}))$ *[commutativity when operations are enabled].*
2. $\forall \bar{y} \Delta_{\alpha,\beta} \wedge en_\alpha(\bar{y}) \rightarrow (en_\beta(\bar{y}) \leftrightarrow en_\beta[f_\alpha(\bar{y})/\bar{y}])$ *[if α is enabled, it does not change the enabledness of β].*

A collapse defines the new independence condition. This independence requires both commutativity of the transformations made by both operations and preserving the enabledness (disabledness) conditions. The latter is less obvious and demands a further explanation. Suppose in one execution sequence α is executed immediately prior to β. Even when f_α and f_β are commutative, it might be the case that if β executes first, it disables α. Another case is that α can execute before β but β cannot execute before α because α enables β, as in the case of the operations $\alpha = \langle true \longrightarrow x := x + 1 \rangle$, $\beta = \langle x > 0 \longrightarrow z := 3 \rangle$ and a state in which $x = 0$.

The predicate $\Delta_{\alpha,\beta}$ is used to identify the context (i.e., the set of global states) where α and β are independent. That is, when $\Delta_{\alpha,\beta}$ is *true*, if both the operations are enabled, their execution order can be reversed, obtaining the same result. Moreover, the execution of one operation does not disable nor enable the other. When $\Delta_{\alpha,\beta}$ is false, the semantics we will define below does not allow changing the order among α and β even if they are commutative. For a program Pr, it is sometimes possible to have many collapses. In verification there is no need to find the weakest possible predicates, and we consider below which ones are appropriate for semantic definitions. Although the predicates in a collapse are symmetric, we shall see that there can be states for which operation α can be switched with β when $\alpha\beta$ occurs, but they cannot be switched when $\beta\alpha$ occurs.

Lemma 2.3 *If $s = \langle \sigma, x\alpha\beta y \rangle$ is a history of Pr, $r = \langle \sigma, x \rangle$ and $fin_r \models \Delta_{\alpha,\beta}$ where $\Delta_{\alpha,\beta}$ is in a collapse of Pr, then $s' = \langle \sigma, x\beta\alpha y \rangle$ is also a history of Pr and $fin_s = fin_{s'}$.*

Proof. Let $r' = \langle \sigma, x\alpha \rangle$. Since β is enabled in $fin_{r'} = f_\alpha(fin_r)$, by the second clause of definition 2.2 it must also be enabled in fin_r. Thus, let $r'' = \langle \sigma, x\beta \rangle$. Again, using the symmetry in the definition of a collapse, en_α holds in $fin_{r''}$. Let now $r_1 = \langle \sigma, x\alpha\beta \rangle$ and $r_2 = \langle \sigma, x\beta\alpha \rangle$. Again from the definition of a collapse (the first condition) it follows that $fin_{r_1} = fin_{r_2}$. The fact that s' is a history and that $fin_s = fin_{s'}$ follows from Definition 2.1 by a simple induction on the length of y. ∎

A collapse induces an equivalence relation on histories of Pr which have the same initial state. Two histories, s and s' are equivalent iff their initial states are the same and one of the strings is obtained from the other by commuting adjacent operations only when the independence among them holds. Thus the semantics of a program is determined by its collection of histories, and by its collapse.

Definition 2.4 *The histories $s = \langle\sigma, v\rangle$ and $s' = \langle\sigma, w\rangle$ are equivalent (denoted $s \equiv s'$) iff there exists a sequence of histories $\langle\sigma, v_1\rangle, \langle\sigma, v_2\rangle, \ldots, \langle\sigma, v_n\rangle$ with $v_1 = v$ and $v_n = w$ and for each $1 \leq i < n$ there exist $x, y \in T^*$, $\alpha, \beta \in T$ such that $v_i = x\alpha\beta y$, $v_{i+1} = x\beta\alpha y$ and for $r = \langle\sigma, x\rangle$, $fin_r \models \Delta_{\alpha,\beta}$. A* conditional trace *is an equivalence class of histories.*

Conditional traces will be called simply *traces* in the sequel. Denote a trace as $t = [\sigma, v]$ where σ is the mutual initial state and $\langle\sigma, v\rangle$ is a member of the equivalence class. The interpretation fin_t is generalized to traces by taking the final interpretation of any member of the equivalence class, as justified by Lemma 2.5 below. Traces will be denoted by $t, t', t_i, \ldots$ Using Lemma 2.5, the length of a trace can be defined as the length of any member of it. We will say that a trace t satisfies φ if $fin_t \models \varphi$.

Lemma 2.5 *If $s \equiv r$ then $fin_s = fin_r$ and the length of the string of s is the same as the string of r.*

Proof. Simple induction on the number of times an operation is commuted when transforming s to r and using Lemma 2.3. ∎

Concatenation between two traces $t_1 = [\sigma, v]$ and $t_2 = [\rho, w]$, denoted $t_1 t_2$, is defined when $fin_{t_1} = \rho$ as $[\sigma, vw]$. The prefix relation $\sqsubseteq$ between conditional traces is defined as $t_1 \sqsubseteq t_2$ iff there exists some t_3 such that $t_1 t_3 = t_2$. It is said that t_1 is subsumed by t_2. If in addition, the length of t_1 is shorter than the length of t_2 by exactly one, it is said that t_2 is an *immediate successor* of t_1.

Two traces t_1 and t_2 of a program Pr are *consistent* iff there exists some t_3 of Pr such that $t_1 \sqsubseteq t_3$ and $t_2 \sqsubseteq t_3$. A *run* of Pr is a maximal set of traces which are pairwise consistent. Denote runs by $\Pi, \Pi', \ldots$ The set of traces of a run Π will be denoted as $traces(\Pi)$. An execution sequence of Π is a maximal sequence of traces $t_0 t_1 t_2 \ldots$ of $traces(\Pi)$ such that for each $i \geq 0$, t_{i+1} is an immediate successor of t_i.

By strengthening or weakening the independence conditions (i.e., the collapse), the traces can shrink or grow, respectively. For example, by choosing $\Delta_{\alpha,\beta} = false$ for each distinct pair of operations, each trace contains exactly a single execution sequence. This is exactly as in linear interleaving semantics, where equivalences among sequences are not explicit on a semantic level. Partial order semantics of traces [20, 21] allows each $\Delta_{\alpha,\beta}$ to be fixed as either *true* or *false*. For such a semantics, $\Delta_{\alpha,\beta}$ will be identically *true* for the pairs of operations generating events that are always commutative and always do not affect each others' enabledness, and will be identically *false* otherwise. (Sometimes operations in the same process are arbitrarily assumed to be ordered, so that the condition for such operations will be *false* even when otherwise it could be *true*.)

Lamport and Schneider [19] also utilize independence to simplify reasoning on concurrent programs. In their formalism, it is said that α *commutes to the right with*

β if whenever β is executed immediately after α, their order can be interchanged, producing the same net effect. This definition is obviously non-symmetric with respect to this pair of operations. Although the definition of a collapse requires that the predicates $\Delta_{\alpha,\beta}$ and $\Delta_{\beta,\alpha}$ are the same, symmetry can be broken by using a predicate which will allow permuting the operations only when they can be executed from this state one after the other in some given order. Furthermore, we show below how to expand commutativity to allow conditional right commutativity.

Assume that it is given that α commutes to the right with β provided that φ_1 holds. Then, $\Delta_{\alpha,\beta} = \varphi_1 \wedge wp_\alpha(en_\beta)$ allows α and β to be commuted exactly in states when φ_1 holds and α can be executed followed by β.

Now, to see why the above formulation of (part of) a collapse captures the property of commuting to the right, observe that histories whose final interpretation satisfies $wp_\alpha(en_\beta)$ are those from which α is enabled and, after executing α, the operation β is enabled. That is, if $s = \langle\sigma, v\rangle$ is a history of Pr and $fin_s \models wp_\alpha(en_\beta)$, then $\langle\sigma, v\alpha\beta\rangle$ is also a history of Pr.

Assume that $\Delta_{\alpha,\beta}$ satisfies the conditions of Definition 2.2. Let $s = \langle\sigma, v\rangle$ be a history of Pr satisfying $\Delta_{\alpha,\beta}$. Then, $s' = \langle\sigma, v\alpha\beta\rangle$ is also a history of Pr. By Lemma 2.3, it holds that $s'' = \langle\sigma, v\beta\alpha\rangle$ is also a history of Pr as required. Conversely, assume that α commutes to the right with β from all the histories which can be extended with $\alpha\beta$ and whose final interpretation satisfies φ_1. Let $r = \langle\sigma, v\rangle$ be a history of Pr where $fin_r \models \varphi_1$ and $r' = \langle\sigma, v\alpha\beta\rangle$ is another history of Pr (hence, $fin_r \models \varphi_1 \wedge wp_\alpha(en_\beta)$). Thus, from right commutativity, $r'' = \langle\sigma, v\beta\alpha\rangle$ is also a history of Pr, with $fin_{r'} = fin_{r''}$. The conditions of Definition 2.2 hold: Condition 2 (for both pairs α,β and β,α) stems from the fact that both r' and r'' exist, and hence α and β are enabled in fin_r, α is enabled after the execution of β, and β is enabled after the execution of α. Condition 1 holds since $fin_{r'} = fin_{r''}$ and α and β are enabled in fin_r.

In a similar manner, if in addition to the conditional right commutativity of α and β discussed above it is also known that β commutes to the right with α when φ_2 holds, then $\Delta_{\alpha,\beta} = (\varphi_1 \wedge wp_\alpha(en_\beta)) \vee (\varphi_2 \wedge wp_\beta(en_\alpha))$ can be used. Notice that nothing is explicitly said about a state s in which φ_1 holds but β can be executed before α (or similarly, a state in which φ_2 holds and α can be executed before β). It is possible that α is not enabled in s and β makes it enabled.

Another definition of independence, by Best and Lengauer [8], is titled *semantic independence.* They show that every pair of events from a pair of operations can be commutative even when the same variables are used in both, because the property needed from each mutual variable is always invariant to events of the other operation. Their definition is however stronger than commutativity (that is, if two operations are semantically independent, then they are commutative) and concerns the possibility of distributed implementation. Their approach might also be generalized to a conditional invariance.

The semantics of a language can either be determined by picking a fixed collapse, as above, and combining it with the basic collection of traces to obtain the equivalence classes above, or by using the *weakest collapse* as the most general default. This collapse is true for α and β exactly in those states for which the two conditions in the definition of a collapse are true. Thus it allows exploiting the independence of events whenever possible. The weakest collapse can be formulated as

$$\begin{array}{rcl}\Delta_{\alpha,\beta} & = & (en_\alpha(\bar{y}) \wedge en_\beta(\bar{y}) \wedge en_\alpha[f_\beta(\bar{y})/\bar{y}] \wedge en_\beta[f_\alpha(\bar{y})/\bar{y}] \wedge f_\alpha(f_\beta(\bar{y})) = f_\beta(f_\alpha(\bar{y})))\\ & \vee & (en_\alpha(\bar{y}) \wedge \neg en_\beta(\bar{y}) \wedge \neg en_\beta[f_\alpha(\bar{y})/\bar{y}])\\ & \vee & (en_\beta(\bar{y}) \wedge \neg en_\alpha(\bar{y}) \wedge \neg en_\alpha[f_\beta(\bar{y})/\bar{y}])\\ & \vee & (\neg en_\alpha(\bar{y}) \wedge \neg en_\beta(\bar{y}))\end{array}$$

The first disjunct gives the positive conditions in Definition 2.2, while the others treat cases where operations are not enabled.

When specific collapses are used, e.g., for verification (as will be seen in Section 3), they must be shown to imply the collapse given for the semantics of the language. That is, whenever the specific collapse is true, so is the collapse of the language semantics.

2.2 Conditional Traces as Partial Orders

A construction that transforms (ordinary) traces into partial order semantics and its opposite companion exist [20]. The existence of these transformations justify the consideration of traces as representing partial order semantics. In this subsection we investigate the conditions under which these transformations may be applied in the context of conditional traces. In the following discussion, for notational convenience we ignore the initial state element of histories and traces, as its explicit occurrence is orthogonal to the transformations. Thus, we denote by $[w]$ a trace where the history $\langle\sigma, w\rangle$ is one of its histories with some initial state σ. Similarly, we may simply write w instead of denoting the above history.

A partial order is a pair $\mathcal{E} = \langle E, \prec\rangle$, where E is a set and $\prec \subseteq E \times E$ is a transitive, irreflexive relation on E. A linearization $\mathcal{L}$ of $\mathcal{E}$ is a total order $\mathcal{L} = \langle E, <\rangle$ where $\prec \subseteq <$.

Let $\#_\alpha w$ be the number of times the symbol α occurs in the string w. The ith symbol in w will be denoted by α_i. Let $\mathcal{T}_w = \{\alpha \mid \alpha \in T \wedge \#_\alpha w > 0\}$ (the set of operations occurring in w). An *occurrence* of w (or, equivalently of $[w]$, because each operation appears the same number of times in each member of the equivalence class) is any pair (α, n) where $\alpha \in \mathcal{T}_w$ and $1 \leq n \leq \#_\alpha w$. Let ξ_w be the isomorphism from $1 \ldots |w|$ to the set of occurrences of w defined as $\xi_w(i) = (\alpha_i, |\{j \mid j \leq i \wedge \alpha_j = \alpha_i\}|)$. For example, $\xi_{\alpha\beta\beta\gamma\alpha}$ will map the integers $1 \ldots 5$ to $(\alpha, 1), (\beta, 1), (\beta, 2), (\gamma, 1), (\alpha, 2)$ respectively. We identify histories with total orders by denoting a history as a sequence of occurrences rather than a simple string (so that no element occurs twice on such a sequence). For each string w, define a total order among its occurrences $<_w$ such that $\xi_w(i) <_w \xi_w(j)$ iff $i < j$. Define now a partial order relation $\preceq_t = \bigcap_{w \in t} <_w$ among the set of occurrences of a trace t.

The opposite construction is to form a trace by taking the set of all the linearizations of the partially ordered events. Then, a string is constructed from each total order by ignoring the number part of each occurrence. For ordinary traces, this transformation is the inverse of the former transformation. Namely, by taking the linearizations of a partially ordered set of occurrences constructed from a trace t, it is guaranteed that t is obtained back. (Obtaining the linearizations of a finite partial order and then applying the transformation which generates a partial order by taking the intersection always returns the original partial order.)

However, for conditional traces, it might happen that by applying the first transformation, and then applying the second on the result of the first, a larger set of histories is obtained. For example, it might happen that an operation γ which can be commuted with both α and β changes the truth value of $\Delta_{\alpha,\beta}$. That is, $\alpha\beta\gamma \equiv \beta\alpha\gamma$ which are also equivalent to $\gamma\alpha\beta$, but these histories are not equivalent to $\gamma\beta\alpha$.

Concretely, let $\alpha : \langle \textit{true} \longrightarrow x := x+2\rangle, \beta : \langle x > 0 \longrightarrow x := x-1\rangle, \gamma : \langle \textit{true} \longrightarrow x := x-2\rangle$, $\Delta_{\alpha,\beta} = (x \neq 0 \wedge x \neq -1)$, $\Delta_{\alpha,\gamma} = \textit{true}$, and $\Delta_{\beta,\gamma} = (x \neq 1 \wedge x \neq 2)$. (This is the weakest collapse, obtained by substituting the appropriate terms and conditions to the formula at the end of the previous subsection.) Starting from an initial state in which $x = 1$, there exists a trace which consists of the strings $\alpha\beta\gamma$, $\beta\alpha\gamma$, $\alpha\gamma\beta$, $\gamma\alpha\beta$, $\beta\gamma\alpha$. When transforming this set of equivalent histories into a partial order, the three occurrences $(\alpha, 1)$, $(\beta, 1)$ and $(\gamma, 1)$ become pairwise unordered, because for each pair of these occurrences there exists a trace in which the first precedes the second, and the other way around. Transforming the partial order back into a set of histories results in $\gamma\beta\alpha$ in addition to the original histories.

To pin down the source of this phenomena, observe that in ordinary traces, each pair of operations is either constantly dependent or constantly independent, while in conditional traces, this is not the case. The key to identifying when conditional traces can be viewed as representations of partial order is to treat histories as total orders (using the mappings ξ defined above) and observe the relative order among *occurrences* (rather than operations) in different histories of a trace.

Two occurrences $o_1 : (\alpha, i)$ and $o_2 : (\beta, j)$ of a trace t can appear in the same order along each of t's histories, or occur in different orders (other occurrences of t involving α and β can have a totally different relative order than o_1 and o_2). The pair of transformations above are inverses precisely if whenever o_1 and o_2 occur adjacent either they never can appear in the opposite order or they always can appear in either order, and commute. That is, the independence of occurences is fixed. This condition, which can be proven sufficient and necessary for the transformations to be inverses, provides an intermediate level between the fixed independence for operations seen in the original traces, and the full generality of collapses. Whether or not the transformations are considered essential is a matter of taste. For purposes of verification and optimization, where the final results are the important consideration, they seem to be extraneous. Note, of course, that global invariants of a system are not affected by the choice of a collapse, since the same collection of states exists in the system, and only the grouping of histories is determined by the collapse chosen.

3 Examples

3.1 Two Programs

The following program (which is a slight modification of a program in [23]) computes the number of possible combinations when choosing k out of n distinct elements using the formula

$$\binom{n}{k} = \frac{n \times (n-1) \times \cdots \times (n-k+1)}{1 \times 2 \times \cdots \times k}$$

The left process repeatedly multiplies the numerator as the values of y_1 range between n and $n-k+1$, while the right process repeatedly divides the denominator as the values of y_2 range between 1 and k. The operation m_3 allows m_4 to be executed only when the number of values multiplied is greater than the number of values divided. This guarantees that m_4 will always produce an integer result (and thus can be implemented as an integer division). The initial condition is

$$\Theta \equiv y_1 = n \wedge y_2 = 0 \wedge y_3 = 1 \wedge l = l_1 \wedge m = m_1$$

l_1:**if** $y_1 = (n-k)$ **then halt**	m_1:**if** $y_2 = k$ **then halt**
l_2:$y_3 := y_3 \times y_1$	m_2:$y_2 := y_2 + 1$
l_3:$y_1 := y_1 - 1$	m_3:**await** $y_2 \leq n - y_1$
l_4:**goto** l_1	m_4:$y_3 := y_3 / y_2$
	m_5:**goto** m_1

Following is a translation of the program into a set of operations. We have used the function

$$\mathtt{if}(cond,\ a,\ b) = \begin{cases} a & \text{if } cond = true \\ b & \text{if } cond = false \end{cases}$$

which returns either its second or third argument, depending on the boolean value of its first argument. The variables l and m represent the program counters. Executing the command **halt** terminates the execution of a process. This is translated as assigning a special value to the process's program counter which disables all its enabledness conditions.

$\langle l = l_1 \longrightarrow l := \mathtt{if}(y_1 = (n-k), halt_l, l_2)\rangle$
$\langle l = l_2 \longrightarrow (l, y_3) := (l_3, y_3 \times y_1)\rangle$
$\langle l = l_3 \longrightarrow (l, y_1) := (l_4, y_1 - 1)\rangle$
$\langle l = l_4 \longrightarrow l := l_1\rangle$

$\langle m = m_1 \longrightarrow m := \mathtt{if}(y_2 = k, halt_m, m_2)\rangle$
$\langle m = m_2 \longrightarrow (m, y_2) := (m_3, y_2 + 1)\rangle$
$\langle m = m_3 \wedge y_2 \leq n - y_1 \longrightarrow m := m_4\rangle$
$\langle m = m_4 \longrightarrow (m, y_3) := (m_5, y_3 / y_2)\rangle$
$\langle m = m_5 \longrightarrow m := m_1\rangle$

Divide the program operations into two sets (the name of an operation and the value of the program counter when the operation is available are the same):

$$L = \{l_1,\ l_2,\ l_3,\ l_4\},\ M = \{m_1,\ m_2,\ m_3,\ m_4,\ m_5\}$$

In every history with operations from L and M, one can commute adjacent pairs of operations from L and M unless the pair is (l_3, m_3) and $y_2 = n - y_1 + 1$. In that case, m_3 cannot be done first, but if l_3 is done first, $y_2 = n - y_1$ and the *await* statement succeeds. We define

$$\Delta_{\alpha,\beta} = \begin{cases} true & \text{if } (\alpha,\ \beta) \in L \times M \setminus \{(l_3, m_3)\} \\ false & \text{if } (\alpha,\ \beta) \in L \times L \cup M \times M \\ y_2 \neq n - y_1 + 1 & \text{if } \alpha = l_3 \wedge \beta = m_3 \end{cases}$$

It is always possible to commute an operation from L with a previous operation from M. The only case which is not obvious is that it is possible to have the operation l_3 precede m_3. That is, if m_3 is executed immediately before l_3, then its enabledness condition $y_2 \leq n - y_1$ implies $y_2 \leq n - y_1 + 1$ or, equivalently, $y_2 \leq n - (y_1 - 1)$. Thus, in that same state, if we now want to execute l_3 first, decrementing y_1 will leave the condition for executing m_3 still true, so that the same result is obtained as previously. Since each execution sequence is equivalent to the sequence in which all the operations from L are executed before all the operations from M, there is a single maximal trace for the program (and hence, a single run).

As another example, consider the following producer/consumer program [19] with a bounded buffer. The program counters of the two processes are p and c, respectively, while n_p and n_c are used to count the number of values produced and consumed, respectively. In this program, the left process P(roducer) generates M values using the function $inp(n_p)$ where $0 \leq n_p < M$. It uses the buffer $buf[0..N-1]$ to communicate the values to the right process C(onsumer). Process C consumes the values from the buffer by executing the procedure $out(y)$ for each y obtained from the buffer.

The initial condition is $\Theta \equiv p = p_1 \land c = c_1 \land n_p = 0 \land n_c = 0$.

p_1:if $n_p = M$ then halt	c_1:if $n_c = M$ then halt
p_2:$x := \texttt{inp}(n_p)$	c_2:await $(n_p - n_c) > 0$
p_3:await $(n_p - n_c) < N$	c_3:$y := buf[n_c \bmod N]$
p_4:$buf[n_p \bmod N] := x$	c_4:$n_c := n_c + 1$
p_5:$n_p := n_p + 1$	c_5:out (y)
p_6:goto p_1	c_6:goto c_1

Since the buffer is bounded, both processes must synchronize so that exactly the values which are produced are finally consumed. Since the producer uses n_p to count the number of values produced, while the consumer uses n_c to count the number of values consumed, when $n_p - n_c = N$, the buffer is full. Hence, the producer has to wait for the consumer to consume some values. On the other hand, when $n_p = n_c$, no new values are ready in the buffer, and the consumer has to wait for the producer to produce new values.

Let P be the producer's operations and C be the consumer operations. Independence predicates can be defined as follows:

$$\Delta_{\alpha,\beta} = \begin{cases} true & \text{if } (\alpha, \beta) \in P \times C \setminus \{(p_3, c_3), (p_5, c_2), (p_4, c_3)\} \\ false & \text{if } (\alpha, \beta) \in P \times P \cup C \times C \\ n_p > n_c & \text{if } \alpha = p_5 \land \beta = c_2 \\ n_p - n_c < N & \text{if } \alpha = p_3 \land \beta = c_4 \\ n_p \bmod N \neq n_c \bmod N & \text{if } \alpha = p_4 \land \beta = c_3 \end{cases}$$

Using these predicates, it can be shown that each execution sequence of the program is equivalent to the sequence of operations in which the the elements are inserted and removed one at a time, i.e., the sequence $p_1\, p_2\, p_3\, p_4\, p_5\, p_6\, c_1\, c_2\, c_3\, c_4\, c_5\, c_6$ appears M times and then p_1 and c_1 appear once. It should be noted that it is not always the case that a single representative sequence can be found, even though this was the case for these two examples.

Although in the above example we followed the convention of having the events from operations in the same process be totally ordered (as seen in the second line of both definitions of $\Delta_{\alpha,\beta}$), this restricts the generality. In the second example Δ_{c_4,c_5} could be *true*. This would require changing the translation from the program to a set of transitions, so that the update of the program counter could be ignored in determining independence. Other possibilities are left as an exercise for the reader.

3.2 An Application: Verifying Total Correctness

The interaction between concurrent segments of a program (usually called *processes*) poses considerable difficulty in verification that does not exist in sequential programs. The basic method is to use assertions that cover all the possible states of the program generated by interleaving independent (concurrent) operations [3]. The assertions are global (referring at the same time to variables of different processes). Considering only the number of possible combinations of values for program counters, this number can grow to the product of the sizes of the different processes (by "size" we mean the number of operations).

It is evident from the works mentioned in the introduction that the following pattern of program verification is appealing: In a first stage, identify the structuring of a concurrent program. That is, independence among various parts. Then, at a second stage, use proof rules which can exploit this independence. Identifying independence does not mean that actual extra structuring is marked or constructed on programs or program models. Merely, some conditions are satisfied that guarantee the soundness of the rules used in the second step. We present a set of proof rules which exploits collapses. These rules are shown to be sound and complete for proving total correctness.

Total correctness of a program Pr with respect to an assertion ψ demands that if Pr started executing from a global state satisfying Θ, then it will eventually terminate in some state which satisfies ψ.

Methods based on linear execution sequences use well-founded induction to show that each sequence is finite and terminates with a correct global state. A parametrized inductive assertion $\varphi(n)$, where n belongs to some domain $\mathcal{W}$ is used to guarantee that from all the intermediate states of the execution satisfying it, each successor state satisfies $\varphi(m)$ for some $m \prec n$ according to some well-founded order '$\prec$' on $\mathcal{W}$. Here, instead of taking care of all the successors of each state, we demand that $\varphi(m)$ with $m \prec n$ will be satisfied by at least one successor of each state satisfying $\varphi(n)$ in every run. By repeatedly choosing successors according to this rule, a set of representative execution sequences (at least one for each run) satisfy the well-founded induction.

Below we prove two lemmas that connect the intuitive notions of termination and total correctness to the conditional trace model.

Lemma 3.1 *If a program does not terminate, there exists an infinite run.*

Proof. If the program does not terminate, there exists an infinite sequence of histories $s_0\, s_1\, s_2 \ldots$ where $s_0 = \langle\sigma, \epsilon\rangle$, $\sigma \models \Theta$ $s_i = \langle\sigma, v_i\rangle$ and for each $i \geq 0$, for some $\alpha \in T$, $fin_{s_i} \models en_\alpha$ and $v_{i+1} = v_i\alpha$. For each $i \geq 0$, let t_i be the set of histories equivalent to s_i, Thus, $t_0\, t_1\, t_2 \ldots$ is a sequence of traces. The set of traces in this sequence is pairwise consistent. It might be the case that this set is not maximal, but then it is contained in a maximal infinite run. ∎

Lemma 3.2 *If a run Π is finite, it has a single maximal trace (according to the trace order '$\sqsubseteq$') and its final interpretation satisfies $Term = \bigwedge_{\alpha \in T} \neg en_\alpha$. Otherwise, no trace of Π satisfies $Term$.*

Proof. Since by definition any two traces of a run must be consistent, there is only one maximal t, since the run is finite. Obviously, $fin_t \models Term$.

Now, assume that an infinite run Π' has a trace t satisfying $Term$. It must also have a trace t' whose length exceeds that of t (because the number of traces with length not more than $|t|$ is finite). Thus, there must exist a trace subsuming both t and t'. However, this is impossible, since t satisfies $Term$. ∎

Thus, total correctness of a program Pr with respect to Θ and ψ holds iff each run Π of Pr is finite and the final interpretations of its maximal trace satisfies ψ.

A notation is needed to describe assertions which use intermediate states, residing on representatives from each equivalence class. Linear Temporal Logic [22] is inadequate here, because it implicitly asserts about all the sequences. The logic ISTL [15] is appropriate. Here, only the subset which is needed for total correctness proofs is used. The rules presented generalize those seen in [16].

Definition 3.3 *Denote $\varphi \to EX\psi$ iff for each run Π of Pr having a trace t with $fin_t \models \varphi$, there exists an immediate successor t' with $fin_{t'} \models \psi$. Denote $\varphi \to EF\psi$ iff for each run Π of Pr having a trace t with $fin_t \models \varphi$, there exists a successor t' with $fin_{t'} \models \psi$.*

Rule 1 SIMP: The following rules are simple properties of 'EX' and 'EF'. They reflect semantic properties of runs.

SIMP1

$$\frac{\varphi \to EX\psi}{\varphi \to EF\psi}$$

SIMP2

$$\frac{\varphi \to \psi}{\varphi \to EF\psi}$$

SIMP3

$$\frac{\begin{array}{c}\varphi \to \varphi_1 \vee \varphi_2 \\ \varphi_1 \to EF\psi \\ \varphi_2 \to EF\psi\end{array}}{\varphi \to EF\psi}$$

SIMP4

$$\frac{\begin{array}{c}\varphi \to EF\varphi_1 \\ \varphi_1 \to EF\psi\end{array}}{\varphi \to EF\psi}$$

Rule 2 IND: Well founded induction can be proved using the following rule. Let $(\mathcal{W}, \prec)$ be a well-founded domain (no infinitely decreasing chains). Let $\varphi(n)$ be a first order formula with a parameter n from the domain of $\mathcal{W}$.

IND

$$\frac{\begin{array}{l}\varphi \rightarrow \exists n\, \varphi(n) \\ \varphi(n) \rightarrow EF(\psi \vee \exists m \prec n\, \varphi(m))\end{array}}{\varphi \rightarrow EF\psi}$$

Rule 3 STEP: Proving $\varphi \rightarrow EX\psi$ is the kernel of the proof method. To choose only representative successors for φ, the set of operations T is partitioned into two complementary sets Q and $\bar{Q}(= T \setminus Q)$. Instead of showing that each $\alpha \in T$ which is enabled when φ holds will produce a state satisfying ψ, the aim is to show that:

1. By executing operations from Q, enough successors for the states satisfying φ are generated.
2. When executing any operation from the set Q from a state satisfying φ, a state satisfying ψ is reached.

A third predicate δ is used to achieve the first goal. It is used to show that from a state satisfying φ, as long as no operation from Q is executed, each operation from $\bar{Q}$ is either disabled or independent of all the operations of Q. By the independence conditions, any operation of Q enabled at s cannot be disabled by an operation of $\bar{Q}$. Thus, there are two cases: One is that there is an infinite sequence of $\bar{Q}$ operations and hence at least one of the successors of s is produced by some element of Q (this *justice–like* property relies on the maximality of the set of traces in each run and will be elaborated in the proof below). The other case is that all the sequences of the class are finite and thus, some element α from Q which is enabled when φ holds is eventually executed. In both cases, by independence (using the collapse), α can be commuted with every previous adjacent operation from $\bar{Q}$ that occurred after s. The last premise of the rule asserts that by executing any operation from Q which is enabled in a state satisfying φ, a state satisfying ψ is reached.

STEP

$$\frac{\begin{array}{ll}\text{S1} & \varphi \rightarrow (\delta \wedge \bigvee_{\alpha \in Q} en_\alpha) \\ \text{S2} & \text{for each } \alpha \in \bar{Q},\ \delta \wedge en_\alpha \rightarrow wp_\alpha(\delta) \\ \text{S3} & \delta \rightarrow \bigwedge_{\alpha \in \bar{Q}}(\neg en_\alpha \vee \bigwedge_{\beta \in Q} \Delta_{\alpha,\beta}) \\ \text{S4} & \text{for each } \alpha \in Q,\ \varphi \wedge en_\alpha \rightarrow wp_\alpha(\psi)\end{array}}{\varphi \rightarrow EX\psi}$$

Theorem 3.4 *The proof rules are sound.*

Proof. The only nonobvious rule is STEP. Assume that all its premises hold. Let t be a trace satisfying φ which belongs to $traces(\Pi)$ for some run Π. By S1, t satisfies δ and at least one operation from Q is enabled at fin_t. Furthermore, by the premise S2, while executing after t (appending to it) only operations from $\bar{Q}$, δ is kept invariant. By S3, when δ holds, each operation of $\bar{Q}$ is either disabled or the conditions for its independence with all the operations from Q hold. Hence, from the conditions of collapses in Definition 2.2, the same operations from Q which are enabled in t remains enabled after executing any number of operations from $\bar{Q}$. Moreover, if an operation from Q is finally executed, it can be commuted with all the operations of $\tilde{Q}$ executed since t. By the premise s4, by executing any operation of Q from a trace satisfying φ, a trace satisfying ψ is obtained.

If Π is a finite run, it is obvious that the maximal trace t' of Π subsuming t cannot avoid executing all the operations from Q after t, because otherwise, at least one operation from Q remains enabled.

Assume now that Π is an infinite run, and all the traces of Π subsuming t avoid executing operations from Q after t. Then, this set of traces is not maximal. To see this, take some operation $\alpha \in Q$ which is enabled in t. Then, δ (using s2 and s3) guarantees that α is enabled in every trace of Π subsuming t. For each such trace, $t' = [\sigma, v]$ form a new trace $\hat{t'} = [\sigma, v\alpha]$. Let $\widehat{traces}(\Pi)$ be the set of newly formed traces. We will show now that for each pair of traces $t_1 \in traces(\Pi)$, $t_2 \in \widehat{traces}(\Pi)$ there exists some trace $t_3 \in \widehat{traces}(\Pi)$ which subsumes both t_1 and t_2. Let $t_4 \in traces(\Pi)$ be the trace satisfying $t_4[fin_{t_4}, \alpha] = t_2$ (t_2 was constructed from t_4 by adding the operation α). Let $t_5 \in traces(\Pi)$ be the trace subsuming both t_1 and t_4. The trace $t_3 = t_5[fin_{t_5}, \alpha]$ subsumes both t_1 and t_2 ($t_5 \models en_\alpha$ because $t \sqsubseteq t_4 \sqsubseteq t_5$). Similarly, consistency among pairs of traces in $\widehat{traces}(\Pi)$ can be shown. Hence, the traces in $traces(\Pi) \cup \widehat{traces}(\Pi)$ are pairwise consistent, which contradicts the maximality of $traces(\Pi)$. ∎

Theorem 3.5 *The proof rules are complete for verifying total correctness.*

Proof. It is always possible to choose $Q = T$, $\tilde{Q} = \emptyset$. That is, we may choose not to exploit the independence. In that case, the proof method is reduced to other methods for proving total correctness, for example to [28]. ∎

Returning to the first example in Section 3.1, the total correctness proof is done using two well-founded inductions. The formula φ_1 describes the states obtained by executing only operations from L. In order to show progress, we have to use a parametric formula where the value of the parameter decreases with each single operation from L which is executed. A closer look at the program reveals that y_1 is decreasing with every traversal of the loop l_1, l_2, l_3, l_4. Thus, a well-founded ordering which decreases with every step of L can be formulated by taking the lexicographical order $\langle \mathcal{N} \times \mathcal{W}_1, \ll_1 \rangle$ where $\mathcal{N}$ is the set of natural numbers with the usual "less than" order, and $\mathcal{W}_1 \equiv \langle L \cup \{halt_l\}, l_4 \succ_1 l_1 \succ_1 l_2 \succ_1 l_3 \succ_1 halt_l \rangle$. Let $\varphi_1(a, b)$ be the parametrized first order formula

$$m = m_1 \wedge n \geq y_1 \geq n - k \wedge y_3 = n \times (n-1) \times \ldots \times (y_1 + \text{if}(l \neq l_3, 1, 0)) \\ \wedge y_2 = 0 \wedge a = y_1 \wedge b = l$$

A second parametric formula is used to show progress from a state in which the left part (the operations in L) has terminated and only operations from M are enabled. Again, a lexicographic order $\langle \mathcal{N} \times \mathcal{W}_2, \ll_2 \rangle$ is used where $\mathcal{W}_2 \equiv \langle M \cup \{halt_m\}, m_3 \succ_2 m_4 \succ_2 m_5 \succ_2 m_1 \succ_2 m_2 \succ_2 halt_m \rangle$. Let $\varphi_2(a, b)$ be the parametrized first order formula

$$l = halt_l \wedge y_1 = n - k \wedge y_3 = \frac{n \times (n-1) \times \ldots \times (n-k+1)}{1 \times 2 \times \ldots \times (y_2 - \text{if}(m = m_3 \vee m = m_4, 1, 0))} \\ \wedge y_2 \leq k \wedge a = k - y_2 \wedge b = m$$

describing states obtained by executing operations from M after none of the operations of L is enabled (a multiplicity of zero elements is defined to be 1).

The proof proceeds as follows:

Using first order logic,

$$\Theta \rightarrow \varphi_1(n, l_1) \tag{1}$$

Using first order logic and (1),

$$\Theta \rightarrow \exists a \exists b\, \varphi_1(a, b) \tag{2}$$

Using STEP with $\delta = true$, $Q = L$, and $\bar{Q} = M$, and the given collapse,

$$((n-k, halt_l) \ll_1 (a, b) \wedge \varphi_1(a, b)) \rightarrow EX\ \exists a' \exists b' ((a', b') \ll_1 (a, b) \wedge \varphi_1(a', b')) \tag{3}$$

Using first order logic,

$$\varphi_1(n-k, halt_l) \rightarrow \varphi_2(k, m_1) \tag{4}$$

Using (3), (4) and the rules SIMP,

$$\varphi_1(a, b) \rightarrow EF(\varphi_2(k, m_1) \vee \exists a' \exists b' ((a', b') \ll_1 (a, b) \wedge \varphi_1(a', b'))) \tag{5}$$

Using (2), (5) and IND,

$$\Theta \rightarrow EF\varphi_2(k, m_1) \tag{6}$$

Using STEP with $\delta = true$, $Q = M$ and $\bar{Q} = L$,

$$((0, halt_m) \ll_2 (a, b) \wedge \varphi_2(a, b)) \rightarrow EX\ \exists a' \exists b' ((a', b') \ll_2 (a, b) \wedge \varphi_2(a', b')) \tag{7}$$

Using first order logic,

$$\varphi_2(0, halt_m) \rightarrow \psi \wedge \bigwedge_{\alpha \in T} \neg en_\alpha \tag{8}$$

Using (7), (8) and the rules SIMP,

$$\varphi_2(a, b) \rightarrow EF((\psi \wedge \bigwedge_{\alpha \in T} \neg en_\alpha) \vee \exists a' \exists b' ((a', b') \ll_2 (a, b) \wedge \varphi_2(a', b'))) \tag{9}$$

Using first order logic,

$$\varphi_2(k, m_1) \rightarrow \exists a \exists b\, \varphi_2(a, b) \tag{10}$$

Using (9), (10) and IND,

$$\varphi_2(k, m_1) \rightarrow EF(\psi \wedge \bigwedge_{\alpha \in T} \neg en_\alpha) \tag{11}$$

Using (6), (11) and applying SIMP4,

$$\Theta \rightarrow EF(\psi \wedge \bigwedge_{\alpha \in T} \neg en_\alpha) \tag{12}$$

4 Discussion

The semantics of conditional traces is a direct extension to trace semantics. As we have shown, a collapse is a formalism that extends independence [20] among operations. Instead of using a fixed relation on pairs of operations (predefined, or easily obtainable from the set of operations using some formation rules), a set of predicates satisfying the independence conditions are used. The motivation for using a collapse is practical: it designates when the order among the occurrence of two operations does not matter and can be exploited according to the convenience of a proof or to improve implementation considerations. In this section we discuss the benefits of using this semantics and compare it to other works.

The concept of *locality* discussed earlier is reflected in the semantics: a specification language, such as the temporal logic ISTL [15] can easily express properties about the existence of execution sequences (in each run). A typical such formula assures the existence of sequences where processes which are executing some local task, independent of the other processes, progress in isolation to the progress of the other processes. The concept of *sequentiality* is also facilitated. Considering communication closed layers, it is possible to assert about the existence of interleaving sequences in which the order of execution progresses layerwise. This was shown in [17] to hold for fixed independence relations and obviously holds for conditional independence, provided that the generated runs obtained by a collapse contain the runs of the fixed independence relation (this is achieved by weakening the fixed independence relation).

Assertions which are written as $\varphi \rightarrow EF\psi$ were shown in [15, 16, 29] to express properties such as concurrency, immediate response, and serializability. However, one should be careful when using conditional independence. Semantic properties such as concurrency rely upon interpreting the independence as "can be executed in parallel". Thus, in this case, the collapse should be chosen to agree with this interpretation. A complete proof system for fixed dependence relations appears in [25] and can also be extended to handle conditional dependence.

The conditional trace notation provides a uniform framework for investigating various strategies for defining collapses, such as those in [19, 8], as aids in verification, implementation, and program optimization. The results of Back and Sere on refining atomicity [4, 5] can also be used to enhance the independence which can be used in program verification. Sometimes it is not possible to find appropriate independence predicates for the atomic operations, but the program behaves as if the atomicity exists at a coarser grain, where independence does hold. Using the techniques of [4, 5], it is sometimes possible to transform a given program into one with coarser atomic operations (although, the aim of those papers is to obtain the opposite, namely, refine the atomicity to achieve more concurrency). A possible extension to conditional traces semantics can allow achieving the effect of coarsening without actually performing the transformation. This is done by allowing independence conditions to be defined on sequences of operations (such as $\Delta_{\alpha\beta\gamma,\mu\zeta}$). Then one sequence can be exchanged with another – even though finer interleavings cannot be done.

Another possibility is to use collapses to prove that a program behaves as if it is constructed from operations of coarser granularity. This can be done within the framework of ISTL, proving properties which are related to *serializability [7]* of database operations. Namely, segments of the program are shown to behave as serializable database transactions. Then, use coarser grained operations and a collapse for these transactions to prove termination.

References

[1] R. Allen, K. Kennedy, Automatic translation of FORTRAN programs to vector forms, Transactions on Programming Languages and Systems, 1987, 491-543.

[2] K. Apt, N. Francez, S. Katz, Appraising fairness in languages for distributed programming, Distributed Computing, Vol 2, No 4, 1988, 226-241.

[3] E. Ashkroft, Proving assertions about parallel programs, Journal of Computer System Science 10(1975), 110-135.

[4] R. J. R. Back, Refining Atomicity in Parallel Algorithms, Åbo Akademi, Reports on computer science and mathematics, Ser. A, No, 57, 1988.

[5] R. J. R. Back, K. Sere, Stepwise refinement of action systems, in J.L.A. van de Snepscheut (ed.), Mathematics of Program Construction, LNCS 375, Springer-Verlag, 1989, 115-138.

[6] A. J. Bernstein, Analysis of programs for parallel processing, IEEE Transactions on Electronic Computers 15 (1966), 757-762.

[7] P. A. Bernstein, V. Hadzilacos, N. Goodman, Concurrency control and recovery in database systems, Addison-Wesley, 1987.

[8] E. Best, C. Lengauer, Semantic independence, Science of computer programming, 13 (1989/90), 23-50.

[9] E.W. Dijkstra, Guarded commands, Nondeterminancy and formal derivation of Programs, Communication of the ACM, 18(1975), 453-457.

[10] H. Gaifman, Modeling concurrency by partial orders and nonlinear transition systems, in J.W. de Bakker, W.P. de Roever, G. Rozenberg (eds.) Linear Time, Branching Time and Partial Order in Logics and Models for Concurrency, LNCS 354, Springer-Verlag, 1989, 467-488.

[11] Tz. Elrad, N. Francez, Decomposition of distributed programs into communication-closed layers, Science of Computer Programming 2(1982), 155-173.

[12] R. T. Gerth, L. Shrira, On proving closedness of distributed layers, in K.V. Nori (ed.) Foundations of Software Technology and Theoretical Computer Science, LNCS 241, Springer-Verlag, 1986.

[13] C. A. R. Hoare, Communicating sequential processes, Communications of the ACM, 21(1978), 666-677.

[14] R. Janicki, M. Koutny, Towards a theory of simulations for verification of concurrent systems, in E. Odijk, M. Rem, J.C. Syre (eds.) PARLE'89, Parallel Architectures and Languages Europe, LNCS 366, Springer-Verlag, 1989, 73-88.

[15] S. Katz, D. Peled, Interleaving set temporal logic, 6th ACM Symposium on Principles of Distributed Computing, Vancouver, Canada, August 1987, 178-190.

[16] S. Katz, D. Peled, An efficient verification method for parallel and distributed programs, in J.W. de Bakker, W.P. de Roever, G. Rozenberg (eds.) Linear Time, Branching Time and Partial Order in Logics and Models for Concurrency, LNCS 354, Springer-Verlag, 1989, 489-507.

[17] S. Katz, D. Peled, Verification of distributed programs using representative interleaving sequences, Manuscript, 1990.

[18] M. Z. Kwiatkowska, Fairness for non-interleaving concurrency, Phd. thesis, Faculty of Sciences, University of Leicester, 1989.

[19] L. Lamport, F. B. Schneider, Pretending atomicity, Research Report 44, Digital Systems Research Center, May 1989.

[20] A. Mazurkiewicz, Trace semantics, in W. Brauer, W. Reisig, and G. Rozenberg (eds.) Petri Nets: Applications and Relationships to Other Models of Concurrency, LNCS 255, Springer-Verlag, 1987.

[21] A. Mazurkiewicz, Complete processes and inevitability, Rept. No. 86-06, Univ. of Leiden, The Netherlands, 1986.

[22] Z. Manna, A. Pnueli, How to cook a temporal proof system for your pet language. Proceedings of the ACM Symposium on Principles on Programming Languages, Austin, Texas, 1983, 141-151.

[23] Z. Manna, A. Pnueli, Adequate proof principles for invariance and liveness properties of concurrent programs, Science of Computer Programming 4 (1984), 257-289.

[24] S. Owicki, D. Gries, An axiomatic proof technique for parallel programs, Acta Informatica 6, 4(1976), 319-340.

[25] D. Peled, A. Pnueli, Proving partial order liveness properties, to appear in Automata, Languages and Programming, Proceedings, 17th Colloquium, University of Warwick, Springer-Verlag, 1990.

[26] C. A. Petri, Kommunikation mit Automaten, Bonn: Institut für Instrumentelle Matematik, Schriften des IIM Nr. 2(1962).

[27] A. Pnueli, Applications of temporal logic to the specification and verification of reactive systems, a survey of current trends, in J.W. de Bakker, W.P. de Roever, and G. Rozenberg (eds.) Current Trends in Concurrency, LNCS 224, Springer-Verlag, 1986.

[28] A. Pnueli, The temporal logic of programs, Proceedings of the 18th Symposium on Foundation of Computer Science, IEEE, Providence, 1977, 46-57.

[29] W. Reisig, Temporal logic and causality in concurrent systems, in F.A. Vogt (ed) CONCURRENCY 88, LNCS 335, Springer-Verlag, 1988.

[30] F. A. Stomp, W. P. De Roever, A formalization of sequentially phased intuition in network protocols, Report 88-15, Department of Informatics, Faculty of science, University of Nijmegen, The Netherlands.

[31] A. Valmari, Stubborn sets for reduced state space generation, 10th International Conference on Application and Theory of Petri Nets, to appear in the Lecture Notes in Computer Science series, Springer-Verlag.

Timed Concurrent Processes

Chris Tofts
Laboratory for the Foundations of Computer Science
Department of Computer Science
University of Edinburgh

Abstract

In this paper two timed calculi for concurrent processes are presented. They differ in their concepts of time cost. We will show that they are strongly related and present a number of natural equivalences and orders over timed processes. Some simple examples are presented.

1 Introduction

Algebraic approaches to the study of concurrent systems [9, 10, 5, 1] and others, have proved effective. Unfortunately they either give no account of the passage of time, or its passage is explained in the form of synchrony [10]. The temporal properties of concurrent processes give an insight into some interesting aspects of concurrent programming. There have been some attempts to provide a formalism within which these concepts can be expressed [16, 7, 8, 6]. However, some of these assume synchrony which results in some of the more interesting temporal properties of process being inexpressible. In a previous paper [18] we provided an extension to CCS which admitted a notion of timing. That approach was unsatisfactory in that the account it gave of time was somewhat eccentric. Processes could only evolve simultaneously by communication, time and action were interleaved otherwise. In order to give a fuller account of time for asynchronous processes we need to simply let time pass, and observe what the processes produce and when they produce it.

In order to give this fuller account the state transitions have been split into two orthogonal parts; one part is our normal notion of action (which can be regarded as computation) and the other part is the passage of time. There are sound reasons for making this separation. Computation involves energy change and there is a result of quantum mechanics which states that energy changes and time cannot be measured simultaneously [4, 17]. Thus it seems reasonable when producing models of time and computation not to permit the simultaneous observance of the two activities.

We therefore assume that actions have no duration; although if we wish to construct actions with duration we can in the manner of [3]. This paper is a reduced version of [19], which contains several more examples and constructions on timed systems.

2 Language Definition

We define a timed extension of the language CCS [9] as follows.

Let Λ be a set of (atomic action) symbols not containing τ or ϵ, and let $Act = \Lambda \cup \{\tau\}$. We also have times t taken from one of the following: positive integers, positive rationals or positive reals, representing the divisions of time. We assume a complementation bijection $\bar{\cdot} : Act \rightarrow Act$ which is its own inverse. The letter λ ranges over Λ, the letter μ over Act, and S over *relabelling functions*, i.e. those $S : Act \rightarrow Act$ such that $S(\overline{\mu}) = \overline{S(\mu)}$ and $S(\mu) \neq \tau$, unless $\mu = \tau$. The languages wTCCS (weakly timed CCS) and sTCCS (strongly timed CCS) consist of an infinite set Var of variables ranged over by X and Y, a constant symbol Nil, unary function symbols $\mu.$, $\backslash\lambda$, $[S]$, and FIX_X ($X \in Var$), and the binary function symbols $+$ and $|$. With unary functions $\mu.$ taking a process and prefixing the process by the given action. In wTCCS the function symbol $[]$, denotes a function which takes a process and a time and yields a process prefixed by that amount of time. The function $()$ takes a process and a time (not zero), and returns the process prefixed by that time, along with the unary function δ which returns a delayed process in the calculus sTCCS.

The set P of wTCCS-expressions ranged over by P is the set given by the following definition:

$$P \ ::= \ Nil \mid \mu.P \mid [t]P \mid P \mid P \mid P+P \mid FIX_X P \mid X \mid P\backslash L \mid P[S].$$

The set P of sTCCS-expressions ranged over by P is the set given by the following definition:

$$P \ ::= \ Nil \mid \mu.P \mid (t)P \mid \delta P \mid P \mid P \mid P+P \mid FIX_X P \mid X \mid P\backslash L \mid P[S].$$

(It will be clear from the context which version of the timing system is being used.) The intention of the time action prefix is as follows. In wTCCS, $[t]P$ means that after a period of time t' where $t' \geq t$ the process P is reached; this is very similar to the *wait* introduced into CSP by Roscoe and Reed [16]. On the other hand, the system sTCCS represents separation of delay from the initial timing so $(t)P$ represents a process that will becomes P in precisely a period of time t. The δ operator provides a way of introducing delays to allow for synchronisation.

2.1 Derivation Laws

The action-evolution of a process can be derived from the operational rules presented in Figure 8-1. The temporal evolutions of wTCCS are derived using the operational rules presented in Figure 8-2. The alternative set of rules presented in Figure 8-3, give the temporal evolutions for sTCCS. The transition relations between processes is the least set of transitions satisfying the set of action laws plus the appropriate set of temporal laws.

Definition 2.1 *We define the operator* $\dot{-}$ *on times as follows;*

$$t \dot{-} t' = \begin{cases} t - t' & \textit{when } t' \leq t \\ 0 & \textit{otherwise,} \end{cases}$$

$$\text{ACT: } \frac{}{\mu.P \xrightarrow{\mu} P}$$

$$\text{SUM0: } \frac{P \xrightarrow{\mu} P'}{P + Q \xrightarrow{\mu} P'} \qquad \text{SUM1: } \frac{Q \xrightarrow{\mu} Q'}{P + Q \xrightarrow{\mu} Q'}$$

$$\text{COM0: } \frac{P \xrightarrow{\mu} P'}{P \mid Q \xrightarrow{\mu} P' \mid Q} \qquad \text{COM1: } \frac{Q \xrightarrow{\mu} Q'}{P \mid Q \xrightarrow{\mu} P \mid Q'}$$

$$\text{COM2: } \frac{P \xrightarrow{\lambda} P' \quad Q \xrightarrow{\overline{\lambda}} Q'}{P \mid Q \xrightarrow{\tau} P' \mid Q'} \qquad \text{REL: } \frac{P \xrightarrow{\mu} P'}{P[S] \xrightarrow{S(\mu)} P'[S]}$$

$$\text{RES: } \frac{P \xrightarrow{\mu} P'}{P \backslash L \xrightarrow{\mu} P' \backslash L} \quad \mu, \overline{\mu} \notin L \qquad \text{REC: } \frac{P_j\{\tilde{P}/\tilde{X}\} \xrightarrow{\mu} P'_j}{FIX_j\{X_i = P_i;\ i \in I\} \xrightarrow{\mu} P'_j}$$

Figure 1: Operational rules for wTCCS and sTCCS

$$\text{TIME: } \frac{}{[t]P \overset{t'}{\leadsto} [t \dot{-} t']P} \qquad \text{IDLE: } \frac{}{P \overset{t}{\leadsto} P}$$

$$\text{TRANS: } \frac{P \overset{t}{\leadsto} P' \quad P' \overset{s}{\leadsto} P''}{P \overset{s+t}{\leadsto} P''}$$

$$\text{COM-TIME: } \frac{P \overset{t}{\leadsto} P' \quad Q \overset{t}{\leadsto} Q'}{P \mid Q \overset{t}{\leadsto} P' \mid Q'} \qquad \text{SUM-TIME: } \frac{P \overset{t}{\leadsto} P' \quad Q \overset{t}{\leadsto} Q'}{P + Q \overset{t}{\leadsto} P' + Q'}$$

$$\text{ACT-TIME: } \frac{P \xrightarrow{\mu} P'}{[0]P \xrightarrow{\mu} P'} \qquad \text{REL-TIME: } \frac{P \overset{t}{\leadsto} P'}{P[S] \overset{t}{\leadsto} P'[S]}$$

$$\text{RES-TIME: } \frac{P \overset{t}{\leadsto} P'}{P \backslash L \overset{t}{\leadsto} P' \backslash L} \qquad \text{REC-TIME: } \frac{P_j\{\tilde{P}/\tilde{X}\} \overset{t}{\leadsto} P'_j}{FIX_j\{X_i = P_i;\ i \in I\} \overset{t}{\leadsto} P'_j}$$

Figure 2: Temporal rules for wTCCS

$$\text{TIME:}\ \frac{}{(t)P \overset{t'}{\rightsquigarrow} (t-t')P} \quad \text{for } t > t'.$$

$$\text{TIME1:}\ \frac{}{(t)P \overset{t}{\rightsquigarrow} P} \qquad \text{TRANS:}\ \frac{P \overset{t}{\rightsquigarrow} P' \quad P' \overset{s}{\rightsquigarrow} P''}{P \overset{s+t}{\rightsquigarrow} P''}$$

$$\text{DELAY:}\ \frac{}{\delta P \overset{t}{\rightsquigarrow} \delta P} \qquad \text{UN-DELAY:}\ \frac{P \overset{\mu}{\longrightarrow} P'}{\delta P \overset{\mu}{\longrightarrow} P'}$$

$$\text{COM-TIME:}\ \frac{P \overset{t}{\rightsquigarrow} P' \quad Q \overset{t}{\rightsquigarrow} Q'}{P \mid Q \overset{t}{\rightsquigarrow} P' \mid Q'} \qquad \text{SUM-TIME:}\ \frac{P \overset{t}{\rightsquigarrow} P' \quad Q \overset{t}{\rightsquigarrow} Q'}{P + Q \overset{t}{\rightsquigarrow} P' + Q'}$$

$$\text{REL-TIME:}\ \frac{P \overset{t}{\rightsquigarrow} P'}{P[S] \overset{t}{\rightsquigarrow} P'[S]} \qquad \text{RES-TIME:}\ \frac{P \overset{t}{\rightsquigarrow} P'}{P\backslash L \overset{t}{\rightsquigarrow} P'\backslash L}$$

$$\text{REC-TIME:}\ \frac{P_j\{\tilde{P}/\tilde{X}\} \overset{t}{\rightsquigarrow} P'_j}{FIX_j\{X_i = P_i;\ i \in I\} \overset{t}{\rightsquigarrow} P'_j}$$

Figure 3: Temporal rules for sTCCS

where − is the usual subtraction operator.

Proposition 2.2 *Let P be a wTCCS process, then whenever we can infer* $P \overset{t}{\rightsquigarrow} P'$*; we can also infer* $P \overset{t'}{\rightsquigarrow} P'$ *for any* $t' \geq t$.

Notation: we will use the abbreviation P^t to represent the derivative of the process P such that $P \overset{t}{\rightsquigarrow} P^t$, whenever it is inconvenient to introduce a new process name for all the timed intermediates of a process.

2.2 Temporal Deadlock

The *Nil* or *deadlocked* process of CCS [9] is one which is capable of no action. There is an equivalent temporal process which can always permit the passage of time, but never produces an action. The following are the simplest definitions for both wTCCS and sTCCS respectively:

$$Nil,$$
$$\delta Nil.$$

There is, however, an infinite variety of processes which are equivalent to this temporal nil. For any P in wTCCS and Q in sTCCS, the following processes are equivalent to the temporal nil:

$$[0][1]P,$$
$$\delta(1)Q,$$

since in neither case can we infer a direct action, and so we cannot remove the leading [0] or the δ operators.

2.3 Deadlock

In sTCCS the Nil processes acts like a *deadlock* [4] with respect to the continuing temporal evolution of the system. If we examine the derivation laws $COM - TIME$ and $SUM - TIME$, we observe that the following are true for any non-zero t.

$Nil + (t)P$ has the same derivatives as Nil and,
$Nil \mid (t)P$ has the same derivatives as Nil.

Thus once we have an unguarded Nil process in any leading binary term *all* further temporal evolution is blocked. Any composite process is stopped immediately; the process cannot evolve further in time. We can use this property to compare the initial time behaviour of any processes.

Definition 2.3 *Given any equivalence [order] we can construct the time pre-fix equivalence [order] simply by composing in parallel both processes we wish to show equivalent [related] with the process* $(t)Nil$.

This is motivated from the preceeding observation. After a period of time t has passed the processes $(t)Nil \mid P$ and $(t)Nil \mid Q$ become equivalent to Nil; until t has passed they exhibit all the possible behaviour of the respective processes within that period.

2.4 Time Actions

There is an interesting distinction between weak and strong time actions.

Proposition 2.4 *Consider two successive time actions in both wTCCS and sTCCS then;*

1. *if* $t_2 > 0$ *then* $[t_1][t_2]P$ *has derivations different from* $[t_1 + t_2]P$,
2. $(t_1)(t_2)P$ *has identical derivations as* $(t_1 + t_2)P$.

3 Strong Time Sensitive Pre-order

It is possible, much as for CCS, to produce two different basic notions of equivalence (strong and weak), which are based on orders with respect to time. The first of these requires that the time taken after any action be matched directly by the time taken after a similar action in the other process, not that the total time taken to go from one state to another via an action is greater.

Definition 3.1 *(Strong pre-order) We will say that* P *is* faster *than* Q *iff there exists a relation* R *with* $(P, Q) \in R$ *iff for all* $\mu \in Act$ *and for all times* t;

1. *if* $P \xrightarrow{\mu} P'$ *then there exists* Q' *such that* $Q \xrightarrow{\mu} Q'$ *and* $(P', Q') \in R$,
2. *if* $P \overset{t}{\leadsto} P'$ *then there exists* Q', t' *such that* $Q \overset{t'}{\leadsto} Q'$ *and* $(P', Q') \in R$ *and* $t' \geq t$,

3. if $Q \xrightarrow{\mu} Q'$ then there exists P' such that $P \xrightarrow{\mu} P'$ and $(P', Q') \in R$,

4. if $Q \overset{t}{\rightsquigarrow} Q'$ then there exists P', t' such that $P \overset{t'}{\rightsquigarrow} P'$ and $(P', Q') \in R$ and $t' \leq t$.

The relation R is called s strong pre-order.

Proposition 3.2 *If R, R' and R_i for $i \in I$ are all* strong pre-orders *then so are;*
1) Id_P, 2) RR', 3) $\bigcup_{i \in I} R_i$.

Definition 3.3 *We define a functional $\mathcal{F}$ on binary relations $R \subseteq P \times P$ such that $(P, Q) \in \mathcal{F}(R)$ iff for all $\mu \in Act$ and for all time t:*

1. *if $P \xrightarrow{\mu} P'$ then there exists Q' such that $Q \xrightarrow{\mu} Q'$ and $(P', Q') \in R$,*
2. *if $P \overset{t}{\rightsquigarrow} P'$ then there exists Q', t' such that $Q \overset{t'}{\rightsquigarrow} Q'$ and $(P', Q') \in R$ and $t' \geq t$,*
3. *if $Q \xrightarrow{\mu} Q'$ then there exists P' such that $P \xrightarrow{\mu} P'$ and $(P', Q') \in R$,*
4. *if $Q \overset{t}{\rightsquigarrow} Q'$ then there exists P', t' such that $P \overset{t'}{\rightsquigarrow} P'$ and $(P', Q') \in R$ and $t' \leq t$.*

Proposition 3.4

- *$\mathcal{F}$ is monotonic,*
- *R is a strong pre-order iff $R \subseteq \mathcal{F}(R)$.*

Definition 3.5 *Call* $\geq \equiv \{ \ \bigcup R \mid R$ *is a* strong pre-order $\}$.

Proposition 3.6 $\geq$ *is the largest strong pre-order.*

Proposition 3.7 $\geq$ *is the least fixed point of $\mathcal{F}$.*

Proposition 3.8 Strong Pre-Order *is substitutive with respect to the finite operators of wTCCS. Thus for $P \geq Q$ the following hold;*
1) $[t]P \geq [t]$, 2) $a.P \geq a.Q$, 3) $P + E \geq Q + E$,
4) $P \mid E \geq Q \mid E$, 5) $P \backslash L \geq Q \backslash L$, 6) $P[S] \geq Q[S]$.

Proof: follows that of [11], Proposition 5.17

Unfortunately this pre-order is *not* substitutive in sTCCS, for consider the following processes;

$$P = (5)a \quad Q = (7)a \quad E = (6)b,$$
$$R = P \mid E \text{ and } S = Q \mid E.$$

Clearly $P \geq Q$ but there does not exists a $t \geq 5$ such that $S \overset{t'}{\rightsquigarrow} S'$ with $a \mid (1)b \geq S'$, since we can *never* reach an S' which can perform an a action without performing a b action first. A similar lack of congruence can be observed with respect to the non-determinism operator.

Strong pre-order is not substitutive with respect to sTCCS, owing to the introduction of causality via timing information. In the system sTCCS the following two processes are equivalent,

$$(5)a \mid (7)b \text{ and } (5)a.(2)b.$$

The process on the left has the causality introduced implicitly by timing, while the other process has the causality explicitly introduced by action-prefix. Any interleaving 'faster than' relation will not preserve timing causality, but will preserve structural causality. Thus to obtain a notion of 'faster than' that will be an order for sTCCS, we shall need to distinguish between the *explicit* introduction of causality through structure and the *implicit* causality introduced by timing.

We will not proceed with further study of the strong pre-order. Since we regard the system sTCCS as the more fundamental we will instead attempt to find an equivalence relation which is substitutive for that system.

4 An Equality for sTCCS

Definition 4.1 *Processes P and Q are* time-equivalent *iff there exists a relationship R between P and Q such that for all $\mu \in Act$ and for all times t;*

1. *if $P \xrightarrow{\mu} P'$ then there exists Q' such that $Q \xrightarrow{\mu} Q'$ and $(P',Q') \in R$,*
2. *if $P \overset{t}{\rightsquigarrow} P'$ then there exists Q' such that $Q \overset{t}{\rightsquigarrow} Q'$ and $(P',Q') \in R$,*
3. *if $Q \xrightarrow{\mu} Q'$ then there exists P' such that $P \xrightarrow{\mu} P'$ and $(P',Q') \in R$,*
4. *if $Q \overset{t}{\rightsquigarrow} Q'$ then there exists P' such that $P \overset{t}{\rightsquigarrow} P'$ and $(P',Q') \in R$,*

the relation R is called a time-equivalence.

Proposition 4.2 *If S, S' and S_i for all $i \in I$, are time-equivalences; then the following are also time-equivalences;*
1) Id_P, 2) SS', 3) S^{-1}, 4) $\bigcup_{i \in I} S_i$.

Definition 4.3 $\sim_T \equiv \bigcup\{S \mid S$ *is a time-equivalence*$\}$.

Proposition 4.4

1. *$\sim_T$ is a time-equivalence,*
2. *$\sim_T$ is the largest time-equivalence.*

Definition 4.5 *T is a time-equivalence up to $\sim_T$ whenever $\sim_T T \sim_T$ is a time-equivalence.*

Proposition 4.6 *If T is a* time-equivalence to $\sim_T$ *then* $T \subseteq \sim_T$.

The usual functional extension in the style of [14] can be used to demonstrate time equivalence well founded; as the details are precisely those of the earlier definition and proof we omit them.

Proposition 4.7 *Time-equivalence is substitutive for the finite operators of sTCCS. In other words, given $P \sim_T Q$ then;*
1) $a.P \sim_T a.Q$, 2) $(t)P \sim_T (t)P$, 3) $\delta P \sim_T \delta Q$,
4) $P + E \sim_T Q + E$, 5) $P \mid E \sim_T Q \mid E$, 6) $P\backslash L \sim_T Q\backslash L$,
7) $P[S] \sim_T Q[S]$.

In order to prove the above we need to demonstrate that appropriate bisimulations can be found. The detail has been presented earlier and is therefore omitted.

Definition 4.8 *Let E and F be two expressions, with free variables $\tilde{X}$. Then we shall say that $E \sim_T F$ iff for all vectors of processes $\tilde{P}$*

$$E[\tilde{P}/\tilde{X}] \sim_T F[\tilde{P}/\tilde{X}]$$

Proposition 4.9 *Let $E \sim_T F$ then $Fix_{\tilde{X}} E \sim_T Fix_{\tilde{X}} F$.*

4.1 Stratified Bisimulations

In his original discription of the language CCS [9], Milner used a stratified notion of bisimulation, in that the bisimulation was given in terms of the number of actions for which two processes were initally equivalent. In the limit this gives the full bisimulation.

In the timed system we have two approaches available to giving a stratified account of bisimulation; one is that for an arbitary number of initial actions of both time and computation our processes match, the other is that for an initial period of time our processes are identical. We should hope that the limiting cases of both these forms of bisimulation give us our original notion of bisimulation. Unfortunately when using time we do not have ordinals and thus can only work with finitely branching processes and do not recover the full bisimulation. In the following we shall be working with the usual ordinal numbers, which we will denote $\mathcal{O}$.

Definition 4.10 *(Action Stratified Bisimulation)*

1. *$P \sim_0 Q$ for all processes P and Q,*
2. *$P \sim_{n+1} Q$ iff*
   - *For all t such that $P \overset{t}{\leadsto} P'$ then there exists Q' such that $Q \overset{t}{\leadsto} Q'$ and $P \sim_n Q$,*
   - *For all a such that $P \xrightarrow{a} P'$ then there exists Q' such that $Q \xrightarrow{a} Q'$ and $P' \sim_n Q'$,*

- *For all t such that* $Q \overset{t}{\leadsto} Q'$ *then there exists* P' *such that* $P \overset{t}{\leadsto} P'$ *and* $P \sim_n Q$*,*
- *For all a such that* $Q \overset{a}{\longrightarrow} Q'$ *then there exists* P' *such that* $P \overset{a}{\longrightarrow} P'$ *and* $P' \sim_n Q'$*,*

3. for each limit ordinal λ $P \sim_\lambda Q$ *iff for all* $\kappa < \lambda$ $P \sim_\kappa Q$.

Proposition 4.11 $\sim = \bigcap_{\kappa \in O} \sim_k$

Definition 4.12 *(Time Stratified Bisimulation(1))* $P \overset{t}{\sim} Q$ *iff*

- *for all* t' *such that* $P \overset{t'}{\leadsto} P'$ *then there exists* Q' *such that* $Q \overset{t'}{\leadsto} Q'$ *and* $P' \overset{t-t'}{\sim} Q'$*,*
- *for all a such that* $P \overset{a}{\longrightarrow} P'$ *then there exists* Q' *such that* $Q \overset{a}{\longrightarrow} Q'$ *and* $P' \overset{t}{\sim} Q'$*,*
- *for all* t' *such that* $Q \overset{t'}{\leadsto} Q'$ *then there exists* P' *such that* $P \overset{t'}{\leadsto} P'$ *and* $P' \overset{t-t'}{\sim} Q'$*,*
- *for all a such that* $Q \overset{a}{\longrightarrow} Q'$ *then there exists* P' *such that* $P \overset{a}{\longrightarrow} P'$ *and* $P' \overset{t}{\sim} Q'$*,*

Definition 4.13 *(Time Stratified Bisimulation (2))* $P \overset{t}{\sim}_i Q$ *iff* $(t)nil \mid P \sim (t)nil \mid Q$.

Proposition 4.14 $P \overset{t}{\sim} Q$ *iff* $P \overset{t}{\sim}_i Q$.

Proposition 4.15 *For finitely branching P and Q;* $P \sim Q$ *iff for all t* $P \overset{t}{\sim} Q$.

Corollary 4.16 *Let P and Q be finitely branching processes and* $t_1, \ldots, t_i, \ldots$ *an infinite strictly increasing sequence of times. Then if for all* t_i $P \overset{t_i}{\sim} Q$ *implies* $P \sim Q$.

5 Equational Characterisation

Consider the following equations.

Given $P \sim_T Q$ and $t_1 \leq t_2$ then the following equations are true of sTCCS processes:

$(t_1)(t_2)P = (t_1 + t_2)P$

$(+_1)\ P + P = P$

$(+_2)\ P + \delta Nil = P$

$(+_3)\ (t)P + Nil = Nil$

$(+_4)\ P + R = R + P$

$(+_5)\ (t_1)P + (t_2)Q = (t_1)(P + (t_2 - t_1)Q)$

$(+_6)\ P + (R + S) = (P + R) + S$

$(+_7)\ (t_1)\delta P + (t_2)\delta P = (t_1)\delta P$

$(+_8)\ \delta a.P + a.P = a.P$

$(+_9)\ \delta P + \delta R = \delta(P + R)$

$(+_{10})\ (t_1)a.P + (t_2)R = (t_1)a.P$

$(+_{11})\ a.P + (t)S = a.P$

$(|_1)\ P \mid \delta Nil = P$

$(|_2)(t)P \mid Nil = Nil$

$(|_3)\ P \mid R = R \mid P$

$(|_4)\ P \mid (R \mid S) = (P \mid R) \mid S$

$(|_5)\ (t_1)P \mid (t_2)Q = (t_1)(P \mid (t_2 - t_1)Q)$

$(\backslash_1)\ a.P\backslash L = Nil \text{ if } a, \overline{a} \in L$

$(\backslash_2)\ a.(P\backslash L) = (a.P)\backslash L \ \ a, \overline{a} \notin L$

$(\backslash_3)(t)(P\backslash L) = ((t)P)\backslash L$

$(\backslash_4)\delta(P\backslash L) = (\delta P)\backslash L$

$(\backslash_5)P = P\backslash L \ \ \forall a \in \mathcal{L}(P) \ \ a \notin L$

$(\backslash_6)P\backslash L_1\backslash L_2 = P\backslash L_1 \cup L_2$

$(\backslash_7)P\backslash L + Q\backslash L = (P + Q)\backslash L$

$(\backslash_8)(P\backslash L) \mid Q = (P \mid Q)\backslash L \ \ \forall a \in \mathcal{L}(Q) \ \ a, \overline{a} \notin L$

We have not given rules for wTCCS since we cannot obtain the same structural identities. But there is no manipulation possible of the temporal operators owing to the property that processes of the form

$$[2][4]P$$

deadlock.

There is no general equation analogous to the expansion theorem, so this equational system is not complete. This results from the problems of introducing unintentional causality. In [12] an extended form of the calculus sTCCS is shown to admit an equational theory which is both sound and complete with respect to strong bisimulation.

6 Process Logic For Timed CCS

We introduce a simple extension of the process logic $\mathcal{PL}$ [17], with a timed modal operator. Since our space of times may be dense, it is not sufficient to add a next operator which is interpreted as at the next instant the proposition holds. A similar logic is presented in [8]. The formulae of our logic ($t\mathcal{PL}$) are defined as follows:

$$F ::= \bigwedge_{i \in I} F_i \mid \neg F \mid < a > F \mid \{t\}F.$$

Definition 6.1 *The satisfaction relation between processes and formulae is defined as follows; $P \models_T F$ iff:*

- $P \models_T \bigwedge_{i \in I} F_i$ *iff for all* $i \in I$, $P \models_T F_i$,
- $P \models_T \neg F$ *iff* $P \models_T F$ *is* false,
- $P \models_T < a > F$ *iff there exists* P' *such that* $P \xrightarrow{a} P'$ *and* $P' \models_T F$,

- $P \models_T \{t\}F$ *iff either*
  - *there exist* a, P' *such that* $P \xrightarrow{a} P'$ *and* $P \models_T F$,
  - *or there exist* P', t' *such that* $P \overset{t'}{\rightsquigarrow} P'$ *with* $t' \leq t$ *and* $P' \models_T F$.

Proposition 6.2 *If* $P \models_T \{t\}F$ *then for all* $t' \geq t$, $P \models_T \{t'\}F$.

Note: since zero times are not permitted in sTCCS the first clause of the temporal modality only applies to delays and these are matched over the equivalence.

6.1 Stratifying $t\mathcal{PL}$

We wish to show that $t\mathcal{PL}$ characterises strong temporal bisimilation. We start by defining the depth of formulae in our logic.

Definition 6.3 *We define the depth of a formula recursively over its structure;*

- $depth(\{t\}F) = 1 + depth(F)$,
- $depth(< a > F) = 1 + depth(F)$,
- $depth(\neg F) = depth(F)$,
- $depth(\bigwedge_{i \in I} F_i) = max_{i \in I}(depth(F_i))$.

Definition 6.4 *The stratified family of formulae* $t\mathcal{PL}_k \stackrel{def}{\equiv} \{F \mid depth(f) \leq k\}$

Proposition 6.5 *For each* $k \in \mathcal{O}$, $P \sim_k Q$ *iff for every* $F \in t\mathcal{PL}_k$

$$P \models F \text{ iff } Q \models F.$$

Corollary 6.6 $P \sim Q$ *iff for all* $F \in t\mathcal{PL}$

$$P \models F \text{ iff } Q \models F.$$

7 Examples

7.1 A Simple Timer

Consider the example of the timed and the timer controlled actions presented in [18].

$$\begin{aligned} E_a &\equiv \tau.a.(t)E_a \\ Timer &\equiv \overline{alarm}.(t)Timer \\ E'_a &\equiv \delta alarm.a.(t')E'_a \\ R_a &\equiv (Timer \mid E'_a)\backslash alarm \end{aligned}$$

We consider the evolutions of the two systems with $t' \leq t$.

$$\begin{aligned} E_a &\xrightarrow{\tau}\xrightarrow{a}\overset{t}{\rightsquigarrow} E_a, \\ R_a &\xrightarrow{\tau}\xrightarrow{a}\overset{t}{\rightsquigarrow} R_a, \end{aligned}$$

It seems that the time of the process R_a is independent of the value of t' provided it remains less than t. It seems that we can achieve an analogous result to the weakness replacement [18]. The following example shows that in these systems weakness replacement will hold only when processes behaviours are much more constrained than the requirements of the original result.

Consider the following processes;

$$P = \bar{b}.(5)P_1 \qquad Q = \bar{b}.(10)Q_1$$
$$E = b.(20)\delta Nil$$
$$R_1 = (E \mid P)\backslash b \qquad R_2 = (E \mid Q)\backslash b$$

In its original form weakness replacement states that the process R_1 and R_2 should be equal. Even if P_1 and Q_1 are identical then R_1 will not be the same as R_2. The former can evolve to a state equivalent to P_1, twice as fast as the latter. Thus the condition for the processes to be made identical by communicating with a slower process must include repeated communication.

7.2 Action Available For a Period

In the following process:

$$(5)\delta a.P + (7)a.P$$

the action a can be inferred at any time between 5 and 7, but it must have been used by at latest 7 or the process will deadlock. This can be used to represent a process that requires a certain time to start and is then only available for a limited period.

7.3 Representing SCCS in sTCCS

We will assume that our action set *Act* is a free abelian group over names with τ as its identity, and $\bar{a}$ as the inverse of a. We can then represent an SCCS [10] process as an sTCCS process using the following translation.

Definition 7.1 *Let P be an SCCS process and $P^\dagger$ its translation into sTCCS, we define $P^\dagger$ as follows:*

SCCS	*sTCCS*
0	*Nil*
$a.P$	$(1)a.P^\dagger$
$P+Q$	$P^\dagger + Q^\dagger$
$P \times Q$	$P^\dagger \mid Q^\dagger$

Definition 7.2 *Let $s \in Act^*$ be a sequence of actions. Then $prod(s)$ is the action $s_1 \times s_2 \times \ldots \times s_n$, where $s = s_1 s_2 \ldots s_n$*

Note, for any permutation s' of a sequence of actions s; $prod(s) = prod(s')$.

Proposition 7.3 *Whenever can infer $P \xrightarrow{a} Q$ in SCCS iff we can infer $P^\dagger \overset{1}{\leadsto} \xrightarrow{s} Q^\dagger$ in sTCCS, with $prod(s) = a$.*

Proof: By an induction over the the structure of the processes.

8 Conclusions

We have presented a temporal model which is an extension of CCS. This system has most of the properties we desire, excepting that we have so far not demonstrated an order over processes. We believe that a substitutive order for sTCCS will have to be given by relativisation techniques; we hope to be able to show that two processes are substitutively faster than one another with respect to some third process, but not globally. The temporal behaviour of the systems sTCCS and wTCCS has little effect on the operational behaviour derived from CCS, and we believe that the methodology of separating action and temporal evolutions can successfully extend any underlying operational reasoning system for computation actions.

Acknowledgements

I would like to thank Robin Milner for his suggestions about the early versions of these systems, and Faro Mallard for his help and discussion throughout.

Bibliography

[1] Bergstra, J.A., J. W. Klop, Algebra of Communicating Processes with Abstraction, Theoretical Computer Science, Volume 37, No 1, 1985.

[2] Cardelli, L., Real Time Agents, in M. Nielsen and E.M. Schmidt (eds), Automata, Languages and Programming, LNCS 140, Springer-Verlag, 1982.

[3] Castellani, I., M. Hennessey, Distributed Bisimulation, Research Report No. 5/87, Sussex University, July 1987.

[4] Dirac, P.A.M., Principles of Quantum Mechanics, 4th. Edition, OUP, 1958.

[5] Hoare, C.A.R., Communicating Sequential Processes, Prentice Hall, 1985.

[6] Jeffrey, A., Synchronous CSP, Techncal Report, Oxford University (to appear).

[7] Koymans, R., J. Vytopil, W.P. de Roever, Real-Time and Asynchronous Message Passing, Technical Report No. RUU-CS-83-9, University of Eindhoven, 1983.

[8] Koymans, R., Specifying Message Passing and Real-Time Systems with Real-Time Temporal Logic, Technical Report, University of Eindhoven, 1987.

[9] Milner, R., A Calculus of Communicating Systems, Springer LNCS 92, Springer-Verlag, 1980.

[10] Milner, R., Calculi for Synchrony and Asynchrony, Theoretical Computer Science 25(3), pp 267-310, 1983.

[11] Milner, R., Communication and Concurrency, Prentice Hall, 1989.

[12] Moller, F., C. Tofts, A Temporal Calculus of Communicating Systems, Research Report No. LFCS-89-104, University of Edinburgh, 1989.

[13] Nielson, H., Hoare Logics for Run Time Analysis of Programs, PhD Thesis, University of Edinburgh, 1984.

[14] Park, D., Concurrency and Automata on infinite sequences, in P. Deussen (ed), Theoretical Computer Science, LNCS 104, Springer-Verlag, 1981.

[15] Plotkin, G.D., A structured approach to operational semantics. Technical Report No. Daimi Fn-19, Computer Science Department, Aarhus University, 1981.

[16] Reed, G.M., A.W. Roscoe, A Timed Model for CSP, in G. Rozenberg (ed), Advances in Petri Nets 1987, LNCS 226, Springer-Verlag, 1987.

[17] Schiff, L.I., Quantum Mechanics, 3rd. edition, Mcgraw Hill, 1982.

[18] Tufts, C.M.N., Temporal Ordering for Concurrency, Research Report No. LFCS-88-49, University of Edinburgh, 1988.

[19] Tofts, C., Timing Concurrent Processes, Research Report No. LFCS-89-103, University of Edinburgh, 1989.

Approaching a Real-Timed Concurrency Theory

David Murphy,
Department of Computing Science,
University of Glasgow,
Glasgow. G12 8QQ
dvjm@uk.ac.glasgow.cs

Abstract

This paper explores a real-timed concurrency theory. The theory is based on the occurrences of events. Each occurrence of an event, or *task* has a start and a finish. Causality is modelled by assigning a partial order to these starts and finishes, while timing is modelled by giving them reals. Hence, it is a 'true concurrency' model in the tradition of Winskel's event stuctures, but where timing has the same status as causality.

The formalism for this theory is developed and its expressive power is examined. All of the traditional notions found in concurrency theories (such as conflict, confusion, liveness, fairness and so on) are seen to be expressible. Four notions of causality arise naturally from the model, leading to notions of safety. These notions of causality also lead to categories wherein structure combinators, such as nondeterministic composition and parallel composition with synchronisation, can be defined.

The theory presented is intended to be suitable for studying the behaviour of real-timed distributed systems. The point of this paper is not only to present the theory, but also to indicate how this concern with behaviour motivates the choice of a formalism.

1 THE NATURE OF CONCURRENCY THEORIES

Concurrency theories have various, often subtly different ways of modelling the notions of 'concurrency,' 'nondeterminism,' and 'causality.' We will be concerned with accurately modelling the *behaviour* of distributed systems, where 'behaviour' will mean 'what can be seen to have happened.' We will show how this concern leads us naturally to particular formalisations of causality, timing etc. The theory is discussed at length in [8], to which the reader is referred for a comprehensive discussion.

1.1 Concurrency Theories as Natural Philosophy

Concurrency theory, in its most fundamental interpretation, is a branch of natural philosophy; it seeks to describe and reason about events happening, and their temporal and causal relationships. There is no reason, then, to suppose that concurrency theory is about computational systems; computation can be seen as an *interpretation* we place on happenings, not an inherent property of them.

It is in this tradition that this paper, with its concern for behaviour, originates. It is important to have concurrency theories with sufficient descriptive power to be able to describe the very rich and subtle behaviours of real systems. If a theory cannot describe a certain behaviour, such as metastability, or synchronisation failure, then a designer can never be sure that a system designed using that theory is free from that kind of behaviour. Pnueli [10], and Olderog both argue that highly descriptive theories are at the bottom of the design hierarchy;[1] one might begin a specification of a distributed system with a descriptively-poor but terse theory, such as linear time temporal logic [10], and move on to a process algebra, such as CSP [5], for detailed design. The model advocated here is one of the most expressive concurrency theories: it lies at the bottom of the hierarchy. This sort of theory often has 'true concurrency;' this means that it has distinct notions of nondeterminism and concurrency.[2]

There seems to be a practical need for a true-concurrency real-timed model. Real time is necessary so that timing considerations can be articulated in a natural way, and discussed *ab initio*; the imposition of timing constraints *post hoc* is often impossible and always undesirable. The model presented here, then, is intended to be used for describing the behaviours of distributed systems subject to hard timing constraints, such as real-time control systems or asynchronous hardware.

1.2 Physical and Abstract Concurrency

Concurrency theorists usually study *reactive, abstractly concurrent* systems. The distinction between reactive and relational systems is made thus in [10];

> *Reactive systems are systems whose behaviours and specification cannot be adequately expressed by* relational *semantics i.e. they cannot be satisfactorily described as maintaining a relation between an input and a corresponding output state. Typically, reactive systems are best described as maintaining an interaction with their environment.*

---

[1] 'Hierarchy' is probably the wrong word, as it indicates a single classifying principle. There are, in fact, several criteria often used to classify concurrency theories, such as the treatment of concurrency, the treatment of nondeterminism, semantics (how much knowledge it is reasonable to demand when assigning meaning) etc. Unfortunately these criteria are not wholly independent; choosing a formalism for nondeterminism, say, can affect what choices of formalism for concurrency are sensible.

[2] In some models, notably *linear time* models, there is no primitive notion of concurrency, the concurrent execution of two transitions being reduced to the choice between their occurrence in either order. Hence 'treatment of concurrency' as a taxonomic criterion.

The distinction between *abstract* and *physical* concurrency is also useful. Abstract concurrency is best described by the title of [5]; "Communicating Sequential Processes." A reactive system displays abstract concurrency when it can be decomposed into at most a countable number of sequential subcomponents each of which communicates a countable message only countably often with other subcomponents. The usual applications of concurrency theory, – transaction processing systems, synchronous digital hardware, vending machines, and so on, – fall roughly into this category.

Physically concurrent systems, on the other hand, continuously or asynchronously exchange real-valued signals. Good examples are general electronic circuits, process control systems and indeed much of physics. The fundamental difference between abstract and physical concurrency is in the signals exchanged; most concurrency theories cannot describe the richness of behaviour introduced by complete asynchrony and real-valued signals. Some pathologies in this area, such as the impossibility of building an arbiter, [7], or chaotic phenomena, [3], have been known by circuit designers for years. No satisfactory theories of physically concurrent systems exist, although there has been some speculation, such as [9]. Real-timed concurrency theories, as well as serving the need for formal techniques for designing real-timed systems, are a start towards theories of physically concurrent systems.

1.3 Partial Order Models

There are two main motivations for constructing a concurrency theory; description and prescription. Being concerned with the former, we shall give scant attention to the latter, and will, instead, concentrate on a class of (implementational) theories known as *partial order* models. We have already indicated that there is a whole spectrum of possible models. It is not yet possible to design a model to do everything, so an area of concern should be selected, and the formalism chosen to suit it. Partial order models suit our need to describe behaviours accurately.

In a partial order model, a set of *transitions* T that a reactive system could engage in is given. (A transition might be thought of as anything that changes the state of the system.) These transitions are endowed with a partial order $<_c$, so that $x <_c y$ is interpreted as the transition x somehow causing the transition y. (The 'c' is for 'causality.') Nondeterminism is modelled by endowing transitions with a symmetric, irreflexive relation, the *conflict relation*, usually written $\#$. The interpretation of $x \# y$ is that the system, in any given execution, can display x, or y, but not both. The choice between the conflicting alternatives x and y is made nondeterministically. Winskel's event structures theory [14] and Gischer's pomset theory [4] are good examples of partial order models.

Partial order models have a notion of *branching time*. If neither $x <_c y$ nor $y <_c x$ nor $x = y$ then x and y are *unrelated*. They could be transitions in different places, or transitions simultaneous with each other, or neither; it doesn't matter. All that is certain is that they do not causally affect each other; they are on different *paths*. A model has branching time if there is a concept of two happenings being causally unrelated.

The partial order framework, with its separate notions of concurrency and nondeterminism, will be the basis for the causal part of the model. Next, timing must be considered.

2 ADDING TIME

Timing is not yet an issue that is much considered in the mainstream of concurrency theory, with the notable exception of timed CSP [2]. However, there are some areas where *when* something happens is as important as *what* happens. This leads us to a timed model. Rather than imposing time *post hoc* on an extant model, timing will be introduced with the same status as causality. In that way, the impact of timing can be understood; if it is imposed *post hoc*, then it will have to fit around the theory, not *vice versa*. The introduction of timing alongside causality, besides providing much-needed descriptive power, gives two further advantages:

- Timing and causality give separate ways of understanding constructions; if a construction made in the theory makes sense both temporally and causally, then it is likely to be sensible. Even untimed models should, in principle be *timeable*; it should be possible to assign consistent timings to transitions.
- There can be two notions of *refinement*. Once tasks have durations, 'event' refinement (replacing one task by a structure of tasks) becomes clean, safe, and entirely separate from process refinement (changing the construction of the structure so as to preserve some behavioural feature).

A notional, omniscient observer who records the time that each task happens will be assumed.[3] Naïvely, it is clear that tasks in nature, like having a twenty-fifth birthday, or eating this apple, have durations, so we will associate a task with an interval of the reals, and so consider both the time a task starts and the time that it finishes.

2.1 Occurrences and their Causality

Suppose that some finite set of events **E** is of interest. These events will be things that can happen more than once, like having a birthday, or eating an apple. Each time an event occurs it will acquire a label taken from a (countable) set **L** so that the pair $(l, e), l \in \mathbf{L}, e \in \mathbf{E}$ is unique.

An occurrence of an event, – a pair $a = (l, e)$, – will be referred to as a 'task,' following the terminology of [4]. Each task has a start and a finish; subscripts will be used for these. Following our previous loose terminology, we will refer to the starts and finishes of tasks as *transitions*, and use a_t for one of a_s or a_f.

[3]This is *not* a global clocks assumption, as the observer's clock cannot influence transitions, only record their times. Even in highly relativistic situations this is not an unreasonable assumption; other observers may disagree with our observer about the times things happen, but their observations can be deduced from those of our observer.

The set of transitions $\mathbf{T}$ was endowed with a partial order $<_c$ representing causality. It will be convenient to enforce the following:

- The beginnings of tasks cause their ends; $\forall a_s, a_f \in \mathbf{T} \,.\, a_s <_c a_f$.
- There is a distinguished task $*$, known as the silent task, the start of which causes everything, and whose finish everything causes.
- Causality is nonambiguous; at most one of $a_t <_c a'_t$ and $a'_t <_c a_t$ holds.

The silent task $*$ should be thought of as an 'on light.' Once we see $*_s$, we know that the structure is active, while $*_f$ tells us that everything is over. It may be important to have tasks beginning at the same time as the on light goes on. For this reason we introduce *causal equality* $=_c$. The statement $a_t =_c a'_t$ indicates that a and a' have the same causality. $=_c$ is a reflexive, symmetric and transitive relation on $\mathbf{T}$. It is a congruence of $<_b$; $a_{t(1)} <_c a_{t(2)} \wedge a_{t(1)} = a_{t(3)} \Rightarrow a_{t(3)} <_c a_{t(2)}$ and $a_{t(1)} <_c a_{t(2)} \wedge a_{t(2)} = a_{t(3)} \Rightarrow a_{t(1)} <_c a_{t(3)}$. Furthermore, causal equality $=_c$ is distinct from causal ordering $<_c$; $a_{t(1)} =_c a_{t(2)} \Rightarrow a_{t(1)} \not\leq_c a_{t(2)} \wedge a_{t(2)} \not\leq_c a_{t(1)}$.

The silent task encompasses all transitions;

$$\forall a_t \in \mathbf{T} \,.\, (*_s <_c a_t \;\vee\; *_s =_c a_t)$$
$$\forall a_t \in \mathbf{T} \,.\, (a_t <_c *_f \;\vee\; a_t =_c *_f)$$

It will be assumed that $*$ is always present, so that $\mathbf{T}$ always contains at least $*_s$ and $*_f$. The set of all tasks is $\mathbf{L} \times \mathbf{E}$. It is related to the set $\mathbf{T}$ thus

$$\mathbf{T} = (\mathbf{L} \times \mathbf{E} \cup \{*\})_s \cup (\mathbf{L} \times \mathbf{E} \cup \{*\})_f$$

2.2 Branching Time

Causality has been modelled by endowing transitions, members of $\mathbf{T}$, with a partial order $<_c$. Timing will be dealt with by assigning them a real. This leaves us with a branching time model incorporating both timing and causality. A point in branching time will be a transition together with the time that transition happened, – a pair (r, a_t) with $r \in \mathbb{R}$ and $a_t \in \mathbf{T}$. For a given set of transitions, $\mathbf{T}$, the set of all possible points in branching time, $\mathbf{BT}(\mathbf{T})$ say, will thus be $\mathbb{R} \times \mathbf{T}$. Points in branching time will be symbolised by t with a subscript, so $t_{s(1)} = (r_{s(1)}, a_{s(1)})$ is the point the task a_1 started. Similarly, $t_{t(1)}$ is either the point in $\mathbf{BT}$ that a_1 started, or the point it finished.

Definition 1 Given a task $a \in \mathbf{L} \times \mathbf{E}$, it will be assumed that projection functions, $\underline{\text{begin}}, \underline{\text{end}} : (\mathbf{L} \times \mathbf{E}) \longrightarrow \mathbf{BT}$ are available to return the points in branching time this task started or finished. We will write $a \equiv [\mathrm{t}_s, \mathrm{t}_f]$ for $\mathrm{t}_s, \mathrm{t}_f \in \mathbf{BT}$ to indicate that a is associated with the 'interval' in branching time $[\mathrm{t}_s, \mathrm{t}_f]$, i.e. that $\underline{\text{begin}}(a) = \mathrm{t}_s$ and $\underline{\text{end}}(a) = \mathrm{t}_f$.

The reals, $\mathbb{R}$, are endowed with $<$ and $=$, whilst transitions have a (causal) partial ordering $<_c$ and causal equality $=_c$, so it seems natural to try to define composite relations on branching time.

Definition 2 Suppose that $a_1 \equiv [(r_{s(1)}, a_{s(1)}), (r_{f(1)}, a_{f(1)})]$, and $a_2 \equiv [(r_{s(2)}, a_{s(2)}), (r_{f(2)}, a_{f(2)})]$. Then define

$$\begin{aligned} (r_1, a_{t(1)}) <_b (r_2, a_{t(2)}) &\iff r_1 < r_2 \wedge a_{t(1)} <_c a_{t(2)} \\ (r_1, a_{t(1)}) =_b (r_2, a_{t(2)}) &\iff r_1 = r_2 \wedge a_{t(1)} =_b a_{t(2)} \end{aligned}$$

The orders $=_b$ and $<_b$ on branching time represent both causality and timing, so that $t_{t(1)} <_b t_{t(1)}$ means that the instant in branching time $t_{t(1)}$ happens before the instant $t_{t(2)}$ and causes it.

There are some obvious things that should be true of our orders:

- Things can't happen before their causes; $a_{t(1)} <_c a'_{t'(2)} \Rightarrow r_{t(1)} < r'_{t'(2)}$. Hence, causal ordering implies temporal ordering.
- Transitions that are causally-equal must be temporally-equal; $a_{t(1)} =_c a'_{t'(2)} \Rightarrow r_{t(1)} = r'_{t'(2)}$.

Any preorder $\preccurlyeq$ on **BT** obeying the restrictions placed on $<_b$ will be called a *branching order*, while an order that looks like $=_b$ will be called a *branching equality.*[4]

2.3 Primitive Concurrency

A rather primitive notion of concurrency is supported by the model as presented thus far. It seems reasonable to say that two tasks are concurrent if there is some point in branching time belonging to one that is not related to a point of the other. We can imagine an instance where a_1 and a_2 are concurrent, but their starts are causally identical, as in $\mathsf{P} \triangleq a_1 \parallel a_2$, where we might expect $a_{s(1)} =_c a_{s(2)}$. This consideration motivates

Definition 3 Suppose $t_{t(1)}, t_{t'(2)} \in \mathbf{BT}$. Then $t_{t(1)}$ and $t_{t'(2)}$ are said to be *incomparable*, written $t_{t(1)}\ \underline{\text{inc}}\ t_{t'(2)}$, iff

$$t_{t(1)} \not<_b t_{t'(2)} \wedge t_{t'(2)} \not<_b t_{t(1)} \wedge t_{t(1)} \neq_b t_{t'(2)}$$

while two tasks, $a_1 \equiv [t_{s(1)}, t_{f(1)}]$ and $a_2 \equiv [t_{s(2)}, t_{f(2)}]$ are said to be *primitively concurrent* if a pair of their times is incomparable, that is, iff

$$t_{s(1)}\ \underline{\text{inc}}\ t_{s(2)} \vee t_{f(1)}\ \underline{\text{inc}}\ t_{s(2)} \vee t_{s(1)}\ \underline{\text{inc}}\ t_{f(2)} \vee t_{f(1)}\ \underline{\text{inc}}\ t_{f(2)}$$

If two tasks a and a' are primitively concurrent then we write $a \ \underline{\text{c}}\ a'$.

2.4 Elementary Interval Event Structures

The model presented here will be called the *interval event structure* (I.E.S.) model, because it is based on Winskel's event structures, and because tasks are associated with intervals of time.

[4]The causal part of this model was influenced by the work of [4]. For a more fundamental look at the relationship between timing and causality, see [13]. This latter work is exploited in [8].

Definition 4 An elementary interval event structure is a triple $(\mathbf{L} \times \mathbf{E}, <_b, =_b)$ consisting of a set of tasks, $\mathbf{L} \times \mathbf{E}$, (together with functions $\underline{\text{begin}}, \underline{\text{end}} : (\mathbf{L} \times \mathbf{E}) \longrightarrow \mathbf{BT}$), a branching order $<_b$, and a branching equality $=_b$.

Before going on to explore the model in more detail, a few small points should be made:

- It is possible have have undefined times in the model; take branching time to be $(\mathbb{R} \cup \{\top\}) \times \mathbf{T}$ instead of $\mathbb{R} \times \mathbf{T}$. It is easiest to make undefined times in the future, so that $\forall r \in \mathbb{R} \, . \, r < \top$.
- If we suppose that concurrency is not observable,[5] then a reasonable model of one execution of an interval event structure is an I.E.S. without unrelated branching times. (This holds when we introduce conflict, too.) Such *linear* I.E.S.s are used in [8] to define an observational semantics.
- If one is only interested in modelling computational systems, then it makes sense to restrict the class of I.E.S.s considered. The following axioms seem sensible for models of computation:

$$\forall r_1, r_2 \in \mathbb{R} \, . \, | \, \{ \, a \mid a \equiv [(r_s, a_s), (r_f, a_f)], [r_s, r_f] \cap [r_1, r_2] \neq \emptyset \, \} \, | \in \mathbb{N}$$

  (The structure is only doing a finite amount at once.)

$$\forall a_t \in \mathbf{T} \, . \, | \, \{ \, a'_{t'} \mid a'_{t'} <_c a_t, a'_{t'} \in \mathbf{T} \} \, | \in \mathbb{N}$$

  (Everything is finitely caused.) Failure to observe these rules may lead to the construction of *Zeno machines*; machines which can do an infinite computation in a finite time. [6] contains some discussion of this point.

3 THE MODEL REFINED

In this section the model will be further developed, and its descriptive power examined by way of an example.

It is useful to be able to express the causal relations between tasks somewhat more abstractly than is possible using $\leq_b$ and $=_b$. For this reason we introduce, in the first section, four causal orders on *tasks*. Then, nondeterminism is introduced via the notion of *conflict*. Finally the example demonstrates how a specification of a class of interval event structures might proceed.

3.1 Orders on Tasks

Definition 5 Suppose that $a_1 \equiv [t_{s(1)}, t_{f(1)}]$ and $a_2 \equiv [t_{s(2)}, t_{f(2)}]$. Then there are four possible causal relationships:

[5] This is not necessarily obvious; if by 'concurrent' we mean 'distributed' then the fact that two transitions are concurrent will be obvious, – they will be in different places.

If $t_{f(1)} \leq_b t_{s(2)}$, then a_1 is *interior-causal* of a_2, written $a_1 \sqsubseteq_i a_2$.

If $t_{s(1)} \leq_b t_{s(2)}$, then a_1 is *head-causal* of a_2, written $a_1 \sqsubseteq_h a_2$.

If $t_{f(1)} \leq_b t_{f(2)}$, then a_1 is *tail-causal* of a_2, written $a_1 \sqsubseteq_t a_2$.

If $t_{s(1)} \leq_b t_{f(2)}$, then a_1 is *exterior-causal* of a_2, written $a_1 \sqsubseteq_e a_2$.

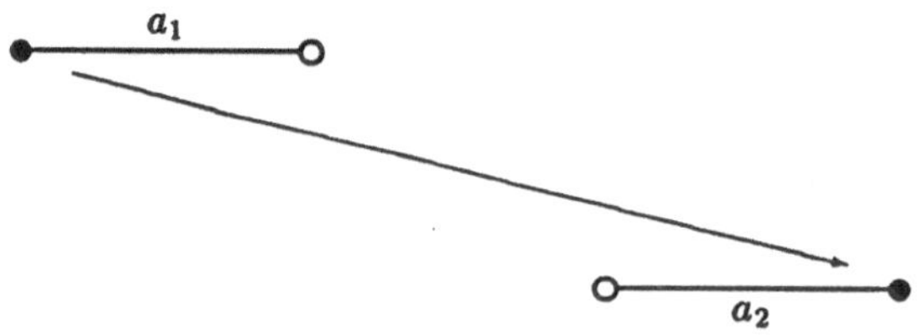

We will write $\sqsubseteq_j$ for one of $\sqsubseteq_i, \sqsubseteq_h, \sqsubseteq_t, \sqsubseteq_e$, and call the relations $\sqsubseteq_j$ *j-morphisms.* The *j*-morphisms $\sqsubseteq_i, \sqsubseteq_h$, and $\sqsubseteq_t$ are partial orders, but $\sqsubseteq_e$ is neither anti-symmetric nor transitive.

There is a simple relationship between the *j*-morphisms; they form a lattice ordered by inclusion:

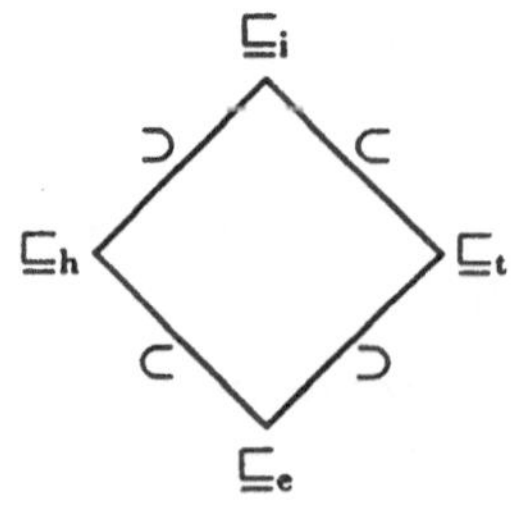

Definition 6 A set of tasks $\{a_1, a_2, \dots\}$ *j-secures* a task a just when $a_1 \sqsubseteq_j a_2 \sqsubseteq_j \dots \sqsubseteq_j a$. An I.E.S. is called *stable* if, given any task a_t and any two j-securings of it $\{a_1, a_2, \dots\}$ and $\{a'_1, a'_2, \dots\}$ the set $\{a_1, a_2, \dots\} \cap \{a'_1, a'_2, \dots\}$ also secures a. This property is required by Winskel (but not here) to ensure that there is a unique minimal sequence of events which leads up to any event.

3.2 Conflict

Conflict will be modelled by the usual partial-order model technique of introducing a set of *consistent sets* of tasks, $\underline{\text{Con}} \subseteq \wp(\mathbf{L} \times \mathbf{E})$. An element of $\underline{\text{Con}}$ is a set of tasks, all of which can happen in the same history, so if $\{a, a'\} \in \underline{\text{Con}}$, then there is some execution in which the tasks a and a' both occur. The $\underline{\text{Con}}$-set tells us where the branches of branching time branch.

If a set of tasks A is consistent, then any subset of it should also be consistent, so we require

$$A \in \underline{\text{Con}} \;\&\; B \subseteq A \Rightarrow B \in \underline{\text{Con}}$$

Two tasks are in conflict, $a \# a'$, just when there is no consistent set containing them

$$a \# a' \iff \{a, a'\} \notin \underline{\text{Con}}$$

Furthermore, it seems sensible to allow two tasks to be in conflict only if they are primitively concurrent; if they are completely causally related, then it is hard to know how they could be in conflict

$$a \# a' \Rightarrow a \,\underline{c}\, a'$$

If two tasks are causally the same, then they should be in the same $\underline{\text{Con}}$-sets

$$\forall c \in \underline{\text{Con}} . (a_1 \in c \wedge a_1 =_b a_2) \Rightarrow a_2 \in c$$

(It is often convenient to require finite nondeterminism; $|\underline{\text{Con}}| \in \mathbb{N}$.)

The introduction of conflict permits a more sophisticated definition of concurrency. Two tasks, a and a', will be *concurrent*, written $a \,\underline{\text{co}}\, a'$, iff they are primitively concurrent and not in conflict;

$$a \,\underline{\text{co}}\, a' \iff a \,\underline{c}\, a' \wedge \{a, a'\} \in \underline{\text{Con}}$$

Definition 7 (Interval Event Structures) An interval event structure $\Im$ is a quadruple $\Im = (\mathbf{L} \times \mathbf{E}, \underline{\text{Con}}, <_b, =_b)$ consisting of a set of tasks, $\mathbf{L} \times \mathbf{E}$, (together with the functions $\underline{\text{begin}}, \underline{\text{end}} : (\mathbf{L} \times \mathbf{E}) \longrightarrow \mathbf{BT}$), a set of consistent sets, $\underline{\text{Con}}$, a branching order $<_b$ and a branching equality $=_b$. The class of all interval event structures will be written **IES**.

3.3 Examples

The expressive power of the interval event structure model will now be demonstrated. In what follows assume that a_1 and a_2 are tasks, and that $a_1 \equiv [(r_{s(1)}, a_{s(1)}), (r_{f(1)}, a_{f(1)})]$, $a_2 \equiv [(r_{s(2)}, a_{s(2)}), (r_{f(2)}, a_{f(2)})]$. The following behavioural features[6] are expressible;

- Sequentiality; the two tasks are sequential if $a_1 \sqsubseteq_i a_2$. That is, a_1 starts wholly before a_2 and is on the same path.
- Temporal overlap; if $\{a_1, a_2\} \in \underline{\text{Con}}$ and $[r_{s(1)}, r_{f(1)}] \cap [r_{s(1)}, r_{f(1)}] \neq \emptyset$ then a_1 and a_2 overlap in time.
- Concurrency; a_1 and a_2 are concurrent if $a_1 \;\underline{\text{co}}\; a_2$. Notice that temporal overlap does not imply concurrency, nor does concurrency imply temporal overlap.
- Local simultaneity; a good example of temporal overlap without concurrency is the situation $a_1 \sqsubseteq_h a_2$ and $a_2 \sqsubseteq_t a_1$ but not $a_1 \;\underline{\text{co}}\; a_2$ or $a_1 \# a_2$. Here a_1 and a_2 are coexisting on the same path.
- The N-poset. This is an important object, since the absence of it embedded in a given poset guarantees that the poset can be decomposed; see [4] for details. Given tasks a_1, a_2, a_3, and a_4, this poset can be described by $a_1 \sqsubseteq_i a_2$, $a_3 \sqsubseteq_i a_4$ and $a_1 \sqsubseteq_i a_4$. This structure displays sequentiality (between a_1 and a_2 for instance), and incomparability (between a_1 and a_3).
- Asymmetric confusion; an I.E.S. displaying asymmetric confusion can be formed from the three tasks a_1, a_2 and a_3 with $a_1 \sqsubseteq_i a_2$, $a_1 \;\underline{\text{co}}\; a_3$ and $a_2 \# a_3$. (The correct Con-set to describe this situation is $\{\{a_1\}, \{a_2\}, \{a_1, a_2\}, \{a_3\}, \{a_1, a_3\}\}$.)
- An I.E.S. without conflict inheritance. Winskel demands that conflict is inherited, that is, if $a \# b$ and $a \sqsubseteq_i c$ then $c \# b$. We will not require conflict inheritance, so that we can describe situations like this; $a_1 \sqsubseteq_i a_2$, $a_3 \sqsubseteq_i a_4$, $a_1 \sqsubseteq_i a_4$, $a_3 \sqsubseteq_i a_2$, $a_1 \# a_3$ but $a_2 \;\underline{\text{co}}\; a_4$.
- An unstable I.E.S. $a_1 \# a_2$, $a_1 \sqsubseteq_i a_3$ and $a_2 \sqsubseteq_i a_3$. Here the Con-set is $\{\{a_1\}, \{a_3\}, \{a_1, a_3\}, \{a_2\}, \{a_2, a_3\}\}$. Confused situations are not necessarily unstable, but unstable situations are always confused.

---

[6]The terminology of this section is that of the Petri net community. See [11] for details.

An extended example should clarify the model further: consider a bar. We will concentrate on drinking, tussling at the bar for a drink, and being served. A set **Hab** of habitués of the bar will be considered, with typical member h, so that the events of interest are $\mathbf{E} = \{drink^h, tussle^h, serve^h \mid h \in \mathbf{Hab}\}$. The integers will serve as labels. Clearly, in order for habitué h to have the nth drink, someone must tussle and be served, so

$$\forall n \in \mathbb{N}, h \in \mathbf{Hab}\,.\,\exists h' \in \mathbf{Hab}, n' \in \mathbb{N}\,.$$
$$\underline{\mathrm{end}}(n', tussle^{h'}) =_{\mathrm{b}} \underline{\mathrm{begin}}(n', serve^{h'}) \;\&\; (n', serve^{h'}) \sqsubseteq_{\mathrm{h}} (n, drink^h)$$

Here we assume that the n'^{th} *serve* always follows the n'^{th} *tussle*; one does not give up tussling until served.

Furthermore, no one tussles more than they drink;

$$\forall n \in \mathbb{N}, h \in \mathbf{Hab}\,.\,(n, drink^h) \sqsubseteq_{\mathrm{i}} (n+1, tussle^h)$$

A somewhat unrealistic requirement is that everyone is served in the order in which they queue

$$\forall n, n' \in \mathbb{N}, \forall h, h' \in \mathbf{Hab}\,.$$
$$(n, tussle^h) \sqsubseteq_{\mathrm{h}} (n', tussle^{h'}) \Rightarrow (n, serve^h) \sqsubseteq_{\mathrm{h}} (n', serve^{h'})$$

Only one person can be served at once

$$\forall n \in \mathbb{N}, h \in \mathbf{Hab}\,.\,\nexists n' \in \mathbb{N}, h' \in \mathbf{Hab}\,.\,(n, serve^h)\ \underline{\mathrm{co}}\ (n', serve^{h'})$$

This assumes the existence of only one barman, of course.

Finally, there are certain obvious performance requirements. The habitués demand that there queueing time is less than a minute:

$$(n, tussle^h) \equiv [(r_{\mathrm{s}(n,tussle^h)}, (n, tussle^h)_{\mathrm{s}}), (r_{\mathrm{f}(n,tussle^h)}, (n, tussle^h)_{\mathrm{f}})] \Rightarrow$$
$$\forall n \in \mathbb{N}, h \in \mathbf{Hab}\,.\,r_{\mathrm{f}(n,tussle^h)} - r_{\mathrm{s}(n,tussle^h)} < 1$$

(assuming the units are minutes). The management, on the other hand, demand that the bar should only serve for five hours:

$$(n, serve^h) \equiv [(r_{\mathrm{s}(n,serve^h)}, (n, serve^h)_{\mathrm{s}}), (r_{\mathrm{f}(n,serve^h)}, (n, serve^h)_{\mathrm{f}})] \Rightarrow$$
$$\forall n \in \mathbb{N}\,.\,\forall h \in \mathbf{H}\,.\,r_{\mathrm{f}(n,serve^h)} - r_{\mathrm{f}(0,serve^h)} < 300$$

Habitué *Harry* can be used to illustrate a recurrent liveness requirement. Consider the occurrences $(n, drink^{Harry}) \equiv [(r_{\mathrm{s}(n,drink^{Harry})}, (n, drink^{Harry})_{\mathrm{s}}), (r_{\mathrm{f}(n,drink^{Harry})}, (n, drink^{Harry})_{\mathrm{f}})]$; we might require that $\forall n < 15$.

$$r_{\mathrm{s}(n,drink^{Harry})} < 10n \qquad \text{and} \qquad r_{\mathrm{f}(n,drink^{Harry})} < 10n + 10$$

4 I.E.S.S, CATEGORIES, & COMBINATORS

It would be nice to have some way of structuring our descriptions of systems: at the moment, I.E.S.s are monolithic. This will be achieved by providing structure-combinators, so that the parallel and nondeterministic combination of I.E.S.s can be represented. The definition of these combinators as limits in appropriate categories will be sketched.[7] The objects of these categories will be I.E.S.s, – what should the arrows represent ?

4.1 j-homomorphisms

The notion of a *bisimulation* has been very productive for CCS; it seems reasonable to investigate what it might mean in the world of I.E.S.s. Two CCS processes bisimulate each other when, whatever state one gets into, the other can always get into a state in which the same actions are possible next.

For I.E.S.s, there is no fundamental notion of state, and we have four notions of causality (the $\sqsubseteq_j$s), so a different definition is needed. A notion, similar to bisimulation, but defineable over I.E.S.s, is *j-homomorphism*. Given two I.E.S.s $\Im = (\mathbf{L} \times \mathbf{E}, \underline{\mathrm{Con}}, <_b, =_b)$ with silent event $*$, and $\Im' = (\mathbf{L}' \times \mathbf{E}', \underline{\mathrm{Con}}', <'_b, ='_b)$ with $*'$, there is an *asynchronous j-homomorphism* f between them if f is a function from $(\mathbf{L} \times \mathbf{E})$ to $(\mathbf{L}' \times \mathbf{E}')$ such that

- Silent events are preserved; $f(*) = *'$.
- The causal precedence order is preserved; $a, a' \in (\mathbf{L} \times \mathbf{E})$ with $a \sqsubseteq_j a'$ implies $f(a) \sqsubseteq'_j f(a')$. (Here $\sqsubseteq_j$ comes from $\leq_b$ and $\sqsubseteq'_j$ from $\leq'_b$.)
- Previously consistent sets must remain consistent. If $c \in \underline{\mathrm{Con}}$ then $\{ f(a) \mid a \in c \} \in \underline{\mathrm{Con}}'$.

Hence, if there is a j-homomorphism from $\Im$ to $\Im'$, there will be a matching j-ordering in $\Im'$ for any in $\Im$, (although this may be the trivial one $a \sqsubseteq_j a'$) so that $\Im'$ can be thought of as *simulating* $\Im$. The arrows, then, will indicate simulation.

Proposition 1 There are four categories whose objects are members of **IES** and whose arrows are asynchronous j-homomorphisms. These categories will be called IES_j. If we replace the second condition defining an asynchronous j-homomorphism by

- if $f(a) = b$ and $a \sqsubseteq_j a'$ then $f(a')$ must be a b' such that $b \sqsubseteq'_j b'$ and $b \neq b'$,

the definition of a *synchronous* j-homomorphism is obtained. The categories whose objects are members of **IES** and whose arrows are synchronous j-homomorphisms will be called $\mathsf{IES}_{syn,k}$. A given $\mathsf{IES}_{syn,k}$ is a wide subcategory of IES_k.

---

[7]It will not be possible to represent all I.E.S.s as combinations of one-task structures because I.E.S.s are not *N-free*. This point is discussed in [1] and [4].

The merits of the particular categories defined here, or, indeed, of category theory *per se* will not be discussed; consult [8] for further details.

The categories defined above concentrated on the simulation of causality. Timing is, however, also of interest, so another category will be useful:

Definition 8 Given two I.E.S.s, $\Im$ and $\Im'$, as usual, a temporal homomorphism is a function, f from $\mathbf{L} \times \mathbf{E}$ to $\mathbf{L}' \times \mathbf{E}'$ such that f is an i-homomorphism (and hence a j-homomorphism for all j) and $\forall a \in (\mathbf{L} \times \mathbf{E})$ if $a \equiv [t_s, t_f]$ and $f(a) \equiv [t_s', t_f']$ then $[t_s, t_f] \supseteq [t_s, t_f]$.

The category whose objects are members of **IES** and whose arrows are temporal homomorphisms will be called tIES. If there is an arrow from $\Im$ to $\Im'$ in tIES then $\Im'$ can do all $\Im$ can, simulating its causality, and in no more time.

4.2 Nondeterministic Composition

The *nondeterministic composition* of two I.E.S.s, $\Im + \Im'$ say, should correspond to a choice between them. We will define a construction for nondeterministic composition and then show that it is a coproduct in all of the categories considered. The construction will essentially stick structures together by their silent tasks, giving a structure that can either behave like $\Im$ or like $\Im'$.

Definition 9 Suppose $\Im = (\mathbf{L} \times \mathbf{E}, \underline{\mathrm{Con}}, <_b, =_b)$ and $\Im' = (\mathbf{L}' \times \mathbf{E}', \underline{\mathrm{Con}}', <_b', =_b')$ are I.E.S.s. Define their nondeterministic composition, or *sum*, as the I.E.S. $\Im'' = (\mathbf{L}'' \times \mathbf{E}'', \underline{\mathrm{Con}}'', <_b'', =_b'')$ where:

1. $\mathbf{L}'' \times \mathbf{E}'' \triangleq \{((0, l_0), e_0),\ ((0, l_1), e_1),\ \ldots \mid (l_0, e_0),\ (l_1, e_1)\ \ldots\ \in \mathbf{L} \times \mathbf{E}\} \cup \{((1, l_0'), e_0'),\ ((1, l_1'), e_1'),\ \ldots \mid (l_0', e_0'),\ (l_1', e_1')\ \ldots\ \in \mathbf{L}' \times \mathbf{E}'\}$

2. There are obvious injections $i_0 : (l, e) \rightarrow ((0, l), e)$ and $i_1 : (l', e') \rightarrow ((1, l'), e')$. Then $\underline{\mathrm{Con}}''$ is just the disjoint union $\underline{\mathrm{Con}}'' \triangleq i_0(\underline{\mathrm{Con}}) \cup i_1(\underline{\mathrm{Con}}')$.

3. Tasks have their times relabelled. For some $(l, e) \in \mathbf{L} \times \mathbf{E}$, suppose that $(l, e) \equiv [(r_s, (l, e)_s), (r_f, (l, e)_f)]$ then $i_0(l, e) \equiv [(r_s, ((0, l), e)_s), (r_f, ((0, l), e)_f)]$, and similarly for $(l', e') \in \mathbf{L}' \times \mathbf{E}'$.

4. One branching time $(r_{t(i)}, ((0, l), e)_{t(i)})$ is $<_b''$ another time $(r_{t(j)}, ((0, l), e)_{t(j)})$ iff $(r_{t(i)}, (l, e)_{t(i)}) <_b (r_{t(j)}, (l, e)_{t(j)})$, and similarly for $(r_{t(i)}, ((1, l), e)_{t(i)})$ & $(r_{t(j)}, ((1, l), e)_{t(j)})$. Things from different 'sides' of the coproduct never compare; it is never the case that $(r_{t(i)}, ((0, l), e)_{t(i)}) <_b (r_{t(j)}, ((1, l), e)_{t(j)})$.

5. A time $(r_{t(i)}, ((0, l), e)_{t(i)})$ is $=_b''$ another $(r_{t(j)}, ((0, l), e)_{t(j)})$ iff $(r_{t(i)}, (l, e)_{t(i)}) =_b (r_{t(j)}, (l, e)_{t(j)})$, and similarly for $(r_{t(i)}, ((1, l), e)_{t(i)})$ & $(r_{t(j)}, ((1, l), e)_{t(j)})$. Clearly $(r_{t(i)}, ((0, l), e)_{t(i)}) =_b (r_{t(j)}, ((1, l), e)_{t(j)})$ never holds.

Proposition 2 The sum construction defines a coproduct in IES_j. By inspection, i_0, i_1 are morphisms. For morphisms $j_0 : \Im \rightarrow \mho$, $j_1 : \Im' \rightarrow \mho$ to some I.E.S.s $\mho$, define $j : \Im + \Im' \rightarrow \mho$ componentwise. It quickly follows that $+$ defines a coproduct. Next note that if j_0 and j_1 are arrows in $\mathsf{IES}_{syn,j}$ then so will j be, so the construction works there, too. A similar argument shows that $+$ also defines a coproduct in tIES.

4.3 Parallel Composition

The parallel composition construction will be broadly described here; see the thesis [8] for a more rigourous approach.

The usual approach to parallel composition, [14], involves the (categorical) product. Consider two I.E.S.s, $\Im = (\mathbf{L} \times \mathbf{E}, \underline{\mathrm{Con}}, <_b, =_b)$ and $\Im' = (\mathbf{L}' \times \mathbf{E}', \underline{\mathrm{Con}}', <'_b, ='_b)$. We wish to form the parallel composition $\Im \parallel \Im'$. Tasks in $\Im \parallel \Im'$ will be pairs of tasks, one member of the pair from $\Im$ and one from $\Im'$. The synchronisation of a task a from $\Im$ with a task a' from $\Im'$ will be modelled by the presence of the pair (a, a') in $\mathbf{L}'' \times \mathbf{E}''$, while asynchronous occurrences will be modelled as synchronisations with the silent task of the other structure, so $(a, *')$ models the asynchronous occurrence of a.

The product is not good enough for us, however, because of timing. A task $a \equiv [(r_s, a_s), (r_f, a_f)]$ from $\mathbf{L} \times \mathbf{E}$ and a task $a' \equiv [(r'_s, a'_s), (r'_f, a'_f)]$ from $\mathbf{L}' \times \mathbf{E}'$ can synchronise just when $[r_s, r_f] \cap [r'_s, r'_f] \neq \emptyset$, yet $\Im \times \Im'$ will contain *all* pairs (a, a'). We can see that timing has a significant impact on which constructions for parallel composition are valid. The set of pairs of tasks which can synchronise, and which we intend to synchronise, will we written as $\Im \updownarrow \Im'$. (Obviously, not all of those synchronisations that can happen are desired; we might want some things to happen asynchronously even though they could synchronise; the synchronisation set allows this to be specified.)

Parallel composition will be defined using $\Im \updownarrow \Im'$, the ***synchronisation set***. Note first that synchronisations are binary; the synchronisation set will contain at most one pair (a, a') for each a and a';

$$\begin{aligned} \forall a \in \mathbf{L} \times \mathbf{E}, a' \in \mathbf{L}' \times \mathbf{E}' . (a, a') \in \Im \updownarrow \Im' \Rightarrow \\ \nexists a'' \neq a' \in \mathbf{L}' \times \mathbf{E}' . (a, a'') \in \Im \updownarrow \Im' \wedge \\ \nexists a''' \neq a \in \mathbf{L} \times \mathbf{E} . (a''', a') \in \Im \updownarrow \Im' \end{aligned}$$

Two structures are necessary to describe the parallel composition $\Im \parallel \Im'$, both derived from the product. The first records information about synchronisations. It just contains the tasks in $\Im \updownarrow \Im'$, and times them with the *intersection* of the component's times, so that $(a, a') \equiv [(\max(r_s, r'_s), (a, a')_s), (\min(r_f, r'_f), (a, a')_f)]$. This information is necessary so that we can interpret multiple parallel compositions correctly; we want to be able to form $((a, b), c)$ only if there is a time *all* of a, b and c are active. This structure, called the ***intersection structure***, will be written $\Im \prod \Im'$.

The second structure records information about asynchronous occurrences and synchronisations. The union of tasks' times is recorded, so that $(a, a') \equiv (\min(r_s, r'_s), (a, a')_s), (\max(r_f, r'_f), (a, a')_f)$ and $(a, *') \equiv [(r_s, a_s), (r_f, a_f)]$. This structure, the ***union structure***, is necessary to record the times that compound tasks actually last. It is written $\Im \coprod \Im'$.

It just remains to state the relationship between the two structures;

Proposition 3 In the category tIES there are projections $p_0 : \Im \coprod \Im' \to \Im$, $p_1 : \Im \coprod \Im' \to \Im'$ and morphisms $k_0 : \Im \to \Im \prod \Im'$, $k_1 : \Im \to \Im \prod \Im'$. Furthermore, k_0 and k_1 are a pushout of p_0 and p_1. [8] contains details of the construction.

5 CONCLUDING REMARKS

The I.E.S. model was an attempt to explore an unconventional point in the concurrency theory design space. A few problems have emerged; it is not clear how to describe sequential composition categorically, for instance, but this is a well-known difficulty. Nevertheless, it seems to be possible to build an expressive partial order model of real-timed concurrent systems. The introduction of real-time is, in some ways, a *simplification*, since it allows fewer constructions. The conclusion is that *this* exploration was successful, but also, less parochially, that exploration *in general* can be profitable. One should *start* from a notion of what the theory should be about, – real-timed truly-concurrent systems in this case, – and proceed to develop the theory around those notions. Most concurrency theories are very limited in their concerns: it is only when we have explored a lot of different theories that we can better understand notions in themselves, rather than as they are expressed in a particular model.

It is important to understand the relationship between models as well as the models themselves. The relationship of I.E.S.s to other models has, thus far, been shamefully neglected, but I hope in the near future to use the descriptive richness of the model presented here to examine the constructions of other models. [12] implies that it is profitable to have a very rich theory for comparing theories; since the I.E.S. model is rich enough to express everything required of it thus far, it might be interesting to see what subclasses of **IES** other theories are capable of specifying.

There has not been space to present many aspects of the theory, such as the semantics of I.E.S.s, a categorical treatment of the relationship between causality and timing, or an I.E.S.-based process algebra: see [8] for further details.

My thanks are due to David Pitt, Mike Shields and Terry Stroup for helpful conversations, and to the Science and Engineering Research Council of Great Britain for support.

REFERENCES

1. Boudol G, Castellani I, Concurrency and atomicity. *Theoretical Computer Science*, Volume 59, Pages 25–84, 1988.

2. Davies J, Schneider S, *An introduction to timed CSP*. Technical Monograph Number 75, Oxford University Computing Laboratory, 1989.

3. Deane J, Johnstone G, Jefferies D, Chaos in Electrical Engineering. *Electronic and Communication Engineers Journal*, March 1989.

4. Gischer J, The equational theory of pomsets. *Theoretical Computer Science*, Volume 61, Pages 199–224, 1989.

5. Hoare C, *Communicating Sequential Processes*. International series on computer science, Prentice-Hall, 1985.

6. Joseph M, Goswami A, *Relating Computation and Time.* Research Report RR 138, Department of Computer Science, University of Warwick, 1985.

7. Mendler M, *Über die Realisierbarkeit von Synchronisationshardware.* Studienarbeit, Lehrstuhl für Rechnerarchitektur und Verkehrstheorie, Universität Erlangen-Nürnberg, April 1987.

8. Murphy D, *Time, causality, and concurrency.* Ph.D. Thesis, Department of Mathematics, University of Surrey, December 1989.

9. Petri C, Prelude. In W. Brauer, W. Reisig and G. Rozenberg (eds), *Petri Nets: Central Models and Their Properties*, (Advances in Petri Nets 1986), Springer-Verlag LNCS 254, 1987.

10. Pnueli A, Linear and Branching Structures in the Semantics and Logics of Reactive Systems. In W. Brauer (ed), *Automata, Languages and Programming*, (12th Coll., 1985), Springer-Verlag LNCS 194, 1986.

11. Reisig W, *Petri Nets: An Introduction.* EATCS Monographs on theoretical computer science, Springer-Verlag, 1985.

12. Shields M, *Elements of a theory of parallelism.* The M.I.T. Press, Forthcoming.

13. Thomason S, On constructing intervals from events. *Journal of Philosophical Logic*, Volume 13, Pages 85–96, 1984.

14. Winskel G, An introduction to Event Structures. In J. de Bakker, W. de Roever, and G. Rozenberg (eds), *Linear Time, Branching Time and Partial Order in Logics and Models for Concurrency*, (REX 1988), Springer-Verlag LNCS 354, 1989.

On Global-Time and Inter-process Communication

Uri Abraham
Department of Mathematics and Computer Science
Ben-Gurion University, Be'er Sheva, Israel

Shai Ben-David
Faculty of Computer Science
Technion, Haifa, Israel

Menachem Magidor
Institute of Mathematics and Computer Science
Hebrew University, Jerusalem, Israel.

Abstract

How should time be represented in models for inter-process communication? The global-time axiom implies that all events can be represented by intervals on one time-axis. Its use simplifies the analysis of protocols and allows for intuitive proofs of their properties. On the other hand,some researchers believe it is too strong an assumption which should be avoided. In order to suggest an answer to this question we study the notion of a system-execution introduced by Lamport. We develop a practical tool which enables the investigation of protocols and allows for intuitive proofs of their properties. We apply our approach to prove that in many cases the global time axiom can be safely used. The main mathematical tool we employ is the theory of interval partial orders and we prove some new results along a line that goes back to the work of Russell and Wiener.

1 Introduction

Since any experience has some duration, the notion of *time-interval* (periods) is prominent in any analysis of 'time'. Starting with Zeno, time-intervals and moments were opposed to one another. Usually a moment, or instant, was considered to be the primitive notion from which time-intervals can be construed. Following the opposite intuition, B. Russell and N. Wiener suggested the period and the precedence relation between events as the primitive notions. They provided an axiomatic frame in which instants can be defined. That is, they defined an instant as the common property of a maximal set of periods such that no period in the set precedes another.

Their definition and theorem was rediscovered by investigators who were unaware of Wiener's [9] pioneering contribution.

While logicians and philosophers are motivated by its ontological aspects, computer scientists analyze time to understand computer systems and programs (see for example the survey [5] by van Benthem). Lamport [7, 8] provides an analysis of time and distributed systems which has influenced this field. His modeling of systems is based on the precedence relation between events, and his axiomatic treatment of the precedence relation resembles the Russell and Wiener axioms. We wish to expose a basic and coherent treatment of these theories of time-intervals and their applications, in addition to our own contribution which is described below.

An interesting philosophical issue, of practical importance, emanates from Lamport [7, 8]: the validity of the Global-Time Assumption in the modeling of distributed systems. Should the flow of time be represented by a linear order, or are there moments incomparable under the precedence relation? The global-time assumption tends to the former assumption (its precise formulation is given in section 2). In practice and in the literature, the design and the analysis of distributed protocols is often done by visualizing events as intervals on a linear order. This presupposes the existence of global-time. On the other hand, many investigators argue that in distributed systems global-time cannot be assumed. Lamport states that "while a global-time model is a valuable aid to acquiring an intuitive understanding of a system, it is better to use more abstract reasoning when proving properties of systems." We believe that formal system should support the intuition, but instead of arguing on philosophical and physical ground for the global-time assumption, we *prove* that (in many cases) conclusions obtained under the global-time assumption can be transferred to the frame where no such assumption is made. So, we argue, why not accept the more intuitive approach? By offering a formal, yet intuitive, frame which incorporate the global-time axiom, we provide here support for pictorial proofs which were hitherto labeled as 'informal'.

Section 2 contains an exposition of interval orders, the Russell-Wiener representation theorem, a definition of Lamport's structures and a proof of the representation theorem for these structures. Our original contribution in this section is an extension (Theorem 2.10) of the representation theorem which is used in section 3. Theorem 2.11 (due to Ben-David [4]) provides a characterization of Lamport's structures in terms of global-time models. Section 3 investigate how the theory can be applied to the analysis of protocols and in particular to the mutual-exclusion problem, and to the register-implementation problem.

2 Interval-orders, Lamport's structures and representations

2.1 Interval-orders

Definition 2.1 *Given a partial order (an irreflexive and transitive relation),* $(L, <)$*, define two relations* $\longrightarrow$ *and* $\dashrightarrow$ *on* $\mathcal{P}(L)$ *(the power-set of* L *but without the empty set): For* $A, B \subseteq L$

1. $A \longrightarrow B$ *iff* $\forall x \in A, \forall y \in B (x < y)$.

2. $A \dashrightarrow B$ *iff* $\exists x \in A, \exists y \in B (x < y \text{ or } x = y)$

Observe that $\longrightarrow$ is irreflexive and transitive.

A case of particular interest is when L is a linear order. Note that in this case $A \dashrightarrow B$ is equivalent to $\neg(B \longrightarrow A)$ and we can confine the discussion to one relation symbol. It can be easily checked that for such L's one can replace each subset A by its convex closure, the interval between its minimal and maximal elements, without changing the $\longrightarrow$ relation. The resulting partial order $\longrightarrow$ on intervals is extensively studied in Fishburn [6].

Definition 2.2 *An irreflexive and transitive relation R on E is called an* interval-order *iff*

$$\forall a, b, c, d \in E (aRb \wedge \neg(cRb) \wedge cRd \Longrightarrow aRd) \tag{1}$$

We shall call statement (1) the *Russell-Wiener axiom.* It is easy to see that, for any linear order $(L, <)$, it holds for the relation $\longrightarrow$ on $\mathcal{P}(L)$.

To understand this formula, define simultaneity as the relation of two events that neither one precedes the other. Intuitively the formula states that if a precedes b and b is simultaneous with c, and c precedes d then a precedes d.

A *representation* of an interval-order (E, R) is a linear order L and a map μ of E into intervals of L such that for all $a, b \in E$, aRb iff $\mu(a) \longrightarrow \mu(b)$.

Theorem 2.3 (Russell and Wiener) *Every interval-order has a representation.*

Proof. The proof follows Russell's intuition which relates a moment to the collection of all intervals in which it occurs. Given an interval-order (E, R) define $X \subseteq E$ to be a *moment* iff X is a maximal (under inclusion) antichain (X is an antichain iff $\forall x \neq y \in X(\neg(xRy)$ and $\neg(yRx)))$. Then let L be the collection of all moments, and define for $X, Y \in L$, $X < Y$ iff $\exists e \in X, \exists f \in Y\ (eRf)$.

It follows that $<$ is a linear order on L (transitivity is an easy consequence of the Russell-Wiener formula, and linearity follows from the maximality of moments). Now define $\mu(e)$ for $e \in E$ to be the collection of all moments X such that $e \in X$.

Lemma 2.4 *For every* $e \in E$ $\mu(e)$ *is convex (an interval in L).*

Proof Assume $X < Y < Z$, and $X, Z \in \mu(e)$. We will prove that $Y \in \mu(e)$. Assume by way of contradiction that $e \notin Y$. By maximality of Y, there is $y \in Y$ such that eRy or yRe. Assume for example that eRy. Since $Y < Z$ there are $y' \in Y$ and $z \in Z$ be such that $y'Rz$. Now the Russell-Wiener formula implies that eRz and this contradicts the fact that the moment Z is an antichain.

Lemma 2.5 *For all* $e, f \in E$, eRf *iff* $\mu(e) \longrightarrow \mu(f)$.

Proof Assume first that eRf. Let be given any $X \in \mu(e)$ and $Y \in \mu(f)$. Then $e \in X$ and $f \in Y$ by definition of μ, and so $X < Y$ by definition of $<$. Thus $\mu(e) \longrightarrow \mu(f)$. Next, let us see that if $\neg eRf$ then $\mu(e) \not\longrightarrow \mu(f)$. Assume $\neg eRf$. If fRe then $\mu(f) \longrightarrow \mu(e)$ as proved above and hence $\mu(e) \not\longrightarrow \mu(f)$ by transitivity an irreflexivity of $\longrightarrow$. If e and f are incomparable under R then a maximal antichain exists which includes both e and f. And again this shows $\mu(e) \not\longrightarrow \mu(f)$.

2.2 Lamport structures

Lamport offers a formalism for the analysis of distributed systems that is based on precedence relations among operation executions. His language consists of two binary relations $A \longrightarrow B$ for strong precedence and $A \dashrightarrow B$ that can be read as "A can causally affect B".

Lamport's Axioms for strong and week precedence relations.

1. $\longrightarrow$ is irreflexive and transitive.
2. $a \longrightarrow b$ implies $a \dashrightarrow b$, and $\neg b \dashrightarrow a$.
3. $a \longrightarrow b \dashrightarrow c$ implies $a \dashrightarrow c$. And similarly $a \dashrightarrow b \longrightarrow c$ implies $a \dashrightarrow c$.
4. $a \longrightarrow b \dashrightarrow c \longrightarrow d$ implies $a \longrightarrow d$.

Anger [3], and independently Abraham [2], have suggested to add the following

Anger's axioms

1. For all x $x \dashrightarrow x$, and
2. $u \dashrightarrow v \longrightarrow x \dashrightarrow y$ implies $u \dashrightarrow y$.

An axiom of much interest is the *global-time* axiom.

The Global-Time Axiom

$$\text{For every } a \text{ and } b \ a \longrightarrow b \text{ iff } \neg b \dashrightarrow a.$$

The global-time axiom is not a consequence of Lamport's four axioms, and the main issue of this paper concerns its validity and usefulness.

The following claims are easily verified.

Claim 2.6 *1. For every partial order the relations $\longrightarrow$ and $\dashrightarrow$ on the collection of its nonempty subsets (Definition 2.1), satisfy Lamport axioms and the Anger axioms.*

2. The global time axiom implies that Lamport axioms are equivalent to the statement that $\longrightarrow$ is an interval order (the Russell-Wiener axiom).

We shall prove the analogue of theorem 2.3 for this context, namely, that any system satisfying the Lamport and Anger axioms can be represented as a collection of subsets of some partial order with the relations of definition 2.1.

Definition 2.7 *We say that $(E, \longrightarrow, \dashrightarrow)$ is a* Lamport's *structure iff it satisfies the axioms listed above and moreover it satisfies the finiteness property: for every $x \in E$ the following set is finite.*

$$\{y \in E \mid \neg x \longrightarrow y\}$$

Note that we are using the symbols $\longrightarrow$ and $\dashrightarrow$ in two modes: in Definition 2.1, these relations derive their meanings from the underlying order relation $<$, but in 2.3, $\longrightarrow$ and $\dashrightarrow$ are arbitrary relations on E satisfying certain axioms. The reader should be careful to distinguish these two modes.

Remark that the finiteness axiom is stronger than the one which states that for any $x \in E$ there are only finitely many $y \in E$ with $y \longrightarrow x$. Lamport [8] distinguishes between terminating and nonterminating events and the finiteness axiom is only stated for terminating events; but we prefer to limit our discussion to terminating events.

Definition 2.8 *Let $S = (E, \longrightarrow, \dashrightarrow)$ be a structure with two binary relations; and let $(L, <)$ be a partially ordered set (not necessarily linear).*

1. *We say that μ is an L-*representation *for S if μ is defined on E with values in $\mathcal{P}(L)$ and such that for all $x, y \in E$*

   (a) $x \longrightarrow y$ iff $\mu(x) \longrightarrow \mu(y)$, and

   (b) $x \dashrightarrow y$ iff $\mu(x) \dashrightarrow \mu(y)$.

   (Of course the arrow relations have different meanings in the right and the left sides of the equivalences.)

2. *We say that a function μ into $\mathcal{P}(L)$ is an L-*representation for $\longrightarrow$ *iff only (a) above holds.*

3. *We say that μ is an L-*homomorphism *of S iff*

   (a) $x \longrightarrow y$ implies $\mu(x) \longrightarrow \mu(y)$, and

   (b) $x \dashrightarrow y$ implies $\mu(x) \dashrightarrow \mu(y)$.

The following is an immediate corollary of theorem 2.3 and part 2 of claim 2.6 above. It was stated without a proof in [8] and then proved in [4] and independently in [3]. What we have here is, by far, the shortest proof for it.

Corollary 2.9 *A structure S satisfies Lamport axioms and the global time axiom iff it has a representation into intervals of some linear order L.*

Given an L-homomorphism μ, it is possible to extend L to a linear order and naturally obtain an homomorphism into intervals of a linear order. However, even if μ is a representation, after the linearization of L, μ needs no longer remain a representation. We are mainly interested in representations into intervals of linear orders, because of the intuition that the linear order is the time-axis and the interval $\mu(a)$ represents the duration of event a. This intuition leads us to the proof of the *representation theorem.* Suppose we want to represent a structure $(E, \longrightarrow, \dashrightarrow)$; then to every $e \in E$ we abstractly attach left and right ends, e_L and e_R, of the purposed interval. If $a \longrightarrow b$ in E then we set $a_R < b_L$; and if $a \dashrightarrow b$ then we set $a_L < b_R$. This intuition is the basic idea in the proof given in Fishburn's book to Wiener's representation theorem and it appears in Anger's paper as well; it leads to the following.

Theorem 2.10 (The representation theorem) *Let $S = (E, \longrightarrow, \dashrightarrow)$ be a structure satisfying all of Lamport's axioms 1 to 4.*

1. *There is a one-to-one L-homomorphism μ of S which is a representation for $\longrightarrow$.*

2. *If S satisfies Anger's axioms then for some partial-order L, it has an L-representation.*

Proof. Let us first prove *1*. Given S as above, let E_L and E_R be two disjoint copies of E and set $F = E_L \cup E_R$. For every $e \in E$ let e_L and e_R be the copies of e in E_L and E_R. We shall define a partial order relation, $<$, on F and set $\mu(e) = [e_L, e_R] = \{f \in F \mid e_L \leq f \leq e_R\}$. (Here $x \leq y$ is $x < y$ or $x = y$.) Define the following relation $<$ on F.

1. For every $e \in E$ set $e_L < e_R$
2. Whenever $x \longrightarrow y$ in S set $x_R < y_L$ and $x_L < y_L$ and $x_R < y_R$.
3. Whenever $x \dashrightarrow y$ in S set $x_L < y_R$.
4. For every triple $u \dashrightarrow v \longrightarrow x \dashrightarrow y$ set $u_L < y_R$.
5. Whenever $x \longrightarrow y \dashrightarrow z$ in S, set $x_R < z_R$.
6. If $x \dashrightarrow y \longrightarrow z$, then set $x_L < z_L$.

It is clear that $<$ is irreflexive. For example, assume $x_R < y_R$ and let us prove $x_R \neq y_R$. If the reason for $x_R < y_R$ is in line 2, then $x \longrightarrow y$ and $x_R \neq y_R$ since $x \neq y$ by irreflexivity of $\longrightarrow$.; if the reason is line 5, then $x \longrightarrow a \dashrightarrow y$ and so $x \neq y$ by Axiom 2 of Lamport.

By checking all possibilities, it can be proved that $<$ is transitive. Suppose that $\alpha < \beta < \gamma$ hold, and let us outline the proof that $\alpha < \gamma$. There are 8 cases to check according to the truth value of $\alpha \in E_L$, $\beta \in E_L$, $\gamma \in E_L$. Suppose, for example, that $\alpha = a_R, \beta = b_L, \gamma = c_R$ for some $a, b, c \in E$. Then $a \longrightarrow b$ as only line 2 can give a relation $x_R < y_L$. Now $b_L < c_R$ can be set in one of the following lines:

1. In line 1, and then $b = c$ so $a \longrightarrow c$, and thus $a_R < c_R$.
2. In line 3, and then $b \dashrightarrow c$ so that $a_R < c_R$ is set in line 5.
3. In line 4, and then $b \dashrightarrow v \longrightarrow x \dashrightarrow c$ so that $a \longrightarrow x$ by the Russell-Wiener property, and hence by line 5 $a_R < c_R$ is introduced.

μ is defined by setting $\mu(a)$ to be the interval $[a_L, a_R] = \{f \in F \mid a_L \leq f \leq a_R\}$. μ is a homomorphism because if $a \longrightarrow b$ then $a_R < b_L$ by line 2, and so $\mu(a) \longrightarrow \mu(b)$; and if $a \dashrightarrow b$ then $a_L < b_R$ in line 3 and so by definition $\mu(a) \dashrightarrow \mu(b)$. since $x_R < y_L$ can hold only by 2 it is a representation for $\longrightarrow$.

To prove *2* suppose that Anger's axioms hold. We prove that μ is now a representation (for both $\longrightarrow$ and $\dashrightarrow$). What needs to be proven is that if $\mu(a) \dashrightarrow \mu(b)$ then $a \dashrightarrow b$ in S. Now $\mu(a) \dashrightarrow \mu(b)$ implies that $a_L < b_R$. This inequality can only be the consequence of lines 1, 3 or 4. If the cause is line 1, then $a = b$ and so $a \dashrightarrow b$, by the first axiom of Anger. If line 3 is the reason for $a_L < b_R$, then $a \dashrightarrow b$

as required. If line 4 is the reason, then for some v and x, $a \dashrightarrow v \longrightarrow x \dashrightarrow b$, and the second Anger's axiom implies that $a \dashrightarrow b$.

Observe that the finiteness axiom was not used in this theorem. If the set E is countable, then the linear-order can be assumed to be the rationales since any countable linear-order is embeddable into the rationales. Now we wish to show that there is some flexibility in finding representations of Lamport's structures. This flexibility is needed in the applications given in section 3.

Theorem 2.11 *Let $\mathcal{S} = (E, \longrightarrow, \dashrightarrow)$ be a structure satisfying the axioms 1-4 of Lamport, and let $a, b \in E$ be given.*

1. *If $a \not\longrightarrow b$ and $b \not\longrightarrow a$ then $\mathcal{S}$ has an L-homomorphism into intervals of a linear order such that $\mu(a) \cap \mu(b) \neq \emptyset$.*

2. *If $a \not\dashrightarrow b$ and $\mathcal{S}$ satisfies Anger's axioms as well, then it has a homomorphism into intervals of a linear order such that $\mu(b) \longrightarrow \mu(a)$.*

Proof. Denote by $x \prec y$ the existence of $u \longrightarrow y$ in $\mathcal{S}$ such that $u = x$ or $x \dashrightarrow u$. It is easy to check that $\prec$ is irreflexive and transitive. Remark also that if μ is a homomorphism into intervals of the form $\mu(x) = [x_L, x_R]$, then $x \prec y$ implies $x_L < y_L$. To prove 1, let a and b be incomparable under $\longrightarrow$. Let D be the set of all $x \in E$ with $x \prec a$ or $x \prec b$ or $x = a$ or $x = b$. Then D is $\prec$ closed. That is, if $d \in D$ and $x \prec d$ then $x \in D$. Now let $F = (E \setminus D) \cup \{a, b\}$. Let us denote by a^D, b^D the copies of a and b in D; and by a^F, b^F their copies in F. Observe that if $x \longrightarrow y$ and $y \in D$ then $x \longrightarrow a$ or $x \longrightarrow b$. In particular $a \not\longrightarrow y$ and $b \not\longrightarrow y$ for $y \in D$ (as a and b are incomparable under $\longrightarrow$).

Use the representation theorem 2.10 to find a homomorphism μ of $\mathcal{S}$ into intervals of a linear-order. We may assume that the homomorphism is into intervals of linear order since otherwise we may extend the partial-order into linear-order and the homomorphism is not spoiled. Let μ_D and μ_F be the restrictions of μ on D and F respectively, and (by taking copies) assume that the ranges of these homomorphisms are disjoint linear orders L_D and L_F respectively.

The first step is to decide that L_D is to the left of L_F and to unite the intervals $\mu_D(a^D)$ with $\mu_F(a^F)$, and similarly for b. That is, define $\mu(a) = [a^D_L, a^F_R], \mu(b) = [b^D_L, b^F_R]$ so that now those two intervals have a non-empty intersection. We claim that the new function, denoted μ as well , is still homomorphism for $\longrightarrow$ that is, if $u \longrightarrow v$ then $\mu(u) \longrightarrow \mu(v)$. Assume $u \longrightarrow v$. If $v \in D$ then $u \in D$ and in this case $\mu(u) \longrightarrow \mu(v)$. (Observe that $a \not\longrightarrow v, b \not\longrightarrow v$ for $v \in D$). So assume $v \in F$, and then $\mu(u) \longrightarrow \mu(v)$ is easily derived.

The second step is to assure that we get a homomorphism for $\dashrightarrow$. For any $x \in (D \setminus \{a, b\})$ and $y \in F \setminus \{a, b\}$, if $y \dashrightarrow x$, then stretch x until y, that is, redefine $\mu(x) = [x_L, y_L]$. If $\mathcal{S}$ is a Lamport structure, then by the finiteness property x may need only finitely many stretches because only finitely many y's can demand that. In the general case one needs to define the appropriate Dedekind cut, the least upper bound of $\{y_L \mid y \dashrightarrow x, \text{and } y \in F\}$, as the new right end point of $\mu(x)$.

We claim that the resulting function μ is a homomorphism. It is easy to see that it is a homomorphism for $\dashrightarrow$. We shall see that if $x, y \in E$ and $x \longrightarrow y$ then $\mu(x) \longrightarrow \mu(y)$. If there is no need to stretch in the second step the interval of x, then there can be no problem; so assume $\mu(x)$ is stretched in the second step. So $x \in D \setminus \{a, b\}$. A moment of thought reveals that the only problem can be in case for some $f \in F \setminus \{a,b\}$ $f \dashrightarrow x$ and $\mu(x) = [x_L, f_L]$ is redefined, but $y_L \leq f_L$. Since $f \prec y$, y is not in D. Indeed, otherwise, $f \in D$. But $f \prec y$ implies $f_L < y_L$ and since both f and y are in F their intervals remain in L_F; this contradicts the assumption $y_L \leq f_L$ made above.

Raz Rafaely has noted that this result extends to arbitrary finite antichains.

Let us now prove 2. So assume that the Anger axioms hold in S, and $a \not\dashrightarrow b$ (and thus $a \neq b$). Let $A = \{x \in E \mid a = x, \text{or } a \prec x\}$. A is upwards $\prec$ closed. Let B be the complement of A. Then $b \in B$. Let μ_A be a homomorphism for A, and let μ_B be a homomorphism for B obtained as the restriction of some homomorphism of S (this assures that if $a \dashrightarrow b \longrightarrow c$ and $a, c \in A$ and $b \in B$ then $a_L < c_L$). Make these homomorphism into disjoint linear orders, and put the linear-order for μ_A above that of μ_B. This to ensure that $\mu(b) \longrightarrow \mu(a)$. Now we must make the necessary corrections. Whenever $x \in A$, $y \in B$ and $x \dashrightarrow y$ we stretch $\mu(y)$ until x_L. Let μ be the resulting function defined on E, and let us check that μ is again a homomorphism. Observe that by Anger's axiom for no $x \in A$ does $x \dashrightarrow b$ holds. Thus $\mu(b)$ is not extended and $\mu(b) \longrightarrow \mu(a)$ for the new The only cause for worry is when $x \longrightarrow y$ and $x \in B$ had to be stretched and perhaps is no longer to the left of $\mu(y)$. In this case, there is some $u \in A$ with $u \dashrightarrow x$ which causes the stretching of $\mu(x)$ to u_L. But then $u \prec y$, and so $y \in A$. Hence $u_L < y_L$, and the new $\mu(x)$ is still to the left of y_L.

Definition 2.12 *Let $\{S_i \mid i \in I\}$ be an indexed family of Lamport structures all with the same set of events E. Define the intersection S of the S_i to be the structure with set of events E and such that: $a \longrightarrow b$ iff for all $i \in I$, $a \longrightarrow b$ in S_i; and $a \dashrightarrow b$ iff in all S_i, $a \dashrightarrow b$ holds.*

Corollary 2.13 *Any structure which satisfies the four Lamport axioms and the Anger's axioms equals the intersection of all of its global-time homomorphic images.*

3 Applications to the analysis of distributed protocols

3.1 Review of system-executions and properties of registers

Lamport introduced the notion 'system-execution' in order to analyze the behavior of computer system runs . We refer the reader to the original papers of Lamport [7, 8], and to the first part of [1] for a discussion of the subject of interprocess communication. In this subsection we briefly review some basic definitions that we shall need later.

A typical system-execution describes the behavior of a particular run of some processes which can communicate between themselves by means of registers and which may operate under the command of some computer programs. The abstract result of this run consists of a set E of events together with some precedence relation $\longrightarrow$, as well as some 'affect' relation $\dashrightarrow$. That is, the system-execution consists of a Lamport structure $(E, \longrightarrow, \dashrightarrow)$ together with further relations and functions which describe the programs, the registers etc.

Any register, R, supports two kinds of events: write onto R, and read of R. If $r \in E$ is a read of R, then a *return* value is associated with r, and we denote with R(r) this value. Any write has also a value, and usually the write value is determined by the program. Lamport [7, 8] assumes that the writes onto a register are linearly ordered by $\longrightarrow$. We do not not make this assumption and so our definitions below are slightly more general. For simplicity assume the existence of some initial write which $\longrightarrow$ precedes all other writes and reads of the register. Lamport assumes (Axiom B1 in [7] Part II]) that, for any read r and write w of the same register in $\mathcal{S}$, w and r are $\dashrightarrow$ comparable, i.e., $w \dashrightarrow r$ or $r \dashrightarrow w$. We accept this assumption (which is implied by the global-time assumption), but we prefer to push it into the following definition of properties of registers.

Definition 3.1 *Let $\mathcal{S} = (E, \longrightarrow, \dashrightarrow, ...)$ be a system-execution.*

1. *Let $w \in E$ be a write onto register* R *. We say that $a \in E$ 'sees' w iff $w \dashrightarrow a$ and whenever $v \in E$ is some other write onto* R *then $v \dashrightarrow w$, or $a \dashrightarrow v$ holds. (In case the write events in E are assumed to be serially ordered by $\longrightarrow$, this definition coincides with the one of Lamport.)*

2. *Register* R *is called 'safe' in $\mathcal{S}$ iff any read and write events in $\mathcal{S}$ of* R *are $\dashrightarrow$ comparable, and, whenever $r \in E$ is a read of* R *, and there is only one write, w, onto* R *such that r sees w, then* R *(r) (the value returned by r) is the value written by w.*

3. *Register* R *is called 'regular' in $\mathcal{S}$ iff any read and write of* R *events are $\dashrightarrow$ comparable, and, whenever $r \in E$ is a read of* R *, there is a write $w \in E$ such that r sees w and* R*(r) is the value that w writes.*

4. *Register* R *is called 'serial' in $\mathcal{S}$ iff all read/write events on* R *in $\mathcal{S}$ are linearly ordered by $\longrightarrow$.* R *is called write-serial iff all write onto* R *events are linearly ordered by $\longrightarrow$. (If the register is process owned–has only one writer–then it is write-serial.)*

Let ω be a function defined on the read of R events in E. We say that ω is *regular* iff $\omega(r)$ is a write of register R in E which writes the value returned by the read r, and such that r sees $\omega(r)$. Thus, a register R is regular iff all read and write events are $\dashrightarrow$ comparable and there exists a regular function on the reads of R.

Definition 3.2 *Register* R *is called 'atomic' in system-execution $\mathcal{S}$ iff there exists a function ω defined on the read of* R *events in $\mathcal{S}$ such that:*

1. *$\omega(r)$ is a write onto* R *of the value returned by r.*

2. *r sees $\omega(r)$.*

3. *there are no cycles in the relation $\prec$ defined on the blocks of ω; where:*

    (a) A block consists of a write, w, onto R *and all reads r such that $w = \omega(r)$.*

    (b) If A and B are blocks, then $A \prec B$ iff for some $a \in A$ and $b \in B$ ($a \longrightarrow b$).

3.2 Absoluteness

Definition 3.3 *We say that system-execution* $\mathcal{H} = (H, \overset{\mathcal{H}}{\longrightarrow}, \overset{\mathcal{H}}{\dashrightarrow}, \ldots)$ *extends a system-execution* $\mathcal{S} = (E, \longrightarrow, \dashrightarrow, \ldots)$ *iff* $E \subset H$ *and* $\longrightarrow \subset \overset{\mathcal{H}}{\longrightarrow}$ *(as sets of pairs) and all other relations and functions in* $\mathcal{S}$*, except* $\dashrightarrow$*, are the restriction on* E *of these relations and functions in* $\mathcal{H}$*.*

That is, in an extension, we are allowed to add events, to know more about the precedence relation on E, and to change the $\dashrightarrow$ relation; but no other information is changed. It follows that, if x is a read event which returns a certain value in $\mathcal{S}$ then this holds for x in $\mathcal{H}$ as well. In many applications, there is no need to add new events ($E = H$) and the $\dashrightarrow$ must be respected. For this reason we define and say that $\mathcal{S}$ *conservatively extends* $\mathcal{H}$ iff $\mathcal{S}$ extends $\mathcal{H}$, and moreover $E = H$ and $\overset{\mathcal{H}}{\dashrightarrow} \subset \dashrightarrow$.

It may seem odd at first that the $\dashrightarrow$ relation is allowed to change in an extension, but the following simple example should clarify the issue. Suppose a system-execution containing only two events, w and r, a write and a read of a register, and suppose that both $w \dashrightarrow r$ and $r \dashrightarrow w$ hold. A possible extension is obtained by deciding that $w \longrightarrow r$, and in this case $r \not\dashrightarrow w$.

Observe that if μ is an L-homomorphism of $\mathcal{S}$ then a natural conservative extension of $\mathcal{S}$ is provided by setting $a \overset{*}{\longrightarrow} b$ iff $\mu(a) \longrightarrow \mu(b)$; and $a \overset{*}{\dashrightarrow} b$ iff $\mu(a) \dashrightarrow \mu(b)$. Thus, any system-execution has a global-time conservative extension.

Definition 3.4 *Let* $\int$ *be some property (with parameters),*

1. *we say that* $\int$ *is upwards absolute for conservative extensions (oof...) iff whenever* $\mathcal{S}$ *is a conservative extension of* $\mathcal{H}$*, and* $\mathcal{H}$ *satisfies property* $\int$*, then* $\mathcal{S}$ *satisfies* $\int$ *too;*

2. *similarly, we define when a property is downwards absolute for conservative extensions;*

3. *and we say that* $\int$ *is* absolute *for conservative extensions iff it is both upwards and downwards absolute for conservative extensions.*

The property of a system-execution of being an execution of a certain program with specific values obtained in specified reads is clearly absolute. All other notions are more delicate, and we rely on the assumption that the register R is write-serial and that for any write and read events w, r on R $w \dashrightarrow r$ or $r \dashrightarrow w$. These assumptions are made by Lamport for any register.

Proposition 3.5 *Assuming register* R *is write-serial and any read/write events are* $\dashrightarrow$ *comparable, the following are upwards absolute for conservative extensions:*

1. r *sees the write* w *onto* R .

2. R *is a safe register.*

3. R *is a regular register.*

Let us only prove 1. Suppose r sees w in $\mathcal{H}$ and $\mathcal{S}$ is a conservative extension of $\mathcal{H}$. As $w \overset{\mathcal{H}}{\dashrightarrow} r$, $w \dashrightarrow r$ in $\mathcal{S}$ too. Now assume that v is another write and, in $\mathcal{S}$, $w \longrightarrow v$. Then $w \overset{\mathcal{H}}{\longrightarrow} v$ as the writes onto R are serial. Thus $r \overset{\mathcal{H}}{\dashrightarrow} v$ and so $r \dashrightarrow v$.

In [4] similar notions are presented and discussed. The analog of being upwards-absolute is called 'distributed' and the analog of being downward-ubsolute is refered to as being 'trasferable'. It is shown there, that for every distributed protocol P, if the assumptions about the regisres it employs are transferable and the specification it has to meet is distributed, then, the correctness of P in Global Time Models implies its correctness in every system execution.

3.3 Two examples for the elimination of the global-time assumption

Let us consider two questions from the theory of communication that drew much attention and are well studied. One is the question of the critical-section or the mutual-exclusion problem, and the other is the question of devising atomic registers out of simpler registers. Suppose a protocol is given and the claim is made that execution of this protocol assures the mutual-exclusion property. Or suppose that a protocol is given and it is claimed that an atomic register is implemented whenever the registers used by the protocol are regular. How are we going to prove these claims? Lamport suggests to derive a formal proof from his axioms and thus ensure that all the possible system-executions resulting from runs of the protocols (and these are well definite mathematical objects) satisfy the desired claim. In practice, however, researchers seldom give a precise definition of the framework within which their proofs is taking place, and moreover some of their basic assumptions (like the global-time axiom) are only tacitly assumed.

We accept Lamport's approach and adopt the use of system-executions for formal definitions of protocol's behavior and for proofs of protocol's properties. To Lamport's minimal frame new axioms can be added, and thus the assumptions used by the proof are clearly stated. However, the four axioms of Lamport do not include the global-time axiom and hence do not allow the use of the temporal intuition. We think that this may be a disadvantage. Many times an argument about the behavior of a protocol is better understood if accompanied by a picture describing the temporal relation of the events on one temporal line. Obviously, such an argument cannot find a formal counterpart unless the global-time axiom is assumed. We wish to bridge this gap between the need for formal proofs and the need for easily pictured intuitive arguments. We shall prove that for many types of protocols the global time axiom can be assumed without losing soundness for any system execution (even those in which this axiom fails).

For concreteness of our discussion, suppose that $\mathcal{P}$ is a protocol and that, in any global-time system-execution which results from a run of the protocol the following holds: If the registers used are regular and process owned, then the mutual-exclusion property holds. That is, if $a, b \in E$ are two events corresponding to the critical-section, then either $a \longrightarrow b$ or $b \longrightarrow a$. Assume, by way of contradiction, that there is a run of the protocol (taking place in a non global-time system-execution) in which the mutual-exclusion property does not hold. Namely, in some system $\mathcal{S}$, there are two event a, b such that $a \not\longrightarrow b$ and $b \not\longrightarrow a$. By theorem 2.11 (1) find a homomorphism μ of $\mathcal{S}$into intervals of a linear-order such that $\mu(a)$ and $\mu(b)$ have a

non-empty intersection. This gives a conservative extension, $\mathcal{S}^*$, in which the global-time axiom does hold, but where $a \not\longrightarrow b$ and $b \not\longrightarrow a$ contradicting the assumption about the protocol.
In order for our counter-argument to be valid, we need to know that (1) system-execution $\mathcal{S}^*$ can still be considered as an execution of protocol $\mathcal{P}$, and (2) that the registers used in $\mathcal{S}^*$ are still regular. This non-trivial transfer of properties is crucial to our argument, and it follows from the absoluteness proposition 3.6.

As a second example suppose that, under the global-time assumption, a protocol $\mathcal{P}$ implements, with regular channels, an atomic register which can be written and read by any process. (A channel is a register which has a single writer and a single reader.) Let $\mathcal{S}$ be an implementation of $\mathcal{H}$ induced by the protocol $\mathcal{P}$, and assume the channels in $\mathcal{S}$ are regular, but these system-executions are not assumed to have the global-time property. We wish to prove that the register implemented is atomic. We will assume that the Anger's axioms hold in $\mathcal{S}$in order to derive the result. This assumption is not necessary, but without it the argument is ad hoc and less interesting. First let us see why there is a problem in a general solution, and why we need to look into the protocol itself.

As before, we can use Theorem 2.11 to find a global-time conservative extension $\mathcal{S}^*$ of $\mathcal{S}$; argue that the registers in $\mathcal{S}^*$ are regular and that $\mathcal{S}^*$ defines executions of the protocol the same way $\mathcal{S}$ does. This naturally and uniquely defines an extension $\mathcal{H}^*$ of $\mathcal{H}$ such that $\mathcal{S}^*$ is an implementation of $\mathcal{H}^*$ induced by $\mathcal{P}$. Hence the register in $\mathcal{H}^*$ is atomic, and this implies that a regular function ω as in Definition 3.3 shows the atomicity of the register. We wish to show that the same function works for $\mathcal{H}$ as well, but we don't know that, in $\mathcal{H}$, $\omega(R) \dashrightarrow R$. The solution to this problem comes from the special form of protocol implementation of a register which we are going to exploit.

We say that protocol $\mathcal{P}$ is a *natural* implementation of an atomic register iff there is some definition D, such that whenever R is an execution of the read protocol of $\mathcal{P}$, then the definition chooses a read, denoted $D(R)$, in R, and such that $\omega(R)$ is defined in the following.

1. $D(R)$ depends only on the values returned by the reads of the registers done in R,

2. Let $\mathcal{S}$ and $\mathcal{H}$ be system-executions where $\mathcal{S}$ is an implementation of $\mathcal{H}$ induced by $\mathcal{P}$, and let ω_E be some regular function defined on the set of events E of $\mathcal{S}$ which are reads of regular registers. Now, for any read execution of the protocol, R, in $\mathcal{H}$, $\omega(R)$ is defined as follows. Let $r = D(R)$. Then, $\omega(R)$ is defined to be that write execution of the protocol $W \in H$ such that $\omega(r) \in W$.

Now under the assumption on $\mathcal{P}$ that it naturally implements an atomic register in global-time system-executions, we can prove that even if the global-time is not assumed the register implemented is atomic. Let $\mathcal{S}$ be an implementation of $\mathcal{H}$ induced by $\mathcal{P}$, with no assumption of the global-time axiom. Let $\prec$ be the resulting relation on the blocks as in Definition 3.3. Two things are to be proved about ω. One is that there are no cycles in $\prec$. But this is obvious as otherwise we shall get cycles in any global-time extension $\mathcal{H}^*$ obtained as above. The second is to show that R sees $\omega(R)$. The fact that $\omega(R) \overset{\mathcal{H}}{\dashrightarrow} R$ follows from the existence of a write $w \in \omega(R)$ such that $w \dashrightarrow D(R)$. Now suppose by contradiction the existence of $V \in H$ such that $W \xrightarrow{\mathcal{H}} V$ but $\neg(R \overset{\mathcal{H}}{\dashrightarrow} V)$. Let $a \in E$ be the first event in R, and let b be the last event in V. Then $a \not\dashrightarrow b$ or else $R \overset{\mathcal{H}}{\dashrightarrow} V$. So by Theorem 2.11(2), there is a global-time conservative extension of S in which $b \longrightarrow a$ holds. This gives a global time implementation in which $W \xrightarrow{\mathcal{H}^*} V \xrightarrow{\mathcal{H}^*} R$ in contradiction to the assumption about the protocol.

References

[1] U. Abraham, On interprocess communication and the problem of common atomic registers, manuscript, 1989.

[2] U.Abraham and S. Ben-David, Informal and Formal Correctness Proofs for Programs, manuscript, November 1987.

[3] F. D. Anger, On Lamport's interprocess communication model, ACM Transactions on Programming Languages and Systems, Vol. 11 No. 3, July 1989, 404-417.

[4] S.Ben-David, The global-time assumption and semantics for concurrent systems, Proceedings of the 7th Annual ACM Symposium on Principles of Distributed Computing, ACM Press, 1988, 223-232.

[5] J. van Benthem, Time, Logic and computation, in Bakker, Roever and Rozenberg (Eds), Linear Time, Branching Time and partial Order in Logics and Models for Concurrency, pp.1-49, Springer, Berlin, 1989.

[6] P. C. Fishburn, Interval orders and interval graphs, Wiley, New-York (Wiley-Interscience series in discrete mathematics), 1987.

[7] L. Lamport, The mutual Exclusion Problem: Part I–A Theory of interprocess Communication; Part II–Statements and Solutions, J. of the A.C.M., Vol 33, No.2(1986), pp. 313-326.

[8] L. Lamport, On Interprocess Communication, Part I: Basic formalism, Part II: Algorithms, Distributed Computing, Vol. 1(1986), pp. 77 - 101.

[9] N. Wiener, A contribution to the theory of relative position, Proc. Camb. Philos. Soc. 17(1914), pp.441-449.

MODELLING REACTIVE HARDWARE PROCESSES USING PARTIAL ORDERS

David K. Probst and Hon F. Li
Department of Computer Science
Concordia University
1455 de Maisonneuve Blvd. West
Montreal, Quebec Canada H3G 1M8
net address: probst@bond.crim.ca

ABSTRACT

There has been considerable recent interest in concurrency modelling of delay-insensitive VLSI systems, which abandon global clocks and rely on communicating asynchronous circuits. We present an approach based on partial-order semantics for abstract specification and composition of reactive hardware processes, and proving the correctness of networks of such processes. Both well-behavedness conditions relating to delay insensitivity, and other conditions that guarantee the finite-state character of these processes, permit practical automatic verification of concurrent systems. Nondeterminism is fully modelled. There is an integrated treatment of safety and liveness properties, although progress requirements and fairness requirements are handled separately. Attempts to provide a reasonable choice structure for sets of pomsets led to the somewhat distinct notion of pomtree. A pomtree differs from a (discrete) set of pomsets precisely in making implicit branching structure explicit. Pomtrees represent a partial compromise with interleaving semantics through the assumption that the nondeterministic choices within a process are serialized. The payoff from this compromise is a pretending-atomicity property (one command "follows" another) in conceptual execution of hardware processes; this leads to a greater focus on states and transitions in our model. A key idea is the use of <u>behavior</u> <u>machines</u> as finite presentations of pomtrees. These machines are transition systems consisting of selected behavior states and commands (socket-extended finite pomsets). Such machines precisely describe the <u>branching</u> and <u>recurrence</u> structure of processes by explicitly distinguishing both concurrency and branching points. Significant advantages in processability result from this local visibility of local structure.

<u>Keywords</u> delay-insensitive systems, reactive hardware processes, partial-order semantics, behavior machines, asymmetry of control, safety, progress, fairness.

This research was supported by the Natural Sciences and Engineering Research Council of Canada under grants A3363, A0921 and MEF0040121.

1. Introduction

Recently, there has been a revival of interest in asynchronous VLSI design methodologies [1-2,7-8,16-20,22-23]. Circuit designers generally agree that clock distribution will be a major problem in future circuit design. A growing number of system architects now agree that composition of components in clocked systems will be a major problem in future systems design. Various alternatives to conventional clocked systems are now being explored as potentially viable replacements in the long run. Research on asynchronous systems is underway at several institutions, almost always with an implicit or explicit concurrency theory underlying efforts in analysis and synthesis. The associated formal representation strategy can have a major impact on efficiency of all sorts. We model reactive hardware processes using partial orders to meet requirements of compositionality, processability and efficiency of model checking. We have been attracted to partial-order semantics as an effective tool for escaping from state explosion in its many forms; we did find, however, that we had to make a slight correction to the sets-of-pomsets model to recover the states and atomicity that "come free" in interleaving semantics.

Similarities between asynchronous circuit components and transmission media suggest that we specify both as asynchronous processes, and model delay-insensitive systems as networks of asynchronous processes that communicate exclusively by direct contact. We present an approach to abstract specification based on partial-order semantics that precisely describes the branching and recurrence structure of processes by banishing any formal notion, including concurrency represented by nondeterministic interleaving, that might masquerade as genuine nondeterministic choice. We view confusion situations resulting from arbiter choice as instances of genuine nondeterministic choice. Other kinds of confusion that arise in asynchronous circuits must be handled by controlled ad hoc deviation from the pomtree model. Problems that typical confusion situations cause in pomset models of true nondeterminism are discussed in [10]. Proper identification of pure choice states in finite-state asynchronous processes is an essential key to practical automatic verification of networks of processes. Our slogan is, combine true concurrency with true nondeterminism to achieve efficient algorithmic processability (more generally, tractable reasoning about concurrent systems).

An asynchronous (hardware) process may be implemented by an asynchronous circuit, which is a sequential digital circuit with no clock. Delay-insensitive systems rely on asynchronous circuit components that communicate through non-isochronic wire and fork interconnections. Delay insensitivity means that system correctness is independent of delays in circuit components and transmission media. A sender process signals a receiver process at some port by causing a voltage transition that the latter can assimilate. The sender process signals again at the same port by causing the complementary transition. In a delay-insensitive system, if the receiver process has not properly assimilated the first transition by the time that the complementary transition arrives, then the future behavior of the receiver process is undefined [4]. After causing a voltage transition, the sender process must receive a (possibly indirect) assimilation completion signal before causing the complementary transition. Communication is asynchronous and unbuffered so that elimination of undesirable inputs is performed by local protocols.

2. Abstract specification of self-contained hardware processes

Specifications of hardware or software modules are abstract when they make no reference to particular implementations [15]. In our model -- sometimes called "process theory" --, each abstract specification consists of the set of complete, externally-visible computational behaviors of an asynchronous process, which may be implemented by an asynchronous circuit. These infinite behaviors are called complete to emphasize that they correspond to some maximal safe use of the process by an environment. An externally-visible computational behavior of an asynchronous process is a temporal abstraction of an infinite execution of the process that contains only the necessary temporal precedences among interface events. The precedences are necessary from the point of view of the process. A computational behavior is therefore an equivalence class of process executions, since each of the latter contains both necessary and accidental temporal precedences. As a formal object, a (possibly incomplete) computational behavior is a partially ordered multiset, or pomset, of interface events that can occur on the input and output ports of the process during one of its infinite executions [14].

An asynchronous system component that has been specified as a self-contained process may be placed in an environment. For good reason, the specification of this environment is not part of the component specification, even though the latter does define the limits of acceptable environment behavior. The (possibly incomplete) behaviors in a particular environment can be computed from the (complete) behaviors corresponding to maximal safe use. Physically, the environment supplies input to the process asynchronously; the environment does not require the consent of the process. Logically, input may be illegal and constitute a failure of the process. Any specification allows the process to behave arbitrarily after failure has occurred. Precise characterization of legal input (that is, the input protocol) is an important part of asynchronous process specification.

An asynchronous process P has a finite number of distinctly named input and output ports. $I = \{a, b, \ldots\}$ is the set of input ports and $O = \{\underline{c}, \underline{d}, \ldots\}$ is the set of output ports. $\Pi = I \cup O$ is the process port set. By convention, port $\hat{p} \in \Pi$ only if $\hat{p}$ is used in some behavior of P. A process action is a (port, transition) pair. A process event is a performance of a process action. The only transitions, which play the role of data in the theory, are rising transitions (denoted +) and falling transitions (denoted $-$); for physical reasons, there is strict alternation between rising transitions and falling transitions at a given port. If $(\hat{p}, t)$ is an action, then $(\hat{p}, -t)$ is the complementary transition at the same port. If $A \subseteq \Pi$, then tA is $A \times \{+, -\}$. $\Sigma = t\Pi$ is the set of process actions. For example, a^+ is a rising transition at input port a. Input events are under the exclusive control of P's environment. Similarly, $\underline{c}^+$ is a rising transition at output port $\underline{c}$. Output events are under the exclusive control of process P. Many "true concurrency" theories simplify their structure by not distinguishing input and output events. However, all real computer systems do have clearly distinguishable input and output. In process theory, this asymmetry of control is central to the modelling of reactive hardware processes.

Two classes of behavioral properties appear in (event-based) abstract specifications; these are safety properties, concerning events that must not occur, and liveness properties, concerning events that must occur [4]. Safety properties (invariance properties) specify what the process is allowed to do (equivalently, what it may not do); they also specify what the environment is allowed to do (equivalently, what it may not do). Liveness properties (inevitability properties) specify what the process is required to do (what it must do); they do not specify what the environment is required to do (what it must do). This asymmetry is a simple consequence of specifying processes as maximal sets of complete behaviors. At the level of processes, progress properties are independent of fairness properties; processes are specified as black boxes, and are unconditionally required to respond to excitations. However, progress properties of systems (that is, open networks of processes) may well depend on the fairness properties of their components. Since (hardware) processes possess direct hardware realizations, there is no notion in process theory of a "scheduler" that selects which of several enabled processes should proceed; they all move forward in parallel (maximal parallelism assumption). Progress properties refer to (output) events that must occur eventually, after some arbitrary but finite delay. If a process does not make nondeterministic choices, then it is subject only to safety and progress requirements. If it does make such choices, then it is generally subject to additional fairness requirements. Conceptually, fairness requirements must be imposed any time a choosing process is (part of) a solution to the mutual exclusion problem; they play no further primitive role in the theory. The mutual exclusion problem, which we view as the ultimate source of nondeterminism in concurrent systems, is discussed in [3]. A safety violation is either a process error (incorrect output by the process) or a process failure (illegal input to the process). Although an asynchronous process may be implemented by an asynchronous circuit, we normally view an asynchronous process as a precise requirements specification, not an abstract model of a particular asynchronous circuit.

At the level of events, there are two primitive notions in process theory: (1) (complete) computational behavior of an asynchronous process, and (2) genuine nondeterministic choice among mutually exclusive sets of events, by either process or environment. A (complete) computational behavior of an asynchronous process is a two-level abstraction of an infinite execution of the process that (1) corresponds to some maximal safe use of the process by an environment, and (2) contains only the necessary temporal precedences among interface events. Events are concurrent when there is absence of necessary temporal relationship among them. When there are conflicts in a process, a particular behavior results from a particular set of conflict resolutions. In the pomtree model, a complete behavior corresponds to a maximal infinite path through the pomtree, while a nondeterministic choice corresponds to selection of a particular branch in the pomtree. Environment choice exists when the latter can apply any one of several mutually exclusive access operators to the process. Process choice is viewed as genuine coin flipping, and ultimately results from arbitration among nearly simultaneous requests. In other words, all output nondeterminism results from race conditions in the presence of arbitration.

Two distinct notions of state are used in the model. States are equivalence classes of sets of events. An execution state is just the process state when the process is viewed as a finite state machine; this (local) state is affected by the performance of process actions in the usual way. A behavior state contains all the information in a conventional execution state plus some additional information about how events in the past are temporally related to events in the future. Using two (distinct) equivalence relations, each finite prefix of each computational behavior of process P is mapped onto both an execution state and a behavior state of process P. An execution state is an equivalence class of behavior states. In this way, behaviors contain any execution state and any behavior state that might have arisen during the computation. At the level of states, however, there is room for a third primitive notion: recurrence (looping) in behavior space. Behavior machines describe how commands (socket-extended finite pomsets) define transitions between selected pairs of behavior states. Like all automata, behavior machines may contain cycles. The primary use of behavior states in our model is to identify cutpoints in loops of computational behaviors. The additional information in behavior states appears to be required for this purpose.

An asynchronous process P is input nondeterminate when P's environment can make mutually exclusive, nondeterministic choices about supplying input to P. P is output nondeterminate when P can make mutually exclusive, nondeterministic choices about producing output from P.

2.1. A brief introduction to pomsets

Pomsets and pomset operations have been studied extensively; we recall and extend some of the relevant definitions here [14]. Just as strings are linearly ordered multisets, so pomsets are partially ordered multisets. In process theory, computational behaviors are represented by infinite pomsets, while partial executions are represented by their finite prefixes. Processes can be represented by (possibly singleton) sets of pomsets. However, since our goal is to characterize choices as discrete selections -- from mutually exclusive alternatives -- that occur after specific enabling conditions, a pomtree model is more appropriate. The definition of pomset proceeds in two stages. A labelled partial order (lpo) is a 4-tuple (V, Σ, Γ, μ) consisting of (i) a countable set V of events in a computational behavior, (ii) a finite set Σ of process actions, (iii) a partial order Γ on V that expresses the necessary temporal precedences among the events in V, and (iv) a labelling function $\mu : V \to \Sigma$ mapping each event $v \in V$ to the process action $\sigma \in \Sigma$ it performs. μ is non-injective. In our model, events at the same port in a given behavior are linearly ordered (concurrent events must be at distinct ports). Since every process has an initial state in which no events have occurred, and since the partial order Γ expresses action enabling (causal dependency among events), Γ must be well-founded (axiom of finite causes) [24]. Formally, a pomset (partially ordered multiset) is the isomorphism class of an lpo, denoted $[V, \Sigma, \Gamma, \mu]$. This distinction is due to the fact that the elements of V are anonymous points (place holders). Events need no identity beyond that of being the n-th performance of a particular action.

Prefix and augment are pomset operations. We write all partial orders Γ as "<". Let p and q be (possibly infinite) pomsets. We say that q is a ρ-prefix of p, written $q \leq_\rho p$, when q is obtainable from p by deleting a subset of the events of p, provided that if event u is deleted and $u < v$, then v is also deleted. $\rho(p)$ is the set of ρ-prefixes of p. We say that α is a π-prefix of p, written $\alpha <_\pi p$, when α is finite, p is infinite, and $\alpha \in \rho(p)$. $\pi(p)$ is the set of π-prefixes of p. We say that q is an augment of p, written $p \leq_{\gamma} q$, when q differs from p only in its partial order, which must be a superset of that of p. $\gamma(p)$ is the set of augments of p. If P is a set of pomsets, then $\pi(P)$ is $\cup\ \pi(p)$, $p \in P$. $\rho(P)$ and $\gamma(P)$ are analogous.

Projection is another pomset operation. Let $p = [V, \Gamma, \Sigma, \mu]$ be a (possibly infinite) pomset and let $V' \subseteq V$. The projection onto V' is $p' = [V', \Gamma', \Sigma, \mu']$, where Γ' and μ' are the restrictions of Γ and μ to V'. Projection, accompanied by renaming of actions, has been used with pomsets to define process composition by relating network computational behaviors to process computational behaviors [13,14]. However, in process theory, (1) processes are prefix and augment free, and (2) communication actions do not require the consent of the receiving process; as a result, a new (process-theoretic) composition operator is required [17]. The effects of asymmetry of control on composition have been insufficiently appreciated.

We use the notion of prefix envelope. Let p be a pomset. $^{\circ}p$ is the set of action labels of initial events of p, that is, the set of $\mu(v)$ of v in p such that $\nexists u$ in p with $u < v$. If $\alpha \in \pi(p)$, then $p - \alpha$ is the projection obtained by deleting the events in α from p. The envelope of α in p, denoted $E_p(\alpha)$, is $^{\circ}(p - \alpha)$. Define $in_p(\alpha) = E_p(\alpha) \cap tI$ and $out_p(\alpha) = E_p(\alpha) \cap tO$. $E_p(\alpha)$ is the set of process actions that are concurrently enabled in behavior p after the events of partial execution α.

Once behavior machines have been defined, pomtrees are simply understood as their acyclic tree-like unwindings. We do, however, sketch the notion of branch point in a pomtree at this time. Consider the following skeleton presentation of a simple finite pomtree. Let α, β_1 and β_2 be finite pomsets, with $^{\circ}\beta_1 \cap {^{\circ}\beta_2} = \{\ \}$. Lay down pomset α. Now, both concatenate β_1 with set Γ_1 of (α, β_1) precedences, and concatenate β_2 with set Γ_2 of (α, β_2) precedences. The pomtree contains one copy each of α, β_1 and β_2. β_1 and β_2 are the two branches. Let p and q be the two (maximal) paths through the pomtree. By construction, $\alpha \in \pi(p)$, $\pi(q)$ is a maximal (under prefix ordering) common prefix of p and q. Also by construction, $E_p(\alpha) \cap E_q(\alpha) = \{\ \}$. We say that α is a branch point. If $E_p(\alpha)$, $E_q(\alpha) \subseteq tI$ (tO), then α is an input (output) branch point. Pomtrees are like computation trees except that arcs are maximal determinate behavior segments, and vertices are input or output branch points.

2.2. Determinate processes

The Muller C-element, which must be implemented as a basic asynchronous circuit, is a determinate asynchronous process. I = {a, b} is the set of input ports and O = {c} is the set of output ports. Suppose that all ports (terminals) have been initialized to low. Fig. 1 shows the safety properties of a C-element initialized in this fashion.

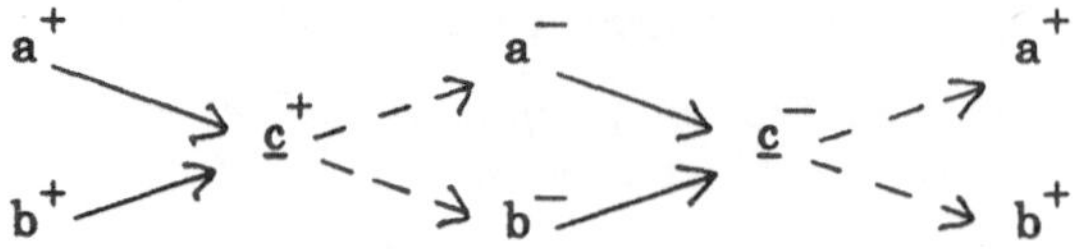

Fig. 1 C-element safety properties generator.

The C-element specification contains a single computational behavior (infinite pomset). The pomset is represented by a generator; it is obtained by concatenating infinitely many copies of the generator, taking care to superimpose (a^+, b^+) pairs. The specified temporal precedences are necessary from the point of view of the C-element.

Fig. 1, which is transitively reduced, contains two kinds of arrows: solid arrows directed from input events to output events, and dashed arrows directed from output events to input events. These arrows represent the *direct temporal orderings* in the behavior. Solid arrows represent direct temporal orderings under the direct control of the process, while dashed arrows represent direct temporal orderings under the direct control of the environment. As illustrated, a computational behavior $p = [V, \Sigma, \Gamma, \mu]$ contains two disjoint partial orders N and Ξ. The *endogenous* (process-controlled) *partial order* N is the relation implied by the solid arrows, while the *exogenous* (environment-controlled) *partial order* Ξ is the relation implied by the dashed arrows. The *behavior partial order* Γ is the transitive closure Ω^+ of a nontransitive *successor* relation $\Omega = N \cup \Xi$. These two components of the successor relation Ω may also be described as the *input protocol* Ξ (of behavior p), and the *output protocol* N. For example, Ξ characterizes legal input that can be supplied to the process during this behavior.

Γ is a set of necessary temporal precedences. If $u < v$, then u must complete before v can begin. If u and v are incomparable (that is, concurrent), then the temporal relationship between u and v does not matter. This means that u and v may be simultaneous (point events), may wholly or partly overlap in time (interval events, space-time regions), may occur in some definite order, and so on. We distinguish (1) u and v are concurrent (the temporal relationship between u and v does not matter) from (2) u and v are not concurrent but may occur in either order (either u must complete before v can begin, or v must complete before u can begin). This distinction between *concurrency* and *nondeterministic interleaving* is easily expressed in partial-order semantics using sets of pomsets, but cannot be expressed in interleaving semantics using sets of linear traces.

We give the semantics of successor arrows. The semantics of *solid* arrows is as follows. The process may produce an output event when all of its solid-arrow predecessors have occurred. The semantics of *dashed* arrows is as follows. The environment may produce an input event when all of its dashed-arrow predecessors have occurred. The semantics can be given more formally. Let $p = [V, \Sigma, \Gamma, \mu]$ be a complete computational behavior and let $v \in V$ be an event. The *preset* of v, denoted $^*v$, is defined as follows: if $\mu(v) \in tO$, then $^*v = \{u : (u, v) \in N\}$; if $\mu(v) \in tI$, then $^*v = \{u :$

(u, v) $\in$ Ξ}. All safety requirements are expressed by the following sentence. If $\alpha \in \pi(p)$, then event v is allowed at α in p if and only if α contains $^*v$ but not v. After initialization, the actions in $^\circ p$ are concurrently enabled.

We define a generally useful operation (input restriction) on complete behaviors. This operation can be used to construct incomplete behaviors of a process P; more precisely, it relates safe uses of processes to maximal safe uses. We say that q is a Ξ-type augment of p when q is obtainable from p by adding a set of dashed arrows to p, and performing transitive closure. Let p be a complete behavior and let q be an infinite pomset. We say that q is an input restriction of p when q is obtainable from p by either (1) deleting a subset of the input events of p to form a ρ-prefix of p, or (2) adding a set of dashed arrows to p and transitively closing to form a Ξ-type augment of p, or both. (Utilization is a synonym of input restriction). This operation is naturally extended to sets of behaviors with input branching structure (equivalently, to behavior machines).

Just as specification P may have many correct implementations, so self-contained process P may be safely placed in many environments. A process is safely placed in an environment (not a symmetric relation) when the latter does not cause the former to fail. Consider the safe placement of process P in some environment. Assume that process P produces output whenever it is allowed to do so. One possibility is that the environment supplies input to P exactly as specified by the input protocol of P. In this case, the set of actual computations carried out by process P in this environment is the specified set of complete computational behaviors. The other possibility is that the environment is more conservative in supplying input to P than required by the input protocol. In this case, the set of actual computations carried out by process P in this environment is an input restriction (or utilization) of the specified set of complete computational behaviors.

2.3. Delay insensitivity

We state the rules that characterize delay insensitivity in partial-order semantics. These well-behavedness conditions are motivated by restrictions that allow asynchronous processes to be used as components of delay-insensitive systems [23]. Assumptions that guarantee delay insensitivity are distinguished from more general assumptions -- not shown in this paper -- that guarantee the finite-state character of asynchronous processes and the bounded-size encoding of behavior states.

Well-behavedness conditions

Rule 0 Every externally-visible computational behavior p of asynchronous process P is infinite (nonterminating). Formally, each $p \in P$ is an infinite pomset on Σ. Example: Fig. 1 represents an infinite pomset of interface events.

Rule 1 Each occurrence of $(\hat{p}, t)$ in asynchronous process P disables $(\hat{p}, -t)$ until an assimilation completion signal or set of signals is either produced by P (if $\hat{p} \in I$) or received by P (if $\hat{p} \in O$) at some other port or set of ports. This prevents the duration of the pulse $[(\hat{p}, t) \ldots (\hat{p}, -t)]$ from becoming arbitrarily small, and allows time for the proper assimilation of $(\hat{p}, t)$ by the receiver process. Formally, any two events with the same port in p $\in$ P are separated in Γ by at least one event with some other port. Example: in Fig. 1, a^+ is separated from a^- by $\underline{c}^+$.

Rule 2 Asynchronous process P directly orders neither its input events nor its output events (see above). Moreover, every port $\hat{p} \in \Pi$ is potentially re-usable. Formally, each line in p $\in$ P consists of an infinite sequence of strictly alternating input and output events. Example: in Fig. 1, there are no arrows directed between symbols of the same type, and there is at least one arrow directed from every symbol in the resulting pomset.

2.4. Progress requirements

We specify the progress properties of a C-element by bracketing certain output events to indicate progress requirements. A determinate process P = {p} does not have alternative (mutually exclusive) progress requirements. As a result, bracketing is an adequate encoding tool. Fig. 2 shows the bracketed output events of the C-element computational behavior.

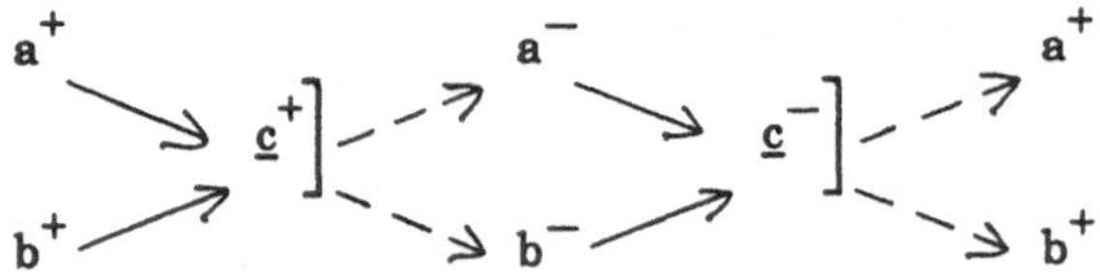

Fig. 2 Complete C-element generator.

In a determinate process, the semantics of bracketing is particularly simple. After partial execution $\alpha \in \pi(p)$, process P = {p} is required to advance to $\beta \in \pi(p)$ that contains all bracketed output events in $E_p(\alpha)$. Since each action in $E_p(\alpha)$ uniquely identifies the event that performs it, we henceforth drop the verbal distinction between action and event in talking about $E_p(\alpha)$ and derived sets. The set of bracketed output events in $E_p(\alpha)$ is denoted $req_p(\alpha)$, where $req_p(\alpha) \subseteq out_p(\alpha)$. We say that the events in $req_p(\alpha)$ are required at α, while the events in $out_p(\alpha) - req_p(\alpha)$ are optional at α. All required events must occur eventually, after some arbitrary but finite delay. Even so, by rule 2, each $v \in req_p(\alpha)$ is at unit distance from α in p.

Separate specification of progress requirements introduces a fourth well-behavedness condition. Let p $\in$ P and let p] $\in \rho$(p) be the ρ-prefix obtained by deleting all nonbracketed output events. If p] $\in \pi$(p), then a network containing P may deadlock (more precisely, permanently block); P's environment may be waiting for an assimilation completion signal that never arrives. By definition, P is allowed to delay any optional output event indefinitely. This motivates the following rule.

Rule 3 Every partial execution α of asynchronous process P is potentially live; after partial execution α, P must allow the environment to supply new input after some arbitrary but finite delay. Formally, if p $\in$ P, then p] is an infinite pomset.

2.5. Nondeterminate processes

We examine variety of computational behavior in nondeterminate asynchronous processes, which have alternative (mutually exclusive) computational behaviors. For example, when there are distinct access operators that can be applied to an abstract data object, then the computational behavior is not fixed a priori, but may vary from one computation to the next [15]. There is variety in safety requirements when, after partial execution α, process P may be willing to accept any of several mutually exclusive (possibly nondisjoint) sets of input events, or may be allowed to produce any of several mutually exclusive (possibly nondisjoint) sets of output events. There is an associated variety in progress requirements. When $P = \{p\}$, each $\alpha \in \pi(p)$ determines three sets $in_p(\alpha) \subseteq tI$, $out_p(\alpha) \subseteq tO$ and $req_p(\alpha) \subseteq out_p(\alpha)$. When P is a set of pomsets, each $\alpha \in \pi(P)$ determines an indexed family $\{(in_p(\alpha), out_p(\alpha), req_p(\alpha)) : p \in P/\alpha\}$ rather than a single 3-tuple $(in_p(\alpha), out_p(\alpha), req_p(\alpha))$. The index set $P/\alpha = \{p \in P : \alpha <_\pi p\}$ is the set of complete computational behaviors of P that are consistent with partial execution α. By extension, $f_P(\alpha) = \{p - \alpha : p \in P/\alpha\}$ is the set of possible futures of P at α.

An important new notion appears in specifying progress requirements of nondeterminate processes: it may be the case, after partial execution α, that event u required in possible future $p - \alpha$ can substitute for event v required in possible future $q - \alpha$ ($u \in req_p(\alpha)$, $v \in req_q(\alpha)$, $v \notin E_p(\alpha)$, $u \notin E_q(\alpha)$, $p, q \in P/\alpha$). We say that events u and v are disjunctively required at α. Sets of pomsets with bracketing allow too much generality in specifying progress requirements. To avoid inconsistency, we adopt the following rule.

Rule 4 After partial execution α of asynchronous process P, event v may not be required in one possible future and optional in another. Let $p, q \in P/\alpha$. Formally, if $v \in req_p(\alpha)$ and $v \in out_q(\alpha)$, then $v \in req_q(\alpha)$; here too, actions uniquely identify events. Moreover, if $req_p(\alpha) \neq \{\ \}$, then $req_q(\alpha) \neq \{\ \}$.

Rule 4 has proved necessary in general process theory. In restricted process theory, both rule 3 and rule 4 are replaced by rule 3′, below.

Rule 3′ Asynchronous process P may not have optional output events. Although there may be nondeterministic choice among disjunctively required events, there is no choice between producing some output and producing no output. Formally, if $p \in P$, then all output events of p are bracketed.

Here, the sets-of-pomsets model begins to show its unwieldiness: processes do not select from infinitely many mutually exclusive alternatives. Finite representations of infinite families are obtained by superset reduction; for example, if $p, q \in P/\alpha$ and $in_p(\alpha) \subseteq in_q(\alpha)$, then we retain only $in_q(\alpha)$. After reduction, we obtain $\mathbf{in}(\alpha) = \{in_j(\alpha) : j \in J\} \subseteq \mathcal{P}(tI)$, $\mathbf{out}(\alpha) =$

$\{out_k(\alpha) : k \in K\} \subseteq \mathcal{P}(tO)$, and $\mathbf{req}(\alpha) = \{req_\ell(\alpha) : \ell \in L\} \subseteq \mathcal{P}(tO)$, where $\mathcal{P}(A)$ is the power set of A. Even now, both branch points (in the sense of section 2.1) and nonbranch points will show up as nonsingleton families, since the sets in a family may or may not be disjoint.

The issue of disjointness merits careful discussion. Consider prefix $\alpha \in \pi(P)$ and the finite set of (reduced) envelopes $E_m(\alpha)$, $m \in M$. If there is some action u that belongs to all $E_m(\alpha)$, then u occurs in all possible futures of α, and should be included in some maximal determinate behavior segment. Branch points can then be used to provide a reasonable choice structure. However, if there are two (independent) concurrent choices at α, then the Cartesian product yields a family of $E_m(\alpha)$ that are sometimes pairwise disjoint and sometimes not. By serializing choice, we recover the pure pomtree structure of section 2.1.

The semantics of nondeterministic choice is much simpler when expressed directly in terms of the pure choice states (branch points) of a behavior machine. Consider a pure output choice state in restricted process theory. Here, each out_k is automatically a req_k. If the process reaches this state as a result of environment excitation, then it has an obligation, within finite time, to choose and produce all events within some out_k. This is the progress requirement in this state. Subtleties arise, for example, in arbiters, when there are (somewhat different) progress requirements in states reached earlier. Suppose that u and v are disjunctively required at α in P. Before P produces either u or v, the environment may supply new input to P so that P advances to β in which u, v and w are disjunctively required; P may then produce w. Formally, if $\alpha \in \pi(P)$, then event v is <u>allowed</u> at α in P if and only if $\exists p \in P/\alpha : v \in E_p(\alpha)$. $E_P(\alpha)$ is $\cup\, E_p(\alpha)$, $p \in P/\alpha$. Moreover, if $\exists p \in P/\alpha : v \in req_p(\alpha)$, then event v is <u>required</u> at α in P, that is, v must occur unless P advances to $\beta \in \pi(P)$ such that $\forall p \in P/\beta : v \notin E_p(\alpha)$. Intuitively, a (possibly disjunctively) required event continues to be required until either (1) it occurs, or (2) the last of the behaviors in which it is allowed drops out. This is an acceptable confusion situation; in an arbiter, an unconditionally required event may become a disjunctively required event after the receipt of new input.

3. <u>State-based abstract specification</u>

Within the interleaving semantics community, there is broad agreement that any computational model of a concurrent system should contain the following features: (1) a set of states, (2) a set of actions, and (3) a set of behaviors [4-5,11]. In this approach, a behavior is either a sequence of states or a sequence of actions. A reasonable way to describe such a system is by specifying, for each action, the set of possible state transitions that are caused by that action. Almost all of the successes of this approach depend on the convention that each action is an operation that is taken to be indivisible. For example, the assumption of atomicity underlies the technique of assertional reasoning, by allowing one to reason separately about individual actions. Since transitions are atomic, attention can be clearly focused on the states. The drawback is that there are too many states.

Within the partial-order semantics community, a clean notion of state is missing [9,12,24]. When the word "state" is used at all, it typically denotes some form of concurrent history. The reason for this is not far to seek. Sequences of actions have a natural equivalence relation familiar from automata theory, defined in terms of sets of sequences that can follow a given sequence. States are then equivalence classes of sequences. When one deals with partially-ordered sets of events, the notion of one set of events "following" another set becomes far more complex. As a result, there is no single -- canonical -- equivalence relation that is universally agreed on. Rather, different equivalence relations may be introduced to solve specific reasoning problems. Our notion of behavior state underlies inductive arguments establishing complete enumeration of pomtrees during automatic verification. We see no way to solve our application problems without a clear focus on states.

3.1 Behavior machines

Behavior machines are finite presentations of pomtrees; they specify nonsequential (hardware) processes that do not control their inputs. A behavior machine consists of a set of selected behavior states, and a set of commands (socket-extended finite pomsets) that can be applied in certain behavior states, producing new behavior states. These machines generate the full set of complete behaviors. One problem that arises in model checking using behavior machines comes from the fact that components of systems are subject to nonmaximal safe use, which may require the encoding of behavior states that were not originally selected. For this reason, it is best to encode all behavior states at specification time. Behavior machines specify both safety and progress properties; fairness properties must be specified by a supplementary condition constraining output choice.

Formally, a behavior machine is a set S of selected behavior states (with a distinguished start state), and a set C of commands. The machine describes the possible state transitions (c takes s to t) produced by each command. For each $c \in C$, there is a relation $\Delta(c)$ on S, where $(s, t) \in \Delta(c)$ if conceptual execution of command c in state s produces state t. The complete behaviors are precisely the infinite sequences of commands generated by the behavior machine. Although a behavior generated in this way does contain an (embedded) infinite sequence of selected behavior states, this has minimal conceptual significance.

Transition systems are beginning to appear in the partial-order semantics community (a recent example is [21]). Because of our requirement of processability, we apply two criteria when assessing these automata. (1) Can we provide an operational semantics for the machine that gives a reasonable account of the branching structure resulting from true nondeterminism, always in the context of asymmetry of control? (2) Is the number of states for which transitions have been identified a small fraction of the actual number of states? The first criterion is used to assess the local visibility of local structure. The second criterion reflects our desire to speak only of selected states, at least during specification; behavior machines are instruments of state reduction.

Fig. 3 shows a behavior machine for a C-element. Each command has the form: behavior state label, socket-extended finite pomset, behavior state label. In constructing behaviors, a new command may be applied provided the command prelabel matches the postlabel of the most recent command. Sockets (denoted o) are explained momentarily; together with their successor arrows, they describe how future behavior follows past behavior. If there is a successor arrow o $\rightarrow$ u, then o is filled by some predecessor of u according to a well-defined rule. More precisely, if command c can follow partial execution α, then there is an injection (produced by simple labelling) from the set of sockets in c to the set of events in α that can still participate in (new) successor arrows.

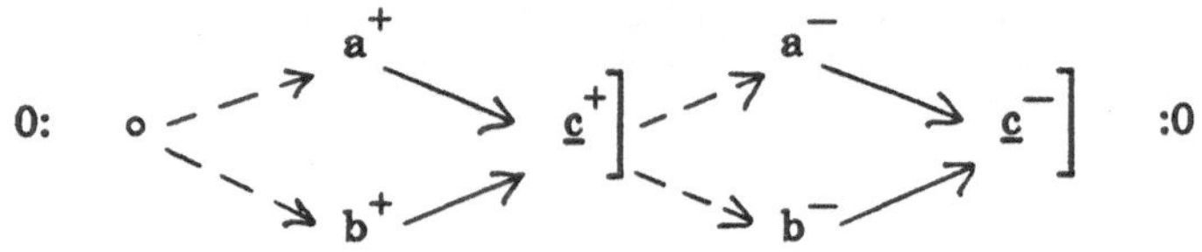

Fig. 3 C-element behavior machine.

The concatenation rule is sequential: every event in one command precedes every event in the next. Behavior machines would be inexpressive if concatenation were always sequential, corresponding to atomic operators. Most behavior machines have commands (finite socket-extended pomsets) that follow one another according to well-defined nonsequential concatenation rules. In Fig. 3, state label 0 denotes both a behavior and an execution state, precisely because the concatenation rule is sequential. By convention, there is an imaginary initialization event • with postlabel 0.

Socket o is filled by • (first command instance) or by $\underline{c}^-$ (all other instances).

Fig. 4 shows a now discarded -- nonbehavior-machine -- unstructured specification of a delay-insensitive arbiter, in the form of a grammar for a set of pomsets. Each of two clients follows a four-cycle protocol. $\langle A \rangle = \underline{c}^+]$ - -> a^- and $\langle B \rangle = \underline{d}^+]$ - -> b^- are the two critical sections. The four small circles are sockets. A finite generator sequence has open sockets; when it is extended, the leftmost actions in the corresponding slots of the next generator fit into these sockets, when such actions exist; otherwise, the sockets remain open. Note that vertical spacing in these grammars is significant: a socket is always filled by a symbol that appears on the same (horizontal) line. This convention was already used in Fig. 3, where we assumed that the default vertical placement of • was "middle". The representation in Fig. 4 was abandoned precisely because it fails to provide a reasonable choice structure for the set of pomsets it generates.

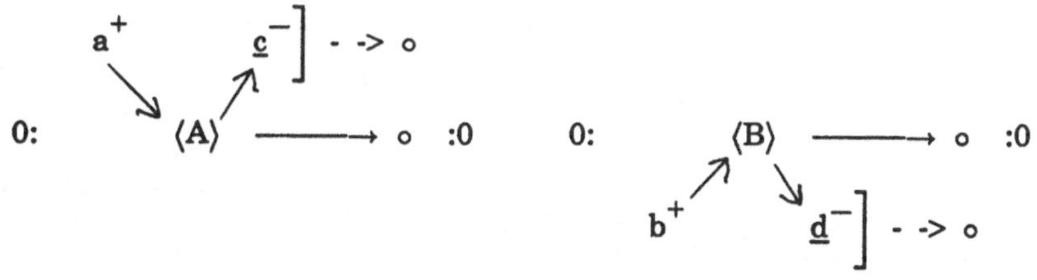

Fig. 4 Unstructured pomset grammar for a delay-insensitive arbiter.

Fig. 5 shows part of a reduced behavior machine for a delay-insensitive arbiter. For space reasons, one command is not shown. This command (command 1) has prelabel 0 and postlabel 1; it contains a leading socket (on the line with state labels), and dashed arrows directed from this socket to a^+ (on the top line) and b^+ (on the bottom line), respectively. For conciseness of presentation -- by clear abuse of notation -- we have included several distinct behavior states under label 1. This label denotes an equivalence class of behavior states that is also an execution state. The two "commands" in Fig. 5 (command 2 and command 3) are also equivalence classes of commands. This is fully explained in the next paragraph. As shown, sockets exist on three horizontal levels. The top o (in command 2) is always filled by a^+ and the bottom o (in command 3) is always filled by b^+. Either middle o can be filled by •, a^- or b^-, perhaps redundantly.

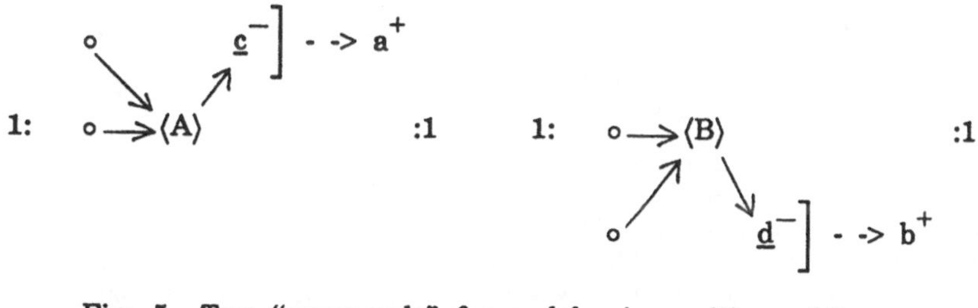

Fig. 5 Two "commands" for a delay-insensitive arbiter.

It turns out that label 1 covers three distinct behavior states, all corresponding to the same execution state. The three may be distinguished as: (1.1) no critical-section entry has occurred (both middle sockets become redundant), (1.2) A's critical-section exit was the most recent (A's middle socket becomes redundant), and (1.3) B's critical-section exit was the most recent (B's middle socket becomes redundant). Behavior states 1.1, 1.2 and 1.3 are output branch points. Behavior states 1.2 and 1.3 form a complete set of loop cutpoints in the full behavior machine; such a set is called a dominator set [6,18]. The full behavior machine is easily obtained. It has four selected behavior states (0, 1.1, 1.2 and 1.3) and seven transitions -- but only five commands (distinct socket-extended pomsets). For example, behavior state 1.2 has a self-loop produced by command 2′ (command 2 minus its middle socket), and a transition to behavior state 1.3 produced by command 3.

Serializing choice is the price we pay for pretending atomicity. If two commands c, $d \in C$ have the same prelabel, then we require that $°c \cap °d = \{ \}$. During conceptual execution, we may imagine cleanly selecting one of these commands via an action performance. A command is always a maximal determinate behavior segment. Hence, commands are either completed or eliminated during conceptual execution, as each event in a selected command appears in all possible futures of the behavior state in which the command was applied.

3.2 Execution states and behavior states

Roughly speaking, a behavior state of an arbitrary process may be identified by the process execution state plus the set of successor arrows crossing from the past to the future, provided only that one has unambiguous names for these successor arrows. In a determinate process P = {p}, one needs an encoding of $\Omega(\alpha, p - \alpha)$, the set of successor arrows with source in α and target in $p - \alpha$, for each $\alpha \in \pi(p)$. One could name these arrows by their endpoints (in simple cases), but it is generally much better to name them directly by recognizing distinct arrows in behavior machines, and assigning appropriate labels. With direct naming and a finite-state determinate process P = {p}, the behavior state $s(\alpha)$ that corresponds to partial execution $\alpha \in \pi(p)$ is uniquely determined by the set (not multiset) $\Omega(\alpha, p - \alpha)$ of successor arrows. This technique can be extended to nondeterminate processes. For example, any behavior state of the arbiter can be encoded by three (small) integers representing the (virtual) successor arrows currently offered by the past to the future. Thus, behavior state 1.2 is encoded as: a^+ (b^+) is currently available to enable the next $\underline{c}^+$ ($\underline{d}^+$) that appears in any downward path through the pomtree, and a^- is currently available to enable the $\underline{d}^+$ that appears in the immediately adjacent B branch.

States of any kind are equivalence classes of partial executions. Some of these classes are refinements of others. Since behavior states remember more of the past than execution states do, they make finer distinctions among partial executions. Two partial executions correspond to the same execution (behavior) state when their sets of possible futures (socket-extended futures) are equal. Formally, each $\alpha \in \pi(p)$ gives rise to a possible future $p - \alpha$. A given α may have several futures $f \in f_P(\alpha)$. We say that two partial executions $\alpha, \beta \in \pi(P)$ are execution equivalent, written $\alpha \equiv_e \beta$, when their sets of possible futures are equal, that is, $f_P(\alpha) = f_P(\beta)$ [15]. This is standard pomset (or pomtree) equality, based on lpo isomorphism. Each $\equiv_e$ equivalence class of partial executions is an execution state of process P. In the same way, each $\equiv_b$ equivalence class ($\alpha \equiv_b \beta$ when their sets of possible socket-extended futures are equal) is a behavior state of process P. More formally, if α and β are prefixes of (possibly distinct) maximal infinite paths through pomtree P, then α and β correspond to the same behavior state of P precisely if the two pomtrees $P//\alpha$ and $P//\beta$ descending from α and β, respectively, are the same, where

P//α and P//β have been extended to include the (α, P//α) and (β, P//β) precedences, respectively, and isomorphism now requires matching both event labels and successor-arrow labels.

3.3 Fairness

We distinguish progress requirements from fairness requirements. Consider a delay-insensitive arbiter P. An $\alpha \in \pi(P)$ indicates which requests, if any, have been received by the arbiter but not yet granted. If there are any outstanding requests, then a live arbiter must grant some request within an arbitrary but finite time; it must also eventually acknowledge each release. Fairness requirements forbid the arbiter to delay granting a request from one client by infinitely often granting a request from the other client. Equivalently, if the arbiter enters its unique output choice state (branch point) an infinite number of times, then it must select both $\underline{c}^+$ and $\underline{d}^+$ an infinite number of times.

4. Correct implementation of reactive hardware processes

An implementation P′ may exceed the minimum safety requirements of the requirements specification P. Intuitively, an implementation may be more liberal in accepting input and more conservative in producing output, but only if all progress requirements are satisfied. The two partial orders N and Ξ give us formal tools for defining "input liberal" and "output conservative". For example, in restricted process theory, so-called corresponding behaviors of implementation P′ are restricted to be Ξ-type augments of ρ-prefixes of corresponding behaviors of specification P.

The notion of corresponding behavior is best explained operationally. Consider specification P and implementation P′. Verification of P′ implementing P is an examination of the actual computations that result when process P′ is placed in an imaginary environment mP, called the mirror of P [2]. mP and P′ behave as coupled coroutines. In process theory, mP is obtained from P by inverting the type of each event, and interchanging dashed and solid arrows. Brackets are preserved unchanged. By convention, each new output (old input) event in mP occurs as soon as it is allowed, while each bracketed new input (old output) event in mP represents a potential progress violation. mP has three useful properties: (1) mP supplies input to P′ exactly as specified by the input protocol of P, (2) process failures in mP precisely correspond to process errors in P, and (3) bracketed input events in mP precisely correspond to potential progress violations in P. When mirror mP and implementation P′ are so coupled, each serves as an environment for the other. Controlled execution of this imaginary closed system yields corresponding partial executions $\alpha \in \pi(p)$ and $\alpha' \in \pi(p')$. We write $\alpha \Longleftrightarrow \alpha'$ to indicate correspondence. When $\alpha \Longleftrightarrow \alpha'$, α and α' contain the same events, but may not agree on which temporal precedences are necessary: α may have more dashed arrows and α' may have more solid arrows. In restricted process theory, the relation becomes even simpler, as stated in the previous paragraph.

We define correctness of safety properties. In specification P, α and p define $in_p(\alpha)$ and $out_p(\alpha)$, the sets of input and output events that are allowed at α in p; similarly, in implementation P′, α' and p′ define $in_{p'}(\alpha')$ and $out_{p'}(\alpha')$, the sets of input and output events that are allowed at α' in p′. By initial definition of correctness, we require that $in_p(\alpha) \subseteq in_{p'}(\alpha')$ and $out_p(\alpha) \supseteq out_{p'}(\alpha')$. In other words, the requirements specification P states that at least $in_p(\alpha)$, and at most $out_p(\alpha)$, is allowed after corresponding α' in any correct implementation P′ of P. This statement generalizes easily to the nondeterminate case.

We define correctness of progress properties. An implementation P′ may exceed the minimum progress requirements of the requirements specification P. Consider P′ = {p′} implementing P = {p}. By further definition of correctness, for $\alpha \in \pi(p)$, $\alpha' \in \pi(p')$ and $\alpha \Longleftrightarrow \alpha'$, we require that $req_p(\alpha) \subseteq req_{p'}(\alpha')$. When all output events in P = {p} are bracketed, the implementation freedom to be output conservative is lost; in other words, when $req_p(\alpha) = out_p(\alpha)$, we require that $out_p(\alpha) = out_{p'}(\alpha') = req_p(\alpha) = req_{p'}(\alpha')$. Specifications with optional output events are rare. When P′ implements P without output restriction (that is, with neither deletion nor delay of output events in P), it can be shown that corresponding partial executions of P and P′ have a very simple relation. Specifically, $\alpha \Longleftrightarrow \alpha'$ if and only if α is a Ξ-type augment of α'.

A network *Net* of asynchronous processes realizes a composite process ℕ(*Net*) [17]. Projection of ℕ(*Net*) onto network ports yields a simple process *P(Net)*. From a formal standpoint, this is just an asynchronous process P′. We summarize what it means for process P′ to implement process P, written P′ imp P. In principle, the composition operator and the implements relation on processes allow us to compute whether a network of processes implements a process; we compose, project onto network ports, and check for correctness. However, it is far more efficient to check the correctness of network *Net* directly by using the input protocol of specification P to compute and verify an input restriction of the composite process ℕ(*Net*).

Consider the case of determinate P and P′ (general process theory). If P′ = {p′} imp P = {p}, then by definition of correctness:

$$\forall \alpha,\alpha' : \alpha \in \pi(p) \wedge \alpha' \in \pi(p') \wedge \alpha \Longleftrightarrow \alpha':$$

$$in_p(\alpha) \subseteq in_{p'}(\alpha') \wedge \qquad (*)$$

$$out_p(\alpha) \supseteq out_{p'}(\alpha') \wedge \qquad (**)$$

$$req_p(\alpha) \subseteq req_{p'}(\alpha') \qquad (***)$$

After corresponding partial executions, the implementation must (1) accept no less input than required by the specification, (2) produce no more output than allowed by the specification, and (3) produce no less output than required by the specification. Conditions (*) and (**) ensure that all safety requirements are satisfied, while condition (***) ensures that all progress requirements are satisfied.

Consider the case of nondeterminate P and P′ (general process theory). Index sets for **in**, **out** and **req** are discussed in section 2.5. If P′ imp P, then by definition of correctness:

$$\forall\alpha,\alpha' : \alpha \in \pi(P) \wedge \alpha' \in \pi(P') \wedge \alpha \Longleftrightarrow \alpha':$$
$$\forall j \quad \exists j' \quad : \mathrm{in}_j(\alpha) \subseteq \mathrm{in}_{j'}(\alpha') \wedge \qquad (*)$$
$$\forall k' \quad \exists k \quad : \mathrm{out}_k(\alpha) \supseteq \mathrm{out}_{k'}(\alpha') \wedge \qquad (**)$$
$$\forall \ell' \quad \exists \ell \quad : \mathrm{req}_\ell(\alpha) \subseteq \mathrm{req}_{\ell'}(\alpha') \qquad (***)$$

The interpretations of (*), (**) and (***) in the nondeterminate case are analogous to those in the determinate case. Specifying and verifying fairness requirements is an additional task best done within restricted process theory.

5. Conclusion

Process theory, based on partial orders, provides a fresh approach to both analysis and synthesis of asynchronous circuits, including delay-insensitive VLSI systems. Like Petri nets, behavior machines model both concurrencies and causal dependencies in a fully explicit and local manner. Unlike Petri nets, behavior machines have fully-encoded selected and unselected behavior states. These machines -- finite presentations of pomtrees -- precisely describe the branching and recurrence structure of processes. Significant advantages in processability result from this local visibility of local structure. Additional details about using process theory to avoid state explosion in model checking of asynchronous systems are available in [19]. We anticipate eventually being able to perform automatic verification of such real-world examples as routing automata [1]. In the past, even the best model-checking approaches have been severely limited by combinatorial explosion.

Of interest for the semantics of concurrency is the fact that pomtrees represent a partial compromise with interleaving semantics, through the assumption that the nondeterministic choices within a process are serialized. A fully general attempt to combine true concurrency with true nondeterminism appears to put the notion of atomicity somewhat at risk, thereby introducing avoidable complexity into our strategies for reasoning about concurrent systems. We have tried to repair this problem by introducing the notions of behavior machine and behavior state. These machines are transition systems consisting of selected behavior states and commands (socket-extended pomsets). Each command defines a transition relation on the set of selected behavior states. Behavior machines preserve atomicity by structuring processes into (1) maximal determinate behavior segments that are either completed or eliminated during conceptual execution, and (2) input or output branch points. In large measure, we recover the states and atomic transitions that "come free" in interleaving semantics.

References

[1] W.J. Dally and C.L. Seitz, "The torus routing chip", Distributed Computing, Vol. 1, No. 4, October 1986, pp. 187-196.

[2] D.L. Dill, "Trace theory for automatic hierarchical verification of speed-independent circuits", Ph. D. Thesis, Department of Computer Science, Carnegie-Mellon University, Report CMU-CS-88-119, February 1988. Also available from MIT Press, Cambridge, MA, 1989.

[3] L. Lamport, "The mutual exclusion problem: Part I - A theory of interprocess communication", JACM, Vol. 33, No. 2, April 1986, pp. 313-327.

[4] L. Lamport, "A simple approach to specifying concurrent systems", DEC System Research Center Report 15, Palo Alto, CA, December 1986. (Revised January 1988).

[5] L. Lamport and N. Lynch, "Distributed computing", in Handbook of Theoretical Computer Science (forthcoming). Also available as Report MIT/LCS/TM-384, Cambridge, MA, February 1989.

[6] Z. Manna and A. Pnueli, "Specification and verification of concurrent programs by ∀-automata", Proc. of 14th ACM Symposium on Principles of Programming Languages, January 1987, pp. 1-12.

[7] A.J. Martin, "Compiling communicating processes into delay-insensitive VLSI circuits", Distributed Computing, Vol. 1, No. 4, October 1986, pp. 226-234.

[8] A.J. Martin, "The limitations to delay insensitivity in asynchronous circuits", In W.J. Dally (ed), Advanced Research in VLSI, Proceedings of the 6th MIT Conference, MIT Press, 1990, pp. 263-278.

[9] A. Mazurkiewicz, E. Ochmanski and W. Penczek, "Concurrent systems and inevitability", Theor. Comput. Sci., Vol. 64, 1989, pp. 281-304.

[10] A. Mazurkiewicz, "Concurrency, modularity and synchronization", In A. Kreczmar and G. Mirkowska (eds), Mathematical Foundations of Computer Science, Proceedings, Lect. Notes in Comput. Sci. 379, Springer-Verlag, 1989.

[11] R. Milner, Communication and Concurrency, Prentice Hall International, London, 1989.

[12] M. Nielsen, G. Plotkin and G. Winskel, "Petri nets, event structures and domains, Part 1", Theor. Comput. Sci., Vol. 13, 1981, pp. 85-108.

[13] V.R. Pratt, "On the composition of processes", Proc. of 9th ACM Symposium on Principles of Programming Languages, January 1982, pp. 213-223.

[14] V.R. Pratt, "Modelling concurrency with partial orders", Int. J. of Parallel Prog., Vol. 15, No. 1, February 1986, pp. 33-71.

[15] D.K. Probst and H.F. Li, "Abstract specification of synchronous data types for VLSI and proving the correctness of systolic network implementations", IEEE Trans. on Computers, Vol. C-37, No. 6, June 1988, pp. 710-720.

[16] D.K. Probst and H.F. Li, "Using a theory of delay insensitivity to prove speed-independent circuits", In D. Pincock (ed), Canadian Conference on VLSI 1988, Proceedings, Halifax, NS, October 1988, pp. 434-443.

[17] D.K. Probst and H.F. Li, "Abstract specification, composition and proof of correctness of delay-insensitive circuits and systems", Technical Report, Department of Computer Science, Concordia University, CS-VLSI-88-2, April 1988 (Revised March 1989).

[18] D.K. Probst and H.F. Li, "Partial-order model checking of delay-insensitive systems", In R. Hobson et al. (eds), Canadian Conference on VLSI 1989, Proceedings, Vancouver, BC, October 1989, pp. 73-80.

[19] D.K. Probst and H.F. Li, "Using partial-order semantics to avoid the state explosion problem in asynchronous systems", In E. Clarke et al. (eds), Workshop on Computer-Aided Verification, Proceedings, Rutgers, NJ, June 1990 (forthcoming).

[20] C.L. Seitz, "Self-timed VLSI systems", In C.L. Seitz (ed), Caltech Conference on VLSI, Proceedings, Caltech Computer Science Department, Pasadena, CA, January 1979, pp. 345-355.

[21] M.W. Shields, "Behavioural presentations", In J.W. de Bakker, W.P. de Roever and G. Rozenberg (eds), Linear Time, Branching Time and Partial Order in Logics and Models for Concurrency, Lect. Notes in Comput. Sci. 354, Springer-Verlag, 1989, pp. 673-689.

[22] J.v.d. Snepscheut, Trace theory and VLSI design, Lect. Notes in Comput. Sci. 200, Springer-Verlag, 1985.

[23] J.T. Udding, "A formal model for defining and classifying delay-insensitive circuits", Distributed Computing, Vol. 1, No. 4, October 1986, pp. 197-204.

[24] G. Winskel, "An introduction to event structures", In J.W. de Bakker, W.P. de Roever and G. Rozenberg (eds), Linear Time, Branching Time and Partial Order in Logics and Models for Concurrency, Lect. Notes in Comput. Sci. 354, Springer-Verlag, 1989, pp. 364-397.

Author Index